The
Hebrew Bible

The
Hebrew Bible

A CRITICAL COMPANION

Edited by
John Barton

PRINCETON UNIVERSITY PRESS

PRINCETON AND OXFORD

221.6
HEB

6-6-16чс

Copyright © 2016 by Princeton University Press
Published by Princeton University Press, 41 William Street, Princeton, New Jersey 08540
In the United Kingdom: Princeton University Press, 6 Oxford Street, Woodstock, Oxfordshire
OX20 1TR

press.princeton.edu

Jacket art: "King David Playing a Harp," *Miscellany of biblical and other texts*. France, Amiens, 1277–86. London, British Library, MS Add. 11639, f. 117v.

Library of Congress Cataloging-in-Publication Data

The Hebrew Bible / edited by John Barton.
    pages cm
  This is a general-interest introduction to the Old Testament from many disciplines. There are
23 essays with 23 individual reference lists.
  Includes bibliographical references and index.
  ISBN 978–0–691–15471–8 (hardcover : alk. paper) 1. Bible. Old Testament—Introductions.
I. Barton, John, 1948– editor.
  BS1140.3.H43 2016
  221.6'1—dc23   2015036308

British Library Cataloging-in-Publication Data is available

This book has been composed in Minion Pro and Novarese Std

Printed on acid-free paper. ∞

Printed in the United States of America

10 9 8 7 6 5 4 3 2 1

Contents

Introduction

John Barton

G uides or introductions to the Bible have traditionally worked through the text book by book, giving the reader information about the date of origin and development of each book in turn. In this guide a different approach is adopted. In part I we look at the Hebrew Bible in its historical and social context, with chapters on the nature of the Hebrew Bible (or should it be Old Testament?) and on the historical, social, and ancient Near Eastern context of the texts. These draw on the most recent developments in scholarship and seek (as does the whole of the book) to make them accessible to the nonspecialist reader. In part II, the biblical books are introduced by genre, with chapters on narrative, prophecy, law, wisdom, and poetry. In part III we turn to the religious themes of the literature—monotheism, creation, the relation between God and humanity, the covenant (God's special relationship with Israel), and ethics—followed by chapters on religious space and structures and on ritual, purity, and diet, which became so central to Judaism as it developed in postbiblical times but are already important within the Hebrew Bible itself. Part IV examines the dissemination and reception of the text, looking at the Bible's reception history, the tradition of historical-critical inquiry into the Bible's origins and development, literary approaches (now growing in importance), theological interpretations, and political and "advocacy" readings of the text (such as liberationist and feminist approaches). Two final chapters consider the transmission of the biblical text and its translation and the mapping of biblical narratives. Each chapter ends by pointing readers to the most important works on the subject of the chapter.

With this approach to the Hebrew Bible we hope to cover more of the questions careful readers will ask than could be done in a simple, serial introduction to each book in turn. The contents of the Hebrew Bible are all dealt with in the book, taken as a whole, but the approach is much more thematic than has been usual. The writers are all specialists in the topics they write on, and they offer an overview of biblical scholarship at this particular moment in the twenty-first century. They were not chosen for any particular religious commitment: some are Jews, some are Christians of various kinds, some have no religious commitment at all. What unites them is deep involvement in biblical study, together with a concern to communicate the results of this study to a wider public.

The nonconfessional character of the book is not simply a negative point but conveys a definite message. Biblical scholarship is traditionally part of theology and has been conducted chiefly by people with a religious commitment. This does not seem likely to change. But the study of the Bible also exists within a broader context of study in the humanities. Even biblical scholars who are religious believers, and who see the Bible as a text to which they are committed by their faith, still recognize that the boundaries between biblical study and the study of other literature, human history, philosophy, social science, and language are porous. Biblical study has always—but perhaps especially since the European Enlightenment—been part of a wider attempt to make sense of human culture. It is continuous with other humanistic study. Biblical study belongs in the university as well as in the church or the synagogue: not in a reductionist sense, as though the religious side were unimportant, but in the positive sense that the Bible is one of the great texts of our culture and needs to be studied with all the rigor and insight that we apply to other texts and their historical and cultural contexts.

The overall aim of this book is thus not simply to provide useful information about the nature and context of the biblical books—though that of course is an aim—but to help reintegrate the study of the Bible into a wider framework of human literature and culture. The time is long past when every educated person in the West knew the contents of the Bible as a matter of everyday cultural knowledge: students of literature now need courses on biblical knowledge in order to understand references in older poetry and prose that were second nature to our forebears. Nowadays general knowledge of the Bible is thin and slight. The Bible is seen as "religious" in a negative sense, as of interest only to religious people and no longer part of the general culture. One of our purposes in writing this guide is to break down this barrier and encourage a wider understanding of the complex, diverse, and above all interesting collection of books that is the Hebrew Bible.

Contributors

❀

John Barton is Emeritus Oriel and Laing Professor of the Interpretation of Holy Scripture, University of Oxford, and Senior Research Fellow of Campion Hall, Oxford.

Assnat Bartor is Lecturer in Biblical Studies in the Department of Hebrew Culture, Tel Aviv University.

Christoph Bultmann is Professor of Biblical Studies, University of Erfurt.

C. L. Crouch is Lecturer in Hebrew Bible, University of Nottingham.

Adrian Curtis is Honorary Research Fellow in Religions and Theology, University of Manchester.

Eryl W. Davies is Professor and Head of the School of Philosophy and Religion, Bangor University, Wales.

Anthony J. Frendo is Professor of Near Eastern Archaeology and the Hebrew Bible, University of Malta.

Susan Gillingham is Professor of the Hebrew Bible, the University of Oxford, and Fellow and Tutor in Theology, Worcester College.

Alison Gray is Director of Studies and Tutor in Old Testament, Westcott House, Cambridge.

Jennie Grillo is Assistant Professor of Old Testament, Duke Divinity School.

David Jasper is Professor of Literature and Theology, University of Glasgow, and Distinguished Overseas Professor, Renmin University of China, Beijing.

R. G. Kratz is Professor for Old Testament, University of Göttingen.

Seth D. Kunin is Vice Principal for Internationalisation, University of Aberdeen.

Dominik Markl is Lecturer, the Pontifical Biblical Institute in Rome.

Hilary Marlow is Course Director of the Faraday Institute for Science and Religion and Affiliated Lecturer in the Faculty of Divinity, University of Cambridge.

Carmel McCarthy is Emerita Professor of Hebrew and Syriac, University College, Dublin.

R.W.L. Moberly is Professor of Theology and Biblical Interpretation, University of Durham.

Thomas Römer is Professor of the Chair "The Bible in Its Environment," Collège de France, and Professor of the Hebrew Bible, University of Lausanne.

Stephen C. Russell is Assistant Professor of Ancient History, John Jay College, City University of New York.

Benjamin D. Sommer is Professor of Bible and Ancient Semitic Languages, Jewish Theological Seminary, New York.

Katherine Southwood is Associate Professor of Old Testament, the University of Oxford, and Fellow of St. John's College, Oxford.

Hermann Spieckermann is Professor of Old Testament, Georg-August-University of Göttingen.

Francesca Stavrakopoulou is Professor of Hebrew Bible and Ancient Religion in the Department of Theology and Religion, University of Exeter.

Part I

The Hebrew Bible in Its
Historical and Social Context

1

❈

The Hebrew Bible and the Old Testament

John Barton

What is traditionally known as the Old Testament is a collection of the main books that were regarded as sacred Scripture in Judaism by the last few centuries BCE. The majority were written in the kingdom of Judah (which later became the Persian province of Yehud) and indeed in its capital, Jerusalem, between the eighth and the second centuries. But there is material in the books that may be much older: some think that there are texts here that go back into the tenth or eleventh century and thus are older than Homer in Greece.[1] So far as actual manuscripts are concerned, the earliest are those found at Khirbet Qumran by the Dead Sea in the twentieth century, normally known as the Dead Sea Scrolls, which contain at least fragments of almost all the biblical books. These manuscripts are in most cases no older than the first century BCE, and thereafter we have nothing before the great codices of the early Middle Ages, the Aleppo Codex and the Leningrad/St. Petersburg Codex. So whereas for the cultures of Mesopotamia and Egypt we possess actual manuscripts from as far back as the third millennium BCE, in the case of the literature of ancient Israel we are dependent on much later texts. It is clear, however, that the contents of the books do in many cases go back into a much earlier period than the extant manuscripts.

The Old Testament is often rightly referred to as a library of books rather than a single book, since it consists of a large variety of texts of different kinds, reflecting different periods in the history of ancient Israel. Though there are stories in the early books that tell of leaders and heroes such as Abraham, Isaac, Jacob, Joseph, Moses, and Joshua, it is not until the eleventh century at the earliest that we can really speak of Israel as a nation, under the reigns of David and Solomon: many biblical scholars think that even these figures are mostly legendary. After the death of Solomon, in the mid-tenth century, "Israel" divided into two, the larger northern kingdom (known variously as Ephraim and, confusingly, Israel) and the smaller southern kingdom of Judah; these kingdoms continued to exist until the 720s, when the northern state was conquered by the Assyrians and became an Assyrian province, and the early sixth century, when Jerusalem fell to the Babylonians under Nebuchadnezzar and many of the population of Judah were deported to Mesopotamia. It is widely believed that many books in the Old Testament came into being during the eighth and seventh centuries: one or two, such as Hosea and Amos, in the north, but far more in the south, where Jerusalem was probably a center of scribal culture. The major ancient traditions about Moses and his predecessors, now in the Pentateuch ("five books of Moses"—Genesis, Exodus, Leviticus, Numbers, Deuteronomy), may have begun to take shape during this period, though they were certainly also worked on after the exile.

The Babylonian Exile of the Judaeans never ended, in that there was a sizable Jewish presence in Mesopotamia from the sixth century onward; but nevertheless a substantial number of the exiles (or their descendents) succeeded in returning to the land once the Babylonians were conquered by the Persian king Cyrus, and Judah was reconstituted as a small Persian province under a native governor, so that Jewish life continued in the homeland. The sixth century, which was so disastrous politically for the Jews, was also an era in which writing seems to have flourished, with significant collections of prophetic texts such as parts of the books of Isaiah, Jeremiah, and Ezekiel taking shape, alongside a major edition of the history of Israel from the settlement under Joshua down to the exile itself, in what are usually called the "historical" books (Joshua, Judges, Samuel, Kings). The postexilic age also saw many important writings, with the collections Psalms and Proverbs (though parts of those books may be older), the book of Job, and large sections of the Pentateuch being written at this time.

In the fourth century Alexander the Great conquered the Persian Empire. Under him and his successors Jewish life continued quietly until the political upheavals of the second century, when Judaism began for the first time to be persecuted by the Syrian king Antiochus IV, provoking revolt by the freedom fighters known as the Maccabees. It is from this "Hellenistic" period, when Greek customs and thought began to make inroads into Jewish life, that we have the book of Ecclesiastes (Qoheleth in Hebrew) and the book of Daniel, as well as a number of what are nowadays often referred to as "Jewish novels," such as Ruth and Esther. Even more important, the Hellenistic age saw the codification of Jewish scripture into a coherent collection, so that something recognizable as the collection we now possess had come into being.

OLD TESTAMENT OR HEBREW BIBLE?

This book is called *The Hebrew Bible*, but so far I have freely used the term *Old Testament*, which is the name by which the collection of books just described is usually known in Western literary culture. It is obvious, however, that it is in origin a Christian term, since it contrasts with the "New Testament," which tells of the acts and words of Jesus in the Gospels and contains an account of the early church in the Acts of the Apostles, as well as early Christian letters and the book of Revelation. We first hear the Jewish scriptures described as books "of the old covenant" in the work of Bishop Melito of Sardis, who died about 190 CE. By this it is meant that God has entered into a new kind of relationship with the human race through Jesus Christ—the "new" covenant, as described in Hebrews 10; and the books of Jewish scripture are witnesses to his previous, or "old," covenant with his people in pre-Christian times. (*Testamentum* is simply the Latin translation of *covenant*.)

From a Christian perspective this would have seemed a merely factual point, but it is easy to see that from a Jewish point of view it might not sound so innocent. The Letter to the Hebrews describes the new covenant in Christ as superseding the old one, so that *old* is not just a temporal but in a sense an evaluative term: "He abolishes the first in order to establish the second" (Heb. 10:9); "In speaking of a 'new covenant,' he has made the old one obsolete. And what is obsolete and growing old will soon disappear" (Heb. 8:13). So in Christian usage, as heard, at least sometimes correctly, by Jews, *old* can have the sense of "superannuated," surpassed, superseded. Hence in modern times many Jews, and Christians sensitive to such matters, have come to think that the term *Old Testament* is somewhat anti-Jewish in tone. It is of course not common on Jewish lips anyway: Jews tend to refer to the collection simply as "the Bible," since for them the "New Testament" is not part of their Bible anyway. (In Israeli universities people who teach the "Old Testament" are called professors of Bible, and the departments in which they work are called departments of Bible, entirely logically.)

In academic circles a popular response to this problem has been to call these books "the Hebrew Bible" (sometimes "the Hebrew Scriptures"). This avoids the problem of the "supersessionism" felt to be implicit in the term *Old Testament*. There are, however, at least three problems about it—not necessarily reasons not to adopt it but revealing, once probed, some important aspects of the books in question. First, "Hebrew Bible" is not strictly accurate, since parts of the collection are in fact in Aramaic rather than Hebrew. Second, "Old Testament" scholars have traditionally been very interested in the Greek and Latin translations of these books, which produces the odd result that there are "Hebrew Bible" scholars who in fact work mainly on Greek or Latin texts. And third, not all of what at least some Christians have included in their Old Testament is part of the scriptures of Judaism, and that includes some texts that never existed in Hebrew or even Aramaic but were in Greek from the beginning. We shall go on next to examine these difficulties.

Meanwhile, however, it is fair to note that the term *Hebrew Bible* does resolve the "supersessionist" difficulty, and in North America it is now the normal term of choice in academic discussion of the Bible. In Britain the usage is more patchy, but "Hebrew Bible" is gaining ground. Within the Christian churches "Old Testament" seems likely to persist on both sides of the Atlantic, though even in Christian liturgy some prefer to speak of "readings from the Hebrew Scriptures." The shift has slightly affected the term *New Testament*, too, since there is little point in that once the term *Old Testament* is abandoned; and it too can sound supersessionist. But there is as yet no agreed alternative. "Early Christian writings" is accurate but does not convey the sense of a fixed canon of texts that is implied in the term *New Testament*.

Some call the two parts of the Christian Bible the "First" and "Second" Testaments, which sounds suitably neutral from a religious perspective, though it is not clear why one should still use the word *Testament* at all in these formulations, given that the reference to two covenants has been abandoned. I think that it will be some time before there is any resolution of these issues. On the face of it the substitution of "Hebrew Bible" for "Old Testament" seems easy and innocent, but as just pointed out it runs into a certain amount of difficulty once we start to think about it more carefully. The next three sections will explore the difficulty from the three points of view mentioned above: the language of the texts, the existence of ancient translations, and the question of the exact contents of the collection.

THE LANGUAGES OF THE OLD TESTAMENT

Most of the "Old Testament" is in Hebrew. Hebrew belongs to the Semitic family of languages, of which the major example in the modern world is Arabic, though there are other important Semitic languages still in use, such as Maltese and the various kinds of Ethiopic. There is a subgroup of Semitic languages called Northwest Semitic, and it is here that Hebrew belongs, along with now-defunct tongues such as Moabite, Phoenician, and Ugaritic. It is the local ancient language of the southern Levant, the area now containing the state of Israel and the Palestinian territories. Of course, Hebrew is not defunct but is the national language of Israel and is also spoken where there are groups of Israelis elsewhere in the world, such as in parts of the United States. Modern Hebrew is a deliberate revival of the ancient language, enriched with grammatical and syntactical borrowings from various European languages and vocabulary from all over the world. But Hebrew had not in fact totally died out even before modern Israel revived it. After the Bible was complete, some rabbis continued to write (and possibly to speak) Hebrew, in the form now known as Mishnaic Hebrew—that is, the language in which the Jewish collection of laws from the first few centuries CE known as the Mishnah is written. Throughout the Middle Ages there continued to be Hebrew speakers both in the land of Israel and in the diaspora communities of Mesopotamia—the descendents of the exiles from the sixth century—as well as in Egypt, where there had long been a Jewish community. Alongside this active use of later forms of Hebrew, the Bible has continued to be read and studied intensively in Hebrew. There has never been a time when Hebrew "died out."

Even within the Bible itself, however, there is some evidence that the Hebrew language developed over time. There are differences between the main narrative books such as Samuel and Kings and the considerably later Chronicles, while Ecclesiastes (probably third century BCE) shows signs of changes that would become more apparent in Mishnaic Hebrew. Linguistic shifts such as these can be of some help in dating the biblical books, though there is a danger of circular arguments, since sometimes it is precisely the supposed dates of the books that enable us to trace the linguistic changes. But there is widespread consent that Hebrew literature written after the exile did begin to show differences from earlier works—not only in its vocabulary, with borrowings from Persian and, eventually, from Greek, but also in its grammar and syntax.

But, as pointed out above, one problem in calling the Old Testament "the Hebrew Bible" is that parts of it are not actually in Hebrew at all. Several sections of the books of Daniel and Ezra are written in Aramaic,[2] which uses the same script as Hebrew but is a distinct language. Because Aramaic had supplanted Hebrew as the language of everyday speech by the second century BCE, and Jesus and his disciples certainly spoke it, it is sometimes thought that Aramaic is a "late" language—even that Hebrew "turned into" Aramaic. But this is not the case. Historically, Aramaic, also a Northwest Semitic language, is a more important language than Hebrew and just as ancient. As Akkadian, the East Semitic chief language of Mesopotamia, declined as an international language in the eighth to seventh centuries BCE, Aramaic came to take its place: Persians communicated with Egyptians through the medium of Aramaic as they had once done via Akkadian and would come to do, from the third century onward, in Greek. Imperial Aramaic, as this lingua franca is known, is close to the "biblical Aramaic" found in Ezra and Daniel.

Hebrew and Aramaic are not mutually comprehensible, but they are very closely related, and anyone who knows one can readily learn the other: they are about as close as German and Dutch, or Spanish and Italian. Once you know which letters in one language correspond to which letters in the other—for example, that words with a *z* in Hebrew will often have a *d* in Aramaic—you can quickly learn to read them both. (Thus "gold" is *zahab* in Hebrew and *dehab* in Aramaic.) Puzzling as it is that Daniel switches from one language to the other in the middle of a chapter, the original readers were probably bilingual and would have had no trouble with the shift. Even the names of the two languages were often confused: when the New Testament refers to words being "in

Hebrew" (Greek *hebraisti*), it means "in Aramaic." But the title "Hebrew Bible" is certainly somewhat misleading in seeming to imply that the collection of books is in one language only and that that language is what we call Hebrew. We ought to say, more precisely, "the Hebrew and Aramaic Bible."

Aramaic survives in the version nowadays known as Syriac—a mainly Christian dialect of Aramaic, which is written in an adapted Arabic script and is used in the Syrian churches to this day. It has a rich religious literature, little of it known to most people in the West.

A peculiarity of the writing of both Hebrew and Aramaic needs to be understood if one is to grasp some of the difficulties in reading the Old Testament. This is that in early times only consonants were recorded, with vowels left to be supplied by the reader. This is not as difficult as it sounds, and it persists today in most Modern Hebrew publications, including Israeli newspapers. Where the material is reasonably familiar, the reader can often guess almost instantaneously what vowels are required: no British reader of English would have the slightest difficulty in decoding *Gd sv th Qn* as "God save the Queen." And this is easier in Semitic languages than in Indo-European ones such as English, since the vowel patterns in words are considerably more predictable.

Even in the earliest Hebrew texts we possess, however, some consonant signs are used also to indicate basic vowels: *y* can be either a consonant or a vowel, just as it can in English, and *w* can stand for *o* or *u* as well as for the consonant we call "double-u." Thus *dor*, "generation," can be written simply as *dr*, with the reader supplying the vowel from the context, or more helpfully as *dwr*. This system was already well developed by the time of the Dead Sea Scrolls, which use a lot of these so-called vowel letters to assist the reader, just as also happens in Modern Hebrew.

Later, however, a more sophisticated system of dots and dashes was invented, written above and below the line to create an absolutely unambiguous guide to pronunciation. These "vowel points," as they are known, were finally codified in the early Middle Ages, and they can be seen in our earliest complete Hebrew Bible, the Leningrad Codex, the work of the scholars known as the Massoretes of Tiberias, whose task was to transmit the Hebrew text in such a way that no one could be in any doubt about its traditional form (*masorah* means "tradition"). In supplying all these vowel signs the Massoretes were not innovating but simply recording what had come down to them through oral reading of the traditional text, and so it is likely that in most cases the Massoretic Text (MT) reflects much earlier reading traditions—the Leningrad Codex often coincides with the evidence of the Dead Sea Scrolls, for example, though it also sometimes differs from it. Partly because the vowel points now do some of the work previously achieved by vowel letters, MT often has fewer vowel letters than the Dead Sea texts—this is technically described by saying that MT often writes "defectively" what the Dead Sea texts record in a "full" way (*defectivum* rather than *plene* spelling, in the traditional Latin terminology).

Nevertheless, the vowel points cannot be regarded as so ancient as the consonantal text, and modern scholars will more often suggest that the Massoretes may have made mistakes in the vowels than that they may have mistransmitted the consonants. As Hebrew has a large number of words that are identical in their consonants but differ in their vowels (like *pan, pen, pin,* and *pun* in English), this can make a difference to the meaning of the text; however, again as in English, often one vocalization is far likelier than another, and the Massoretes much more often than not got it right. (In English *th pn s mghtr thn th swrd* could conceivably mean "the pun is mightier than the sword" but hardly "the pan" or "the pin"; and in fact we recognize "the pen" as correct partly because the saying then makes more sense and partly, of course, because we probably know it already.) The different age of the consonants and the vowel signs is a reminder, though, that the text of the Bible is not an absolute given but developed over time even after the books were written.

ANCIENT TRANSLATIONS OF THE BIBLE

To call the Old Testament the "Hebrew Bible" may be a bit misleading, given that some of it is in Aramaic, but it does register the fact that it existed in ancient Semitic languages before it became part of the scriptures of the Christian church. In treating as authoritative this collection of books, the church was accepting an already existing body of material, not creating or inventing one itself. The relationship in the new "covenant" the church believed God had entered into with "his people," and indeed with the human race, through Jesus Christ had always to be related to a Scripture that already existed. This relationship, sometimes one of continuity but also sometimes one of dialogue or tension, existed from the very beginning of the Christian movement. But another important factor that may give us pause in using the term *Hebrew Bible* for the older collection of Scripture is this: early Christians in many cases read or used the Jewish scriptures not in Hebrew (or Aramaic) at all but, rather, in Greek.

Jesus presumably read the Bible in Hebrew (and Aramaic), and Paul certainly knew the languages and could read them. But all the sayings of Jesus that we have referring to the Old Testament have come down to us in the Gospels in Greek, despite the fact that Aramaic was his daily language; and Paul wrote only in Greek. One explanation would be that Paul and the Gospel writers made their own translations from the Hebrew and Aramaic text of the Bible, but in fact this is both unnecessary and unlikely because a Greek translation already existed.

Our only evidence about its origins lies in a legend preserved in a document called the *Letter of Aristeas*, which tells how Pharaoh Ptolemy II (309–246 BCE) arranged for the Jewish laws (which may mean the Pentateuch or Torah) to be translated into Greek, so that he might understand the laws under which his Jewish subjects lived and so that Jews not fluent in Hebrew might be able to read them. There were seventy-two translators, and by a miracle they all produced the same translation. Their version was thereafter known as the Septuagint (Latin for "Seventy" and sometimes abbreviated LXX). In reality we do not know for sure when and where the Septuagint was produced, but it was definitely between the fourth and the first century BCE and almost certainly in Egypt, where there was the highest concentration of Greek-speaking Jews.

Whether the Pentateuch was indeed the first part of the Bible to be translated is not known, but it is a reasonable conjecture: by this time it was regarded as preeminent among the Jewish Scriptures and was certainly more important for the regulation of Jewish life than other parts of the Bible. But translations of the other biblical books followed, and by the time of Jesus and Paul, in the first half of the first century CE, many Greek-speaking Jews knew their Bible primarily through the Greek translation. Paul was almost certainly bilingual in Hebrew and Greek (and no doubt could also speak Aramaic): he had had the equivalent of a university education. But Jesus himself may have spoken at least some

Greek, even if he could not read it. The Gospel writers were all Greek speakers and very often, like Paul, cite the Bible in Greek according to the LXX version, not in accordance with the original Hebrew or Aramaic.

Thus, whatever the origins of the Greek translation of the Hebrew and Aramaic texts, by the time of the New Testament writers it was already an established fact, and all, or virtually all, of the biblical books were available in Greek—indeed, as we shall go on to see, the Greek version actually contained more books than the Hebrew. In studying the "Hebrew Bible" today scholars therefore need to know Greek as much as they need to know Hebrew, since sometimes the Greek will contain wording that differs from the MT but which may attest an older underlying Hebrew text. In one notable case, the Greek text of the book of Jeremiah is much shorter than the Hebrew, and the evidence of the Dead Sea Scrolls suggests that the shorter version may reflect the fact that there was an older edition in Hebrew, which the LXX translators had in front of them. The present Hebrew text is, then, a lengthened version of the original, and the Greek is a better guide to the original book of Jeremiah than the Hebrew we encounter in printed Bibles. We cannot assume that the Hebrew we have is always older than the Greek we have, even though there is no doubt that the books were originally written in Hebrew. Sometimes the "original" text may be represented better by the Greek than by the Hebrew of the MT that has come down to us. For some religious believers, this raises questions of biblical authority: In such cases, which is the *real* Bible? Or is that a meaningless question?

The Greek Bible is assumed by many to be simply a translation of the truly authoritative Hebrew text. But for early Christians, many of whom could not read Hebrew, any authority the Hebrew original possessed was very theoretical, since they only ever encountered the Old Testament in Greek and treated its wording as the authority for faith and life. Since the LXX is at many points a faithful rendering of the Hebrew, so far as we can tell, this may not seem to matter very much. But if one starts to press the *exact* wording of the text, matters become more complicated. To take one of the most famous examples: Isaiah 7:14 refers in the LXX to a virgin becoming pregnant, and this became an important "proof text" for Christians who believed in the virgin birth of Jesus. But the Hebrew word underlying the translation means simply a young woman. In the original Hebrew the verse therefore contributes nothing to the doctrine: it probably refers to the imminent birth of a son to King Ahaz of Judah. In the Greek, it has wide doctrinal implications. Which text is "authoritative" for the Christian church? The question is hard to answer; but if authority lies with the Greek, then one needs some theory of the inspiration of the Greek translators, a little like that in the *Letter of Aristeas*, perhaps. In modern times the issue has hardly been discussed: most Christians who think about the matter assume that authority lies with the original Hebrew, and modern biblical translations are always made from that, though the evidence of the LXX is allowed to influence decisions in places where it might reflect an earlier Hebrew text. For early Christians, with no access to the Hebrew at all, the matter appeared in a different light.

As Christianity spread from Greek-speaking circles to those where Latin was the everyday language, Latin translations were made—but always from the Greek. It is only with Jerome (347–420) that we encounter a translator who sought to weigh the evidence of the Hebrew text in producing a Latin version, and his translation (traditionally called the Vulgate) may again in places preserve traditional readings in the Hebrew that are older than our MT. The older Latin translations (*vetus Latina*, "old Latin") cannot help us with the Hebrew but can sometimes point to old traditions in the Greek Bible that are older than the Greek we now possess, in just the same way as the Greek can attest to earlier Hebrew readings. Biblical scholars need to be able to consider Hebrew, Greek, and Latin versions if they are to establish the earliest versions of the biblical books. Even so, to get back to the *original words* written by the authors of the books is no more than a pipe dream. The best we can ever do is to establish what may be the earliest version that can be reconstructed.

THE APOCRYPHA

A further problem is that the Greek Bible contains more books than the Hebrew one. The additional books can be found in English Bibles that contain a section called "The Apocrypha," which since the Reformation has been understood by Protestants to mean the majority of books either that never had a Hebrew original (such as the Wisdom of Solomon, composed in Greek) or whose Hebrew original was lost (such as Tobit or Sirach [= Ecclesiasticus], large parts of the original Hebrew of which have now been found). *Apocrypha* means "hidden books," and in the early church the term was used to describe "secret" books, often those used by sects such as the Gnostics, of which orthodox Christians disapproved; there was also a theory that there were certain divinely inspired books that God had chosen to keep hidden (see 2 Esdr. 14:45–46). The Protestant Reformers borrowed the term to refer to biblical books that were not accepted by the Jews as inspired, which they excluded from the list of books fully approved by the church; some Protestants, such as Lutherans and Anglicans, continued to read them and think highly of them, while others, such as Calvinists, rejected them altogether.

In the early church, as soon as contact with the Hebrew Bible was lost, the books in question were mostly treated as simply part of Scripture: most people did not know that Jews did not accept them or would not have cared if they had known. Early Christian writers quote freely from some of them as if they were wholly on a par with all other biblical books. An awareness that they did not form part of the Jewish "canon" can be found as early as Melito of Sardis, who made a fact-finding journey to the Holy Land to discover Jewish attitudes to Scripture. But in the fifth century a row erupted about them between Jerome and Augustine (354–430). The former, in touch with Jews and, as we have seen, knowing Hebrew, became acutely aware that Christians were using books not accepted in Judaism and not extant in Hebrew, and he argued that they should stop doing so. The latter contended that these books had always been regarded as holy, and should continue to be so regarded, within the church. The matter was tacitly resolved in Augustine's favor, since the "apocryphal" books continued in use from then on. At the time of the Reformation Jerome's view of the matter resurfaced and resulted in a move to assert that only the Jewish canon of the Bible should count as the church's Old Testament. Catholics, however, continued to affirm the inspiration of the Apocrypha, and in Catholic Bibles today they do not appear in a supplementary section but, rather, integrated among the other Old Testament books, standing next to those they most resemble— thus Tobit and Judith are next to Esther, and the Wisdom of Solomon and Ecclesiasticus are next to Proverbs, Job, and Ecclesiastes. Though they are sometimes referred to as "deuterocanonical," "belonging to a second order of the canon," they are treated in both theology and liturgy as entirely on a par with other biblical books. And there the question rests: the extent of the Old Testament canon never seems to be on the agenda for ecumenical discussion, and it is simply accepted that different churches have different Old Testaments. Indeed, the Orthodox churches recognize a few additional books (Psalm 151, 3 and 4 Maccabees, the Prayer of Manasses) that are not even in the Catholic Bible; while the church in Ethiopia has an even more expansive canon of Scripture. Whereas all Christians agree on every detail of the New Testament, the Old Testament remains a gray area.

So far I have written about the "early church," meaning the church from about the second century onward, in which Greek was the standard language and access to Scripture in Hebrew was barely available to most Christians. But what was the situation if we go back still earlier, into the age of the New Testament? What was the biblical canon (i.e., the authoritative list of scriptural books) for Jesus or Paul or their immediate followers? Here the issues become complicated. It is a natural assumption that Scripture for Jews—and Jesus and Paul were Jews—comprised only the books that exist in Hebrew (and Aramaic) and that the Greek books cannot have been regarded as canonical. But, as we saw, many Jews were bilingual in Hebrew and Greek even in that period, and Jews in Egypt may in many cases have been monolingual in Greek and unable to read the Hebrew books at all: that is why the LXX was made in the first place. So it is not at all a matter of course that Jews would have regarded only the Hebrew books as holy.

An old theory was that the shorter Hebrew canon of Scripture was authoritative in Palestine but the longer Greek one was authoritative in Egypt, and there was sense in such a conjecture. But it now seems likelier that in both areas the Bible, rather than being a tightly defined set of books in which a given book was definitively "in" or "out," consisted of a central core and a penumbra. The central core contained the Torah or Pentateuch and many of the historical and prophetic books, especially perhaps Isaiah (which is referred to so plentifully in the New Testament), together with the Psalms. The penumbra consisted of various other books, including some that are now in the Hebrew Bible (e.g., Job, Ecclesiastes) and others that are only in the Greek Bible (e.g., Wisdom of

Solomon, Judith). Some Jews revered some of the penumbral books more than others, but there had been no definite rulings on the exact extent of the canon. It may be that some Jewish groups were clearer than others about these questions. It has recently been argued that the Pharisees tended toward the Hebrew canon and were followed in this by the Jewish historian Josephus; while the Dead Sea community, for example, probably had a more expansive Scripture, which included books such as *1 Enoch* and *Jubilees*, which did not in the end make it into the main Jewish or Christian canons (though *1 Enoch* is canonical in Ethiopia).

If this is broadly correct, then the word *canon* itself may be a bit anachronistic for the very early period. Most Jewish communities knew and revered the main books that are now in the Hebrew Bible, but they did not positively reject other books, and the boundary between scripture and nonscripture was not a clear one. (New Testament writers nowhere discuss which books they regarded as Scripture; we can only work it out by seeing which books they cite.) Though there is no record of any formal canonization process in Judaism, it is perfectly clear by the time of the Mishnah (second and third centuries CE) that the Bible was taken to include the books that are now in the Hebrew canon: only they are cited as scriptural. (This accords with what Melito established.) Very occasionally we hear of discussions of canonicity: the main example is Sirach (Ecclesiasticus), which was widely approved of but regarded as too recent to be part of Scripture. Some think (though I disagree) that there were disputes about Ecclesiastes and the Song of Songs. But no one ever *decided* that Genesis, say, should be regarded as Scripture: it had been so for as long as memory stretched back. Christians in later times were much more prone than Jews to discuss the issue of what belonged in the Bible, but even among them decisions about the canon were mostly a matter of endorsing what had come down from the past, not creating a canon from first principles, as it were. And doubts were only ever expressed about books on the margins; there was a very large fixed core.

To return to the issue of terminology: If we use "Hebrew Bible," does that include or exclude the books some call Apocrypha? On the face of it, it excludes them, since they exist in Greek, not Hebrew. Or worse still, it includes any such books for which an original Hebrew turns up, as it did for Sirach, but excludes Wisdom of Solomon, which is plainly Greek in its whole conception and never existed in Hebrew. In practice, biblical scholars who say that they study "the Hebrew Bible" are quite likely to be interested in the "Apocrypha," and indeed one cannot be a biblical scholar without knowing about these books. But "Hebrew Bible" is, then, a very inexact way of describing the subject of study. "Old Testament" also has the drawback that it does not clearly indicate whether or not the apocryphal/deuterocanonical books are included. In the end there is no ideal term, but of the two under consideration, *Hebrew Bible* is the more restrictive and less informative, even though it avoids the danger of supersessionism, which we have seen to be a major concern and which probably tips the scales for most scholars today.

It is sometimes said that, whatever the theoretical position, in practice New Testament writers only appeal at all substantially to the books now in the Hebrew canon, not to those in the Apocrypha. In terms of actual quotation this is generally true, though there is the remarkable fact that the Letter of Jude quotes from *1 Enoch*, which, as we have seen, is not even in the larger Greek canon as that has come down to us.[3] (Arguments that it is not quoted "as Scripture" are usually special pleading on behalf of a conservative theory of the canon.) But Paul shows extensive knowledge of the Wisdom of Solomon in his argument about human sin in the first chapter of Romans—or at least of something very like it; and when he discusses the origins of sin as lying with Adam, he cannot be dependent on the Hebrew Bible alone (which never reflects on Adam's sin after Genesis 3) but, rather, more on the traditions to be found in Wisd. of Sol. 1:12–16 and Sir. 25:24, which clearly identify Adam and Eve as the source of universal human sinfulness and death in exactly the same way as Paul does. On a traditional understanding of the matter, we should have to say that Paul was deeply indebted to some noncanonical books. But a better way is probably to say that Paul knew many Jewish books, some nearer the center of Scripture than others, which he drew on for his ideas. Unless we have a heavy personal investment in knowing exactly which books are to be counted as "The Bible," we can best express this by saying that for Paul, as for many early Jews and Christians, many books that were known to be ancient exercised a certain authority and influence. The question "Is this book part of the canon of Scripture or not?" was not one that exercised their minds: no one had yet formulated it in those terms. For the modern "biblical scholar" any books from ancient Israel are similarly of interest and concern, and it does not matter very much whether or not they were "canonical." Accordingly it probably also does not matter much for the discipline of biblical scholarship whether we call the subject of study "Hebrew Bible," "Old Testament," "First Testament," or something else. Within religious communities, however, it may matter a good deal; and finding a term that will not be offensive to other religious groups is an important aim.

THE HEBREW BIBLE/OLD TESTAMENT IN JUDAISM AND CHRISTIANITY

Both Judaism and Christianity regard the Old Testament/Hebrew Bible as possessing special authority, which is implied by calling the collection of books "Scripture." But in both cases the authority is not exactly like that of a legal document or constitution or of a creed or "confession" in the Christian case (such as the Augsburg Confession for Lutherans or the Westminster Confession for Presbyterians). In both communities the authority of the Old Testament is subject to various complicated checks and balances, different in character in the two cases and different, indeed, in different branches of the two religions.

In Judaism the books of the Hebrew Bible are organized differently than what is familiar from the Christian Old Testament. There are three divisions: the Law or Torah (the Pentateuch); the Prophets (which includes not only what everyone calls the prophetic books, such as Isaiah and Hosea, but also the "historical books," Joshua, Judges, Samuel, and Kings); and the Writings, a miscellaneous section including Psalms, Proverbs, Job, and Ezra–Nehemiah but also Chronicles, which does not therefore appear alongside the other historical books as it does in the Christian Bible. The threefold division is reflected in the name sometimes used in modern Judaism for the Bible, "Tanakh," an acronym from the initial letters of *Torah*, *Nebi'im*, and *Ketubim*, the Hebrew words for Law, Prophets, and Writings. It is possible that the threefold division reflects the historical realities of "canonization" and that in the Greek Bible, which is arranged more according to the types of literature (history, wisdom, prophecy), an ancient order has been disturbed; or it may be that the Jewish and Christian arrangements are roughly contemporary and simply represent different ways of ordering the material. If the

Jewish system is older, however, it may indicate that the Pentateuch was the first section to be universally accepted as holy scripture in ancient Israel (possibly as early as the fourth century BCE), and some think that the Prophets came next and then finally the Writings, which were still fluid into the first century BCE or even CE. On the model suggested above, it is perhaps more likely that the Prophets and Writings were both still in flux down almost into the age of the New Testament and that the division between them occurred in rabbinic times (after the end of the first century CE). This may be suggested by the fact that the New Testament seems to attest more to a twofold distinction ("the law and the prophets") and that early rabbinic sayings also differentiate the Law from the rest but do not point to a division between Prophets and Writings. But as things now stand, the threefold division is regarded as standard in Judaism, and printed Hebrew Bibles, following the earliest evidence for the MT in the Aleppo and Leningrad codices, adopt this pattern.

Sometimes it has been suggested that the threefold division reflects the contents of the books. The Torah is the word of God spoken directly by him; the Prophets represent God's word mediated through human vehicles; the Writings are human reflection on the word of God. This scheme works more or less well in practice, but with some inconsistencies: Deuteronomy, for example, within the Torah, is presented very much as mediated through Moses, while, on the other hand, there are places in Job—in the Writings—where God is represented as speaking directly. However, it is very unlikely to be historically the reason for the division: it is more a homiletic account of the given fact, trying to make it fruitful for religious faith.

The distinctions are definitely functional liturgically in Judaism. In the synagogue liturgy, the whole Torah is read through annually in large sections; and to each section there corresponds a second reading, always from the Prophets, though they are read only very selectively. Five of the Writings (Lamentations, Esther, Song of Songs, Ecclesiastes, and Ruth) are read at various festivals, and parts of the Psalms are used regularly in worship, but other books in the Writings do not appear in the liturgy at all. The reading of the Torah is surrounded by ceremonial, and the scrolls from which it is read must be handwritten and occupy the holiest place in the synagogue; the other scriptural books can be read from simple printed editions. Just when these usages all became established is not known for certain, but in modern times they are certainly more or less universal in Judaism and attest to the functional importance of the threefold division.

Does the division have any importance for interpretation? It is overwhelmingly the Torah that matters for questions of *halakhah*, that is, for how life is to be lived. Texts from the Prophets and Writings may be adduced in support, but the Torah reigns supreme. In the Mishnah, material from the Writings, especially from Proverbs, is rather more plentiful than that from the Prophets, but overall in Jewish texts, especially the two Talmuds, all of the Prophets and Writings certainly contribute to rabbinic discussions, and in principle any text can clinch an argument, whichever section it comes from. Furthermore, the canon is clearly "closed": that is, there is no fluidity about which texts count as Scripture, since only those from the Hebrew Bible are ever cited with the formula "as it is written" or "as it is said."

But to speak of the authority of the Bible in rabbinic discussion can give a misleading impression. In Talmudic discourse—and even in the Midrash, where texts are commented on serially—the biblical text is appealed to as an authority, but the rulings and arguments presented often exist in a world more controlled in reality by what is called the *Oral Torah*—that is, the accumulated teachings and speculations of generations of rabbis. True, every opinion must be traced back to a scriptural text; but it is not often the biblical text itself that calls the tune. In theory, the written Torah has absolute jurisdiction; in practice, it is the accumulation of traditional interpretation that determines what is taught. Citations from the Torah (or from the rest of the Bible) come in to underscore what is taught, but they are not its true origin.

Thus there is a paradox, a paradox that tends to characterize many religions that appeal to fixed scriptures. Precisely because the scriptures are so central, they tend to be read in such a way as to endorse what is already believed as part of the religion in question. Yet that religion would not be what it is without the scriptures. Judaism would not be Judaism without the Hebrew Bible, from which in many ways it derives. Yet it reads the Bible in accordance with norms that themselves are postbiblical. As religious believers, we read our sacred texts in the light of what we already believe, yet what we already believe does to some degree arise from those same sacred texts.

Christianity is no exception to this rule. In desperate attempts to extract the doctrine of the Trinity from the Bible, for example, one sees the same tug-of-war between what the text appears to mean and the meaning that the religion it supports needs to derive from it. Traditional Catholicism has in some measure avoided this problem by stressing that the essence of the faith derives from tradition rather than from Scripture, though that solution then takes its own revenge by leading people to read the documents of the tradition—creeds and bulls and encyclicals—in the same "creative" way, so as to make sure that they speak with the voice of later orthodoxy. And even then it has often had to interpret the Bible in accordance with tradition, since it has not been willing simply to abandon the idea that the Bible is authoritative, even if functionally it occupies a more secondary role than it apparently does in Judaism. But Protestantism, which has traditionally invested all authority in the Bible, has been very strongly constrained to read all it wanted to believe out of the Bible and has done so by reading at least some of it into the Bible in the first place.

Christianity, however, has a more complicated relationship than Judaism to the Old Testament in particular. There are varieties of Protestantism, and, indeed, of traditional Catholicism, for which the Old Testament is seen as exactly on a par with the New in terms of its authority. In principle, for them, the laws in Leviticus are as binding on Christians as they are on Jews, though in cases such as the food laws they tend to be interpreted metaphorically rather than literally. But most kinds of Christianity see the relation of the faith to the Old Testament more dialectically. The Old Testament presents the basic picture of God to which Christians are committed—as one, as the creator, as the deity whose chose Israel, as the preserver of all humanity; yet in the light of the revelation in Christ some of what it affirms needs modification, and some is perhaps even abrogated. Thus many Christians would think that the more vengeful aspects of the Old Testament God have to be moderated in the light of what is revealed of God in Christ, and most would see some of at least the so-called ceremonial laws as no longer applicable in the Christian dispensation.

How far down this road Christians should be prepared to go is a matter of opinion. The mainstream churches have always rejected "Marcionism," the belief (attributed to Marcion of Sinope, ca. 85–160 CE), that in Christ the Old Testament is revealed as the scriptures of a hostile and alien God. Yet many (and perhaps especially in Lutheranism) have contrasted the Testaments to the detriment of the Old, rather than seeing the Old as flowing seamlessly into the New (as Calvinists are more likely to do). How much these various approaches can be justified is perhaps one of the biggest issues dividing Christians today. It bears on all manner of social and moral issues, not least the (among Christians) hugely controversial area of homosexuality, where so many of the biblical prohibitions (though not all of them) occur in Old Testament texts. Biblical conservatives regard any attempt to give the Old Testament a second rank in Christianity as a form of "liberalism"; those whose tradition has always done this regard those who equalize the Testaments as fundamentalists (the ancient church would probably have called them "Judaizers," a term of abuse that thankfully is no longer used). Though the interpretation of the Old Testament, like the question of its exact contents, is seldom on the agenda at ecumenical conferences, in truth it is a very contentious issue. The Old Testament's place in Christianity is a complex one, entirely unlike its unproblematic status in Judaism, and large theological issues hinge upon it.

NOTES

1. The "Song of Deborah" in Judges 5 is widely thought to go back into the eleventh century BCE, and some think that there is a very early "core" to the Song of Moses in Exodus 15. On the other hand, it is most unlikely that the Ten Commandments, for example, are earlier than the time of the Hebrew monarchies, since they reflect a settled, agrarian lifestyle, not at all the desert milieu from which they purport to come.

2. Ezra 4:8–6:18, 7:12–26; and Dan. 2:4b–7:28.

3. See Jude 14–15.

FURTHER READING

On the textual history of the Hebrew Bible, see the full discussion in Emanuel Tov, *Textual Criticism of the Hebrew Bible*, 3rd ed. (Minneapolis: Fortress Press, 2012). On its development through time, a good guide is John J. Collins, *Introduction to the Hebrew Bible* (Minneapolis: Fortress Press, 2004).

For further reflections on the question of terminology (Old Testament or Hebrew Bible?), see John J. Collins, *Hebrew Bible or Old Testament? Studying the Bible in Judaism and Christianity* (Notre Dame, Ind.: University of Notre Dame Press, 1990); J.F.A. Sawyer, "Combating Prejudices about the Bible and Judaism," *Theology* 94 (1991): pp. 269–78; J. A. Sanders, "First Testament and Second," *Biblical Theology Bulletin* 17 (1987): pp. 47–49; R.W.L. Moberly, *The Old Testament of the Old Testament* (Minneapolis: Fortress Press, 1992).

For the character and development of the Hebrew language, an excellent guide is Angel Sáenz-Badillos, *A History of the Hebrew Language*, J. F. Elwolde, trans. (Cambridge: Cambridge University Press, 1993).

On the Greek Bible, an accessible guide is T. M. Law, *When God Spoke Greek: The Septuagint and the Making of the Christian Bible* (New York: Oxford University Press, 2013).

Canonical questions are discussed in L. M. McDonald and J. A. Sanders, *The Canon Debate* (Peabody, Mass.: Hendrickson, 2002); and J. Barton, *Oracles of God: Perceptions of Ancient Prophecy in Israel after the Exile*, 2nd ed. (London: Darton, Longman and Todd, 2007). For the question of the Pharisaic canon, see T. Lim, *The Formation of the Jewish Canon* (New Haven, Conn.: Yale University Press, 2013). For a general overview of the variety in the Old Testament canon, see J. Barton, "The Old Testament Canons," in J. Schaper and J. Carleton Paget, eds., *The New Cambridge History of the Bible*, vol. 1, *From the Beginnings to 600* (Cambridge: Cambridge University Press, 2013), pp. 145–64.

2

⚜

The Historical Framework

Biblical and Scholarly Portrayals of the Past

Francesca Stavrakopoulou

G iven its long-lived and privileged place in Western culture, the Bible remains one of the most influential collections of ancient literature. Although its stories about the origins of the world and the beginnings of humanity have been eclipsed in the Western intellectual tradition by widely accepted scientific theories, the Bible's continued status not only as a sacred book but as a cultural icon has gifted its other stories about the past an *assumed* historical reliability denied other ancient texts.

To a certain extent, the persistent tendency to uphold traditional claims about the historical reliability of the Bible over and against other stories about the distant past might be argued to derive as much from the Western quest for a cataloged cultural identity as from a confessional reverence of Scripture as the "true" word of God. In essence, the Bible tells a story in which its readers and hearers are urged to identify themselves as the inheritors of a historically rooted and exclusive relationship God makes with a group specially selected from among all the peoples of the world. In the Tanakh (the Hebrew Bible), membership of this group is defined according to the socioreligious precepts of earliest Judaism. In the Christian Bible (which adopts the books of Tanakh and couples them with other early Jewish and Christian writings), the group accorded privileged status as the benefactors of a special relationship with God are to define themselves as followers of Christ.

In the history of the Christian-dominated West, an enduring belief in the essential "historicity" of the biblical story thus underlies a number of the cultural dynamics of Western identities. The Bible has been used not only as a book of religious instruction within families and communities but as an authoritative account of a much broader but distinct religio-cultural lineage, stretching back through time. While perceptions of the nature and legitimacy of this biblically derived cultural identity have frequently been contested, both within and beyond the West, it has nonetheless been used to "other," oppose, and subjugate vast numbers of people across the world over the centuries, playing a notable part (for example) in the colonial projects of European nation-states and the ongoing wars and conflicts in the Middle East.

More than simply a religious manual or a collection of socially endorsed ethical preferences, and whether for better or for worse, the Bible remains a cultural icon of Western identity. As such, contemporary debates about the historicity of its story of the past are heavily freighted—whether explicitly acknowledged or not—with the weight of a cultural and intellectual privileging not credited to other ancient accounts of the past.

THE PROBLEM WITH "HISTORY"

In both the Hebrew Bible (Old Testament) and the New Testament, religious events and the belief claims they foster are firmly located in specific historical contexts: the rebuilding of Yahweh's Temple in Jerusalem is said to occur during the reigns of the Persian kings Cyrus, Darius, and Artaxerxes[1]; the death of Jesus of Nazareth is claimed to have taken place during the tenure of Pontius Pilate as Roman prefect of Judea.[2] The correlation of various biblical traditions with externally verifiable figures and events of broader imperial politics has been used by generations of scholars to plot the historical time frame of the Bible—and often, therefore, to endorse the plausibility, if not the veracity, of its claims. But while the writings of the New Testament appear to reflect—and to have been composed over—a relatively short period (a century or so), the texts of the Hebrew Bible not only tell a story stretching over vast spans of time (indeed, from the beginning of the world to the Hellenistic era) but were likely composed and reworked over many generations. For this reason, questions concerning the historical reliability of the Hebrew Bible (notwithstanding its theological claims) have come to play a major role in modern scholarship.

The modernist challenge to the authority of the Hebrew Bible as a historical source was already anticipated in the debates among its ancient commentators, many of whom were themselves Jewish or Christian adherents to its theological and historical claims. As is well known, uncertainties, inconsistencies, or apparent contradictions in the biblical texts themselves have given rise in both the ancient and modern worlds to a variety of methods employed to smooth or settle these seemingly problematic aspects of the biblical portrayal of the past.[3]

In the wake of the Enlightenment-inspired colonial projects of the West, in which the gathering and cataloging of material artifacts pertaining to the past became closely tied to the "scientific" interrogation of both history and religion, the archaeological verification of biblical events came to dominate analyses of the Hebrew Bible's veracity. However, by the latter half of the twentieth century, the certainties of the so-called Bible-and-spade approach to biblical history had collapsed,[4] giving way not only to more sophisticated and nuanced methods of archaeological inquiry in the discipline but also to a more nuanced and self-reflexive intellectual sensitivity to the cultural dynamics of biblical scholarship.[5] In the wake of Edward Said's seminal work *Orientalism*,[6] an increasing number of scholars began to recognize that the Western quest for the "historical" Israel had perpetuated the marginalization and vilification of peoples (ancient and modern) for whom the Bible was neither a sacred text nor a cultural icon but a dangerous tool of colonialism and sociopolitical oppression.[7]

This was an important shift closely related to postmodern critiques of the nature of "history" itself.[8] As Neville Morley remarks of "history":

> Traditionally, it has been argued that the role of the historian is to "leave the facts to speak for themselves" without imposing anachronistic theories or personal prejudices on them; only thus is it possible to discover "how it really was" in the past. However, facts *don't* speak for themselves. The facts have to be identified, selected, translated, interpreted and contextualised by the historian before we can learn anything from them; they acquire meaning only when incorporated into the historian's framework of interpretation.[9]

"History," then, is a *portrayal* or a *version* of the past, not an accurate "record" or description. This is an observation just as appropriately directed at contemporary scholarly reconstructions of the past as it is to the biblical testimony.[10] But this raises two important questions: What explains the biblical writers' particular portrayal of the past, and what—if anything—can contemporary scholars agree on about the period the biblical writers seek to portray? It is to the first of these questions that the discussion will now turn.

PRESENTATIONS OF THE PAST IN THE HEBREW BIBLE

At first blush, the Hebrew Bible presents what appears to be a seemingly coherent narrative about the past. The story of the people commonly known in the texts as "Israel" spans their descent from a shared ancestor, Abraham (in the book of Genesis), through their escape from forced labor in Egypt (Exodus) and on to Canaan, the land divinely promised to Abraham (Leviticus–Deuteronomy), where they conquer the indigenous inhabitants and form a tribal polity (Joshua and Judges) and finally emerge as a kingdom (1 and 2 Samuel). The fracturing of the kingdom into two monarchic neighbors, Israel in the north (governed by a series of short-lived rulers) and Judah in the south (reigned over by the descendents of David), gives rise to a period of intermittent cooperation and conflict (both with each other and with their neighbors), which is eventually brought to an end first by the destruction of the northern kingdom of Israel and the forced migration of its people at the hands of the Neo-Assyrians and then by the destruction of Judah and the exile of its elites by the Neo-Babylonians (1 and 2 Kings). Under the imperial reign of the Persian kings Cyrus and Darius, a group of Judahite exiles return to their capital city, Jerusalem, to rebuild their community as an obedient province of the Persian Empire (Ezra and Nehemiah).

The apparent coherence of this story derives in part from its presentation as a lengthy series of narratives spanning the Torah (Pentateuch) and the so-called historical books of the Hebrew Bible. However, as scholars have long recognized, coherence need not imply historical reliability, and a closer reading suggests that it is neither as comprehensive nor as coherent as it might initially appear. Rather, the texts collectively present a series of narratives and traditions shot through with jarring contradictions and striking absences. From confusion over the names and number of Israelite tribes,[11] to inconsistencies in the portrayal of the settlement in Canaan (particularly in Joshua and Judges), to the mysterious silence concerning the fate of the ark of the covenant (cf. 1 Kings 8:8; Jer. 3:16), a closer reading of the biblical texts suggests that the narratives cannot be interpreted as a reliable or straightforward "record" of the past.

Nor can they be reliably dated to periods contemporaneous with the events they present. The confidence of older generations of scholars in a hypothetical model of early literary sources (underlying the traditions about patriarchs, exodus, land settlement, and the emergence of monarchy) dating from roughly the tenth to the eighth centuries BCE and edited together to form a broad narrative has been widely challenged and broadly rejected.[12] Instead, and at best, piecemeal details in certain texts are subjected to intense philological and historical scrutiny in the hope that some fossils of the past might be uncovered or that evidence of a text's latest point of composition might be discerned. The result is that the biblical story spanning the books of Genesis–2 Kings appears to have been shaped and reworked a good deal later than the long period it seeks to describe. Indeed, a critically rigorous reading of the story presented suggests that the biblical story of the past appears to function as a written manifesto or memorialization of a particular cultural and social identity, for the past is more often than not presented by the biblical writers with a view to informing their own present—and their own theological and ideological preferences.

This is well illustrated in the book of Deuteronomy, in which the writing and remembering of the past is explicitly presented as a distinctly religious activity of social consolidation. Set at the edge of the promised land, on the eve of Moses's death, Deuteronomy presents itself as Moses's final teaching, in which the recitation, writing, and active remembrance of his words are promoted as the means by which the Israelites and their descendents will successfully endure as a people in the land of Canaan:

> [4] Hear, O Israel: Yahweh is our God, Yahweh alone. [5] You shall love Yahweh your God with all your heart, and with all your soul, and with all your might. [6] Keep these words that I am commanding you today in your heart. [7] Recite them to your children and talk about them when you are at home and when you are away, when you lie down and when you rise.

[8] Bind them as a sign on your hand, fix them as an emblem on your forehead, [9] and write them on the doorposts of your house and on your gates. [10] When Yahweh your God has brought you into the land that he swore to your ancestors, to Abraham, to Isaac, and to Jacob, to give you—a land with fine, large cities that you did not build, [11] houses filled with all sorts of goods that you did not build, hewn cisterns that you did not hew, vineyards and olive groves that you did not plant—and when you have eaten your fill, [12] take care that you do not forget Yahweh, who brought you out of the land of Egypt, out of the house of slavery. [13] Yahweh your God you shall fear; him you shall serve, and by his name alone you shall swear. [14] Do not follow other gods, any of the gods of the peoples who are all around you, [15] because Yahweh your God, who is present with you, is a jealous God. The anger of Yahweh your God would be kindled against you and he would destroy you from the face of the earth. (Deut. 6:4–15)

In this text, appeals to the ancestral past—from patriarchal origins, through the exodus from Egypt, to the conquest of Canaan—are presented as the basis on which the Israelites' social identity is constructed (6:10–12); these appeals are ritualized by means of recitation and ritualized writing across successive generations in order to perpetuate this shared identity through time (6:6–8; cf. 11:18–25). Traditions about the past are thus brought into the present and form the ideological foundation on which life in the land is to be lived and the continued existence of the Israelites is to be ensured.

The teaching (*torah*) of Moses is also the lens through which the biblical writers view subsequent episodes in the story of Israel: certain political leaders and Davidic kings are praised because they adhere to the theological precepts of Moses (Josh. 4:14, 8:35, 11:15; 1 Kings 2:1–4; 2 Kings 18:5–7, 23:25), while the eventual destruction of the two kingdoms, and the exile of their people from the land, is understood as the result of punishment from Yahweh for the religious disobedience against which Moses warned (2 Kings 18:12, 21:7–15; cf. 2 Kings 17:7–18, 22:8–17; Jer. 15:1–4). For many scholars, this is evidence of a determined attempt by a particular group or school of writers to bring diverse and competing traditions about the past into a more systematic and programmatic account, in order to render more authoritative and archaic the scribal emphasis on the notion of Torah.[13]

However, Deut. 6:4–15 also illustrates a more complex and pervasive ideology that not only permeates the historical books but extends in less systematized ways into the majority of Hebrew Bible compositions. This overarching trope is a seemingly dichotomous distinction between "insiders" and "outsiders." Whether territorial, social, or religious, this distinction heavily underscores the biblical portrayal of the past. But it is a dichotomy in the Hebrew Bible that is neither fixed nor uniform. Instead, it indexes a shifting, fluid construction of identity and is employed to demonstrate and define who the biblical story is about and who it is for: the people identified as "Israel."

In the text above, the distinction between the Israelites as "insiders" and other peoples as "outsiders" is made clear in the portrayal of Israel as a group separate from and unlike all others: this is a cross-generational familial group, defined by an exclusive and personal relationship with Yahweh, as the repeated and emphatic use of pronouns suggests ("Yahweh is our God," "You shall love Yahweh your God," "Yahweh your God … is present with you"). According to this passage, the "other" people surrounding Israel have "other" gods, all of whom are to be avoided and rejected by the Israelites (Deut. 6:13–14). This construction of Israelite identity is also built on the notion of land. The "otherness" of the indigenous inhabitants of Canaan is underscored in the explicit claim that Israel has taken over and occupied the houses and fields of the Canaanites (6:10–11). This indexes a broader paradox at the heart of the biblical ideology of the past: whether geographically, politically, or ideologically staked out, the dichotomy of being "inside" or "outside" the land frames the presentation of the past. Here, Israel is cast as the "insider" group because they have come from "outside" the land (6:10–12).

Indeed, in many biblical texts, the identity of Israel is predicated on its being an "outsider" in relation to the land. Set within its current narrative frame, Israel is a people whose beginnings lie in Mesopotamia: in the book of Genesis, the ancestor Abraham is presented as a migrant from Ur in Chaldea, who settles first in Haran (11:27–32) and then in Canaan (11:27–12:9), a land Yahweh repeatedly vows he will give to Abraham's descendents (e.g., 12:7, 13:15–17, 17:8). The same trope is also attested in the exodus tradition. In numerous texts, Israel is a people who have escaped captivity and oppression in Egypt and are led into the land of Canaan, gifted to them as incomers by Yahweh (e.g., Exod.

3:17, 6:6–8; Num. 15:41, 22:5; Deut. 5:6, 15). Tracing their lineage back to both Abraham and the exodus generation, the people of Israel are thus presented in the Hebrew Bible as the archetypal "outsiders," distinct from the seemingly indigenous Canaanite communities of the land that Abraham and his descendents make their own (Gen. 12:6; Deut. 7:1–8; cf. Isa. 51:1–2; Ezek. 33:24). Being an "insider" in the community of Israel is thus couched in the conceptual terms of having come from "outside" the land, suggesting to many scholars an "exilic" or "postexilic" context for the compilation of these traditions.

These biblical portraits of the distant past appear to be employed to support the assertions made of the biblical writers' own circumstances. Notwithstanding contested arguments for the very early origin of some poetic texts and mythic tropes, most scholars now agree that the bulk of narratives constituting the biblical story of Israel was composed, reworked, and compiled at various points during and after the period of the two kingdoms of Israel and Judah—most probably within a time frame stretching from as early as the ninth/eighth century BCE (for those adhering to a more conservative view) to as late as the third or second century BCE (for those adopting a more radical perspective). As such, the colonial imperatives of a broader ancient West Asian imperialism shape the cultural landscape against which the urbanite biblical writers memorialize the identity of Israel in their texts. Within this context, the forced migrations of conquered communities—a useful tool of political and economic control employed by successive empires in the region—inform the biblical writers' perspectives on both the past and the present.

Consequently, the destruction of the northern kingdom of Israel, and the displacement of its high-status communities, at the hands of the Neo-Assyrians in the late eighth century BCE (2 Kings 17:5–18), as well as the invasion of Judah and the subsequent exile of its elites by the Neo-Babylonians in the sixth century BCE (2 Kings 21:2–15; 24:1–4, 20), are presented both as a punishment from Yahweh for religious malpractice and as a confirmation of the identity of "Israel" as an "outsider" people who have failed to "separate" themselves from the indigenous religious practices of the land in which their ancestors made their home. The people thereby find themselves outside the land once again.

This in turn endorses the biblical claim that those tasked by the Persians to journey from Babylon to Jerusalem in the fifth century BCE are an exclusive "remnant" of the people of Israel, who have been blessed by Yahweh to come out of exile and into the land (Ezra 9:8–15; cf. Isa. 37:31, 46:3–13). These "insiders" of the Yahweh community, with a Persian-approved claim to the land, are identified as those who have come from outside the land (Ezra 2:1–64, 4:1–3; Neh. 7:6–73), a claim explicitly aligned in some texts with the traditions about the archetypal incomers: the patriarchs and the exodus generations (Isa. 51:1–3, 10–11; Ezra 7:1–10; cf. Isa. 41:8–10, 48:20–21; Ezek. 28:25, 33:24; Neh. 9).[14] Across a number of these and other texts, a commitment to the Mosaic demand for the exclusive and obedient worship of Yahweh, and a corresponding rejection of the gods and religious practices of "other" peoples, consolidates Israel's identity as a distinctive "insider" group.

The biblical presentation of this group identity, and the lengthy story of its formation and consolidation, is thus carefully plotted along a seemingly historical continuum, according to which key moments in imperial and domestic politics are firmly pitched in both theological and ideological terms. The story has its heroes, from cultural founders (Abraham, Moses, Aaron, David) to pious traditionalists (Hezekiah, Josiah, Ezra), and also its villains, whether religious deviants (the Canaanites, Jeroboam ben Nebat, Ahab, Manasseh) or hostile oppressors (Egypt, Assyria, Babylonia). However, the extent to which this portrayal of the past can be considered historically verifiable, or even broadly reliable, is a matter of great dispute among scholars, for whom disentangling a more objective reality from a highly subjective biblical ideology has proved fraught— but not altogether fruitless.

PRESENTATIONS OF THE PAST IN BIBLICAL SCHOLARSHIP

Most scholarly histories of Israel begin with a discussion of the patriarchs, before moving forward, in accordance with the biblical chronology, to discuss the exodus tradition and the emergence of Israel in Canaan, the rise and fall of the kingdoms of Israel and Judah, and then the period of Persian imperial rule, during which the Jerusalem Temple was rebuilt. This close adherence to the biblical time line, even among most of the recent histories of Israel, which are more cautious in ascribing even a loose historicity to the stories of Israel's earliest origins, demonstrates the pervasive extent to which the Hebrew Bible has been privileged as a heavyweight historical anchor, fixing the historian to a predetermined area of exploration. But as scholars have increasingly recognized, there are a great many aspects of the past that the biblical writers ignore or address only in passing. These include the histories of the rural communities that made up the majority of populations in ancient West Asia and the socioreligious, economic, and political contexts of women. Both these demographic groups have been ignored, marginalized, or misrepresented in a biblical story that is instead heavily focused on what used to be approvingly described by older generations of scholars as the "great men and movements" of Israel's past.[15]

While the recent interest in those underrepresented in the biblical history of Israel has greatly enriched scholarly understanding of the diversity of ancient Israelite society, the greatest assaults to the Hebrew Bible's claims about the past have been launched from the platforms constructed by the biblical writers themselves. That supporting the claim of an ancient ancestral pedigree came crashing down in the 1970s and 1980s, when texts from the early second-millennium societies of Mari and Nuzi, which had been used to verify the corresponding antiquity of certain names, customs, and migration activities in the patriarchal narratives, were shown to be less distinctive than had previously been assumed; instead, they offered only localized snapshots of customs and practices that had a much longer and more widespread history, extending down well into the Iron Age.[16] When this was combined with intrabiblical evidence attesting to the composition and compilation of the patriarchal narratives in the sixth–fourth centuries BCE, the historicity of their stories was rendered increasingly improbable. The patriarchs could no longer be taken as historical figures of the Middle Bronze Age. At best, they were literary creations, based at most on fragmented legends and disparate traditions.

A similar fate befell the biblical claim that Israel's origins as a polity were consolidated in the experience of a mass exodus from a lengthy captivity in Egypt into the Syro-Palestinian region commonly designated Canaan in the Hebrew Bible. Despite inconsistencies in the Hebrew Bible's internal dating method, earlier generations of scholars agreed that the biblical writers understood the exodus event to have occurred in the fifteenth century BCE. But even circumstantial archaeological evidence to corroborate this is entirely lacking. Indeed, scholarly attempts to harmonize the traditions and redate them to a couple of centuries later have similarly fallen flat, for extrabiblical evidence for any kind of Israelite exodus out of Egypt and into the desert regions bordering Canaan in the Mid- to Late Bronze Age is agreed to be absent.[17] Although a small minority of scholars has sought to argue for the plausibility of the traditions on the basis of social and political mechanisms in Egypt,[18] others have argued more persuasively for a much later dating of these loose analogies—weakening further the case for a historical exodus.[19]

Instead, scholars have been forced to rely on a critical appraisal of the biblical writers' own material. However, this material is not only contradictory within the Pentateuch and piecemeal outside it; it also suggests regional variations and diversities across differing periods in the Iron Age that appear to indicate localized rituals, skirmish legends, and combat myths about the gods, relating to either political and social oppression by Egypt, a conflict with an Egyptian force in Syro-Palestine, or a journey from Egypt.[20] An increasing number of scholars now agree that the exodus narratives in Exodus–Deuteronomy represent a carefully crafted synthesis of diverse and unrelated traditions about Egypt, harmonized in the sixth or fifth century BCE (or later) to provide a foundation myth of "outside" origins for the biblical Israel, in response to the experience of Judah's exile.[21]

As the discussion thus far implies, scholarly inquiry into the historical reliability of the biblical traditions can be conducted with a degree of confidence only in the face of corroborating data external to the Hebrew Bible. More often than not, this demands direct evidence of figures, places, and events attested in the biblical texts. Thus, for example, while a number of settlements that emerged in the central hill country of Palestine in the Late Bronze/Early Iron Age period might be plausibly identified as the rural communities from which the kingdoms of Israel and Judah would later emerge, their designation in this early period as distinctively (or even ethnically) "Israelite" remains conjectural—at least until more robust evidence is found.[22]

Within this context, historians are generally on firmer ground when nonbiblical evidence offering explicit and reasonably plausible information can be used to support or to contest the biblical portrayal of the past. All archaeological artifacts demand careful contextualization and interpretation, and some material is better understood than others. To this end, monumental inscriptions, administrative documents, and other epigraphic artifacts from the empires of ancient West Asia remain the richest resource for historical discussion.

Certain events around which the broad chronology of the story in the Hebrew Bible is reconstructed are evidenced in these materials. They include references to the tributes sent by the eighth-century kings Menahem of Samaria and Ahaz of Judah to the Neo-Assyrian king Tiglath-Pilesar III (cf. 2 Kings 15:19–20, 16:7–8), who also claims to have engineered King Pekah's replacement in Samaria with Hoshea (cf. 2 Kings 15:27–30); the fall of Samaria in about 721 BCE and the exile of a number of its people at the hands of the Neo-Assyrian kings Shalmaneser V and his successor, Sargon II (cf. 2 Kings 17:3–6, 23–24; 18:9–11); the Neo-Assyrian attack on Judah, and the subjugation of Jerusalem, during the reign of Hezekiah in about 701 BCE (cf. 2 Kings 18:13–19:37); and the capture of Jerusalem, the deportation of its elites, and the replacement of its king in 597 BCE in a Neo-Babylonian military campaign led by King Nebuchadnezzar (2 Kings 24).[23] Neo-Babylonian sources also attest to a community of Judahites living in Babylonia in the sixth century BCE,[24] while some administrative documents, coins, stamps, and seals include the names of certain Persian-endorsed governors of Samerina and Yehud during the fifth–third centuries BCE.[25]

This material goes some way toward supporting in the broadest terms the historicity of certain figures and events shaping the biblical story of the past. However, by contrast, nonbiblical material of this nature also evidences activities undertaken by particular figures and communities that are unattested by the biblical writers: King Jehu, for example, pays tribute to Shalmaneser III and is perhaps depicted prostrating himself at the Neo-Assyrian king's feet on the famous Black Obelisk—events that go unmentioned in the book of Kings, which simply infers a territorial disempowerment by claiming instead that Jehu's lands were "trimmed" by Yahweh (2 Kings 10:32).[26] Similarly, King Manasseh is said to have assisted in the building campaigns of the Neo-Assyrian king Esarhaddon (ca. 677 BCE) and to have paid homage to his successor, Assurbanipal—even joining him on his imperial journey to Egypt—in about 667 BCE. Again, no mention of this occurs in the detailed (and damning) description of Manasseh's reign in 2 Kings 21:1–18.[27] It may be that either the biblical writers were unaware of these events, which might imply that the texts were produced a considerable time afterward, or they were uninterested in certain events, which points to the selective and ideological nature of their writing.

This latter possibility is indicated by the fleeting nature of biblical references to the Judahite city of Lachish. The handful of texts to mention Lachish would suggest that it was a fortified town of relatively minor significance.[28] Its most notable role occurs in the traditions about the siege of Jerusalem and Hezekiah's subsequent capitulation to the Neo-Assyrian king Sennacherib: Lachish is the city in which Sennacherib and his army take up temporary residence following his subjugation of Judah (2 Kings 18:14–17, 19:8; cf. 2 Chron. 32:9; Isa. 36:2, 37:8). By contrast, Sennacherib's own reflections on his campaign against Phoenicia, Philistia, and Judah appear to glory in the heroic capture of Lachish, for sophisticated reliefs decorating the walls of Room XXXVI in his Southwest Palace in Nineveh portray its defeat in lavish detail. For many commentators, this demonstrates that Lachish was a city of far greater significance and sociopolitical value than the biblical texts would allow.[29] This apparent biblical lack of interest is likely related to the dominant privileging and prioritizing of Jerusalem and its traditions throughout the Hebrew Bible, cautioning against historians' uncritical acceptance of its version of the past—even when that version seems to tally with non-biblical sources of evidence.

Perhaps most intriguing, however, is evidence suggestive of the deliberate misrepresentation of the past in the Hebrew Bible. According to the biblical writers, Omri is just one among a series of kings in the northern kingdom to come to power by means of a coup (1 Kings 16:15–23). Only two aspects of this king's reign merit comment by the biblical writers—the formulaic dismissal of his kingship, applied to all northern monarchs in the book of Kings, as a period of religious deviance (1 Kings 16:25–28) and a brief remark about a building project: "He bought the hill of Samaria from Shemer for two talents of silver; he fortified the hill, and called the city that he built, Samaria, after the name of Shemer, the owner of the hill" (1 Kings 16:24). The brisk account of his reign, and this fleeting reference to the founding of Samaria, suggests that Omri was only of marginal significance in the history of the northern kingdom of

Israel. But nonbiblical texts offer a very different appraisal. The famous stele of King Mesha, a Moabite ruler of the ninth century BCE, bears an inscription celebrating the regaining of sizable portions of Moabite territory from "Omri king of Israel," who had "oppressed Moab for a long time," a policy continued by his unidentified son, who had also said, "I will oppress Moab."[30] This inscription not only suggests that Omri had successfully pursued a powerful and expansionist policy in the region in the ninth century BCE but also demonstrates that his dynastic and territorial legacy continued after his death and into the reign of his successor. The longevity of this legacy is further reflected in a number of Neo-Assyrian inscriptions of the ninth and eighth centuries, in which the kingdom conventionally known as "Israel" in the Hebrew Bible and in scholarship is frequently designated "Omri-land," and several of its various kings as "sons of Omri," long after Omri and his son had died.[31]

This epigraphic evidence demonstrates that Omri was a king of great significance, whose name was synonymous with his kingdom well beyond its borders. By contrast, the sketchy portrayal offered in the book of Kings looks deliberately low key. Indeed, closer attention to its form encourages the suspicion that Omri's profile has been deliberately downplayed, or even suppressed, in the biblical account: an unusual passing remark, buried in the formulaic epilogue to his reign, refers obliquely but significantly to "the rest of the acts of Omri, *and the power that he showed*" (1 Kings 16:27; emphasis added).[32]

Archaeological excavations and demographic studies further support the historian's perception that Omri and his successor were accomplished and powerful kings. Material evidence from the period signals a sizable increase in settlements and agricultural hubs in the northern hill country; the construction of major urban centers at Samaria and Jezreel, plus the redevelopment of Hazor, Megiddo, and Gezer; and sustained, profitable regional trade routes. The region rapidly became the heartland of a well-organized state: Samaria appears to have controlled the main roads crossing the area, and concentrated efforts to fortify the highways and regional borders, as well as the cities, are evident in the remains of fortresses, military posts, and towers, all indicating the political and economic strength of the territory.[33] The scholarly consensus is that this, then, is the period in which the northern polity can be properly considered a developed "state."[34] For this reason, this is the point at which scholars can most confidently begin to speak of the ninth century BCE as the beginning of the real history of ancient Israel.

But this scholarly view is at odds with the Hebrew Bible's portrayal of the past, in which the biblical Israel achieved the political, territorial, and economic stature of a fully fledged state in the period of David and Solomon. According to this portrayal, the center of power was originally Jerusalem, not Samaria, and the development of Megiddo, Hazor, and Gezer as economic and administrative bastions of the state was the work of Solomon (1 Kings 9:15–17), not Omri and his successors. These claims form a part of the Hebrew Bible's larger portrait of the kingdoms of Israel and Judah as the two halves of an originally larger kingdom, reigned over by David and his successor, Solomon, and fractured when the religious deviancy of the northern communities led to political rebellion (1 Kings 12:1–33).

Evidence of the long-standing separateness of Israel and Judah from the ninth century BCE onward is attested by what some archaeologists describe as a "shatter zone," evident in the remains of material culture lying north of Jerusalem along the Gezer-Bethel line; for many, this is strongly suggestive of a cultural and political border.[35] This raises questions about whether or not the northern and southern areas were a unified polity before this. However, archaeological evidence for the existence of a developed "state" in Judah in the tenth century BCE (the period associated with the "united monarchy" of David and Solomon), and also the ninth century BCE (when the kingdom of Judah was supposed to have coexisted alongside its northern neighbor), is tenuous at best.

Previous generations of scholars cited as evidence the remains of monumental architecture in support of the Hebrew Bible's claim that monarchy first emerged in the period identified—on the basis of the biblical chronology—as the tenth century BCE. Their arguments focused on the biblical assertion that Solomon embarked upon extensive building projects:

[15] This is the account of the forced labour that King Solomon conscripted to build the house of Yahweh and his own house, the Millo and the wall of Jerusalem, Hazor, Megiddo, Gezer [16] (Pharaoh king of Egypt had gone up and captured Gezer and burned it down, had killed the Canaanites

who lived in the city, and had given it as dowry to his daughter, Solomon's wife; [17] so Solomon rebuilt Gezer), Lower Beth-horon, [18] Baalath, Tamar in the wilderness, within the land, [19] as well as all of Solomon's storage cities, the cities for his chariots, the cities for his cavalry, and whatever Solomon desired to build, in Jerusalem, in Lebanon, and in all the land of his dominion. [20] All the people who were left of the Amorites, the Hittites, the Perizzites, the Hivites, and the Jebusites, who were not of the people of Israel—[21] their descendents who were still left in the land, whom the Israelites were unable to destroy completely—these Solomon conscripted for slave labour, and so they are to this day. [22] But of the Israelites Solomon made no slaves; they were the soldiers, they were his officials, his commanders, his captains, and the commanders of his chariotry and cavalry. (1 Kings 9:15–22)

This text presents Solomon as a powerful monarch with the military, territorial, economic, and human resources at his disposal to fortify and develop urban centers throughout his kingdom, subdue and control "outsider" elements within the population, enter into a profitable diplomatic marriage with a powerful nation, and transform Jerusalem into a beacon of architectural monumentality suitable for both his god and him to reside in.

Initially, archaeological studies appeared to support this image of Solomon as a successful royal builder, for excavations at Hazor, Megiddo, and Gezer revealed defense systems exhibiting almost identical architectural features. From this sprang the persistent supposition that one central authority must have been responsible for these seemingly parallel fortification patterns. Given the biblical material, Solomon was widely credited with instigating these tokens of statehood.[36]

However, the biblical concept of Israel and Judah as one state divided into two is increasingly considered historically improbable. This position draws strength from three significant developments within scholarship since the late 1980s and 1990s: the reevaluation of archaeological evidence, the considerable contribution of social-scientific investigations, and the increasing consensus arguing for the later dating of the biblical texts well beyond the ninth and eighth centuries BCE, all of which have undermined the assumption of the basic historicity of the biblical description of a united-then-divided monarchy.[37]

Accordingly, while architectural features of ancient Megiddo, Hazor, and Gezer were formerly understood to reflect a shared and unified process of development and fortification within the tenth century, their reinterpretation now challenges this view: the similarities and dates of the monumental six-chambered gates are questioned, and the citing of casemate walls as an indicator of tenth-century fortification is disputed.[38] These architectural features thus no longer signify what they once did.[39] Their testimony to the existence of a common, centralized political power in the tenth century is not indisputable. With the challenging of the older interpretation of these data, the bedrock of archaeological evidence supporting the united monarchy of David and Solomon has suffered serious erosion.

Closely related to this reinterpretation of monumental architecture is Israel Finkelstein's extensive argument for the redating of many of the archaeological strata at several sites, including Megiddo, Hazor, and Gezer.[40] His proposal of an alternative, "low chronology" is based upon a more comprehensive classification of strata discernible across the board among the major sites and is supported by the dating of Philistine pottery and refined methods in carbon 14 dating.[41] This new chronology redates to later periods some strata at sites that were previously held to be eleventh, tenth, or ninth century, without impacting eighth-century strata, thus maintaining the current dating of most material remains known from the kingdoms of Israel and Judah.[42] Accordingly, Finkelstein rejects the traditional identification of material remains with a supposed Davidic–Solomonic kingdom of the tenth century and instead relocates most of the northern monumental architecture, fortifications, and public buildings previously dated to the tenth century to the ninth century—the period in which Omri and his immediate successors are already firmly attested as building a powerful kingdom.

As such, Finkelstein and his supporters now argue for the formation of the states of Israel and Judah as distinct episodes, separated both chronologically and territorially. Though Finkelstein's low chronology has not been accepted by all scholars in the field, the breadth and depth of his arguments have encouraged the modification of the conventional chronology used by more conservative scholars and symbolize another blow to the biblical assertion of a united monarchy.[43]

Settlement patterns also suggest that statehood came later to the Judahite region than the Hebrew Bible would suggest. Archaeological surveys indicate that until the eighth century, the settlement system in the Judahite highlands was neither extensive nor developed, consisting of only a few poor, small sites, thereby negating the possibility that Judah was a state in the tenth and ninth centuries.[44] Indications of some form of a developed state would include medium and large sites alongside the smaller ones evident in the Judahite hills at this time.[45] Importantly, though this does not preclude the possibility that a small Jerusalemite kingdom might have existed in the tenth and ninth centuries,[46] it does argue against the "statehood" of the larger Judahite region during this period.

Clear archaeological support from Jerusalem itself for a united monarchy or an early Judahite state is also lacking. The few architectural features recovered from the tenth- and ninth-century remains of Jerusalem are highly ambiguous. In particular, the large stepped-stone structure, popularly identified with the *millo* built by Solomon in 1 Kings 9:15 (cf. 2 Sam. 5:9; 1 Kings 11:27; 1 Chron. 11:8), and more recently associated with what building excavator Eilat Mazar describes as a palace,[47] has been redated by most to the Late Bronze Age, rendering its association with the Davidic–Solomonic period untenable.[48] In general, the increasing opinion is that in the tenth and ninth centuries BCE, Jerusalem was a small, poor, and remote highland stronghold with little—if anything—to distinguish it from other small fortified settlements in the Palestinian highlands.

It would appear that it was not until relatively late in the eighth century that Jerusalem expanded quite rapidly and became surrounded by wide, fortified walls.[49] This concurs with the results of David Jamieson-Drake's extensive and influential socioarchaeological analysis of Judah. In his assessment of the cultural nature and political status of this region, Jamieson-Drake argues that the production of luxury items is a fair indication of a centralized political establishment, reflecting a developed and complex economic system. Setting that alongside his analysis of demographic patterns and archaeological evidence, he argues that unambiguous evidence for developed statehood in Judah cannot be found before the eighth century BCE, complementing the conclusions of many other scholars.[50]

These summary observations indicate that the kingdoms of Israel and Judah developed independently and at different rates. Israel probably emerged as a state at least a century earlier than Judah: the northern region appears to have attained monarchic statehood by the ninth century BCE, growing rapidly into a prospering and powerful kingdom by the eighth century, whereas during the ninth century the Judahite region was little more than a collection of rural settlements and a few scattered strongholds, one of which was Jerusalem. Though this small fortified compound may well have had a "king" of sorts, it was not until at least the eighth century that the economic and political power of Jerusalem's elites brought about the city's regional domination in Judah.

The one dominant feature of the biblical portrait of a Davidic–Solomonic kingdom to remain a part of the modern historian's vista is David himself. The discovery in the 1990s of an Aramaic inscription on a broken stela at the ancient northern city of Dan is among the most celebrated archaeological discoveries of the past century. The so-called Tel Dan inscription is widely agreed to date to the late ninth or early eighth century BCE.[51] Although it is fragmentary and worn, its significance is found in its mention of a "king of Israel" and what is widely understood as a reference to the "House of David," (perhaps) presenting both as the losers in a battle won by an Aramaean king.[52] The latter designation is often understood to refer to the dynastic or assumed name of the kingdom of Judah,[53] and it is thought to offer the earliest nonbiblical attestation of the name David. As such, it has been used by some to support the case for the historicity of David himself.

However, the translation and interpretation of the inscription remains highly contested. Even if it is to be understood as referring to the "House of David," it testifies neither to the historicity of David nor to the cooperative coexistence of the kingdoms of Israel and Judah in the late ninth/early eighth century BCE. Rather, the designation "House of David" may refer simply to the city of Jerusalem or to the ruling family of the small, fortified settlement of Jerusalem and its dependent villages,[54] whose (perhaps legendary) ancestral founder was believed to be named David or perhaps "Beloved" (Hebrew *dwd*). It does not logically lead to the assumption that David was a historical figure; nor does it support the biblical claim that he and his son reigned over an expansive kingdom. Moreover, the mention of the "House of David" within an inscription that also mentions a "king of Israel" need not indicate the paralleling of their political stature or the fully fledged statehood of the "House of David." Simply put, the Tel Dan inscription can add little, if anything, to support the assumption that a verifiable archaeological history of Israel begins with David and his kingdom.

Instead, the historian is left with an uneven collection of archaeological material with which to attempt to reconstruct, even in its broadest outlines, a "history" of Israel. Some of this material might appear to be more reliable than other aspects—thus inscriptions and other written sources tend to be valued (whether explicitly acknowledged or not) above nonepigraphic evidence. But the historian is also aware that any archaeological data are only rendered "evidence" by means of interpretation, so that both the material and cultural contexts of any artifact must be considered and evaluated. Thus an inscription may appear to offer a direct testimony of an event, but any ancient inscription is also a product of the social, cultural, and ideological dynamics of its own context and is subsequently subject to the ideologies of the contexts in which it is received or "read," whether ancient or modern. In this sense, for example, Neo-Assyrian, Neo-Babylonian, or Persian texts are no less ideological than the literature of the Hebrew Bible.[55]

The use of the famous Cyrus Cylinder in historical reconstructions of Israel's past is a good example of the need for a critical approach to all available material. This inscription celebrates the conquest of Babylon by Cyrus the Great of Persia in 539 BCE and in a first-person narrative asserts that Cyrus himself permitted the restoration of Babylonian gods to their temples and the return of displaced communities to their native territories.[56] This inscription has been widely used to smooth conflicting biblical traditions about the timing and nature of a return of Judah's exiles and the rebuilding of the Temple in Jerusalem.[57] However, the Cyrus Cylinder neither refers to the Judahites nor gives any indication that the displaced peoples offered repatriation were any other than the Babylonian communities who had fallen victim to what is portrayed as the oppressive policies of the Neo-Babylonian regime. Rather, it is an example of ancient Persian propaganda, designed to legitimize Cyrus as the benevolent new ruler of Babylon, and can offer no explicit evidence about the nature of the early history of Yehud.[58] Instead, direct information about this period derives either from the biblical texts themselves, which are notoriously complex and contradictory in their presentation of the Persian era, or from the sparse and piecemeal material remains of communities in and around Yehud.

Any historian is thus faced with a choice as to how to adduce and weigh "evidence" of the past. While the extant material evidence for Israel's past from nonbiblical sources can provide a very rough framework of political events associated with the societies from which the biblical texts emerged, from the ninth century BCE through to the late Persian/ early Hellenistic period, major gaps and uncertainties remain. Beyond that, the extent to which the biblical literature could or should be used to fill these gaps largely depends on the individual scholar's judgment as to the perceived reliability of the texts and those who produced them.

CONCLUSION

The Hebrew Bible locates the earliest origins of Israel first in Eden and then in Abraham, the ancestor of the people, and the exodus, a journey from captivity to a homeland that is repeated in the experience of a return from exile. In contrast, historians locate the clearest *discernible* historical origins of Israel as a distinctive sociopolitical group among the northern highland communities of the ninth century. Both the Hebrew Bible and biblical scholarship agree that the northern kingdom of Israel was destroyed in the eighth century, with the final demise of the kingdom of Judah, and the deportation of its elites, following in its wake in the sixth century. Beyond this, there is little consensus. Most agree that a community identifying itself as the descendents of the deported Judahites established itself in and around Jerusalem in the fifth and fourth centuries and that their Temple in the city would eventually emerge as the politically and culturally dominant religious center of the new "Israel." This is the group by whom, and for whom, most of the texts of the Hebrew Bible were compiled, in roughly the form they are found today.

As such, these biblical texts can only offer a version of the past, just as scholarly reconstructions of the history of Israel can only provide their readers with alternative versions of that past. Both types of writing are shaped by the priorities and preferences of their authors. For the writers and compilers of the biblical texts, one of those priorities was the construction of a religious portrait of a people they called "Israel," whose identity, longevity, and culture were authoritatively inscribed by a particular theological and ideological worldview. For biblical scholars, the "authoritative" inscribing of Israel's past depends on the relative worth of archaeological evidence over biblical testimony. Some take this testimony reasonably seriously and cast the Hebrew Bible as a primary—if theologically loaded—historical source; others prefer to privilege the witness of nonbiblical sources and archaeological artifacts and to view the biblical literature as a secondary resource, to be handled with caution. Ultimately, it is up to each reader of the past to decide.

NOTES

1. See, for example, 2 Chron. 36:22–23; Ezra 1:1–11, 4:3–11, 6:14; Neh. 2:1, 12:22; Isa. 44:28; 45:1, 13.

2. Matt. 27:1–24; Mark 15:1–15, 43; Luke 3:1; 23:1–25, 52; John 18:29–40, 19:1–38; Acts 3:13, 4:27, 13:28; 1 Tim. 6:13.

3. See further J. D. Levenson, *The Hebrew Bible, the Old Testament, and Historical Criticism* (Louisville, Ky.: Westminster/John Knox, 1993); J. Barton, *The Nature of Biblical Criticism* (Louisville, Ky.: Westminster John Knox, 2007), pp. 117–36.

4. T. W. Davis, *Shifting Sands: The Rise and Fall of Biblical Archaeology* (Oxford: Oxford University Press, 2004).

5. See T. Levy, ed., *The Archaeology of Society in the Holy Land* (New York: Continuum, 1998); I. Finkelstein and N. A. Silberman, *The Bible Unearthed: Archaeology's New Vision of Ancient Israel and the Origins of Its Sacred Texts* (New York: Free Press, 2001).

6. E. Said, *Orientalism: Western Conceptions of the Orient* (London: Routledge, 1978).

7. See especially K. W. Whitelam, *The Invention of Ancient Israel: The Silencing of Palestinian History* (London: Routledge, 1996).

8. E.g., P. R. Davies, *In Search of "Ancient Israel,"* Journal for the Study of the Old Testament Supplement 148 (Sheffield: Sheffield Academic Press, 1992); T. L. Thompson, *Early History of the Israelite People from the Written and Archaeological Sources*, Studies in the History of the Ancient Near East 4 (Leiden: Brill, 1992); L. L. Grabbe, *Can a "History of Israel" Be Written?* Journal for the Study of the Old Testament Supplement 245 (Sheffield: Sheffield Academic Press, 1997).

9. N. Morley, *Writing Ancient History* (Ithaca, N.Y.: Cornell University Press, 1999), p. 15.

10. Cf. M. B. Moore, *Philosophy and Practice in Writing a History of Ancient Israel*, Library of Hebrew Bible/Old Testament Supplement 437 (New York: T&T Clark, 2006); P. R. Davies, *Memories of Ancient Israel: An Introduction to Biblical History—Ancient and Modern* (Louisville, Ky.: Westminster John Knox, 2008).

11. Note, e.g., the discrepancies among Gen. 48:5; Num. 2–3; Deut. 27:12–13, 33:6; Judg. 5:14–18; 2 Sam. 19:43; 1 Kings 11:31.

12. For a discussion of the so-called Documentary Hypothesis, see J. Barton, *Reading the Old Testament: Method in Biblical Study* (London: Dartman, Longman and Todd, 1984); J. Van Seters, *The Edited Bible: The Curious History of the "Editor" in Biblical Criticism* (Winona Lake, Ind.: Eisenbrauns, 2006). For a recent defense of the theory, see J. S. Baden, *The Composition of the Pentateuch: Renewing the Documentary Hypothesis*, Anchor Yale Bible Reference Library (New Haven, Conn.: Yale University Press, 2012).

13. See further K. van der Toorn, *Scribal Culture and the Making of the Hebrew Bible* (Cambridge, Mass.: Harvard University Press, 2007).

14. See further M. Liverani, *Israel's History and the History of Israel*, C. Peri and P. R. Davies, trans. (London: Equinox, 2003), pp. 250–91.

15. R. Kittel, *Great Men and Movements in Israel* (London: Williams and Norgate, 1925); cf. H.G.M. Williamson, ed., *Understanding the History of Ancient Israel*, Proceedings of the British Academy, 143 (Oxford: Oxford University Press, 2007), p. xiii.

16. T. L. Thompson, *The Historicity of the Patriarchal Narratives: The Quest for the Historical Abraham*, Beihefte zur Zeitschrift für die alttestamentliche Wissenschaft 133 (Berlin: de Gruyter, 1974); J. Van Seters, *Abraham in History and Tradition* (New Haven, Conn.: Yale University Press, 1975).

17. See further M. B. Moore and B. E. Kelle, *Biblical History and Israel's Past: The Changing Study of the Bible and History* (Grand Rapids, Mich.: Eerdmans, 2011), pp. 77–95.

18. J. K. Hoffmeier, *Israel in Egypt: The Evidence for the Authenticity of the Exodus Tradition* (Oxford: Oxford University Press, 1997); K. A. Kitchen, *On the Reliability of the Old Testament* (Grand Rapids, Mich.: Eerdmans, 2003).

19. D. B. Redford, "An Egyptological Perspective on the Exodus Narrative," in A. F. Rainey, ed., *Egypt, Israel, Sinai: Archaeological and Historical Relationships in the Biblical Period* (Tel Aviv: Tel Aviv University Kaplan Project on the History of Israel and Egypt, 1987), pp. 137–61; D. B. Redford, *Egypt, Canaan and Israel in Ancient Times* (Princeton, N.J.: Princeton University Press, 1992).

20. S. C. Russell, *Images of Egypt in Early Biblical Literature: Cisjordan-Israelite, Transjordan Israelite, and Judahite Portrayals*, Beihefte zur Zeitschrift für die alttestamentliche Wissenschaft 403 (Berlin: de Gruyter, 2009); cf. K. L. Noll, "An Alternative Hypothesis for a Historical Exodus Event," *Scandinavian Journal of the Old Testament* 14 (2000): pp. 260–74.

21. N. P. Lemche, *The Israelites in History and Tradition* (Louisville, Ky.: Westminster John Knox, 1998), pp. 86–95; Liverani, *Israel's History and the History of Israel*, pp. 277–82.

22. For some, a reference to a group called "Israel" on the Merneptah Stela (late thirteenth century BCE) is thought to be related to these settlements. However, the extent to which the stela offers any information about the social or topographical location of this "Israel" is limited; see further D. V. Edelman, "Ethnicity and Early Israel," in M. G. Brett, ed., *Ethnicity and the Bible* (Leiden: Brill, 1996), pp. 25–55. On the problems of ascribing and claiming the "ethnic" distinctiveness of Israel and Judah, see R. Kletter, "Can a Proto-Israelite Please Stand Up? Notes on the Ethnicity of Iron Age Israel and Judah," in A. M. Maeir and P. de Miroschedji, eds., *"I Will Speak the Riddle of Ancient Times": Archaeological and Historical Studies in Honor of Amihai Mazar on the Occasion of His Sixtieth Birthday* (Winona Lake, Ind.: Eisenbrauns, 2006), pp. 573–86. On the

vexed issue of ethnicity in ancient societies more generally, see S. Jones, *The Archaeology of Ethnicity: Constructing Identities in the Past and Present* (London: Routledge, 1997).

23. See further A. R. Millard, "Kings and External Textual Sources: Assyrian, Babylonian and North-West Semitic," in B. Halpern, A. Lemaire, and M. J. Adams, eds., *The Books of Kings: Sources, Composition, Historiography and Reception*, Vetus Testamentum Supplement 129 (Leiden: Brill, 2010), pp. 185–202.

24. L. L. Grabbe, *Ancient Israel: What Do We Know and How Do We Know It?* (London: T&T Clark, 2007), p. 190.

25. "Yehud" and "Samaria/Samerina" are the names given to the Persian provinces of the regions roughly related to the former kingdoms of Judah and Israel. See L. L. Grabbe, *A History of the Jews and Judaism in the Second Temple Period*, vol. 1, *Yehud: A History of the Persian Province of Judah* (New York: T&T Clark, 2004).

26. On Jehu, see J. M. Robker, *The Jehu Revolution: A Royal Tradition of the Northern Kingdom and Its Ramifications*, Beihefte zur Zeitschrift für die alttestamentliche Wissenschaft 435 (Berlin: de Gruyter, 2012). On the debates surrounding the iconography of the Black Obelisk, see C. Uehlinger, "Neither Eyewitnesses, Nor Windows to the Past, but Valuable Testimony in Its Own Right: Remarks on Iconography, Source Criticism and Ancient Data-Processing," in Williamson, *Understanding the History of Ancient Israel*, pp. 173–228.

27. The claim in 2 Chron. 33:11–12 that Manasseh was captured by Neo-Assyrians and taken to Babylon has been cited by some scholars to argue that this tradition was known in some biblical circles but suppressed for theological purposes in the account of his reign in Kings. See further F. Stavrakopoulou, *King Manasseh and Child Sacrifice: Biblical Distortions of Historical Realities*, Beihefte zur Zeitschrift für die alttestamentliche Wissenschaft 338 (Berlin: de Gruyter, 2004).

28. Josh. 10:3, 5, 23, 31–35; 12:11; 15:39; 2 Kings 14:19; 2 Chron. 11:9, 25:27; Jer. 34:7; Mic. 1:13; Neh. 11:30.

29. See further Uehlinger, "'Neither Eyewitnesses, Nor Windows to the Past, but Valuable Testimony in Its Own Right," pp. 211–19; cf. D. Ussishkin, *The Conquest of Lachish by Sennacherib* (Tel Aviv: Institute of Archaeology/Tel Aviv University, 1982).

30. K.A.D. Smelik, "Moabite Inscriptions," in W. W. Hallo and K. L. Younger Jr., eds., *The Context of Scripture*, 3 vols. (Leiden: Brill, 1997–2003), 2.137–38. See also A. Dearman, ed., *Studies in the Mesha Inscription and Moab*, Archaeology and Biblical Studies 2 (Atlanta: Scholars Press, 1989); A. Lemaire, "West Semitic Inscriptions and Ninth-Century BCE Ancient Israel," in Williamson, *Understanding the History of Ancient Israel*, pp. 279–303.

31. Millard, "Kings and External Textual Sources," pp. 189–90.

32. This remark is made of only one other king, the Judahite monarch Jehoshaphat (1 Kings 22:45).

33. A. Zertal, "The Heart of the Monarchy: Pattern of Settlement and Historical Considerations of the Israelite Kingdom of Samaria," in A. Mazar, ed., *Studies in the Archaeology of the Iron Age in Israel and Jordan*, Journal for the Study of the Old Testament Supplement 331 (Sheffield: Sheffield Academic Press, 2001), pp. 38–64.

34. See the summaries in I. Finkelstein and A. Mazar, *The Quest for the Historical Israel: Debating Archaeology and the History of Early Israel*, B. B. Schmidt, ed., Society of Biblical Literature Anchor Bible 17 (Atlanta: Society of Biblical Literature, 2007);

A. Mazar, "The Spade and the Text: The Interaction between Archaeology and Israelite History in Relating to the Tenth–Ninth Centuries BCE," in Williamson, *Understanding the History of Ancient Israel*, pp. 143–71.

35. W. G. Dever, *What Did the Biblical Writers Know, and When Did They Know It? What Archaeology Can Tell Us about the Reality of Ancient Israel* (Grand Rapids, Mich.: Eerdmans, 2001), p. 130. See further R. Kletter, "Pots and Polities: Material Remains of Late Iron Age Judah in Relation to Its Borders," *Bulletin of the American Schools of Oriental Research* 314 (1999): pp. 19–54.

36. Y. Yadin, *Hazor, the Head of All Those Kingdoms*, Schweich Lectures of the British Academy 1970 (London: Oxford University Press, 1972), pp. 135–64; W. G. Dever, "Solomon and the Assyrian 'Palaces' at Gezer," *Israel Exploration Journal* 35 (1985): pp. 217–30; J. S. Holladay, "The Kingdoms of Israel and Judah: Political and Economic Centralization in the Iron IIA–B," in T. E. Levy, ed., *The Archaeology of Society in the Holy Land* (London: Leicester University Press, 1995), pp. 368–98; B. Halpern, *David's Secret Demons: Messiah, Murderer, Traitor, King* (Grand Rapids, Mich.: Eerdmans, 2003), pp. 433–50.

37. See further Moore and Kelle, *Biblical History and Israel's Past*, pp. 165–92.

38. E.g., D. Milson, "The Design of the Royal Gates at Megiddo, Hazor, and Gezer," *Zeitschrift des Deutschen Palästina-Vereins* 102 (1986): pp. 87–92; D. Ussishkin, "Was the 'Solomonic' City Gate at Megiddo Built by King Solomon?" *Bulletin of the American Schools of Oriental Research* 239 (1980): pp. 1–18; G. W. Ahlström, *The History of Ancient Palestine* (Minneapolis: Fortress Press, 1993), pp. 525–26; H. M. Niemann, "Megiddo and Solomon: A Biblical Investigation in Relation to Archaeology," *Tel Aviv* 27 (2000): pp. 61–74.

39. Mazar, "Spade and the Text," pp. 155–57.

40. Finkelstein has published a number of scholarly and popular works on this. For convenience, see I. Finkelstein, "The Archaeology of the United Monarchy: An Alternative View," *Levant* 28 (1996): pp. 177–87; I. Finkelstein, "State Formation in Israel and Judah," *Near Eastern Archaeology* 62 (1999): pp. 35–52; Finkelstein and Silberman, *Bible Unearthed*; Finkelstein and Mazar, *Quest for the Historical Israel*.

41. Finkelstein, "State Formation in Israel and Judah," pp. 36–39.

42. Ibid., p. 39.

43. See Mazar, "Spade and the Text," pp. 148–49.

44. See further Moore and Kelle, *Biblical History and Israel's Past*, pp. 300–302.

45. Finkelstein, "State Formation in Israel and Judah," p. 42.

46. M. Steiner, "Jerusalem in the Tenth and Seventh Centuries BCE: From Administrative Town to Commercial City," in Mazar, *Studies in the Archaeology of the Iron Age in Israel and Jordan*, pp. 280–88, esp. 283; A. Ofer, "The Monarchic Period in the Judaean Highland: A Spatial Overview," in Mazar, *Studies in the Archaeology of the Iron Age in Israel and Jordan*, pp. 14–37; E. A. Knauf, "Jerusalem in the Late Bronze and Early Iron Ages: A Proposal," *Tel Aviv* 27 (2000): pp. 75–90.

47. This view is summarized in E. Mazar, "Did I Find King David's Palace?" *Biblical Archaeology Review* 32 (2006): pp. 16–27, 70.

48. Finkelstein, "State Formation in Israel and Judah," p. 40. See further J. M. Cahill and D. Tarler, "Respondents," in A. Biran and J. Aviram, eds., *Biblical Archaeology Today* (Jerusalem: Israel Exploration Society, 1993), pp. 625–26; L. E. Stager, "The Archaeology

of the East Slope of Jerusalem and the Terraces of Kidron," *Journal of Near Eastern Studies* 41 (1982): pp. 111–24; Y. Shiloh, "Jerusalem," in E. Stern, ed., *The New Encyclopedia of Archaeological Excavations in the Holy Land* (Jerusalem: Israel Exploration Society; and New York: Simon and Schuster, 1993), 2.705–8.

49. M. Steiner, "A Note on the Iron Age Defence Wall on the Ophel Hill of Jerusalem," *Palestine Exploration Quarterly* 118 (1986): pp. 27–32.

50. D. W. Jamieson-Drake, *Scribes and Schools in Monarchic Judah: A Socio-archaeological Approach*, Social World of Biblical Antiquity 9/Journal for the Study of the Old Testament Supplement 109 (Sheffield: JSOT Press, 1991); E. A. Knauf, "From History to Interpretation," in D. V. Edelman, ed., *The Fabric of History: Text, Artifact and Israel's Past*, Journal for the Study of the Old Testament Supplement 127 (Sheffield: JSOT Press, 1991), pp. 26–64; Thompson, *Early History of the Israelite People from the Written and Archaeological Sources*, pp. 407–12.

51. A. Biran and J. Naveh, "An Aramaic Fragment from Tel Dan," *Israel Exploration Journal* 43 (1993): pp. 81–98; A. Biran and J. Naveh, "The Tel Dan Inscription: A New Fragment," *Israel Exploration Journal* 45 (1995): pp. 1–18; G. Athas, *The Tel Dan Inscription: A Reappraisal and a New Interpretation*, Journal for the Study of the Old Testament Supplement 360 (Sheffield: Sheffield Academic Press, 2003).

52. The inscription is frequently (and all too hastily) related to the description of Jehu's coup in 2 Kings 9–10. For a useful discussion of this point, see Lemaire, "West Semitic Inscriptions and Ninth-Century BCE Ancient Israel," pp. 293–97.

53. Although the reference to a "king of Israel" is fairly secure, the rendering of the phrase *bytdwd* as "House of David" is disputed, not least because it occurs without the expected word dividers, which are employed elsewhere throughout the inscription. Alternative interpretations of *bytdwd* include the interrelated renderings of *dwd* as a toponym or as a divine name or epithet. For a detailed discussion of these possibilities, see Athas, *Tel Dan Inscription*, pp. 217–26.

54. Ibid., pp. 223–24, 275–81.

55. See the discussion in D. C. Polaski, "What Mean These Stones? Inscriptions, Textuality and Power in Persia and Yehud," in J. L. Berquist, ed., *Approaching Yehud: New Approaches to the Study of the Persian Period* (Atlanta: Society of Biblical Literature, 2007), pp. 37–48.

56. M. Cogan, "Achaemend Inscriptions," in W. W. Hallo and K. L. Younger Jr., eds., *The Context of Scripture*, 3 vols. (Leiden: Brill, 1997–2003), 2.314–16.

57. On the complexity of biblical material pertaining to the communities in Yehud, and the scarcity of archaeological evidence, see Grabbe, *History of the Jews and Judaism in the Second Temple Period*; O. Lipschits and M. Oeming, eds., *Judah and the Judeans in the Persian Period* (Grand Rapids, Mich.: Eerdmans, 2006); D. V. Edelman, *The Origins of the "Second" Temple: Persian Imperial Policy and the Rebuilding of Jerusalem* (London: Equinox, 2005).

58. A. Kuhrt, "The Cyrus Cylinder and Achaemenid Imperial Policy," *Journal for the Study of the Old Testament* 25 (1983): pp. 83–97.

FURTHER READING

Ahlström, G. W., *The History of Ancient Palestine* (Minneapolis: Fortress Press, 1993).

Athas, G., *The Tel Dan Inscription: A Reappraisal and a New Interpretation*, Journal for the Study of the Old Testament Supplement 360 (Sheffield: Sheffield Academic Press, 2003).

Baden, J. S., *The Composition of the Pentateuch: Renewing the Documentary Hypothesis*, Anchor Yale Bible Reference Library (New Haven, Conn.: Yale University Press, 2012).

Barton, J., *The Nature of Biblical Criticism* (Louisville, Ky.: Westminster John Knox, 2007).

Barton, J., *Reading the Old Testament: Method in Biblical Study* (London: Dartman, Longman and Todd, 1984).

Biran, A., and J. Naveh, "An Aramaic Fragment from Tel Dan," *Israel Exploration Journal* 43 (1993): pp. 81–98.

Biran, A., and J. Naveh, "The Tel Dan Inscription: A New Fragment," *Israel Exploration Journal* 45 (1995): pp. 1–18.

Cahill, J. M., and D. Tarler, "Respondents," in A. Biran and J. Aviram, eds., *Biblical Archaeology Today* (Jerusalem: Israel Exploration Society, 1993), pp. 625–26.

Davies, P. R., *In Search of "Ancient Israel,"* Journal for the Study of the Old Testament Supplement 148 (Sheffield: Sheffield Academic Press, 1992).

Davies, P. R., *Memories of Ancient Israel: An Introduction to Biblical History—Ancient and Modern* (Louisville, Ky.: Westminster John Knox, 2008).

Davis, T. W., *Shifting Sands: The Rise and Fall of Biblical Archaeology* (Oxford: Oxford University Press, 2004).

Dearman, A., ed., *Studies in the Mesha Inscription and Moab*, Archaeology and Biblical Studies 2 (Atlanta: Scholars Press, 1989).

Dever, W. G., "Solomon and the Assyrian 'Palaces' at Gezer," *Israel Exploration Journal* 35 (1985): pp. 217–30.

Dever, W. G., *What Did the Biblical Writers Know, and When Did They Know It? What Archaeology Can Tell Us about the Reality of Ancient Israel* (Grand Rapids, Mich.: Eerdmans, 2001).

Edelman, D. V., "Ethnicity and Early Israel," in M. G. Brett, ed., *Ethnicity and the Bible* (Leiden: Brill, 1996), pp. 25–55.

Edelman, D. V., *The Origins of the "Second" Temple: Persian Imperial Policy and the Rebuilding of Jerusalem* (London: Equinox, 2005).

Finkelstein, I., "The Archaeology of the United Monarchy: An Alternative View," *Levant* 28 (1996): pp. 177–87.

Finkelstein, I., "State Formation in Israel and Judah," *Near Eastern Archaeology* 62 (1999): pp. 35–52.

Finkelstein, I., and A. Mazar, *The Quest for the Historical Israel: Debating Archaeology and the History of Early Israel*, B. B. Schmidt, ed., Society of Biblical Literature Anchor Bible 17 (Atlanta: Society of Biblical Literature, 2007).

Finkelstein, I., and N. A. Silberman, *The Bible Unearthed: Archaeology's New Vision of Ancient Israel and the Origins of Its Sacred Texts* (New York: Free Press, 2001).

Grabbe, L. L., *Ancient Israel: What Do We Know and How Do We Know It?* (London: T&T Clark, 2007).

Grabbe, L. L., *Can a "History of Israel" Be Written?* Journal for the Study of the Old Testament Supplement 245 (Sheffield: Sheffield Academic Press, 1997).

Grabbe, L. L., *A History of the Jews and Judaism in the Second Temple Period,* vol. 1, *Yehud: A History of the Persian Province of Judah* (New York: T&T Clark, 2004).

Halpern, B., *David's Secret Demons: Messiah, Murderer, Traitor, King* (Grand Rapids, Mich.: Eerdmans, 2003).

Hoffmeier, J. K., *Israel in Egypt: The Evidence for the Authenticity of the Exodus Tradition* (Oxford: Oxford University Press, 1997).

Holladay, J. S., "The Kingdoms of Israel and Judah: Political and Economic Centralization in the Iron IIA–B," in T. E. Levy, ed., *The Archaeology of Society in the Holy Land* (London: Leicester University Press, 1995), pp. 368–98.

Jamieson-Drake, D. W., *Scribes and Schools in Monarchic Judah: A Socio-archaeological Approach,* Social World of Biblical Antiquity 9/Journal for the Study of the Old Testament Supplement 109 (Sheffield: JSOT Press, 1991).

Jones, S., *The Archaeology of Ethnicity: Constructing Identities in the Past and Present* (London: Routledge, 1997).

Kitchen, K. A., *On the Reliability of the Old Testament* (Grand Rapids, Mich.: Eerdmans, 2003).

Kittel, R., *Great Men and Movements in Israel* (London: Williams and Norgate, 1925).

Kletter, R., "Can a Proto-Israelite Please Stand Up? Notes on the Ethnicity of Iron Age Israel and Judah," in A. M. Maeir and P. de Miroschedji, eds., *"I Will Speak the Riddle of Ancient Times": Archaeological and Historical Studies in Honor of Amihai Mazar on the Occasion of His Sixtieth Birthday* (Winona Lake, Ind.: Eisenbrauns, 2006), pp. 573–86.

Kletter, R., "Pots and Polities: Material Remains of Late Iron Age Judah in Relation to Its Borders," *Bulletin of the American Schools of Oriental Research* 314 (1999): pp. 19–54.

Knauf, E. A., "From History to Interpretation," in D. V. Edelman, ed., *The Fabric of History: Text, Artifact and Israel's Past,* Journal for the Study of the Old Testament Supplement 127 (Sheffield: JSOT Press, 1991), pp. 26–64.

Knauf, E. A., "Jerusalem in the Late Bronze and Early Iron Ages: A Proposal," *Tel Aviv* 27 (2000): pp. 75–90.

Kuhrt, A., "The Cyrus Cylinder and Achaemenid Imperial Policy," *Journal for the Study of the Old Testament* 25 (1983): pp. 83–97.

Lemaire, A., "West Semitic Inscriptions and Ninth-Century BCE Ancient Israel," in H.G.M. Williamson, ed., *Understanding the History of Ancient Israel,* Proceedings of the British Academy 143 (Oxford: Oxford University Press, 2007), pp. 279–303.

Lemche, N. P., *The Israelites in History and Tradition* (Louisville, Ky.: Westminster John Knox, 1998).

Levenson, J. D., *The Hebrew Bible, the Old Testament, and Historical Criticism* (Louisville, Ky.: Westminster/John Knox, 1993).

Levy, T., ed., *The Archaeology of Society in the Holy Land* (New York: Continuum, 1998).

Lipschits, O., and M. Oeming, eds., *Judah and the Judeans in the Persian Period* (Grand Rapids, Mich.: Eerdmans, 2006).

Liverani, M., *Israel's History and the History of Israel,* C. Peri and P. R. Davies, trans. (London: Equinox, 2003).

Mazar, A., "The Spade and the Text: The Interaction between Archaeology and Israelite History in Relating to the Tenth–Ninth Centuries BCE," in H.G.M. Williamson, ed.,

Understanding the History of Ancient Israel, Proceedings of the British Academy 143 (Oxford: Oxford University Press, 2007), pp. 143–71.

Mazar, E., "Did I Find King David's Palace?" *Biblical Archaeology Review* 32 (2006): pp. 16–27, 70.

Millard, A. R., "Kings and External Textual Sources: Assyrian, Babylonian and North-West Semitic," in B. Halpern, A. Lemaire, and M. J. Adams, eds., *The Books of Kings: Sources, Composition, Historiography and Reception*, Vetus Testamentum Supplement 129 (Leiden: Brill, 2010), pp. 185–202.

Milson, D., "The Design of the Royal Gates at Megiddo, Hazor, and Gezer," *Zeitschrift des Deutschen Palästina-Vereins* 102 (1986): pp. 87–92.

Moore, M. B., *Philosophy and Practice in Writing a History of Ancient Israel*, Library of Hebrew Bible/Old Testament Supplement 437 (New York: T&T Clark, 2006).

Moore, M. B., and B. E. Kelle, *Biblical History and Israel's Past: The Changing Study of the Bible and History* (Grand Rapids, Mich.: Eerdmans, 2011).

Morley, N., *Writing Ancient History* (Ithaca, N.Y.: Cornell University Press, 1999).

Niemann, H. M., "Megiddo and Solomon: A Biblical Investigation in Relation to Archaeology," *Tel Aviv* 27 (2000): pp. 61–74.

Noll, K. L., "An Alternative Hypothesis for a Historical Exodus Event," *Scandinavian Journal of the Old Testament* 14 (2000): pp. 260–74.

Ofer, A., "The Monarchic Period in the Judaean Highland: A Spatial Overview," in A. Mazar, ed., *Studies in the Archaeology of the Iron Age in Israel and Jordan*, Journal for the Study of the Old Testament Supplement 331 (Sheffield: Sheffield Academic Press, 2001), pp. 14–37.

Redford, D. B., *Egypt, Canaan and Israel in Ancient Times* (Princeton, N.J.: Princeton University Press, 1992).

Redford, D. B., "An Egyptological Perspective on the Exodus Narrative," in A. F. Rainey, ed., *Egypt, Israel, Sinai: Archaeological and Historical Relationships in the Biblical Period* (Tel Aviv: Tel Aviv University Kaplan Project on the History of Israel and Egypt, 1987), pp. 137–61.

Robker, J. M., *The Jehu Revolution: A Royal Tradition of the Northern Kingdom and Its Ramifications*, Beihefte zur Zeitschrift für die alttestamentliche Wissenschaft 435 (Berlin: de Gruyter, 2012).

Russell, S. C., *Images of Egypt in Early Biblical Literature: Cisjordan-Israelite, Transjordan Israelite, and Judahite Portrayals*, Beihefte zur Zeitschrift für die alttestamentliche Wissenschaft 403 (Berlin: de Gruyter, 2009).

Said, E., *Orientalism: Western Conceptions of the Orient* (London: Routledge, 1978).

Shiloh, Y., "Jerusalem," in E. Stern, ed., *The New Encyclopedia of Archaeological Excavations in the Holy Land*, 4 vols. (Jerusalem: Israel Exploration Society; and New York: Simon and Schuster, 1993), 2.705–8.

Smelik, K.A.D., "Moabite Inscriptions," in W. W. Hallo and K. L. Younger Jr., eds., *The Context of Scripture*, 3 vols. (Leiden: Brill, 2000), 2.137–38.

Stager, L. E., "The Archaeology of the East Slope of Jerusalem and the Terraces of Kidron," *Journal of Near Eastern Studies* 41 (1982): pp. 111–24.

Stavrakopoulou, F., *King Manasseh and Child Sacrifice: Biblical Distortions of Historical Realities*, Beihefte zur Zeitschrift für die alttestamentliche Wissenschaft 338 (Berlin: de Gruyter, 2004).

Steiner, M., "Jerusalem in the Tenth and Seventh Centuries BCE: From Administrative Town to Commercial City," in A. Mazar, ed., *Studies in the Archaeology of the Iron Age in Israel and Jordan*, Journal for the Study of the Old Testament Supplement 331 (Sheffield: Sheffield Academic Press, 2001), pp. 280–88.

Steiner, M., "A Note on the Iron Age Defence Wall on the Ophel Hill of Jerusalem," *Palestine Exploration Quarterly* 118 (1986): pp. 27–32.

Thompson, T. L., *Early History of the Israelite People from the Written and Archaeological Sources*, Studies in the History of the Ancient Near East 4 (Leiden: Brill, 1992).

Thompson, T. L., *The Historicity of the Patriarchal Narratives: The Quest for the Historical Abraham*, Beihefte zur Zeitschrift für die alttestamentliche Wissenschaft 133 (Berlin: de Gruyter, 1974).

Toorn, K. van der, *Scribal Culture and the Making of the Hebrew Bible* (Cambridge, Mass.: Harvard University Press, 2007).

Uehlinger, C., "Neither Eyewitnesses, Nor Windows to the Past, but Valuable Testimony in Its Own Right: Remarks on Iconography, Source Criticism and Ancient Data-Processing," in H.G.M. Williamson, ed., *Understanding the History of Ancient Israel*, Proceedings of the British Academy 143 (Oxford: Oxford University Press, 2007), pp. 173–228.

Ussishkin, D., *The Conquest of Lachish by Sennacherib* (Tel Aviv: Institute of Archaeology/Tel Aviv University, 1982).

Ussishkin, D., "Was the 'Solomonic' City Gate at Megiddo Built by King Solomon?" *Bulletin of the American Schools of Oriental Research* 239 (1980): pp. 1–18.

Van Seters, J., *Abraham in History and Tradition* (New Haven, Conn.: Yale University Press, 1975).

Van Seters, J., *The Edited Bible: The Curious History of the "Editor" in Biblical Criticism* (Winona Lake, Ind.: Eisenbrauns, 2006).

Whitelam, K. W., *The Invention of Ancient Israel: The Silencing of Palestinian History* (London: Routledge, 1996).

Williamson, H.G.M., ed., *Understanding the History of Ancient Israel*, Proceedings of the British Academy 143 (Oxford: Oxford University Press, 2007).

Yadin, Y., *Hazor, the Head of All Those Kingdoms*, Schweich Lectures of the British Academy 1970 (London: Oxford University Press, 1972).

Zertal, A., "The Heart of the Monarchy: Pattern of Settlement and Historical Considerations of the Israelite Kingdom of Samaria," in A. Mazar, ed., *Studies in the Archaeology of the Iron Age in Israel and Jordan*, Journal for the Study of the Old Testament Supplement 331 (Sheffield: Sheffield Academic Press, 2001), pp. 38–64.

3

❀

The Social and Cultural History of Ancient Israel

Katherine Southwood

METHODS OF APPROACHING ISRAEL'S SOCIAL AND CULTURAL HISTORY

Much of what we know regarding Israel's social and cultural history has emerged through the use of social scientific methods. Such approaches are usually interdisciplinary, looking to information from the social sciences (e.g., anthropology, economics, psychology, politics, sociology) and using them as a means of understanding the Hebrew Bible. Although this method has gained increasing popularity within the last thirty years, the approach itself is actually rather more long-standing. During the nineteenth century, William Robertson-Smith (1885, 1889) published work on kinship, marriage, and ethnicity. Two publications were particularly important, as can be seen from the numerous reprints of the works, and these are *Kinship and Marriage in Early Arabia* (Robertson-Smith 1885, reprinted in 1903, 1907, and 1967) and *Lectures on the Religion of the Semites* (Robertson-Smith 1889, reprinted in 1894, 1927, 1956, 1969, and 1997). Similarly, ethnicity was the topic of Causse's (1937) work, which argued that Israel began as an ethnic pastoral nomadic community but gradually lost its organic solidarity, a change that was principally due to the pressure and attraction of Canaanite civilization. However, although the social sciences remain in use among modern scholars, greater attention is now devoted to the question of method. Nowadays, the approach is designed to generate new insights into the Hebrew Bible; as Esler argues, "Social-scientific interpretation undertaken by the overwhelming majority of its practitioners is a heuristic process. It fires the social-scientific imagination to ask new questions of data" (2006:3).

However, it should be recognized that those making use of the social sciences nowadays acknowledge that the method hinges on certain presuppositions. First, "the text has a certain ideology. . . . [I]t is a meaning-ful instrument of communication" (Botha 2002:1407). Thus, the "social features of the form and context of texts and the conditioning factors and intended consequences of the communication process" can be ex-amined (Elliott 2001:10). Second, the biblical material contains encoded information regarding the social and cultural systems in which it origi-nated (Elliott 1993:50). Thus, the text acts as a reflection of, and response to, a specific construction of a social and cultural situation. Therefore, social scientific investigation aims to expose the social and cultural di-mensions of a text and to correlate these matters with its literary features in order to determine how and what it was intended to communicate (Elliott 1993:70). However, increasing awareness of the Hebrew Bible's socially constructed nature has accompanied the increased awareness of methods and theories. Thus attention is paid to the possible social loca-tions of those writing and editing the texts, sometimes resulting in the argument that what we have in biblical literature hardly represents the interests and concerns of the general society but, rather, the concerns of the tiny literate elite, that is, those in power (Frick 2002).

Several serious methodological problems have led to skepticism re-garding the method's validity. The most popular of these is anachronism; if modern theories such as those emerging within ethnicity, for example, are applied to the Hebrew Bible, then surely the level of correlation will be low owing to the temporal distance that separates the material from modern times. As Sadler explains, "To ask the Bible to speak to issues of race is like asking it for instruction on airplanes, cellular phones, and cable television" (2006:387). Many responses to the charge of anachro-nism exist; simply because the Hebrew Bible does not speak directly about issues such as race, it does not mean that such issues do not exist. There are plenty of terms, if we use ethnicity as an example, that refer to foreigners or foreignness in the Hebrew Bible and in the Greek Septua-gint. For example, Hebrew terms exist to describe "foreigners," includ-ing *necar* (foreigner), *zar* (stranger), and *ger* (sojourner, one who stands somewhere between a "native" [*ezrach*] and a foreigner). In the niphal and *hithpael* forms, the root *ncr* means to "dissemble/conceal one's iden-tity" (Prov. 26:24; Gen. 42:7; 1 Kings 14:5ff.), and in the *piel* form it can mean "alienate" (Jer. 19:4; Sir. 11:12). This difference is also echoed in the Septuagint's selection of words. The niphal is rendered with the Greek term *epineiein*, "nod to" (Prov. 26:24); the *piel*, with the Greek term *apallotrioun*, "alienate"; and the *hithpael*, with the Greek terms *apochenoun*, *allotrioun*, and *diestrammenos*. Similarly, there are plenty of features in the material that correlate to modern definitions of ethnicity. For example, a wealth of biblical scholars utilizing ethnicity cite Hutchinson and Smith's (1996:6–7) list of ethnicity's distinguishing features (such as groups with a common proper name, common ancestry, shared historical memories, elements of common culture, links to the homeland, and a sense of solidarity) and are able to find such features of society in parts of the Hebrew Bible.

Nevertheless, the concerns pertaining to anachronism must be taken seriously if it is to be avoided. A similar problem is that of spatial distance. Many concepts emerge from Westernized studies that have little relevance to ancient Israel. One means of avoiding this problem that is adopted, especially by anthropologists, is to aim for models that are cross-culturally continuous, that is, those whose relevance is not undermined by cultural distance.[1] As Frick notes, "There is among anthropologists a constant focus on the assessment of the extent to which their ethnographic data are truly comparable, especially in view of the drive for holism which characterizes the functionalist approach to human society" (1986:11).

A further problem, relating again to distance, concerns the inaccessibility of ancient Israel. Scholars cannot collect data through "participant observation" (that is, by observing a group through becoming involved within the group, sometimes over an extended period of time)[2] but must rely on textual and archaeological evidence, which is often incomplete or ideological. Effectively, this makes a scholar using anthropology as a tool for understanding the social and cultural history of ancient Israel vulnerable to the accusation of being an "armchair anthropologist," who does not actually meet the people he or she is studying but depends "on data that is variously incomplete or unreliable or making too much of data that is available" (Gilders 2009:235). One way of avoiding this problem is to emphasize that the Hebrew Bible is not an ethnographic account and instead to understand it as analogous to a native informant— that is, a character whose statements about the society and its culture must be recorded, organized, compared, collated, and interpreted. A native informant will provide an emic perspective and thus when quizzed about why he or she does something may suggest that "it's traditional." It is the task of the anthropologist to interpret this information, thus providing an etic perspective. For example, the "tradition" might actually play a role in reaffirming the group's identity. Likewise, the information provided within a certain biblical text may be treated as the emic perspective of a native informant, but it is the task of the scholar using anthropology to apply an etic evaluation of the evidence. Admittedly, the Hebrew Bible is permeated with ideological bias, and the danger of reconstructing such bias as ancient Israel's social and cultural "reality" exists (Meyers 1988:13). Nevertheless, it could be argued that native informants are equally as unreliable, often providing interpretations of practices that explain little regarding their meaning. As Leach commented, "The observer must distinguish between what people actually do and what people say that they do.... [H]e must distinguish behaviour from ideology" (1982:130; cf. Gilders 2009).

The use of models is also often the subject of criticism. Applying models sometimes arouses suspicions about reductionism and oversimplification. Admittedly, reductionism is indeed a danger for the interpreter since, by their very nature, models are "essentially simplifications, exemplifications, and systemizations of data" (Esler 2006:3). However, reductionism is not a necessary result of using social scientific criticism. The aim of models is to enable comparisons between a vast array of data and the material within the Hebrew Bible. Thus, models cannot be accused of being "false" as a result of being simplified; they are either helpful or unhelpful for exegesis. McNutt provides a useful summary of the advantages of the method: those who "risk" using the social sciences have "generated new theories and fresh ways of conceptualizing the nature of, and interrelationships among, various types of social phenomena in Ancient Palestine," launching new perspectives "in a way that traditional approaches do not." The significance of this approach lies, therefore, "in providing 'tools' for analysing and raising questions about the ancient information" (McNutt 1999:215–16). Essentially, therefore, the use of models that are extrapolated from data that emerge within social scientific studies allows the biblical scholar to achieve a new and creative approach to the material and to examine ancient Israel's social and cultural history in new and fresh ways.

APPROACHES TO ISRAEL'S SOCIETY AND CULTURE:
EARLY ISRAEL

In the middle of the twentieth century interest in social scientific approaches to the Hebrew Bible began to gain momentum. Frick (2002) labels this a "second wave" of interest in the topic, although, as Wilson (2009) argues, the trend cannot be traced to a single source, and it was not well coordinated enough to be considered a movement. Gottwald's landmark book *The Tribes of Yahweh* (1979b) was one of the initial publications that explicitly used methods and models derived from the social sciences.[3] Gottwald (1979a:69) describes the difference between historical methodology and sociological methodology, stating that historical methods employ literary criticism, form criticism, tradition history, rhetorical criticism redaction history, history, history of religions, and biblical theology, while sociological method is associated with anthropology, sociology, political science, and economics. He reconstructs premonarchic society using synchronic and diachronic readings of biblical texts and their social structure. Gottwald argues that early Israel was a peasant society that endeavored for liberation from economic and political domination. Through focusing on the social structure, Gottwald argues that an indigenous conflict emerged between Canaanites, causing a retribalization of marginalized groups. Thus, an internal social evolution of Canaanite society occurred, rather than struggles between ethnic groups. Eventually, the growing Israelite groups became powerful enough to take the land; nevertheless, they maintained egalitarian forms of government (until the rise of the monarchy, *pace* Gottwald 1986a). Using this point of departure, Gottwald applies theories concerning tribal structures to Israel. He does not follow a single sociological approach. Anthropology, archaeology, history, and Marxism are all used as comparative sources.

Despite the popularity of Gottwald's arguments, his theories were nevertheless critiqued. Lemche, for example, criticized Gottwald for attempting to reconstruct "entire social systems" rather than selected portions of societies (Lemche 1985:21). Similarly, Thompson (1978) was wary of Gottwald's use of the Mari people, who were understood as very different from those in early Palestine, and he also criticized Gottwald's lack of distinction between cities and villages. Later, Brandfon (1981) questioned the justification of using the revolt model and questioned whether it was possible to differentiate between a source that is appropriate to sociological analysis and one that is suitable for historical analysis. Nevertheless, Gottwald's reconstruction of ancient Israel's social and cultural history was enormously influential and was later developed by a range of scholars. For example, Frick (1986) examines literature on state origins through looking at African sociopolitical systems as described by Fortes and Evans-Pritchard (1940). Similarly, Chaney (1983) develops a socioeconomic sketch of the rise of Israel, suggesting that the adoption of monarchy occurred in response to the threat of a Philistine bid to dominate the Israelite economy (also refer to Coote and Whitelam 1987; Flanagan 1981).

Attempts to reconstruct Israel's social and cultural history have been affected over the last thirty years by corresponding debates concerning how and whether the Hebrew Bible can be used as a historical source. We can acknowledge that history is a social construct, that is, it is intended not for antiquarian agendas or to present facts "but to answer questions that people ask about their relationship—relationships to the land on which they live, to the ethnic group with which they identify, and to their religious myths and rituals that undergird their sense of identity" (Frick 2002:29). One means of answering such questions has been to use archaeology to reconstruct the social world. While many studies focus on the urban elite, some also examine the everyday life of the average village dweller (Wood 1990). Debates concerning the history of the monarchy became particularly polarized in the last decade between those labeled maximalists and minimalists. Maximalists argue for the historicity of the biblical accounts of the United Monarchy (Dever 2001; Kitchen 2003; Provan, Long, and Longman 2003). Minimalists emphasize the ideological characteristics of the accounts and view much of the narrative as later constructions that may contain fragments of historical memories but should be doubted (Davies 1992; Finkelstein and Silberman 2001; Lemche 1998b; Thompson 1992; Whitelam 1996). Part of the problem is how one writes a history of Israel and if such a history can be written at all (Grabbe 1997, 2006; Hess, Klingbeil, and Ray 2008). A further problem is that before harmonization can occur, if it can occur at all, between archaeological data and the biblical accounts there are initially vast differences in opinion concerning archaeological data themselves and between interpretations of accounts within the Hebrew Bible. This is partly because scholars in each field use different research methods and are driven by different agendas. Another aspect of the issue is context; what researchers learn from material remains is sometimes rooted in their own conceptions of culture.

Many of the problems that characterize debates concerning the history of the monarchy have reemerged in more recent discussions of Israelite ethnicity during the premonarchic era. These include problems associated with harmonizing biblical texts and archaeological data, as well as differing opinions and methods concerning the interpretation of each set of information. However, to add to the complication, scholars also approach ethnicity in various ways and using differing methods. For example, primordialists attribute ethnicity to ties of religion, blood, race, language, region, and custom and consider it to be a fundamental, indefinable aspect of populations (Geertz 1963). In contrast, instrumentalists define ethnicity as a tool for the pursuit of material interests and power by competing cultural groups who use identity as a social and political resource (Hutchinson and Smith 1996:8). Killebrew, who examines the ethnicity of Egyptians, Canaanites, Philistines, and early Israel from the Late Bronze Age to Iron Age I, argues that "ethnicity ... can be identified under certain circumstances in the archaeological record" (2005:2). She focuses on Israel's ethnogenesis during this period and argues that Israel is best understood through the context of regional developments such as the decline of Late Bronze Age empires, which resulted in social and political disintegration. Such circumstances enabled a rise in kinship-based societies and facilitated greater movement among indigenous Canaanite populations. As a result, settlements grew in the central highlands, and Israel gradually emerged (Killebrew 2005:37–42). Israel at the time had a distinctive material culture; Killebrew states that villages were characterized by modest numbers of domestic structures such as "the three- or four-room pillared house; few, if any, public structures or fortifications; a proliferation of silos; the appearance of cisterns and agricultural terraces; absence of pig bones; paucity of burials; and, most notably, a very limited repertoire of utilitarian ceramic containers that continue the tradition of Late Bronze Age pottery shapes" (2005:157; cf. Meyers 1998:202). Killebrew also argues that Israel at the time had a particular ethnic myth or epic narrative concerning the Exodus from

Egypt. Like Killebrew, Brett (2003) argues that "Israel" emerged as an ethnic network, or informally linked groups, among indigenous populations of the hill country. Likewise, Dever (1995) claims that we can recognize early Israel from the material culture, particularly ceramics such as the collared-rim jar. Thus, Dever claims that this early group of Israelites should be understood as "progenitors" of biblical Israel (1993:24).[4]

In contrast, Bloch-Smith doubts that the search for Israelite ethnicity during this period is viable since the ethnic identifiers used (such as the collared-rim jar, the four-room house) "cannot be identified as exclusively 'Israelite'" (2003:406). A similar view was expressed by Edelman, who claimed that "nothing definitive can be said about the ethnicity of pre-monarchic Israel" (1996:25). Nevertheless, Bloch-Smith chooses to emphasize ethnic differences between Israelites and Philistines, rather than attempting to distinguish between Israelites and Canaanites. Thus, Bloch-Smith (2003) claims that hostility between Israelites and Philistines fueled ethnic affiliation.

ANCIENT ISRAEL'S SOCIETY AND CULTURE: ETHNICITY

In recent decades, approaches to ancient Israel's social and cultural history have started with the question of the formation of Israelite ethnicity. Numerous prominent studies of ethnicity have emerged within the last ten years. Sparks (1998), who surveys ethnicity, focuses on the monarchic period and analyzes, in particular, ethnicity within the prophets and selected parts of Deuteronomy.[5] Despite Sparks's focus on the monarchic period, he nevertheless argues that ethnic sentiments only became really important during the exilic and postexilic periods as a result of the perceived dangers of assimilation and the loss of ancestral land. In order to come to terms with this, the exilic community adopted Abrahamic traditions through which to promote a claim to the land. More recently, in contrast, Crouch (2014) argues that the monarchic period was a major period for the formation of Israelite ethnic identity. Although, as Miller explains, Sparks's "decision about dating texts" would be regarded as "idiosyncratic" by many scholars, Sparks's work has nevertheless been influential (Miller 2008:193). Sparks maintains that the ancestor and migration traditions evident among the prophets act as forerunners for Israelite ethnic identity and should be viewed as the first firm evidence for ancient Israelite ethnicity. However, it was not until the destruction of the Northern Kingdom in 722 that ethnicity became important, after refugees migrated south to Judah, resulting in a more diverse population (Sparks 1998). Of particular significance for Sparks is the impact that Deuteronomy had on ethnicity.[6] Sparks argues that Deuteronomy contains a number of features that betray the importance of ethnicity, such as the emphasis on a common history via repeated references to Israel's ancestors, worship of Yahweh alone, connections with the land (Deut. 7:1–6, 16–26; 18:9), fictive kinship through the emphasis on the brotherhood of all Israel, distinctions between Israel and other nations (and sojourners), and pervasive treaty language (Deut. 4:13, 23, 25–31; 5:2; 7:12; 8:1, 6, 11; 11:8, 13, 22; Weinfeld 1972).

Similar to Sparks, in his initial monograph Mullen (1993) also focuses on Deuteronomy and the Deuteronomistic History through the lens of ethnicity (cf. Mullen 1997). Mullen suggests that Deuteronomy emerged during the crisis of the exile and functioned in the building of shared historical memories that formed the foundation of a new ethnic identity. Perceived threats to ethnic identity among the exiles were, according to Mullen, the danger of cultural assimilation and dissolution, especially as later generations of exiles began to forget the homeland and ancestral traditions. As such Jerusalem's destruction becomes a variety of "national and ethnic myths cast in the form of a history" (Mullen 1993:284).

Finally, the evidence for the significance of ethnicity during the post-exilic period is considerable. Numerous monographs and articles have appeared on the topic. Heard (2001), for example, argues that Genesis (which he dates as a postexilic work) reveals that immigrant elites in Yehud composed the patriarchal narratives as a means of emphasizing their ethnic identity and using this ethnic identity as an instrument that could be applied in order to manufacture a claim to the land. One means of achieving this objective, Heard argues, was through endogamous marriage with women from those who remained in exile. Kessler also emphasizes the significance of those who remained in exile for ethnicity during the postexilic period, arguing that the exiles functioned as a "Charter Group," that is, an ethnic elite that moves into a geographic region and "creates a sociological and cultural structure distinct from the one existing in that region" (2006:99). Ethnicity has also been analyzed during this period through looking at the book of Ezra–Nehemiah, especially in relation to the question of migration and of intermarriage (Esler 2003; Southwood 2011, 2012).

Ethnicity is also clearly a feature of the book of Ruth, as the repeated epithet "Ruth the Moabite" indicates (Ruth 1:22, 2:2, 2:21, 4:5, 4:10). Glover (2009) argues that toward the end of the narrative, when Ruth is simply called "Ruth," Ruth's Moabite ethnic identity has shifted so that she has become more Israelite through ethnic transfer. This highlights the impact that different approaches to ethnicity have on decisions about its role within texts; an approach to the topic based on the fact that Ruth is a new migrant who accompanies Naomi, a return migrant, to Naomi's homeland prioritizes the problem that assimilation may render different results (Southwood 2014). Finally, the question of group unity, especially relating to the dynamics of honor and shame, has been examined in Psalm 129 (Botha 2002). Botha, who dates the psalm to the postexilic period, argues that two distinct groups can be discerned within it: Israel and a hostile out-group of "wicked ... haters of Zion" who humiliate Israel. Unity is established within the psalm through reference to the in-group's common history and divine support (Botha 2002:1410).

As has been demonstrated, despite methodological difficulties concerning how it can be used, ethnicity is nevertheless one of the central topics for examining Israel's cultural and social history. As Coote argues, "Discourse on ethnicity in biblical studies continues to deal with subjects that have long been invoked to define ethnicity, like phonotypical features, language, and religion, but that are, like ethnicity itself, highly variable, and, for antiquity, usually anachronistic" (2006:45). Nevertheless, ethnicity, if applied with methodological clarity and caution, can provide interesting new perspectives on the existing material, and, as such, it is becoming an increasingly popular means of approaching the texts within the Hebrew Bible.

ANCIENT ISRAEL'S SOCIETY AND CULTURE: KINSHIP

Another central topic within Israel's social and cultural history is kinship.[7] At approximately the same time that Gottwald developed his theories concerning early Israel, Malamat (1968) suggested the use of social anthropology in order to understand the social structure of early Israel as a lineage-based society.[8] Since then numerous studies on kinship have emerged (Bendor 1996). Initially, the fluidity of kinship terminology should be acknowledged. A good example of this is the narrative in Joshua 7, where the term for "tribe" (*shebet)* can also refer to subgroups within tribes (Num. 4:18; Judg. 20:12; 1 Sam. 9:21) and *mishpachah* can refer to the tribe as a whole (Judg. 17:7; 1 Sam. 9:21; Jer. 8:3; Amos 3:1–2; Mic. 2:31; Coote 2006:41).[9]

During the premonarchic period Israelite society would have consisted of agrarian families with permanent ties to their landholdings. The *beth av* was a primary point of affinity within the kinship structure. Subsequently, families banded together in a clan (*mishpachah*). The clan would have invoked a concept of fictive kinship to enhance its cohesion despite the fact that the network was not based upon biological ties (Meyers 1997:37–38). In addition, an equally prominent social unit is the tribe (*shebet* or *mateh*). As Bautch argues, "Historically the tribe was not as important as the clan; the tribe was merely the collective that resulted when members of nearby villages might join forces *ad hoc* to provide military protection or large-scale agricultural work" (2012:362). This suggests localized and heterogeneous religions of the clans. Furthermore, in an earlier article, Bautch argues, "On average … a family covered four generations with between 50 and 100 closely related people living in a cluster of dwelling units with their labourers and resident aliens" (2009:89). However, similar problems to those encountered in ethnicity concerning lack of evidence hinder the study of kinship at such an early period. Later, during the monarchic period, Bautch argues that the Deuteronomic reform "consolidated and stabilized the concept of Israel as 'a people,' thereby laying the groundwork for a more robust understanding of theological concepts such as land and covenant" (2012:363). As Coote argues, "Politics explains descent sooner than descent explains politics" (2006:47). However, one outcome of this for kinship was that existing traditions were compromised, such as the connection between the *beth av* and an inherited plot of land. As a consequence of this, and a series of intrusions from the state, the *beth av* eventually diminished (Bautch 2012:363). Nevertheless, the term did not fade away. Rather, with its meaning transformed to refer to various close-knit voluntary organizations, the *beth av* remained current (Blenkinsopp 1997:91; cf. Bautch 2009:89).

By the postexilic period kinship terminology such as *tribe* and *clan* was particularly significant, not least because of the loaded history connected to such terms. The changes in language suggest new understandings of the operative family unit, now the clan (*mishpachah*), rather than the *beth av*. Furthermore, kinship language was appropriated by the state in order to bolster social policy, and kinship was connected to honor and identity (Leeb 2006). For example, in Ezra little distinction is made between the *beth avoth* (house of the fathers) and the *bene hagolah* (sons of the exile) (Ezra 10:16; Bautch 2009:116). Similarly, the term for "brother" (*ach*) is repeated in Nehemiah in order to cloud class boundaries and to unify the community in action (Neh. 5:1, 5, 7, 8, 10, 14). One result of the centrality of family and fictive kinship during the postexilic period is its support for the rise of Jewish nationalism (Goodblatt 2006:108–15; cf. Cohen 1999; Mendels 1997; Weeks 2002). Coote's cautionary observation, referring not to nationalism but to ethnicity, should be acknowledged: "Ethnicity does not automatically relate to tribalism in the modern period and there is no reason to think it did in antiquity" (2006:45). The terms *ethnicity* and *nationalism* are not necessarily interchangeable. Nevertheless, at this point, the principle at stake is caution concerning automatically connecting two separate ideas. Despite the rise in nationalism, the importance of kinship relations never diminished. At a later period, for example, in the Greek version of Tobit, eleven kinship terms are employed within the first chapter: *sperma* (1:1), *phule* (1:1), *adelphos* (1:3), *ethnos* (1:3), *pater* (1:4 [in the wider sense of "ancestor"]), *oikos* (1:5; especially in the combination *oikos tou patros mou*, which reflects the standard Hebrew term *beth av*), *patria* (1:9), *genos* (1:10), *oi hioi Israel* (1:18), *exadelphos* (1:22), *suggeneia* (1:22; Faßbeck 2005:177). Within Tobit, Faßbeck argues, the seriousness of proper conduct in obedience to the rules of kinship relations is evidenced in the narrative figure of the demon, who is "employed as a boundary marker" (2005:180); only endogamous marriages will not result in the appearance of the demon.

Not only do terminology and kinship boundaries change, but some scholars point out that kinship can be described as "disintegrating" in certain parts of the biblical material (Oeste 2011). For example, Niditch's (1982:371–72) work on Judges 19–20 illustrates precisely such a breakdown of relationships at multiple levels of Israelite society including the household (*beth av*), the clan (*mishpachah*), the tribe (*shebet*), and even the people (*am Israel*; cf. Niditch 2008).

The language describing kinship relations, and indeed the boundaries between such relations, has changed as a result of time, political context, and exile and through local social factors. As Faust observes, "Israelite ... terminology is so plastic, the lines between different levels of tribal organization often blur" (2000:29). However, while recognizing this, it is also important to remember that kinship boundaries, similar to ethnic boundaries, are subjective, malleable, and socially constructed. As Coote argues, "Tribal structures and identities are fluid even as specified by members" (2006:48).[10] Kinship terminology and relations are as much a product of the human imagination as they are of "real" bonds between individuals. In many ways, therefore, such changes are to be expected.

Death should not be disregarded when examining kinship within the Hebrew Bible, since on many occasions it fails to stop individuals from returning to the world of the living (1 Sam. 28; 1 Kings 17:21–22; Isa. 8:19, 14:9–10). As such, proper burial was crucial. Bodies would be interred within family tombs, upon family land (2 Kings 9:10; Jer. 8:2, 16:4). The lack of burial of the dead is one of the problems that the book of Tobit contends with (Tob. 1:18). Nevertheless, the Hebrew Bible displays a degree of revulsion concerning death. Dead bodies are understood to be unclean and are sources of contamination. As such, care for the dead is the duty of the family and clan, but priests, and the broader Israelite community, are defiled by contact with corpses (Num. 19:11–22; Lev. 10:6, 21:1–2; Ezek. 39:14–16, 44:25; cf. Frymer-Kensky 1983).

In an interesting study on death and kinship, Cook uses ethnographic evidence from traditional African societies to construct a provisional social scientific model for illuminating the problem of death. He shows that "in traditional African thought, death is always and everywhere unnatural and preventable. When someone dies, the people immediately suspect some evil force to be at play: most likely magic, sorcery, or witchcraft. For the Akan of Ghana, death is never anything other than a curse and a wicked destroyer" (2009:108). Furthermore, Cook demonstrates that this interpretation of death is also prevalent in East Africa, in places such as Tanzania, Kenya, and Uganda. For example, the Madi of Uganda "equate death with fear, sorrow, and the dreadful dissolution of the body" (Cook 2009:108). Cook uses this evaluation of ideas about death in Africa as a model through which to explain many of the negative interpretations of death in the Hebrew Bible.[11] He argues that "in the mind of the Hebrews, injury, sickness, and death were forces that cut off the person from the land of the living, from blessings, and from Yahweh, God of the living" (2009:108). Thus, similar to the understandings of death among communities within Africa, such as the Akan of Ghana, the interpretation of death within the Hebrew Bible displays fear and revulsion (Pss. 69:1–3, 14–15; 88:4–7, 10–12; 116:3; Isa. 66:3; Jer. 19:51; Ezek. 23:37; Cook 2009:108), to the extent that Death is considered to be a demonic power (2 Kings 3:27; Jer. 32:35; Ps. 106:37–38; Cook 2009:109).

Most importantly, death has the potential to isolate an individual, therefore breaking any ties of kinship. If things went well, one would be gathered (*asaph*) to one's ancestors and rest peacefully, as Yahweh's instructions to Moses at the end of Deuteronomy illustrate: "There on the mountain that you have climbed you will die and be gathered [*weteaseph*] to your people, just as your brother Aaron died on Mount Hor and was gathered [*wayeaseph*] to his people" (Deut. 32:50).[12] However, if things did not go well, one risked ending up being cut off (*gazar*, usually in the niphal form) from kinfolk and from territory (Lam. 3:54; Pss. 31:22, 88:6). Alongside this possibility is the horror and dread of ending up in Sheol. As Cook points out, "In biblical thought, death and *Sheol* are parallel concepts" (2009:110). This is explicit through Death's placement in parallelism with Sheol within the Psalms:

> For in Death there is no remembrance of you
> In *Sheol* who will give you thanks? (Ps. 6:5; cf. Pss. 18:5, 55:15, 89:48)

Effectively, death has the potential to break kinship ties and ties with land and can isolate individuals from God. Although ideas about death are not cross-culturally continuous and can vary vastly, the comparison of ideas about death in traditional African societies and in the Hebrew Bible is immensely helpful as a starting point for understanding some of the ideas that underpin concepts such as Sheol and the organization of ancestral graves for kin.

ANCIENT ISRAEL'S SOCIETY AND CULTURE:
WOMEN, MARRIAGE, FERTILITY, AND RAPE

Another important aspect of ancient Israel's social and cultural history is the regulation of kinship through marriage and the role of women. Although ancient women are often traditionally interpreted as being occupied with domestic duties and with procreating, Meyers (2007), who also uses ethnographic data in order to construct cross-cultural comparisons, illustrates that women played many other important roles in Israelite society. These roles included musical traditions, prophetic roles (some of which may have been linked to health care and fertility), funerary services (Jer. 9:19; 1 Kings 20:35), midwifery (Exod. 1:15–20), and psychological care. Therefore, women would have participated in organizational structures that had their own internal hierarchies. Particularly important to Meyers is the notion of women's informal networks, for which she finds archaeological evidence of Iron Age dwellings: "The positioning of the implements and the installations used in bread production, a female task, shows that women from several households would have worked together in the tedious series of processes required to change grain into bread. The same is probably true for some components of domestic textile production" (2007:92).

As a consequence of working together in close-knit groups, Meyers argues, female solidarity and companionship would have been strong. Meyers also emphasizes the importance of women's networks at the end of the book of Ruth, which refers to *hashecenoth*, "a group of connected women gathered for socio-medical purposes, namely, facilitating childbirth and the naming of the newborn" (Meyers 2007:93; Ruth 4:17; cf. Meyers 1999). Therefore, alongside other more recognized roles, women also played an important part in the social structure.

However, undeniably, one of the most significant roles played by women in ancient Israel was childbirth. Evidence of this includes the range of laws, prohibitions, and mores concerning marriage (Deut. 21–22). What is surprising here is the sheer range of marriage options and practices that appear within the Hebrew Bible. Although the second narrative of creation suggests something similar to the type of marriage practiced in modern Westernized society (Gen. 2:24), numerous other types of marriage existed. A man could take many wives (polygamy), as well as concubines; marriage was sometimes encouraged within the group, especially in texts where Israelite ethnicity is important (endogamy)[13]; levirate marriage also occurred. A soldier was permitted to marry a prisoner of war, if the correct rituals were undertaken (Num. 31:1–18; Deut. 21:28–29), marriage by capture occurred (Judg. 21; cf. Southwood forthcoming), and a rapist could marry his victim (Deut. 22:28–29; Fleishman 2002, 2004). Part of the reason for the variety is because marriage was as much a distribution of wealth as it was an instrument of personal and political alliance. As Guenther states, "All the parties stood to benefit from astutely and strategically arranged marriages. The extended family and clan had vested interests as represented in the (direct) dowry and indirect dowry (bride-price *mohar*). The direct dowry consists of the bride's trousseau, personal furniture, and a gift to her by her family in the amount of 5–25 per cent of the total family wealth" (2005:388).[14] As such, the legislations concerning marriage are complex, sometimes appearing to be contradictory, and confusing. Part of the problem in this case is the sheer variety of practices and attempting to understand why, aside from protection from illegitimate offspring, such customs gained the status of mores or norms. Virginity was expected at marriage, especially for priests (Gen. 24:16, 43; Lev. 21:3, 14; Frymer-Kensky 1998, 2002). Similarly, Leeb argues that one might expect that polygamous marriages, alongside their instrumental value (through forging alliances and distributing wealth), occurred in order to control access to women by creating a virtual excess. However, it is not easy to detect such reasoning in the Hebrew Bible, since "the texts which we have received may tell us less about Israel's actual past than about a presumed past" (Leeb 2006:53).

As well as being difficult to legislate, many types of marriage appear to have been troublesome on a more social level, mainly as a result of their connections with honor and shame. One example is levirate marriage (Gen. 38; Deut. 25:5–10; Ruth 4; cf. Willis 2001). Levirate unions generally occur within pastoral societies that are patrilocal, exogamous, and polygynous and where inheritance is patrilineal or, in some cases, there is joint fraternal inheritance. However, that is where the commonalities end. As Weisberg (2009) illustrates, they are sometimes employed out of a concern for the family's investment of a bride-price; other times, out of concern for the widow and her offspring; and yet other times, out of respect for the dead. Furthermore, despite the apparent goal of Deuteronomy's legislation, to ensure that a childless widow has a home and the possibility of childbearing, Weisberg emphasizes the significance of the resistance to act as a *levir* by Onan, Judah, and Ruth's nearest kinsman. One of the reasons for the reluctance to marry wives of deceased brothers may have been that levirate marriage runs the risk of being misinterpreted by emic actors and onlookers as very close to incest (Lev. 18:16, 20:21), albeit a type of "sanctioned" incest. As Weisberg demonstrates, such incest anxiety has some interesting cross-cultural comparisons. For example, the Luo of Kenya encourage levirate marriage but recognize that a *levir* may want to invest his time and resources in his more immediate family. Similarly, for the Swazi of Africa "it is dangerous to show too much friendliness during the husband's lifetime lest they be accused of causing the death," and this anxiety is also evident in Hindu texts where "psychologically, the last person you want to have sex with your wife, even when you are dead, is your brother, because of sibling rivalry" (Weisberg 2004:421). Failure to take up the role of the *levir* is represented as shameful within Genesis 38:9–10, 26, and Ruth 4:7–8. However, when contextualized through the lens of levirate marriage in other parts of the world, such reluctance is understandable.

Another aspect of Israel's social and cultural history wherein honor and shame play a significant role is in relation to rape. In response to Dinah's rape, her brothers are angry and distraught (Gen. 34:7).[15] A big part of the reason for this anger is the humiliation (*cherpah*) not only of Dinah but of the whole family (Gen. 34:14). Despite the points of comparison with Genesis 34, a very different account of rape occurs in 2 Samuel 13. Esler (2011) evaluates this account using a model of patrilinearity, polygyny, and patrilocality. Tamar's rape, like Dinah's, may be interpreted as shameful, for her but more significantly within the narrative, for Absalom, her brother. By raping but not marrying Tamar, Amnon not only assaults his half sister but also consigns her to "a form of social death" (Esler 2011:344). It is important that Absalom is Tamar's brother (from the same mother) while Amnon is a half brother, since Esler (2011) argues on the basis of various anthropological examples that siblings with the same mother exhibit a greater sense of solidarity than those of only the same father. However, in both cases male honor is inextricably connected to female sexuality, and rape not only humiliates the woman involved but also symbolizes the rapist's power over her brothers and father and the family's inability to control their women.

Also connected to the issue of honor and shame within the Hebrew Bible is infertility (Gen. 16; 1 Sam. 1–2). In a polygamous setting, such as is envisaged within 1 Samuel 1–2, favoritism on the part of the male often results in tension and rivalry between cowives, as can be seen through comparisons with polygynous Palestinian Arab men (Esler 2011). Child-bearing, however, was a mark of honor; thus with each birth, Peninah's authority and status within the household is increased despite Hannah's place as Elkanah's favorite. Such honor was not confined to the house-hold, as Peninah's public provocation of Hannah at Shiloh illustrates (1 Sam. 1:6). Clearly, therefore, infertility was linked to shame; as Esler comments, "The experience of a woman's childlessness and shame were closely connected" (2011:77). Thus, it is unsurprising that Hannah weeps and fasts. Neufeld interprets this as a trance state, claiming that "weep-ing and food abstention are well known in the world of antiquity to trigger ecstatic states" (2006:139). The same can be said about the ri-valry between Sarai and Hagar. As Neufeld comments, "Infertility in an honor/shame-based society would have reflected negatively not only upon Abram but Sarai. She would have been deeply humiliated, perhaps scorned by her husband and his extended kin along with inquisitive tribal neighbours…. In a patrilineal system, the pressure upon Sarai to produce an heir to the promise would have been intense" (2006:136).

Thus, although, as Meyers (1999, 2007) emphasizes, many important social and cultural roles were played by women in ancient Israel, it must be acknowledged that procreation was a central role. Despite this obser-vation we should also bear in mind the social value of children as repre-sented within the Hebrew Bible. Sarai's need for a child "appears to be based on the child's social value" and its ability to raise *her* status, thus providing Abraham "with the preferred heir he needs to continue his lineage after his death" (Steinberg 2009:263). Furthermore, a child would have served as a protector to a mother in her old age and would have been economically valuable. Nevertheless, as Steinberg points out, ill-behaved children could be killed (Deut. 21:18–20), and sons could be taken by creditors to pay off debts (2 Kings 4:1). Moreover, some children were orphans, as the repetition of the "orphan and the widow" throughout Deuteronomy illustrates. For example, Steinberg makes a case for the prevalence of child abandonment in ancient Israel, arguing that "child abandonment was a reality in ancient Israel" (2009:264): for example, Ishmael is doubly abandoned; "first Abraham abandons Ishmael and Hagar" (Gen. 21:14) and "then Hagar abandons Ishmael" (Gen. 21:15; see also Exod. 1:22; Ezek. 16:5).

ANCIENT ISRAEL'S SOCIETY AND CULTURE: HOSPITALITY

A final, happier, area for consideration of Israel's cultural and social history is hospitality. Although there is no term for hospitality within the Hebrew Bible, the social importance of hospitality is easy to recognize. For example, in Genesis 18, three strangers approach Abraham, who rushes out to greet them and makes a feast for them.[16] Similarly, in Genesis 24, Abraham's servant is invited in for a meal, and his camels are cared for (Gen. 24:32–35). However, such hospitality was not motivated purely by kindness and humanity. Two key reasons for hospitality, aside from generosity, occur. First, hospitality is a means of returning to God a portion of what has been given (Deut. 16:17; Exod. 16–17). Second, hospitality is a means of protecting property and community from possible violence through transforming a stranger into a guest. Indeed, the term most often associated with hospitality in the LXX and the NT is *xenos*, meaning "foreigner," "stranger," and sometimes "enemy." As Matthews argues, "Reciprocal actions and expectations form out of this need allowing the stranger to be welcomed into an encampment, village, or town. This stranger was given new status as a guest, thereby removing hostile overtones associated with the different and the unfamiliar. However, if at any point the pattern of ritual which governed the relationship between the host and guest were violated, by either party, then overt hostility could occur" (1991:13).

The risks associated with not offering hospitality can be illustrated through the story of Nabal and Abigail and the dynamics of honor and shame that underpin the narrative. Honor prevents David and his men from begging for provisions. Indeed, if they are not offered such provisions, food, and shelter, then these things will be taken by force (1 Sam. 25:13). Nabal's foolish and undiplomatic failure to recognize the importance of hospitality puts the entire household at risk. Not only is no hospitality offered, but insults are hurled at David's men (1 Sam. 25:10), and Nabal questions the entire code of hospitality itself, asking, "Why should *I* take *my* bread and *my* water, and the meat *I* have slaughtered for *my* shearers, and give it to men coming from who knows where?" (1 Sam. 25:11; emphasis added). The syntax illustrates Nabal's selfish and foolhardy actions in dismissing the hospitality code; first-person pronominal suffixes and verbs are repeated throughout, as the italics highlight. Abigail's immediate reaction illustrates the seriousness of the breach of honor; there is a swift succession of verbs that describe her action, including the note that she "hurried" (*mahar*; 1 Sam. 25:23). Thus, while Abigail discerns social and cultural norms at work, Nabal is characterized by a complete lack of social awareness. We should also note that Esler discerns the politics of honor and shame within the narrative. However, Esler (2011) explains theses by analogy with "protection" rackets offered to isolated farms and estates such as are exemplified through Block's (1988) study of the Mafia in isolated rural estates in Sicily during the 1920s.

Because of the importance of hospitality, certain obligations fence the code around. To maintain the host's honor "the guest must be careful not to ask for or even look longingly at anything in the host's house" since by asking, the host's right to offer is usurped and the implication is that the host has been too stingy or slow (Matthews 1991:15). However, the relationship is reciprocal; guests are expected to express gratitude and to show that they are enjoying the hospitality through praising the host's generosity and honor. As Matthews comments, "The principles of reciprocity upon which the hospitality code is based make it clear that the extension of protection and service to strangers is a necessary qualification for maintenance of honor in the ancient Near East" (1991:20; cf. Pitt-Rivers 1968). He goes so far as to state that "the sense of reciprocity … is at the heart of the hospitality ritual" (1991:20). However, while hospitality is clearly of significant social and cultural importance, more evidence would be required to substantiate a case to classify it as "ritual." Nevertheless, hospitality was extremely socially and culturally important in ancient Israel. Although it does not permeate all of the texts within the Hebrew Bible, being found mostly in Judges and in the patriarchal narratives, it nevertheless can be understood as an essential part of ancient Israelite society.

CONCLUDING REMARKS

This brief survey of Israel's social and cultural history began by examining the then-new ideas and methods found within Gottwald's *The Tribes of Yahweh*. Despite criticisms regarding the use of the social sciences within biblical studies, this chapter has illustrated their importance for understanding some aspects of Israel's social history, including the emergence of ancient Israel, ethnicity, kinship, death, the role of women, various marriage practices, infertility, children, and hospitality. Nevertheless, there are a number of areas that also fall into the broad category of social and cultural history that have not been discussed. These include, among myriad others, primogeniture, masculinity, the importance of migration and return migration, food, and humor. Naturally, more remains to be said. However, using studies that apply theories from the social sciences, in particular anthropology, plays a key part in broadening out and contextualizing our understandings of ancient Israel's social and cultural history. While we still do not have "instruction on airplanes, cellular phones, and cable television" (Sadler 2006:387), we have gained, despite their anachronism at first glance, important insights into some of the aspects of Israel's social and cultural history through referring to the social sciences.

NOTES

1. The validity of *applying* models cross-culturally is, nevertheless, problematic. Refer to the debate between Esler (2000) and Horrell (2000).

2. Refer to DeWalt and DeWalt (2011). Participant observation is by no means infallible; various problems hinder data collection, such as, for example, the anthropologist's impact on the community.

3. Although this approach was part of the reason for the book's success, it must also be recognized that Gottwald's theories were appealing to students of liberation theology.

4. Nowadays, very few scholars refer to "Israelites" in discussing the Iron Age I. Instead, terms such as *proto-Israelites* have become more prevalent (Dever 1995:206–7; Williamson 1998:147), and many prefer to avoid *Israelites* altogether (Finkelstein 1996; Lemche 1998a; Thompson 1999).

5. Hagedorn points out that redaction of the prophetic material greatly complicates this task. In the case of Nahum, he argues that notions of ethnicity "change over time and correspond to different stages in the development of the book." However, Hagedorn also insists that "the stereotypes employed to characterize the Other remain stable and do not seem to be affected by the change of the reference group" (2006:239). Thus, while the context changes, the concept of ethnicity is expressed using consistent means of categorizing.

6. Deuteronomy's social functions had been acknowledged long before Sparks's analysis of the text from an ethnic perspective. For example, McBride (1987), arguing that Deuteronomy was a constitution of the Deuteronomic State, recognized its emphasis on group unity and the features that distinguish Israel from the surrounding nations (cf. Dion 1984; Wilson 2005).

7. It should be acknowledged that there is some overlap between ethnicity and kinship. Chapman, for example, argues that breast milk should be understood as a kinship-forging substance within the Hebrew Bible: thus the process of breastfeeding transfers tribal identity. Such narratives, therefore, establish a character's inside ethnic identity (Chapman 2012).

8. Concerning genealogy within the Hebrew Bible, consult Knoppers 2001a, 2001b, 2003a, 2003b, 2009 (again, some overlap with ethnicity); and Wilson 1977.

9. Indeed, Zevit (2001) argues that the term for "clan," *mishpachah*, was replaced by *beth av* during the postexilic period (cf. Coote 2006:41).

10. Carsten, examining the Malays in Pulu Langkawi, challenged axiomatic assumptions such as "blood is thicker than water" through arguing that kinship can also be established through communal eating and sharing a single substance (food). As Carsten concludes, "Ideas about relatedness in the Langkawi show how culturally specific is the separation of the 'social' from the 'biological' and the reduction of the latter to sexual reproduction. In Langkawi relatedness is derived both from acts of procreation and from living and eating together. It makes little sense in indigenous terms to label some of these activities as social and others as biological" (2007:322). The essays in Parkin and Stone (2007) illustrate effectively the extent to which kinship is socially constructed through offering a variety of perspectives concerning kinship in different cultures and contexts.

11. It should be acknowledged that not everyone agrees that death is a negative force in the Hebrew Bible (Barr 1992).

12. *'-s-ph* is repeated as a niphal imperative and then a niphal imperfect with *waw* consecutive. Other examples of the dead being gathered, usually in the niphal, to their ancestors include Gen. 25:8, 35:29; Judg. 2:10; 2 Kings 22:20.

13. Ethnic and religious endogamy remained an important social and cultural practice until quite a late period. It represents a dominant value throughout the book of Tobit; for example, Tobit marries a kinswoman and urges his son to do the same (Tob. 6:12, 7:10), and Tobias is only entitled to take Sarah as his wife "because he is *closest* in kin to her" (Tob. 8:7; emphasis added; Faßbeck 2005:179).

14. Numerous technical terms concerning marriage and divorce also occur within the Hebrew Bible and the Aramaic Elephantine Papyri (Southwood 2012:163–89).

15. *'ß-ts-v*, or *hithpael* (grieve). As Blyth points out, this verb occurs only here "and in Gen. 6:6, where it describes God's lamenting over his creation" (2010:119).

16. Despite his later incest, Lot is often interpreted positively as a result of his hospitality in Genesis 19. Lot's willingness to entertain strangers features as an important element in Pirqe R. El. 25 and, to a lesser extent, in 1 Clem. 11:1. 1 Clem. 11:1 merely commends Lot for his hospitality and piety (Alexander 1985:289).

FURTHER READING

Davies, P. R., and D. V. Edelman, eds. 2010. *The Historian and the Bible: Essays in Honour of Lester L. Grabbe*. New York: T&T Clark International. [A good collection of essays by established scholars on topics such as the Bible and history, sources, archaeology, memory, religious culture, and the origins of Judaism.]

Dutcher-Walls, P., ed. 2009. *The Family in Life and in Death. The Family in Ancient Israel: Sociological and Archaeological Perspectives*. Library of Hebrew Bible/Old Testament Studies 504. New York: T&T Clark International. [A good collection of essays by established scholars on topics such as social identity, deceit, house size, cult practices, death, community, afterlife, and birth.]

Esler, P., ed. 2006. *Ancient Israel. The Old Testament in Its Social Context*. Minneapolis: Fortress Press. [This collection of essays is an excellent resource for placing Israel in its social context. Chapters are arranged in three sections ("Themes," "Texts," and "Hermeneutics") and explore a wide range of issues in light of the advantages of a social scientific approach to the Hebrew Bible.]

Goodblatt, D. 2006. *Elements of Ancient Jewish Nationalism*. New York: Cambridge University Press. [This is a thoroughly researched, consistently and carefully referenced book concerning Jewish nationalism that is in dialogue with the work of Doron Mendels and Seth Schwartz. Goodblatt illustrates how Jewish nationalism evolved, transformed, and was reinterpreted.]

Gottwald, N. K. 1979. *The Tribes of Yahweh: A Sociology of the Religion of Liberated Israel, 1250–1050 B.C.E.* Maryknoll, N.Y.: Orbis Books. [A pioneering book that was one of the initial publications that explicitly used methods and models derived from the social sciences.]

Grabbe, L. L. 2006. *Ancient Israel: What Do We Know and How Do We Know It?* London: T&T Clark. [A good, thoroughly researched overview and analysis of sources and biblical texts, which are organized temporally.]

Overholt, T. W. 1996. *Cultural Anthropology and the Old Testament*. Minneapolis: Fortress. [Overholt applies cultural anthropology to Israelite social roles and institutions and to the Elijah and Elisha cycle. The initial chapter discussing method is thoughtfully and clearly argued. Overholt's work is a good starting point for understanding the social and cultural history of ancient Israel.]

Robertson-Smith, W. 1889. *Lectures on the Religion of the Semites. Fundamental Institutions. First Series*. London: Adam and Charles Black. [One of the earliest contributions from an anthropological perspective to the social and cultural history of ancient Israel.]

Sparks, K. L. 1998. *Ethnicity and Identity in Ancient Israel: Prolegomena to the Study of Ethnic Sentiments and Their Expression in the Hebrew Bible*. Winona Lake, Ind.: Eisenbrauns. [A useful summary of ethnicity followed by a discussion of ethnicity in the monarchic period that focuses on the prophets and Deuteronomy. A book that activated numerous later inquiries into ethnicity within the Hebrew Bible.]

BIBLIOGRAPHY

Alexander, T. D. 1985. "Lot's Hospitality: A Clue to His Righteousness." *Journal of Biblical Literature* 104/2: pp. 289–91.

Anderson, C. B. 2009. "Reflections in an Interethnic/Racial Era on Interethnic/Racial Marriage in Ezra." In R. Bailey, C. Liew, B. S. Tat-siong, and F. Fernando, eds., *They Were All Together in One Place? Toward Minority Biblical Criticism*, pp. 47–64. Society of Biblical Literature Semeia Studies 57. Leiden: Brill.

Bailey, L. R. 1979. *Biblical Perspectives on Death*. Overtures to Biblical Theology. Philadelphia: Fortress.

Baker, J. C. 2008. "New Covenant, New Identity. A Social-Scientific Rereading of Jeremiah 31:31–34." *Bible and Critical Theory* 4/1: pp. 1–11.

Barr, J. 1992. *The Garden of Eden and the Hope of Immortality*. Read-Tuckwell Lectures for 1990. London: SCM.

Bautch, R. J. 2009. *Glory and Power, Ritual and Relationship: The Sinai Covenant in the Postexilic Period*. New York: T&T Clark.

Bautch, R. J. 2012. "Biblical Antecedents of the Kinship Terms in 1QSa." In E. F. Mason, S. I. Thomas, A. Schofield, and E. Ulrich, eds., *A Teacher for All Generations. Essays in Honor of James C. VanderKam*, vol. 1, pp. 359–77. Journal for the Study of Judaism Supplement. Leiden: Brill.

Bendor, S. 1996. *The Social Structure in Ancient Israel: The Institution of the Family (Beit 'ab) from the Settlement to the End of the Monarchy*. Jerusalem: Simor.

Blenkinsopp, J. 1997. "The Family in First Temple Israel." In L. G. Perdue, J. Blenkinsopp, J. J. Collins, and C. Meyers, *Families in Ancient Israel*, pp. 48–103. Louisville, Ky.: Westminster John Knox Press.

Blenkinsopp, J. 2003. *Isaiah 56–66: A New Translation with Introduction and Commentary*. Anchor Bible 19B. New York: Doubleday.

Bloch-Smith, E. 2003. "Israelite Ethnicity in Iron I: Archaeology Preserves What Is Remembered and What Is Forgotten in Israel's History." *Journal of Biblical Literature* 122: pp. 401–25.

Block, A. 1988. *The Mafia of a Sicilian Village, 1860–1960: A Study of Violent Peasant Entrepreneurs*. Long Grove, Ill.: Waveland.

Blyth, C. 2010. *The Narrative of Rape in Genesis 34: Interpreting Dinah's Silence*. Oxford: Oxford University Press.

Botha, P. J. 2002. "A Social-Scientific Reading of Psalm 129." *HTS Theological Studies* 58/4: pp. 1401–14.

Brandfon, G. R. 1981. "Norman Gottwald on the Tribes of Yahweh." *Journal for the Study of the Old Testament* 21: pp. 101–10.

Brett, M. G. 2003. "Israel's Indigenous Origins: Cultural Hybridity and the Formation of Israelite Ethnicity." *Biblical Interpretation* 11/3: pp. 400–412.

Carr, D. M. 2010. *An Introduction to the Old Testament: Sacred Texts and Imperial Contexts of the Hebrew Bible*. Oxford: Wiley-Blackwell.

Carsten, J. 2007. "The Substance of Kinship and the Heat of the Hearth: Feeding, Personhood, and Relatedness among the Malays in Pulu Langkawi." In R. Parkin and L. Stone, eds., *Kinship and Family: An Anthropological Reader*, pp. 309–28. Oxford: Blackwell.

Causse, A. 1937. *Du groupe ethnique à la communauté religieuse*. Paris: Alcan.

Chaney, M. 1983. "Ancient Palestinian Peasant Movements and the Formation of Premonarchic Israel." In D. N. Freedman and D. F. Graf, eds., *Palestine in Transition: The Emergence of Ancient Israel*, pp. 39–90. Sheffield: Almond Press.

Chaney, M. L. 1986. "Systemic Study of the Israelite Monarchy." In N. K. Gottwald, ed., *Social Scientific Criticism of the Hebrew Bible and Its Social World: The Israelite Monarchy*, pp. 53–76. Semeia 37. Decatur, Ga.: Scholars Press.

Chapman, C. R. 2012. "'Oh That You Were Like a Brother to Me, One Who Had Nursed at My Mother's Breasts.' Breast Milk as a Kinship-Forging Substance." *Journal of Hebrew Scriptures* 12/7: pp. 1–41.

Cohen, S.J.D. 1999. *The Beginnings of Jewishness: Boundaries, Varieties, Uncertainties*. Hellenistic Culture and Society 31. London: University of California Press.

Cook, S. L. 2009. "Death, Kinship, and Community: Afterlife and the חסד Ideal in Israel." In P. Dutcher-Walls, ed., *The Family in Life and in Death. The Family in Ancient Israel: Sociological and Archaeological Perspectives*, pp. 106–21. Library of Hebrew Bible/Old Testament Studies 504. New York: T&T Clark International.

Coote, R. B. 2006. "Tribalism: Social Organization in the Biblical Israels." In P. F. Esler, ed., *Ancient Israel: Ancient Israel in Its Social Context*, pp. 35–49. Minneapolis: Fortress Press.

Coote, R. B., and K. W. Whitelam. 1987. *The Emergence of Early Israel in Historical Perspective*. Sheffield: Almond.

Crook, Z. A. 2005. "Reflections on Culture and Social-Scientific Models." *Journal of Biblical Literature* 124/3: pp. 515–20.

Crouch, C. L. 2014. *The Making of Israel: Cultural Diversity in the Southern Levant and the Formation of Ethnic Identity in Deuteronomy*. Leiden: Brill.

Davies, P. R. 1992. *In Search of "Ancient Israel."* Sheffield: JSOT Press.

Davies, P. R., and D. V. Edelman, eds. 2010. *The Historian and the Bible: Essays in Honour of Lester L. Grabbe*. New York: T&T Clark International.

Day, J. 1989. *Molech: A God of Human Sacrifice in the Old Testament*. Cambridge: Cambridge University Press.

Dever, W. G. 1993. "Cultural Continuity, Ethnicity in the Archaeological Record and the Question of Israelite Origins." *Eretz-Israel* 24: pp. 22–33.

Dever, W. G. 1995. "Ceramics, Ethnicity, and the Question of Israel's Origins." *Biblical Archaeologist* 58: pp. 200–213.

Dever, W. G. 2001. *What Did the Biblical Writers Know and When Did They Know It? What Archaeology Can Tell Us about the Reality of Ancient Israel*. Grand Rapids, Mich.: Cambridge.

DeWalt, K. M., and B. R. DeWalt. 2011. *Participant Observation: A Guide for Fieldworkers.* Lanham, Md.: AltaMira Press.

Dion, P. E. 1984. "Israël et l'étranger dans le Deutéronome." In M. Gourgues and G. D. Mailhoit, *L'Altérité, vivre ensemble différents: Approches pluridisciplinaires*, pp. 211–33. Montreal: Bellarmin; and Paris: Cert.

Dutcher-Walls, P., ed. 2009. *The Family in Life and in Death. The Family in Ancient Israel: Sociological and Archaeological Perspectives.* Library of Hebrew Bible/Old Testament Studies 504. New York: T&T Clark International.

Edelman, D. V. 1996. "Ethnicity and Early Israel." In M. G. Brett, ed., *Ethnicity and the Bible*, pp. 25–56. Leiden: Brill.

Elliott, J. H. 1993. *What Is Social Scientific Criticism?* Guides to Biblical Scholarship, New Testament Series. Minneapolis: Fortress Press.

Elliott, J. H. 2001. "On Wooing Crocodiles for Fun and Profit: Confessions of an Intact Admirer." In J. J. Pilch, ed., *Social Scientific Models for Interpreting the Bible*, pp. 5–20. Leiden: Brill.

Esler, P. F. 2000. "Models in New Testament Interpretation: A Reply to David Horrell." *Journal for the Study of the New Testament* 78: pp. 107–13.

Esler, P. F. 2003. "Ezra–Nehemiah as a Narrative of (Re-invented) Israelite Identity." *Biblical Interpretation* 11/3–4: pp. 413–26.

Esler, P. F. 2006. "Social-Scientific Models in Biblical Interpretation." In P. Esler, ed., *Ancient Israel. The Old Testament in Its Social Context*, pp. 3–14. Minneapolis: Fortress Press.

Esler, P. F. 2011. *Sex, Wives, and Warriors: Reading the Old Testament Narrative with Its Ancient Audience.* Cambridge: James Clarke.

Faßbeck, G. 2005. "Tobit's Religious Universe between Kinship Loyalty and the Law of Moses." *Journal for the Study of Judaism* 36/2: pp. 173–96.

Faust, A. 2000. "The Rural Community of Ancient Israel during Iron Age II." *Bulletin of the American Schools of Oriental Research* 317: pp. 17–39.

Faust, A. 2010. "Future Directions in the Study of Ethnicity in Ancient Israel." In T. Levy, ed., *Historical Biblical Archaeology and the Future. The New Pragmatism*, pp. 55–68. London: Equinox.

Finkelstein, I. 1996. "Ethnicity and the Origin of the Iron I Settlers in the Highlands of Canaan: Can the Real Israel Stand Up?" *Biblical Archaeologist* 59/4: pp. 198–212.

Finkelstein, I., and N. A. Silberman. 2001. *The Bible Unearthed. Archaeology's New Vision of Ancient Israel and the Origin of Its Sacred Texts.* New York: Simon and Schuster.

Flanagan, J. W. 1981. "Chiefs in Israel." *Journal for the Study of the Old Testament* 20: pp. 47–73.

Fleishman, J. 2002. "*Exodus* 22:15–16 and *Deuteronomy* 22:28–29—Seduction and Rape? or Elopement and Abduction Marriage?" *Jewish Law Association Studies* 14: pp. 60–74.

Fleishman, J. 2004. "Shechem and Dinah—in the Light of Non-biblical and Biblical Sources." *Zeitschrift für die alttestamentliche Wissenschaft* 116: pp. 12–32.

Fortes, M., and E. E. Evans-Pritchard. 1940. *African Political Systems.* London: Oxford University Press.

Frevel, C. 2011. *Mixed Marriages: Intermarriage and Group Identity in the Second Temple Period.* London: T&T Clark.

Frick, F. S. 1985. *The Formation of the State in Ancient Israel: A Survey of Models and Theories*. Decatur, Ga.: Almond.

Frick, F. 1986. "Social Science Methods and Theories of Significance of the Study of the Israelite Monarchy: A Critical Review Essay." In N. K. Gottwald, ed., *Social Scientific Criticism of the Hebrew Bible and Its Social World: The Israelite Monarchy*, pp. 9–52. Semeia 37. Decatur, Ga.: Scholars Press.

Frick, F. S. 2002. "Norman Gottwald's *The Tribes of Yahweh* in the Context of 'Second-Wave' Social-Scientific Biblical Criticism." In R. Boer, ed., *Tracking "The Tribes of Yahweh": On the Trail of a Classic*, pp. 17–34. Journal for the Study of the Old Testament Supplement 351. London: Sheffield Academic Press.

Frymer-Kensky, T. 1983. "Pollution, Purification, and Purgation in Biblical Israel." In C. Meyers and M. P. O'Connor, eds., *The Word of the Lord Shall Go Forth: Essays in Honor of David Noel Freedman in Celebration of His Sixtieth Birthday*, pp. 399–414. Winona Lake, Ind. Eisenbrauns.

Frymer-Kensky, T. 1998. "Virginity in the Bible." In V. H. Matthews and B. M. Levinson, eds., *Gender and Law in the Hebrew Bible and the Ancient Near East*, pp. 79–96. Journal for the Study of the Old Testament Supplement 262. Sheffield: Sheffield Academic Press.

Frymer-Kensky, T. 2002. *Reading the Women of the Bible: A New Interpretation of Their Stories*. New York: Schocken.

Geertz, C. 1963. "The Integrative Revolution: Primordial Sentiments and Civil Politics in the New States." In C. Geertz, ed., *Old Societies and New States: The Quest for Modernity in Asia and Africa*, pp. 105–57. New York: Free Press.

Gilders, W. K. 2009. "Anthropological Approaches: Ritual in Leviticus 8, Real or Rhetorical?" In J. M. LeMon and K. H. Richards, eds., *Method Matters: Essays on the Interpretation of the Hebrew Bible in Honor of David L. Petersen*, pp. 233–50. Society of Biblical Literature Resources for Biblical Study 56. Atlanta: Society of Biblical Literature.

Glover, Neil. 2009. "Your People, My People: An Exploration of Ethnicity in Ruth." *Journal for the Study of the Old Testament* 33/3: pp. 293–313.

Goodblatt, D. 2006. *Elements of Ancient Jewish Nationalism*. New York: Cambridge University Press.

Gottwald, N. K. 1979a. "Sociological Method in the Study of Ancient Israel." In M. J. Buss, ed., *Encounter with the Text: Form and History in the Hebrew Bible*, pp. 69–81. Missoula, Mont.: Scholars Press.

Gottwald, N. K. 1979b. *The Tribes of Yahweh: A Sociology of the Religion of Liberated Israel, 1250–1050 B.C.E.* Maryknoll, N.Y.: Orbis Books.

Gottwald, N. K. 1986a. "The Participation of Free Agrarians in the Introduction of Monarchy to Ancient Israel: An Application of H. A Landsberger's Analysis of Peasant Movements." *Semeia* 37: pp. 77–106.

Gottwald, N. K., ed. 1986b. *Social Scientific Criticism of the Hebrew Bible and Its Social World: The Israelite Monarchy*. Semeia 37. Decatur, Ga.: Scholars Press.

Grabbe, L. L. 1997. *Can a "History of Israel" Be Written?* Journal for the Study of the Old Testament Supplement 245. Sheffield: Sheffield Academic Press.

Grabbe, L. L. 2006. *Ancient Israel: What Do We Know and How Do We Know It?* London: T&T Clark.

Guenther, A. 2005. "A Typology of Israelite Marriage: Kinship, Socio-economic, and Religious Factors." *Journal for the Study of the Old Testament* 29/4: pp. 387–407.

Hagedorn, A. C. 2006. "Nahum—Ethnicity and Stereotypes. Anthropological Insights into Nahum's Literary History." In P. Esler, ed., *Ancient Israel: The Old Testament in Its Social Context*, pp. 223–39. Minneapolis: Fortress Press.

Heard, R. C. 2001. *Dynamics of Diselection: Ambiguity in Genesis 12–36 and Ethnic Boundaries in Post-exilic Judah*. Semeia Studies. Atlanta: Society of Biblical Literature.

Hess, R. S., G. A. Klingbeil, and P. J. Ray. 2008. *Critical Issues in Early Israelite History*. Winona Lake, Ind.: Eisenbrauns.

Horrell, D. G. 2000. "Models and Methods in Social-Scientific Interpretation: A Response to Philip Esler." *Journal for the Study of the New Testament* 78: pp. 83–105.

Hutchinson, J., and A. D. Smith, eds. 1996. *Ethnicity*. Oxford Readers. Oxford: Oxford University Press.

Jackson, B. S. 2010. "Marriage and Divorce: From Social Institution to Halakhic Norms." In C. Hempel, ed., *The Dead Sea Scrolls: Texts and Context*, pp. 339–64. Studies on the Texts of the Desert of Judah 90. Leiden: Brill.

Johnson, W. M. 2011. *The Holy Seed Has Been Defiled: The Interethnic Marriage Dilemma in Ezra 9–10*. Sheffield: Sheffield Phoenix Press.

Kennedy, E. R. 2011. *Seeking a Homeland: Sojourn and Ethnic Identity in the Ancestral Narratives of Genesis*. Leiden: Brill.

Kessler, J. 2006. "Persia's Loyal Yahwists: Power Identity and Ethnicity in Achaemenid Yehud." In O. Lipschits and M. Oeming, eds., *Judah and the Judeans in the Persian Period*, pp. 91–121. Winona Lake, Ind.: Eisenbrauns.

Killebrew, A. E. 2005. *Biblical Peoples and Ethnicity*. ABS 9. Atlanta: Society of Biblical Literature.

Kirkpatrick, S. 2005. *Competing for Honor. A Social-Scientific Reading of Daniel 1–6*. BIS 74. Leiden: Brill.

Kitchen, K. 2003. *On the Reliability of the Old Testament*. Grand Rapids, Mich.: Cambridge.

Knoppers, G. N. 2001a. "The Davidic Genealogy: Some Contextual Considerations from the Ancient Mediterranean World." *Transeuphratène* 22: pp. 35–50.

Knoppers, G. N. 2001b. "Intermarriage, Social Complexity and Ethnic Diversity in the Genealogy of Judah." *Journal of Biblical Literature* 120/1: pp. 15–30.

Knoppers, G. N. 2003a. "The Relationship of the Priestly Genealogies to the History of the High Priesthood in Jerusalem." In O. Lipschits and J. Blenkinsopp, eds., *Judah and the Judeans in the Neo-Babylonian Period*, pp. 109–35. Winona Lake, Ind.: Eisenbrauns.

Knoppers, G. N. 2003b. "Shem, Ham and Japheth: The Universal and the Particular in the Genealogy of Nations." In M. P. Graham, S. L. McKenzie, and G. N. Knoppers, eds., *The Chronicler as Theologian. Essays in Honor of Ralph W. Klein*, pp. 13–31. Journal for the Study of Old Testament Supplement 371. London: T&T Clark.

Knoppers, G. N. 2009. "Ethnicity, Genealogy, Geography, and Change: The Judean Communities of Babylon and Jerusalem in the Story of Ezra." In G. Knoppers and K. A. Ristau, eds., *Community Identity in Judean Historiography. Biblical and Comparative Perspectives*, pp. 147–71. Winona Lake, Ind.: Eisenbrauns.

Lang, B. 1985. "Anthropology as a New Model for Biblical Studies." In B. Lang, ed., *Anthropological Approaches to the Old Testament*, pp. 1–20. Issues in Religion and Theology 8. London: SPCK.

Leach, E. R. 1982. *Social Anthropology*. Oxford: Oxford University Press.

Leeb, C. S. 2006. "Polygyny: Insights from Rural Haiti." In P. Esler, ed., *Ancient Israel: The Old Testament in Its Social Context*, pp. 50–65. Minneapolis: Fortress Press.

Lemche, N. P. 1985. *Early Israel: Anthropological and Historical Studies on the Israelite Society before the Monarchy*. Leiden: Brill.

Lemche, N. P. 1998a. *The Israelites in History and Tradition*. Louisville, Ky.: Westminster John Knox Press.

Lemche, N. P. 1998b. "The Origin of the Israelite State—A Copenhagen Perspective on the Emergence of Critical Historical Studies of Ancient Israel in Recent Times." *Scandinavian Journal of the Old Testament* 12: pp. 44–63.

Lewis, T. J. 1989. *Cults of the Dead in Ancient Israel and Ugarit*. Harvard Semitic Monographs 39. Atlanta: Scholars Press.

Mace, D. R. 1953. *Hebrew Marriage: A Sociological Study*. London: Epworth Press.

Malamat, A. 1968. "King Lists of the Old Babylonian Period and Biblical Genealogies." *Journal of the American Oriental Society* 88: pp. 163–73.

Matthews, V. 1991. "Hospitality and Hostility in Judges 4." *Biblical Theology Bulletin* 21: pp. 13–21.

Matthews, V. H., and D. C. Benhamin. 1993. *Social World of Ancient Israel 1250–587 BCE*. Peabody, Mass.: Hendrickson.

McBride, S. D. 1987. "Polity of the Covenant People: The Book of Deuteronomy." *Interpretation* 41/3: pp. 229–44.

McNutt, P. 1999. *Reconstructing the Society of Ancient Israel*. Library of Ancient Israel. Louisville, Ky.: Westminster John Knox Press.

Mendels, D. 1997. *The Rise and Fall of Jewish Nationalism*. Grand Rapids, Mich.: Eerdmans.

Mendenhall, G. E. 1962. "The Hebrew Conquest of Palestine." *Biblical Archaeologist* 25: pp. 66–87.

Meyers, C. 1988. *Discovering Eve: Ancient Israelite Women in Context*. New York: Oxford University Press.

Meyers, C. 1997. "The Family in Early Israel." In L. G. Perdue, J. Blenkinsopp, J. J. Collins, and C. Meyers, *Families in Ancient Israel*, pp. 1–47. Louisville, Ky.: Westminster John Knox Press.

Meyers, C. 1998. "Kinship and Kingship: The Early Monarchy." In M. Coogan, ed., *The Oxford History of the Biblical World*, pp. 165–205. New York: Oxford University Press.

Meyers, C. 1999. " 'Women of the Neighbourhood' (Ruth 4:17): Informal Female Networks in Ancient Israel." In A. Brenner, ed., *Ruth and Esther*, pp. 110–29. Sheffield: Sheffield Academic Press.

Meyers, C. 2007. "Contesting the Notion of Patriarchy: Anthropology and the Theorizing of Gender in Ancient Israel." In D. W. Rooke, ed., *A Question of Sex? Gender and Difference in the Hebrew Bible and Beyond*, pp. 84–105. Hebrew Bible Monographs 14. Sheffield: Sheffield Phoenix Press.

Miller, G. D. 2011. *Marriage in the Book of Tobit*. Berlin: Walter de Gruyter.

Miller, J. C. 2008. "Ethnicity and the Hebrew Bible: Problems and Prospects." *Currents in Biblical Research* 6/2: pp. 170–213.

Moffat, D. P. 2013. *Ezra's Social Drama: Identity Formation, Marriage and Social Conflict in Ezra 9 and 10*. New York: Bloomsbury.

Mullen, E. T. 1993. *Narrative History and Ethnic Boundaries: The Deuteronomistic Historian and the Creation of Israelite National Identity*. Society of Biblical Literature Semeia Series. Atlanta: Scholars Press.

Mullen, E. T. 1997. *Ethnic Myths and Pentateuchal Foundations*. Society of Biblical Literature Semeia Series. Atlanta: Scholars Press.

Neufeld, D. 2006. "Barrenness: Trance as a Protest Strategy." In P. Esler, ed., *Ancient Israel: Ancient Israel in Its Social Context*, pp. 128–41. Minneapolis: Fortress Press.

Niditch, S. 1982. "The 'Sodomite' Theme in Judges 19–20: Family, Community and Social Disintegration." *Catholic Biblical Quarterly* 44: pp. 365–78.

Niditch, S. 2008. *Judges*. Old Testament Library. Louisville, Ky.: Westminster/John Knox Press.

Oeste, G. 2011. "Butchered Brothers and Betrayed Families: Degenerating Kinship Structures in the Book of Judges." *Journal for the Study of the Old Testament* 35/3: pp. 295–316.

Overholt, T. W. 1996. *Cultural Anthropology and the Old Testament*. Minneapolis: Fortress.

Parkin, R., and L. Stone, eds. 2007. *Kinship and Family: An Anthropological Reader*. Oxford: Blackwell.

Perdue, L. G. 1997. "The Israelite and Early Jewish Family: Summary and Conclusions." In L. G. Perdue, J. Blenkinsopp, J. J. Collins, and C. Meyers, *Families in Ancient Israel*, pp. 163–222. Louisville, Ky.: Westminster John Knox Press.

Pitt-Rivers, J. 1968. "The Stranger, the Guest, and the Hostile Host." In J. G. Peristiany, ed., *Contributions to Mediterranean Sociology*, pp. 13–30. Paris: Mouton.

Provan, I. W, P. V. Long, and T. Longman. 2003. *A Biblical History of Israel*. London: Westminster John Knox Press.

Robertson-Smith, W. 1885. *Kinship and Marriage in Early Arabia*. Cambridge: Cambridge University Press.

Robertson-Smith, W. 1889. *Lectures on the Religion of the Semites. Fundamental Institutions. First Series*. London: Adam and Charles Black.

Rogerson, J. W. 1986. "Anthropology and the Old Testament." *Proceedings of the Irish Biblical Association* 10: pp. 90–102.

Sadler, R. S. 2006. "Can a Cushite Change His Skin? Cushites, 'Racial Othering' and the Hebrew Bible." *Interpretation* 60/4: pp. 386–403.

Southwood, K. E. 2011. "'And They Could Not Understand Jewish Speech': Ethnicity, Language, and Nehemiah's Intermarriage Crisis." *Journal of Theological Studies* 63/1: pp. 1–19.

Southwood, K. E. 2012. *Ethnicity and the Mixed Marriage Crisis in Ezra 9–10: An Anthropological Approach*. Oxford Theological Monographs. Oxford: Oxford University Press.

Southwood, K. E. 2014. "Will Naomi's Nation Be Ruth's Nation? Ethnic Translation as a Metaphor for Ruth's Assimilation within Judah." Translation as the Foundation for Humanistic Investigations, special issue. *Humanities* 3: pp. 102–31.

Southwood, K. E. Forthcoming. *Marriage by Capture in Judges 21: An Anthropological Approach*. Society of Old Testament Studies Supplement 1. Cambridge: Cambridge University Press.

Sparks, K. L. 1998. *Ethnicity and Identity in Ancient Israel: Prolegomena to the Study of Ethnic Sentiments and Their Expression in the Hebrew Bible*. Winona Lake, Ind.: Eisenbrauns.

Stansell, G. 2011. "David and His Friends: Social-Scientific Perspectives on the David-Jonathan Friendship." *Biblical Theology Bulletin* 41/3: pp. 115–31.

Steinberg, N. 1993. *Kinship and Marriage in Genesis: A Household Economics Perspective*. Minneapolis: Fortress Press.

Steinberg, N. 2009. "Sociological Approaches: Toward a Sociology of Childhood in the Hebrew Bible." In J. M. LeMon and K. H. Richards, eds., *Method Matters: Essays on the Interpretation of the Hebrew Bible in Honor of David L. Petersen*, pp. 251–70. Society of Biblical Literature Resources for Biblical Study 56. Atlanta: Society of Biblical Literature.

Thompson, T. L. 1978. "Historical Notes on Israel's Conquest of Palestine: A Peasants' Rebellion?" *Journal for the Study of the Old Testament* 7: pp. 20–27.

Thompson, T. L. 1992. *Early History of the Israelite People: From the Written and Archaeological Sources*. Leiden: Brill.

Thompson, T. L. 1999. *The Bible in History: How Writers Create a Past*. London: Jonathan Cape.

Weeks, S. 2002. "Biblical Literature and the Emergence of Ancient Jewish Nationalism." *Biblical Interpretation* 10/2: pp. 144–57.

Weinfeld, M. 1972. *Deuteronomy and the Deuteronomistic School*. Oxford: Clarendon.

Weisberg, D. E. 2004. "The Widow of Our Discontent: Levirate Marriage in the Bible and Ancient Israel." *Journal for the Study of the Old Testament* 28/4: pp. 403–29.

Weisberg, D. E. 2009. *Levirate Marriage and the Family in Ancient Judaism*. Waltham, Mass.: Brandeis University Press.

Whitelam, K. W. 1996. *The Invention of Ancient Israel: The Silencing of Palestinian History*. London: Routledge.

Williamson, H.G.M. 1998. "The Origins of Israel: Can We Safely Ignore the Bible?" In S. Ahituv and E. D. Oren, eds., *The Origins of Early Israel—Current Debate: Biblical, Historical, and Archaeological Perspectives*, pp. 141–51. Beersheba: Ben Gurion University of the Negev.

Willis, T. 2001. *The Elders of the City*. Atlanta: Society of Biblical Literature.

Wilson, R. R. 1977. *Genealogy and History in the Biblical World*. New Haven, Conn.: Yale University Press.

Wilson, R. R. 2005. "Deuteronomy, Ethnicity, and Reform: Reflections on the Social Setting of the Book of Deuteronomy." In J. T. Strong and S. S. Tuell, eds., *Constituting the Community. Studies on the Polity of Ancient Israel in Honor of S. Dean McBride Jr.*, pp. 107–23. Winona Lake, Ind.: Eisenbrauns.

Wilson, R. R. 2009. "Reflections on Social-Scientific Criticism." In J. M. LeMon and K. H. Richards, eds., *Method Matters. Essays on the Interpretation of the Hebrew Bible in Honor of David L. Petersen*, pp. 505–22. Society of Biblical Literature Resources for Biblical Study 56. Atlanta: Society of Biblical Literature.

Wilson, R. R. 2012. "Forced Migration and the Formation of the Prophetic Literature." In J. J. Ahn and J. Middlemas, eds., *By the Irrigation Canals of Babylon. Approaches to the Study of the Exile*, pp. 125–38. Library of Hebrew Bible/Old Testament Studies 526. London: T&T Clark.

Wood, B. 1990. *The Sociology of Pottery in Ancient Palestine: The Ceramic Industry and the Diffusion of Ceramic Style in the Bronze and Iron Ages.* Sheffield: JSOT Press.

Yee, G. A. 1999. "Gender, Class, and the Social-Scientific Study of Genesis 2–3." *Semeia* 87: pp. 177–92.

Zevit, Z. 2001. *The Religions of Ancient Israel: A Synthesis of Parallactic Approaches.* London: Francis Pinter.

4

Israel in the Context of the Ancient Near East

Anthony J. Frendo

Virtually every word in the title of this chapter needs to be clarified. For the reader of the Old Testament, the meaning of the word *Israel* might seem obvious given the fact that it is a commonplace that its significance is tantamount to the twelve tribes of Israel (or to their geographic area) mentioned in the Bible. In fact things turn out to be somewhat more nuanced than that, for the simple reason that the word *Israel* has various meanings in the Old Testament itself.[1] Moreover, we must also reckon with the fact that Israel is mentioned for the first time in an extrabiblical text on the famous stela of Merneptah dating to 1207 BC.[2] However, in this case there is a twofold problem: in the first place, not all scholars agree that this Israel is to be identified tout court with the Israel mentioned in the Bible,[3] and, second, it is in fact still a moot question whether on this stela this word stands for a geographic term or whether it refers to a nomadic group in the process of settling down. In this latter case, I am convinced by the arguments of the minority group who hold that on Merneptah's stela the word *Israel* is used as a geographic term.[4] However, this does not militate against the fact that we can view the reference on Merneptah's stela as ultimately pointing to a group of people called Israelites, whom we later encounter in the Old Testament and whom we can call "Proto-Israelites."[5] Indeed, it is self-evident that a group of people living in an area called "Israel" are Israelites. In this study, *Israel* refers to members of ancient Israel mentioned in the Old Testament and whose direct and more immediate precursors are the "Proto-Israelites" just referred to.

The preposition *in* in the title of this chapter needs to be given special attention, since it helps underscore the fact that Israel was part and parcel of the ancient Near East. The distinctive hallmarks of Israel in the

Old Testament will be addressed shortly below, but at this stage it is sufficient to say that such qualities do not in any way deny the fact that the ancient Near East, too, forms an integral part of Israel's own identity.

What is the ancient Near East? Scholars agree that the chronological parameters referred to in this phrase range from the appearance of human beings in the Near East down to the beginning of the Hellenistic period in 323 BC in this region. But which areas does this region include in modern geographic terms? It is accepted that *Near East* is a term that stems from a Eurocentric viewpoint of the world. In the fifteenth century AD, the European maritime powers split the Asian continent into three parts: (a) the Near East, which comprised the western regions of the Ottoman Empire and which included the Balkans, Greece, Turkey, and the eastern Mediterranean; (b) the Middle East, which ranged from Iraq right up to Burma and Ceylon; and (c) the Far East, which included eastern and southeastern Asia but which primarily referred to China and Japan. Nowadays we encounter a development in the use of these terms, especially with reference to the "Middle East," which stands for Turkey, Syria, Lebanon, Israel, Jordan, Egypt, the Arabian Peninsula, Iraq, and Iran.[6] The upshot is that in modern politics and economics, we speak of the Middle East as just defined, whereas today in universities one still refers to the areas just mentioned as the "Near East," with the exception that strictly speaking in this case Egypt is not included under this heading. However, given the well-known fact that Egypt played a crucial role in the history and culture of the ancient Near East, it will be taken into consideration in this study, just as happens in many universities where one speaks of Egypt and the ancient Near East.

As signaled above, the preposition *in* in the title of this chapter shows clearly that the Israel that we encounter in the Old Testament was one of the various protagonists of the ancient Near East. Indeed, "the frequent use in modern studies of a rubric like 'the Bible *and* the Ancient Near East,' is an historical absurdity in its implication that somehow the Bible is not a product or part of the ancient Near East."[7] When we speak of "Israel in the context of the ancient Near East" we are stating that we can only really understand the hallmarks of ancient Israel if we put this people and their land in their proper context, namely, that of the ancient Near East. The identity of ancient Israel can be properly appreciated if its characteristics are considered on a par with its proper context, namely, the ancient Near Eastern one. Just as the human personality can be viewed as the outcome of both heredity and environment on an equal basis,[8] so in the same manner Israel's identity can only be properly grasped once we give equal weight to the special qualities that it inherited, as well as to the ancient Near Eastern world of which it formed an integral part.

So in order to better appreciate ancient Israel, we must try to get at its own particular characteristics while simultaneously putting them in the context of the ancient Near Eastern world. Since both variables are equally important, and since therefore we can never get to know Israel properly unless these two variables are taken into consideration, both the Bible and the other sources (those written as well as the nonwritten material remains) recovered in the archaeological exploration of Egypt and the ancient Near East have to be taken into account. When we make a comparison and contrast of ancient Israel with these two areas just mentioned, we realize that the special hallmarks of Israel as it features in the Old Testament are two: its status as a newcomer in the land of Canaan and its marginal status.[9] In ancient Egypt, these two qualities meant that someone was "a barbarian, immoral, and chaotic,"[10] while in the Bible being a newcomer and marginal was tantamount to a proof of being chosen by God.[11] But why did God choose Israel in the first place? To this query the Old Testament does not furnish a proper answer; the special relationship between Yahweh and the people whom he chose is "a mystery" to the extent that this relationship ends up by highlighting Yahweh's "uniqueness" (Isa. 43:10).[12]

Besides the two qualities just discussed that Israel inherited, we must also look at its environment, namely, the context of Egypt and of the ancient Near Eastern world of which it formed an integral part, if we really want to understand this people and its culture. In this context, the archaeology of Egypt and of the ancient Near East plays a crucial role. Thanks to the archaeological work done in these regions, we now possess a great amount of data that throws light on the Israelites and their customs and which helps us to get a better understanding not only of the broad outline of their history and culture but also of specific biblical passages. The famous British orientalist Samuel Rolles Driver had insisted already a long time ago that Old Testament scholars should make it a point to take into consideration the results of archaeology as they impinge on the Old Testament and to learn how to evaluate them properly. However, it is important to be very careful when linking the results of archaeology with those of critical biblical investigation. Indeed, Driver underscored "the need to beware of attempts to set archaeology against higher and historical criticism, and to make exaggerated claims about the degree to which archaeological discovery vindicates the truth of biblical statements."[13] In this respect, the main point at issue is to learn how to properly link and integrate the results of a critical analysis of the biblical texts with those of archaeological excavations undertaken according to the rules of archaeology and which include the critical study of both written and nonwritten data retrieved in the excavations.[14] Therefore, the whole enterprise ultimately boils down to integrating in a proper fashion textual and artifactual evidence.[15] With respect to ancient Israel, this means integrating the results of a critical analysis of the Old Testament texts with the results of the relevant archaeological research in Egypt and the ancient Near East *after each type of data has been studied separately.*[16] It is only then that the results of the textual analysis of the Old Testament can be compared and contrasted with the archaeological results (both of the inscriptions and of the nonwritten artifacts).

However, for the purposes of this study, the upshot of the foregoing points is for me to consider select results of the archaeology of ancient Egypt and of the ancient Near East so as to throw light on the land and the people of ancient Israel as they appear in the Old Testament and to even understand better the formation processes of the latter. Before proceeding any further, it is important to realize that many biblical scholars are engaged in a discussion as to whether they should be concentrating on a diachronic study of the Bible or on a synchronic one. Simply put, the former type of study deals with the biblical texts through time, and therefore it takes into consideration, among other things, matters such as the sources used, the formation of the texts, and their various editions. On the other hand, in a synchronic study of the Bible scholars concentrate on the final version of a particular book of the Bible, and they purport to make sense of the text as it stands in front of them in its final version. Which of these two approaches is the better one? If we want to understand the meaning of a given biblical text, we need to use both types of analysis. The analogy of personality viewed as the outcome of both heredity and the environment, which was used above to illustrate the importance of the special hallmarks that ancient Israel inherited *and* of its being an integral part of the ancient Near East, can be applied to the *equal importance* that both the diachronic study and the synchronic study of texts have when it comes to determining the meaning of the latter. The debate is endless, but it must be made clear that, although in the last analysis students of the Bible must get at the meaning of the text in its final edition, this does not preclude the fact that they must also seriously take into account the telltale clues of the sources and of the editorial processes that helped to bring forth a particular text and which do throw light on the meaning of its final edition. Both approaches are important for the simple reason that ultimately they both stem from attempts to understand texts. Indeed, the diachronic exercise of source analysis itself originates from efforts to grasp the biblical narratives (especially those of the Pentateuch) "as finished wholes" but which "the texts themselves seemed systematically to frustrate."[17] Indeed, "biblical criticism is not a matter of *processing* the text, but of *understanding* it."[18]

All this makes it clear that the Old Testament took time to reach its present format and that, although biblical scholars are bound to unfold the meaning of texts as handed down to us in their final edition, still the points just discussed demonstrate that they can only fulfill this task properly if they also take the origin and growth of texts as well as their various editions into consideration. However, the desire to account for the biblical texts from a synchronic point of view has led some scholars to overstate their point that the telltale clues for various editions of certain narratives do not warrant the conclusion that such editions ever existed unless the latter are actually extant. Thus, for example, Arthur Gibson states that "unless there is proof from within early texts for the existence of two historically distinct narratives, the absence of unedited narrative is absence of requisite proof for editing."[19] Although this is true in a certain sense, it is not the whole truth, since it is equally true to say that the absence of edited narratives, for example, in the Pentateuch, is not tantamount to there not having ever been such narratives, for the simple reason that the absence of evidence is not identical to evidence of absence.[20] Indeed, the hypothesis held by a number of biblical scholars that certain biblical literary writings, such as the Pentateuch, must have been written on the basis of preexisting sources is strengthened by the evidence regarding the composition of Mesopotamian literature. However, it is true that this conclusion can be certain only "in very clear cases" or when (as in the case of the Epic of Gilgamesh, which circulated in Mesopotamia) "variant copies" of a literary piece are extant.[21] The extant copies of the very popular Epic of Gilgamesh are an eye-opener to biblical scholars because they can throw light on the formation of the Pentateuch. There are two extant copies in Sumerian of this epic that were freely retold in Mesopotamia; this oral transmission must have been joined to material that is no longer extant, thus leading to the formation of the Babylonian version of this epic dating to circa 1700 BC. It is also highly interesting to note that a "comparison of different copies of Sumerian incantations and Babylonian translations of them" allows us to find "modifications creeping into the wording in a manner quite like the hair-splitting analysis of even single sentences in the Hebrew Bible proposed by scholars in the wake of Wellhausen."[22] So the hypothesis that a number of Old Testament narratives that we have were composed on the basis of different sources and that these stories are at times found in different editions becomes ever more likely when we consider that Mesopotamia has furnished us with hard evidence of such practices. The Israelite authors were simply composing their literature in the manner that was customary in the world of which they formed a part.

The ancient Near Eastern practice of editorial expansions of texts (parallel to a similar usage that obtained in ancient Israel) is not confined to myths or epics. The practice can also be found in historical documents from Mesopotamia, thus showing us that (just as happens in biblical scholarship) we must exercise historical criticism by comparing the different versions of stories dealing with historical events if we want to reconstruct the latter. The military campaigns of the Assyrian king Sennacherib (704–681 BC) are relayed in his Annals as well as in an inscription found in the Walters Art Museum. A detailed comparison and contrast of the information about this king's campaigns as relayed in these two documents led to the conclusion that the original events were registered in *two sources* that were *independent of each other*.[23] According to the Annals of Sennacherib, this king conducted eight military campaigns, whereas according to his inscription in the Walters Art Gallery he conducted only five such campaigns![24] The Old Testament, too, contains similar conundrums (on a micro- as well as on a macrolevel), which scholars try to grapple with by exercising the art and science of the "historical critical method."[25] Thus, for example, 1 Sam. 17:49 states

that David is the hero who killed "the Philistine," with the overall context of the final version of the narrative where this text is found implying that "the Philistine" was Goliath; yet in 2 Sam. 21:19 we are told very
clearly that it was a certain Elhanan who killed Goliath. Another example can be found in the book of Joshua, which portrays the entry of the
Israelites in Canaan as a quick military campaign, whereas the first two
chapters of the book of Judges depict it as piecemeal, largely peaceful,
and protracted in time.[26] It is clear that Old Testament scholars and
those of ancient Mesopotamia face similar problems when it comes to
reconstructing past historical events on the basis of the available documents, and they therefore have to read the relevant texts in the same
critical manner if they want to extract the required historical information. This is so because the "production" of texts in Israel was similar to
that in Mesopotamia.

The documents retrieved in the ancient Near East can not only help
Old Testament scholars to understand better the processes of how texts
were expanded and edited; they can also throw light on specific aspects
of the history of ancient Israel itself. Thus, for example, the documents
found at the important ancient site of Mari (which scholars reckon as
falling within the field of Mesopotamian archaeology, although the site
is actually located in modern Syria, right on the border with Iraq) help
us to put in better perspective the rule of King David: just as Zimri-Lim
governed "a Sim'alite tribal state" after he had taken over the "city seat"
and the administrative structure of Samsi-Addu, so, too, David is portrayed in the biblical texts as ruling over the northern and the southern
tribes of Israel after having taken over Jerusalem, which functioned as
a "neutral capital." In this sense, Mari offers an analogy "to early tribal
Israel."[27] In fact, the Mari documents help us to appreciate much better
the "tribal-nomadic" remote origins of the Israelites; in these documents
there are two words that in English could be rendered as "king": *malikum*, which per se refers to "sheikhs still at the tribal-nomadic stage of
society" and which is the cognate of the Hebrew word *melek*, the word for
"king" in the Old Testament; and *šarrum*, which indicates a sedentary
king.[28] There is one document from the Mari Archive that mentions the
"*malikum* ritual," and this led Abraham Malamat to ask whether in this
particular case *malikum* could be referring to "contacting the ancestral
spirits of the kings,"[29] which in its own turn led him to propose a similar

meaning for the cognate word *mlk* in Isaiah 57:9, which he translates thus: "You have given offering to the *mlk* [the deceased king?] with oil, and you have provided many perfumes; and you have sent your envoys far, you sent down to Sheol."[30] The standard Hebrew text of the Old Testament (known as the Masoretic Text) vocalizes the consonants *mlk* as *melek*, namely, "king," but (given the context of this biblical passage) scholars generally vocalize it as *Moloch*, with reference to the cult of this west Semitic god of the underworld. Malamat's proposal fits the context of Isaiah 57:9 perfectly, without the need of changing the vowels of the Masoretic Text in a way that ends up by unnecessarily introducing the god Moloch.

The Mari Archive has also yielded letters from the royal palace there that show us that in the eighteenth century BC the city of Emar (located in modern Syria) had no kings. These letters speak of the "assembly," of the elders, or simply of Emar. We find a different situation five centuries later, since the thirteenth-century BC archive from Emar itself shows us that this city had a limited type of kingship and that it had not been able to oust the previous well-established forms of authority there. Indeed, at this time at Emar we encounter elders and clans, as well as religious traditions that did *not* give the king a primary function.[31] This scenario helps us to put in its proper context and to understand much better the situation in early Israel when kingship was introduced circa 1000 BC. When the Israelites introduced kingship they did so in such a way as to let it "overlie an existing tribal system." It is interesting to note that Emar "provides a rare view of 'limited kingship' in the ancient Near East,"[32] and it therefore throws precious light on the way in which the early Israelites introduced the institution of kingship into what was up to then a loose confederation of tribes in the central hill country of Palestine.

It is a commonplace that monotheism played a crucial role in ancient Israel. Although the issues of the origins and of the development of monotheism in Israel are quite complex (and they cannot be dealt with here), still it is important to state that most scholars agree that Moses was responsible for an incipient monotheism and that in its formative period Israel was officially bound to monolatry; it was only in the exilic period that Israel professed and was bound to strict monotheism in the way we understand it today. The documents unearthed in Mesopotamia can also throw light on this complex point. It is a well-known fact that religion in Mesopotamia was polytheistic; however, it should also be pointed out that as time went by "some gods were being further glorified by swallowing up their rivals. The supreme example of this occurs in a small god list ... devoted to Marduk alone," which "has every claim to present Marduk as a monotheistic god."[33] However, at the same time we must assume that the compiler of this list would not have denied the existence of Zarpānîtum, Marduk's spouse in his temple in Babylon.[34] At first sight this might seem to militate against the list in question being viewed as providing any light on monotheism in Israel; and yet, a closer look at the evidence reveals that in reality the list is tantamount to stating that there was one god (Marduk), who had a spouse. The focal point would still be the god Marduk. In this sense, this evidence from Mesopotamia offers us an excellent context for the much-debated inscriptions from Israel that speak of "Yahweh and his a/Asherah," where the latter could be understood as referring either to Asherah (one of the many west Semitic goddesses of fertility) or to her symbol, namely, a wooden pole or tree.[35] I think that the same pattern obtained both in Mesopotamia and in Israel, namely, that a monotheistic trend centering on a male god was itself not annulled via the mention of his consort. Be that as it may, however, it is clear that this practice was not sufficiently orthodox in Israel, and we can understand why, when the monotheistic trend there was fully developed by the sixth century BC, Yahweh was presented as unambiguously enjoining explicit monotheism when we read: "I am Yahweh, and there is no other; besides me there is no god" (Isa. 45:5).

Mesopotamia has also yielded many legal documents that help us to put in a much clearer context the various legal texts found in the Old Testament. This is applicable to collections of laws as well as to particular customs. Thus, for example, in Judg. 11:1–2 we learn that Gilead was the father of Jephthah, who was born of a prostitute. However, Gilead "also had sons by his wife," and these sons excluded Jephthah from their father's inheritance. This passage seems to echo the Sumerian law code of Lipit-Ishtar, which allowed the sons a man had by a harlot to be able to inherit from him, but only when he had had no sons by his wife.[36] On a broader scale, we find a very close parallelism between the collection of biblical laws known as "the Book of the Covenant" in Exod. 21–23 and various ancient Near Eastern legal traditions. Exod. 21:28–32, for example, presents a law dealing with two various instances of a goring ox. It is highly interesting to note that this biblical law is worded virtually in an identical manner to a similar law found in sections 53–55 of the Eshnunna law code.[37]

The numerous texts in Akkadian that archaeologists have unearthed in various parts of the Near East as well as in Egypt can also help us to better understand certain idioms in Hebrew.[38] Thus, for example, in the Old Testament there are three instances (1 Sam. 24:15; 2 Sam. 9:8, 16:9) where we find the phrase "dead dog." The context of these passages allows us to comprehend that this phrase is denoting something negative about the person it refers to, without, however, allowing us to get at its full nuance and meaning. In Akkadian "dead dog" is used as a "disparagement of oneself, in letters, to denote humility."[39] Indeed, in Neo-Assyrian, it also clearly refers to a poor person—thus, we read: "I used to be a poor man, a dead dog."[40] Overall, the evidence from Akkadian indicates that the phrase "dead dog" is used as a disparagement of oneself or to show that someone is unimportant or poor.[41] With all this in mind, readers can appreciate much better the meaning of the three passages from the books of Samuel just referred to.

Ancient Egypt, too, has yielded a great deal of material that can help Old Testament scholars to place the texts they study in their proper context. It goes without saying that when the Old Testament and Egypt are mentioned, it is the narratives about the Exodus that first come to mind. It is a well-established fact that the biblical narratives about the liberation of the Hebrew slaves from Egypt play a pivotal role in most of the Old Testament and that they provide the background to various types of biblical texts, whether historical, prophetic, or hymnic. On the other hand, the historicity of the Exodus narratives is a very moot question. And yet, the majority of scholars (including those who are quite skeptical) are of the opinion that behind the narratives that describe the liberation of the Hebrews from Egypt there must be historical events, although their precise details escape us. Indeed, Alan H. Gardiner expressed all this very aptly way back in 1922 when he wrote: "That Israel was in Egypt under one form or another no historian could possibly doubt; a legend of such tenacity representing the early fortunes of a people under so unfavourable an aspect could not have arisen save as a reflexion, however much distorted, of real occurrences."[42]

The fact that in the Egyptian records we have no direct explicit evidence about this particular event does not mean that the latter never occurred: first, because it is unsound to argue from silence and, second, because we do have proof of Egyptian pharaohs who erased the evidence of rulers before them, whose memory they wanted to simply delete from history. Thus, for example, Thutmosis III erased the names of his mother-in-law and of his uncle, and he also "altered" inscriptions. If the information in the book of Exodus is true with respect to the fact that Moses had held an important official position at the Egyptian court, whichever pharaoh was involved at the time of the exodus of the Hebrews from Egypt "would have had special reasons for wishing excise [sic] any reference" to Moses.[43] Different scholars hold different opinions regarding the date of this event, although the most commonly held view is that it would have taken place sometime in the second half of the thirteenth century BC.

Egyptian records provide more detailed and explicit information that throws light on the history of Israel (and on the related biblical passages) when it comes to the first millennium BC. Thus, for example, in 2 Kings 19:9 and Isaiah 37:9 we find mention of "Tirhakah king of Cush," who is presented as an ally of Hezekiah, king of Judah, in his war against Sennacherib in 701 BC. Scholars generally dismiss this piece of biblical information on the grounds that Tirhakah (= Egyptian Taharqa) only became king of Egypt in 690 BC and therefore he could not have been Hezekiah's ally in 701 BC! However, there is another side to this issue, since we should remember that the second book of Kings as well as the first Isaiah had not received their present form before 681 BC for the simple reason that they record the death of Sennacherib, which took place in that year (see 2 Kings 19:37 and Isa. 37:38). Thus, it stands to reason that the narrator of 2 Kings 19:9 and Isaiah 37:9 would have labeled Tirhakah by his current title of 681 BC or thereafter.[44] Hence, the biblical title that the Bible gives to Tirhakah as "king of Cush" seems to make perfect sense. Moreover, epigraphic evidence from Iran supports this. An Assyrian text from Tang-i Var in Iran dating to 706 BC at the latest mentions "Shapataka, King/Ruler of Nubia/Kush ('Meluhha')." It is highly probable that this shows that the kings of Cush had resorted to the custom of appointing two rulers to govern the vast area of Egypt and Nubia: there would have been a senior king, ruling from Memphis, and his helper (who would be his future successor), ruling from Napata in Nubia. Thus it appears that when Shabako consolidated Nubian rule over Egypt in 715 BC, he appointed Shebiktu (= Shapataka, mentioned in the Assyrian text just referred to) as his coruler in Cush. In 702 BC, Shebiktu became the chief ruler of Egypt, and he appointed Taharqa "as ruler of Kush in turn—which is what we have (for 701) in Kings and Isaiah."[45] Hence in 701 BC Taharqa was indeed ruler of Cush but not yet of all Egypt, exactly as this situation is pictured in 2 Kings 19:9 and Isaiah 37:9.

Ancient Egyptian literature has also shed important light on various literary genres of the Old Testament, and the latter's hymnic literature is certainly no exception. It has long been known, for example, that the famous Egyptian hymn known as "Akhenaten's Great Hymn" has had a great influence on Ps. 104. Recently John Day has argued convincingly that Ps. 104:20–30 is directly dependent on this Egyptian hymn to the sun; this is true even of the one instance (Ps. 104:24) out of a total of six parallels "where the psalm reference is out of sequence with Akhenaten's hymn."[46] Indeed, the psalm's discourse on God's creation as a whole would be more appropriately located somewhat later, namely, after verses 25–26, as had already been argued by some biblical scholars and as is in fact appropriately found in Akhenaten's hymn itself. Thus the dependence of the scribe of Ps. 104:20–30 on this Egyptian hymn is so great that in fact the latter has helped biblical scholars to find confirmation for their hypotheses that account for a better sequence and exegesis of the biblical text![47] Akhenaten's Great Hymn to the Sun would have reached Canaan in the brief Amarna period, and "eventually an Israelite author [would have] combined motifs from Akhenaten's Sun hymn with other motifs originating in the Canaanite storm god (vv. 1–18), thus producing the psalm we now have."[48]

The points discussed thus far have shown that the archaeological remains from Egypt and the ancient Near East help us to understand the overall context of the Old Testament much better and that thereby they contribute to our accounting in a more appropriate manner for the documents that it contains. Although certain problems linked with the historical information found in the Old Testament were already taken into consideration above, I would like to conclude this study by discussing further the question of the historical reliability or otherwise of the Old

Testament. I am doing this in view of the fact that it is well known that many readers of the Old Testament are very concerned as to whether these biblical documents are historical or not. In this regard, it is important to first point out that the work of many biblical scholars over the centuries has clearly established the fact that the Bible as a whole is not a historical book per se but a religious one. However, this does not mean that it lacks a historical basis or indeed at times very precise historical information. Biblical scholars can reach proper conclusions in this regard only if they examine the texts critically. Prime importance should be given to establishing the genre of a particular text before any conclusions can be reached. Indeed, this is the only way whereby scholars can establish the "plain sense" of a particular Old Testament text, thereby *eventually* establishing whether it is historical or not: "Critical scholarship requires attention to the type of text being studied. What is its plain sense will depend on that."[49] The "plain sense" is the sense of the text that is unfolded when the latter is read critically. In fact, the plain sense of a particular text or book of the Old Testament could turn out to be an allegorical one, just as in the case, for example, of the Song of Songs, the plain sense of which is not historical.[50] The point is that "biblical criticism, in its quest for this plain sense, is a semantic or linguistic and a literary operation first and foremost, only indirectly concerned with the original, the intended, the historical, or the literal meaning."[51] However, even if the plain sense of a given text turns out to be nonhistorical, that particular text could still contain precious historical details that scholars can glean from a close reading of the text and which could help them to uncover certain important historical information pertaining to ancient Israel. This is achieved by reading "documents obliquely," and this allows us to glean historical information even from a text whose plain sense is not historical.[52] Ultimately the Old Testament is a religious book that contains historical documents embedded in narratives, the overall plain sense of which is not historical, as well as nuggets of historical information found in texts that do not even contain any archival details.

This type of historical information happens to be corroborated by the results of Egyptian and ancient Near Eastern archaeology. Time and time again archaeologists have unearthed many remains that include inscriptions containing very specific historical information about ancient Israel and which allow us to conclude that the Old Testament is essentially a theological reflection that is largely based on historical experience. In simple terms one can say that the Old Testament is not a history book but that it certainly contains historical information that is often corroborated by the archaeological remains of Egypt and of the ancient Near East. Thus, for example, the Neo-Assyrian Annals mention the names of various Israelite kings such as Ahab, Jehu, Menahem, Pekah, Hosea, and Manasseh while also giving us certain details about them. This very simple fact itself allows us to infer that it is highly probable that even other events in the Old Testament that have no extrabiblical corroboration could very well have a historical basis.[53]

An interesting example is provided by the case of the Egyptian king Sheshonq I, who conducted a campaign in Egypt's province of Canaan in 925 BC with the intent of renewing Egypt's hold on this province. This campaign is recorded mainly in a large triumphal relief of his on the walls of the temple in Karnak, but it is also reported in an inscription from the temple of Amun at El-Hibeh and on a fragmentary stela in Hall K also at Karnak.[54] These Egyptian sources list "180 or so" places that Sheshonq overcame.[55] Some of the toponyms in these sources are damaged, either totally or partially, but from those that can be read it appears that Sheshonq attacked the regions of the Negev, the Shepelah, the hills of Ephraim, and Gilead—Jerusalem and other places in the Judaean hills do not feature in the legible extant Egyptian sources.[56] But an attack on Jerusalem is mentioned in the Old Testament, namely, in 1 Kings 14:25–26 (see also 2 Chron. 12:2–9), where the pharaoh's name is registered as Shishak. The most likely explanation for this situation is the fact that the Egyptian sources list the cities that Sheshonq actually *conquered*—which was not the case with Jerusalem. This explains why this city is not mentioned in the Egyptian sources. The biblical texts just cited describe Sheshonq's going up against Jerusalem with the intent of conquering it, but no actual attack or victory over the city is mentioned. Instead we are told that Shishak carried off the treasures of the Temple and of the royal house. This seems to be best explained as a move by Rehoboam, king of Judah at the time, to pay a heavy ransom to Sheshonq, thereby averting an actual military attack that the pharaoh had planned. Be that as it may, archaeologists of Palestine have linked the destruction layers of sites in the region of Canaan with Sheshonq's campaign of 925 BC, and it is these synchronisms that have led scholars to set up the generally accepted chronology of the first three kings of Israel, namely, Saul (ca. 1025–1005 BC), David (ca. 1005–965 BC), and Solomon (968–928 BC).[57]

The two foregoing cases, namely, the mention of various Israelite kings in the Neo-Assyrian Annals and the Egyptian record of Sheshonq's campaign in Canaan, provide us with further interesting examples of how extrabiblical information helps us to appreciate certain important historical personages and events that are mentioned in the Old Testament and which have been molded into narratives that are replete with theological concerns. Hence in the narratives found in 1 and 2 Samuel as well as in 1 Kings 1–11, we encounter the narrator's "pervading interest in the characters of the narrative—the tragically inadequate Saul, the heroic David, the ambitious but flawed Solomon—and the intrigues of the royal court."[58] And yet, a close reading of these Old Testament narratives has allowed scholars to conclude that we can glean from them "archival and other details" that can be linked with the results of archaeological research in Palestine and which in no way militate against the structure of the events assumed by the biblical narrators. Indeed, we can conclude that "the skepticism of some modern historians, who argue that the biblical accounts of the United Monarchy are fictional retroversions from a later time, seems unwarranted."[59]

The examples adduced above together with their relative discussions should have shown that there is indeed an essential link between ancient Israel as depicted in the Old Testament and Egypt and the ancient Near Eastern world of which it formed a part. Indeed, as already pointed out above, in order to understand Israel in a more comprehensive manner that does justice to the historical events as well as to the theological reflections upon them, one should give equal weight to the critical reading of the Old Testament texts and to a similar critical assessment of Egypt and of the ancient Near Eastern world as revealed by the material and textual remains that archaeologists have been unearthing for more than two centuries. When this is done, we can place the linguistic, the historical, the legal, the literary, the mythological, the religious, the geographic, and the political hallmarks of Israel as it is presented in the Old Testament in their proper context. Moreover, the evidence marshaled above also indicates that when Old Testament exegetes come to grips with the world of Egypt and of the ancient Near East, they can benefit a great deal even with respect to the understanding of the formation of the biblical texts that they study and with respect to the editorial processes that led to their composition. Only then can they combine the results of both a diachronic and a synchronic analysis of these religious texts and, together with all those who read the Old Testament with a critical eye, address Yahweh with the words of the psalmist: "Your word is a lamp to my feet and a light to my path" (Ps. 119:105).

NOTES

1. *Israel* could refer to all Israel, and therefore to both the northern and the southern kingdoms, as in Deut. 34:10 and 2 Kings 24:13, but it could also simply signify the northern kingdom of Israel, as in Hosea 1:1 and 2 Sam. 3:10. Finally there is the rare case when *Israel* is used with reference to the southern kingdom of Judah, as in 2 Chron. 11:3 and 21:2.

2. John A. Wilson, "Hymn of Victory of Mer-ne-Ptah (The 'Israel Stela')," in James B. Pritchard, ed., *Ancient Near Eastern Texts Relating to the Old Testament*, 3rd ed. with supplement (Princeton, N.J.: Princeton University Press, 1969), pp. 376–78.

3. The most logical inference backed by archaeological evidence is that of seeing a link between the "Israel" mentioned on the Merneptah Stela and the later Israel of the Old Testament, but for caution's sake preferably labeling the Israelites of the twelfth century BC as "Proto-Israelites." See William G. Dever, "Archaeology and the Emergence of Early Israel," in John R. Bartlett, ed., *Archaeology and Biblical Interpretation* (London: Routledge, 1997), pp. 20–50 (especially pp. 43–45).

4. Anthony J. Frendo, "Back to Basics: A Holistic Approach to the Problem of the Emergence of Ancient Israel," in John Day, ed., *In Search of Pre-exilic Israel: Proceedings of the Oxford Old Testament Seminar* (London: T&T Clark International, 2004), pp. 41–64 (especially pp. 52–53 and references there). Unfortunately James Hoffmeier has virtually glossed over the discussion on this complex problem surrounding the determinative that the Egyptian scribe used for the word *Israel*; see James K. Hoffmeier, "The (Israel) Stela of Merneptah," in William W. Hallo, ed., *The Context of Scripture*, vol. 2, *Monumental Inscriptions from the Biblical World* (Leiden: Brill, 2000), pp. 40–41, where he takes the word *seed* on the stela to mean "human offspring" rather than "grain" while affirming that "it has long been noted that the writing of Israel uses the determinative (semantic indicator) for an ethnic group, and not for a geographic region or city."

5. Dever, "Archaeology and the Emergence of Early Israel," p. 43.

6. Ann C. Gunter, "Asia and the Ancient Near East," *Asian Art* 1, no. 2 (1988): pp. 3–5 (especially p. 3). Indeed, in modern parlance, especially in that of the media, *Middle East* turns out to be a fluid term, seeing that sometimes it includes even North African places, such as Libya, and subcontinental countries, such as Pakistan (p. 3).

7. Peter Machinist, "The Question of Distinctiveness in Ancient Israel: An Essay," in Mordechai Cogan and Israel Eph'al, eds., *Ah Assyria ... : Studies in Assyrian History and Ancient Near Eastern Historiography Presented to Hayim Tadmor* (Jerusalem: Magnes Press, 1991), pp. 196–212, at p. 197; emphasis added.

8. Indeed, "*personality*—or any of its subsystems, such as habit, trait, sentiment = *f* (heredity) × (*environment*). The two causal factors are not added together, but are related as multiplier and multiplicand. If either were zero there could be no personality"; see Gordon W. Allport, *Pattern and Growth in Personality* (New York: Holt, Rinehart and Winston, 1961), p. 68.

9. Although the Old Testament itself tells us that some of the components of ancient Israel stemmed from within the land of Canaan, still overall the Bible underscores the fact that the origins of Israel are from outside Canaan. Indeed, Israel enters Canaan "as an outsider"; see Machinist, "Question of Distinctiveness in Ancient Israel," pp. 209–10. God took Israel "from the midst of another nation" (Deut. 4:34), and he tells Israel: "The land will not be sold irretrievably, for the land is mine, [and] you are aliens and sojourners" (Lev. 25:23).

10. Machinist, "Question of Distinctiveness in Ancient Israel," p. 211.

11. Ibid., p. 211; see also Deut. 7:7–8.

12. Machinist, "Question of Distinctiveness in Ancient Israel," p. 206.

13. J. A. Emerton, "Samuel Rolles Driver, 1846–1914," in C. Edmund Bosworth, ed., *A Century of British Orientalists: 1902–2001* (Oxford: Oxford University Press, 2001), pp. 122–38, at p. 133.

14. For a thorough and lucid discussion of the nature of biblical criticism, see John Barton, *The Nature of Biblical Criticism* (Louisville, Ky.: Westminster John Knox, 2007).

15. For a recent treatment of this problem from the methodological point of view, see Anthony J. Frendo, *Pre-exilic Israel, the Hebrew Bible, and Archaeology: Integrating Text and Artefact* (New York: T&T Clark International, 2011).

16. Roland de Vaux, "On Right and Wrong Uses of Archaeology," in James A. Sanders, ed., *Near Eastern Archaeology in the Twentieth Century: Essays in Honor of Nelson Glueck* (Garden City, N.Y.: Doubleday, 1970), pp. 64–80 (especially p. 70).

17. Barton, *Nature of Biblical Criticism*, p. 63.

18. Ibid., p. 57.

19. Arthur Gibson, *Text and Tablet: Near Eastern Archaeology, the Old Testament and New Possibilities* (Aldershot: Ashgate, 2000), p. 132.

20. Indeed, "the weakness of the *argumentum e silentio* is its presumption that the evidence available to us is complete"; Stanley Mayer Burstein, "The *Babylonica* of Berossus," *Sources from the Ancient Near East* 1, no. 5 (1978): pp. 141–81, at p. 173.

21. W. G. Lambert, "Ancient Near Eastern Studies: Mesopotamia," in J. W. Rogerson and Judith M. Lieu, eds., *The Oxford Handbook of Biblical Studies* (Oxford: Oxford University Press, 2006), pp. 74–88, at p. 83.

22. Ibid.

23. A. K. Grayson, "The Walters Art Gallery Sennacherib Inscription," *Archiv für Orientforschung* 20 (1963): pp. 83–96 (especially pp. 84, 87, 89).

24. Ibid., p. 84.

25. I use the phrase "historical critical method" simply because it is so common in the literature on the Old Testament. However, as such my stance is identical to that of Barton when the latter states that "it is not a concern for history per se, but in a particular style of studying history that biblical scholars have been 'critical.' Historical study, where that is the concern, can be either critical or noncritical; and critical study can be historical or nonhistorical. This suggests that the term 'historical-critical method' is an awkward hybrid and might be better avoided" (*Nature of Biblical Criticism*, p. 39).

26. For one critical overview of how Israel probably emerged in history, see Frendo, "Back to Basics."

27. Daniel E. Fleming, "Mari and the Possibilities of Biblical Memory," *Revue d'Assyriologie et d'Archeologie orientale* 92 (1998): pp. 41–78, at pp. 44, 47.

28. Abraham Malamat, *Mari and the Early Israelite Experience* (Oxford: Oxford University Press, 1989), p. 102.

29. Ibid.

30. Ibid., p. 108; see also p. 103.

31. Daniel E. Fleming, "A Limited Kingship: Late Bronze Age Emar," *Ugarit-Forschungen* 24 (1992): pp. 59–71 (especially pp. 67, 70).

32. Ibid., p. 71.

33. W. G. Lambert, "The Historical Development of the Mesopotamian Pantheon: A Study in Sophisticated Polytheism," in Hans Goedicke and J.J.M. Roberts, eds., *Unity and Diversity: Essays in the History, Literature, and Religion of the Ancient Near East* (Baltimore: Johns Hopkins University Press, 1975), pp. 191–200, at pp. 197–98).

34. Ibid., p. 198.

35. William G. Dever, *Did God Have a Wife? Archaeology and Folk Religion in Ancient Israel* (Grand Rapids, Mich.: Eerdmans, 2005) (especially pp. 101–2, 196–208).

36. Yairah Amit, "Judges," in Adele Berlin and Marc Zvi Brettler, eds., *The Jewish Study Bible* (Oxford: Oxford University Press, 2004), pp. 508–57 (especially p. 535); articles 25–27 of Lipit-Ishtar's law code—see S. N. Kramer, "Lipit-Ishtar Lawcode," in Pritchard, *Ancient Near Eastern Texts Relating to the Old Testament*, pp. 159–61 (especially p. 160).

37. Lambert, "Ancient Near Eastern Studies," p. 82; Albrecht Goetze, "The Laws of Eshnunna," in Pritchard, *Ancient Near Eastern Texts Relating to the Old Testament*, pp. 161–63 (especially p. 163).

38. An archive of 382 documents discovered at Tell el-Amarna in Egypt mainly consisted of letters to the pharaoh written in Akkadian that were sent to him by various rulers of the Near East, mostly by the local rulers of the Levant who were subservient to him; see William L. Moran, ed. and trans., *The Amarna Letters* (Baltimore: Johns Hopkins University Press, 1992).

39. A. Leo Oppenheim, editor-in-charge, *The Assyrian Dictionary of the Oriental Institute of the University of Chicago*, vol. 8 (Chicago: University of Chicago, 1971), p. 72.

40. Ibid.

41. Ibid.

42. Alan H. Gardiner, "The Geography of the Exodus," in *Recueil d'études Égyptologiques dédiées à la Mémoire de Jean-Francois Champollion* (Paris: Librairie Ancienne Honoré Champion, 1922), pp. 203–15, at p. 204.

43. Gibson, *Text and Tablet*, p. 146.

44. Kenneth Kitchen, "Ancient Near Eastern Studies: Egypt," in J. W. Rogerson and Judith M. Lieu, eds., *The Oxford Handbook of Biblical Studies* (Oxford: Oxford University Press, 2006), pp. 89–98 (especially p. 94).

45. Ibid., p. 95.

46. John Day, "Psalm 104 and Akhenaten's Hymn to the Sun," in Susan Gillingham, ed., *Jewish and Christian Approaches to the Psalms* (Oxford: Oxford University Press, 2013), pp. 211–28, at p. 215.

47. Ibid.

48. Ibid., p. 224.

49. Barton, *Nature of Biblical Criticism*, p. 109.

50. Ibid., pp. 97–98.

51. Ibid., p. 101.

52. Ziony Zevit, *The Religions of Ancient Israel: A Synthesis of Parallactic Approaches* (London: Continuum, 2001), p. 39.

53. Friedrich Vinzenz Reiterer, "Geschichtsschreibung," in Franz Kogler, ed., *Herders neues Bibellexikon* (Freiburg: Herder, 2008), pp. 249–50 (especially p. 250).

54. Leo Depuydt, "Egypt, Egyptians," in Bill T. Arnold and H.G.M. Williamson, eds., *Dictionary of the Old Testament Historical Books* (Leicester: InterVarsity Press, 2005), pp. 237–46 (especially p. 243).

55. Ibid., p. 243. For a select list of the places in western Asia taken by Sheshonq, see John A. Wilson, "Lists of Asiatic Countries under the Egyptian Empire," in Pritchard, *Ancient Near Eastern Texts Relating to the Old Testament*, pp. 242–43.

56. Carolyn Higginbotham, "Shishak," in Katharine Doob Sakenfeld, ed., *The New Interpreter's Dictionary of the Bible*, vol. 5, *S–Z* (Nashville: Abingdon Press, 2009), pp. 241–42 (especially p. 242); see also Depuydt, "Egypt, Egyptians," p. 243.

57. Michael D. Coogan, "Cultural Contexts: The Ancient Near East and Ancient Israel to the Mid-First Millennium BCE," in Michael D. Coogan, ed., *The New Oxford Annotated Bible*, 4th ed. (Oxford: Oxford University Press, 2010), pp. 2236–42 (especially p. 2240). In order to get a more precise and refined picture in this regard, it should also be pointed out that in the case of Sheshonq I, Egyptian chronology is actually derived from biblical chronology, which is in turn derived from ancient Near Eastern sources anyway, in the sense that the date of ca. 930 BC as the beginning of Rehoboam's reign is based on "counting back about ninety years from synchronisms of Ahab of Israel and Jehu 'son' of Omri of Israel with Shalmaneser III" (Depuydt, "Egypt, Egyptians," p. 243).

58. Coogan, "Cultural Contexts," p. 2240.

59. Ibid., p. 2241.

FURTHER READING

The classic source books for the texts and artifacts retrieved from Egypt and the ancient Near East relevant to the Old Testament remain the editions by James B. Pritchard—*Ancient Near Eastern Texts Relating to the Old Testament*, 3rd ed. with supplement (Princeton, N.J.: Princeton University Press, 1969) and *The Ancient Near East in Pictures Relating to the Old Testament*, 2nd ed. with supplement (Princeton, N.J.: Princeton University Press, 1969)—which (together with material from other publications edited by him) have been recently abridged in one volume with a foreword by Daniel E. Fleming and entitled *The Ancient Near East: An Anthology of Texts and Pictures* (Princeton, N.J.: Princeton University

Press, 2011). For a more updated source book on the texts, see William W. Hallo, ed., *The Context of Scripture*, vol. 1, *Canonical Compositions from the Biblical World* (Leiden: Brill, 1997); William W. Hallo, ed., *The Context of Scripture*, vol. 2, *Monumental Inscriptions from the Biblical World* (Leiden: Brill, 2000); William W. Hallo, ed., *The Context of Scripture*, vol. 3, *Archival Documents from the Biblical World* (Leiden: Brill, 2002). For a comprehensive overview of the ancient Near East, see Wolfram von Soden, *The Ancient Orient: An Introduction to the Study of the Ancient Near East* (Grand Rapids, Mich.: Eerdmans, 1994). A thorough history of the ancient Near East is Amélie Khurt, *The Ancient Near East: c. 3000–330 BC*, 2 vols. (London: Routledge, 1995); for a recent solid historical overview, see Marc van de Mieroop, *A History of the Ancient Near East: ca. 3000–323 BC*, 2nd ed. (Oxford: Blackwell, 2007). Very good essays relevant to the topic of Israel in its Egyptian and ancient Near Eastern context together with very useful notes on the specific relevant biblical passages can be found in two important study Bibles, namely, Adele Berlin and Marc Zvi Brettler, eds., *The Jewish Study Bible* (Oxford: Oxford University Press, 2004); and Michael D. Coogan, ed., *The New Oxford Annotated Bible: An Ecumenical Study Bible*, 4th ed. (Oxford: Oxford University Press, 2010).

Part II

Major Genres of Biblical Literature

5

⚜

The Narrative Books of the Hebrew Bible

Thomas Römer

THE NARRATIVE BOOKS: AN OVERVIEW

There is almost no doctrine in the Hebrew Bible (HB) or Old Testament (OT) but a lot of narration. Statistically around half of its content is narrative. The first part of the HB/OT, the Torah or Pentateuch, can be read as an ongoing narrative starting with the creation of the world and ending with the death of Moses. The reader can easily perceive a will to organize the narration as a chronological sequence, a succession of different periods: the time of the origins of the world and humanity (Gen. 1–11) is followed by the era of the patriarchs, Abraham, Isaac, and Jacob (Gen. 12–36). The story of Joseph's descent to Egypt and his rise as second to the Egyptian king (Gen. 37–50) offers a transition to the next episode, the deliverance of the Israelites through Moses from Egyptian oppression (Exod. 1–15). After the exodus begins the time of the Israelites' sojourn in the wilderness and God's revelation on Mount Sinai, which constitutes the very center of the Pentateuch. All the legislation as well as the instructions for the construction of the mobile sanctuary are embedded in the second half of the book of Exodus, the whole book of Leviticus, and the first part of Numbers (Exod. 20–Num. 9). In the middle of the Torah the narration is thus interrupted by different collections containing legal, ritual, and ethical prescriptions. However, all these collections are reworked in such a way that they fit into the narrative framework. The instructions for the construction of the sanctuary and its building are interrupted by the narrative of Israel's first apostasy (the golden calf story in Exod. 32–34), and inside the book of Leviticus the narration of the illegitimate sacrifice presented by two sons of the first priest Aaron (Lev. 10) illustrates the danger of not respecting the sacrificial ritual. The narration continues in the book of Numbers, reporting the time of Israel's wandering in the desert, which is presented as a time of ongoing revolts against Yhwh (Yahweh[1]), Moses, and Aaron. Because of this behavior the adult generation has to die in the wilderness (Num. 10–20), but they are finally able to conquer territory in Transjordan before arriving on the plain of Moab (Num. 21–36), where Moses delivers his last speech to Israel before he dies without entering the land. He is, however, buried by Yhwh himself and proclaimed to be forever the incomparable mediator (Deut. 34).

Again, in Deuteronomy, the narration includes a very long—sometimes interrupted—speech in which Moses recapitulates episodes from the time in the wilderness and also announces coming events such as the crossing of the River Jordan, the conquest of the land, the institution of monarchy, and the possible exile in case of disobedience to the divine Law. That means that despite the canonical distinction between the Torah (Pentateuch) and the Prophets (which in the HB comprises the "Former Prophets," the so-called historical books, and the "Latter Prophets," the prophetic books), the narration goes on until the book of Kings. The book of Joshua takes up where Deuteronomy has ended: Yhwh confirms Joshua as Moses's successor and grants him victory over the inhabitants of the Promised Land, which can therefore be conquered and distributed among the Israelite tribes. At the end of the book Joshua delivers two speeches that conclude the times of the conquest. The statement that a new generation arose, who did not know Joshua anymore and therefore turned away from Yhwh, worshipping other gods (Judg. 2), introduces the next period, the time of the "judges" or saviors. This era is depicted as a time of Israel's continuous forsaking of its God. Each time Yhwh punishes his people by sending enemies who oppress them, but then the Israelites invoke him again, so that he sends saviors to deliver them. But when the savior dies, apostasy starts again. The time of the judges is therefore depicted as a cyclic one. The cycle ends in the book of Samuel with the figure of Samuel, who is presented as the last judge but also as a prophet through whom Yhwh will give Israel its first king, Saul. After several different stories about the establishment of the Israelite monarchy (1 Sam. 8–12), Samuel also pronounces a speech in which he presents the opportunities and dangers for Israel to live under the reign of a king (1 Sam. 12). This speech opens the time of Israel's first kings (Saul, David, Solomon), which concludes with Solomon's construction of the Jerusalemite Temple, on the occasion of which he announces the possible deportation of the people in later days (1 Kings 8).

Solomon's death starts a new era, the time of the two kingdoms, Judah in the south and Israel in the north. The narration here alternates episodes dealing with the situation in the north (Israel) with episodes from the south (Judah). It focuses on the good and mostly bad behavior of the kings but also includes stories of prophets, such as Elijah and Elisha. Since Jeroboam, the first king of the north, founds competing sanctuaries to Jerusalem in Bethel and Dan in which Yhwh is worshipped in the form of a calf (1 Kings 12), the northern kingdom is strongly criticized by the narrators. The destruction of Samaria and Israel's incorporation into the Assyrian Empire are therefore presented as the result of Yhwh's anger against the northern kings (2 Kings 17). The last episode of the narration (2 Kings 18–25) concerns the remaining kingdom of Judah, in which King Josiah undertakes a religious reform. But this reform cannot prevent the destruction of Jerusalem and its Temple by the Babylonians as well as the deportation of King Jehoiachin and parts of the Judaean upper class to Babylon. The narration ends in 2 Kings 25 with a short note about the improvement of Jehoiachin's situation in Babylon: he is admitted at the table of the Babylonian king. The narrative clearly comes to an end since the following book, according to the order of the HB, Isaiah, brings the reader back to the situation of the time of the two kingdoms.

It has therefore been argued that one should speak of an "Enneateuch" (Greek *ennea* = "nine"), a narrative unit binding together the five books of the Torah and the four of the Former Prophets (Genesis, Exodus, Leviticus, Numbers, Deuteronomy, Joshua, Judges, Samuel, and Kings). One may observe indeed a narrative continuity that covers the whole time span from the loss of Paradise to the loss of the land, or from the exile out of the garden to the exile out of the Promised Land. However, one needs to explain why, despite this continuity, the books of Genesis to Deuteronomy have been considered as a separate unit, the Torah, distinct from the books of Joshua to Kings that constitute now the first part of the *Nebiim*, the Prophets.

Even the large narrations of the Pentateuch and the Former Prophets can easily be recognized as composite units, a combination of former independent narrations. It is quite clear that the stories about the creation of the world and the Flood once existed independently of the patriarchal narratives. And it is also quite plausible that the Abraham narratives were not linked from the very beginning to the Jacob narratives. Further, the Joseph story is so different in style and theology that one may also think that it was conceived as an autonomous novella. The Exodus story was certainly also told in the beginning without the stories of the book of Genesis. In the Former Prophets, the conquest stories were originally not followed by the savior narratives in the book of Judges. The narratives in Samuel and Kings were originally not related with the stories about the conquest and the judges. Thus, the so-called Enneateuch is the result of a long and complex process implying different groups of scribes and redactors.

Besides the Enneateuch, the Old Testament contains more narratives. The book of Chronicles recounts the books of Genesis–Kings in a very different way, by summarizing the time from the origins to the beginning of monarchy through genealogies. The time of the monarchy is here related in quite a different manner than in the books of Samuel and Kings. Contrary to Kings, Chronicles does not end with the destruction of Jerusalem and the reign of the Babylonians but, rather, with the arrival of the Persian king Cyrus, who defeated the Babylonians. The end of Chronicles is an exhortation of Cyrus to the Judaean exiles to go back to Jerusalem and to rebuild the Temple (2 Chron. 36:22–23). The story about the restoration of Jerusalem is continued in the books of Ezra and Nehemiah. The book of Ezra opens where 2 Chronicles ends, with the edict of Cyrus, and then recounts the rebuilding of the Temple and the publication of the Law brought by Ezra from Babylon, whereas the book of Nehemiah relates the difficult reconstruction of the city wall as well as the reading of the Law.

The canon of the HB, and the Protestant OT, which comprises the same books as the HB, contains a number of other narrative books. Among the prophetic books, Jonah is more a narrative than a classical prophetic book. It narrates the story of a reluctant prophet who finally understands that God can change his mind and act differently by not realizing the prophetic oracles. The book of Daniel, which belongs in the Hebrew canon to the *Ketubim* (Writings) and in the Christian canons to the Prophets, contains in its first part (Dan. 1–6) a "court tale" about the dangers and triumphs of young Daniel and his friends living in exile in

Babylon. The books of Esther and Ruth are two novellas about heroic women. The book of Ruth has a rural setting and narrates how a Moabite woman became the ancestor of King David. The book of Esther tells the story of how a Jewish girl planned to become the wife of the Persian king in order to save the Jews living in the Diaspora from mortal danger.

The OT of the Roman Catholic Church contains more narrative books (which in many Protestant Bibles are printed as "apocryphal" or "deuterocanonical" books). The book of Judith again tells the story of a heroic woman who saves her people by killing a (fictional) Assyrian king. The book of Tobit is again a Diaspora tale. Like Judith the story is placed in the Assyrian period and recounts two parallel stories about the pious Tobit and his son Tobias, who, with the help of the angel Raphael, is able to exorcise a demon that threatens a young girl, who will become Tobias's spouse at the end. Finally, the first and second books of Maccabees narrate the fight of Judas Maccabeus ("the hammer") and his descendants against the hellenization of Judaea.

THE BIBLICAL NARRATIVES IN THEIR ANCIENT NEAR EASTERN CONTEXT

Narratives are universal; they make it possible to entertain an audience, to teach, to legitimate or to criticize, to create cohesion among a group, and so on. In ancient times, many narratives were not the work of individual authors; they were first transmitted orally before they were written down. Thus one should be careful when comparing biblical narratives with modern novels as is done sometimes in "narrative criticism." The biblical stories were transmitted anonymously; no narrative book of the Hebrew Bible is signed. Biblical literature is not a literature of authors but a literature made up from tradition. The same holds true for narratives from ancient Mesopotamia and the Levant. From time to time we have the name of a scribe, who indicates at the end that he copied or wrote down the text, but he never presents himself as the author. As in ancient Israel and Judah, narratives played a major role in everyday life but also among elites and at the court. The major difference between the biblical narratives and the narrative material we know from the Levant and Mesopotamia is that the biblical narratives were canonized and transmitted as "Holy Scriptures," whereas the ancient Near Eastern texts, although some of them had an "official" status, did not become part of a "holy book" and disappeared before being rediscovered in the nineteenth and twentieth centuries by archaeologists. That also means that we have most of these narratives only in a fragmentary form; but in many cases we can reconstruct the sense of the stories despite the gaps.

The most popular narrative in the ancient Near East was undoubtedly the epic of Gilgamesh.[2] This epic is very important not only because of its content but also because of the history of its composition, which parallels in a certain sense the history of the formation of some of the biblical narrative material. The oldest written documents about Gilgamesh are tablets from the early second millennium BCE written in Sumerian. These tablets do not belong to one coherent narrative but are independent tales that focus on different exploits of a hero called Gilgamesh. In the second half of the second millennium the Gilgamesh tradition became very popular, and the different stories were combined into an epic. At the end of the second millennium a scribe named Shin-leqi-unninni organized the epic on twelve tablets and gave it more or less its standard form, in which it was recopied during the first centuries of the first millennium and found in the library of the Assyrian king Assurbanipal. The Babylonians, who succeeded the Assyrians, considered Shin-leqi-unninni the "author" of the epic. In fact, he probably recopied an older text, but he also introduced major changes and added new passages, such as the prologue and the epic's end, and probably also an abbreviation of the Flood myth, thus recasting a poem that originally told about the glorious deed of a mighty king into a meditation on the fragility and difficulty of the human condition.

The standard version of the poem presents Gilgamesh, the mighty king of Uruk (located in present-day Iraq), as being two-thirds divine and one-third human. But the mighty Gilgamesh is alone, and therefore the inhabitants ask the gods to create someone like him, a vis-à-vis. The goddess Aruru creates with clay a being named Enkidu. But he is not a real human yet: he lives with the animals and behaves like an animal, until he encounters the prostitute Shamhat and has sex with her. After that, the animals abandon him, and he becomes a human; according to the poem, he had acquired reason (I, 201–2). Shamhat introduces Enkidu to Gilgamesh, and they become inseparable friends or even lovers. Gilgamesh is prepared for this encounter by his dreams, which his mother explains to him as meaning that he will meet someone who will be his "equal" (I, 256–58 and 283–85). Both friends accomplish a heroic exploit by killing the mighty Humbaba, guardian of a mysterious cedar forest. After their return Ishtar, the goddess of sexuality, offers herself to Gilgamesh, but he refuses. Furious, she wants to kill him in revenge by dispatching the Bull of Heaven—the constellation Taurus—but Enkidu and Gilgamesh are able to kill the bull. In order to punish Gilgamesh, the gods decide that his counterpart Enkidu has to die.

After Enkidu's death, Gilgamesh undertakes a dangerous journey to the end of the world because he wants to encounter Utnapishti, the hero of the Flood, to whom, together with his wife, the gods gave immortality. Gilgamesh assumes that Utnapishti knows the remedy against death. Before arriving at this place, which no human being can normally reach, Gilgamesh comes to a mysterious garden full of precious stones (very similar to those of the garden described in Ezek. 28) in which he encounters a woman, named Shiduri, a tavern keeper by the edge of the ocean, the waters of Death, which Gilgamesh has to cross. Shiduri already tells him that death is the destiny of mankind and that he should enjoy life (Fragment Meissner iii, 1–13), a piece of advice that comes very close to a passage in the biblical book of Qoheleth (9, 7–10). However, Shiduri helps Gilgamesh to meet Utnapishti, who tells him the whole story of the Flood and confirms that the gods have decided that death is the destiny of all humans. But pushed by his wife, Utnapishti finally reveals to Gilgamesh a mysterious plant at the bottom of the ocean, which may have the property of rejuvenation or preventing death. Gilgamesh is able to find this plant, but on his way home, when he is taking a bath, a serpent emerges and swallows it; after that the serpent immediately sheds its skin, a sign of its "immortality." Gilgamesh has to accept death as being part of the human condition and return to Uruk. He must learn that humans are mortal, though humankind may be immortal, through the generations that succeed each other.

This epic was largely known all over the ancient Near East, as is shown by the fragments and mentions of Gilgamesh found from Palestine to Babylon. And even in a fragment of the "book of the Giants" (a part of the book of Enoch) found at Qumran, Gilgamesh is still mentioned (4Q530, col. 2). The epic of Gilgamesh served for the training and instruction of young men in Mesopotamia and probably also in the Levant. It seems quite obvious that the epic was known to the biblical writers, who picked up several themes and expressions from it, for instance, the role of the snake in the loss of immortality (Gen. 3), the link between sexuality and "knowledge," and the anthropological statement that a human being cannot be alone but needs a vis-à-vis (Gen. 2). The homoerotic friendship of Gilgamesh and Enkidu may have inspired the biblical story of David and Jonathan (see the elegies of Gilgamesh and David in *Gilgamesh* VIII:44–60 and 1 Sam. 1:25–27). Thus, although we have no parallel epic to Gilgamesh in the HB, the biblical writers were certainly influenced by this narrative and, consciously or subconsciously, used several themes and motifs from it.

The parallels between biblical narratives and ancient Near Eastern myths are stronger in regard to the creation and Flood stories. It is quite widely accepted that the biblical authors of the two creation accounts in Gen. 1:1–2:3 and of Gen. 2:4–3:24 were familiar with the Babylonian accounts of Athrahasis and Enuma Elish. *Athrahasis* (The Very Wise One) is a diptych telling of the creation of human beings and the Flood story.[3] More than twenty copies of this epic exist; the oldest can be dated to the seventeenth century BCE, but the epic was still popular in the Neo-Babylonian period (sixth century BCE). It explains the creation of human beings as a means for the minor gods to avoid having to work for the more important gods. One of the minor gods is killed, and his blood is mixed with clay in order to create humans. But the gods do not appreciate the multiplication of the humans or their noise and decide to annihilate them with a flood. The god Ea, however, warns the pious Athrahasis, who builds a huge boat, by which he saves his family and the animals. After the Flood Athrahasis offers a sacrifice, which marks the reconciliation between humans and the gods, who, however, invent different means to reduce the multiplication of humankind (infertility, stillbirths, sexual abstinence for certain women).

Enuma Elish (named after its beginning, "When above . . .") was a very popular myth relating the creation of the world and humankind, since more than sixty copies have been discovered.[4] The oldest date from the beginning of the first millennium BCE, many manuscripts come from the Neo-Assyrian period, and the epic was copied even after the fall of Babylon in 539 BCE and translated into Greek in the third century BCE.

The epic narrates the creation of the world via the victory of the god Marduk over Tiamat, a dragon or sea monster. Marduk uses her corpse in order to create heaven and earth. As in the Athrahasis epic, humankind is created by killing the god Kingu, Tiamat's ally. His blood is added to the soil, and humans are formed out of this mixture. The poem ends with the praise of Marduk as the most powerful of all gods.

It seems quite evident that the biblical creation and Flood accounts borrow from these epics. Like *Enuma Elish*, Gen. 1 tells of the creation as a "victory" of the creator god over the watery chaos (the Hebrew word *tehom* may be related to the Akkadian term *tiamat*). But unlike the Babylonian poem, in Gen. 1, there are no more traces of a fight (Pss. 74 and 89, however, still reflect the idea of a victory of Yhwh against sea monsters). In Gen. 1, man and woman are created in the "image of god," whereas in Egypt and Mesopotamia this appellation is reserved for the king, such that the biblical account could be understood as a democratization of ancient royal ideology. In Gen. 2 the creation of the first human being using clay also recalls Athrahasis and Enuma Elish. In the biblical account, no god is killed to mix his blood with the clay; note, however, that Yhwh breathes into the man's nostrils his breath or spirit, so that in Gen. 2, the humans also have something divine in them. One may even detect an allusion to the blood theme: Gen. 2 explains the name of Adam with the statement that he is made out of the *'adamah* (soil). The name *'adam* may, however, also evoke the Hebrew term for blood, *dam*.

According to the creation account in Gen. 1, the human being, as the image of God, should govern the world, like a king, and multiply. In the Athrahasis epic, the multiplication of humans is also an issue but, contrary to the Bible, an issue that the gods try to prevent. And in the version of the Flood according to the epic of Gilgamesh, we find the same idea: the Flood is considered a disproportionate means by which the gods limit the growth of humans. The two biblical versions of the Deluge, which are contained in Gen. 6–9, display an opposite concern. Even after the Flood, Yhwh exhorts Noah and his family to become numerous and multiply (Gen. 9:1 and 7). The divine command, given to humankind at the time of creation and repeated after the Flood in Gen. 1 and 9, is therefore a redefinition of the Babylonian myths. Humanity is called to multiply and fill the earth, and this fact no longer causes the wrath of the gods. This difference between Athrahasis and the biblical account probably reflects significant economic, political, and theological changes and a different view of humanity and its destiny. The biblical writers' knowledge of the Babylonian creation and Flood epics can easily be explained by the fact that after the destruction of Jerusalem by the Babylonians (587 BCE), Judaean intellectuals were deported to Babylonia, where they could easily acquire knowledge of those texts.

For the following narratives in the Pentateuch (Patriarchs, Exodus, wilderness) we have no direct parallels in the narrative material of the ancient Near East. As for the patriarchal stories, some comparable elements can be found in epics from Ugarit, a wealthy city-state during the second half of the second millennium BCE.[5] As in Gen. 12–36, the fragmentary epic of King Kirta (or Keret) is concerned with the question of offspring. The god El intervenes in order to give Kirta a son and to heal him from a dangerous illness. The figure of Danel, who is the hero of another Ugaritic myth, was certainly known by the Judaean scribes, since Danel is referred to in Ezek. 14:12–20. In the Ugaritic narrative, Danel, who is also a king, is childless. He is finally healed from his infertility by El, who gives him a son, Aqhat. But Aqhat dies very quickly, and the king is again without offspring. Since the epic is incomplete, its end is still unknown. Perhaps El intervened again in favor of Danel by restoring Aqhat to him or by giving him another son. The Abraham narratives are also very much concerned with the absence of an heir and with the danger that the living heir can be lost. Interestingly, Yhwh is identified in the patriarchal narratives with El more often than in other texts of the Pentateuch. Contrary to the Ugaritic myths, however, the patriarchs are not kings. This is a similar phenomenon as observed in the creation narrative of Gen. 1: the democratization of royal ideology. Although the Ugaritic narratives are at least five hundred years older than the biblical accounts, it is quite possible that the themes of the Ugaritic epics were still circulating in the Levant in the first half of the first millennium BCE.

As for Moses, there exists one clear extrabiblical parallel in regard to his birth account in Exod. 2: the birth legend of King Sargon, the mythical founder of the Assyrian dynasty. This text, which refers to the Sargon from the third millennium BCE, was written under Sargon II (722–705 BCE) in order to legitimate this king, who was probably a usurper.[6] Sargon and Moses are both exposed by their mothers, who are both in some way related to the priesthood. Sargon's mother is a priestess, and Moses's mother is the daughter of Levi, the ancestor of Israel's priestly tribe. Their fathers do not intervene. Both children are set adrift on a river in a basket, found, and adopted. In both cases, the adoption alludes to royal adoption: Sargon is "loved" by Ishtar, and Moses becomes the son of Pharaoh's daughter. According to the biblical account, Moses is depicted as Israel's founder, as important as the founder of the Assyrians, Sargon. It is tempting, then, to understand the first written story about Moses to be a reaction to Neo-Assyrian royal ideology, elaborated during the seventh century BCE. The tradition about the Exodus may, however, have been older and come from an old Israelite memory, since no similar narratives can be found in the ancient Near East. There is a very fragmentary Hittite poem called "Song of Release"[7] in which a storm god demands the release of his worshippers who are kept in slavery in the city of Ebla. The elders of the city, contrary to the king, insist that they need these slaves. Unfortunately the text breaks off so that its outcome is unknown. It is, however, possible that the deity destroyed the city of Ebla and liberated his people. This text was probably unknown to the biblical scribes who put the Exodus narrative into shape. However, it shows the existence of similar motifs in the ancient Near East and illustrates that the idea of a god delivering his people is not an absolute specificity of the biblical tradition.

The conquest accounts in the book of Joshua display strong parallels with Assyrian military narratives, relating the victorious campaigns of the Assyrian kings and their armies and the intervention of the Assyrian gods against their enemies. There is an interesting parallel between a "Letter to the God" written on behalf of Sargon II and an episode from Joshua 10:10–11. The Assyrian text relates the victory of the Assyrian army thanks to an intervention of the storm god Adad. The Assyrian and the biblical texts relate a slaughter of enemies on the descent or ascent of a mountain, and both episodes are followed by divine military intervention: "The rest of the people, who had fled to save their lives ... Adad, the violent, the son of Anu, the valiant, uttered his loud cry against them; and with flood cloud and stones of heaven, he totally annihilated the remainder."[8] In a similar way, Joshua 10:11 reports: "As they fled before Israel, while they were going down the slope of Beth-Horon, Yhwh threw down huge stones from heaven on them as far as Azekah, and they died; there were more who died because of the hailstones than the Israelites killed with the sword." There may be a subversive component in these parallels. Apparently the biblical writers took over the Assyrian narratives in order to show that Yhwh is indeed stronger than the Assyrians and all their gods.

The story of David's rise in the book of Samuel displays some parallels with royal legends of the ancient Near East, especially the epic of Zimri-Lîm, who in the eighteenth century BCE became king of Mari (a city-state located in Syria) after returning from a forced exile and ousting his rival. He campaigned extensively and broadened the territory of his kingdom. The inscription of King Idrimi of Alakha (a city-state located in the south of Turkey) from the fifteenth century BCE recounts how he regained kingship by rejoining the "Habiru people" in Canaan. He became their chief, and after seven years he led them to war against Alakha, where he was acclaimed king. Like the David narrative, these royal documents legitimate the rise to power of a king who first had to flee before coming back and taking the throne.

The story of the two kingdoms of Israel (the northern kingdom) and Judah (the southern kingdom) resembles Assyrian and Babylonian royal chronicles.[9] However, contrary to this kind of literature, the stories about the kings of Israel and Judah are evaluated according to theological criteria, regarding fidelity or infidelity toward the god of Israel and his exclusive worship in the Jerusalemite Temple. Unlike the Mesopotamian chronicles, the books of Kings also contain an important number of prophetic narratives.

Summing up, the different narrative traditions gathered in the Enneateuch (Genesis–Kings) are not without parallels. For some of the stories, especially the creation and Flood narratives, Moses's birth story, and the conquest accounts, it seems plausible that the biblical authors took over ancient Near Eastern narratives and adapted them to their own theological agenda. Other Near Eastern narratives (such as the tales about the rise of exiled kings or the Ugaritic material about childless kings healed by El) display similar narrative features as the biblical narratives, but the authors of Genesis or Samuel probably did not know them. The major difference between the biblical and the ancient Near Eastern narratives is the fact that the different epics, novellas, and stories in Genesis–Kings have been compiled into one meganarrative and have in a long process become "Holy Scripture."

THE FORMATION OF THE PENTATEUCHAL NARRATIVE

According to Jewish and Christian tradition, Moses was the author of the whole Pentateuch. This idea is inspired by some texts in the Torah according to which God asks Moses to write down some events or laws (Exod. 24:4; Deut. 1:1 and 4:45). But there is no biblical text that states explicitly that Moses wrote the whole Torah. Very soon some rabbis wondered whether Moses could have written down his own death. They concluded that the last verses of the Torah were added later by Joshua, Moses's successor (this idea can be found in a passage of the Talmud, a compilation containing rabbinic discussions of the Pentateuch, *Baba Bathra* 12[10]). This theory was in a certain way the beginning of the critical investigation of the Torah.[11] In the seventeenth century, the philosopher Baruch Spinoza, in his *Theologico-political Treatise* (1670), claimed that Moses could not be the author of the Pentateuch, since the narration that starts in Genesis does not come to an end in Deuteronomy but continues in the books of Joshua to Kings, so that the author of the story must have lived after the destruction of Jerusalem in 587 BCE. For a long time the denial of Mosaic authorship of the Pentateuch was considered to be a heresy (Spinoza was ejected from his synagogue), and only in the eighteenth century did a critical and scientific investigation about the formation of the Pentateuch find its place in (Protestant) faculties of theology.

A critical investigation of the Pentateuchal narrative revealed an important number of contradictions, tensions, and repetitions: for example, there are two different creation accounts in Gen. 1:1–2:3 and 2:4–3:21. In the first account, man and woman are created at the same time, whereas in Gen. 2, Adam is created first, then the animals, and only then the woman. There are also indications that Gen. 6–9 combine two originally separate Flood accounts. According to Gen. 7:15, Noah introduces onto the ark one pair of every kind of animal, whereas in Gen 7:2 he takes seven pairs of all clean animals and one pair of the unclean animals. According to Gen. 4:26, the name of Yhwh was known to all humans from the very beginning, whereas according to Exod. 6:2–3, God reveals his name only at the time of Moses. There are also an important number of repetitions: in the patriarchal narrative, the story of a patriarch presenting his wife as his sister because he fears being killed by the foreign king is told three times (Gen. 12:10–20, Gen. 20, Gen. 26:1–14), and the call of Moses is repeated twice (Exod. 3:1–4:18 and Exod. 6). These observations led to the establishment of a "Documentary hypothesis," which was first envisaged by a French physician, Jean Astruc, in 1753. His aim was to save the Mosaic authenticity of the Pentateuch by claiming that Moses had two different documents at his disposal, the first using the divine name "elohim" (god) and the second using "Jehova" (as Astruc, with many others, pronounced the name Yhwh). This observation was the base of a scholarly theory that became dominant in biblical research from the end of the nineteenth century until the 1970s and which is still used by many scholars, especially in North America.

In the last decades of the nineteenth century, the Dutch scholar Abraham Kuenen and his German colleague Julius Wellhausen gave this model a widely accepted form. The formation of the Pentateuch was explained in the following way: The Torah results from the compilation of three formerly independent and parallel sources or documents and the addition of a fourth document, the book of Deuteronomy. The oldest sources were the Yahwist (in German "J," because the author of this document mostly uses "Yahweh" when referring to the god of Israel) and the Elohist ("E," because of the document's preference for the term *elohim*— god). J and E were dated to the time of the monarchy—J sometimes even under the reign of Solomon (according to Gerhard von Rad), and E in the eighth century BCE, often in the northern kingdom. Already in the beginning of the nineteenth century Wilhelm M. L. de Wette located the original form of the book of Deuteronomy ("D") at the time of the religious reform of King Josiah, around 622 BCE, because his cult centralization (Jerusalem was declared the only legitimate Yahwistic sanctuary, and all non-Yahwistic cultic symbols in Jerusalem and Judah were destroyed) corresponds to the requirements of the book of Deuteronomy. The last of the four documents is the so-called Priestly source ("P"), which was written by priests after the destruction of Jerusalem during the time of the Babylonian exile (587–539 BCE) or at the beginning of the Persian period (539–515).

Thus, according to the Documentary hypothesis, the Pentateuch is the result of the bringing together of three parallel narrative documents from different times and the adjunction of the book of Deuteronomy. One may imagine this procedure as if several redactors or compilers wanted to unite the three synoptic gospels (Mark, Matthew, and Luke) and the gospel of John into one megagospel, like the Diatessaron ("Out of four"), a gospel harmony of the second century CE in which the Christian theologian Tatian tried to combine all the narratives that exist in the four gospels into one coherent narrative of Jesus's life and death. But contrary to the case of the Diatessaron, there is no evidence for the existence of three or four independent documents that are supposed to constitute the material out of which the Pentateuch was made up. Although the Documentary hypothesis was and is still quite popular, no scholar has succeeded in reconstructing the four documents J, E, D, and P entirely and in their original form. For each of the four documents one had to postulate gaps and omissions. And it was also very difficult to decide whether a text should belong to J, E, or D (the criteria for the P-texts seemed somewhat more clear-cut). For these and other reasons the Documentary hypothesis was challenged around 1975 by several scholars, especially John Van Seters, Hans Heinrich Schmid, and Rolf Rendtorff. Whereas Van Seters and Schmid denied that the so-called Yahwist (as well as the Elohist[12]) could be much older than the D-source, Rendtorff challenged the idea of an original narrative that comprised all major themes of the Pentateuch or Hexateuch (according to the Documentary hypothesis, some of the sources continued in the book of Joshua, since the conquest account is a better narrative conclusion than the death of Moses). He pointed out that many of the narrative units of the Pentateuch, the primeval history (Gen. 1–11), the Patriarchs (Gen. 12–36), and the Moses and Exodus narrative existed independently before they were brought together, probably not before the sixth century BCE. As a consequence of these challenges, many scholars modified or abandoned the classical Documentary hypothesis. For some of them J is so close to the D-texts that the formation of the Pentateuch should be explained as the result of the merging of two "compositions," a deuter-onomistic and a priestly, that were combined at the beginning of the Persian period. Other scholars hold that during a long time the patriar-chal narrative and the Exodus story were two independent (perhaps even competing) foundation myths, which were brought together only by priestly redactors.

Despite quite different models for the formation of the Torah, there are nevertheless important points on which many scholars would agree:

the Pentateuchal narrative is the result of a long process of transmission and editing of formerly independent "documents" or narratives. The "priestly texts" can quite easily be detected (at least in the books of Genesis–Leviticus), and the priestly group may have been the first who tried to combine the primeval, patriarchal, and Exodus narratives. The Torah came into being in the first half of the Persian period (between 539 and 400 BCE), when different elite factions of Judah and Samaria decided to collect their different narrative and legal traditions in order to construct one great narrative that could be accepted by all groups and serve as the foundation document of a new religion based on regular reading of the Pentateuch. The fact that the Pentateuchal narrative ends in Deut. 34 with the death of Moses, who has to die outside the land, is easily understandable in a context in which most Jews were living in a Diaspora situation and could easily identify themselves with Moses. The most important thing for Judaism was not the possession of the land but, rather, the Torah (which should be translated as "Instruction" and not as "Law"), which God had handed down to them. For that reason, the Torah remains to this day in Judaism the most important part of the tripartite Hebrew Bible.

THE FORMATION OF THE BOOKS OF DEUTERONOMY TO KINGS AND THE THEORY OF THE "DEUTERONOMISTIC HISTORY"

As we have seen, the book of Deuteronomy constitutes the end of the Pentateuch, but it also contains many links to the following books. In Moses's final speech the conquest of the land that is narrated in Joshua is already mentioned several times. But Deuteronomy also contains allusions to the time of the Judges (compare Deut. 6:12–15 and Judg. 2:12–14) and the history of the rise and fall of the Israelite and Judaean monarchies (see the law of the king in Deut. 17:14–20 and the exile announced in the curses of Deut. 28). These close relations between Deuteronomy and Joshua–Kings had already led Spinoza (see above) to the theory that all these books should be considered as the work of one single author who lived after the events of 587 BCE and who wanted to produce with his narration an explanation of the fall of Judah. Reading this narrative it becomes obvious that the events are explained according to the theological options of the book of Deuteronomy. For that reason, the German scholar Martin Noth elaborated in 1943 his theory of the "Deuteronomistic History."[13] According to Noth, the books of Deuteronomy and Joshua–Kings should be considered the work of an anonymous author, the "Deuteronomist," who shortly after 560 BCE composed a historical work in order to explain the collapse of Judah. The Deuteronomist integrated older sources and independent narratives in his work, such that he should be seen as the author of a complex tradition; for the first time, he conceived a thoroughgoing history of Israel and Judah from the Mosaic beginnings until the destruction of Jerusalem. The Deuteronomist's closest relatives are those historians of Hellenistic and Roman times who, using older and mostly anonymous narrative material, wrote a history of former times in order to explain the present. According to Noth, the Deuteronomist wrote his history to point out that the exile was a punishment by Yhwh for the continuous disobedience of his people and their kings, who did not follow the laws contained in the book of Deuteronomy.

Noth's theory was well received in scholarship but soon underwent two major modifications. The first modification goes back to Frank M. Cross, who pointed out that there are several indications of an older Deuteronomistic History written before the Babylonian exile under the reign of King Josiah (640–609 BCE). According to Cross, two main themes characterize the Deuteronomistic History: the "sin of Jeroboam" (1 Kings 12), the first northern king, who built Yhwh sanctuaries outside Jerusalem in the cities of Dan and Bethel, and the promise of an everlasting Davidic dynasty in 2 Sam. 7. Those two lines come to a conclusion in the narration of Josiah's reform (2 Kings 22–23): Josiah destroys the sanctuary of Bethel (2 Kings 23:15), bringing the sins of Jeroboam to an end. Furthermore, Josiah is presented as a "new David," the best of all kings. Consequently, Cross claimed that the original Deuteronomistic narration ended in 2 Kings 23:25a. He distinguished between Dtr¹ (the redactor of the Josianic edition) and Dtr², who added 2 Kings 24–25 and other texts after the fall of Jerusalem in 587 BCE. This model is still used today by most scholars in the Anglo-Saxon world.

Rudolf Smend from Göttingen altered Noth's theory in a different way. Analyzing the divine speech to Joshua that opens the book of Joshua, he observed that verse 6 of Josh. 1 draws a first conclusion. In verses 7–9 there is an addition, also in a Deuteronomistic style, that transforms the military speech into an exhortation to obedience toward the Mosaic Law. According to Smend, these verses are the work of a later redactor, whom he calls "DtrN," a Deuteronomistic "nomist," who wanted to strengthen the necessity to be obedient in all circumstances to the divine law. His student Walter Dietrich added a "DtrP," a prophetic Dtr, responsible for the insertion of the main prophetic histories in the books of Kings, promoting a theory of prophetic announcement and fulfillment. Contrary to Cross, the so-called Göttingen model, which is largely used in Continental scholarship, assumes like Noth that the compilation of the Deuteronomistic History only started after the events of 587 BCE. However, Noth's idea of a single author or redactor is definitely given up. Other scholars even added more Deuteronomistic layers, diluting in this way the idea of a coherent Deuteronomistic narrative. Indeed, in the last few decades the whole theory of the Deuteronomistic History has been criticized, especially in European scholarship (A. Graeme Auld, E. Axel Knauf, Kurt Noll). The opponents of Noth's idea insist on the old observation that the Deuteronomistic texts in the different books of the Former Prophets are extremely different from one another and cannot be assigned to one or two coherent Deuteronomistic editions: the condemnation of the "high places," very important in the books of Kings, never appears in Deuteronomy, and the theme of cult centralization only plays a role in Deuteronomy and Kings. For these reasons, some scholars claim that one should definitely reject the idea of a Deuteronomistic History. However, they do not offer a clear alternative model, so the best solution is to try to combine observations from Noth and from the Cross and Smend schools as well as from the critical voices.

The idea of a multilayered edition of the Deuteronomistic History should be preferred to Noth's, whose assumption of an individual author writing on his own initiative is quite anachronistic. "Private writing" outside the temple, palace, or scribal schools can hardly be assumed before Hellenistic times. Against the opponents of a Deuteronomistic History it should be recalled that the books of Deuteronomy–2 Kings create a chronologically coherent narrative in order to narrate a history from the Mosaic beginnings to the collapse of Israel and Judah. Since the books of Deuteronomy and Joshua display important parallels with Assyrian vassal treaties and military narratives, they may have been composed for the first time in the seventh century BCE as a "counterhistory" responding to Assyrian imperial ideology. The first edition of Samuel and Kings may also have taken place during this time as an attempt to present Josiah as a new David. We may therefore assume a Deuteronomistic "library" in the Jerusalem Temple composed of several scrolls. In the Babylonian period, and probably in Babylon, where the scribes and the older scrolls had been taken, a new edition developed explaining the reasons for the destruction of Jerusalem and for the exile. The Deuteronomistic History came to an end when, in the middle of the Persian period, the decision was taken to promulgate a Pentateuch (see above). Deuteronomy was cut off from the following books and became the end of the Torah, without, however, losing its links to the Former Prophets. Deuteronomy is therefore the hinge that holds together the Pentateuch and the Former Prophets in the so-called Enneateuch.

THE FORMATION OF THE BOOKS OF CHRONICLES AND EZRA–NEHEMIAH

Since the books of Ezra and Nehemiah seem to follow the narrative of the books of Chronicles—Ezra starts exactly where Chronicles ended by quoting an edict of the Persian king Cyrus, exhorting the Jews to restore Jerusalem—biblical scholarship since the beginning of the nineteenth century (Leopold Zunz in 1832) assumed the same author for those books.[14] In analogy to the Deuteronomistic History, Martin Noth coined the term "Chronistic History." The Chronicler would have written his work in the second half of the Persian period to glorify the reconstruction of Jerusalem and to condemn the Samaritans, the inhabitants of the former northern kingdom. This theory is, however, problematic for several reasons. As Sara Japhet has shown, theology as well as vocabulary and style are quite different in Chronicles and Ezra–Nehemiah.[15] Whereas Ezra and Nehemiah display a segregationist ideology, the books of Chronicles seem more "integrative." Although the narration in Chronicles is focused on the southern kingdom, the Judaean kings often appeal to their "brethren in the north" to join the legitimate Yhwh worship in Jerusalem. One should therefore consider the books of Chronicles and Ezra–Nehemiah as two independent narratives. This is also the case in most manuscripts of the Hebrew Bible, in which Ezra and Nehemiah are placed, against chronological logic, before the books of Chronicles.

The books of Ezra and Nehemiah are probably based on a "Nehemiah memoir" (containing parts of Neh. 1–7, 12, and 13), written in the first person, in which Nehemiah legitimated his activities of restoring and repopulating Jerusalem. If this memoir was written by the historical Nehemiah, it could be dated in the middle of the fifth century. Another source could be an "Ezra narrative," which contained the story of the promulgation and the reading of the Torah in Jerusalem (parts of Ezra 1–6 and Nehemiah 8–10). Both sources were then combined in a quite complex process of editing and revising before the book was completed at the end of the Persian or perhaps beginning of the Hellenistic period.[16] The popularity of the figure of Ezra is reflected in the Greek version of the Hebrew Bible, which has another book of Ezra (Esdras α), a rewriting of narratives from Ezra and Nehemiah with some additional stories; in the English translation this book is often called 1 Esdras or the Greek Esdras. The Latin Bible even has a fourth book of Ezra, which contains various apocalyptic texts from the Christian era.

The books of Chronicles are generally considered a rewriting of the Enneateuch. The long genealogy in 1 Chron. 1–9 summarizes the narrative from Adam to Saul, and 1 Chron. 10–2 Chron. 36 narrates the story from David to the arrival of the Persians in a quite different perspective than the Enneateuch. The exodus and the conquest are hardly mentioned, such that the reader gets the impression that Israel has always been in its land. The kings are more interested in taking care of the Temple and the celebrations of festivals than in waging war. Therefore most scholars believe that the author of Chronicles presupposes the Pentateuch and the books of Samuel and Kings, although not in their final form. This view has been challenged by A. Graeme Auld and Ray Person,[17] who think that Samuel–Kings and Chronicles both depend on the same source (a story about the kingdoms of Israel and Judah), which they used with different theological perspectives. Many stories of Chronicles seem, however, a theological correction of the accounts in Samuel–Kings: in 1 Sam. 24, it is Yhwh himself who pushes David to undertake a census for which he is later punished; in 1 Chron. 21, however, the instigator is not Yhwh's anger but "satan"; in 2 Kings the worst king of Judah, Manasseh, has the longest reign of all (fifty-five years; 2 Kings 21:1–2), and so the Chronicler tries to explain this by inventing a story about a deportation of Manasseh and his conversion to Yhwh, who then rewarded him with many years of reign. Therefore the traditional view that Chronicles is an interpretation of Samuel–Kings still seems quite plausible. The books of Chronicles were written either at the end of the Persian or more likely at the beginning of the Hellenistic period.[18]

THE EMERGENCE OF JEWISH NOVELLAS

During the Persian period short narratives became popular. The book of Ruth was written, maybe in reaction to Ezra–Nehemiah, in order to legitimate the integration of foreign women, for the quite idyllic story narrates the adhesion of the Moabite Ruth to the people of Yhwh and her exemplary fidelity, which enable her to become an ancestress of King David.[19] In the Greek Bible, Ruth is placed between the book of Judges and Samuel, which seems quite logical, since the story is situated at the time of the Judges. Perhaps the book of Ruth was indeed conceived as an insertion between Judges and Samuel in order to correct the Deuteronomistic theology of these books.

The book of Esther reflects the first problems Jews could face in a Diaspora situation. The book is less idyllic than Ruth, but both heroines use ruses, and their respective marriages are beneficial for the people of Yhwh. The Esther narrative was very popular; we have three different versions of it, two in Greek, which may be a translation from a Hebrew text different from the canonical one. Since the views about the Persians in the book of Esther reflect Greek stereotypes it is plausible that the Esther story dates from the Hellenistic era.[20] The book of Esther may be called a Diaspora novella, like the first part of the book of Daniel and the Joseph story (Gen. 37–50), which all share some literary motifs and narrate the dangers but above all the possibilities of integration for Jews living in the Diaspora.[21]

NOTES

1. The name of the god of Israel is often pronounced "Yahweh." But Judaism does not pronounce anymore the name of the god of Israel, so that we cannot be sure about the original vocalization. For that reason I refer to the god of Israel by the four consonants written in the Hebrew Bible, called the tetragrammaton.

2. The best English translation and introduction available is Andrew R. George, *The Babylonian Gilgamesh Epic. Introduction, Critical Edition and Cuneiform Text*, 2 vols. (Oxford: Oxford University Press, 2003).

3. English translation: Wilfred G. Lambert and Alan R. Millard, *Atra-ḫasīs: The Babylonian Story of the Flood* (Winona Lake, Ind.: Eisenbrauns, 1999).

4. For an English translation, see W. G. Lambert, *Babylonian Creation Myths*, Mesopotamian Civilizations 16 (Winona Lake, Ind.: Eisenbrauns, 2013).

5. An English translation of the Ugaritic myths can be found in Johannes Cornelis de Moor, *An Anthology of Religious Texts from Ugarit*, Nisaba 16 (Leiden: Brill, 1987), pp. 199–223 (*Kirta*), 224–73 (*Danel* and *Aqhat*).

6. For a presentation and translation of this text, see Brian Lewis, *The Sargon Legend. A Study of the Akkadian Text and the Tale of the Hero Who Was Exposed at Birth*, American Schools of Oriental Research Dissertation Series 4 (Cambridge, Mass.: American Schools of Oriental Research, 1980).

7. An English translation is available in Harry Angier Hoffner, *Hittite Myths*, 2nd ed., Writings from the Ancient World 2 (Atlanta: Scholars Press, 1998), pp. 65–80.

8. In K. Lawson Younger Jr., *Ancient Conquest Accounts. A Study in Ancient Near Eastern and Biblical History Writing* (Sheffield: JSOT Press, 1990), p. 210.

9. For an English translation, see Jean-Jacques Glassner, *Mesopotamian Chronicles*, Benjamin R. Forster, trans., Writings from the Ancient World 19 (Atlanta: Society of Biblical Literature, 2004).

10. *Baba Bathra* means "the last gate."

11. For the quite complicated history of research concerning the formation of the Pentateuch, see Jean Louis Ska, *Introduction to Reading the Pentateuch* (Winona Lake, Ind.: Eisenbrauns, 2006), a book that also contains the bibliographical references of the works of the scholars mentioned in this paragraph.

12. The Elohist was from the beginning a very fragmentary source, so that many scholars spoke of "Elohistic fragments" or considered the E-texts as later additions to the J-source.

13. An English translation of this important study is available: Martin Noth, *The Deuteronomistic History* (Sheffield: Sheffield Academic Press, 1991). For the following presentation and bibliographical indications, see also Thomas Römer, *The So-Called Deuteronomistic History: A Sociological, Historical and Literary Introduction* (London: T&T Clark; and New York: Continuum, 2007).

14. For an orientation on research on the Chronicles, see Matt Patrick Graham, Kenneth G. Hoglund, and Steven L. McKenzie, eds., *The Chronicler as Historian* (Sheffield: JSOT Press, 1997).

15. Sara Japhet, *The Ideology of the Book of Chronicles and Its Place in Biblical Thought* (Frankfurt/Main: P. Lang, 1997).

16. Jacob L. Wright, *Rebuilding Identity: The Nehemiah-Memoir and Its Earliest Readers*, Beihefte zur Zeitschrift für die alttestamentliche Wissenschaft 348 (Berlin: W. de Gruyter, 2004).

17. A. Graeme Auld, *Kings without Privilege. David and Moses in the Story of the Bible's Kings* (Edinburgh: T&T Clark, 1994); Raymond F. Person Jr., *The Deuteronomistic History and the Books of Chronicles. Scribal Works in an Oral World*, Ancient Israel and Its Literature 6 (Atlanta: Society of Biblical Literature, 2010).

18. Hans-Peter Mathys, "Chronikbücher und hellenistischer Zeitgeist," in *Vom Anfang und vom Ende: Fünf alttestamentliche Studien* (Frankfurt/M.: Peter Lang, 2000), pp. 41–155.

19. Irmtraud Fischer, "The Book of Ruth: A 'Feminist' Commentary to the Torah?" in Athalya Brenner, ed., *Ruth and Esther*, A Feminist Companion to the Bible Second Series (Sheffield: Sheffield Academic Press, 1999), pp. 24–49.

20. Jean-Daniel Macchi, "The Book of Esther: A Persian Story in Greek Style," in Ehud Ben Zvi, Diana V. Edelman, and Frank Polak, eds., *A Palimpsest: Rhetoric, Ideology, Stylistics, and Language Relating to Persian Israel*, Perspectives on Hebrew Scriptures and Its Contexts 5 (Piscataway, N.J.: Gorgias Press, 2009), pp. 109–27.

21. Michael J. Chan, "Joseph and Jehoiachin: On the Edge of Exodus," *Zeitschrift für die alttestamentliche Wissenschaft* 125 (2013): pp. 566–77.

FURTHER READING

A good introduction to the question of the narrative units in the books of Genesis to Kings can be found in the volume Thomas B. Dozeman, Thomas Römer, and Konrad Schmid, eds., *Pentateuch, Hexateuch, or Enneateuch? Identifying Literary Works in Genesis through Kings*, Ancient Israel and Its Literature 8 (Atlanta: Society of Biblical Literature, 2011). The question of narrative, history, and ideology is presented in Yairah Amit, *History and Ideology. Introduction to the Historiography in the Hebrew Bible* (Sheffield: Sheffield Academic Press, 1999). A good overview on the current discussion about the formation of the Pentateuch can be found in Jean Louis Ska, *Introduction to Reading the Pentateuch* (Winona Lake, Ind.: Eisenbrauns, 2006). How the Pentateuch was read and understood in the Persian period is exposed in Diana V. Edelman, Philip R. Davies, Christophe Nihan, and Thomas Römer, *Opening the Books of Moses*, BibleWorld (Sheffield: Equinox, 2012). The history of the idea that the Pentateuch is a compromise of two competing foundation myths is brilliantly exposed in Konrad Schmid, *Genesis and the Moses Story. Israel's Dual Origins in the Hebrew Bible*, Siphrut 3 (Winona Lake, Ind.: Eisenbrauns, 2010). An introduction to the debate about the Deuteronomistic History and the formation of the narrative in the books of Joshua to Kings is given in Thomas Römer, *The So-Called Deuteronomistic History: A Sociological, Historical and Literary Introduction* (London: T&T Clark; and New York: Continuum, 2007). It is useful to consult a synopsis that permits one to read the books of Samuel–Kings and Chronicles in parallel: John C. Endres, William R. Millar, and John Barclay Burns, eds., *Chronicles and Its Synoptic Parallels in Samuel, Kings and Related Texts* (Collegeville, Minn.: Liturgical Press, 1998). One of the best presentations of the books of Chronicles is Sara Japhet, *The Ideology of the Book of Chronicles and Its Place in Biblical Thought* (Frankfurt/Main: P. Lang, 1997); for Ezra and Nehemiah one should consult Lester L. Grabbe, *Ezra–Nehemiah*, Old Testament Readings (London: Routledge, 1998). Finally, Carolyn J. Sharp, *Irony and Meaning in the Hebrew Bible*, Indiana Studies in Biblical Literature (Bloomington: Indiana University Press, 2009), pp. 43–83, gives a good overview of the genre of Diaspora novellas and their themes and motifs.

6

※

The Prophetic Literature

R. G. Kratz

1. PROPHETS IN THE ANCIENT NEAR EAST

There were prophets throughout the ancient Near East. Their activity is attested in various places over about two millennia. The two most important archives in which evidence of prophets is to be found are the royal archive of Mari (Tell Hariri) on the upper Euphrates (from the eighteenth century BCE) and the royal library in Neo-Assyrian Nineveh (from the seventh century BCE).[1] In Mari there were thousands of letters, including about fifty that also contained prophetic oracles to the king, Zimri-Lim, who was absent at the time. Often the edges of the prophet's or scribe's garment, or locks of his hair, are mentioned: they were evidently sent with the letter to authenticate the document. In Nineveh some thirty oracles of the goddess Ishtar of Arbela, and occasionally of other deities, were discovered, addressed to the kings Esarhaddon (681–669 BCE) and Asshurbanipal (669–627 BCE) and concerned principally with the accession of these two kings. Additionally, prophets are mentioned in many inscriptions of Assyrian kings.

From the documents from Mari and Nineveh a clear profile of the prophets (who quite often included women) emerges. They bore various job descriptions, such as "ecstatic," "speaker," "oracle priest," "seer," "soothsayer," or "prophet." As a rule they were cultic officials working in the name of the imperial god for the king in office at the time and advised him on political, military, cultic, or ethical issues. They inquired of the gods and received replies in the form of auditions or visions, which they passed on. The sources from Mari also speak of spontaneous revelations to various people who then repair to the court and communicate what has been revealed to them. The messages of the prophets might sometimes contain a certain criticism of the kings for a too-lax practice of the cult or carelessness in waging war; but taken as a whole, the messages served to confirm and support the king, and this can especially be seen in the Neo-Assyrian prophecies. In the ancient Near East prophecy was a vehicle of politics and propaganda.

Some witnesses to prophetic activity have also survived from the more immediate surroundings of Israel and Judah.[2] The inscription of King Zakkur of Hamath, from around 800 BCE, describes the usual scenario: surrounded by a coalition of hostile kings, King Zakkur raises his hands to the "god of heaven," Baal-shamayim, and consults seers and soothsayers. They reply with the typical oracle of salvation, "Do not fear," which also occurs very frequently in Neo-Assyrian prophecy, and they promise the king victory over his enemies. The inscription was then placed on a stela to commemorate the victory.

Yet prophets did not always announce only good tidings. From Deir 'Alla in the land of Gilead (the territory of Moab in Transjordania) come the words of Balaam the son of Beor, the seer of the gods.[3] This is no other than the Balaam of the Bible (Num. 22–24), only we encounter him here in his original context and time (around 800 BCE), before he was adopted for Israel by the biblical tradition. The inscription was written on a whitewashed wall in red and black ink, so the writing is literally on the wall! Balaam announces to his people, with weeping, a dreadful catastrophe decreed by the gods. From the badly preserved remains it is not possible to say unambiguously what the occasion of the announcements of doom and the curses was or why they were written down. They are most readily understood as warnings and exhortations to reform. In this way the gods who had been angered (Shamash, perhaps also El, and the assembly of the Shaddin; cf. Num. 24:4, 16) were to be appeased, in the hope that the catastrophe that was impending, or had even been survived by the time the text was written down, might be averted through fasting and weeping.

The oracles or visions of the prophets were uttered in a concrete historical situation and were not primarily devised in order to be written down and transmitted to later generations. And yet written testimony of them does survive. Records in the form of letters served for communication and were placed in archives for this purpose (Mari). Mention in inscriptions meant that the message or activity of the prophets was retained for posterity (Zakkur). Collecting and recording the Neo-Assyrian prophetic oracles on tablet collections, deposited in the royal library (Nineveh), set in motion a regular transmission of prophetic oracles. They served to prove the legitimacy of the Neo-Assyrian kings. We do not know what purpose was served by the wall inscription of Deir ʿAlla, though in a sense this is the first and only "book" that a seer has left behind.

There were also prophets in ancient Israel and Judah. The evidence for this is not only the stories about prophets in the books of Samuel and Kings, or in the books of the prophets, in the Old Testament; there is also very occasional epigraphic testimony. Not long before 587 BCE, when the Babylonian king Nebuchadnezzar II and his troops were besieging Jerusalem for the second time in about ten years, in order to capture it and, this time, to destroy it, the commandant of a Judaean outpost named Joash received a letter from a subordinate called Hoshayahu. The letter is written on an ostracon (fragment of pottery), which together with twenty further ostraca of the same kind was discovered between 1935 and 1938 during excavations in Lachish, southwest of Jerusalem. It is moving to read these texts, which convey an authentic impression of the chaotic situation shortly before the fall of Jerusalem. The people were communicating through smoke signals, and by messengers bringing letters, and were trying through every possible means to avert the impending disaster.

An attempt to do this was also the mission of a general called Koniyahu, who (as we learn from the letter from Hoshayahu to his superior officer Joash) had traveled to Egypt, presumably to forge an alliance against the Babylonians, on the orders of the last Judaean king, Zedekiah. As we know from the Bible, in the ninth year of his reign Zedekiah rebelled against the Babylonian king, which led to the siege and then in the end to the fall of Jerusalem (2 Kings 25). In the same letter Hoshayahu mentions a letter from a certain Tobiyahu, who quotes from a prophetic oracle the words "take heed, beware!" This expression is common in prophetic speech and usually introduces a warning, for example, of an enemy trap (2 Kings 6:9); but it can also be the opening of an oracle of salvation conveying a coming victory over the enemies. Thus, in a similar situation, when toward the end of the eighth century BCE Judah was attacked by a Syro-Israelite coalition, we hear: "Take heed, be quiet, do not fear, and do not let your heart be faint because of these two smouldering stumps of firebrands, because of the fierce anger of Rezin and Aram and the son of Remaliah" (Isa. 7:4). Both types match what we know about prophets from the ancient Near Eastern parallels.

To date, the quotation in the letter from Lachish is the only prophetic oracle from Israel and Judah we know of that was transmitted outside the Bible. It raises many puzzles for us. We do not know who the author of the oracle was or exactly to what event it related; we know only the general political situation around 587 BCE. But is the oracle intended as an exhortation or as an oracle of salvation? Is it a literal quotation or an abbreviated version, a freely formulated approximation to the contents, made by the writer of the letter Hoshayahu is quoting from, or by Hoshayahu himself? The original senders and addressees of the news will not have been troubled by such questions—they knew the answers, and so a mere indication will have sufficed. We, on the other hand, remote as we are from the events and having (by archaeological accident) only the hint in the letter, need to reconstruct the historical situation and try to fit the oracle into it.

This epigraphic example prepares us for the task that awaits us in the Old Testament. For the writers of the biblical texts were themselves in a similar position to ours. No doubt they knew a good deal more, but they, too, had to decode the message themselves when they came upon a prophetic oracle in an archive or by some other means and wanted to put it into a narrative or a prophetic book. This chapter will deal with how they did this and what the result was. I shall first examine the stories of the prophets to establish what a prophet was understood to be in ancient Israel, and then address the question why prophetic books were written.[4]

2. PROPHETIC TALES IN THE OLD TESTAMENT

What was a prophet in ancient Israel and ancient Judah? The question can best be answered through a study of the prophetic stories, by reading them somewhat against the grain, that is, contrary to their own intentions. My first example is the stories about the prophet Jeremiah (Jer. 26–45), which deal with the same period as the one that produced the Lachish ostracon. They provide a great deal more detailed information about the events of the time than does the ostracon and allow the reader direct access to the activity and the sufferings of the prophet. Indeed, it has even been suggested that the prophet of the Lachish ostracon should be identified with Jeremiah or with one of his opponents, though there is no ground for this in the text.

The element of truth in this historical combination is that, in the time of the anonymous prophet in the ostracon and of Jeremiah, there were various different ideas as to what the will of Yhwh was and of how the threatening catastrophe could perhaps be avoided. The political situation was unreadable, and so the prophets took up party positions in diverse ways. Many—probably the majority—took the side of the ruling kings, Jehoiakim, Jehoiachin, and Zedekiah, and supported political alliances with the great power that was Egypt against their Babylonian enemies. Others—and Jeremiah seems to have been among them—advised against this. They held to an older political doctrine that had prevailed under King Josiah, when Assyria and Egypt had still exercised rule over Judah. They saw the future of Judah as a Babylonian vassal state, freed from Assyria, as a buffer against Egypt. The first group saw in Babylon the enemy; the other, a protecting power, even if this was not a matter of choice. Both parties, with equal justification, supposed that they had the imperial God, Yhwh, on their side.

For the stories about Jeremiah this disagreement had been long decided. They do show that Jeremiah, like his opponents, was implicated in the politics of the day in the last years of Judah in the sixth century BCE; but they are looking back on the events from a great temporal distance. The destruction of Jerusalem had shown that it was those with whom Jeremiah stood who were in the right. The others—such as the prophet Hananiah, once an opponent of Jeremiah (Jer. 27–28)—hence come to be explained as "lying prophets." Additionally, the events back then acquire a new meaning: according to the stories, they were a punishment by God for the sins of Judah and Jerusalem, which had caused Yhwh to give the city into the hands of the Babylonians. This explanation is an ex post facto rationalization of the catastrophe that had happened and at the same time a theological interpretation of the historical facts. Rather than political strategy and human acts of power, according to the narrative God—and God's word in the mouth of the (true) prophet—is responsible for the course of history. The narrative thus derives a deeper theological sense from the historical events.

It is no different in the stories in the historical books of the Old Testament, Samuel and Kings as well as Chronicles. From a phenomenological perspective, the prophets in biblical narratives differ little from their fellows in the ancient Near East. But from the point of view of content, these narratives take a quite different road, presenting the prophets as heralds of divine judgment and teachers of the law.

To begin with the phenomenology: in the stories we meet both men and women who are called "prophet" or "prophetess," "seer," "man of God," "soothsayer," "magician," or "necromancer." In terms of gender, the male prophets are dominant. Yet there are also examples of female prophets: Miriam (Exod. 15:20), Deborah (Judg. 4:4), Huldah (2 Kings 22:14; 2 Chron. 34:22), the wife of Isaiah (Isa. 8:3), and Noadiah (Neh. 6:14). However, there is no prophetic book named after a woman. Most prophets are to be found in the circle of the court and the Temple (2 Sam. 24:11; 1 Kings 1:8; 2 Kings 22:14). Others live at local sanctuaries or are organized in a kind of religious order (Judg. 4:4–5; 1 Sam. 9:6; 1 Kings 13:11). Often priests and prophets are mentioned in the same breath, which shows that we are dealing with various classes of cult functionaries. Apart from their mantic abilities, many are attributed with the ability to work miracles (Elijah, Elisha). In the ancient Near East manticism and magic were not greatly differentiated, and even the tradition could not make much of the difference (1 Sam. 9:9). Only in biblical law do we find most mantic and magical practices forbidden (Deut. 18:9–22), thus introducing the difference between "true" and "false" prophets—the former being those sent by Yhwh and the latter being those who prophesy "lies" and seduce Israel to worship idols (Jer. 23, 27–29; Ezek. 13).

Like their ancient Near Eastern counterparts, prophets in Israel and Judah received their messages in dreams and visions (1 Kings 22:17, 19; Isa. 6:1; Amos 7–9; Zech. 1–6) or in auditions (1 Sam. 3:9, 9:15; 2 Sam. 7:4). Groups of prophets, but not only they, are said to have fallen easily into ecstasy and then to have behaved like people possessed (1 Sam. 10:5–6, 10–13; 19:20–21; 1 Kings 18:25–29, 22:10–12). For that reason prophets might sometimes be regarded as *meshugge*, that is, "mad" (2 Kings 9:11; Isa. 29:26; Hosea 9:7). They communicated their message in short or long sayings. Sometimes this communication was accompanied by symbolic acts, such as wearing horns as a sign of coming victory over enemies (1 Kings 22:11), or wearing/breaking a yoke as a sign of the outcome of the rule of the Babylonian enemy (Jer. 27–28), or the shattering of a pot to stand for the fate of Judah and Jerusalem (Jer. 18–19).

If we move from a phenomenological to a historical point of view, there is again much in the stories of Israelite and Judaean prophets to remind us of the ancient Near Eastern parallels; but at the same time differences appear. The Old Testament sees the genealogy of the prophets as beginning in remote antiquity. Named examples are Abraham (Gen. 20:7), Miriam (Exod. 15:20), Moses (Num. 12:6–8; Deut. 18:15, 18; 34:9), the foreign seer Balaam (Num. 22–24), and Deborah (Judg. 4). These are, indeed, projections—reflections from a later period. Israel and Judah emerged into history no earlier than the rise of the monarchy around 1000 BCE.[5] The seer Balaam, from whom we have authentic texts (see above, section 1), is attested in the ninth or eighth century BCE at the earliest, before he was claimed for Israel and its mythical prehistory, the time of the wanderings in the wilderness. Thus Israelite-Judaean prophecy cannot be traced back further than the time of the two kingdoms, the northern kingdom of Israel and the southern kingdom of Judah. Even in postexilic times prophets appeared (Neh. 6:7, 10–14; Zech. 13), but not all entered the literature and became part of the biblical tradition.

The principal task of the prophets consisted in appointing, accompanying, and advising the kings. According to an old tradition Saul, on his way to search for his father's escaped donkeys, was anointed as king by a man of God called Samuel, in a place in the land of Zuph where the latter was settled (1 Sam. 9–10). The story is not historical in our sense and competes with the more realistic version of 1 Sam. 11: it is a legend about the foundation of the kingdom of the house of Saul. Yet in terms of phenomenology the scenario—asking a local expert in divination about all sorts of daily life problems—is well chosen and shows what the task of the "men of God" consisted of. We learn of similar things about the court of David, in the southern kingdom, where the prophet Nathan was active and is supposed to have prophesied to David the eternal duration of his dynasty (2 Sam. 7). The information that he was implicated in the intrigues surrounding the succession to David is most likely reliable. Together with the priest Zadok and other officials he sided with the younger Solomon, the son of Bathsheba, against Adonijah, David's older son (2 Sam. 11–12; 1 Kings 1–2).

Thus right from the beginning, in the Old Testament stories, we see the prophets of Israel and Judah concerned with installing and deposing kings; giving advice on matters of war and peace (1 Sam. 22:5; 1 Kings 12:22–25; 20; 22; 2 Kings 3; 6–7; 13:14–19; 18–20); and taking a position on cultic (2 Sam. 7; 1 Kings 13), ethical, or legal questions (2 Sam. 11–12, 24; 1 Kings 21). All of this accords with the findings in extrabiblical, ancient Near Eastern witnesses from the second and first millennia. Once there was no longer a king in Israel (722 BCE) or Judah (587 BCE), however, the prophets changed their character in Old Testament narratives: as the voice of God they became decided opponents of the kings and the monarchy as such.

In the place of the monarchy there arose not democracy but theocracy, the rule of God and his pious ones. The law of the theocracy is the Decalogue, and especially the First Commandment, in whose light the kings of Israel and Judah cut a poor figure. They are all charged with the "sin of Jeroboam"—Jeroboam was in fact installed by a prophet (1 Kings 11:26–40) but dissolved the unity of kingdom and cult in Jerusalem, multiplied altars, and venerated "other gods" (1 Kings 12–14). The few exceptions among the kings confirm the rule: in the time without kings hopes fastened on David and Josiah. The former, as founder of the Judaean dynasty, and the latter, as the reformer of cultic life, became the bearers of messianic expectation and models of "*torah* piety," trusting not in their own institution and its ideology but in God alone. Like the stories of Jeremiah, the narratives in the historical books reflect the older circumstances, yet at the same time work to overcome precisely these circumstances.

This ambivalence also characterizes the stories about Elijah and Elisha (1 Kings 17–19, 21; 2 Kings 1–10, 13). Elisha was the head of a group of prophetic disciples who lived in rather miserable conditions and whose survival he achieved through his power to work miracles (2 Kings 2:19–22, 4:1–44, 6:1–7). No less is true of Elijah, who in the tradition has been made into Elisha's predecessor (1 Kings 19:16, 19–21; 2 Kings 2). The story is told (made famous through a scene in Felix Mendelssohn's oratorio *Elijah*) that in the presence of King Ahab, Elijah put his head between his knees and compelled it to rain, after a long drought (1 Kings 18:41–46). He is the type of wonder-worker such as we still (or again) meet in the tradition about Jesus. This type derives from a rural milieu in which people believed in hidden forces that pervade nature and in supernatural abilities to control these forces. Both these charismatics are also active on occasion as political advisers to kings and as soothsayers in the wars against Moabites and Aramaeans (2 Kings 3, 6:8–7:20). Here, too, their magical abilities play their part (2 Kings 13:14–19).

These memories of the men of God are recorded in the biblical tradition but interpreted theologically in a new way. The wonder-workers are turned into representatives of the word of God, and the wonders themselves into signs that authenticate that word. Elijah becomes a contender for the First Commandment—which he carries in his name: *Elijah* = "My God is Yhwh." As such the prophet becomes the opponent of king and kingdom. In the sacrificial contest on Mount Carmel, which ends with the slaughter of 450 prophets of Baal (1 Kings 17–18), Elijah prepares the bloody work that (in accordance with his prophecy) King Jehu completes by completely wiping out the dynasty of his predecessor, Omri (2 Kings 9–10). At the time of Elijah, in the ninth century BCE, the First Commandment did not yet exist, yet the tradition dates it back into his time and turns the prophet (as Julius Wellhausen once so beautifully put it) into "a bird that sings before the dawn."

From the example of Elijah it becomes especially clear what the biblical tradition in the books of Samuel, Kings, and Chronicles—but also in the stories in the prophetic books (Isa. 36–39; Jer. 26–45; Amos 7:10–17)—is up to, forcing us to distinguish between the *historical* and the *biblical* prophets. The tradition is not interested in the historical phenomenon of prophecy but, rather, in its theological meaning. The texts we have before us have been worked over with many literary revisions, which have introduced into the narrative the law of Moses, the First Commandment, and many other theological interests. Thus the biblical stories have turned the onetime kingmakers and wonder-workers into preachers of the law, who call people to obedience to God and warn them of the impending downfall of Israel and Judah that they announce—a downfall that in reality had already arrived long ago and now lay in the past. The theological reworkings of the older narrative material had the catastrophe behind them and draw lessons from it for the future. They trust in God, rather than in prevailing circumstances, and thus open up a perspective that outlasts changing political systems, ideologies, and fashions.

3. FROM PROPHETIC ORACLE TO PROPHETIC BOOK

Besides the stories about prophets, fifteen books named after prophets have been transmitted in the Old Testament: the three Major Prophets (Isaiah, Jeremiah, Ezekiel) and the twelve Minor Prophets (Hosea, Joel, Amos, Obadiah, Jonah, Micah, Nahum, Habakkuk, Zephaniah, Haggai, Zechariah, and Malachi). In most editions of the Bible Daniel also appears among the prophetic books—this was already the case in the ancient (Greek and Latin) translations and is traceable back to the second century BCE. Already in the community of Qumran, the settlement on the Dead Sea, Daniel was reckoned to belong to the prophets. But in the Hebrew canon things are different: there Daniel appears in the third part of the canon, the "Writings" (*ketubim*), after the "Law" (*torah*) and the "Prophets" (*nebi'im*).

The existence of such prophetic books is in some ways astonishing. Prophets in the ancient Near East did not, so far as we know, write books. Once they had received their oracles, they conveyed them either orally or in writing through the medium of a professional scribe. Most of their oracles are lost forever; only a very few were retained in letters and inscriptions and conserved in the royal archives. We know them only through accidents of archaeology, which has brought them to light again, just like the Lachish ostracon (see section 1 above). But, with rare exceptions (Neo-Assyrian prophecies, Balaam at Deir 'Alla), there clearly never developed a regular prophetic *literature*. With the decline of the ancient Near Eastern monarchies, and their archives and inscriptions, the prophetic tradition also regularly broke off. All that has survived is the religio-historical *phenomenon* of ancient Near Eastern prophecy, which sprang up recurrently at various times—mostly times of crisis—and in various places in the Syro-Mesopotamian area.

The Old Testament, too, mentions the setting in writing of prophetic oracles. Thus Isaiah is told to write on a tablet the saying "The spoil speeds, the prey hastens," so that everyone can see it and check its coming true (Isa. 8:1–2; cf. Isa. 30:8; Hab. 2:2). In the case of Jeremiah there is a record of correspondence with the exiles in Babylon (Jer. 29 and the Greek Letter of Jeremiah), and it is reported that he wrote his words in a "book" (at that time, a scroll) or else got Baruch to do it for him (Jer. 30:2; 36; 51:59–64; cf. Isa. 30:8, 34:16; Ezek. 2:8–3:3). Setting oracles in writing was not purely for the purpose of communication; it also had a magical meaning. The written word stood for the event that it announced and was meant to guarantee its actualization. Yet we would know nothing of all this had not occasional writings and other oracles been retained "forever" in the books of the prophets and copied out again and again. In the Old Testament, contrary to ancient Near Eastern practice, transmission took a form that was resistant to the changes and chances of history. The tradition survived the downfall of the kingdoms of Israel and Judah and the destruction of the Second Temple in Jerusalem and still survives to this day. Why this happened only here, and nowhere else, it is hard to say. One can only describe the stages by which it happened and what came of it.

At the beginning stand one or more oracles of a prophet—as a rule the prophet who gave his name to the book. There was no idea at all of producing a prophetic book. Take, for example, the saying "The spoil speeds, the prey hastens," with which Yhwh entrusted Isaiah of Jerusalem.[6] This saying derives from Egyptian military speech and promises Judah, toward the end of the eighth century BCE, victory over its enemies, a coalition of Aram and Israel. The word was transmitted in two different scenarios. Once it appears as the inscription on a tablet that Isaiah is to prepare: "Then the LORD said to me, Take a large tablet and write on it in common characters, 'The spoil speeds, the prey hastens'" (Isa. 8:1). This is a matter of a symbolic act that creates publicity and at the same time has a magical meaning. The other time the same word appears in connection with the birth of a child: "And I went to the prophetess, and she conceived and bore a son. Then the LORD said to me, Name him 'The spoil speeds, the prey hastens'; for before the child knows how to call 'My father' or 'My mother,' the wealth of Damascus and the spoil of Samaria will be carried away by the king of Assyria" (Isa. 8:3–4).

These two scenes support the policy of King Ahaz, who, as we know from the books of Kings, appealed to the major power, Assyria, for help against the coalition of Aram and Israel and paid tribute for it (2 Kings 16:5, 7–9). The prophet makes it clear that the liberation of Jerusalem from its northern enemies through Assyria is Yhwh's work. In the present text of Isaiah 8:1–4 the two scenes are narrated one after the other and bolted together by the shared expression. The first-person report by Isaiah conforms in this to what one would also expect from any ancient

Near Eastern prophet. If we had only these four verses, it would occur to no one to think that they formed the oldest part, and the basic stem, of the book of Isaiah.

By way of comparison we may take an example from ancient Near Eastern prophecy, an oracle of the god Dagan of Terqa, which similarly occurs three times in letters from the archive from the Old Babylonian city of Mari.[7] It reads: "Beneath straw water runs." The saying is directed against an alliance of the king of Mari with the king of Eshnunna, a city on the Tigris. It is repeated in a varying form by three prophets who had appeared at the court of Mari, as advice against the alliance. The first derives from it an exhortation to the king to obtain another oracle first. A prophetess finds in it the political advice that the king should mistrust the king of Eshnunna and his flattering speeches. Finally, the third promises the king of Mari unequivocal victory. There is no difference in the substance: Dagan of Terqa desires peace, not through an alliance but, rather, through victory. But the prophets, or the letter writers who forwarded the prophets' words, clothed the message from the god (except for the basic metaphor "Beneath straw water runs," which occurs in all three versions) in differing words, in their own words as much as in those of the god Dagan of Terqa. So far as we know no prophetic book arose from this.

It is different with Isaiah's saying "The spoil speeds, the prey hastens." The two scenes of the first-person report, which prophesy that Judah's enemies will fall to Assyria, take on a surprising twist in what follows:

> The LORD spoke to me again: Because this people has refused the waters of Siloah that flow gently, and melt in fear before Rezin and the son of Remaliah; therefore, the LORD is bringing up against it the mighty flood waters of the River, the king of Assyria and all his glory; it will rise above all its channels and overflow all its banks; it will sweep on into Judah as a flood, and, pouring over, it will reach up to the neck. (Isa. 8:5–8)

The "River" is the Euphrates; its "mighty flood waters," which "overflow all its banks," are the Assyrian armies, which are marching from east to west and from north to south. After Damascus and Samaria, they are to reach Judah and Jerusalem themselves. What has happened here?

The text is quite obviously formulated with hindsight. It presupposes that the original prophetic saying has come true and that Assyria has overrun the enemy in the north. The tribute to the Assyrian king must therefore have paid off and led to the liberation of Judah from its northern enemies. This must have been how the king and the majority of Judaeans—presumably including the prophet Isaiah—took the announcement of the end of Samaria in 732 and the end of the northern kingdom of Israel in 722 BCE, at least as long as the kingdom of Judah still stood.

But the scribes who wrote the book of Isaiah saw it differently. For them the end of the kingdom of Israel spelled principally that the God of Israel—Yhwh of Samaria—and his institutions had fallen to the Assyrians. Responsibility for this event lay with the God of Judah—Yhwh of Jerusalem—in whose name Isaiah had uttered the oracle "The spoil speeds, the prey hastens." When, after 722, and especially in 701 BCE, the danger that the Assyrian armies would advance on Judah threatened, the scribes—against Isaiah's intention!—drew the astonishing implication that Yhwh had determined on judgment not only against Israel but also against Judah and Jerusalem. They held absolutely fast to the God of the prophet and in consequence gave up not only on the enemy in the north but on their own people. The violent impression made by the Assyrian progress to Syria-Palestine meant that they saw less significance in the local differences and rivalries between Israel and Judah. In Yhwh of Samaria and Yhwh of Jerusalem they discovered the same God and in Israel and Judah the one people of God, which is called "Israel"; that is how this people, "Israel," came in the Bible to be the object of belief and confession. The prophet of salvation—the historical Isaiah—became in biblical tradition a prophet of judgment, whose book has a single motto: "If you will not believe, you will not be established" (Isa. 7:9; cf. 30:15).

Thus the transition from prophetic oracle to prophetic book is connected with a far-reaching reinterpretation of the historical prophet in the literary tradition. This reinterpretation explains the downfall of both kingdoms—Israel in 722 BCE, Judah in 587 BCE—as an act of God, his judgment on his people. Correspondingly, the books of the prophets in the Old Testament contain almost exclusively prophecies of judgment. And even where the books speak (once more) of God's salvation (as, for example, in the second half of the book of Isaiah [Isa. 40–66]), the act of salvation is always preceded by divine judgment. But even the proclamation of the end implies a new beginning: it forces a rethink. God's judgment on his people, and the faith that the prophets of the prophetic books demand, set new standards in relation to God, just as among human beings.

Of these new standards set by the prophetic books any number of examples might be given. Just two must suffice here: Hosea's criticism of the cult and Amos's social criticism.[8] Only a few fragments have survived of the original oracles of these two historical prophets, from the last years of the northern kingdom of Israel toward the end of the eighth century BCE. These fragments—which in their own day would have been immediately comprehensible—no longer make it possible to judge whether they originally related (in the interests of Israel) to a survival of the northern kingdom or (in Judaean interests) took their stand against the enemy in the north. Sayings on both fronts, from the time of the Syro-Ephraimite war (also the setting for the saying "The spoil speeds, the prey hastens" in Isa. 8:1–4), appear to have found their way into Hosea 5:8–11. The authentic sayings of the prophet Hosea, however, have been integrated and worked over in Hosea 6:8–7:7 and bemoan the imminent downfall of the kingdom of Israel, which came true in 722 BCE. The same circumstances gave rise to Amos's metaphors (Amos 3:12; 5:2, 3, 19) and the woe-sayings in Amos 3–6 (Amos 5:18, 6:1ff.; compare the participles in Amos 3:12, 4:1, 5:7). They set down the end of Samaria as unavoidable—whether they lament this, from an Israelite perspective, and might even be intended to avert it or, from a Judaean perspective, welcome it and are even meant in some way to help to bring it about. The tradition has set this lack of clarity aside and found in the oracles of both prophets an accusation against, and judgment on, "Israel," understood to mean the one people of God. In the grounds it offers for the disaster, however, the tradition gives different accents to Hosea and Amos.

In the book of Hosea the people are reproached for a false cult. Yhwh's dictum is, "I desire steadfast love and not sacrifice, the knowledge of God rather than burnt-offerings" (Hosea 6:6). It is not obvious from this what was "false" in the Israelite cult or why Yhwh suddenly no longer wanted the usual sacrifices. The later scribes explained the matter by implying that it was not Yhwh who was worshipped in the Israelite cult but Baal and the "other gods," so that the sacrifice was therefore not acceptable to Yhwh. At any rate Yhwh demands more than regular sacrifices and thus puts the relationship between God and people, founded on and mediated by the cult, on a new footing. What is demanded is complete commitment to God and the knowledge of God, which renders everything else of secondary importance. This does not lead to a new ordering of worship or community: yet the demand does have in it the potential to relativize traditional religious orders, if not indeed to blow them up and then remake them, with God rather than human needs in mind.

In the book of Amos social critique dominates. This has been attached to the prophet's old metaphors, which originally simply foresaw a great disaster coming on Israel: "As the shepherd rescues from the mouth of the lion two legs, or a piece of an ear, so shall the people of Israel be rescued, who sit in Samaria on the corner of a couch and the head of a bed" (Amos 3:12). In other words, they will *not* be rescued but will be totally consumed by the lion. Attached to this is a saying that was originally directed only against the upper class in Samaria but now has been generalized and turned against Israel as a whole, as if all Israelites spent the whole day lolling on divans. And in order to make it quite clear who has brought on this disaster—and that it is a punishment from God—the tradition adds a word of judgment that is directed against the material basis for the evil: "I will tear down the winter house as well as the summer house, and the houses of ivory shall perish, and the great houses shall come to an end, says the LORD" (Amos 3:15).

What on the face of it seems just a small-scale polemic against luxury turns out, on closer inspection, to be an innovation in social and legal history. The social and legal inequalities that have always existed and always will exist come to be explained as the reason for Yhwh's judgment, and this turns them into sins against God. "Justice and righteousness" (Amos 5:7, 6:12; cf. Isa. 5:7) become God's main demand, which he makes primarily for himself but also for human beings among themselves, through the prophets and, later, in the law. We cannot derive from this a comprehensive reform program for home and foreign policy in order to solve the problems of this world; yet, presented with a divine demand, the old standards of justice and righteousness in the human polity acquire a higher valuation and become a possible means of changing the world: "No one can serve two masters.... You cannot serve God and Mammon" (Matt. 6:24; Luke 16:13).

4. THE BOOKS OF THE PROPHETS

As soon as the end of the kingdom of Israel (722 BCE; in the books of Isaiah, Hosea, and Amos) and thereafter the end of the kingdom of Judah (587 BCE; in the book of Jeremiah) had been interpreted as an act of Yhwh, the history of the prophetic literature began to take its course. Over time new books kept appearing, and in them the process began that in German is called *Fortschreibung*—a process that seemed never to want to end, of interpretation, adaptation, and actualization, in which one word led to another. It is not unfair to the Bible to say that none of the prophetic books was written by a single prophet in one sitting; every book grew little by little until it reached its present compass, and interpretation then shifted to other writings outside the prophetic books.

The history of the prophetic books cannot be completely told here, only adumbrated briefly.[9] It lasted from the eighth to the third century BCE. But since the individual books grew within this time period, they cannot be unambiguously assigned to any one moment; only the beginning of their transmission (or terminus a quo) can be determined by examining the contents. Any further dating is possible only by means of literary-critical analysis, which leads to a relative chronology. Thus, as we have seen, the end of the kingdom of Israel under Assyria in the late eighth century BCE was the stimulus for the prophetic tradition in the books of Isaiah, Hosea, and Amos.

The Judaean prophet Isaiah's original oracles of salvation (Isa. 7:4, 7–9; 8:1–4; 17:1–3) were first reformulated in the context of the so-called memorandum (*Denkschrift*) of Isaiah (Isa. 6–8) to become oracles of disaster against Israel and Judah, that is, against "Israel, the people of God." Both kingdoms, Israel and Judah, become the objects of the judgment that Yhwh has pronounced against his people (Isa. 6, 7:9b, 8:5–8). The memorandum of Isa. 6–8 was the starting point for the development of all the rest of the book: for the ring-structured composition of the "vision" or the "words about Judah and Jerusalem" (Isa. 1:1, 2:1) in Isaiah 1–12; for the so-called Assyrian cycle, Isa. 28–32, which centers on the fate of Zion and represents a parallel version or, perhaps, rather, a *Fortschreibung* of Isaiah 5–10; for the oracles against the nations in Isaiah 13–23; and for the scenario of world judgment in Isaiah 24–27 and 33–35. From a thematic point of view the book of Isaiah, which was set into being by the siege of Jerusalem in 701 (Isa. 36–39, paralleled in 2 Kings 18–20) and the destruction of the Temple in 587 BCE, is dominated by the theme of Zion—not only in the first part of the book but also in the second, from chapter 40 onward. Jerusalem is the center of the world: the nations either attack it or, having converted to the one God, turn to it.

In a similar way the original oracles of the prophet Hosea, which went to make Hosea 4–9, and those of the prophet Amos, which can be found in Amos 3–6, were put together, worked over, and given a theological meaning. The announcements of coming disaster on Israel turned into intimations of divine judgment; laments turned into accusations, justifications for the judgment; the ill fortune that was lamented, and the misdeeds that were criticized, turned into sins against God. And in all this the political boundaries between the monarchies of Israel and Judah were dissolved: "Israel" stands for the whole of the people of God, implicitly or explicitly including Judah. The fall of the two kingdoms means the end of Yhwh's people Israel, which he had foretold. In the two books of Hosea and Amos the tradition reflects intensively on this end. This theological reflection was recorded above all in the framing sections, which seem to have been added later: the history of Hosea's marriage and the historico-theological reflections in Hosea 1–3 and 9–14 and the cycles about the nations and the visions in Amos 1–2 and 7–9 (compare also Amos 4:6ff.).

The consequences for the picture of God are obvious. Yhwh is no longer the imperial God of the two monarchies, locally differentiated into Yhwh of Samaria and Yhwh of Judah-Jerusalem. He is seen much more as the one God of the one people of God, who reveals his true being and his will in judgment. It is the end of Israel that reveals the past and future of its relationship to God; the criterion that, according to the theological interpretation of the prophets, led to the breach with God becomes the criterion by which the people of God should have guided their past and should guide their future. Reconstituting the broken relationship with God presupposes repentance, according to this criterion.

After the end of the kingdom of Israel at the end of the eighth century BCE, the end of the kingdom of Judah (under Babylon) in the sixth set in motion a second phase in the literary production of the prophetic books. Happiness at the decline of foreign rule by the Assyrians, which is reflected in the original oracles of the prophet Nahum, did not last long. Shortly after the fall of Nineveh in 612 BCE the prophet Jeremiah begins his laments over the decline of Judah, which was already becoming apparent, in 597–587 BCE. These laments break out of the innermost being of the prophet, full of engagement with the people's fate (Jer. 4:7, 11, 13, 19–21; 6:1, 22–23). In these laments it is Jeremiah who speaks, not Yhwh. He is appalled by what he sees and hears coming. What this is, he only hints at, presumably because he does not know exactly himself, but so much is clear: for Jeremiah himself it is not Yhwh who is punishing Judah and Jerusalem for their sins but an immense war machine, marching on Judah and Jerusalem, the ominous "foe from the north." Alongside Jeremiah's laments we may set Zephaniah's word about the "Day of Yhwh" (Zeph. 1:14–16), which recalls the world turned upside down in the disaster visions of Balaam of Deir 'Alla.

But on the model of the older prophetic tradition in Isaiah, Hosea, and Amos, Jeremiah's laments have been subsequently turned into predictions of divine judgment on (Israel and) Judah (Jer. 4–6; cf. 4:5–6 with 6:1, 22). Here, too, a core tradition, the songs about the "foe from the north" in Jeremiah 4–6, forms the starting point for the literary development of the book. We find the same addition of further sayings material—symbolic actions, speeches in prose, stories of suffering, the prophet's personal confessions, and not least the substantial oracles against the nations, which stand in the middle of the book in its Greek recension but at the end in the Hebrew version. The center of the book of Jeremiah is the demand for obedience to the word of God and to his law and the personal fate of the prophet in his relationship to his God, which represents the relationship of the people to God.

The next crucial point is marked by the rebuilding of the Second Temple in Jerusalem, which provided the impulse for the tradition in the books of Haggai, Zechariah (1–8), and Malachi and introduced a third and powerful drive toward literary production in the transmission of the prophets. Dated to the second year of a King Darius (presumably Darius I, i.e., 520 BCE), there are two oracles transmitted in the book of Haggai that call for the rebuilding of the Temple and proclaim the entry of the glory of Yhwh (Hag. 1:1, 4–8, and 1:15b/2:1, 3, 9a). Here the building of the Temple is unambiguously understood as a sign of dawning salvation. However, for others the Persian permission to build, and financial support for the Temple, amounted to no more than a continuation of foreign domination, and they expected more: the building of the Second Temple and the inner constitution of Israel, the people of God, were not enough for them.

It is to this attitude that many insertions in the older prophetic books are to be attributed, above all oracles against the nations and oracles of salvation for Israel, which in many books have the upper hand (Isa. 40–66; Micah; Hag. 1–2; Zech. 1–8). They link back to the old, preexilic tradition of salvation prophecies, or onto more recent oracles of this old sort (such as Hag. 1:1, 4, 8, and 1:15b/2:1, 3, 9a), but completely presuppose the fall of the two kingdoms and the literary tradition of judgment prophecy and develop their visions of the future salvation of Israel on this basis. This is also true of the book of Ezekiel, a sort of midrash on the prophets, which to a great extent makes a literary use of older prophetic books that already existed, and indeed other biblical books, in order to develop the ideal picture of a prophet's life. The book of Ezekiel deals with the destruction of Jerusalem, and ends with the vision of the new Jerusalem, in order to demonstrate the unity, uniqueness, and holiness of Yhwh (or of his "name").

The later prophetic literature is characterized by scriptural learning and the use of scripture. This tendency can be seen in all the prophetic books, but especially in those that have a very concealed, or even no, old core and are purely literary (Joel, Obadiah, Habakkuk, and for considerable stretches Micah, Nahum, and Zephaniah). In the same way the next historical caesura was reflected in the prophetic literature, that is, the collapse of the Persian Empire after the death of Alexander the Great (330 BCE), whose successors, the *diadochoi*, fought over his inheritance. From this period derive the texts that speak of a universal judgment on all peoples and a universal salvation: that proclaim a new heaven and a new earth on which the pious in Israel and the nations will find shelter and deliverance (Isa. 24–27, 34–35, 63–66; Zech. 9–14; Joel; and others). The mention of "Javan" (Greece) in Isaiah 66, Ezek. 27, and Zech. 9 (cf. Dan. 8:21) most probably points to a dating in the third century and in any case demonstrates that we have to envisage the possibility of late, third-century additions and supplements in the books of the prophets.

Toward the end of the third century BCE literary production in the books of the prophets came gradually to be exhausted. On the one hand, this had technical causes: a book in the form of a scroll cannot be just however long one wishes. On the other hand, the challenges of Hellenism, then spreading, necessitated a certain stability in authoritative tradition. Thus the *corpus propheticum* took shape, the collection of the three Major and twelve Minor Prophets, and finally the section of the canon called *nebi'im*, "Prophets." The earlier part of this includes the books Joshua to Kings; the later, the prophetic books proper (compare the brackets Josh. 1:7 and Mal. 3:22). Thus "Prophets" took its place alongside the first, and older, section of the canon, the Torah. This does not mean that these two sections of the Hebrew canon were already fixed and absolutely invariable. On the contrary, the text of both the Torah and the (Former and Latter) Prophets was still fluid in terms of shaping and textual variation, as the evidence of the Septuagint and the Qumran manuscripts demonstrates.

The combination of the historical and the prophetic books into a more or less fixed section of the canon presupposes the theory of the Chronicler—shared also by Josephus[10]—that each epoch had its prophets and that the prophets were the chroniclers of their times. Thus prophets were declared to be history writers, and history writers to be prophets. Ben Sira's "Praise of the Fathers" (Sir. 44–49) is a witness to the section of the canon "Prophets" as a history of the saints in the early second century BCE; the prologue to the Greek translation of the book of Ben Sira, the instruction 4QMMT (a halakhic letter on "some issues of the works of the Torah" from the community at Qumran), and the New Testament call it so by name. The interpretation of the prophets, which until then had taken place within the books themselves, continued in other books: in the book of Daniel and in Jewish apocalyptic, in commentaries such as the *pesharim* at Qumran, and in other Jewish writings of the Greco-Roman period—and not least in the New Testament and the Christian literature that connected with it.[11]

There is an immense cost to the transmission and interpretation of the prophetic books, which began with their literary genesis and continues to this day, and it is by no means self-explanatory. It rests on the conviction, which must have been determinative from the beginning, that in the prophets and their books God is present. "Then the LORD put out his hand and touched my mouth; and the LORD said to me, 'Now I have put my words in your mouth'" (Jer. 1:9) and "I am watching over my word to perform it" (Jer. 1:12)—this is how the book of Jeremiah begins. We may also think of Ezekiel, whom God first gives a scroll to eat, in order to prepare him for his task (Ezek. 2:8–3:3).

The presence of the word of God in the mouths and in the books of the prophets guarantees them a lasting meaning that transcends the times. For the authors and tradents of the prophetic books, the word of God has the characteristic of eternity: "The grass withers, the flower fades; but the word of our God will stand for ever" (Isa. 40:8). This means that it does not display its effect just once but, rather, repeatedly, over and over again: "For as the rain and the snow come down from heaven, and do not return there until they have watered the earth, making it bring forth and sprout, giving seed to the sower and bread to the eater, so shall my word be that goes out from my mouth; it shall not return to me empty, but it shall accomplish that which I purpose, and succeed in the thing for which I sent it" (Isa. 55:10–11; cf. also 9:7).

For this reason scribes and interpreters of the prophetic literature feel justified, indeed compelled, repeatedly to bring the word of God in the books of the prophets to bear on themselves and their time. They do this sometimes with and sometimes against the wording of the text that has been transmitted to them, since, they believe, it contains the full truth and therefore is relevant to them even if it does not explicitly say so. *Fortschreibung* and commentary make explicit what the interpreters find implicitly in the text for their own time.

This way of proceeding is not easy to understand, especially because it joins together two things that to our sensibility seem mutually exclusive: unconditional faithfulness toward the transmitted, inspired text and the freedom to intervene in it at will. Yet for the authors of the prophetic books this was clearly not a contradiction. For them, prophetic inspiration and interpretation based on scriptural learning coincided. The interpretation within the prophetic books is not less inspired than the interpreted text, inasmuch as the interpretation that is written in the text derives its force from the inspiration of the transmitted text. Interpretation outside the books, on the other hand, does mostly require a supplementary revelation to guide the understanding of the transmitted prophetic text (cf. Dan. 9; 1QpHab VII). In the New Testament it is the revelation of God in Jesus Christ that determines the delivery of the interpretation of the law and the prophets.

That the immensely costly business of interpretation was practiced, and continues to be practiced, thus has its reason in the fact that the books of the prophets (like the Bible as a whole) understood themselves to be the word of God and were so regarded by those who were attached to them. After the loss of kingdom and Temple, the word of God remained in the form of Torah and Prophets, and the other biblical books, as the only source of divine revelation and as the mediator between God and his people. In the book of Isaiah this mediating role of the word of God is expressed with the theological metaphor of the "covenant," a term otherwise reserved for the law: "This is my covenant with them, says the LORD: my spirit that is upon you, and my words that I have put in your mouth, shall not depart out of your mouth, or out of the mouths of your children, or out of the mouths of your children's children, says the LORD, from now on and for ever" (Isa. 59:21). It was a small step, yet one with vast consequences, when early Christians derived from such incorporation of the word of God the belief that this word had become flesh in Jesus Christ, as we read in John 1:14. The law and the prophets of the Old Testament are not thereby overtaken but, on the contrary, become, under these new premises, more meaningful and topical than ever. The liberating anger and the healing consolation of the word of God in the prophets of the Old Testament thereby give not only to Judaism but also to Christianity the once-and-for-all chance to serve God rather than man.

NOTES

1. See M. Nissinen, *Prophets and Prophecy in the Ancient Near East*, Writings from the Ancient World 12 (Atlanta: Society of Biblical Literature, 2003), with contributions from Choon-Leong Seow and Robert K. Ritner; cf. R. G. Kratz, *Die Propheten Israels*, Beck'sche Reihe Wissen 232 (Munich: Beck Verlag, 2003), pp. 21–28 (English version: *The Prophets of Israel*, Critical Studies in the Hebrew Bible 2 [Winona Lake, Ind.: Eisenbrauns, 2015]); J. Stökl, *Prophecy in the Ancient Near East: A Philological and Sociological Comparison*, Culture and History of the Ancient Near East 56 (Leiden: Brill, 2012).

2. Nissinen, *Prophets and Prophecy in the Ancient Near East*, pp. 201ff.

3. Ibid., pp. 207ff. See recently E. Blum, "Die aramäischen Wandinschriften von Tell Deir 'Alla," in *Texte zur Umwelt des Alten Testaments, Neue Folge 8* (Gütersloh, Germany: Gütersloher Verlagshaus, 2015), pp. 459–77.

4. For what follows, see Kratz, *Propheten*; R. G. Kratz, *Prophetenstudien: Kleine Schriften II*, Forschungen zum Alten Testament 72 (Tübingen: Mohr Siebeck, 2011);

K. Koch, *Die Propheten*, vol. I (Stuttgart: Kohlhammer, 1978; 3rd ed., 1995), vol. II (Stuttgart: Kohlhammer, 1980; 2nd ed., 1988) (English version: *The Prophets*, 2 vols. [Philadelphia: Fortress, 1982–83]); J. Blenkinsopp, *A History of Prophecy in Israel* (Louisville, Ky.: Westminster John Knox, 1983; 2nd ed., 1996); O. H. Steck, *Die Prophetenbücher und ihr theologisches Zeugnis: Wege der Nachfrage und Fährten zur Antwort* (Tübingen: J.C.B. Mohr [Paul Siebeck], 1996) (English version: *The Prophetic Books and Their Theological Witness*, James D. Nogalski, trans. [St. Louis: Chalice Press, 2000]); O. H. Steck, *Gott in der Zeit entdecken: Die Prophetenbücher des Alten Testaments als Vorbild für Theologie und Kirche*, Biblisch-Theologische Studien 42 (Neukirchen-Vluyn, Germany: Neukirchener Verlag, 2001); J. Barton, *Oracles of God: Perceptions of Ancient Prophecy in Israel after the Exile* (Oxford: Oxford University Press, 2007); J. Day, ed., *Prophecy and Prophets in Ancient Israel: Proceedings of the Oxford Old Testament Seminar*, Library of the Hebrew Bible/Old Testament Series 531 (London: T&T Clark International, 2010).

5. Cf. R. G. Kratz, *Historisches und biblisches Israel: Drei Überblicke zum Alten Testament* (Tübingen: Mohr Siebeck, 2012) (English version: *Historical and Biblical Israel: The History, Tradition, and Archives of Israel and Judah* [Oxford: Oxford University Press, 2015]).

6. For what follows, see Kratz, *Prophetenstudien*, pp. 49–70; M. J. de Jong, *Isaiah among the Ancient Near Eastern Prophets: A Comparative Study of the Earliest Stages of the Isaiah Tradition and the Neo-Assyrian Prophecies*, Vetus Testamentum Supplement Series 117 (Leiden: Brill, 2007), pp. 67–73. For a different view, see H.G.M. Williamson, "Isaiah: Prophet of Weal or Woe?" in R. P. Gordon and H. M. Barstad, eds., "*Thus Speaks Ishtar of Arbela*": *Prophecy in Israel, Assyria, and Egypt in the Neo-Assyrian Period* (Winona Lake, Ind.: Eisenbrauns, 2013), pp. 273–300. On Isaiah, see J. Barton, *Isaiah 1–39*, Old Testament Guide (Sheffield: Sheffield Academic Press, 1995).

7. See Nissinen, *Prophets and Prophecy in the Ancient Near East*, pp. 28–29, 31, 34–35.

8. Cf. Kratz, *Prophetenstudien*, pp. 273–379. On the ethical principles in Amos, see also J. Barton, *Amos's Oracles against the Nations*, Society for Old Testament Study Monograph Series 6 (Cambridge: Cambridge University Press, 1980).

9. For the details, see the literature referred to above in note 4, which offers surveys with varying perspectives.

10. On the theory, compare R. G. Kratz, *Das Judentum im Zeitalter des Zweiten Tempels. Kleine Schriften I*, 2nd ed., Forschungen zum Alten Testament 42 (Tübingen: Mohr Siebeck, 2013), pp. 157–80; Josephus Flavius, *Contra Apionem* I 7, 37–41.

11. Compare on this Barton, *Oracles of God*; Kratz, *Prophetenstudien*. On the *pesharim*, see Kratz, *Prophets of Israel*.

FURTHER READING

Classics of research on prophecy from the nineteenth century come from three scholars, unfortunately not translated into English yet—Heinrich Ewald, Bernhard Duhm, and Gustav Hölscher:

Duhm, Bernhard, *Die Theologie der Propheten als Grundlage für die innere Entwicklungsgeschichte der israelitischen Religion*. Bonn, 1875.

Duhm, Bernhard, *Israels Propheten*. Tübingen: J.C.B. Mohr (Paul Siebeck), 1916; 2nd ed., 1922.

Ewald, Heinrich, *Die Propheten des Alten Bundes*, 2 vols. Stuttgart, 1840–41; 2nd ed., 1867–68.

Hölscher, Gustav, *Die Propheten: Untersuchungen zur Religionsgeschichte Israels*. Leipzig: Hinrichs, 1914.

Ewald was the teacher of Julius Wellhausen, who in his account of his life wrote that Ewald "aroused him from sleep." One reason for this impression was certainly the sympathetic, highly emotional view of the individual figures of the prophets that Ewald expresses in his work. Following this view Duhm is also interested in the heroic individuality and personal inner life of the prophets. However, he goes a step further and maps the prophet in the new picture of the history of ancient Israel's religion as it was reconstructed on the historical books by Julius Wellhausen in his famous *Prolegomena to the History of Israel*, 6th ed. (Berlin: Reimer, 1905; English version: *Prolegomena to the History of Israel*, translated from the 2nd ed., 1883 [Atlanta: Scholars Press, 1994]). Within this picture the prophets of the eighth century BCE play a key role. By means of literary and redactional criticism Duhm separates the authentic oracles from secondary additions and thus reaches his view of the historical prophet. Hölscher's book is more interested in the religious historical and anthropological phenomenon of prophecy and thereby initiates a new perspective of research.

The new perspective, which dominated the first half of the twentieth century and lasted until the 1970s, is still oriented toward the great, individual figures but introduces a novel dimension: the flow of tradition in which the prophets moved. Sigmund Mowinckel and Gerhard von Rad are exemplary for this perspective:

Mowinckel, Sigmund, *Prophecy and Tradition: The Prophetic Books in the Light of the Study of the Growth and History of the Tradition*. Oslo (Kristiania): Jacob Dybwad, 1946.

Mowinckel, Sigmund, *Psalmenstudien III: Kultprophetie und prophetische Psalmen*. Oslo (Kristiania): Jacob Dybwad, 1923.

von Rad, Gerhard, *Old Testament Theology*, vol. 2: *The Theology of Israel's Prophetic Traditions*, D.M.G. Stalker, trans.; introduction by Walter Brueggemann. Old Testament Library. Louisville, Ky.: Westminster John Knox Press, 2001. (German original version: *Theologie des Alten Testaments II: Die Theologie der prophetischen Überlieferung Israels*. Munich: Chr. Kaiser, 1960.)

While Mowinckel explains the prophets and the prophetic books more with the stream of (mainly oral) tradition, von Rad sees them as great theologians and interpreters of tradition who turned the tradition up-side down and reformulated it in a particular way. Both approaches have in common that they recognize the prophets as part of a process of oral and literary tradition that covers the general religious historical back-ground of prophecy, the oral prehistory of the prophetic oracles, and their literary history (*Nachgeschichte*) in the books of the prophets.

Klaus Koch and Joseph Blenkinsopp choose a middle course between historical prophet and tradition:

Blenkinsopp, Joseph, *A History of Prophecy in Israel.* Louisville, Ky.: Westminster John Knox, 1983; 2nd ed., 1996. (German translation: *Geschichte der Prophetie in Israel,* Erhard S. Gerstenberger, trans. Stuttgart: Kohlhammer, 1998.)

Koch, Klaus, *The Prophets,* 2 vols. Philadelphia: Fortress, 1982–83. (German original version: *Die Propheten.* Stuttgart: Kohlhammer, vol. I: 1978, 3rd ed., 1995; vol. II: 1980, 2nd ed., 1988.)

These two overviews summarize the consensus of the second half of the twentieth century, which remains common and widespread today. Ac-cording to this consensus the biblical prophets are deeply rooted in the ancient Near East and thus represent nothing unusual: they distinguish themselves, however, as historical personalities through their social and religious message and initiated a literary tradition that lasted until Per-sian and Hellenistic times. Also in regard to the differentiation between authentic oracles and secondary additions these two overviews take the usual pragmatic path: what cannot be proved secondary is supposed to be authentic.

Research in the second half of the twentieth century received new stimulus from three angles: first, from the investigation of Near Eastern analogies from Mesopotamia (Mari, Assyria). A thorough religious his-torical comparison revealed the similarities as well as the fundamental differences between the ancient Near Eastern (including Israelite-Judahite) phenomenon of prophecy, on the one hand, and the biblical prophets, on the other, more clearly than before. The relevant sources with a short commentary are provided by Martti Nissinen. Jonathan Stökl gives an overview of the phenomena and discusses the secondary literature. As a case study I would like to recommend the pathbreaking book of Mat-thies de Jonge on Isaiah:

de Jonge, Matthies J., *Isaiah among the Ancient Near Eastern Prophets: A Comparative Study of the Earliest Stages of the Isaiah Tradition and the Neo-Assyrian Prophecies.* Vetus Testamentum Supplement Series 117. Leiden: Brill, 2007.

Nissinen, Martti, *Prophets and Prophecy in the Ancient Near East*. Writings from the Ancient World 12. Atlanta: Society of Biblical Literature, 2003. With contributions from Choon-Leong Seow and Robert K. Ritner.

Stökl, Jonathan, *Prophecy in the Ancient Near East: A Philological and Sociological Comparison*. Culture and History of the Ancient Near East 56. Leiden: Brill, 2012.

A second impulse was the (re)discovery of the prophetic book as literature. Here, the insight is decisive that the prophetic oracles are preserved exclusively in a literary form (as a "book") and we are not able to trace back the oral prehistory of the book or even the original, authentic voice of the prophet (*ipsissima vox*). Furthermore, scholarship partly gave up the (far-too-)simple differentiation between "authentic" and "inauthentic" and turned to the book itself, that is, the literary form of the prophetic tradition. Consequently, even the "inauthentic" passages (which usually cover more than half of a book) take center stage. Instead of the oral prehistory, this approach is interested either in the literary history of the prophetic books, which represents a kind of inner-biblical interpretation, or in the final shape. For the former the works of Odil Hannes Steck are representative, and for the latter the introduction of Martin Sweeney, for instance, is characteristic:

Steck, Odil Hannes, *Gott in der Zeit entdecken: Die Prophetenbücher des Alten Testaments als Vorbild für Theologie und Kirche*. Biblisch-Theologische Studien 42. Neukirchen-Vluyn, Germany: Neukirchener Verlag, 2001.

Steck, Odil Hannes, *The Prophetic Books and Their Theological Witness*, James D. Nogalski, trans. St. Louis: Chalice Press, 2000. (German original version: *Die Prophetenbücher und ihr theologisches Zeugnis: Wege der Nachfrage und Fährten zur Antwort*. Tübingen: J.C.B. Mohr [Paul Siebeck], 1996.)

Sweeney, Marvin A., *The Prophetic Literature*. Interpreting Biblical Texts. Nashville: Abingdon Press, 2005.

The third stimulus came from the findings from the Dead Sea. Among the Dead Sea Scrolls numerous manuscripts of prophetic books (completely extant or fragmentarily preserved) and many interpretations were found. Both led attention (again) to the broad reception history that the prophets experienced, not only in Qumran but also in ancient Judaism in general and in early Christianity. In a way this renewed interest in reception history is seamlessly connected to the previous approach: both approaches are focused on interpretation, be it interpretation within the prophetic books and their literary growth (*Fortschreibung*) or in the history of the text and its reception in the form of revision, rewriting, and reception. Perception of the prophets in ancient Judaism is the focus of an important monograph by John Barton, two articles by George Brooke, and a volume with collected articles, all of which are recommended for the situation in the Dead Sea Scrolls:

Barton, John, *Oracles of God: Perceptions of Ancient Prophecy in Israel after the Exile.* Oxford: Oxford University Press, 2007.

Brooke, George, J., "The Place of Prophecy in Coming Out of Exile: The Case of the Dead Sea Scrolls." In Anssi Voitila and Jutta Jokiranta, eds., *Scripture in Transition: Essays on Septuagint, Hebrew Bible, and Dead Sea Scrolls in Honour of Raja Sollamo*, pp. 535–50. Leiden: Brill, 2008.

Brooke, George J., "Prophecy and Prophets in the Dead Sea Scrolls: Looking Backwards and Forwards." In Michael H. Floyd and Robert D. Haak, eds., *Prophets, Prophecy, and Prophetic Texts in Second Temple Judaism*, pp. 151–65. Library of the Hebrew Bible/Old Testament Series 427. London: T&T Clark International, 2006.

De Troyer, Kritin, and Armin Lange, eds., *Prophecy after the Prophets? The Contribution of the Dead Sea Scrolls to the Understanding of Biblical and Extra-biblical Prophecy.* Contributions to Biblical Exegesis and Theology 52. Leuven: Peeters, 2009.

I, too, am committed to the approach of connecting inner- and extra-biblical interpretations or, speaking in methodological terms, text and literary histories as an ongoing process of reception history:

Kratz, Reinhard G., *Prophetenstudien: Kleine Schriften II.* Forschungen zum Alten Testament 72. Tübingen: Mohr Siebeck, 2011.

Kratz, Reinhard G., *The Prophets of Israel.* Critical Studies in the Hebrew Bible 2. Winona Lake, Ind.: Eisenbrauns, 2015. (German original version: *Die Propheten Israels.* Beck'sche Reihe Wissen 232. Munich: Beck Verlag, 2003.)

A couple of volumes with collected essays by different scholars, mostly conference proceedings, document the current discussion:

Day, John, ed., *Prophecy and Prophets in Ancient Israel: Proceedings of the Oxford Old Testament Seminar.* Library of the Hebrew Bible/Old Testament Series 531. London: T&T Clark International, 2010.

Gordon, Robert P., and Hans M. Barstad, eds., *"Thus Speaks Ishtar of Arbela": Prophecy in Israel, Assyria, and Egypt in the Neo-Assyrian Period.* Winona Lake, Ind.: Eisenbrauns, 2013.

Köckert, Matthias, and Martti Nissinen, eds., *Propheten in Mari, Assyrien und Israel.* Forschungen zur Religion und Literatur des Alten und Neuen Testaments 201. Göttingen: Vandenhoeck & Ruprecht, 2003.

Nissinen, Martti, ed., *Prophecy in Its Ancient Near Eastern Context: Mesopotamian, Biblical, and Arabian Perspectives.* Society of Biblical Literature Symposium Series 13. Atlanta: Society of Biblical Literature, 2000.

Nissinen, Martti, and Charles E. Carter, eds., *Images and Prophecy in the Ancient Eastern Mediterranean.* Forschungen zur Religion und Literatur des Alten und Neuen Testaments 233. Göttingen: Vandenhoeck & Ruprecht, 2009.

7

※

Legal Texts

Assnat Bartor

INTRODUCTION: WHAT DO WE MEAN WHEN
WE SAY "LEGAL TEXTS"?

There is more than one answer to the question of which biblical texts should be classified as legal texts. According to the minimalist approach, biblical legal literature includes three types of texts. First, there are the laws of the Pentateuch—hundreds of laws appearing in codes, in collections, or individually, especially in the books of Exodus–Deuteronomy. Examples are the law of the Hebrew slave (Exod. 21:2–6), the dietary laws (Lev. 11), the law concerning a woman suspected of adultery (Num. 5:11–31), and the law of warfare (Deut. 20:1–9). Second, there are narratives dealing with legal issues, for example, Solomon's ruling (1 Kings 3:16–28), Moses's appointment of judges (Exod. 18:13–27; Deut. 1:12–18), Jeremiah's trial (Jer. 26), and the divvying of spoils after David's victory over Amalek (1 Sam. 30:22–25)—a story that ends with a clear legal utterance: "From that day forward he made it a statute and an ordinance for Israel; it continues to the present day." Third, there is the collection of laws composed by the prophet Ezekiel—future laws pertaining chiefly to ritual matters, to be implemented after the redemption (Ezek. 40–48).

The maximalist approach adds to these three categories texts from biblical narrative, prophecy, and the wisdom literature that mention or allude to the laws of the Pentateuch, citing either the extant text or a different version, or which contain other legal elements. These texts are instances of the phenomenon known as "law in literature"—an appearance of legal materials in the context of other literary genres, as, for example, in the famous story of the Gibeonites (Josh. 9:3–27). The false pretenses that the Gibeonite-Canaanites presented to the Israelites, as if they had come "from a far country," which allowed them to escape death, mirror the distinction made in the law of *herem* between "the towns of the nations here," which should be destroyed unreservedly, and "the towns that are very far from you," with which a covenant may be entered into (Deut. 20:10–18). The narrative, therefore, alludes to one of the laws of the Pentateuch.

An even more explicit reference appears in one of Jeremiah's prophecies. In likening the relationship between God and Israel to the relationship between husband and wife, the prophet describes a case derived from the law of marriage and divorce: "If a man divorces his wife and she goes from him and becomes another man's wife, will he return to her?" (Jer. 3:1); the answer to the (rhetorical) question presented by the prophet is also part of the law: "Her first husband, who sent her away, is not permitted to take her again to be his wife" (Deut. 24:4).

The world of law is also represented in biblical narrative and prophecy in another way, through three literary patterns that appear to reflect common principles and conceptions of ancient Israel's legal system: the "juridical dialogue," the "juridical parable," and the "*rib* pattern." The "juridical dialogue" contains no elements defining the situation as an institutional trial. However, its content, language, and apparent intentions indicate an attempt to convey the character of a judicial proceeding. Examples are the "trial" of Adam and Eve (Gen. 3:9–19) and Saul's "trial" after the Amalekite War (1 Sam. 15:13–31).[1] The "juridical parable," apparently an actual "case," which is brought before the king, the supreme judge, is a rhetorical scheme aiming to spur a perpetrator into awareness and acknowledgment of his sin. The most famous is Nathan's parable of the poor man's ewe lamb (2 Sam. 12:1–4).[2] And finally the "*rib* pattern"[3] is one of the popular literary patterns in prophetic literature. In several prophetic speeches God and the people of Israel are represented as participants in a legal process. God's accusations toward Israel are presented with the metaphorical use of a model of legal confrontation. Thus, for example: "The LORD rises to argue his case; he stands to judge the peoples" (Isa. 3:13); "O people of Israel; for the LORD has an indictment against the inhabitants of the land" (Hosea 4:1).[4]

The laws of the Pentateuch are also represented in wisdom literature. Some of the didactic instructions in the book of Proverbs—aphorisms that are meant to guide humans on the right path—are paralleled by laws of the Pentateuch. The topics are diverse: theft, adultery, commerce, land, slavery, and even ritual. The instruction "Honor the Lord with your substance and with your first fruits of all your produce" (Prov. 3:9) is parallel to the commandment: "The best of the first fruits of your ground you shall bring to the house of the Lord your God" (Exod. 34:26). The following two verses are also quite similar: "Do not remove the ancient landmark that your ancestors set up" (Prov. 22:28); "You must not move your neighbor's boundary marker, set up by former generations" (Deut. 19:14).

The maximalist approach may create the impression that the Bible abounds in legal texts, from the book of Genesis, which begins with two foundational stories about "crime and punishment," up to the book of Job, which presents a judicial confrontation between man and God,[5] and within the four Pentateuchal books, which are made up chiefly of laws. The present chapter will focus on the latter.

THE LAWS OF THE PENTATEUCH—OVERVIEW

There are various ways to begin an overview of the laws of the Pentateuch. One can begin with the question of where and in what framework the laws appear or with the question of when they were authored and by whom. To answer the first question, it is sufficient to read the Pentateuch consecutively. A few isolated laws (three or perhaps four) appear in the book of Genesis, while in Exodus, and almost through the end of Deuteronomy, their presence is overwhelming, in the form of hundreds of laws appearing in small collections or in larger textual units—"law codes." The answer to the second question, however, cannot be answered just by reading through the Pentateuch. The answers (since there is more than one) belong, rather, to the domain of the critical study of the Pentateuch and of the Bible. I choose to start the overview differently, more ceremoniously—with God, the origin of the laws.

The biblical view of the divinity of the law has no parallel in other ancient Near Eastern cultures,[6] in which the authority to legislate was the province of kings. The kings presented themselves as those chosen by the gods to impose law and justice, and this granted them the mandate to give laws. The gods' involvement was limited to appointing the kings to their mission and granting them authority, but the laws themselves were laws of the king—he determined their content. The Bible's innovation was the transfer of legislative authority from the king to God. It is more than likely that, historically, Israelite kings, like other ancient Near Eastern kings, promulgated laws and ordinances, but this is not reflected in scripture. On the contrary, scripture reflects the ideological and theological stance that laws are divine. They came into being, therefore, long before the establishment of the Israelite monarchy, before the Israelites' arrival in Canaan, in the desert. This is how the Pentateuch presents the story.

This juridico-theological position has several implications. First, laws whose origin is divine are intended not only to maintain the social order—a typical function of the law—but also to establish and regulate the relationship between the lawgiving God and his addressees. Therefore, a violation of the law is not only a civil infringement but a religious sin, which sometimes also entails divine punishment (see, e.g., Lev. 20:2–5). Second, the lawgiver's identity influences and even dictates the contents of the law. Hence, alongside the "usual" civil laws, biblical law also includes a number of moral commandments and a great many ritual rules and regulations. The combination of these three normative planes—the civil-secular, the moral, and the ritual-religious—does not of course exist in modern legislation, but nor does it exist in ancient monarchic lawmaking, which was secular in nature.

The following nine laws illustrate this normative triad. The first group includes three civil laws in three different legal areas: the laws of homicide (Exod. 21:12–14), honesty in trade (Deut. 25:13–16), and incest (Lev. 18:7). The second group includes three moral commandments: "Keep far from a false charge" (Exod. 23:7); "Justice, and only justice, you shall pursue" (Deut. 16:20); "You shall love your neighbor as yourself" (Lev. 19:18). And the third group includes three ritual instructions: the prohibition against sacrificing to other gods (Exod. 22:20), the consecration of firstling males of oxen and sheep (Deut. 15:19), and the donation of bread (Num. 15:19).

Note the locations of these laws in the Pentateuch and notice that in the three groups enumerated, the laws from Deuteronomy are presented before the laws from Leviticus and Numbers (unlike their sequence in the Pentateuch). This leads us back to the questions with which we began our discussion (where and in what framework the laws appear, when they were authored, and by whom) and to the insights of critical scholarship.

According to the leading theory of classical biblical criticism, called the "Documentary Hypothesis," the Pentateuch was created through the combination of four independent source documents: the Yahwist (J), the Elohist (E), the Deuteronomist (D), and the Priestly (P). Each of these sources was composed in a different era, by a different scribal school: E and J are considered the most ancient sources, from the eighth or seventh century BCE; D is intermediate and is associated with the seventh century BCE; and the latest source is P, dated to the sixth or fifth century BCE (although some scholars believe that it preceded D). Each of these sources represents a particular orientation and has unique characteristics, in terms of both content and style, and each has its own law collection, which reflects its orientation and authorial perspective. It is therefore customary to present the laws and the law collections according to their identification with one of the documentary sources. I have also followed this scheme in presenting the abovementioned nine laws.

The law of homicide, the command to keep far from a false charge, and the prohibition against sacrificing to other gods all belong to "The Book of the Covenant," the first law collection that appears just after the Decalogue and is considered the most ancient of the Pentateuch's law collections.[7] This collection begins with ritual instructions mainly relating to the altar—"You need make for me only an altar of earth and sacrifice on it" (Exod. 20:23–26)—and ends with blessings addressed to those who keep the laws, for example: "No one shall miscarry or be barren in your land; I will fulfill the number of your days" (Exod. 23:20–33). Later in the book of Exodus there is another law collection, known as "The Cultic Decalogue." The first collection was formerly thought to belong to E, while the second was considered part of J, but today they are regarded as independent collections that were composed independently of the Pentateuch's document sources. The first is more ancient, while the second, which echoes the first's themes and language (and is therefore also called "The Little Book of the Covenant"), is later.

The law prohibiting trespassing and the injunctions to pursue justice and to dedicate the firstlings of one's livestock to God all belong to the Deuteronomic Code. This law collection appears as part of Moses's oration to the Israelites on the plains of Moab, constituting the main part of the speech and occupying chapters 12–28. It also begins with a ritual law, the law of cultic centralization—"Take care that you do not offer your burnt-offerings at any place you happen to see. But only at the place that the LORD will choose in one of your tribes" (Deut. 12:1–19)—and ends with blessings for those who keep the commandments, such as "The LORD will make you the head, and not the tail; you shall be only at the top, and not at the bottom" (Deut. 28:13), and with imprecations against those who neglect or violate them, for example: "The LORD will send upon you disaster, panic, and frustration in everything you attempt to do" (Deut. 28:20).

The final three laws—the prohibition of incest, the command to love your neighbor, and the order to donate bread to God—all belong to the Priestly legislation. The priestly laws are distributed throughout the books of Exodus, Leviticus, and Numbers (e.g., Exod. 13, Lev. 7, Num. 19), but the Priestly source also has its own comprehensive law collection, "The Book of Holiness," in Leviticus 17–26. It, too, as expected, begins with ritual instructions on slaughter and sacrifice—"And anyone of the people of Israel . . . who hunts down an animal or bird that may be eaten shall pour out its blood and cover it with earth" (Lev. 17:13)—and ends with blessings and imprecations (Lev. 26).[8]

It is important to understand that the distinction among the law collections is neither technical nor formalistic; each has its own distinguishing characteristics, in terms of both style and content. One can discern the essential difference among the three annual pilgrimages in "The Book of the Covenant" (Exod. 23:14–19), in "The Cultic Decalogue" (Exod. 34:17–26), and in the parallel laws in Deuteronomy 16 and Leviticus 23. And yet, despite the difference, there are several common features shared by all the law collections. One of these is stylistic diversity. None of the collections is couched in a uniform style (as are other law collections from the ancient Near East); rather, they combine several different formulaic patterns. The two most prominent styles are the casuistic and the apodictic.[9]

Casuistic law presents a case (*casus* in Latin) and states the outcomes or sanctions proceeding from it. For example: "When someone delivers to a neighbor money or goods for safe keeping, and they are stolen from the neighbor's house, then the thief, if caught, shall pay double. If the thief is not caught, the owner of the house shall be brought before God, to determine whether or not the owner had laid hands on the neighbor's goods" (Exod. 22:7–8). The law discusses two alternative cases, both arising from a case of theft, each of which is treated differently.

Unlike the casuistic law, apodictic law (from the Greek *apodeiktikos*—"incontrovertible") presents an absolute injunction, unaccompanied by any sanction. A sanction is apparently deemed unnecessary because obedience to the law is absolute, as, for example, in the Decalogue (Exod. 20:1–17) and also, with a difference, in the injunction: "You shall not plough with an ox and a donkey yoked together" (Deut. 22:10).

In each law collection, alongside the central models, we also find hybrid models, such as the "participle" form: "*Whoever strikes* father or mother shall be put to death" (Exod. 21:15; emphasis added). There are also some patterns exhibiting unique characteristics. One of these, considered the hallmark of the Deuteronomic Code, is the "if you" form: "When *you* come into the land that the Lord *your* God is giving *you, you* must not learn to imitate the abhorrent practices of those nations" (Deut. 18:9; emphasis added).[10] The direct address (in second person) to the law's addressee, indicative of an "I-Thou" relationship, is not merely a formal matter of style but attests to the way in which the authors perceived the relationship between the lawgiver and his audience.[11] This is related to another element in biblical lawmaking—its "face-to-face" nature. The laws are delivered to the Israelites in direct speech. God speaks the Ten Commandments to their ears, and the remaining commandments are delivered by Moses, the go-between, after receiving them directly from God. The direct address is a natural outcome of this encounter, which is sometimes referenced within the law itself, as, for example, in the events described in the law protecting the rights of the weak: "If *you* do abuse them, when they cry out to *me, I* will surely heed their cry; *my* wrath will burn, and *I* will kill you with the sword, and *your* wives shall become widows and *your* children orphans" (Exod. 22:21–24; emphasis added).

LAW AND NARRATIVE IN THE PENTATEUCH

In quantitative terms, most of the Pentateuchal texts are laws. In spite of this the Pentateuch is not a law book. It includes stories, poems, and genealogies, and these literary genres, of which law and narrative are indeed the most salient, are intertwined and inseparable. The inextricable connection between law and narrative in the Pentateuch—only one of the many links between law and literature in the Bible—is chiefly a structural connection. The laws usually appear in codes or collections, but unlike modern legislation, where laws appear in law books, that is, in a separate domain, in the Pentateuch they are set within a story—the narrative frame.[12] Judging from our familiarity with the Hebrew Bible, a different structure could easily have been imagined. Just as it contains books devoted to a specific genre—the Psalms for hymns, Lamentations for dirges, the Former Prophets for historiography, Prophets for prophetic speeches, Proverbs and Ecclesiastes for proverbs and sayings of wisdom—the Pentateuch could thus have included two or three self-standing law books, containing all the laws and nothing but laws. The redactors of the Pentateuch did not have this in mind.

The melding of prose and law is not unique to the Bible. Other ancient Near Eastern law collections that predate the Pentateuch—the Sumerian law collections of Ur-Namma and Lipit-Ishtar as well as the laws of Hammurabi—include two prose sections each, a prologue and an epilogue, where the kings, the lawgivers, present, inter alia, their legal and social credo. And yet, despite its lack of originality, the biblical model, which is a narrative continuum, interspersed with laws that appear at various intersections in the plot, is more developed than the "original model" and is certainly more interesting.[13]

This model will be outlined in brief. The Israelites wandered in the desert, moving from one station to the next; repeatedly complained about the hardships; battled the Amalekites; and arrived at Mount Sinai. They camped at the foot of the mountain and prepared for the divine revelation. And God revealed himself in an outburst of natural elements. From the midst of this spectacular outpouring he sounded with his own voice the Decalogue, both negative and positive commandments. The Decalogue is ostensibly a separate textual unit, but from a literary point of view it is an utterance that God, the main character in the narrative frame, addressed to the Israelites, another protagonist. We are immediately told of the effect that the divine speech had on them, of their fear and their reluctance to receive the following laws directly. This led to the mediating role of Moses, also a chief protagonist of the story. From this point onward, only Moses, with his human voice, would deliver the divine laws to the Israelites. After having heard the Ten Commandments, the people received the first collection of laws, entitled "The Book of the Covenant," and when God renewed his covenant with them, after they had violated it by creating the golden calf, they received a second collection of laws, known as "The Cultic Decalogue."

And the story goes on. The Israelites wandered in the desert, and on occasion Moses would enter the Tent of Meeting to receive additional laws from God. First he heard them from God, and later he repeated them to the people. This is in essence the description offered in the books of Leviticus and Numbers. Finally, when the Israelites were encamped in the plains of Moab, on the eastern bank of the Jordan River, just as they were about to enter the land of Canaan, they received the final collection of laws, which is part of Moses's oratory. This, in a nutshell, is the combined structure.

The redactors of the Pentateuch chose a structure that combines law with narrative for ideological-theological (as well as rhetorical) reasons, because only this structure could illustrate their central approach that laws are part of a contractual relationship, part of a covenant; they are the stipulations of the covenant.[14] God—one partner to the covenant—bestowed loving-kindness on the other partner, the Israelites: he released them from bondage, took them out of Egypt, led them in the desert, and enabled them to conquer Canaan. All of this is recounted in the narrative framework (which begins in the Pentateuch but extends beyond it). Because of these many acts of loving-kindness, the beneficiaries accrue debt to their benefactor, which they must repay by observing the laws they were given. This is the condition for the perseverance of the covenant, on which the sustained existence of the people is contingent. It follows that the laws play a crucial role in the plot of the narrative; they, or to be precise, the attitudes toward them, determine the course of events and the ill or good fate of the people. (According to biblical historiography, the land was devastated and the people were exiled because they did not observe the divine laws.)

The narrative and the laws are not only combined together—at times they are actually merged. A noted example is the laws related to the Passover festival—the Passover sacrifice and the feast of unleavened bread—which arise almost naturally out of the narrative continuum (Exod. 12).

The narrative present and future legal stratum are completely merged together without any formal boundary or separating device.

Another type of connection between law and narrative in the Pentateuch is a case of an utter symbiosis between the two, such as the story of the daughters of Zelophehad (Num. 27:1–11). A private case concerning the inheritance of female progeny became a general rule.[15] Therefore the story of Zelophehad's daughters is a story about the birth of a law. It is an etiologic story, aiming to explain the source of a particular legal custom, and like all etiological stories it most probably did not reflect reality.[16] Alongside the story of Zelophehad's daughters, the Pentateuch includes three other stories about the birth of laws. These also appear in Priestly sections, and they are commonly ascribed by scholarship to "The Book of Holiness" source.[17] They are the stories of oracular inquiries concerning the blasphemer (Lev. 24:10–23), the second Passover (Num. 9:1–14), and the man who collected firewood on the Sabbath (Num. 15:32–36). In these passages the laws have no independent standing, for without the stories they would never have come into being. In addition, they present a different model of legislation, unlike the "standard" model in which laws are given at God's initiative (he decides when and chiefly which laws will be handed down). According to the view reflected in the four stories—a less dogmatic, more practical, and indeed more human approach—the law is not imposed on humans "from above" (perhaps even arbitrarily) but, rather, serves needs arising from "below." Although it is of divine origin, the law comes forth out of human reality, and its purpose is to provide solutions to problems encountered by human beings. Law is fundamentally a gift, not a burden, and narrative helps to show that.

The links between narrative and law presented so far relate only to structural aspects—to the way in which the laws appear in the Pentateuch, to their place and position vis-à-vis the narrative frame. However, the connection between the two also pertains to aspects of content that reveal the way in which the story affects the substance of the laws and the way in which the laws respond to the narrative, are motivated by it, and serve its needs. A considerable number of laws in the Pentateuch refer to events that occurred in the past as well as to future events. The purpose of these historical references is to explain the background or reason for the legal norm established by law.[18] It is impermissible to mistreat and oppress a foreigner not because it is immoral or inhuman but, rather, "for you were strangers in the land of Egypt" (Exod. 22:21). The recent memory of being a stranger and being deprived of rights is meant to bolster a sense of empathy toward the stranger. The lawgiver invokes a personal and collective experience to justify the law. He makes an analogical use of the familiar historical tradition, which appears in narrative. Law and narrative interact for the purposes of persuasion.

An interesting use of historical events is tied to the concept of *imitatio dei*—imitation of divine deeds. The law does not draw an analogy between different human behaviors but, rather, between divine and human behaviors, basing the legal norm on acts performed by God. This, for example, is the justification for the commandment to observe the Sabbath, which appears in the Decalogue (in the Exodus version): "For in six days the Lord made heaven and earth . . . and rested the seventh day" (Exod. 20:11).[19] Law is understood as a way in which the people respond to what God has done on their behalf. The law is an exegesis of the divine action, of the narrative. However, the laws not only mention foundational cosmic events such as the creation of the world and the Exodus but also include references to less "important" stories, as long as they are part of the narrative. Such, for example, is the mention of the leprosy of Miriam, which is meant to justify the injunction to obey the priests, who possess the authority and expertise for dealing with leprous infections (Deut. 24:8–9).

Alongside the explicit historical references, the laws also contain some veiled allusions. This occurs in a few cases where the law does not explicitly mention the historical or narrative tradition, and yet the skilled and attuned reader can perceive the allusion. One example is the law of the firstborn, which prohibits a man who is married to two women—one loved and the other unloved—to prefer the child of the loved one over the firstborn, who is the son of the unloved woman (Deut. 21:15–17). It is not unlikely (although questioned by quite a few scholars) that this law echoes the story of Jacob, who of course loved Rachel and disliked Leah, a sentiment that led to his preference of Joseph, Rachel's son, over the firstborn Reuben, Leah's child. The law appears to engage polemically with this narrative tradition and perhaps even with the broader literary pattern of preferring the younger son over the firstborn. The law of the firstborn seems a clear example of the hidden allusions to a narrative tradition. But there may be other, more subtle cases where narrative traditions are encoded in the laws.[20]

ASSOCIATIONS, LACUNAE, AND MARGINAL, UTOPIAN, AND CONTRADICTORY LAWS—SOME CHARACTERISTICS OF THE LAW COLLECTIONS

Anyone examining the law collections in the Pentateuch will notice that, unlike modern legislation, they are not organized systematically but, rather, bounce from one topic to another. This is not due to lack of skill or sloppiness on the part of the biblical scribes; rather, it reflects the deliberate choice of a different mode of organization—not by topic or type but by association. Although the arrangement of some follows a categorization of contents (Deut. 20–21 contain four laws of warfare; Leviticus 13–14 deal with leprosy in a clearly systematic manner; Exodus 21 presents a continuum of laws concerning bodily injuries), it is more often the case that laws that have no common legal thread are placed side by side.[21] It is sometimes difficult to discern a reason for the association between laws, but in several cases one can surmise what led the author or redactor to link them—a repeated word or shared concept that appears in both laws. Thus, for example, "an ox," one of the animals mentioned in the law about falling into an uncovered pit (Exod. 21:33–34), is the hook by which this law is interpolated into the laws on the goring ox (vv. 28–32, 35–36). Another type of hook is the phonetic similarity of different words; for example, the Hebrew תַטֶּה (*taṭeh*—"distort") and תִטַּע (*tiṭa* = "plant") may have been the reason for the consecutive arrangement of the prohibition against distorting justice (Deut. 16:19–20) and the prohibition against planting any tree as an *asherah*, beside God's altar (v. 21). There are many other delightful examples of such an associative organizing principle in action, which prove that literary imagination and creativity are integral features of the Pentateuch's laws.

The next features to be presented raise a central question in regard to the laws of the Pentateuch: What was their status, and were they considered binding? In other words, what was the function of these texts, and how and to what extent did they reflect the legal reality of ancient Israelite life? The first characteristic is deficiency (lacunae). The laws of the Pentateuch do not cover all areas of the law—and not even the central ones (that would be relevant to the historical period in question). There are virtually no procedural laws pertaining to judicial processes; there are no laws of marriage, contract, or sales; and when one of these topics is addressed, the treatment is usually partial and insufficient. Ancient Israelite society had of course its own customs and binding norms. People knew what was acceptable, what was prohibited, and what was permitted, and judges made decisions based on accepted norms and familiar legal procedures. But the laws by which legal disputes were settled and by which commerce was conducted were not the laws of the Pentateuch but other, unwritten laws. The law of the king (Deut. 17:14–20) is a typically deficient law. It sets down various rules of conduct but does not address two of the king's most important roles—judge and military leader. This means nothing else than that, similar to the king's other roles and authorities, these functions were anchored in the unwritten, customary laws. Moreover (and this is another characteristic of the laws), in law collections that lack vital laws and in which many topics are only partially treated, there appear no small number of "unimportant" or even "marginal" laws. Thus we have, for example, the laws of rendering assistance to animals in distress (Deut. 22:1–4). They are so important to the biblical lawmakers that they appear twice (first in Exod. 23:4–5).

Alongside such esoteric laws are other laws that are impracticable, utopian laws. Such are the laws of year of release and year of Jubilee, which appear in three versions (Exod. 23:10–11; Deut. 15:1–11; Lev. 25) and contain, jointly, four main instructions: the prohibition against cultivating the land during the seventh year and the obligation to release debts, to manumit slaves, and to return lands to their original owners. Even if we ignored the lack of agricultural and economic sense in a complete cessation of agricultural activity, the idyllic image of harmony and fertility pictured in this law is far from realistic. Nor are the other injunctions realistic, because a social-economic upheaval of this scale (remission of all debts, return of all lands, and wholesale manumission of slaves) could not take place in isolation from the social and economic realities, merely in accordance with a calendar cycle. The biblical lawmakers adopted a royal practice that was prevalent throughout the ancient Near East—under specific political and social circumstances, kings granted their subjects certain social and economic privileges[22]—and imbued this practice with a religious-symbolic rationale pertaining to the relationship among humans, God, and the world.

An additional characteristic of the Pentateuch's laws involves the differences found between parallel laws, such as the three laws of the Hebrew slave (Exod. 21:2–6; Deut. 15:12–18; Lev. 25:39–46). They are explained by the hypothesis that these laws derive from different sources (either from one of the Pentateuch's documentary sources or from an independent source). The laws establish different, and even contradictory, norms because their authors held divergent views. The differences may also have been the product of historical development, of social and political changes that evolved over time. Either way, whether the differences are rooted in distinct worldviews or in varying social circumstances, the contradictory laws are accorded identical status and validity, as they are all the living word of God. And this would seem to present a problem.

Should the Hebrew slave be manumitted on the seventh year, as written in Exod. 21:2 and Deut. 15:12, or on the Jubilee year, as in Lev. 25:40? Are his wife and children released together with him, as implied by the Deuteronomic law and as written explicitly in the Priestly law (Lev. 25:41), or must they remain in the home of the owner (Exod. 21:4)? And there are other differences among the three laws, making it impossible to determine which norm is binding and how one ought to behave. Given this state of affairs, these texts cannot fulfill their ostensible purpose; they cannot be considered laws.

THE INFLUENCE OF ANCIENT NEAR EASTERN LAW ON THE LAWS OF THE PENTATEUCH

Hundreds of years before the laws of the Pentateuch were composed various ancient Near Eastern cultures had produced law collections. The most ancient of these are the Sumerian Laws of Ur-Namma, from the end of the third millennium BCE, and the Laws of Lipit-Ishtar, from the beginning of the second millennium BCE. The Babylonian law collections were authored in the eighteenth century BCE—the Laws of Eshnunna and, fifty years later, the Laws of Hammurabi. Some two hundred years later, the Hittite Laws were written, and the Middle Assyrian Laws were composed at the end of the eleventh century BCE.[23]

Despite the time gap, which apparently cannot easily be bridged (some 1,300 years separate the Sumerian Laws of Ur-Namma, the earliest law code discovered to date, and "The Book of the Covenant," the Pentateuch's earliest law collection), there are many similarities between these law collections and the laws of the Pentateuch.[24] If, in addition to the time gap, we take into account the differences that certainly existed among the different societies of the ancient Near East, this is a surprising fact, for laws are supposed to reflect the social, economic, political, ideological, and religious profiles of the society in which they were formulated. The similarities, in both content and style, among the ancient Near Eastern law codes is usually explained by assuming that they belong to a common tradition of legal writing. They are a literary genre, like other literary genres that characterized ancient Near Eastern cultures, and do not necessarily reflect a living legal reality.

Following are several examples that indicate the similarity, beginning with formal similarities. The casuistic model, one of the two main patterns for formulating the laws of the Pentateuch, is the central, practically exclusive pattern for formulating laws in the other ancient Near Eastern law collections. As a reflection of the scientific thinking of the ancients, it also appears in what can be considered the scientific literature of those eras: predictions, medical diagnostics, and dream interpretation. The biblical authors, who were familiar with the pattern, made use of it, conventionally, as dictated by the genre. In addition to adopting this typical style, in many cases it is clear that the biblical authors borrowed or even copied the content of the "foreign" laws, sometimes without any modifications, sometimes by adapting them to their own worldview, and sometimes polemically, with the biblical law establishing opposite norms to those set down in the other laws. The entire gamut of these possibilities can be seen, for example, in two laws: the law concerning injury to a pregnant woman (Exod. 21:22–25), which exists in almost every ancient Near Eastern law code—the Laws of Lipit-Ishtar (d–f), Laws of Hammurabi (209–14), Hittite Laws (17–18), and Middle Assyrian Laws (A 50–52)[25]—and the laws on the goring ox (Exod. 21:28–32, 35–36), also appearing in the Laws of Eshnunna (53–54) and the Laws of Hammurabi (250–52).[26] Does the fact that the law on the pregnant woman victim is so popular in ancient Near Eastern law codes indicate that injuries to pregnant women were frequent and that the ancient lawmakers sought a response to a "societal plague"? This would not seem to be the case. Otherwise it would be difficult to explain why, among the thousands of legal documents discovered throughout the ancient Near East—documents describing legal disputes and legal proceedings—not a single record dealing with injury to a pregnant woman has been found. Nor has any record of a goring ox ever surfaced.

WHAT WAS THE STATUS OF THE SO-CALLED LAW CODES?

In order to foreground the doubts concerning the binding status of ancient Near Eastern laws as well as the laws of the Pentateuch, some scholars have preferred to label them "the so-called 'law-codes,'"[27] given the broad consensus among researchers that the ancient law collections were *not* books of law that actually served the rendering of justice in court settings. Rather, they are a reflection of a literary genre—legal literature. This opinion has emerged with even greater conviction since it has become apparent that among the thousands of legal documents discovered in the region—records of legal proceedings and lawsuits, contracts, and other documents that reflect legal dealings between people—not even once is there a reference to or citation of "the so-called 'law codes.'" The conclusion drawn is that there seems to have been a "separation" between the law collections, namely, "the written law," and the law that was actually practiced in day-to-day affairs. This insight, which has been found to be instructive also in respect to the laws of the Pentateuch, is reinforced by acquaintance with some of the characteristics of the laws: the existence of impracticable laws and of moral injunctions that cannot be enforced; the absence of many laws that would be vital for the ordering of social life and, conversely, the existence of laws for which there is no real need; and last, parallel and contradictory laws, which cannot possibly fulfill their purpose. The final support for this position concerns the stylistic element. The unmistakable "literariness" of the laws and the various artistic devices they employ (repetitions, word-play, parallelism), including their "associative" arrangement and the stylistic affinities with moral-didactic wisdom instruction in the book of

Proverbs, all reinforce the view that the law collections were authored primarily as literary texts and not as laws.

There are three main opinions regarding the formation of the ancient Near Eastern "legal literature." First, the "monumental" position argues that the laws were part of royal propagandistic literature—royal apologia—which extolled the king and presented him as one whose path was illuminated by law and justice.[28] The laws did not have any practical value, and their only use was ceremonial and archival. Analogously, the laws of the Pentateuch were meant to reflect divine law and justice and were mainly meant to be recited publicly at festivals and ceremonies. Second, the "practical" position views the laws as part of scientific literature. They were an outgrowth of a systematic effort to collect particular cases that were brought before judges and became precedents and eventually came to be used as professional literature—as a legal textbook.[29] Third, the "scribal-wisdom" position contends that the laws were a literary genre that emerged out of scribal schools. The "legal writing" was meant to instill moral precepts and to develop legal thinking, and the laws served as theoretical study texts.[30] Only at a later stage, during the fifth century BCE, under Persian rule, at the time of Ezra the Scribe, did their status change, and they were transformed from general principles of moral advice to a binding set of laws.[31] Later they became the primary source of Jewish law.

RESEARCH ON BIBLICAL LEGAL LITERATURE

The following is a brief survey of the main research topics in the study of legal texts. Since the very beginnings of biblical criticism, the law collections have been at the center of discussion concerning the process of the formation of the Pentateuch. The association of each of the collections with one of the documentary sources, the dating of the collections, the intertextual relations and dependencies among them, and the links between the law collections and the narrative frameworks within which they are embedded are central topics that have been and continue to be addressed by biblical research.[32] An additional topic is the connection between the laws and other literary genres in the Bible, especially the ways in which the legal traditions are reflected in biblical narrative.[33] An-

other genre of research is concerned with topics of historical, sociological, and anthropological interest. The laws, which are assumed to reflect
features of the society that produced them, are a window to an understanding of "biblical society" and allow us to describe the main tenets
of belief, religious practices, and the development of social institutions
in ancient Israel.[34] Another area, among the most fertile in the research
on biblical law, is the comparative study of the laws of the Pentateuch and
the ancient Near Eastern law collections.[35] Finally, the recognition of the
law collections as a literary genre has led to an engagement with their
literary, stylistic, and rhetorical features.[36] In addition, some studies have
examined the laws through the prism of theories and models from other
fields of knowledge (e.g., semiotics, orality and literacy studies, narratol-
ogy).[37] Biblical law is indeed fertile soil for interdisciplinary research.

NOTES

1. Assnat Bartor, "The 'Juridical Dialogue': A Literary-Judicial Pattern," *Vetus Testamentum* 53 (2003): pp. 445–64.

2. Uriel Simon, "The Poor Man's Ewe-Lamb: An Example of a Juridical Parable,"
Biblica 48 (1967): pp. 207–42.

3. The primary sense of the Hebrew *rib* is strife or dispute, which may involve
bodily struggle as well as verbal contention. Its restricted meaning is conducting a legal
process or making an accusation.

4. Berend Gemser, "The *Rib-* or Controversy-Pattern in Hebrew Mentality," in *Supplement to Vetus Testamentum* 3 (Leiden: Brill, 1955), pp. 120–37; Kirsten Nielsen, *Yahweh as Prosecutor and Judge: An Investigation of the Prophetic Lawsuit* (*Rib-Pattern*)
(Sheffield: University of Sheffield, 1978).

5. See F. Rachel Magdalene, *On the Scales of Righteousness: Neo-Babylonian Trial
Law and the Book of Job* (Providence, R.I.: Brown Judaic Studies, 2007).

6. On this topic, see two foundational articles, presenting opposing views: Moshe
Greenberg, "Some Postulates of Biblical Criminal Law," in Menahem Haran, ed., *Yehezkel Kaufmann Jubilee Volume* (Jerusalem: Magnes Press, 1960), pp. 5–28; Bernard S.
Jackson, "Reflections on Biblical Criminal Law," *Journal of Jewish Studies* 24 (1973): pp.
8–38.

7. According to the classic approach the Decalogue belongs to the Elohist, but in
recent years several scholars have rejected this view. See Yair Hoffman, "The Status of the
Decalogue in the Hebrew Bible," in Henning G. Reventlow and Yair Hoffman, eds., *The
Decalogue in Jewish and Christian Tradition*, Library of Hebrew Bible/Old Testament
Studies 509 (New York: T&T Clark, 2011), pp. 32–49.

8. The inclusion of blessings and imprecations in the law collections is derived from
international treaty law. International covenants and contracts, which were formulated

by kings in the ancient Near East, concluded with blessings for those who would observe the stipulations of the covenant and with curses against those who would violate them. Since the laws of the Pentateuch were given within a contractual framework, as part of the covenant between God and the Israelites, the laws were naturally appended with this important and integral part of covenantal agreements. See Rolf Rendtorff, *The Covenant Formula: An Exegetical and Theological Investigation*, M. Kohl, trans. (Edinburgh: T&T Clark, 1998).

9. These terms were first coined by Albrecht Alt in his foundational study about the patterns of legal formulation in the Pentateuchal laws ("The Origins of Israelite Law," in *Essays on Old Testament History and Religion*, R. A. Wilson, trans. [Garden City, N.Y.: Doubleday, 1967], pp. 79–132).

10. See Harry Gilmer, *The If-You Form in Israelite Law* (Missoula, Mont.: Scholars Press, 1975).

11. It should be noted that this formulation is unique to biblical lawmaking. The laws in other ancient Near Eastern law collections are couched in the third person.

12. Harry P. Nasuti, "Identity, Identification and Imitation: The Narrative Hermeneutics of Biblical Law," *Journal of Law and Religion* 4 (1986): pp. 9–23; David Damrosch, *The Narrative Covenant: Transformations of Genre in the Growth of Biblical Literature* (San Francisco: Harper and Row, 1987).

13. Adele Berlin, "Numinous Nomos: On the Relationship between Narrative and Law," in Saul M. Olyan and Robert C. Culley, eds., *"A Wise and Discerning Mind." Essays in Honor of Burke O. Long* (Providence, R.I.: Brown Judaic Studies, 2000), pp. 25–31.

14. Edward L. Greenstein, "Biblical Law," in Barry W. Holtz, ed., *Back to the Sources. Reading the Classic Jewish Texts* (New York: Summit Books, 1984), pp. 83–103.

15. The common law of the Anglo-Saxon legal system arose in precisely the same manner, following the method of "binding precedent." Judicial decisions, which originally were only binding for the parties to the legal process, received the status of law.

16. The inheritance of daughters was a recognized legal right in several ancient Near Eastern societies. It appears, for example, in Sumerian documents from the third millennium BCE, such as the Laws of Lipit-Ishtar and in will tablets from the city of Nuzi, dated from the second millennium BCE. See Zafrira Ben-Barak, *Inheritance by Daughters in Israel and the Ancient Near East. A Social, Legal and Ideological Revolution* (Jaffa: Archaeological Center Publications, 2006). At the same time, it may be that the story of Zelophehad's daughters has a kernel of historical truth, for in the Samaria Ostraca (clay shards from the end of the ninth century BCE), which document shipments of wine and oil from different provinces in the kingdom of Israel, the names of the Manassean families appear, and two of these names—Hogla and Noa—are known as the daughters of Zelophehad.

17. Simeon Chavel, " 'Oracular Novellae' and Biblical Historiography: Through the Lens of Law and Narrative," *Clio* 39 (2009): pp. 1–27.

18. Rifat Sonsino, *Motive Clauses in Hebrew Law: Biblical Forms and Near Eastern Parallels* (Chico, Calif.: Scholars Press, 1980).

19. In the Deuteronomic version, a different, socially motivated, justification is given, and therefore the law does not mention the creation of the world but, rather, the enslavement in Egypt to explain why the slave is entitled to a day of rest on the seventh day (Deut. 5:15).

20. See Calum Carmichael, *Law and Narrative in the Bible: The Evidence of the Deuteronomic Laws and the Decalogue* (Ithaca, N.Y.: Cornell University Press, 1985); and *Illuminating Leviticus: A Study of Its Laws and Institutions in the Light of Biblical Narratives* (Baltimore: Johns Hopkins University Press, 2006).

21. See, for example, Exod. 22:16–18 (a law concerning the seduction of a virgin and a law of capital punishment for a female sorcerer) and Deut. 22:4–7 (a law of rendering assistance to animals in distress, a prohibition against wearing a garment of the opposite sex, and a law of sending away a mother's bird).

22. These privileges were awarded in the framework of royal edicts called *mišarum* and *andurarum*.

23. Other legal collections have been discovered in the region: royal regulations and instructions (e.g., the edict of the Babylonian king Ammisaduka from the seventeenth century BCE) and laws dealing with specific topics (e.g., the Sumerian Laws about Rental Oxen from the eighteenth century BCE).

24. Raymond Westbrook, "Biblical and Cuneiform Law Codes," *Revue Biblique* 92 (1985): pp. 247–64; David Wright, "The Laws of Hammurabi as a Source for the Covenant Collection (Exodus 20:23–23:19)," *Maarav* 10 (2003): pp. 11–87.

25. Stanley Isser, "Two Traditions: The Law of Exodus 21:22–23 Revisited," *Catholic Biblical Quarterly* 52 (1990): pp. 30–45.

26. Raymond Westbrook, *Studies in Biblical and Cuneiform Law* (Paris: Gabalda, 1988), pp. 83–88.

27. See Westbrook, "Biblical and Cuneiform Law Codes," p. 247; Jean Bottéro, "The 'Code' of Hammurabi," in *Mesopotamia, Writing, Reasoning, and the Gods* (Chicago: University of Chicago Press, 1992), pp. 156–57.

28. Victor Avigdor Hurowitz, *Inu Anum ṣirum: Literary Structures in the Non-juridical Sections of Codex Hammurabi* (Philadelphia: University Museum, 1994).

29. Westbrook, "Biblical and Cuneiform Law Codes"; Bottéro, "'Code' of Hammurabi."

30. Anne Fitzpatrick-McKinley, *The Transformation of Torah from Scribal Advice to Law* (Sheffield: Sheffield Academic Press, 1999).

31. Note the message of Artaxerxes, king of Persia, to Ezra: "All who will not obey the law of your God and the law of the king, let judgment be strictly executed on them, whether for death or for banishment or for confiscation of their goods or for imprisonment" (Ezra 7:26).

32. See, e.g., Calum Carmichael, *The Spirit of Biblical Law* (Athens: University of Georgia Press, 1996); John Van Seters, *A Law Book for the Diaspora. Revision in the Study of the Covenant Code* (Oxford: Oxford University Press, 2003); Bernard M. Levinson, "The Manumission of Hermeneutics: The Slave Laws of the Pentateuch as a Challenge to Contemporary Pentateuchal Theory," in André Lemaire, ed., *Congress Volume Leiden 2004* (Leiden: Brill, 2006), pp. 281–324.

33. David Daube, *Studies in Biblical Law*, 2nd ed. (New York: KTAV Publishing House, 1969), pp. 1–73; Pamela Barmash, "The Narrative Quandary: Cases of Law in Literature," *Vetus Testamentum* 54 (2004): pp. 1–16.

34. See Raymond Westbrook, *Property and the Family in Biblical Law* (Sheffield: JSOT Press, 1991); Frank Crüsemann, *The Torah. Theology and Social History of Old Testament Law*, Allan W. Mahnke, trans. (Minneapolis: Fortress Press, 1996); Pamela

Barmash, *Homicide in the Biblical World* (Cambridge: Cambridge University Press, 2005).

35. Shalom M. Paul, "Biblical Analogues to Middle Assyrian Law," in Edwin B. Firmage, Bernard G. Weiss, and John W. Welch, eds., *Religion and Law: Biblical-Judaic and Islamic Perspectives* (Winona Lake, Ind.: Eisenbrauns, 1990); Bernard M. Levinson, ed., *Theory and Method in Biblical and Cuneiform Law: Revision, Interpretation and Development* (Sheffield: Sheffield Academic Press, 1994); Moshe Weinfeld, *Social Justice in Ancient Israel and in the Ancient Near East* (Minneapolis: Fortress Press, 1995).

36. Joe Sprinkle, *"The Book of the Covenant." A Literary Approach* (Sheffield: JSOT Press, 1994); Baruch Schwartz, *The Holiness Legislation: Studies in the Priestly Code* [in Hebrew] (Jerusalem: Magnes Press, 1999); James Watts, *Reading Law: The Rhetorical Shaping of the Pentateuch* (Sheffield: Sheffield Academic Press, 1999).

37. Bernard S. Jackson, *Studies in the Semiotics of Biblical Law* (Sheffield: Sheffield Academic Press, 2000); Assnat Bartor, *Reading Law as Narrative: A Study in the Casuistic Laws of the Pentateuch* (Atlanta: Society of Biblical Literature, 2010).

FURTHER READING

General Studies of Biblical Law

Pietro Bovati, *Re-establishing Justice, Legal Terms, Concepts and Procedures in the Hebrew Bible* (Sheffield: Sheffield Academic Press, 1994).

Gershon Brin, *Studies in Biblical Law from the Hebrew Bible to the Dead Sea Scrolls* (Sheffield: Sheffield Academic Press, 1994).

Bernard M. Levinson, *"The Right Chorale": Studies in Biblical Law and Interpretation* (Tübingen: Mohr Siebeck, 2008).

Yochanan Muffs, *Love and Joy: Law, Language and Religion in Ancient Israel* (New York: Jewish Theological Seminary of America, 1992).

Dale Patrick, ed., *Thinking Biblical Law*, Semeia 45 (Atlanta: Scholars Press, 1989).

The Biblical Legal System and Legal Principles

Hans J. Boecker, *Law and the Administration of Justice in the Old Testament and Ancient East* (London: SPCK, 1980).

Baruch Halpern and Deborah W. Hobson, eds., *Law and Ideology in Monarchic Israel* (Sheffield: JSOT Press, 1991).

Raymond Westbrook and Bruce Wells, eds., *Everyday Law in Biblical Israel: An Introduction* (Louisville, Ky.: Westminster John Knox Press, 2009).

Ancient Near Eastern Legal Texts

Jonathan Ben-Dov, "The Poor's Curse: Exodus XXII 20–26 and Curse Literature in the Ancient World," *Vetus Testamentum* 56 (2006): pp. 431–51.

Bruce Wells, "The Cultic versus the Forensic: Judahite and Mesopotamian Judicial Procedures in the First Millennium B.C.E.," *Journal of the American Oriental Society* 128 (2008): pp. 205–32.

Raymond Westbrook, ed., *A History of Ancient Near Eastern Law*, 2 vols. (Leiden: Brill, 2003).

Law and Narrative

Assnat Bartor, "The Representation of Speech in the Casuistic Laws of the Pentateuch: The Phenomenon of Combined Discourse," *Journal of Biblical Literature* 126 (2007): pp. 231–49.

Chaya Halberstam, "The Art of Biblical Law," *Prooftexts* 27 (2007): pp. 345–64.

The Book of the Covenant

Bernard S. Jackson, *Wisdom-Laws: A Study of the Mishpatim of Exodus 21:1–22:16* (Oxford: Oxford University Press, 2006).

Shalom M. Paul, *Studies in the Book of the Covenant in the Light of Biblical and Cuneiform Law* (Leiden: Brill, 1970).

Deuteronomic Code

Eckart Otto, *Gottes Recht als Menschenrecht: Rechts- und literaturhistorische Studien zum Deuteronomium* (Wiesbaden: Harrassowitz Verlag, 2002).

Moshe Weinfeld, *Deuteronomy and the Deuteronomic School* (Winona Lake, Ind.: Eisenbrauns, 1972; reprint, 1992).

The Priestly Legislation

Mary Douglas, *Leviticus as Literature* (Oxford: Oxford University Press, 1999).

Jacob Milgrom, *Leviticus: A Book of Ritual and Ethics. A Continental Commentary* (Minneapolis: Fortress Press, 2004).

James Watts, *Ritual and Rhetoric in Leviticus: From Sacrifice to Scripture* (Cambridge: Cambridge University Press, 2007).

8

❀

The Wisdom Literature

Jennie Grillo

"Wisdom literature" as a category has no currency in the Old Testament or, so far as we can tell, in any ancient Near Eastern literary culture. A notion of biblical wisdom literature goes back to antiquity, but the unifying conceit for this kind of wisdom was simply the figure of Solomon; thus for the early rabbis and church fathers, Proverbs and Ecclesiastes belonged with Song of Songs as "Solomonic books," while Job, on the other hand, was still being read as the work of Moses as late as the great eighteenth-century Hebrew scholars Robert Lowth and Johann David Michaelis.[1] However, by the time of the ninth edition of the *Encyclopaedia Britannica* in 1881, Julius Wellhausen could write of "the so-called 'Wisdom'" of Job, Proverbs, Sirach, and Ecclesiastes,[2] and that scholarly category of "wisdom literature" has now replaced the various canonical arrangements for many readers while still intersecting with them: the Protestant and Jewish canons have only Proverbs, Job, and Ecclesiastes/Qohelet, while Roman Catholic and Orthodox Bibles also include Sirach and Wisdom of Solomon. But while "wisdom literature" is strictly speaking a scholarly construction, it is a scholarly discovery too: the books thus gathered together share a pool of family resemblances, and while—as in any family—particular traits may be stronger, or weaker, or missing in individual family members (or present in others outside the family), nevertheless by some combination of these traits all display a basic kinship with the group. First, these texts all share a common vocabulary of wisdom, including a habit of thinking about thinking. Most obvious is the Hebrew *ḥokmah*, usually translated "wisdom": more than half of its attestations appear in Proverbs, Job, and Ecclesiastes, and other words in the semantic fields of understanding and of education also sprinkle these texts thickly. Second, biblical wisdom literature is marked by particular literary forms: most obviously the short proverb of various kinds but also refinements such as acrostics and riddles, dialogues, discourses, and what Giorgio Buccellati has called "lyric introspection."[3] Third, these books share the desire to learn from the way the world works in order to live a successful life, though with varying degrees of confidence about that task.

WISDOM IN THE ANCIENT NEAR EAST

The emergence of wisdom literature as a scholarly category has been closely tied to archaeological discoveries in Egypt and Mesopotamia in the nineteenth and twentieth centuries; texts such as the Egyptian teaching of Amenemope (found in 1923) and fragments of the wisdom of Ahiqar in Aramaic (found in 1906) seemed to offer close parallels from neighboring cultures. But the appeal to wisdom as an international literary phenomenon has an inbuilt circularity: the newly discovered texts tended to be classified as wisdom literature precisely because they resembled certain biblical books. In reality, the differences are just as illuminating as the similarities. For example, biblical wisdom literature is frequently characterized as secular, and the more explicit religious motivations found in parts of Proverbs tend to be regarded as late developments that are somehow not quite true to the wisdom ethos; yet ancient Near Eastern wisdom is irreducibly religious in orientation. Egyptian scribes worked in a "House of Life" attached to large temples; practices such as divination and exorcism were part of the expertise of the wise Mesopotamian scribe. Similarly, the source of wisdom in Mesopotamian mythology was heavenly revelation: divine wisdom was mediated by the seven primordial sages or *apkallus* who passed on their antediluvian knowledge to a chain of scholars linked to the Babylonian school. These comparisons challenge the idea that revealed wisdom is a secondary digression in the Hebrew environment and make traditions such as the antediluvian sage Enoch look less tangential.[4]

The closest ancient Near Eastern parallel to the main stream of biblical wisdom literature is the "instruction" genre. Instructions are texts addressing a younger man in the voice of an elder, passing on wisdom in proverbial form and sometimes reflecting on a lifetime's work; their nearest analogues in the Bible are Proverbs and Ecclesiastes. The greatest number come to us from Egypt: they are regularly fictional, like the Instruction of Amenemhet (Egyptian, Middle Kingdom), who warns his son from beyond the grave about palace intrigues such as those that killed him. The subject matter of the teaching can include preparation for death, moderation in eating, discretion in speech, respect for parents, love of learning, the dangers of quarrelling, the way to choose a wife, and how to succeed and to enjoy peace. The speakers and their addressees are often royal, as in the Instruction to King Merikare by his father (Egyptian, First Intermediate Period), or at least members of the ruling classes, like the vizier Ptahhotep delivering maxims to his son (Egyptian, Middle Kingdom). These instructions are not secular either: running beneath their counsel is the Egyptian belief in Maʿat, usually translated as a blend of justice and truth. As a goddess, Maʿat is the daughter of the sun god Re; the instructions teach this divine principle of justice and truth and enable their hearers to discern it in the world. In the words of Michael V. Fox, "Put positively, the place of Maʿat in Egyptian Wisdom shows that practical advice with utilitarian incentives *can* have a religious foundation and express a religious ethos. Hence so can Israelite Wisdom, though it is rooted in a very different religion."[5]

Outside Egypt, we find the Sumerian Instructions of Shuruppak (versions date from 2500 BCE to 1100 BCE), in which a legendary wise man advises his eldest son, Ziusudra (the Sumerian Noah), in short proverbial commands. The Instruction of Ahiqar (sixth century BCE, Aramaic), which was transmitted by Jewish communities, fits sapiential material within a tale of a wise courtier. Without the personal frame of the instructions, proverb collections also transmitted sayings; more than twenty-four collections of Sumerian proverbs are known, which include also fables and jokes.[6] Just north of Israel, Babylonian wisdom texts have been found in Akkadian at Ugarit, but there is also evidence of wisdom style within Canaanite literature, such as a phrase from the Baʿal cycle that uses the graded numerical saying familiar from Proverbs and Ahiqar: "Now there are two (kinds of) feasts (that) Baʿalu hates, three (that) Cloud-Rider (hates): An improper feast, a low-quality feast, and a feast where the female slaves misbehave."[7] Other ancient texts especially comparable to individual biblical wisdom books will be noted below.

PROVERBS

The book of Proverbs is the classic expression of wisdom literature in the Old Testament. It opens with a sustained exposition of the ambitions of that genre, which reveals the many facets of the wisdom on offer:

> The proverbs of Solomon son of David, king of Israel:
> For learning about wisdom and instruction,
> for understanding words of insight,
> for gaining instruction in wise dealing,
> righteousness, justice, and equity;
> to teach shrewdness to the simple,
> knowledge and prudence to the young—
> Let the wise also hear and gain in learning,
> and the discerning acquire skill,
> to understand a proverb and a figure,
> the words of the wise and their riddles. (Prov. 1:1–6)[8]

Here, wisdom involves simultaneously a body of knowledge ("wisdom and instruction," "words of insight"), an intellectual faculty ("to understand," "for learning"), a practical aptitude ("skill," "shrewdness"), a set of virtuous practices ("righteousness, justice, and equity"), and a moral tendency ("prudence"). As an aggregate, this wisdom generally has a morally positive character, though it can include skills that in other contexts are ethically neutral (*taḥbulot*, "skill") or even dubious (*'ormah*, "shrewdness," or *mezimmah*, here "prudence" but elsewhere "scheming"). As Fox puts it, the wisdom of Prov. 1–9 "is a disposition of character, a configuration of knowledge, fears, expectations, and desires, that enables one to identify the right path and keep to it. Wisdom means not only knowing but also *desiring* to do what is right."[9]

Forms

The book of Proverbs displays the range of formal features at the disposal of wisdom literature. Chapters 1–9 open the book with a series of instructions or lectures: these are highly crafted poetic lessons cast in the first person, which address a child from the standpoint of a parent ("Hear, my child, your father's instruction, and do not reject your mother's teaching," 1:8). Interspersed with these instructions, and perhaps reflecting on them, are pieces that apostrophize wisdom as an eloquent woman calling out for followers (8:1–36) or paint a lush verbal picture of the fruits of her service (9:1–6). The main body of the book, chapters 10–31, is in turn arranged in several collections, and here the great mass of the material takes the form of proverbs. These are typically two-part sayings that exploit Hebrew poetic parallelism ("Hatred stirs up strife, but love covers all offenses," 10:12), but within this framework there are numerous characteristic forms. Many proverbs are simple but shrewd aphorisms observing how things are ("The heart knows its own bitterness, and no stranger shares its joy," 14:10), which can in turn be ordered as a comparison ("Like vinegar to the teeth, and smoke to the eyes, so are the lazy to their employers," 10:26). Comparison is strengthened persuasively in the "better than" saying ("Better to be despised and have a servant, than to be self-important and lack food," 12:9) and "how much more" or "how much less" sayings ("Fine speech is not becoming to a fool; still less is false speech to a ruler," 17:7). Numerical sayings list phenomena grouped by surprising points of similarity ("Three things are never satisfied; four never say, 'Enough': Sheol, the barren womb, the earth ever thirsty for water, and the fire that never says, 'Enough,'" 30:15); many proverbs trade on an anomaly (the beautiful woman without discretion, the flattering neighbor with evil intention, the satisfied buyer loudly complaining). Other proverbs take the form of admonitions ("Do not be among winebibbers, or among gluttonous eaters of meat," 23:20), precepts ("Commit your work to the LORD, and your plans will be established," 16:3), or rhetorical questions of the type "Who can find?" or "Who can say?" ("Many proclaim themselves loyal, but who can find one worthy of trust?" 19:6). In general, proverbs are compressed, vivid, frequently paradoxical, require a pause for thought, and demand an often rueful assent; as pedagogical devices, they engage a mentally active style of learning, and their form follows the bounded and patterned world that they reflect.

Literary Layers

The clearly distinguished divisions in the overall arrangement of the book, and the self-reflexive character of the introductory chapters, point toward a literary history behind Proverbs; one schema that has commanded broad assent suggests three stages. A first layer of pithy sayings survives from family or clan origins in Israel's history; as comparative evidence for this kind of popular setting, proverbs are a feature of folk tradition across countless cultures and periods.[10] A second stage might be the royal court as a workshop for the gathering and generating of more proverbs: the collection beginning at 25:1 with the heading "These are other proverbs of Solomon that the officials of King Hezekiah of Judah copied" has a particular concern with life in a royal household ("With patience a ruler may be persuaded, and a soft tongue can break bones," 25:15). Kings' courts as theaters of wisdom persist in the collective memory of the ancient Near East, from Solomon to the tale of the three clever pages in 2 Esdras. If some of the sayings in the book of Proverbs have reached us through a royal court in Jerusalem, then perhaps it is into that setting—better internationally networked than the old family circles trading oral wisdom—that we could fit the non-Israelite borrowings that are a feature of the book of Proverbs, in particular the close relationship that exists between Proverbs and the Instruction of Amenemope. This is an Egyptian collection of wise sayings in thirty chapters (cf. Prov. 22:20, "Have I not written for you thirty sayings of admonition and knowledge?"), closely paralleled in wording and order in Prov. 22:17–23:11 and echoed elsewhere in the book. Most scholars now agree that the direction of borrowing is from the Egyptian text to the Hebrew book, and this is an instance of wisdom's easy eclecticism: there is no suspicion about learning from non-Israelite sources and no felt incongruity in framing the words of those foreign sages as "what is right and true."

That framing brings us to the third literary layer of the book, consisting of the introductory chapters 1–9 (and perhaps much more proverbial material too), probably dating to the Persian or Hellenistic periods, and with its own complex history of development; the final pieces of chapters 30 and 31 may have been added later still. In the introduction furnished by chapters 1–9, a confident Yahwism repurposes and re-presents the borrowed riches inside, so that "apples of gold in settings of silver" (Prov. 25:11) could stand as an appropriate image for the whole book. The editors of the collection have placed the deeply pious chapters 1–9 as an interpretive guide to the earlier wisdom materials: "The fear of the Lord is the beginning of wisdom" stands as an almost shocking claim over the mixed bag of Egyptian lore and common sense that follows it. To a certain extent this leitmotif is a claim made over against the wisdom materials it encompasses, and yet the sages' invitation to embrace the proverbial wisdom that follows in the light of the fear of the Lord is a real one. For these editors, the universalistic genius of wisdom literature is capable of being accommodated, unaltered, within the particularistic ethos of Israelite religion.

Moral Reasoning

The moral reasoning of the book of Proverbs is multiple, not single, and is certainly not reducible to the crude eudaemonism with which it is sometimes caricatured: for example, "what God hates" (*to 'evah*, "abomination") is one common way of describing actions intolerable to a wisdom way of looking at the world (e.g., 20:23, "Differing weights are an abomination to the LORD, and false scales are not good"), and while this is an appeal to order, it is not straightforwardly self-interested. But a strong and central line of argument is nevertheless based on the benefits of wisdom: "She is a tree of life to those who lay hold of her; those who hold her fast are called happy" (3:18). This is equally true in the theological rationale of chapters 1–9 and in the older proverbial wisdom of the body of the book: throughout, wise or foolish choices play out in what has been called an "act-consequence relationship."[11] Wisdom and folly (or righteousness and wickedness—the two frameworks are often interchangeable) carry within themselves their own rewards or punishments, sometimes demonstrated in slapstick effects: "Whoever digs a pit will fall into it, and a stone will come back on the one who starts it rolling" (26:27). The wise life, then, is one of diligent work leading to prosperity, discretion in speech leading to respect, faithfulness between husband and wife leading to a happy home, and just dealings leading to an equitable society. Their opposites are folly, laziness, stupidity, ignorance, and thoughtlessness, but these are dynamic opposites. In some instances the failings of unwisdom are reversible ("Folly is bound up in the heart of a boy, but the rod of discipline drives it far away," 22:15), and a central character in the book is the simple youth, who hovers between wisdom and folly and possesses the moral agency to go either way: "O simple ones, learn prudence; acquire intelligence, you who lack it" (8:5). The force of the act-consequence relationship, then, is as an invitation rather than as a mechanism. There is also a large reserve of inscrutability in God's dealings with people, experienced as contingency by life's actors: "The lot is cast into the lap, but the decision is the Lord's alone" (16:33). Proverbs acknowledges the possibility of perplexity and sorrow as a part of the human condition that no amount of wise planning is bulwark against: "There is a way that seems right to a person, but its end is the way to death. Even in laughter the heart is sad, and the end of joy is grief" (14:12–13). And while the sages insist that wisdom is within reach, it is never facile: the hardship of the quest is written into the metaphors for seeking wisdom (education, romantic pursuit, treasure hunting), and the difficulty of finding wisdom becomes overwhelming near the close of the collection in the proverbs of Agur son of Jakeh (chap. 30).

The argument from consequences encodes a worldview rooted in a theology of creation; in fact, creation has become a central category in the study of wisdom literature (though we should be cautious about importing ideas of a separate realm called "creation" or "nature" into the book of Proverbs, since human society is a large part of its focus and not differentiated from the nonhuman world). "The Lord by wisdom founded the earth, by understanding he established the heavens" (3:19)—this is the wisdom teachers' rationale for their project, discerning in the world the orderliness with which God made it. In formulating it this way, the later sages seek to identify and explain the intuition implicit in the interweaving of "religious" and "secular" material within the earlier collections of proverbs: the wise of old discovered patterns in the world because God created it orderly and thus "readable." The fullest expression of this mirroring of wisdom and creation comes in Prov. 8:22–31, and here in addition the possibility of a more personal, less simply deductive relationship to wisdom opens up: wisdom is now personified. Both the text itself and the philosophical background of this personification are difficult to be sure of, but Wisdom here (*hokmot*) seems to be both a female figure hosting a sumptuous banquet and a favorite child playing alongside (or possibly a master craftsman working alongside) God in the task of creating the world. An illuminating parallel for this relationship to creation is the account of the Temple decoration in Exod. 35:30–36:1, where the work of the artisans, empowered by divinely given wisdom, mimics that of God himself: working with wisdom, they embellish the Temple as a miniature cosmos that mirrors the real created cosmos. The emphasis there is on *their* wisdom as they work, not a wisdom embedded within the Temple. In a similar way, the wisdom of Prov. 8 is not an abstract principle lurking within the creation to be discovered but an aspect of God's own creating activity, which is at the same time available to anyone who now seeks to interpret and understand that world; this tilts the view of Proverbs away from either deism or pantheism.

Epistemology

The discourse of the book of Proverbs is based on observation: "Go to the ant, you lazybones; consider its ways, and be wise" (6:6). The sayings ground their claims on experience, and thus knowledge seems to be arrived at experimentally, rather than accepted on authority: "I passed by the field of one who was lazy, by the vineyard of a stupid person; and see, it was all overgrown with thorns; the ground was covered with nettles, and its stone wall was broken down. Then I saw and considered it; I looked and received instruction" (24:30–32). Against this, Fox has argued that such gestures to visual examples are purely rhetorical and that the real source of knowledge in Proverbs is already-established tradition.[12] Certainly there is a sense of shared experience in the appeals to discovery: a proverb gets its wide circulation from the fact that what is discovered by living and learning is what everyone always discovers, and this comes close to being a pool of common knowledge or even tradition. But perhaps we need a somewhat phenomenological account of the interplay between latent knowledge and the shock of experience: in the book of Proverbs, what the imagined observer sees does confirm known principles, but this is felt as a realization, and sometimes it brings the principle to consciousness for the first time. There is a characteristic "Aha!" in the explosive impact of a proverb, not simply "I knew it all along," so that the rhetoric of discovery is not purely illustrative.

JOB

The book of Job is the Old Testament's *King Lear*; it assaults its audience with the sustained anguished shriek of a solitary sufferer, whirlwind-tossed, who presses the force of his personality on the reader as he rages against his losses in words very like King Lear's claim that "I am a man more sinned against than sinning." And yet Job is also the model of fortitude behind Lear's resolve to be "the pattern of all patience," and the book itself is diverted from tragedy to comedy by an ending that restores to Job riches, his position in family and society, and especially daughters in place of those ripped from him. This varied texture is partly the result of the generically diverse pieces that have been stitched together to make the final book of Job: the dialogues of Job and his friends are set within a prose tale (chaps. 1–2 and 42:7–17), which narrates at the beginning God's decision in the heavenly council to allow Satan to test the blameless Job by destroying his property, family, and health and at the end God's rebuke of Job's friends and the restoration of Job. The dialogues themselves (chaps. 3–27) exchange prose for poetry and are arranged in three cycles of speeches between Job and his friends Eliphaz, Bildad, and Zophar, though the third cycle is cut off after only two of the friends speak. There follows a poem in praise of wisdom (chap. 28, perhaps still in the mouth of Job); Job's final self-defense (chaps. 29–31); speeches from a new character, Elihu (chaps. 32–37); the voice of God from the whirlwind (chaps. 38–41); and Job's reply (42:1–6). The poetic language of Job and of God is some of the most dazzling in the Hebrew Bible, in its anatomy of suffering, the rhetorical appeal of its forensic language, and the sheer beauty of its sweep through creation.

Job as Wisdom

The book of Job has not always been read as wisdom literature: the highly individualized figure of Job, vividly dramatized in the psychological realism of the speeches, had a strong exemplary role in the earliest Jewish and Christian readings and later a typological one. Until the beginnings of modern critical study, Job was widely thought to be the work of Moses (it is placed after Deuteronomy in the Syriac Peshitta), in a reading that takes its pre-Israelite setting and its historical narration as the determinative generic markers; later, the book was amenable to reading against a more philosophical grid. Differently, Job had always belonged with Psalms and Proverbs as "poetical books" for the Hebrew reading tradition predominant in the West; others have seen its closest family resemblances to lament.[13] Certainly Job does make startlingly creative use of a common fund of language and imagery for individual suffering that gave voice to the human stricken by the gods across many ancient Near Eastern texts: these poetic resources for lament are known to us from biblical psalms of complaint and from Mesopotamian texts such as *Ludlul bel nemeqi* ("By day sighing, by night lamentation, / Monthly, trepidation, despair the year. / I moaned like a dove all my days, / Like a singer, I moan out my dirge").[14]

However, the identification of Job as wisdom literature is also based on some real affinities between this text and others that share its searching orientation toward a moral universe where the innocent inexplicably suffer. One of these, the "Babylonian Theodicy," is framed in the dialogue form of Job 3–27 and draws on sapiential language as it tells of the exchange between a sufferer, who complains, "Those who seek not after a god can go the road of favor, / Those who pray to a goddess have grown poor and destitute," and his friend, a "sage," who objects that "you have overthrown wisdom," "you have scorned divine design."[15] Both the "Babylonian Theodicy" and the dialogues of Job seem to participate in a genre that worries away at perennial human dilemmas as questions of wisdom and which does so in the back-and-forth conversations of scholars and sages. Job is at home in the wisdom tradition in other ways too: the book is studded with wisdom vocabulary and forms. The friends speak in proverbs ("Surely vexation kills the fool, and jealousy slays the simple," 5:2) and give voice to the perspective of traditional wisdom, as Job recognizes ("No doubt you are the people, and wisdom will die with you," 12:1); the poem of chapter 28 asks the question "Where shall wisdom be found?" and closes with the place of wisdom within God's primordial work of creation in a manner reminiscent of Prov. 8, before summing up in the terms of Proverbs: "The fear of the Lord, that is wisdom, and to depart from evil is understanding" (Job 28:28). The test (and eventual reward) of Job happen to someone who is the consummate blameless and upright man of the book of Proverbs, fearing God and turning away from evil (Job 1:1; see Prov. 2:7, 2:21, 3:7). Thus the book of Job speaks from within the wisdom tradition; however, many have heard in it a critical voice.

Job against Wisdom?

A great deal of debate has focused on the book of Job's exact stance toward conventional wisdom. Job himself returns obsessively to the act-consequence relationship, which he insists has stopped functioning: "How often is the lamp of the wicked put out? How often does calamity come upon them?" (21:17); instead he, an innocent man, has become God's target. The whole sensibility of Job's speeches, as he spills forth his furious demands for justice from God, is opposed to the measured cadences of Proverbs. One example of the complicated clash between the two books might be Job's attitude to death: life is perhaps the highest good in the wisdom literature, but Job longs for death (the poetic part of the book opens with his "Let the day perish on which I was born," 3:2); and yet the specific agony of his back-and-forth closeness to wisdom is also clear, as he in turn mourns the prospect of being torn away from the familiar things of life ("As the cloud fades and vanishes, so those who go down to Sheol do not come up; they return no more to their houses, nor do their places know them any more," 7:9–10). In particular, discussion has focused on Job's friends as stock examples of the shortcomings of conventional wisdom. On one view, they mistake Job's innocence for guilt and speak the right words at the wrong time, failing in the wisdom task of discerning the proper time for action. On another view, they speak accurately as faithful representatives of the wisdom tradition and thus expose the bankruptcy of the act-consequence nexus: it cannot handle a case such as Job's. In this way the book of Job, like Ecclesiastes, is taken as evidence of a "crisis of wisdom"; a historical background often proposed for such a crisis is the Babylonian Exile and beyond, when belief in the justice of retribution began to break down as a result of the nation's defeat (though it should be said that large swathes of other, diverse biblical traditions found it possible to understand the Exile within the paradigm of acts and their consequences). This crisis-of-wisdom model certainly finds some support in the text: God says in the final chapter that Job's friends "have not spoken of me what is right, as my servant Job has" (42:7). Throughout the dialogues, the imaginative power of the text is not with the friends but with Job, whose poetry makes theirs pale by comparison; equally spectacular is the final answer given by God, which differs completely from the friends' wisdom in reorienting Job's and the reader's gaze toward the breathtaking otherness of a wild world.

A Polyphonic Book

However, a more sympathetic understanding of the friends is possible, especially in view of the amount of space given to their speeches: including Elihu, they occupy fully fifteen out of forty-two chapters, or more than a third of a rather long biblical book; for most readers throughout Jewish and Christian history all this has not been read only to dismiss it. At least in the first cycle and arguably also in the second, the friends insist that "God will not reject a blameless person" (Job 8:20) in order to comfort Job rather than to condemn him; for them the logic of retribution means that a righteous man's suffering is only temporary, not that it is deserved. Perhaps the different perspectives of Job, the friends, God, and the narrator each have their part to play in a "polyphonic" book: the phrase is from Carol Newsom, who invokes Mikhail Bakhtin's category of the "dialogic imagination" to account for the unresolved but real coexistence of conflicting voices in the book.[16] In many readers' experience, these jostling moral perspectives are individually reinforced by the very different aesthetic experiences of each, the jagged textures of the poetry of Job and of God playing as a counterpoint to the soothingly traditional rhythms of the prose tale from long ago and far away. The book of Job, then, can be read as a complication and a deepening of the wisdom tradition, rather than a sharp break with it.

ECCLESIASTES

Ecclesiastes scrutinizes the sorrow and also the sweetness of life "under the sun," though it is everywhere a bittersweetness; the book takes its place in a long line of works that have wrestled with the question of where to find meaning in human existence. Like much wisdom literature, the book has a strong Egyptian connection: somewhere behind Qohelet, though at several removes, stands a poem such as the *Harper's Song from the Tomb of King Intef*, where skepticism about any lasting memory for the passing generations is met by advice to "follow your heart and your happiness"; the refrain urges, "Make holiday, / Do not weary of it! / Lo, none is allowed to take his goods with him, / Lo, none who departs comes back again!"[17]

Qohelet and Solomon

Ecclesiastes aligns itself with an existing body of Hebrew wisdom literature by invoking the famously wise figure of Solomon: the narrative of the book begins with an autobiographical sketch in which the speaker recalls his splendid accumulation of wisdom and wealth (1:12–2:11), "surpassing all who were over Jerusalem before me" (1:16). Coming from one who calls himself "the son of David, king in Jerusalem," these claims of riches, wisdom, exotic palaces, and lush gardens have been read alongside the accounts of Solomon's reign in 1 Kings 3–5; until the modern era, Solomon was thought to be the author of Ecclesiastes. But the royal guise in the book is held at arm's length: the wisest of all kings is reduced to despair when death levels the wise and the foolish (Eccles. 2:12–17), and the name of Solomon is never used. Instead, Solomon's oblique presence in the book makes a critical argument: as an archetype of wisdom and royal splendor, he provides the focus for a searching examination of both of these. The real author is hidden still further behind a layer of third-person narrative and the voice of the character Qohelet, the name or title by which the voice in the text identifies itself. This word comes from the Hebrew root qhl, meaning "assemble," and may allude to the assemblies convened by Solomon and many kings of Israel and Judah besides him; whether qohelet would be the speaker in an assembly (Luther's *Prediger*) or a member (the Septuagint's *ekklesiastes*) is hard to decide, though the form of the word may suggest someone with a job to do in the assembly.

Ecclesiastes and Wisdom

As well as the Solomon connection, Ecclesiastes has formal ties to the wisdom tradition: whole stretches of the book are written in aphoristic style, and Qohelet thematizes wisdom from several angles. Wisdom is better than folly, as light is better than darkness (2:13); it protects and gives life to the one who possesses it (7:12), gives strength to the wise

(7:19), and makes the face shine (8:1); but it also brings vexation (1:18), remains elusive (7:23), goes unheeded (9:16), and is easily outweighed by folly (10:1). Like Job, Ecclesiastes has often been read as the product of a crisis in wisdom thinking; in the words of James L. Crenshaw, Qohelet "had seen the assumptions of the intelligentsia and the practical guidelines of ordinary citizens give way under the heavy questioning of poets such as the genius behind the book of Job and the vicissitudes of history."[18] The reputation of Qohelet as a skeptic or a pessimist is often driven by the destructive force of his "vanity" exclamations, which demolish every accomplishment and value; the word often translated "vanity," *hebel*, reactivates a dead metaphor of breath or vapor and has connotations of fleetingness, insubstantiality, and futility. The use of *hebel* certainly has a bearing on Qohelet's valuation of wisdom: it tends to function as a protest against things that disrupt the act-consequence relationship, such as death ("How can the wise die just like fools?" Eccles. 2:16), the unpredictable returns of labor ("The lover of money will not be satisfied with money," 5:10), the fickleness of memory ("I saw the wicked buried . . . and they were praised," 8:10), and injustice ("There are righteous people who are treated according to the conduct of the wicked, and there are wicked people who are treated according to the conduct of the righteous," 8:14). Qohelet is dogged by the nagging possibility that you can toil and build up riches but fail to enjoy them (6:1–2); being able to enjoy them depends not on hard work but on God's gift, and that seems dangerously arbitrary. Does Qohelet, then, reject the wisdom project of identifying predictable outcomes for actions in the world? Fox suggests instead that "Qohelet's complaints are not an attack on wisdom, but a complaint against life on wisdom's behalf"[19]; Qohelet speaks passionately from *within* the wisdom tradition and rails at a world that fails to reward its observance. Much of his strangeness is simply his anguished personal involvement; Stuart Weeks has pointed out how many of Qohelet's perspectives already find a place in earlier wisdom.[20] Wisdom remains a value in Ecclesiastes, although vulnerable; Qohelet still offers proverbs, even if they are often cautionary tales rather than confident expectations. Recognizing this, the epilogists who close the book from an orthodox perspective still find it possible to frame Qohelet's words within the wisdom tradition: he "taught the people knowledge" and "wrote words of truth plainly" (12:9–10). They offer two summaries, both partial and yet both capturing something present within the book: "Vanity of vanities, says the Teacher; all is vanity" (12:8); "Fear God, and keep his commandments" (12:13).

The Recovery of Meaning

The question posed by Ecclesiastes is "What do people gain from all the toil at which they toil under the sun?" (1:3); Qohelet stages his whole investigation solely so that he "might see what was good for mortals to do under heaven during the few days of their life" (2:3). He despairs over many frustrated routes to gain or good, but these expressions of despair are punctuated by a series of "joy sayings," beginning at 2:24: "There is nothing better for mortals than to eat and drink, and find enjoyment in their toil." These sayings offer the simple pleasures of food, drink, work, clothing, marriage, and merriment as instances of "what is good" in the midst of disillusion, and as Qohelet's words unfold, the commendation of joy gets stronger and stronger.[21] Qohelet answers his own question by saying that there *is* something good to do in life; he has flirted with hatred of life, but there is nothing in the book like the settled embrace of death expressed in one poem from a text often compared with Ecclesiastes, the *Dispute between a Man and His Ba*: "Death is before me today / Like the fragrance of myrrh, / Like sitting under sail on breeze day."[22] Some also detect in Ecclesiastes a drift toward a more confident embrace of life's contingencies over the course of the book: by chapter 11, a string of positive exhortations seem to accept risk and to urge confident and carefree action (11:1–10). In gauging the book's overall tone, much depends on how we read its three poetic passages at 1:4–11, 3:1–8, and 12:1–8: there is in all of these a cinematic eye for small things that crystallize the beauty of the natural world and, in the latter two, a pleasure in life and in language that seems to run counter to Qohelet's dark streak.

WISDOM ELSEWHERE IN THE OLD TESTAMENT

If "wisdom literature" is something of a constructed category, then discovering wisdom outside its boundaries comes as no surprise: the themes and expression of these three Old Testament books find echoes across many others. Explaining these correspondences as the definite influence of wisdom on other texts has not always been fruitful, nor has the attempt to claim other writings (Esther, the Joseph story, the narrative of David's rise) as wisdom literature.[23] The search for influence assumed that wisdom was a discrete intellectual enterprise, housed in a particular context of schools for training court bureaucrats, on the model of other ancient Near Eastern cultures; a historical backdrop for this flurry of state-sponsored wise activity was found in von Rad's "Solomonic enlightenment." However, the archaeological and epigraphic evidence for all this school-centered wisdom production has not stood up well to scrutiny, and without this institutional framework it becomes harder to imagine wisdom literature as the product of a self-segregating movement wielding a distinctive influence.[24]

Rather, it may be more fruitful to see wisdom as a widespread intellectual current in Israel—what Giorgio Buccellati calls a "cultural tradition"—not confined to any one social group or structure.[25] Several biblical books bear the imprint of this widely dispersed wisdom. Language characteristic of the book of Deuteronomy resonates with the wisdom literature: Israel's laws, Moses tells the people, "will show your wisdom and discernment to the peoples, who, when they hear all these statutes, will say, 'Surely this great nation is a wise and discerning people!'" (Deut. 4:6).[26] Wisdom has affinities not just with Deuteronomy but with Deuteronomism: the act-consequence relationship illuminates Deuteronomistic structures of thought, a moral equivalence that stands out in clearer relief when wisdom later turns its explicit attention to history. Differently, the Joseph story (Gen. 37–50) has long been compared with wisdom literature because it narrates the success of the wise courtier, a proverbial motif also given story form in Ahiqar, Esther, and Daniel 1–6; it is noteworthy that the wise men Joseph and Daniel are interpreters of dreams, like other ancient Near Eastern practitioners of wisdom but unlike the wise man of the classic biblical wisdom literature. Some psalms are suggestive of wisdom themes and concerns: Ps. 73 puzzles over undeserved suffering like Job and Qohelet; Ps. 49 invokes a proverb and a riddle to meditate on the fate of the wise and the foolish (cf. also Pss. 1, 32, 34, 37, 112, 128).[27] Prophetic books make use of wisdom forms such as proverbs and riddles (for instance, Isaiah's vineyard parable and Amos's lists of impossible things); narratives embed wise sayings in dialogue

("As the ancient proverb says, 'Out of the wicked comes forth wicked-ness,'" 1 Sam. 24:13); and wisdom from an altogether different source is at the heart of the second creation narrative in Gen. 2–3.

Revisiting the question of schooling, David Carr has instead pro-posed an educational milieu in which wisdom literature mingled with other texts in the enculturation of Israel's elites, without modern disci-plinary boundaries: proverbs and instructions were learned and copied alongside songs and poems, ritual texts, narratives, and administrative documents.[28] This account of wisdom literature as just one of many agents in the transmission of cultural memory explains the cross-pollination between wisdom literature and other streams of what would become the Old Testament. It also sharply relativizes the perceived theo-logical distinctiveness of the wisdom literature: wisdom may be alone in lacking a focus on exodus, conquest, and the great traditions of Israel's history, but in the experience of its ancient readers, wisdom never was alone.

WISDOM LITERATURE AS A TRADITION

"Many great teachings have been given to us through the Law and the Prophets and the others that followed them, and for these we should praise Israel for instruction and wisdom. Now, those who read the scrip-tures must not only themselves understand them, but must also as lovers of learning be able through the spoken and written word to help the outsiders" (Sir. Prologue)—so wrote the grandson of Jesus Ben Sira sometime not long after 132 BCE, in a colophon to his translation of his grandfather's book—Ben Sira in Hebrew, Sirach in Greek, and later Ecclesiasticus in Latin. In presenting the work to an Alexandrian Jewish audience with this particular flourish, the translator is a witness to many of the shifts by which wisdom literature in the Hellenistic age reoriented itself.[29] One of the hardest to calibrate is the shift from composition to interpretation: the grandfather is still a collector-composer in the style of the authors of Proverbs, gathering wisdom materials (proverbs, poems, instructions) new to the Hebrew corpus; however, his collection is framed by a growing awareness of an existing body of written literature, the "great teachings" already given and now to be interpreted "through the spoken and written word," even though the exact status, boundaries, and textual form of that body of literature were still in flux in this period. Ben Sira himself expresses this dual task eloquently when he likens his work to a canal drawing from the mighty Nile or the Euphrates, in a rhetorical figure where previous scripture is the headwater and his own teaching is a tributary: "As for me, I was like a canal from a river, like a water channel into a garden.... And lo, my canal became a river, and my river a sea" (39:30–31). A passage praising the wisdom of a scripture scholar makes the authorial task dependent on the prior interpretive task: "If the great Lord is willing, he will be filled with the spirit of understanding; he will pour forth words of wisdom of his own, and give thanks to the Lord in prayer" (39:6).

A further shift is the enlarged scope of wisdom. In the grandson's prologue, the "instruction and wisdom" that a wise man such as Ben Sira interprets includes not only the biblical wisdom literature but "the Law and the Prophets and the others that followed them": all scriptures are now the business of the wisdom teacher. Sir. 39 paints a fuller pen portrait of the ideal scribe, who "seeks out the wisdom of all the ancients" and "penetrates the subtleties" of parables and proverbs but is also "concerned with prophecies" and above all "devotes himself to the study of the law of the Most High" (38:34–39:3). The most profound integration of wisdom with other streams of tradition comes in the poem of Sir. 24, building on Prov. 8: the fair and fragrant personified wisdom now journeys from heavenly places and primordial times to take up her dwelling place within the Jerusalem Temple and to be identified with the law of Moses just as she, too, first came forth from the mouth of the Most High. Israel's wisdom is finely poised here between an ambitious universalism ("Over every people and nation I have held sway," Sir. 24:6) and a deepened particularism ("And so I was established in Zion," 24:8). This chapter's mythic pattern of wisdom's preexistence, descent, and embodiment as the word of God would become influential in works such as the deuterocanonical Baruch and on into Christianity and rabbinic Judaism. Although the equation of law and wisdom is not absolutely new here (see on Deuteronomy above or possibly proverbs such as Prov. 28:4, 7, 9; 29:18), it is now explicitly at the heart of the wisdom enterprise, and *torah* here is a more clearly defined body of text than the framers of either Deuteronomy or Proverbs knew. Writing wisdom literature now means self-consciously belonging to a written tradition, while the "wisdom" within that tradition encompasses far more than the sayings of the sages.

This new orientation toward wide-ranging scriptural interpretation also marks Wisdom of Solomon, though that book is saturated with the categories of Greek philosophy and rhetoric, which filter and frame its presentation of Israel's wisdom. Wisdom of Solomon was probably written in Alexandria, in the Greek language, and most likely in the first century BCE. The author begins with the question of justice for the ungodly and the righteous in language reminiscent of Qohelet, or at least an Epicurean caricature of Qohelet, but dissolves Qohelet's and Job's problem into the promise of immortality. The book likewise maintains a fiction of Solomon's voice, woven into an encounter with a beloved Lady Wisdom, but the main work of scriptural interpretation in the book is a history of the human race culminating in a long retelling of the Exodus plagues. Sacred history has become the pattern book of wisdom's action in the world.[30]

Wisdom has several distinctive notes in those books that emerged from more apocalyptic early Jewish circles. The book of Daniel is not cast in the forms of wisdom literature, but it brings the wise-courtier tale of the older, international wisdom into contact with a newly energized form of sapiential scribal activity more sharply defined around scriptural interpretation. Daniel's wisdom in the earlier tales is his God-given gift for mantological exegesis of dreams and mysterious writing (e.g., 2:20–23, 5:11–12); in the later literary stages of the book, divinely given wisdom becomes the revelation that unlocks scriptural prophecies (9:1–3, 22–23), the knowledge of the hidden future (10:12–14), and the ministry of instructing the faithful for endurance and martyrdom (11:33–35, 12:3). Like Sirach, the book of Daniel is marked by a deep integration of wisdom with a priestly sensibility; differently to Sirach, in Daniel wisdom is combined with apocalyptic urgency and a more radical dependence on divine revelation.

Further examples of Second Temple Jewish wisdom literature have also emerged among the Dead Sea Scrolls: copied at Qumran but predating the sect there, works such as 4QBeatitudes (4Q525) and 4QWiles of the Wicked Woman (4Q184) mirror the forms (proverbs, instructions, macarisms) and themes (the two ways, the feminine appeal of wisdom and of folly) of Israel's older wisdom literature, though with a more de-cisive orientation toward Torah and toward heavenly revelations and rewards. In the composition known as 4QInstruction, the search for wisdom takes on notes of inscrutability reminiscent of Ecclesiastes, as the hiddenness of wisdom is bound up with the hardships of life under the sun: "Investigate the mystery of existence, and consider all paths of truth, and observe closely all the roots of injustice. Then you will know what is bitter for a human being and what is sweet for a man" (4Q416 2 iii). This work combines a pedagogical format with an insistence on the heavenly "mystery that is to be" or "mystery of existence" (*raz nihyeh*); here, the imagery and advice of Proverbs meet a strictly apocalyptic worldview.[31] In the eclectic intellectual culture of Second Temple Juda-ism, categories such as "wisdom," "prophecy," "law," and "cult" increas-ingly blur into one another; as the wisdom tradition weaves itself more tightly around scriptural memories of Solomon and the sages, so, too, do its latest scribes spin a web of connections to many other books.

NOTES

1. For the idea of Solomonic literature, see Origen's prologue to his commentary on the Song of Songs in *Origen. The Song of Songs: Commentary and Homilies*, R. P. Lawson, trans. (New York: Paulist Press, 1956).

2. Julius Wellhausen, "Israel," reprinted in *Prolegomena to the History of Israel*, J. Sutherland Black and Allan Menzies, trans. (Edinburgh: Adam & Charles Black, 1885), p. 501.

3. Giorgio Buccellati, "Wisdom and Not: The Case of Mesopotamia," *Journal of the American Oriental Society* 101 (1981): pp. 35–47.

4. See Richard J. Clifford, ed., *Wisdom Literature in Mesopotamia and Israel* (Atlanta: Society of Biblical Literature, 2007).

5. Michael V. Fox, "World Order and Ma'at: A Crooked Parallel," *Journal of the Ancient Near Eastern Society* 23 (1995): pp. 37–48.

6. For a convenient summary of all these and other ancient Near Eastern wisdom literature, see Richard J. Clifford, *The Wisdom Literature* (Nashville: Abingdon Press, 1998), pp. 23–41.

7. "The Ba'alu Myth," *CTA* 4.iii.17–21, Dennis Pardee, trans., in William W. Hallo, ed., *The Context of Scripture*, vol. 1 (Leiden: Brill, 2003), p. 258. For the different kinds of wisdom compositions found at West Semitic sites, see Yoram Cohen, *Wisdom from the Late Bronze Age* (Atlanta: Society of Biblical Literature, 2013).

8. All biblical translations are from the NRSV.

9. Michael V. Fox, *Proverbs 1–9* (New York: Yale University Press, 2000), p. 133.

10. For an early, oral layer in Proverbs, see Claus Westermann, *The Roots of Wisdom*, J. D. Charles, trans. (Louisville, Ky.: Westminster John Knox, 1995).

11. In German, *Tat-Ergehen Zusammenhang*. The foundational inquiry into this principle is that of Klaus Koch, "Gibt es ein Vergeltungsdogma im Alten Testament?" *Zeitschrift für Theologie und Kirche* 52 (1955): pp. 1–42; English translation as "Is There a Doctrine of Retribution in the Old Testament?" in James L. Crenshaw, ed., *Theodicy in the Old Testament* (Philadelphia: Fortress, 1983), pp. 57–87.

12. Michael V. Fox, *Proverbs 10–31* (New Haven, Conn.: Yale University Press, 2009), pp. 963–76.

13. Claus Westermann, *Der Aufbau des Buches Hiob* (Tübingen: Mohr Siebeck, 1956).

14. "The Poem of the Righteous Sufferer," Benjamin R. Foster, trans., in Hallo, *Context of Scripture*, pp. 486–92, at p. 488.

15. "The Babylonian Theodicy," Benjamin R. Foster, trans., in ibid., pp. 492–95, at pp. 493–94.

16. Carol A. Newsom, *The Book of Job: A Contest of Moral Imaginations* (Oxford: Oxford University Press, 2003).

17. Translated in Miriam Lichtheim, *Ancient Egyptian Literature,* vol. 1, *The Old and Middle Kingdoms* (Berkeley: University of California Press, 1975), pp. 194–97, at p. 197.

18. James L. Crenshaw, *Qoheleth: The Ironic Wink* (Columbia: University of South Carolina Press, 2013), p. 1.

19. Michael V. Fox, *A Time to Tear Down and a Time to Build Up: A Rereading of Ecclesiastes* (Grand Rapids, Mich.: Eerdmans, 1999), p. 92.

20. Stuart Weeks, *Ecclesiastes and Scepticism* (New York: T&T Clark, 2012), especially the conclusion on pp. 170–79.

21. The classic study of these "joy sayings" is R. N. Whybray, "Qoheleth, Preacher of Joy," *Journal for the Study of the Old Testament* 23 (1982): pp. 87–98.

22. Translated in Lichtheim, *Ancient Egyptian Literature*, pp. 163–69, at p. 168.

23. For an early critique, see J. L. Crenshaw, "Method in Determining Wisdom Influence upon 'Historical' Literature," *Journal of Biblical Literature* 88 (1969): pp. 129–42.

24. Stuart Weeks, *Studies in Early Israelite Wisdom* (Oxford: Oxford University Press, 1994), thoroughly examines the old model and finds it wanting.

25. Buccellati, "Wisdom and Not," p. 44.

26. See Moshe Weinfeld, *Deuteronomy 1–11* (New York: Doubleday, 1991), pp. 55–57, 62–65; and for legal traditions more broadly, David Daube, *Law and Wisdom in the Bible: David Daube's Gifford Lectures,* vol. 2, Calum Carmichael, ed. (West Conshohocken, Pa.: Templeton Press, 2010).

27. This list, except for Ps. 73, is that suggested by Roland E. Murphy in his "A Consideration of the Classification 'Wisdom Psalms,'" in James L. Crenshaw, ed., *Studies in Ancient Israelite Wisdom* (New York: KTAV, 1976), pp. 456–67.

28. David M. Carr, *Writing on the Tablet of the Heart: Origins of Scripture and Literature* (Oxford: Oxford University Press, 2005).

29. For more on the cultural context of these books and their task, see John J. Collins, *Jewish Wisdom in the Hellenistic Age* (Louisville, Ky.: Westminster John Knox, 1997).

30. For the interplay of scriptural interpretation with wisdom in these two works, see Benjamin G. Wright III, "Biblical Interpretation in the Book of Ben Sira," and Peter Enns, "Pseudo-Solomon and His Scripture: Biblical Interpretation in the Wisdom of

Solomon," both in Matthias Henze, ed., *A Companion to Biblical Interpretation in Early Judaism* (Grand Rapids, Mich.: Eerdmans, 2012), pp. 363–88 and 389–412.

31. For a critical edition, translation, and commentary, see Matthew J. Goff, *4QInstruction* (Atlanta: Society of Biblical Literature, 2013).

FURTHER READING

Useful introductions to biblical wisdom literature include Roland E. Murphy, *The Tree of Life: An Exploration of Biblical Wisdom Literature*, 3rd ed. (Grand Rapids, Mich.: Eerdmans, 2002); and James L. Crenshaw, *Old Testament Wisdom: An Introduction*, 3rd ed. (Louisville, Ky.: Westminster John Knox, 2010). Still the most penetrating study, though flawed, is Gerhard von Rad, *Wisdom in Israel*, James D. Martin, trans. (London: SCM, 1972). For ancient Near Eastern wisdom literature in translation, a few collections are referred to in the notes. A classic text is W. G. Lambert, *Babylonian Wisdom Literature* (Oxford: Oxford University Press, 1960), to which should be added Bendt Alster's *The Proverbs of Ancient Sumer* (Bethesda, Md.: CDL Press, 1997) and *The Wisdom of Ancient Sumer* (Bethesda, Md.: CDL Press, 2005). For Egyptian texts, including the Instruction of Amenemope, see the three-volume collection of Miriam Lichtheim. The best detailed English commentary on Proverbs is that of Fox. The standard works on Ecclesiastes are Thomas Krüger, *Qoheleth*, O. C. Dean Jr., trans. (Minneapolis: Fortress, 2004); and Choon-Leong Seow, *Ecclesiastes* (New Haven, Conn.: Yale University Press, 1997). And the older study of Robert Gordis, *Koheleth: The Man and His World* (New York: Jewish Theological Seminary, 1951), is still very much worth consulting. Shorter commentaries full of insights from earlier Jewish and Christian readers are Michael V. Fox, *Ecclesiastes* (Philadelphia: Jewish Publication Society, 2004); and Ellen F. Davis, *Proverbs, Ecclesiastes and the Song of Songs* (Louisville, Ky.: Westminster John Knox, 2000). The Hebrew of Job is some of the most difficult in the Bible, and the Greek translation of the Septuagint has a correspondingly complex relation to the Hebrew: a full treatment with much else besides is David Clines, *Job*, 3 vols. (Waco, Tex.: Thomas Nelson, 1989–2011). A major commentary with attention to the text's "history of effects" in religion, art, music, literature, and beyond is C.-L. Seow, *Job 1–21* (Grand

Rapids, Mich.: Eerdmans, 2013). Wisdom's developments in Jewish literature outside the Old Testament can be very conveniently studied in Daniel Harrington, *Wisdom Texts from Qumran* (London: Routledge, 1996), which includes a good selection of primary texts; for longer analysis, see Matthew Goff, *Discerning Wisdom: The Sapiential Literature of the Dead Sea Scrolls* (Leiden: Brill, 2007). For studies of biblical wisdom that engage fruitfully with theological questions and the history of interpretation, see Stephen C. Barton, ed., *Where Shall Wisdom Be Found? Wisdom in the Bible, the Church and the Contemporary World* (Edinburgh: T&T Clark, 1999); David W. Ford and Graham Stanton, eds., *Reading Texts, Seeking Wisdom* (London: SCM Press, 2003); and Paul Fiddes, *Seeing the World and Knowing God: Hebrew Wisdom in a Late-Modern Context* (Oxford: Oxford University Press, 2013).

9

❀

The Psalms and Poems of the Hebrew Bible

Susan Gillingham

This survey falls into five parts. Two parts deal with historical issues, on the origins and use of the psalms. Because these days these are among the most contentious issues, they will be considered in some detail. Two parts deal with more literary concerns, on the compilation of the psalter and biblical poetry in general. The final section outlines a more recent interest in psalm study, namely, the reception history of psalmody.

1. THE ORIGINS OF THE PSALMS

It is impossible to assign a date to any single psalm. The poetic medium does not always make it easy to contextualize the contents, and the superscriptions refer to later use rather than to any origins. For example, the superscription (over seventy-three psalms) that is usually translated "*of* David" (*ledawid*) really means "for" or "dedicated to" David, rather than "by David." The prefix *l* is also used in psalm titles that are translated as "to" or "for" the choirmaster (*lamnaṣṣeᵃḥ*), where it never denotes authorship but informs us about the use of the psalm in Second Temple worship. So it is most unlikely that all the so-called Davidic psalms were written by David. Even the thirteen psalms that are set specifically in the life of David indicate that they were read, after the exile, as prayers in which David's life was a paradigm of obedient faith when suffering persecution: these psalms tell us little about their actual setting.[1]

During most of the nineteenth century it was popular to date many of the psalms as late as the Maccabean period (second century BCE).[2]

However, by the middle of the twentieth century most were dated during the time of the monarchy (tenth to sixth century BCE).[3] Such a swing of interpretation confirms the difficulty of ascertaining the origins of the psalms. Today the more acceptable view is that most of the psalms, with a few exceptions, were composed in the Persian period (sixth to fourth century BCE). However, it is difficult to believe that such a diverse phenomenon as psalmody actually originated in the postexilic period, under Persian rule, so it is important to establish some criteria that might enable us to consider the origins of the psalms within three very different forms of worship—namely, the state religion of the preexilic period (up to the sixth century BCE), the nonsacrificial cult of the exilic period (circa 597–538 BCE), and the theocratic liturgy of the postexilic period (sixth to second century BCE).

a. Preexilic Psalms and "State Religion"

Some of the very earliest psalms exhibit an interaction with the mythologies of the surrounding cultures, not least those of neighboring Canaan.[4] Their early origins are further confirmed by evidence of what can only be termed "opaque poetry": the many archaisms make the translation of the Hebrew a challenging task. Some psalms echo the nationalistic and military concerns found in preexilic prophets, such as Isaiah of Jerusalem, where Israel's and Judah's fate is seen in the context of other nations: these concerns are very different from those in the postexilic period, when the people were subservient to Persian rule. References to the king and allusions to the Ark also suggest a preexilic setting, given that both king and Ark were taken captive by the Babylonians. Finally, fragments of prophetic liturgy that echo the form and content of earlier prophecy also suggest an early date. By identifying psalms that exhibit one or more of these features it is possible to date some psalms (perhaps nearly one-third of the Psalter) to preexilic times. Together they reflect the diverse features of an emergent "state religion."

Psalm 68 arguably contains some of the earliest fragments of psalmody in the Psalter. It displays many archaisms, making the Hebrew difficult to interpret, and its vocabulary has several correspondences with Ugaritic words and phrases.[5] Furthermore, there are allusions to the Ark in verse 1 ("Let God rise up, let his enemies be scattered"), using a formula also found in Numbers 10:35 concerning a procession where God took on the role of a divine warrior alongside the Ark. This psalm also reflects several instances of the use of ancient mythology to interpret an emergent Israelite faith. It describes, in anthropomorphic terms, how "the God of Sinai" made his new home on Mount Zion: He appears from the heavens (verse 4) and marches through the wilderness and creates a storm (verses 7–8); having left Mount Sinai he moves to Mount Bashan (verses 15–18); he engages in a battle against the depths of the sea (verse 22), and he rides on the clouds of heaven (verses 4 and 33–34). All these are themes found in Canaanite poetry.[6]

Psalms that use mythological language to describe how God is greater than all the other deities presume an early view that other deities actually exist. They, too, are likely to be preexilic. Psalm 82:1, for example, speaks of God taking his place in a divine council, holding judgment in the midst of other deities; it then describes how God (Elohim) demotes these gods (*elohim*) for their lack of justice and compassion (verses 2–7). Psalm 29 also starts with God in a heavenly council: here he is to be both praised and feared as he brings about a storm. Several verses have correspondences with various references to Baʿal Hadad, the Canaanite storm deity. See, for example, verses 1 and 3: "Ascribe to the Lord, O heavenly beings, ascribe to the Lord glory and strength.... The voice of the Lord is over the waters, the God of glory thunders, the Lord, over mighty waters."

Thunder is also represented as the voice of Baal in the Ugaritic texts (*KTU²* 1.4: VII: 29–31). The voice of God's thunder is heard seven times in this psalm; Baal also appears "seven times" in the lightning and "eight times" in the thunder, and he, too, is seated enthroned over the waters. For example, in *KTU²* 1.101: 1–4 Baal is the one who brings about

[3b] *šb ʿt. brqm.* [[.*ṯ*]] ... seven lightnings ...
[4] *ṯmnt. ʾiṣr r ʿt. ʿs. brq. y*[ ] Eight storehouses of thunder.
      The shaft of lightning[7]

In the same way, several hymns celebrate God's world rule by comparing him with other deities and declaring him sovereign over them. This again suggests sometime before the more monotheistic faith of the Persian period. Psalms 95:3 ("The Lord ... is a great king above all gods"), 96:4 ("The Lord ... is to be feared above all gods"), and 97:9 ("You are exalted far above all gods") are typical examples.[8]

Other early psalms suggest the international and military concerns of preexilic prophets, with their interests in the role of the king and Zion and the affairs of foreign nations. One example is Psalm 2, which begins by announcing some threatening alliance of enemy nations (verses 1–3), in order to affirm, perhaps by way of a prophetic voice, God's protection of Jerusalem and its king (verses 4–9), ending with a warning to other nations to fear Yahweh, Israel's God (verses 10–12).[9] Psalms 46 and 48, which focus on the protection of Jerusalem rather than the king, speak of the attacks of foreign nations along the lines of Psalm 2, and here there are other general correspondences with verses in Isaiah 6–8.[10] These two psalms also suggest an early date because of their use of Canaanite mythology: Psalm 46, for example, addresses God as "El Elyon" (translated in verse 4 as "the Most High"), the name of the Canaanite deity associated with ancient Jebus (later to become Jerusalem). There are also references to God calming the chaotic seas (verses 2–3); he is a heavenly warrior who protects his people (verses 8–9). In Psalm 48:2 Zion is called "mount Zaphon" (the translation is usually "the far north"), which is the name of the mountain where El, the supreme Canaanite deity, was believed to dwell. So all three psalms use ancient mythology to describe an attack of enemy nations being repulsed by "the Lord of Hosts," Israel's heavenly warrior.

Like Psalm 2, other psalms display nationalistic concerns as they affirm, somewhat idealistically, the king's power over other nations. Psalm 18 is almost identical to 2 Samuel 22 as a victory song of the king. Psalm 20 seems to be a prayer before the king ("the anointed") sets out to battle, while Psalm 21 is another victory song after the battle has been won. In fact, all the psalms with military concerns are more likely to come from preexilic times rather than during Persian rule, when battles with foreign peoples were hardly known: so Psalms 44 and 60, which refer to Yahweh "going out with our armies" (44:9 and 60:10), may also be preexilic psalms, echoing the same spirit of the preexilic prophets, even though they do not refer to the king.

Other psalms refer to the king without emphasizing warfare. Psalm 72 proclaims the king as responsible for maintaining a just social order:

this was a common theme in the preexilic prophets and in the ancient Near East. The first verse proclaims:

> Give the king your justice, O God,
> and your righteousness to a king's son.
> May he judge your people with righteousness,
> and your poor with justice.

This may well have been used on the anniversary of the king's accession to the throne.

Psalm 45 also refers explicitly to the king, but here the occasion is quite different. The contents reveal a wedding celebration involving the king and his (foreign) bride. This seems to have been a composition by a royal official, as seen in the first verse:

> My heart overflows with a goodly theme;
> I address my verses to the king;
> my tongue is like the pen of a ready scribe.[11]

Psalms 110 and 132 testify to the king's role in worship. Psalm 110, like Psalms 2 and 68, presents God as Israel's divine warrior; it seems to be another very early, albeit composite, psalm and has several puzzling archaisms, like Psalm 68: verses 3, 4, and 6 are notoriously difficult to translate. As in Psalm 2, there is also evidence of some prophetic mediation. Psalm 110:1 cites an oracle about the king's special place at God's right hand, which assures him of victory in battle.[12] Verse 4 cites another ancient oracle about the king representing a sacral order whose ancient high priest was the Jebusite king Melchizedek. Psalm 132 is also a composite psalm that contains prophetic elements (verses 11–12, 14–18). It adapts ancient sayings about King David bringing the Ark to Jerusalem, an act that confirmed the city as God's dwelling place (verses 7 and 14). Given the disappearance of the Ark after the exile, this suggests a preexilic liturgical composition, perhaps to accompany some procession involving the king (see Psalm 68:1, discussed earlier). The Ark may also be alluded to in Psalm 24, which also refers to some procession into the city, for example, in verses 7 and 9:

> Lift up your heads, O gates!
> and be lifted up, O ancient doors!
> that the King of glory may come in.

Although many of these psalms would have been brought into a final form after the exile, there is a good deal of evidence of the vestiges of psalmody from the period of the monarchy.

b. Exilic Psalms

Books such as Lamentations and Ezekiel reflect the devastation caused by the Babylonians in the early sixth century BCE, which resulted in the end of the monarchy, the destruction of the Temple, the invasion of the land, and the exile to Babylon. A few psalms also echo this period of desolation. The most obvious psalm that testifies to this is 137, which begins: "By the rivers of Babylon—there we sat down and there we wept when we remembered Zion. On the willows there we hung up our harps. For there our captors asked us for songs, and our tormentors asked for mirth, saying, 'Sing us one of the songs of Zion!'" (verses 1–3).

The citation of the taunt "Sing us one of the songs of Zion!" suggests that earlier hymns about God's protection of Jerusalem were being sung in exile. Psalms 46 and 48, with their focus on Zion, could have been such psalms. So Psalm 137 gives us insights into how preexilic psalms might have been used by the exiles, when singing was a vital part of their worship, the sacrificial cult having terminated with the Temple's destruction. Despite their experience of the loss of Jerusalem and the king, they sang these earlier psalms to remind themselves of the promises of the past and to give themselves new hope for the future.

Other psalms that may well reflect this national crisis include parts of Psalms 44, 74, 79, and 89. Psalm 74 begins: "O God, why do you cast us off forever? Why does your anger smoke against the sheep of your pasture? ... Remember Mount Zion, where you came to dwell. Direct your steps to the perpetual ruins; the enemy has destroyed everything in the sanctuary" (verses 1–3). It continues to describe in detail the attacks of the enemy, who set fire to the "holy place" and placed there signs of foreign deities (verses 4–9). The second half of the psalm recalls the ancient roots of Israel's faith by using mythological language to show how in primordial times God fought the dragon of the chaotic waters, Leviathan (verses 12–15); hence he is able to control the power of chaos now (verses 16–23). This could suggest an adaptation of the Canaanite account of the battle between Leviathan and the gods Baal and Anat and of the victory of Baal over Yam, the god of the sea; but its exilic context would suggest that its influence could also be Babylonian, adapting the myth of Marduk's victory over the sea monster Tiamat, as recorded in the *Enuma Elish*.

Psalm 89 is a composition in three parts. The first part (verses 5–18) suggests an early hymn, again using mythological motifs of God at the head of a heavenly council (verses 5–8), who calms raging waters by crushing Rahab the dragon like a carcass (verse 10). The second part (verses 1–4, 19–37) recalls the promises of God about the permanence of the Davidic dynasty. The third part is more clearly exilic, with three subsections (verses 38–45, 46–48, 49–51).[13] Here we see a satirical contrast to the earlier parts: just as Psalm 74 laments the loss of the Temple, this lament is of the end of the Davidic line. In Psalm 89, verses 38–40 read: "But now you have spurned and rejected him; you are full of wrath against your anointed. You have renounced the covenant with your servant; you have defiled his crown in the dust. You have broken through all his walls; you have laid his strongholds in ruins."

So a few psalms reveal a situation of crisis, with the loss of the city, Temple, and king. It is likely that they all refer to the Babylonian captivity.

c. Postexilic Psalms

This leaves about a hundred psalms that could have been composed in Persian and Hellenistic times. Some of these suggest the influence of Persian religion.[14] Most of our evidence, however, has to be gleaned by comparing psalms with what we know of this period from other biblical works of this time. Here we find a greater interest in the individual, such as in the stories of Ruth, Esther, and Daniel 1–6; some texts refer to God in more explicitly monotheistic terms, such as Genesis 1, Isaiah 40–55, and Job 38–41. Other pertinent works are those that are concerned with the identity of the community—such as in Haggai, Zechariah, Isaiah 55–66, Ezra, and Nehemiah—and literature that questions the purposes of God amid suffering, such as the book of Job.

A large number of psalms are intensely personal, and their contents contrast starkly with the interests of earlier psalms. Some seek forgiveness from God, such as Psalms 32 and 51. In Psalm 51:2–4, for example, the supplicant prays: "Wash me thoroughly from my iniquity, and cleanse me from my sin. For I know my transgressions, and my sin is ever before me. Against you, you alone, have I sinned, and done what is evil in your sight." The superscription reads "A Psalm of David, when the prophet Nathan came to him, after he had gone in to Bathsheba." This is a good illustration of how David becomes an exemplar of piety: with the psalm being credited to David, other supplicants are reminded that even the great King David needed to plead for forgiveness.

Other psalms (for example, Psalms 22:1–21 and 38:1–22) speak of an illness that alienates supplicants from their community. Yet others speak of some spell that has been cast upon them by "workers of evil": Psalms 6:8, 91:1–6, 139:19–22, and 140:1–3 are relevant examples.[15] Others speak of party strife, of people finding themselves at odds with other members of the community: Psalms 54–59 form a collection in this respect.

Other psalmists lament that they are separated from the Temple and long to return to it (Psalms 42–43 and 63). Other supplicants take issue with God about the success of the wicked, who, according to the teaching of, for example, Deuteronomy and Proverbs, should be punished for their sins, while the suffering righteous should be rewarded. Psalms 49 and 73, for example, each reflect on the disparity between the righteous and the wicked. They partly resolve this issue by reflecting on some restitution in life beyond death (a belief that is found only rarely and then only in the latest literature of the Bible, such as Isaiah 25:8 and Daniel 12:1–3). Psalm 49 expresses this as follows: "Like sheep they are appointed for Sheol; Death shall be their shepherd; straight to the grave they descend, and their form shall waste away; Sheol shall be their home. But God will ransom my soul from the power of Sheol, for he will receive me" (verses 14–15).

Other psalmists affirm an unwavering faith. Psalm 23 reflects on the presence of God in times of danger: he is both Shepherd and Host. Psalm 8, which has affinities with Genesis 1:26–28, rejoices in the creator of both the cosmos and the individual. Psalm 1 (as well as the second part of Psalm 19 and also Psalm 119) speaks of an ideal individual who reads and keeps the Law and who is accordingly rewarded by God.

Although not every psalm that suggests a more personal faith is necessarily a late composition, most of the psalms cited above reflect the need to express Jewish identity with individual acts of piety. Several psalms may have been composed away from the official Temple cult; they are thus very different from those psalms that are more concerned with affairs of the king and official religion. These may well have been compositions by skilled poets, writing for anyone to use them; many, however, suggest that they are prayers emerging from a genuine particular experience. Whatever the reasons for their composition, their inclusion in the Psalter was because of their potential for universal appropriation. Some of the psalms in the "Songs of Ascents" (Psalms 120–34) show how profoundly personal prayers were included in a collection whose focus is on a pilgrimage to the Jerusalem Temple.[16]

Not all postexilic psalms are individual in outlook. During this period there was also a pressing concern about the identity of the whole community of faith. Psalms that recall the people's history, echoing, for example, Isaiah 63:7–14 and Nehemiah 9, whose backgrounds appear to be a liturgy of penitence, may well come from this period. Two pairs of psalms, 105/106 and 135/136, review the people's history through confession (Psalm 105) or praise and thanksgiving (Psalms 106, 135, 136; Psalm 106:27 and 47 even refers to the people having been "scattered ... over the lands," soon to be "gathered among the nations"). The emphasis in these psalms is no longer on David and Zion but on earlier traditions popularized by later writers about the promises of the land to Abraham (for example, 105:9–11) and especially about God's rescue of his people from Egypt, a belief that became a later paradigm about the people's restoration to the land.

These historical psalms serve a didactic purpose, teaching the community about the origins of their faith. Personal psalms, too, serve an instructional purpose: Psalms 37, 111, and 112, for example, teach about the rewards for righteousness despite the apparent success of the wicked. Other suppliants testify to the community about what God has done for them: Psalms 32, 34, 92, 107, and 138 are all different examples of this. A number of these psalms also suggest a specific scribal culture, for they are acrostic psalms, structured line by line according to the twenty-two letters of the Hebrew alphabet: Psalms 34, 111, and 112 fall into this category.[17] Other didactic psalms appear to be a pastiche of formulaic expressions found in earlier psalms. Psalm 144, for example, uses Psalm 8 in verses 3–4 and Psalm 18 in verses 5–11.

Many hymns of praise declare God's "world rule." Like Second Isaiah and Job, they affirm him as the one and only God, and in style and content they seem later than the creation psalms 29, 19A, and 104, noted earlier. Psalms 93–99 form an interesting collection. We have seen how parts of Psalm 93 (verse 3), 96 (verse 4), and 97 (verse 9) may be early because they acknowledge the existence of other deities. However, as a collection they have been adapted to create a more monotheistic outlook: they suggest the influence of Second Isaiah, for example, in the references to the "new song" in Psalms 96:1 and 98:1 (see Isaiah 42:10) and the renunciation of idols in Psalms 96:5 and 97:7 (as in Isaiah 40:18–20). Psalms 145–50 also affirm God's rule as creator and king: paradoxically, like Psalms 93–100, they also serve to express faith and hope at a time when morale was low, under foreign rule.[18]

A time of dissonance is also reflected in other psalms that consider the theme of the everlasting might of God and the fragility of human life. Psalm 90:4–6 is a good example of this: "For a thousand years in your sight are like yesterday when it is past, or like a watch in the night. You sweep them away; they are like a dream, like grass that is renewed in the morning; in the morning it flourishes and is renewed; in the evening it fades and withers."[19]

Postexilic psalmody, therefore, appears to have more emphasis on the community than the nation and on the individual within the community. Furthermore, its belief in one and only God accords with what we know of the developing Jewish faith after the exile.

Observations and Implications

This overview of the diverse origins of psalmody leads to some important observations. First, it is clear that those who compiled the Psalter were not really interested in historical origins; they certainly did not arrange psalms in any chronological order. The fact that Psalm 1, an example of "Torah piety," which reflects a postexilic date, precedes Psalm 2, a preexilic "royal psalm," suggests that this lack of chronological interest is apparent from the very beginning of the Psalter. Throughout the Psalter early psalms are frequently set alongside later ones: for example, some of the "psalms of Korah" (Psalms 44–48) suggest preexilic or exilic times, while other Korahite psalms (42–43 and 49) are much later. Similarly Psalms 74, 89, and 137, which all reflect on the effects of the exile, are scattered throughout the Psalter.

Second, from a literary point of view, it is not always possible to classify a psalm according to a specific form or type. For example, my discussion of psalms about the king was determined by the psalms' contents, not by any specific genre, while my discussion of later psalms of instruction was similarly based upon their contents rather than on any shared form (some are complaints, others are thanksgivings, and others are simply reflections on the conflict of faith and experience). Although it is clear that personal laments and hymns of praise are the two prominent psalm types, with the former occurring more in the first part of the Psalter and the latter occurring nearer the end, even laments and hymns

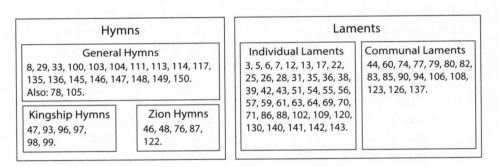

Figure 9.1. An outline of the Psalms according to their forms.

use several other elements, such as thanksgivings, curses, blessings, and proverbial sayings. Many psalms—for example, those illustrating some prophetic liturgy, such as 50 and 81—do not fit any psalm category at all. This suggests that the classification of psalms according to their forms, which was such a prominent feature of psalms scholarship throughout the last century, popularized by Hermann Gunkel, might be a helpful guide, but it has many shortcomings. Certainly the compilers of the Psalter were not very concerned with such categorization. For example, a hymn of praise (Psalm 8) is found in the heart of a sequence of psalms (3–7 and 9–13) that are mainly personal laments, and laments (139–44) preface the final paean of praise (145–50). Or again, to take just three psalms in sequence, Psalm 72, a royal psalm, is followed by 73, a psalm of instruction, and then 74, a lament over the destruction of the Temple. Furthermore, the Songs of Ascents (Psalms 120–34) comprise laments, instructions, hymns, thanksgivings, confessions, blessings, and expressions of trust—some of which even occur in the same psalm.

2. THE USE OF PSALMODY

The Psalter is a complex anthology, spanning in time perhaps seven hundred years, from the time of David up to and even beyond the Persian period. Despite this, many studies of the Psalms have argued that the use of a particular form implies a specific liturgical context and purpose.

Sigmund Mowinckel, for example, understood the prominent setting of psalmody to be the royal cult, with its great ritual drama, the Enthronement Festival, which celebrated the rule of God at the time of the New Year. One of Mowinckel's later publications actually ascribed more than 140 psalms to preexilic times. Only Psalms 4, 25, 70, 100, 111, 141, 143, 147, and 148 receive no mention in the index of his 1962 publication, whose focus is this Enthronement Festival.[20] Mowinckel's mentor, Hermann Gunkel, used a form-critical classification to propose a very different view: Gunkel understood most of the psalms (the royal psalms being exceptions) to be imitations of now lost preexilic psalms, reflecting a piety independent of the cult, eventually to be brought into postexilic Temple worship.[21]

During the last century psalms scholars built their various theories on these two views. Following Mowinckel's emphasis on preexilic worship, Hans-Joachim Kraus, for example, proposed that the psalms were composed for an early Royal Zion Festival (also at the New Year, which would have been in autumn), which celebrated God's choice and protection of Jerusalem. Artur Weiser, meanwhile, understood the majority of psalms to have been composed for an early but very different (New Year) Covenant Renewal Festival.[22] By contrast, scholars such as Klaus Seybold and Erhard Gerstenberger, following Gunkel, understood the psalms as compositions that served the needs of dispersed communities throughout the Persian period. Seybold accepted the preexilic origins of some psalms, but his main emphasis was on the use of psalms of sickness at local sanctuaries in postexilic times. Gerstenberger, meanwhile, who views the Persian period as seminal for the literature of the entire Bible, has argued that the majority of psalms were composed at local cultic centers, serving the needs of families and clans, while the Temple served the needs of the priests and other personnel.[23]

We have already observed that any theory that tries to superimpose too monolithic a view onto the use of the psalms falls short of the evidence: the Psalter defies dating and classification in this way. As Mowinckel, Weiser, and Kraus have indicated, some of the psalms do seem to tell us something about the preexilic royal cult and its nationalistic concerns, as well as its dependence upon ancient Near Eastern myth and ritual as a means of expressing them. And as Gunkel, Seybold, and Gerstenberger have argued, many of the psalms echo postexilic concerns, not only of the Temple under Persian rule but also of individuals composing more personal psalms, which were eventually used in Temple worship as well.

Whether speaking about preexilic Temple royal liturgy, or exilic "Templeless" psalmody, or postexilic worship at the Second Temple and in dispersed communities, one common characteristic is evident. At all stages of evolution we see the importance of words alongside cultic rituals—words that were spoken but also words that were sung. To speak of the use of psalmody in both early Israelite and later Jewish worship is to imply a singing cult.

The psalms actually have very little interest in the cultic legislation of the Pentateuch: even the word for "festival" (*ḥag*) occurs only once,

and not one of the festivals listed in the cultic calendars is mentioned—
neither Unleavened Bread nor Passover, neither Weeks nor Tabernacles.
Indeed, Psalm 81:3, which refers to blowing the trumpet at "the full
moon," is the only pertinent reference, but even this does not give information about the actual cultic occasion. Furthermore, with a few exceptions (including Psalms 72:10 and 96:8), there are no positive references
to the term for a sacrificial offering (*minḥah*) and only a handful of references to more specialized sacrifices, such as freewill offerings, burnt
offerings, and memorial offerings (exceptions include Psalms 54:6; 20:3,
50:8, and 51:19; and 66:13, 15). And where guilt and penitence are expressed, there is little evidence of how the rituals advocated in priestly
legislation might "atone" for them: there is no reference to the guilt
offering (*ašam*), for example, so popular in priestly codes, and the one
reference to sin offering (*ḥaṭṭat*) in Psalm 40:6 is a negative one. Instead,
a more spiritualized view prevails, whereby a "song of thanksgiving" is
more pleasing to God than the act of sacrifice (Psalms 40:5–8; 50:7, 15,
23; 51:16–18; 69:29–31; 116:17; and 141:2–3).

Because the psalmists show little explicit interest in the actions that
might accompany the words, it is important not to reconstruct what
cannot be known and, instead, to stress what we do know: that is, the
importance of liturgical song at all stages of the evolution of psalmody.
Singing the psalms was a crucial practice in the exilic period, when a
sacrificial cult was all but impossible: we saw this in relation to Psalm
137. And psalm-singing was a popular practice in the postexilic period,
particularly in Temple liturgy, as is evidenced by the number of musical
superscriptions—over some seventy-five psalms—and by the contents
of the many psalms that refer to "singing praises" and "making music"
to God.[24] The Chronicler describes the preexilic cult through postexilic
eyes, and this is quite different from the account in 1 and 2 Kings: it is,
essentially, a singing cult. Although the Chronicler only cites a handful
of psalms, they are all used in the context of music and song.[25]

3. THE COMPILATION OF THE PSALTER

The Psalter evolved in several overlapping phases. The first involves compilations from fragments of psalmody into the individual compositions

we have today. The second is the inclusion of individual psalms in collections of psalms, where earlier psalms were adapted for later use. The third is the amalgamation of collections to create whole books. The final stage is the compilation of five books, comparable to the five books of Moses, to create the "Psalter of David."

a. Individual Compositions

We have already observed that some of the oldest psalms contain ancient fragments. In Psalms 68, 110, and 132, for example, it is possible to see how layers of liturgy lie behind each psalm as a whole. Psalm 132, for example, has many temporal breaks, not only between the two parts (David's oath to God, in verses 1–10, and God's oath to David, in verses 11–18) but between the two oracles in the second part. Psalms 50 and 81 are also likely to have grown in this way; Psalm 81, for example, consists of a hymn and festal instructions in verses 1–5b, with two very different prophetic elements in verses 5c–16: one (verses 6–10) is a traditional oracle, while the other (verses 11–16) is a divine speech in a lament form.

There are several other examples of this process. For instance, some personal psalms have been given a more communal conclusion. In the Songs of Ascents, several psalms were given an "Israelite" orientation, with a final call to praise, for example, "Peace be upon Israel!" (Ps. 128:6; see also 131:3). Other personal psalms, such as 51 and 69, which both advocate the value of prayer over sacrifice, have conclusions that bring the psalms more in line with Temple orthodoxy. Psalm 51, for example, ends with a prayer for the restoration of Jerusalem, where sacrifices will be offered in profusion (verses 18–19).

Other psalms comprise elements that were probably added at different times. Psalms 40 and 41, for example, start unusually with a thanksgiving (40:1–10, 41:1–3), which is followed by a prayer for healing (40:11–17, 40:4–12): the thanksgiving is likely to be a later addition. The latter part of Psalm 40 (verses 13–17) has even been used as an independent lament in the five verses of Psalm 70.

Psalms 19A and 19B are completely different psalms, probably from very different periods in Israel's history. The first praises God for the gift of the sun (verses 1–6), and the second, for the gift of the law (verses

7–14). Psalm 108 appears to have been compiled from two separate psalms (57:7–11 are in verses 1–5, and 60:5–12 are in verses 6–13).

Occasionally psalms paired together seem to have been redacted in order to highlight mutual concerns: Psalm 2:12, for example, has several linguistic correspondences with the beginning and end of Psalm 1 ("Lest you perish in the way") and echoes Psalm 1:6 ("For the way of the wicked will perish"). Its final phrase, "Happy are all who … ," echoes Psalm 1:1 ("Happy are those who …"). So whether in smaller additions or larger compilations, some individual psalms appear to have evolved over time.

b. Larger Collections

As I noted earlier, many psalms with more personal concerns have been read in the light of David's piety and given the title "for David" (*ledawid*). Psalms 1–41 form an entire large collection in this way. Only Psalm 10, which is really part of Psalm 9, as it shares the same acrostic form, and Psalm 33—probably a much later psalm—do not have these headings. The hallmark of this Davidic collection is the predominant use of the name "Yahweh" for God.

Alongside this, a number of other, also mainly personal, psalms were collected together with headings "for David" (although here many have liturgical superscriptions as well). The hallmark, however, is the use of the name Elohim for God, thus creating a second Davidic Psalter (Psalms 51–72). Other, smaller Davidic collections developed that were never incorporated into either of these two collections: the largest comprises Psalms 138–45, but other small groups of twos, threes, and fours are evident in the latter part of the Psalter.[26]

Other collections are more obviously liturgical. Those with the heading "For the sons of Asaph" form a collection of mainly older psalms, some even suggesting northern associations with their references to Joseph and Ephraim (see, for example, Psalms 78:67 and 80:1–2). Many express a sense of the judgment of God. Twelve in all, these were designated for the Asaphite choir guild in the postexilic Temple cult. One (Psalm 50) introduces the second Davidic Psalter; the other eleven follow it (Psalms 73–83). Another twelve-psalm choir collection, with the heading "For the sons of Korah," whose main theme is a longing for the Temple, was also added to this evolving collection—with eight psalms

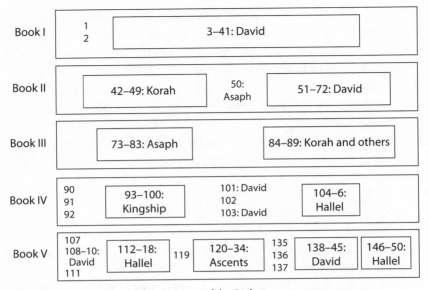

Figure 9.2. An overview of the structure of the Psalter.

(42–49) prefacing it and four (Psalms 84–85, 87–88) following it. In another self-contained liturgical collection, Psalms 120–34, each psalm is headed "a song of ascents" (šîr hama'alôt), as the group appears probably to have served pilgrims "going up" to the Jerusalem Temple.

The headings to these psalms are all taken from the Hebrew version. There are several differences between these and the later Greek translation (called the LXX), possibly undertaken by the end of the second century BCE, and these reflect the fluidity of the final form of the text at this time. The LXX attributes thirteen more psalms to David (and actually takes away this attribution in Psalms 122 and 124). It also attributes a psalm with an exilic context to Jeremiah (Psalm 137), while Psalm 65 is credited to both Jeremiah and Ezekiel, and Psalms 146, 147, and 148 are credited to the prophets Haggai and Zechariah. The LXX also adds new liturgical headings, such as which days of the week the psalms should be sung on (e.g., Psalm 24—for the first day of the week; Psalm 48—for the second day of the week; see also, for the subsequent days, Psalms 82, 94, 81, and 93). Furthermore, it sometimes translates liturgical terms in the Hebrew eschatologically: the most obvious is the phrase "for the choirmaster," which in the Greek is rendered "for the end [of time]."

Other collections (mostly without superscriptions in the Hebrew original) were brought together on account of shared themes: for example, the psalms celebrating the kingship of God (93–99) and the psalms celebrating God as creator (145–50). A miscellaneous collection, 111–18, with its various themes of God's deliverance of his people from Egypt, may well have come together because of its use at the Passover Festival.

Clearly in this process there were some "orphan psalms." Some seem to have been brought together as pairs (105/106, 135/136), and some seem to have a singular place at the seams of various parts of the Psalter (89, 119). The reasons for placing some of the others (e.g., 33, 86) are unclear.[27]

c. Complete Books

It would seem that books I–III were formed first, out of the two Davidic collections, the Asaphite and Korahite collections, and a few miscellaneous psalms. The very similar doxologies in Psalms 41:13, 72:18–19, and 89:52, which are calls to bless the God of Israel, mark out one book from another. Comparing these three books with psalms scrolls found at Qumran, most of those that contain books I–III follow the same order as the Hebrew Bible, but other scrolls—such as 11QPs[a]—follow a different order in books IV to V, and 11QPs[a] even includes several hitherto unknown psalms. Scholars are now inclined to suppose that books I–III were completed in the Persian period, while books IV–V were not in a final form until near the end of the Greek period in the second century BCE. Psalm 2 may well have headed up books I–III, with its great confidence in the monarchy, while Psalm 89 forms its conclusion, with its despair about the monarchy's demise.

d. The Final Form of the Psalter

So exactly how books IV and V evolved is unclear. It may be that book IV originally ended with Psalm 119 and that this lengthy psalm about the Torah, along with Psalm 1, a contrastingly brief psalm also about the Torah, reshaped the Psalter so that it would begin and end with the covenant with Moses. Certainly the heading to Psalm 90, "A Prayer of Moses, the man of God," points to this. The fourth doxology (Psalm 106:48) is longer and different from the other three, and it may have been added when further Davidic collections (e.g., 138–45), the Songs of Ascents (120–34), and the so-called Great Hallel (145–50) were included, thus embedding Psalm 119 in the heart of book V. The addition of books IV and V certainly give the Psalter a new and positive theological dimension of hope in God's protection of Jerusalem and his sovereignty over all peoples.

It is impossible to know for certain the identity of those who brought the Psalter together in these various stages. The book of Chronicles as well as later writers, such as Philo and the rabbis who compiled the Mishnah, write about how the Levitical singers played a vital part in the delivery and preservation of psalmody. Certainly these final compilers had respect not only for the Davidic dynasty but also for the importance of the Mosaic Law, and they were concerned about teaching and preaching the psalms and with the efficacy of cultic song as well as ritual and sacrifice. The traditional picture of the Levites (who later became Temple singers) reflects these interests. The final arrangement of the psalms also points to an interest in how they served as prophecies pointing to some future fulfillment: in Chronicles, for example, this also accords with Levitical prophetic interests. Furthermore, divested of land and property, the Levites would have been concerned for the "poor and needy," a theme in many of the psalms: one example is in Psalms 135–37, where the reference to the "house of Levi" in Psalm 135:20 and the refrain "For he is good, for his steadfast love endures for ever" in Psalm 136 (which, in Ezra 3:10–11, is sung by the Levites) suggest their influence. Last, the compilers would have had to belong to the Temple community, working at the center of Judaism rather than at the periphery, bringing together psalms from outlying communities into an organized whole. In all these ways the Levitical singers do appear to be likely candidates: their Psalter served as an "identity marker" for a people under foreign domination.[28]

4. POEMS OUTSIDE THE PSALTER

The boundaries between Hebrew prose and poetry are often blurred. Poetic conventions do not follow those of what we would normally term "poetry," with obvious rhyme and rhythm. Hebrew poetry depends more on sense than sound. It uses what is often termed "synonymous" or "antithetic" parallelism, whose essence lies in either repeating a phrase in different words or using contrasting ideas.[29] Hebrew poetry, even in translation, thus provides a rich resource for an exploration of the power of metaphorical discourse.[30] Below are two accounts of poems outside the Psalter: first, small units, probably quite old, set in prose narratives and, second, more expansive literary imitations. Both, in different ways, have some associations with the psalms.

a. Briefer Poems

The smallest poetic units may have been adapted from ancient oral tradition; the use of mythology and warfare imagery has correspondences with some of the psalms discussed earlier (for example, Psalms 68 and 110 and Psalms 2, 46, and 48). One example, noted earlier, is Numbers 10:35–36, with its associations of the Ark with victory in battle: "Arise, O Lord, let your enemies be scattered, and your foes flee before you."

A lament at defeat in battle, ascribed to David (2 Samuel 1:19–27), cites its origins in the *Book of Jashar* (see 2 Samuel 1:18), and a contrasting victory song (Joshua 10:12–13) also cites this book (verse 13). This may well allude to a genuine collection of war poetry. Other victory songs have more correspondences with the psalms: they include Exodus 15:2–3, 17–18; Judges 5:12–30 (a complex poem that has several links with Psalm 68); and parts of Habakkuk 3:2–19 and of Deuteronomy 32:1–43. Incorporated into narrative texts, these units were used for reading and teaching rather than singing and public worship.

Other poetic fragments suggesting some oral tradition include legal pronouncements, working songs, and ballads. An example of legal poetry, with the purpose of ratifying blood revenge, is in Genesis 9:6. Another is Genesis 4:23–24: "Adah and Zillah, hear my voice; you wives of Lamech, listen to what I say: I have killed a man for wounding me, a young man for striking me. If Cain is avenged sevenfold, truly Lamech seventy-sevenfold." A typical working song is Numbers 21:17–18: "Spring up, O well! Sing to it! The well that the leaders sank, that the nobles of the people dug, with the scepter, with the staff."

An example of a short blessing is in Numbers 6:24–26: "The LORD bless you and keep you; the LORD make his face to shine upon you, and be gracious to you; the LORD lift up his countenance upon you, and give you peace." This has been discovered on a seventh-century amulet, so the date must be earlier than that. Even the expanded blessings of Genesis 49:3–27, Numbers 23:7–10, 18–24, and 24:3–9, 15–24, and Deuteronomy 33:2–29, purported to come from the lips of Jacob and Moses, probably adapt fragments of older oral poetry.

b. Literary Imitations of Psalms

Most of these examples concern the piety of particular individuals: they are therefore similar to the more personal thanksgivings and laments in the Psalter and might be dated after the exile. Hannah's prayer in 1 Samuel 2:1–10 seems originally to have been a community thanksgiving, but its imagery of the poor and needy being exalted and rewarded provided some associations with Hannah's situation after Samuel's birth. Hezekiah's thanksgiving in Isaiah 38:10–20 serves a similar purpose: it could have been a psalm, but its narrative context about the king's recovery from illness makes it more particular and didactic. Jonah 3:2–9 is a pastiche of cultic formulas thanking God for release from danger: given Jonah's plight, this is somewhat anachronistic, but the water imagery in verses 3, 5, and 6 fits well with his being in the belly of a whale. David's prayer in 2 Samuel 23:1–7 adopts the language of psalmody, although its reference to David as "the sweet psalmist of Israel" (verse 1) suggests a later date overall. Similarly some of the hymns, laments, and royal oracles in the prophetic books are later literary imitations of the psalmic tradition: the creative uses of hymns in, for example, Amos 5:8–9, Isaiah 6:3, and Zephaniah 3:14–15 are pertinent examples, and the laments in, for example, Amos 5:2, Micah 7:1, Jeremiah 9:1, 10:19, 14:17, and Isaiah 61:1–12 are others; the use of royal oracles in, for example, Isaiah 9:6, Micah 5:2, and Jeremiah 23:5–6 similarly suggest variations of some of the royal psalms.[31]

c. Two Poetic Scrolls

Two entire books deserve mention here, as they provide contrasting poems about the depths and heights of human experience. The contents of Lamentations reveal an exilic setting in that they are dirges over a fallen city; the acrostic form in the first four laments is, as I have noted, a scribal device used in several psalms. The contents of the twenty-five lyric poems of Song of Songs, interwoven to create a dialogue between two lovers with interjections from a stylized "chorus," suggest adaptations of early wedding poems into a dramatic exploration of human love; there may even be evidence of Hellenistic influence through the role of the chorus. The eroticism troubled the rabbis, whose response was to interpret the poetry allegorically and to read the two voices as those of God and Israel, with the chorus serving as a didactic commentary on this relationship.

d. Later Poetry outside the Bible

The finding of the Dead Sea Scrolls from 1947 onward has opened up another window on our understanding of Hebrew poetic texts. 11QPs[a], which was noted earlier, includes some fourteen additional psalms in books IV and V of the Psalter: four of these were previously known in a Syriac version, and one is preserved in Ben Sirach 51:13–19, but the others—such as "Apostrophe to Zion" and the "Hymn to the Creator"—were completely unknown. Other scrolls found in Caves 1 and 4 contain some twenty-five "Thanksgiving Psalms," and these, too, were previously unknown. Also in Cave 4 were two other scrolls (termed 4Q380 and 4Q381) that contained early (perhaps third-century BCE) poetic fragments in a similar prosodic style to the psalms. At the end of 11QPs[a], in column 27, we find a curious poem describing David's poetic skills:

> And David, the son of Jesse, was wise
> and a light like the light of the sun, and literate,
> and discerning and perfect in all his ways before God and men.
> And the Lord gave him a discerning and enlightened spirit.
> And he wrote three thousand six hundred psalms.

This again shows the fluidity of the tradition about the poetry of the psalms: 3,450 other psalms, not contained in our Hebrew Psalter, apparently have yet to be discovered!

This leads to one final observation. Poetry that is embedded in narrative has a particularity in its attribution to a specific setting or particular character, while the psalms, which are context-free, are more open to a universal appropriation through liturgical recitation. For example, we read 2 Samuel 22:2–51, which is presented at the end of Samuel as David's thanksgiving for being released from Saul, as part of the story of David; whereas we read the almost identical royal psalm, Psalm 18, with a similar heading, as set amid the laments and praises of the Psalter. Its additional liturgical instruction ("for the choirmaster") reminds us that David, the prolific psalms composer in ancient memory, has become "everyman," a figure who invites us to pray with him rather than read about him.

5. RECEPTION OF PSALMS IN JEWISH AND CHRISTIAN TRADITION

We have already seen how earlier psalms—royal psalms, psalms about Jerusalem, psalms about military defeat and victory—were performed in different ways during and after the exile: we would know nothing about these older psalms had they not been taken up and sung in later liturgy. The Chronicler's use of psalms to illustrate the way the postexilic cult is as much about song as sacrifice is another mode of reception. So "reception history" belongs to the early history of psalmody, even before the Psalter itself was fully formed.

Although reception history in practice is almost as old as the psalms themselves, the study of their reception is a fairly recent phenomenon. There have been two key reasons for this development. One is the recognition that text-critical studies have obvious limitations, especially given the rich cultural history of performing the psalms through the centuries. For example, we see the words in a new light when we view the psalms visually through artistic representation in illuminated manuscripts and in modern art, and we hear the words differently when they are interpreted through music, both sacred and secular. Despite the obvious importance of their words since their inception, the psalms have the ability to transcend the literary medium: analytic studies of the text of the psalms are important, but there is more to the impact of the text than this.

A second reason is the renewed interest in Jewish and Christian relations: because the psalms have provided many conflicting readings in the past, scholars interested in the convergence of these traditions are concerned to trace the history of Jewish and Christian reception of the psalms. For example, by comparing the different ways the psalms were used in the earliest communities, through early "commentaries" in Jewish works such as the Dead Sea Scrolls and, by Christians, in the New Testament, we see the beginning of the divide between the two traditions: Christians read the psalms as prophecies in the process of fulfillment through the person of Christ. By comparing the use of the psalms by the early church fathers, who often interpreted individual verses and phrases allegorically in the light of Christ, and their use by the early rabbis, who often read the psalms as narrative poems about their own history, we are able to trace this divide even further. Translations are also an early form of reception, and the early (Jewish) Greek and early Latin (Christian) versions illustrate the different ways each faith tradition understood particular psalms.

Jews and Christians also used the psalms very differently in liturgy, where they became a vital means of shaping the beliefs and practices of each community of faith during persecution and change. In Jewish tradition psalms were read and chanted rather than sung, in deference to the fallen Temple, while in Christian tradition they were sung, ironically picking up ancient Jewish traditions of Temple and synagogue chant. Through examining the liturgical uses of the psalms we also get a sense of the differences within each tradition, as well as the differences between them.

By the early Middle Ages their liturgical use inspired interpretations through Christian art, and hundreds of illuminated manuscripts give us vivid examples of a visual exegesis of earlier Christian commentaries on the psalms. Jewish illustrations from the late Middle Ages, albeit more cautious in their representation of the human form, nevertheless offer us similar visual insights into the way they understood the rabbinic commentary tradition. By the sixteenth century we have access to the psalms in a vast array of musical scores—metrical psalmody composed for the laity to sing, chants for cathedral choirs, songs of celebration or lament from the Jewish ghettos—and again we see how yet another form of psalmody shapes Christian and Jewish identities in very different ways.

Also from the sixteenth century onward poetic imitations of psalms, usually in the vernacular, offer us an aesthetic appreciation, as each tradition "performs" psalmody not only in the church and synagogue but in salons and concert halls, family homes, and theaters. By the twenty-first century, this concern to "perform" the psalms beyond the confines of a particular confessional community has served to bring the two traditions closer together, whether in music, art, or contemporary imitation and translation, where the anti-Jewish or anti-Christian sentiments that were so prevalent in early, medieval, and Reformation reception history are mainly absent.

So after three thousand years, it is not too much of an exaggeration to claim that Psalms has preoccupied Jews and Christians more than any other book in the Hebrew Bible, and an account of the reception history of psalmody tells us as much about the cultural history of Judaism and Christianity as it does about the psalms themselves.[32] Even though their origins and use and even compilation process might sometimes perplex us, their adaptation through the centuries illustrates just how much these once-ancient prayers now have a universal and multivalent life of their own.

NOTES

1. These are Psalms 3, 7, 18, 34, 51, 52, 54, 56, 57, 59, 60, 63, and 142. The psalm numbering, psalm versification, and citations are taken from the NRSV unless otherwise stated.

2. For example, see Julius Wellhausen, in Harold Furness, *The Book of Psalms: A New English Translation (with Explanatory Notes and Appendix by J. Wellhausen)*, Polychrome Bible 14 (Cambridge: James Clark and Co., 1898), pp. 162–63; Charles Briggs and Grace Briggs, *A Critical and Exegetical Commentary on the Book of Psalms*, vol. 1 (Edinburgh: T&T Clark, 1906), §§37–38, pp. lxxx–lxxxi, and §43, pp. lxxxix–xcii.

3. A seminal figure here is Sigmund Mowinckel; see his *Offersang og Sangoffer* (Oslo: H. Aschehoug and Co., 1951); translated by D. R. Ap-Thomas as *The Psalms in Israel's Worship*, 2 vols. (Oxford: Basil Blackwell, 1962).

4. On Canaanite mythology as it relates to the psalms, see John Day, *Yahweh and the Gods and Goddesses of Canaan* (Sheffield: Sheffield Academic Press, 2000), pp. 91–127.

This criterion is, admittedly, controversial: for example, Daniel 7 has many Canaanite allusions and is usually dated very late. But Daniel uses ancient mythology as a literary device: the psalms, by contrast, are mainly liturgical texts, and some poetic fragments appear to be a genuine interaction with the ever-present Canaanite culture, rather than a faded recollection of it.

5. Verses 5, 14, 15, 17, and 30 are particularly controversial, but the entire psalm is full of corruptions, using terms that occur nowhere else.

6. Verse 4 ("Lift up a song to him [or make a highway for him] who rides upon the clouds" [*larokeb baarabôt*]) has correspondences with descriptions of the Canaanite warrior deity Baal, who is also the "rider of the clouds" (*rkb ʿrpt*), for example, in Manfried Dietrich, Oswald Loretz, and Joaquin Sanmartín, eds., *Die Keilalphabetischen Texte aus Ugarit* (*KTU*) (Neukirchen-Vluyn, Germany: Neukirchener Verlag, 1976), 1.19: I: 38–46 and 1.2: IV: 7–9. See also Manfried Dietrich, Oswald Loretz, and Joaquin Sanmartín, eds., *The Cuneiform Alphabetic Texts from Ugarit, Ras Ibn Hani and Other Places*, 2nd ed. (*KTU²*) (Munster: Ugarit-Verlag, 1995).

7. See the discussion in Day, *Yahweh and the Gods and Goddesses of Canaan*, pp. 95–98.

8. Two other "creation psalms" may well be preexilic, borrowing more from Babylonian and Egyptian mythology. Psalm 19A, which describes God (El) creating a tent for the sun in the heavens (verse 4) and being like a bridegroom and strong man (verse 5), is very like a Babylonian hymn to the sun god Shamash (James B. Pritchard, ed., *Ancient Near Eastern Texts Relating to the Old Testament*, 3rd ed. [Princeton, N.J.: Princeton University Press, 1969], pp. 387–89). Psalm 104 has several affinities not only with Canaanite mythology but also with an Egyptian hymn to Aton by Pharaoh Akhenaten (pp. 369–71). On this latter psalm, see John Day, "Psalm 104 and Akhenaten's Hymn to the Sun," in Susan E. Gillingham, ed., *Jewish and Christian Approaches to the Psalms. Conflict and Convergence* (Oxford: Oxford University Press, 2013), pp. 211–28.

9. Typical texts in Isaiah that refer to God's protection of Zion include 29:1–8 and 31:4–5. A text that concerns God's promises to the king, part of which may go back to the prophet himself, is Isaiah 9:2–7.

10. For example, the reference to God being exalted in his sanctuary has correspondences with Isaiah 6:1–5; the refrain that "the Lord of Hosts is with us" (Psalm 46:7, 11) echoes Isaiah 7:14 (Immanuel: "God is with us"); and the imagery of divine control over the threatening waters is found in Isaiah 8:5–8. This is not to claim any specific influence from one text to the other but to observe that these motifs may well come from a similar context.

11. Four other psalms also refer to the king (or to "the anointed"), but the liturgical context is more difficult to ascertain. Such a reference may have been added to a psalm composed for other reasons. They are Psalms 28 (verse 8), 61 (verses 6–7), 63 (verse 11), and 84 (verse 9).

12. This is a motif in Canaanite mythology: for example, of Kothar and Baal, in *KTU* 1.4: V: 45, we read, "A seat was prepared and he was seated at the right hand of the Valiant Baal."

13. Each ends with the Hebrew word *selah*, meaning "pause" or "interlude."

14. Erhard Gerstenberger offers examples such as the noniconic views of God; the dualistic thinking about truth and falsehood, good and evil, light and darkness; and the affirmation of a high deity, who, like Ahura Mazda, is the guardian of all wisdom and

order in the world. Erhard Gerstenberger, *Israel in der Perserzeit: 5. Und 4. Jahrhundert v.Chr.* (Stuttgart: W. Kohlhammer GmbH, 2005); translated by S. S. Schatzman as *Israel in the Persian Period: The Fifth and Fourth Centuries B.C.E.*, Biblical Encyclopedia/ Biblische Enzyklopädie, vol. 8 (Atlanta: Society of Biblical Literature, 2011), pp. 251–52.

15. For an account of the postexilic setting of this phenomenon, see Erhard Gerstenberger, *Der bittende Mensch: Bittritual und Klagelied des Einzelnen im Alten Testament* (Neukirchen-Vluyn, Germany: Neukirchener, 1980), pp. 64–112.

16. Examples include Psalms 120, 121, 123, 127, 128, 130, and 131.

17. Other acrostic psalms include 9, 10, 25, 37, 119, and 145. That this is a later device might be illustrated by the fact that other acrostic forms occurring outside the psalms are mainly found in exilic or postexilic texts, including Lamentations 1–4, Proverbs 31:10–31, and the Greek text Ecclesiasticus 51:13–20.

18. Note the reference to the "new song" in Psalm 149:1. This collection may also reflect Persian influence in its elevation of God over the entire cosmos: see Gerstenberger, *Israel in the Persian Period*, pp. 250–51.

19. See also Psalms 39:4–6 and 103:14–16. This idea is found in Isaiah 40:6–8 and is prevalent throughout Job.

20. For a discussion of Mowinckel's work and influence, as well as an expanded discussion of other scholars referred to here, see Susan E. Gillingham, *Psalms through the Centuries*, vol. 1 (Oxford: Wiley-Blackwell Publishing, 2008), pp. 269–75.

21. See Hermann Gunkel and Joachim Begrich, *Einleitung in die Psalmen: Die Gattungen der religiösen Lyrik Israels*, Göttinger Handkommentar zum Alten Testament (Göttingen: Vandenhoeck & Ruprecht, 1933); translated by J. D. Nogalski as *Introduction to the Psalms: The Genres of the Religious Lyric of Israel* (Macon, Ga.: Mercer University Press, 1998), pp. 15–21.

22. See Hans-Joachim Kraus, *Psalmen 1. Teilband Psalmen 1–59* (Neukirchen-Vluyn, Germany: Neukirchener Verlag, 1960); translated by H. C. Oswald as *Psalms 1–59*, vol. 1 (Minneapolis: Augsburg Fortress Press, 1978), pp. 62–81, 86–89; and Artur Weiser, *Die Psalmen* (Göttingen: Vandenhoeck & Ruprecht, 1959); translated by H. Hartwell as *The Psalms* (London: SCM, 1962), pp. 35–52.

23. See Klaus Seybold, *Die Psalmen. Eine Einführung* (Stuttgart: Verlag W. Kohlhammer, 1986); translated by R. Graeme Dunphy as *Introducing the Psalms* (Edinburgh: T&T Clark, 1990), pp. 34–58, 80–108; and Gerstenberger, *Israel in the Persian Period*, pp. 216–52, 355–64.

24. For example, Psalms 95:1–2; 96:1–2; 98:1, 4–6; and 135:2–3. See John A. Smith, "Which Psalms Were Sung in the Temple?" *Music and Letters* 71 (1990): pp. 167–86.

25. For example, in 1 Chronicles 16, which describes David bringing the Ark to Jerusalem, Psalm 105:1–5 is used in verses 8–22; Psalm 96:1–3, in verses 23–33; Psalms 106:1/136, in verse 34; and Psalm 106:46–47, in verses 35–36. On the use of psalmody in Chronicles, see Adele Berlin, "Psalms in the Book of Chronicles," in M. Bar-Asher, D. Dom-Shiloni, E. Tov, and N. Wazana, eds., *Shai le-Sara Japhet. Studies in the Bible, Its Exegesis and Its Language* (Jerusalem: Bialik Institute, 2007), pp. 21–36.

26. See also James C. McCann, ed., *The Shape and Shaping of the Psalter* (Sheffield: Sheffield Academic Press, 1993).

27. Recent scholarship has sought to explain the inclusion of every psalm; see, for example, Frank-Lothar Hossfeld, *Psalmen 51–100, 2. Teilband*, Frank-Lothar Hossfeld

and Erich Zenger, eds. (Freiburg: Herder, 2000); translated by L. M. Maloney as *Psalms 2: A Commentary on Psalms 51–100* (Minneapolis: Fortress Press, 2005).

28. See Susan E. Gillingham, "The Levitical Singers and the Editing of the Hebrew Psalter," in Erich Zenger, ed., *The Composition of the Book of Psalms* (Leuven: Peeters Publishing, 2010), pp. 91–123.

29. See Susan E. Gillingham, *The Poems and Prayers of the Hebrew Bible* (Oxford: Oxford University Press, 1994), pp. 18–43 (on poetry and prose) and pp. 44–88 (on meter and parallelism).

30. William Brown traces metaphors of refuge, pathways, sun, water, trees, and animals in the poetry of the psalms. There are also interesting associations here between the personal and impersonal metaphorical descriptions of God and the use of ancient mythology. See William P. Brown, *Seeing the Psalms: A Theology of Metaphor* (Louisville, Ky.: Westminster John Knox Press, 2002).

31. The book of Job is another example of creative interplay with the psalms. Job 7:17–19, for example, serves as a parody of Psalm 8:4–8. For other examples of this device in Job, see William Kynes, *My Psalm Has Turned into Weeping. Job's Dialogue with the Psalms* (Berlin: de Gruyter, 2012).

32. For a general survey of these different forms of reception of the Psalter as a whole, see Gillingham, *Psalms through the Centuries*; and for a more specific account of the reception of just the first two psalms, see Susan E. Gillingham, *A Journey of Two Psalms: The Reception of Psalms 1 and 2 in Jewish and Christian Tradition* (Oxford: Oxford University Press, 2013).

FURTHER READING: TEN BOOKS ON THE PSALMS

For one of the best compendiums on the market of recent approaches to the psalms, see W. P. Brown, ed., *The Oxford Handbook of the Psalms* (New York: Oxford University Press, 2014), which contains forty-two essays from international scholars on the ancient Near Eastern backgrounds to psalmody, on language, poetry, translation, composition, reception history, interpretive approaches, culturally based interpretations, theologies, anthropologies, and the practice of the psalms.

Students cannot understand psalms studies today without reading two seminal works by Hermann Gunkel and Sigmund Mowinckel. Gunkel's *Introduction to the Psalms: The Genres of the Religious Lyric of Israel* was translated by James Nogalski from the 1933 German original and published in 1988 by Mercer University Press and shows the innovative nature of his form-critical approach to the individual psalms. Sigmund Mowinckel's Norwegian original published in 1951 was translated into two volumes by D. R. Ap-Thomas as *The Psalms in Israel's Worship* by

Basil Blackwell Publishers in 1962: it is a fascinating imaginative reconstruction of Israel's early cultic life through the window of the psalms. Both works have come under heavy fire over the past two decades or so, but without these scholars' insights, psalms studies over the last century would have taken a very different turn.

Of the most recent commentaries that I turn to first, that by Frank-Lothar Hossfeld and Erich Zenger is the most detailed and original: their German commentary has been translated by Linda Maloney, in the Hermeneia series, and to date Psalms 51–100 and 101–50 have been published (2005 and 2011). This excellent commentary looks at the connections between neighboring psalms and gives priority to the Psalms as a book. John Goldingay has also produced a fresh and theologically astute commentary in the Baker Academic series, divided into three volumes according to the books of the Psalter (*1–41*: 2005; *42–89*: 2007; *99–150*: 2009). A third commentary, which is somewhat idiosyncratic but which I always find stimulating, is Samuel Terrien's *The Psalms: Strophic Structure and Theological Commentary*, published in the Eerdmans Critical Commentary series (2003); it has an interesting introduction on the musical use of the psalms, and the different Jewish and Christian readings, and looks at individual psalms not so much verse by verse as strophe by strophe.

For a specifically Jewish reading of the psalms, my own preference is Rabbi Avrohom Chaim Feuer's *Tehillim: The Book of Psalms* (published in two volumes in 1977, revised in 1985 and 1995), which has the Hebrew text on one side of the page and the translation on the other, with a running commentary below. For specifically Christian readings, Walter Brueggemann's prolific output still commands the field. One example is his *Praying the Psalms. Engaging Scripture and the Life of the Spirit*; the second edition was published by Cascade Books in 2007. This takes a more experience-centered approach to the Psalter, focusing on issues such as life and death in the psalms and how to read those psalms that speak of vengeance, both human and divine.

Finally, my own interest in the reception history of psalmody has resulted to date in two publications. *Psalms through the Centuries* was published in the Wiley-Blackwell series in 2008 and looks at how the Psalter as a book has been used by Jews and Christians over the last two millennia, focusing not only on the commentary tradition and the different translations but also on their liturgical use, artistic representation, musical interpretation, and literary imitation. As the title suggests, *A Journey of Two Psalms: The Reception of Psalms 1 and 2 in Jewish and Christian Tradition*, published by Oxford University Press in 2013, looks at these issues through the lens of just two psalms.

Part III

Major Religious Themes

10

Monotheism

Benjamin D. Sommer

The fact that scholars pose the question, "Is the Hebrew Bible monotheistic?" surprises many people. Isn't monotheism one of the great contributions of biblical Israel to civilization? Aren't the Israelites renowned for believing in only one God? The Decalogue famously commands: "You shall have no gods other than Me" (Exodus 20:3; Deuteronomy 5:7).[1] The Shema, a verse that serves as the most important liturgical text in Judaism and introduces what Jesus (in Matthew 23:35–38 and Mark 12:28–30) calls "the great commandment," teaches: "Hear, O Israel: the LORD your God, the LORD is one!" (Deuteronomy 6:4).

A closer look reveals that the issue is less clear-cut than many presume. The Decalogue's wording does not deny the existence of "other gods"; it merely directs Israelites to have no relationship with them. The Shema's language is obscure: What does it mean to say that "the LORD is one"? According to some modern scholars, this line merely asserts that the God of Israel does not subdivide into local manifestations in the way many ancient Near Eastern deities did. In Mesopotamia there was a goddess Ishtar of Nineveh, an Ishtar of Arbela, and an Ishtar of Carchemish; in Canaan there were dozens of local Baal-Hadads; but, the Shema tells us, the LORD, the God of Israel, exists only in a single manifestation.[2] Even if one rejects this interpretation of Deuteronomy 6:4, understanding it instead to mean "The LORD is our God, the LORD alone,"[3] this verse may teach not that no other gods exist but that they are not Israel's deity. Further, in the Hebrew original the Shema, like the Decalogue, speaks not of "the LORD" but of "Yhwh,"[4] which is the personal name of the God of Israel. The use of a name to refer to this deity suggests that there may be other deities out there; names are necessary when we talk about a particular member of a larger class. In allowing for the possibility that additional heavenly beings exist, these two verses are not alone. The Hebrew Bible often refers to heavenly creatures other than Yhwh, calling them "gods" (Genesis 6:2; Psalms 29:1, 82:6, 86:8, 89:7; Job 1:6), "angels" (Numbers 20:16; 2 Samuel 24:16; 1 Kings 13:18; Zechariah 1:11–12; Psalm 78:49; Job 33:23), and "the council of holy ones" (Psalm 89:6–8).

Consequently, many modern biblical scholars contend that Israelite religion prior to the Babylonian exile was basically polytheistic. Pre-exilic texts from the Hebrew Bible, according to these scholars, are not genuinely monotheistic; the first monotheistic text in the Hebrew Bible is the block of material beginning in Isaiah 40, which was composed at the end of the Babylonian exile. Other scholars recognize the existence of a small minority of monotheists or protomonotheists late in the pre-exilic period but stress that the vast majority of ancient Israelites were polytheists before the exile. Another group of scholars, however, maintain that exclusive worship of Yhwh as the only true deity not only existed but was widespread in ancient Israel well before the exile.

In what follows, I enter this fray to argue that the Hebrew Bible is a monotheistic work and that its monotheism was not unusual for Israelite religion in the preexilic era. Even more importantly, however, I hope to give readers a sense of why this debate exists and why the evidence is subject to more than one interpretation. Before turning to that evidence, however, I need first of all to discuss how the term *monotheism* is most usefully defined. Further, I must explain the difference between asking whether ancient Israelite religion was monotheistic and asking whether the Hebrew Bible is monotheistic.

DEFINING MONOTHEISM

If *monotheism* means the belief that no heavenly beings exist other than the one God (as a common definition proposes), then the texts cited above make clear that the Hebrew Bible is not a monotheistic work. We may ask, however, how useful this definition of monotheism is. After all, Judaism, Christianity, and Islam all exhibit a belief in angels, beings who reside in heaven and who do not normally die. In the case of Catholic and Orthodox Christianity, we can also note a belief in saints residing in heaven, that is, humans whose death had no long-term impact on their continued existence and activity; death for them constituted nothing more than a change of venue from earth to heaven. Similar beliefs are attested, albeit in a less formalized way, in Judaism and Islam (especially in its Shiite and Sufi forms). Many Jews, Christians, and Muslims believe that one can direct prayer to these beings with realistic hope of the prayer's efficacy. The common definition of monotheism would require us to classify not only the Hebrew Bible but most forms of Judaism, Christianity, and Islam as polytheism. Such a definition fails to capture something essential that distinguishes these religions from classical Greek religion, Hinduism, and Shintoism. A category of polytheism that includes both Hinduism and Judaism, both the worship of the Greek pantheon and the worship of the biblical God, is so large as to be meaningless.

The neo-Kantian philosopher Hermann Cohen (1842–1918) and the biblical scholar Yehezkel Kaufmann (1889–1963) proposed a definition of monotheism that is more helpful. For Cohen, God's uniqueness rather than God's oneness is the essential content of monotheism.[5] What distinguishes the Bible from other religious texts known from the ancient world is not that the Bible denies that Marduk and Baal and Zeus exist—it does not—but that it insists that Yhwh is qualitatively different from all other deities: Yhwh is infinitely more powerful. Monotheism, then, is the belief that one supreme being exists, whose will is sovereign over all other beings. These other beings may include some who live in heaven and who are in the normal course of events immortal; but they are unalterably subservient to the one supreme being, except insofar as that being voluntarily relinquishes a measure of control by granting other beings free will. It is appropriate to term the supreme being the one God and the other heavenly beings gods or angels. In this definition of monotheism, it is not the number of divine beings that matters but the relations among them. A theology in which no one deity has ultimate power over all aspects of the world is *polytheistic*. A theology in which all power ultimately resides in one God is *monotheistic*—even if people pray to various heavenly beings to intercede on their behalf with the one God in whom all power ultimately resides.

One might be surprised at a definition of monotheism that allows for many gods, but further reflection shows that this definition is much more sensible than the common one. Let us imagine two theologies that recognize one supreme being as well as other beings who have some degree of free will. In one of these theologies, the other beings are immortal and live in heaven. In the other, they are mortal and live on earth, or they may be both mortal and immortal—that is, they may achieve immortality after dying. In both theologies the supreme being is not the only being who can have some effect on the universe; in both the subservient beings' free will constitutes a limitation, though a voluntary one, on the omnipotence of the supreme being. Now, according to the common definition, the first of these theologies is not monotheistic because the nonsupreme beings happen to live in heaven and are termed "gods" or "angels," but the second is monotheistic because these nonsupreme beings live on earth and are called "humans." The second definition sketched out above is more consistent: both theologies I just described are monotheistic, regardless of where the subservient beings live. There is no reason that we should find the existence of subservient beings in heaven any more surprising in monotheism than the existence of subservient beings on earth. It is this second definition of monotheism that I adopt in this essay.

I should note another term: *monolatry*, which scholars define in a number of ways. In this essay, I use it to refer to any religious system in which people worship one deity alone. As I use the term, monolatry is a broad category that can overlap with monotheism or with polytheism: monolatrous worshippers are exclusively loyal to one deity, whether or not they believe that deity is the only one with unalterable power. Thus a monolatrist as I use the term is either a *monotheistic monolatrist* (if he or she worships only one God because that God is unique in holding ultimate power) or a *polytheistic monolatrist* (if he or she worships a single deity while recognizing the genuine power of other deities and forces in the universe).

ISRAELITE RELIGION VERSUS BIBLICAL RELIGION

Ancient Israelite religion and the Hebrew Bible's religion are not the same thing. The latter represents a subset of the former or several closely related subsets. It is possible that the vast majority of ancient Israelites were polytheistic, while a small minority whose writings are preserved in the biblical canon were monotheistic. Consequently, in what follows I ask two questions. The first is, "Were the ancient Israelites monotheists?" To answer this question, we turn to biblical and archaeological data. The Hebrew Bible presents a picture of the religion practiced by Israelites, and that picture contains useful information (even though, as with any primary source, the data it presents must be viewed critically). The findings of archaeologists are also crucial for anyone attempting to portray the religious reality lived by men and women in ancient Israel (even though the data archaeology provides are much less explicit than the biblical data). The second question is, "Are the documents found in the Hebrew Bible monotheistic?" Answering this question is a matter of investigating the religious practices and beliefs the Hebrew Bible *prescribes* rather than the practices and beliefs it *describes*.

WERE THE ANCIENT ISRAELITES MONOTHEISTS?

Biblical texts provide a consistent answer to our first question: many Israelites—at times, most Israelites—were polytheistic. The book of Judges narrates a cycle of polytheistic worship by the Israelites, followed by punishment by Yhwh, forgiveness from Yhwh, and further polytheism on the people's part. The book of Kings emphasizes the polytheism of Israelites both north and south. It portrays some kings (Hezekiah and Josiah in the south, Jehu in the north) as exclusively loyal to Yhwh but describes others (Manasseh in the south, Ahab in the north) as encouraging the worship of many deities. Prophetic books from the era of the monarchy excoriate Israelites north and south for worshipping Baal and other gods and goddesses.

It is important to emphasize that the biblical texts largely portray the Israelites as polytheists because many modern scholars somehow assume that the biblical texts must say that the Israelites were monotheists. A depressingly large amount of scholarly writing on Israelite religion attempts to debunk the Bible by demonstrating something the Bible itself emphasizes: that Israel before the exile worshipped many gods. For example, William Dever asks why the biblical authors do not discuss the many female figurines found by archaeologists in Israelite sites, which

he understands to be images of a goddess. He maintains that their failure to mention these figurines results from their deliberate attempt to
suppress any reference to them: "They did not wish to acknowledge the
popularity and the powerful influence of these images."[6] However, biblical authors constantly acknowledge the widespread polytheism of Israelites, and they mention Israelite goddess worship specifically on a number of occasions (e.g., Jeremiah 7:18, 44:17–19). Israelite authors (rather
like many later Jewish and contemporary Israeli authors) love talking
about how awful their own people are; self-criticism, sometimes of an
exaggerated sort, is one of the most prominent hallmarks of biblical (and
later Jewish) literature. Consequently, the Bible's failure to discuss these
figurines may indicate that they did not portray a goddess (more on this
shortly). When Dever portrays the Bible as whitewashing Israelite history, he fails to attend to the fact that biblical authors are obsessed with
tarnishing Israelite history. Although they do not always realize it, scholars who argue that preexilic Israelites were polytheists seek not to overturn the biblical picture of Israelite religion but to confirm it. Conversely,
scholars who minimize the extent of preexilic polytheism reject the biblical picture as inaccurate or vastly overstated.[7]

What of the archaeological evidence? It is more mixed. Two types of
archaeological data suggest that polytheism was extremely rare in preexilic Israel, though not unheard of, while a third type may suggest that
Israelites worshiped a goddess.

The first sort of evidence comes from ancient Israelite inscriptions
(that is, from what scholars call *epigraphic* evidence) and especially
from the personal names they mention (that is, from what scholars call
onomastic evidence). Ancient Semites often gave their children names
that contain a statement about or prayer to a deity: thus in Mesopotamia
we know the name "Esarhaddon" (Akkadian, "Ashur-aḫa-idin"), which
means "[The god] Ashur has given a brother," and in Israel, "Jonathan"
(Hebrew, "Yehonatan"), which means "Yhwh has provided." (Names of
this sort are called *theophoric* names.) Several decades ago Jeffrey Tigay
studied the theophoric names Israelites gave their children throughout
the preexilic era, as evidenced not only in books of the Hebrew Bible but
also in archaeological finds that mention personal names (such as letters,
official documents, and personal seals).[8] The results, at least for someone inclined to trust the picture the Hebrew Bible paints of consistent

disloyalty to Yhwh, were surprising. Already centuries before the exile, personal names that mention the names of gods other than Yhwh are exceedingly rare. This finding suggests that worship of gods other than Yhwh may have been less common than the biblical texts lead us to believe. The censures of prophets and scribes whose work is found in the Bible, Tigay surmises, must have exaggerated the extent of the problem. Similarly, Patrick Miller has noted that even outside the evidence of personal names, "the weight of epigraphic data from the ninth through the sixth centuries BCE testifies in behalf of the 'Yhwh only' stream of Israelite religion, particularly but not only in the south. From the Mesha stele to the finds from Arad, Lachish, and Ramat Rachel, for example, Yhwh is the only named deity in Israelite inscriptions, and Yhwh's name is mentioned over 30 times."[9]

The second sort of evidence comes from ancient Israelite art. Over several decades, Othmar Keel built up a database of Israelite iconography, especially as evidenced by stamp seals. In ancient times people pressed seals over wax or clay to close a legal document that had been rolled up, thus protecting it from being tampered with, since one would have to break the seal to make any alteration to the document. These seals contained a short text (usually the name of the seal's owner), or some decoration, or both. Keel's database includes more than 8,500 seals from the area of ancient Canaan; some belonged to Israelites, and some to Phoenicians, other Canaanites, and Arameans. Comparing the Israelite and non-Israelite seals, Keel and his student Christoph Uehlinger noted a startling pattern. Non-Israelite seals portray a wide variety of deities; a single seal often portrays more than one deity. But Israelite seals tend not to portray more than one deity. This finding suggests that preexilic Israelites tended to obey the command, "You shall not have any gods other than Me" (Exodus 20:3; Deuteronomy 5:7). Further, Israelite seals almost never provide a picture of their deity; rather, the deity is represented symbolically, most often by a sun disk. This finding suggests that preexilic Israelites tended to obey the command, "You should not make any sculpted image or picture" of a deity (Exodus 20:4; Deuteronomy 5:8). Evidence of polytheism in ancient Israel does crop up here and there, especially in seals from the seventh century BCE, but much less frequently than in seals from other cultures. Other forms of art (statuary, graffiti on walls) provide similar evidence.[10] Precisely as Israel begins to emerge in the highlands of Canaan at the beginning of the Iron Age, anthropomorphic representations of deities become vastly less common in those highlands, though they never disappear completely.[11]

What would happen if we wrote a history of Israelite religion exclusively on the basis of the epigraphic, onomastic, and iconographic evidence, and not on the basis of the Hebrew Bible's testimony? A comparison of Israelite and non-Israelite artifacts would show a pronounced difference between Israelite religion and the religions of other ancient Near Eastern peoples.[12] This evidence suggests that, with important exceptions, Israelites tended to pray only to one deity, whereas other peoples—at least those peoples for whom we have sufficient epigraphic, onomastic, and iconographic evidence to come to a conclusion—prayed to many. These kinds of evidence suggest that Israelites were largely monolatrous. They do not allow us to decide whether their monolatry was monotheistic or polytheistic in nature.

Epigraphic, onomastic, and iconographic data are not the only types of archaeological evidence available, however. Small statues of female figures have been uncovered from ancient Israelite sites, and many scholars believe they demonstrate that Israelites worshipped a goddess or goddesses. These statues are found overwhelmingly in remains of Israelite homes, sometimes in graves, not in cultic sites or temples. They inform us about how religion was practiced in the ancient Israelite family, rather than about public or official cults sponsored by the king or by communal leaders. Three types of statues have been identified.[13]

First, a small number of figurines have been found in Israelite sites from the early Iron Age (thirteenth through eleventh century), the era in which Israel first began to emerge in the highlands of Canaan. These figurines depict a frontally nude woman whose genital triangle and labia are portrayed very prominently. These figurines resemble Canaanite statues of goddesses from the Late Bronze Age, and there is little doubt that, like their Late Bronze forebears, they represent a goddess who brings fertility. Statues of this kind from Israelite sites are rare, however, and they disappear as we get further into the Iron Age (when Israelite culture had solidified in central Canaan). The few found in the central areas of Canaan as late as the ninth century come from Philistine, not Israelite, sites. In light of these figurines it is clear that some of the earliest Israelites worshipped a goddess at the time of the Israelites' appearance in Canaan.

Second, figurines portraying a woman, usually clothed, holding a circular object have been found in Israelite sites from the tenth century on; most date to the seventh century. Scholars disagree about who this woman is and what she is holding. Dever argues that she is a goddess. Identifying the disk as a bread cake, he connects her with the worship of the Queen of Heaven condemned by the sixth-century prophet Jeremiah in 7:18 and 44:17–19.[14] Keel and Uehlinger, however, believe that these figurines depict a human female worshipper; the disk, they suggest, is a tambourine such as those used by Israelite women in song (Exodus 15:20; Judges 11:34; 1 Samuel 18:6). Thus these women depict human cult participants, not objects of worship. They do not provide evidence of Israelite worship of a goddess.[15]

Third, by far the most common figurines—literally hundreds have been found—depict a woman with prominent, often pendulous, breasts; unlike the figurines from the first category, these figurines do not display the woman's genitalia. At the bottom of these figurines one finds a sort of pedestal that resembles either a tree trunk or a woman's robe. It seems clear that they are associated not with sexual fertility but with nursing and maternal care. In the eyes of the ancients, these pendulous breasts were associated more with nursing than with sexuality.[16] These figurines, made of terra-cotta or clay, first appear in the archaeological record later than the first two types of figurines; most date to the eighth and seventh centuries BCE.

How did figurines of this third type function, and what did they depict? Keel and Uehlinger, who elsewhere highlight the monolatrous nature of Israelite worship, consider these objects to be representations of a goddess and hence of Israelite worship of more than one deity.[17] If so, the polytheism they evince was quite widespread in the eighth and seventh centuries (a finding that dovetails perfectly with the testimony of eighth- and seventh-century prophetic texts from the Hebrew Bible). Dever regards these figurines as talismans that worked magic, especially in difficult moments such as childbirth and caring for infants.[18] He sees this magical use as further evidence of Israelite polytheism, but here caution is called for. It is not clear that such a talisman in fact depicts a goddess; it is just as likely that it depicts a human female whose large breasts symbolize (or engender through sympathetic magic) a woman's ability to give birth and to nurture. Carol Meyers points out significant differences between these figurines and statues of goddesses known from ancient Canaan. Statues of the divine, Meyers notes, "normally exhibit some symbols of divine identity in headdress, garb, pose, or attached object. One should be skeptical about identifying any of these terracotta statues or related clay plaques with goddesses at all, let alone with any specific goddess such as Ishtar, Anat, or Asherah."[19]

If the iconography of these figurines imitated depictions of a goddess elsewhere in Canaan or the Near East, or if they were made from materials usually used for the production of divine images, we could confidently identify the figurines as a goddess. However, Keel and Uehlinger point out that no transition from other objects to these objects is evident (a point that opposes their own conclusion that the figurines represent a goddess).[20] Consequently, we should follow Meyers in identifying these objects as representations of human females or of the concept of the female and especially the maternal. Similarly, Tikva Frymer-Kensky maintains that "they are a visual metaphor, which shows in seeable and touchable form that which is most desired … a … tangible prayer for fertility and nourishment."[21]

Of course, if the objects depict human women (or represent their hopes to nurture) but were used for magical purposes, we may still ask whether their magical use provides evidence of Israelite polytheism. A moment's reflection will show that it does not. Within monotheistic religions magic is often condemned (see Exodus 22:17; Deuteronomy 18:10), but it is just as often practiced—by people who consider themselves (and are considered by others) loyal monotheists. Prominent rabbis, for example, have gained fame for producing amulets. Many rigorously religious Jews believe that unfortunate events in their lives result from having a defective *mezuzah* on their doorposts and can be reversed by repairing it. Some voices in Jewish tradition have condemned such practices and beliefs, but subsequent Jews who practiced what to outsiders appears to be magic managed to consider what they were doing as outside the category that earlier authorities had censured. Because most monotheistic authorities in antiquity and the Middle Ages did not deny magic's reality or effectiveness, many monotheists have practiced some magic. If the figurines in this third category were in fact used as Dever suggests, then their owners may have been no less monotheistic than enormous numbers of religious Jews, Christians, and Muslims in the postbiblical world.

Asherah Worship in Ancient Israel?

Another possible indicator of Israelite polytheism from the archaeological record should be addressed: the possibility that the goddess Asherah was popular among ancient Israelites. This Northwest Semitic goddess appears prominently in the Late Bronze Age texts from the northern Canaanite city of Ugarit. Devotion to Asherah declined precipitously at the end of the Late Bronze Age and in the Early Iron Age among Northwest Semites generally.[22] (This decline was part of a larger phenomenon throughout the Near East in the Late Bronze Age: the role of goddesses in polytheistic systems shrank in a widespread purge of the feminine from the realm of divinity.[23]) Consequently, some scholars wonder whether most Israelites even knew of the goddess's existence. The term *asherah* in the Bible in scripture usually refers to a wooden cult object (a pole or a tree), but in rare cases (1 Kings 18:19 and 2 Kings 23:4) it clearly refers to the goddess, showing that at the very least some Israelites knew that this word was the name of a goddess. Did Israelites worship her? Biblical verses like the two just cited maintain that some Israelites did. In addition, two pieces of archaeological evidence are especially relevant.

First, several eighth-century inscriptions from Kuntillet 'Ajrud and Khirbet el-Qom refer to "Yhwh and His *'asherah*." Does the term translated "His *'asherah*" in these Israelite inscriptions refer to the goddess or to the more commonly known wooden pole or tree? A number of scholars argue (to my mind convincingly) that the term cannot mean "His Asherah"—that is, it cannot consist of the goddess's name with the pronominal suffix meaning "His" attached. Pronominal suffixes never attach to proper names in Hebrew or other Canaanite languages. But this point is debated among scholars. If the term does refer to the goddess, then these inscriptions show that some eighth-century Israelites from both the north and the south regarded the goddess Asherah as Yhwh's wife, and the authors of these inscriptions present fine examples of Israelite polytheists.[24] If, as is more likely, the term refers to the cult object, then the eighth-century inscriptions do not provide direct evidence of Asherah worship among Israelites—though the mere fact of a cultic pole of a type that must once have been sacred to Asherah (as its name indicates) shows that Asherah worship must have played a role at some earlier stage in the religion of the Israelites or their forebears.

A second piece of evidence is a cult stand dating to the tenth century. (Cult stands were used in temples and other sacred sites to support bowls into which liquids or other gifts could be poured. Alternatively, they may have been used for burning incense.) This cult stand comes from Taʿanakh, a northern Israelite town. The Taʿanakh cult stand has four levels (see Figure 10.1). The lowest or first level depicts a female with

Figure 10.1. The Taʿanakh cult stand. Drawing by Ellen Holtzblatt.

prominent breasts and upraised arms touching two lions, one on each side. The next level as one moves up depicts two mixed creatures. They are known in Hebrew as *kerubim*, or cherubs; their bovine form, human faces, and wings match the description of cherubs in Ezekiel 1:5–11 and 10:15. They stand on each side of an empty space in the middle of this register. The third level depicts the same two lions found on the bottom level, but this time, in between them we find a tree with three leafy branches on each side of the trunk; two goats, one on each side, nibble the leaves. The fourth level shows two spiral scrolls next to the remains of another cherub on each side. In between the scrolls is a horse, on top of which sits a sun disk surrounded by rays of light.

Ruth Hestrin and John Glen Taylor suggest that the first and third levels depict one deity (who is surrounded by lions in both cases) while the second and fourth levels depict another deity (flanked by cherubs both times).[25] The second and fourth levels, with their cherubs, depict Yhwh. Many biblical texts associate Yhwh with cherubs: Yhwh rides on top of cherubim (1 Samuel 4:4; 2 Samuel 22:11; Ezekiel 9:3, 10:4; Psalms 80:2, 99:1), and Yhwh sits above statues of cherubim in the tabernacle and the Jerusalem Temple (Exodus 25–26; Numbers 7:89; 1 Kings 6–7). More specifically, in the top register Yhwh is represented symbolically by a sun disk. (The symbolic representation of Yhwh with the sun is widespread in the archaeological record; it is also known from a few biblical passages, such as Psalm 84:10–12.[26]) Taylor makes the brilliant proposal that the empty space surrounded by cherubs in the second level also represents Yhwh, "the unseen God who resides among the cherubim."[27] The portrayal of this Israelite deity, after all, is insistently prohibited in biblical law, and it is also exceedingly rare in the archaeological record. The large-breasted figure on the first level is a goddess who is associated with fertility and especially with maternal roles. In the third register we find the same goddess, this time depicted symbolically as a tree. Both because of the connection of the term *asherah* with trees and because of Asherah's maternal role (she is known as "mother of the gods" in Ugaritic literature), it is clear that the goddess on the first and third levels is Asherah.

The Ta'anakh cult stand is a fascinating example of early Israelite religion. It evinces the refusal to portray Yhwh's form so characteristic of biblical religion, but its aniconic religiosity is not monotheistic or even monolatrous. The cult stand pairs Yhwh with the goddess Asherah. Such a pairing is not surprising: Asherah was the wife of El in Ugarit, and both the name El and the imagery associated with him are attributed to Yhwh throughout the Hebrew Bible.[28] It is to be expected that some Israelites loyal to Yhwh assumed that Asherah must be His wife. If this interpretation of the cult stand is correct (I find it quite compelling), then at an early stage of Israelite history and at least in the north, the goddess Asherah was worshipped alongside Yhwh.

Were the Ancient Israelites Monotheists?

Both the archaeological evidence and biblical evidence give complex answers to the question, "Were the Israelites monotheistic?" While the Hebrew Bible claims that the ideal of monolatry or monotheism existed in the early preexilic period, it also claims that loyalty to this ideal was consistently inadequate. On the other hand, a great deal of archaeological evidence (epigraphic, onomastic, and iconographic data) suggests that most Israelites in the preexilic period worshipped only one deity. These data render plausible the biblical claim that the ideal of monolatry existed at an early period, but they shed doubt on the biblical claim that loyalty to the ideal was rare. By their nature, these archaeological data cannot make clear whether Israelites practiced monotheistic monolatry or polytheistic monolatry. Some of the pillar figurines may support the biblical picture of widespread polytheism among Israelites, especially in the eighth and seventh centuries—if we accept the suggestion that the figurines depict a goddess. But if they depict a human female and were used in sympathetic magic, then they do not provide evidence of polytheistic worship in domestic settings in ancient Israel. The tenth-century Taʿanakh stand and the thirteenth- through eleventh-century figurines of a naked fertility goddess clearly point to Israelite polytheism at the earliest stage of Israelite history. According to one interpretation of inscriptions from two sites, this worship may have persisted into the eighth century. This interpretation is linguistically problematic, but it may be bolstered by seventh-century biblical passages that condemn goddess worship among Israelites (2 Kings 23:4; Jeremiah 7:18, 44:17–19). In spite of differences, all this evidence allows us to speak of Israelite polytheism (whether it was rare or common, it clearly existed) and thus allows us to note areas of continuity between ancient Israel and the cultures of its neighbors. At the same time, the archaeological record allows us to speak of early preexilic Israelite monolatry as well and thus to note areas of discontinuity between Israel and most of its neighbors.

IS THE HEBREW BIBLE MONOTHEISTIC?

The Hebrew Bible demands that the Israelites render to Yhwh exclusive loyalty; the documents in this anthology repeatedly and insistently endorse monolatry. The question facing us is whether the monolatry they intend exemplifies what I referred to above as monotheistic monolatry or polytheistic monolatry. Do biblical texts imagine Yhwh to be unique among heavenly beings and in exclusive control of all powers in the universe? Or do they imagine Yhwh to be one among many deities, to whom, for a variety of historical reasons, the Israelites have pledged undivided fealty?

Poor Evidence for Biblical Monotheism

Some biblical texts seem at first glance to present Yhwh as genuinely unique and thus to exemplify monotheism. "Who is like you among the gods, Yhwh? Who is like you, exalted in holiness, acknowledged as awesome, performing wonders?" Moses and the Israelites sing at the shore of the Reed Sea (Exodus 15:11; cf. 1 Kings 8:23; Isaiah 40:18; Jeremiah 10:6–7; Psalms 35:10, 71:19, 89:9). Such a verse sounds tailor-made to exemplify monotheism as I have defined it, since it posits an essential distinction between Yhwh and all other heavenly beings. Indeed, this line appears in the daily liturgy of rabbinic Judaism, where it functions in a genuinely monotheistic way. But a line such as this does not always function in that way. Other ancient peoples (for example, in Sumerian and Akkadian liturgical texts) also laud various gods as incomparable.[29] This is the case not only in prayers to the heads of pantheons such as Ashur in Assyria and Marduk in Babylon but in prayers to other gods and goddesses as well. Consequently, we cannot cite verses such as

Exodus 15:11 as proof of early monotheism in Israel. Such a verse could have been recited by a monotheistic monolatrist, by a polytheistic monolatrist, or even by a nonmonolatrous polytheist.

The same may be said of biblical texts that stress Yhwh's kingship over the gods (such as Psalms 47:2–3, 95:3–5, and 96:4–5) and perhaps even those that maintain that Yhwh assigned other gods their roles (Deuteronomy 4:19; Deuteronomy 32:8–9 as preserved in the Dead Sea Scrolls and the Septuagint). These passages stress Yhwh's power in contrast to the relative weakness of other deities. Additional passages require other gods to praise the one true God (see Psalms 29:1–2, 103:20–22, 148:1–3). But similar lines occur regarding high gods of polytheistic pantheons. Thus in the Babylonian creation epic known as *Enuma Elish* the gods themselves praise Marduk as unrivaled and supreme (4:3–15). One might want to take the description of Marduk in these lines literally and therefore suggest that Marduk is being raised to the sort of level we associate with a monotheistic God. However, earlier in *Enuma Elish* the goddess Tiamat had spoken of Qingu in nearly identical terms when she acclaimed him king of the gods in 1:153–58. Qingu's command, which Tiamat claimed was unchangeable, did not in fact endure: like Tiamat, he died at the hand of Marduk. That the gods' guarantee of eternal power to Marduk is phrased in the same language as Tiamat's short-lived guarantee to Qingu suggests that we should read this sort of language with a grain of salt. This language is an exaggerated form of praise for whatever deity happened to be on the throne. As a result, we cannot be sure that similar lines from the book of Psalms and Deuteronomy are intended to posit an essential distinction between Yhwh and other gods of the sort that Hermann Cohen and Yehezkel Kaufmann require for their definition of monotheism.

One can imagine two models of divine kingship: a monotheistic one, in which members of a divine retinue praise the only God who has ever ruled and carry out that God's wishes; and a polytheistic one, in which the king is first among equals, mightiest to be sure, but in control of the universe neither automatically nor permanently. The divine retinue of the monotheistic God resembles the American cabinet, where secretaries of various departments carry out the president's policies and serve at the president's whim. The polytheistic pantheon recalls the British cabinet, in which each minister may have an independent power base, and all cabinet members, the prime minister included, may be dismissed by lower-ranking politicians in Parliament—though this will involve struggle; ministers can also be dismissed (at least in theory) by a higher and more august, if otiose, authority. The conceptual distinction is clear, but which model do we have in a given piece of literature? The pantheons of Canaan, Greece, and Mesopotamia were clearly polytheistic. Each had a high god, but none of their gods would be called supreme or all-powerful in the monotheistic sense. Even the high god or goddess could be seriously challenged, and indeed kingship did pass from one god to another, sometimes peacefully (from Enlil and Anu to Marduk, as described in the preface to Ḥammurapi's legal collection), sometimes violently (from Baal to Mot and vice versa in the Ugaritic *Baal Cycle* or from Tiamat to Marduk in *Enuma Elish*). But what of the biblical material? Because the vocabulary describing the divine retinue known to us from the Hebrew Bible resembles language depicting the pantheon of Canaanite religion, and because the Israelite conception grew out of the Canaanite, the possibility that biblical texts describing a divine council are polytheistic must be taken seriously.

Strong Evidence for Biblical Monotheism

Two sorts of evidence, however, can demonstrate the monotheism of the biblical authors: first, consistent differences between biblical depictions of other gods and Canaanite and Mesopotamian depictions of gods; and second, the different ways these literatures describe the relationship of their high gods to the world. My reasoning in this matter largely follows the still unsurpassed discussion of this issue by Yehezkel Kaufmann.[30]

The divine retinue we know from the Hebrew Bible differs from those of Mesopotamian, Canaanite, and Greek literature because lower beings never successfully or even realistically challenge Yhwh in the Hebrew Bible. Numerous texts from non-Israelite cultures narrate conflicts in which a high god is either seriously threatened or overthrown. At the beginning of the Akkadian *Atraḫasis* epic, the lower-ranking Igigi gods revolt against the higher-ranking Anunnaki gods. The first half of the Babylonian creation epic, *Enuma Elish*, tells the stories of two successive revolts by younger gods against older ones, whom the younger ones kill. The Ugaritic *Baal Cycle* describes the conflicts of a young god, Baal, with his peers Yam (whom he slays) and Mot (at whose hands he dies, though he comes back to life when his sister Anat kills Mot). In Hesiod's *Theogony* Kronos violently usurps the kingship of his father, Ouranos, only to be deposed by his own son Zeus. Especially revealing in these texts are scenes of fear and trembling in the councils of the gods. In *Atraḫasis* 1:193–95, the lowly Igigi genuinely frighten mighty Enlil. The older and younger gods are terrified of each other in *Enuma Elish* 1:57–58; 2:5–6, 49–52; 3:125–29; 4:67–70, 87–90, and 107–9. Yam's demands provoke real dismay at the council of El (see *Baal Cycle* 1.2.i.21–25).[31] These battles among gods and goddesses are real struggles; none of the deities involved knows the outcome in advance, because both sides have genuine power.

The divine council depicted in the Hebrew Bible is something else altogether. In Psalm 29 and Isaiah 6, the divine retinue exists to praise Yhwh, not to battle Him. In Genesis 1:26, they are informed, but not really consulted, regarding the creation of humanity. In 1 Kings 22, Isaiah 6, and Isaiah 40, the retinue is called on to relay Yhwh's messages. It is significant that in these three last texts (and also Zechariah 3) a human being sits in on the council's meeting—a circumstance that underscores the fact that humanity and the gods/angels are basically on the same level in Hebrew scripture, linked with each other in their ontological difference from Yhwh. This differentiation, in which Yhwh stands unique on one side and humans and other gods are together on the other, is the essence of monotheism. This ontological similarity of humanity and the gods becomes apparent in Psalm 29:1–2 and Psalm 103:20–22, in which humans call out to the gods to praise Yhwh, just as humans call on each other to praise Yhwh in most psalms of praise. Here the human beings are on the same level as the gods or angels; indeed, the humans are a little higher than the angels, whom they lead in worship.

Even a large sample of biblical literature fails to turn up any examples of genuine struggle on Yhwh's part against those who rise up against Him, while Canaanite, Mesopotamian, and Greek literatures abound with examples of real combat among the gods. To be sure, biblical texts describe a conflict between Yhwh, on the one hand, and the Sea and his helpers, on the other: famous examples include Isaiah 27:1, 51:9–11; Habakkuk 2:8–9; Psalms 74:13–15, 89:6–14; and Job 26:5–13. These passages use terms that also appear in the Ugaritic myth in which Baal defeats Yam or Sea. The biblical texts differ from their Ugaritic parallels in crucial respects. They describe a doomed revolt against a deity who is already in charge, a revolt Yhwh puts down without any difficulty. These passages lack drama, for they convey no sense that Yhwh has to exert Himself to suppress the insurrection. Baal and Marduk, Zeus and Kronos, toil in order to attain an exalted status; Yhwh has that status to begin with and retains it with ease. The texts describing Yhwh's conflict with the Sea in Isaiah, Habakkuk, Psalms, and Job remind us of the older myth in order to make clear to us precisely what story is *not* being told: to wit, a genuine theomachy.

Thus it is difficult to imagine Yhwh, confronted by any other being, smiting His thigh and biting His lip like Anshar when he hears of Tiamat's war plans (*Enuma Elish* 2:50). Yhwh never feels threatened by a workers' revolt to the point of bursting out in tears like Enlil (*Atraḥasis* 1:167). Nor can one imagine Yhwh being intimidated into agreeing to another being's demand by threats of violence against Yhwh, in contrast to El in the Baal texts (*Baal Cycle* 1.2.i.30–38 and 1.3.v.19–29).[32] God can be moved to action by prayer, but this involves no threat against Yhwh. In sum, similar terminology is used to describe Yhwh's council and pagan pantheons, but this resemblance hardly shows that the respective theologies are identical. In almost no biblical texts is there any sense that Yhwh's authority, like Tiamat's or Enlil's, El's or Baal's, is contingent. There may be hints of such a view in the Bible here and there. Yhwh seems to feel threatened by humankind in Genesis 11:6 (an obscure verse in any event) and in Genesis 6:1–4. Even these verses, however, do not regard any other force as superior to or mightier than Yhwh. Further, when reading narratives that give a sense that some being or force opposes Yhwh, we need to recall that we are in fact reading narrative—a text with a plot and, hence, with conflict. If there is to be a monotheistic narrative, it is inevitable that this narrative will give some sense that the one God's power is at least temporarily challenged.[33]

Similarly, we are never told that Yhwh ascended at some point in time to the role He has throughout the Hebrew Bible.[34] It is important to stress this point, since without it one could formulate a facile argument that Yhwh is merely another high god like Marduk, Baal, or Zeus. Mesopotamian, Canaanite, and Greek texts tell us that the high god took over his role at some point in time, whereas Yhwh is the high god from the opening verses of the Hebrew Bible. In Mesopotamia and Canaan, the primary sources themselves tell us that the high god received another god's office; to take one example, the prologue to Ḥammurapi's Laws announces that Anu and Enlil have raised up Marduk to leadership of the gods. As a result, Babylonian texts speak of Marduk (and other deities and even temples of these deities) as possessing what they call "Enlil-status" and "Anu-status" (*illilūtu* and *anūtu*, both of which are usually translated as "authority"). These texts openly describe one deity taking over the functions of another because from their point of view both gods exist, even if practically speaking Marduk is the one who primarily matters for the present. In the case of the Hebrew Bible, modern scholars had to work to discover how Israelites applied to Yhwh vocabulary once associated with other gods. The biblical texts themselves do not reveal this theological background, because as far as they are concerned this theological background does not exist.

Kaufmann emphasizes a further difference between the gods of pagan religions and Yhwh in the Hebrew Bible.[35] Pagan gods were created or born from something prior to them. All the gods to whom hymns and sacrifices are offered are younger than the world itself. The regnant gods never belong to the earliest generation of beings. In *Enuma Elish* Apsu and Tiamat give rise to Laḫmu and Laḫahamu, who generate Anshar and Kishar; they beget Anu, whose son Ea kills his great-grandfather Apsu; subsequently, Ea's son Marduk kills Tiamat to gain dominion over the cosmos. In Hesiod's *Theogony*, Gaia (Earth) mates with her eldest son, Ouranos (Sky), to produce the generation of Titans, of whom the youngest is Kronos; Kronos, plotting with his mother against his father, achieves dominion by castrating him; Kronos then maintains control by eating his own children, the Olympians; his son Zeus is saved, however, and grows up to lead the Olympians in warfare against the Titans, whom Zeus eventually imprisons in Tartarus, whereupon he gains sovereignty. Similar narratives are found, with various permutations, in Sumerian and Hittite mythology. What is striking is not only the recurring motif of patricidal, matricidal, and filicidal conflict but the youth of the gods who are described as currently holding power. The gods in charge of the world are part of creation rather than older than it, for all these gods had a moment of origin; the world once existed without them. But in Hebrew scripture, the world never exists without Yhwh. The Bible contains no stories of this deity's birth to another god or generation from earlier matter.

Kaufmann emphasizes the special importance of the relationship between Yhwh and matter and, more broadly, between Yhwh and other forces in the universe.[36] In polytheistic theologies, the gods are subject to matter and to forces stronger than themselves. The gods' power is great, but that power largely derives from their ability to manipulate matter through special techniques, especially the use of language and ritual. Thus Ea and Belet-ili use incantations to create humanity in *Atraḥasis*. These same techniques, usually termed magic, are available to humanity as well. Of course human beings' mastery of these techniques pales in comparison with that of the gods, but the difference is one of quantity rather than quality. In Mesopotamian religion, there exists a realm of power independent of, and greater than, the realm of divinity. It is for this reason that in some Mesopotamian texts, humans attempt to ward off evil without turning in any significant way to the gods. In texts such as the *Namburbi* rituals humans attempt not to influence gods but to control powers inherent in the stuff of the universe. In omen literature such as *Šumma izbu*, humans attempt to gain access to information about the future by attending to unusual events or by examining entrails of animals slaughtered for this purpose. Such information is part of the complex and intricately interconnected structure of the cosmos rather than information inscribed into the universe by the gods: thus a particular oddity might be present in the liver of a calf not because a god put it there to warn humanity of a coming famine but because that particular oddity happens to correlate with crop failures for reasons beyond our understanding. The role of the gods, when they are mentioned in texts of this kind, is merely to aid the humans in accessing those powers, which transcend even the gods' realms but are better understood by the gods than by humans.[37]

Classical Greek sources articulate the same idea more explicitly. A proverb cited by Herodotus (*History* 1.91.1) states that nobody, not even a god, can escape his or her destined lot (μοῖραν). Plato quotes the same proverb (*Laws* 5.741), using the term *necessity* (ἀνάγκην) rather than μοῖρα. The character Prometheus states baldly in Aeschylus's *Prometheus*

Bound 515–20 that Zeus is less powerful than the three Fates (Μοῖραι) and the Furies (Ἐρινύες), who are the controllers of necessity (ἀνάγκης). Thus Walter Otto can assert:

> Sometimes it is said that the gods "can do all things," but a glance at the stories of the gods shows that this is not to be taken literally. Their one-ness with nature would of itself contradict their ability to do all things.... There is a fixed limit to their power, a basic "so far and no farther." ... In the *Odyssey* Athena herself says: "Death is certain, and when a man's fate (Moira) has come, not even the gods can save him, no matter how they may love him" [*Odyssey* 3:236].... [The gods] themselves sometimes avow that they are subject to destiny's decree. This decree is not only with-drawn from the gods' sphere of authority once and for all; it is essentially different from the functions of the gods.[38]

Fate, like matter, precedes the gods. When personified, it is usually asso-ciated with the pre-Olympians. Thus Hesiod tells us (*Theogony* 217) that Fate is the daughter of Night, indicating that Fate is older than Zeus and the gods who are his siblings and children. The relationship is not completely straightforward; Hesiod also tells us that the Fates can be described as Zeus's daughters (*Theogony* 904). Hesiod does not contra-dict himself here; rather, he acknowledges the great power of the gods, who can on occasion decree a fate, even as he makes clear that ultimately the gods themselves are subject to its decrees and cannot overturn them even when their own favorites are concerned.

The Hebrew Bible presumes an entirely different sort of relationship between divinity and powers present in the cosmos. Yhwh's will is never frustrated by forces of nature, by matter, or by other gods. Only in one area can Yhwh be thwarted: by human free will. This exception results from Yhwh's own decision to create beings who can choose for good and for ill. Yhwh's single limitation in the Hebrew Bible is self-imposed, but the limitations on the gods in polytheistic texts are often the result of forces beyond themselves. There may be one additional limit to Yhwh's will that Kaufmann did not acknowledge, but it, too, is rooted in Yhwh's own person. Moshe Halbertal and Avishai Margalit point out:

> The God of the Bible is free from nature and fate, but he is not free from emotional tendencies. In modern terms we would say that he is free of

physics and biology, but not of psychology.... In recognizing that God is independent from the world in terms of nature and fate Kaufmann discovered a deep and important distinction between paganism and the monotheistic religions.... There is, however, an emotional interdependency that involves God in a complex relationship with the world.... This dependency is not a causal subjection like the subjection of the gods to nature and fate in myth, and so Kaufmann's significant distinction remains intact.[39]

The Hebrew Bible's distinctive account of the relationship between divinity and powers inhering in the cosmos stands behind its rejection of the entire category of magic. The nature of this rejection needs to be carefully described, however, if we are to avoid misunderstanding. The authors of the Hebrew Bible did not regard magic as nonsense. Like everyone else in the ancient world, they believed that magic was real: human beings could use specific language and behaviors to gain access to powers inhering in the universe. The biblical authors believed that these powers were limited, however, because Yhwh was in no way subject to them. (Contrast the devastating effect of incantations on Tiamat or Qingu in *Enuma Elish* 4:60–62 and 153.) Biblical authors insisted that followers of Yhwh should not use magic (Exodus 22:17; Deuteronomy 18:10), because using magic was an act of disloyalty toward the God whose power outshone it. Magical practices among followers of Yhwh are not necessarily from the biblical point of view indications of polytheism; they are, rather, indications of sin. (Similarly, an Israelite or a Jew might eat pork, but this does not demonstrate that this person is a polytheist; rather, he or she may be a monotheist who is missing a mark.)

One final contrast between polytheistic literature and the Hebrew Bible is arresting. While the Hebrew Bible mentions the existence of other gods, those other gods never appear in biblical narrative as independent actors.[40] The gods of other nations are real; their authority over those nations, according to texts such as Deuteronomy 4:19–20 and 32:8–9 (LXX), is genuine. But these gods are never sufficiently important to appear as characters with their own names. It is within the realm of the imaginable that Moab's Kemosh is one of the members of the divine council portrayed in 2 Kings 22 or that Assyria's Ashur is among those called on to shout out Yhwh's praises in Psalm 29. Nevertheless, the biblical text portrays them only as part of an anonymous mass. Never do other nations' deities interact with Yhwh or contact human beings on their own in biblical narrative. Even the few apparent exceptions to this rule are instructive: Kemosh is described as a real actor twice, in Numbers 21:29 and Judges 11:24. In both cases it is not the biblical narrator who speaks; rather, Israelite characters in the narrative mention Kemosh when addressing a foreign audience (in the former, anonymous bards address the Moabites; in the latter, Jephthah addresses the Ammonites).[41] Second Kings 3:27 is the closest the Hebrew Bible comes to acknowledging real power from another god; even this verse, which describes a rite of child sacrifice performed by a Moabite king, does not give the name of the god and does not state that it was that god who dictated the final outcome of the events. A crucial text that acknowledges the existence of these beings, Deuteronomy 4, not only refuses to give us their names but refrains from applying the term *god* to them at all, thus removing them from the realm of the sacred and reducing them to mere secular beings.

What I have constructed in this section is an argument from silence: the absence of crucial elements found in the polytheistic religions of Israel's neighbors leads me to conclude that the Hebrew Bible exemplifies monotheism and not merely monolatry. In regard to any one text, such an argument lacks validity. We cannot say definitively that Exodus 15:11, or Exodus 20:2–3, or Psalm 82 or 96, on its own, must be a monotheistic text. But when we examine a wide variety of biblical texts from several genres (narrative, law, prophecy, prayer), the consistent omission of unambiguous polytheistic themes is revealing, and in such a case, an argument from silence is legitimate. Here a caveat is necessary: we cannot enter the head of every Israelite who uttered or heard these texts. Were there worshippers of Yhwh who understood some of these texts in a polytheistic manner? No doubt there were. Some texts within the Hebrew Bible on their own can be understood in a polytheistic fashion if one so chooses. But the fact that the Hebrew Bible as a whole fails to attest any examples that *must* be read in a polytheistic fashion justifies the conclusion that this anthology as a whole is a monotheistic one and that all these texts in their canonical context are monotheistic.[42]

MONOTHEISM, POLYTHEISM, AND OTHER POLARITIES

In spite of the similarities of language, poetic style, narrative structure, and ritual program so manifest between biblical documents and other ancient Near Eastern texts, a scholar who attends to large amounts of texts from both sets of cultures cannot but be struck by the failure of the former to display a host of motifs repeatedly present in the latter. It is precisely the strong similarities between these corpora that make the absence so striking. The motifs in question center around the issue of how the cosmos and its powers relate to divinity. Attending to these motifs, we can identify two types of thinking in these bodies of literature. In one, which I term polytheism, divinity is subject to the cosmos and its powers, even if it excels at manipulating those powers; this sort of thinking pervades nonbiblical literature from the ancient Near East. In the other type of thinking, which I term monotheism, divinity is not subject to the cosmos and its powers, except when divinity voluntarily limits its might to allow freedom of action for some of the creatures it has fashioned; this thinking pervades the Hebrew Bible.

The question addressed here, then, is one of distinction: Are there respects in which the Hebrew Bible differs fundamentally from its environment? Biblical scholars in the first three-quarters of the twentieth century tended strongly to stress discontinuities between Israel and its surrounding cultures, and this overpronounced tendency left subsequent scholars wary of this question. But a past obsession with this theme need not lead us to slight its importance. Biblical religion does in fact distinguish itself from other religions of the ancient Near East in its perception of one God as the exclusive creator of a world over which that God has complete control.

At the same time, noting an element that distinguishes biblical religion from the religions of Canaan, Greece, and Mesopotamia should not blind us to other possible distinctions and connections, which we might miss if we simply lump Canaanite, Greek, and Mesopotamian religion under the broad category of "polytheism." It is just as important to ask what makes a given polytheistic religion distinctive, what elements link certain polytheistic religions to each other and not to others, or what elements link a polytheistic religion and a monotheistic one. For example, one might argue that Canaanite and Sumerian polytheisms share significant features that are largely lacking in Assyrian and Babylonian religion; these include a stress on fertility and repetition and the vulnerability or even mortality present in the realm of the divine. Similarly, in significant respects some forms of biblical monotheism are very close to Canaanite and Mesopotamian polytheism. Elsewhere I have shown that biblical texts debate each other regarding the nature of God's body; biblical texts on one side of this debate share core theological insights with Canaanite and Mesopotamian texts, while biblical traditions on the other side share an approach found in classical Greek religion.[43] That debate, then, defies the basic polarity between monotheism and polytheism. The term *monotheism* can be meaningfully employed in discussing Israelite religion: this term has explanatory power that helps us see how Israelite religion differs crucially from its environment. Nevertheless, studying the Hebrew Bible within its own cultural context also suggests that the polarity between monotheism and polytheism is of less explanatory value than many students of religion suppose—or at least that it can obscure connections of great interest that cross over that division. The terms *monotheist* and *polytheist* are useful starting places for a historian of religion, but they are no more than that.

NOTES

This essay is based on the appendix of Benjamin Sommer, *The Bodies of God and the World of Ancient Israel* (New York: Cambridge University Press, 2009), pp. 145–74. The most apt comment on the secondary literature relevant to this essay is found in the Bible itself, at Ecclesiastes 12:12. Consequently, the items cited here, and even the 251 items cited in the appendix to my earlier book, are intended to give readers some sense of the secondary literature; they are in no way comprehensive.

1. All biblical translations are mine.

2. For this reading of Deuteronomy 6:4, see, e.g., William Bade, "Der Mono-yhwhwismus des Deuteronomiums," *Zeitschrift für die alttestamentliche Wissenschaft* 30 (1910): pp. 81–90; Peter Höffken, "Eine Bemerkung zum religionsgeschichtliche Hinterngrund von Dtn 6,4," *Biblische Zeitschrift* 28 (1984): pp. 88–93.

3. As do medieval commentators such as Rasbham and ibn Ezra, as well as many modern scholars; see, e.g., S. R. Driver, *Deuteronomy*, 3rd ed. (Edinburgh: T&T Clark, 1902), pp. 89–90.

4. Following Jewish tradition, I do not pronounce this name out loud, nor do I write it out completely, instead writing only its consonants. The vowels in the name were an *a*, as in "father," after the *Y* and an *e*, as in "red," after the *w*.

5. Hermann Cohen, *Religion of Reason out of the Sources of Judaism*, Simon Kaplan, trans. (Atlanta: Scholars Press, 1995), pp. 35–49. Detailed references to Kaufmann appear below.

6. William Dever, *Did God Have a Wife? Archaeology and Folk Religion in Ancient Israel* (Grand Rapids, Mich.: William B. Eerdmans, 2005), p. 184.

7. This is in fact the claim of Yehezkel Kaufmann, *Toledot Ha-Emunah Ha-Yisraelit*, 4 vols. (Jerusalem: Mosad Bialik and Devir, 1937–56), 1:661–63; and of Jeffrey Tigay, "Israelite Religion: The Onomastic and Epigraphic Evidence," in P. D. Miller, P. D. Hanson, and S. D. McBride, eds., *Ancient Israelite Religion: Essays in Honor of Frank Moore Cross* (Philadelphia: Fortress Press, 1987), pp. 179–80. See also William Propp, "Monotheism and 'Moses': The Problem of Early Israelite Religion," *Ugarit-Forschungen* 31 (1999): pp. 546–51.

8. Tigay, "Israelite Religion," pp. 157–94.

9. Patrick D. Miller, "The Absence of the Goddess in Israelite Religion," in *Israelite Religion and Biblical Theology* (Sheffield: Sheffield Academic Press, 2000), p. 198 n. 2.

10. Othmar Keel and Christoph Uehlinger, *Gods, Goddesses, and Images of God in Ancient Israel* (Minneapolis: Fortress Press, 1998), esp. pp. 173–74, 277–81, 306–16, 323–49, 354–67.

11. William Dever, "Material Remains and the Cult of Ancient Israel," in Carol L. Meyers and Michael O'Conor, eds., *The Word of the Lord Shall Go Forth: Essays in Honor of David Noel Freedman* (Winona Lake, Ind.: Eisenbrauns, 1983), pp. 574, 582–83 n. 12; Ronald S. Hendel, "The Social Origins of the Aniconic Tradition in Early Israel," *Catholic Biblical Quarterly* 50 (1988): p. 367. On early Israelite aversion to image worship, see the classic study of Tryggve Mettinger, *No Graven Image? Israelite Aniconism in Its Ancient Near Eastern Context* (Stockholm: Almqvist och Wiksell, 1995), and references in the "Further Reading" section of this chapter.

12. Propp, "Monotheism and 'Moses.'"

13. This classification follows Dever, *Did God Have a Wife?*, pp. 176–79.

14. Ibid., pp. 177–79.

15. Keel and Uehlinger, *Gods, Goddesses, and Images of God in Ancient Israel*, pp. 164–66.

16. Carol Meyers, *Discovering Eve: Ancient Israelite Women in Context* (New York: Oxford University Press, 1988), p. 162; Dever, *Did God Have a Wife?*, p. 187.

17. Keel and Uehlinger, *Gods, Goddesses, and Images of God in Ancient Israel*, pp. 333–36.

18. Dever, *Did God Have a Wife?*, pp. 187–88.

19. Meyers, *Discovering Eve*, p. 162.

20. Keel and Uehlinger, *Gods, Goddesses, and Images of God in Ancient Israel*, p. 329. Contrast the clear continuity, albeit with specific areas of innovation, between the naked figurines (from category 1 above) with Late Bronze Canaanite figures; see ibid., p. 163.

21. Tikva Frymer-Kensky, *In the Wake of the Goddesses. Women, Culture, and the Biblical Transformation of Pagan Myth* (New York: Free Press, 1992), p. 159.

22. Saul M. Olyan, *Asherah and the Cult of Yhwh in Israel* (Atlanta: Scholars Press, 1988), pp. 36–37.

23. Keel and Uehlinger (*Gods, Goddesses, and Images of God in Ancient Israel*, pp. 96–97, 128–31, 174–75) document this phenomenon in the Northwest Semitic sphere

using iconographic evidence; Frymer-Kensky (*In the Wake of the Goddesses*, pp. 70–80) documents the phenomenon in Mesopotamia using literary evidence.

24. Kuntillet ʿAjrud was a caravan station in the Sinai desert utilized by northern Israelite traders; Khirbet el-Qom is located in Judah.

25. Ruth Hestrin, "The Cult Stand from Taʿanach and Its Religious Background," in E. Lipiński, ed., *Phoenicia and the East Mediterranean in the First Millennium B.C.* (Leuven: Uitgeverij Peeters, 1987), pp. 67–71, 74; and John Glen Taylor, *Yhwh and the Sun: Biblical and Archaeological Evidence for Sun Worship in Ancient Israel* (Sheffield: JSOT Press, 1993), pp. 28–37.

26. Mark Smith, "The Near Eastern Background of Solar Language for Yhwh," *Journal of Biblical Literature* 109 (1990): pp. 29–39; Bernd Janowski, "JHWH und der Sonnengott. Aspekte der Solarisierung JHWHs in vorexilischer Zeit," in *Die rettende Gerechtigkeit* (Neukirchen, Germany: Neukirchener, 1999), pp. 192–219; Taylor, *Yhwh and the Sun*, pp. 24–26; Martin Arneth, *"Sonne der Gerechtigkeit": Studien zur Solarisierung der Jhwhe-Religion im Lichte von Psalm 72* (Wiesbaden: Harrassowitz, 2000), pp. 1–17, 109–31. Biblical authors describe solar worship in the Jerusalem Temple in several passages (2 Kings 23:11; Ezekiel 6:1–7 and 8:16). The authors of Kings and the prophet Ezekiel regard this worship with horror, but the worshippers they condemn for disloyalty to Yhwh probably did not see themselves as worshipping a foreign deity. Rather, they may have intended to bow down to Yhwh as a sun-god or in His manifestation in the sun.

27. Taylor, *Yhwh and the Sun*, pp. 29–30. See further Judith Hadley, *The Cult of Asherah in Ancient Israel and Judah* (Cambridge: Cambridge University Press, 2000), pp. 169–76.

28. Frank Moore Cross, *Canaanite Myth and Hebrew Epic* (Cambridge: Harvard University Press, 1973), pp. 44–60; Mark Smith, *The Origins of Biblical Monotheism: Israel's Polytheistic Background and the Ugaritic Texts* (New York: Oxford University Press, 2001), pp. 139–48.

29. C. J. Labuschagne, *The Incomparability of Yhwh in the Old Testament* (Leiden: E. J. Brill, 1966), pp. 34–66; Morton Smith, "The Common Theology of the Ancient Near East," *Journal of Biblical Literature* 71 (1952): pp. 138–40.

30. Kaufmann, *Toledot*, 1:221–417; English abridgment: Yehezkel Kaufmann, *The Religion of Israel: From Its Beginnings to the Babylonian Exile*, Moshe Greenberg, trans. and abr. (Chicago: University of Chicago Press, 1960), pp. 7–149.

31. For translations, see the rendering of Dennis Pardee in William Hallo and Lawson Younger, eds., *The Context of Scripture: Canonical Compositions from the Biblical World* (Leiden: Brill, 2003), p. 246b; and that of Mark Smith in Simon Parker, ed., *Ugaritic Narrative Poetry* (Atlanta: Scholars Press, 1997), p. 99.

32. See El's capitulation to Yam, in Pardee's translation in Hallo and Younger, *Context of Scripture*, p. 246b; and in Mark Smith's translation in Parker, *Ugaritic Narrative Poetry*, pp. 100–101. See also El's capitulation to Anat's threat of violence in Pardee, in Hallo and Younger, *Context of Scripture*, p. 254b; and Smith, in Parker, *Ugaritic Narrative Poetry*, p. 105.

33. Propp, "Monotheism and 'Moses,'" p. 566 n. 142.

34. A single biblical exception may appear in Psalm 82, if one follows the reading suggested by Mark Smith (*Origins of Biblical Monotheism*, pp. 155–57). In Smith's plausible reading, Psalm 82 is genuinely polytheistic. But if one follows the equally plausible

reading of the poem put forward in Matitiahu Tsevat, "God and the Gods in Assembly," in *The Meaning of the Book of Job and Other Biblical Studies* (New York: Ktav Publishing House, 1980), pp. 155–76, Psalm 82 is monotheistic. Within the context of the Psalter, the latter reading is stronger.

35. Kaufmann, *Toledot*, 1:245, 419–22.

36. Ibid., 1:245, 447–48.

37. H. W. F. Saggs, *The Encounter with the Divine in Mesopotamia and Israel* (London: Athlone Press, 1978), pp. 131–33.

38. Walter F. Otto, *The Homeric Gods*, Moses Hadas, trans. (New York: Thames and Hudson, 1979), pp. 263–64. See also Albert Henrichs, "Moira," in *Der Neue Pauly. Enzyklopädie der Antike* (Stuttgart: J. B. Metzler, 2000), 8:340–43.

39. Moshe Halbertal and Avishai Margalit, *Idolatry*, Naomi Goldblum, trans. (Cambridge: Harvard University Press, 1992), pp. 72–73. See further Yochanan Muffs, *The Personhood of God* (Woodstock, Vt.: Jewish Lights, 2005).

40. Kaufmann, *Toledot*, 1:276.

41. Propp, "Monotheism and 'Moses,'" p. 553 n. 73.

42. Thus it is possible that some texts (e.g., Exodus 15:11; Psalm 82) now found in the anthology called the Hebrew Bible functioned polytheistically for some Israelites. But in the absence of clear examples of polytheism in the anthology, when read in their current setting (as opposed to a hypothetical earlier setting we can imagine), they are monotheistic.

43. Sommer, *Bodies of God and the World of Ancient Israel*, pp. 12–79, 173–74.

BIBLIOGRAPHIC ESSAY

Many readers find overviews of the history of Israelite religion a useful resource. A judicious summary is Patrick D. Miller, *The Religion of Ancient Israel* (Louisville, Ky.: Westminster John Knox Press, 2000). Also useful is Rainer Albertz, *A History of Israelite Religion in the Old Testament Period*, vol. 1 (Louisville, Ky.: Westminster John Knox Press, 1994).

The most productive definition of monotheism for biblical studies is found in Hermann Cohen, *Religion of Reason out of the Sources of Judaism*, Simon Kaplan, trans. (Atlanta: Scholars Press, 1995), pp. 35–49. A similar idea, termed "diffused monotheism," is discussed in E. Bolaji Idowu, *Olódùmarè: God in Yoruba Belief* (London: Longmans, 1962), pp. 202–4 and, in greater detail, pp. 48–70 and 140–43. The classic application of this approach to biblical texts is Yehezkel Kaufmann, *The Religion of Israel: From Its Beginnings to the Babylonian Exile*, Moshe Greenberg, trans. and abr. (Chicago: University of Chicago Press, 1960), pp. 7–149. Individual arguments Kaufmann makes for the early dating of biblical monotheism have been critiqued, sometimes justifiably. Other issues, such as the place of myth in Israelite religion, could be stated in a more nuanced form. Nevertheless, Kaufmann's fundamental insight about the distinction between polytheism and monotheism and the absence of the former in biblical texts remains compelling. On Kaufmann's approach and his connection with Hermann Cohen, see Job Jindo, "Concepts of Scripture in Yehezkel Kaufmann," in Benjamin Sommer, ed., *Jewish Concepts of Scripture* (New York: New York University Press, 2012), pp. 230–46; Eliezer Schweid, "Biblical Critic or Philosophical Exegete?" [in Hebrew], in Michal Oron and Amos Goldreich, eds., *Massu'ot: Studies in Qabbalah and Jewish Thought in Memory of Professor Efraim Gottlieb* (Jerusalem: Mosad Bialik, 1994), pp. 414–28; and Menahem Haran, "Judaism and Scripture in the Outlook of Yehezkel Kaufmann" [in Hebrew], *Madda'ei Ha-Yahadut* 31 (1991): pp. 69–80. On scholarly works in recent decades (such as Albertz's book cited above) that independently come to conclusions in some ways comparable to Kaufmann's but often in a more realistic and flexible manner, see Benjamin Sommer, "Kaufmann and Recent Scholarship on Monotheism," in Thomas Staubli, Benjamin Sommer, and Job Jindo, eds., *Yehezkel Kaufmann and the Reinvention of Jewish Biblical Scholarship* (Freiburg, forthcoming).

On this approach to biblical monotheism, see further James Barr, "The Problem of Israelite Monotheism," *Glasgow University Oriental Society* 17 (1957–58): pp. 52–62; José Faur, "The Biblical Idea of Idolatry," *Jewish Quarterly Review* 69 (1978): pp. 1–15; David Petersen, "Israel and Monotheism," in Gene Tucker, David Petersen, and Robert Wilson, eds., *Canon, Theology, and Old Testament Interpretation: Essays in Honor of Brevard S. Childs* (Philadelphia: Fortress Press, 1988), pp. 92–107; Adrian Schenker, "Le monothéisme israélite: Un dieu qui transcende le monde et les dieux," *Biblica* 78 (1997): pp. 436–48; and Nili Fox, "Concepts of God in Israel and the Question of Monotheism," in Gary Beckman and Theodore Lewis, eds., *Text, Artifact, and Image: Revealing Ancient Israelite Religion* (Providence, R.I.: Brown Judaic Studies, 2006), pp. 326–45. This approach is not new; it was articulated by the thirteenth-century rabbinic commentator Nachmanides; see Alon Goshen-Gottstein, "Other Gods in Ramban's Thought" [in Hebrew], in U. Ehrlich, H. Kreisel, and D. Lasker, eds., *'Al Pi Ha-Be'er: Studies in Jewish Philosophy and in Ha-*

lakhic Thought Presented to Gerald Blidstein (Beersheba: Ben-Gurion University Press, 2008), pp. 28–62.

Closely related to monotheism is the Bible's prohibition of representing the Israelite deity in physical form, or scripture's *aniconism*. The classic study dating Israelite aniconism early in the preexilic era is Tryggve Mettinger, *No Graven Image? Israelite Aniconism in Its Ancient Near Eastern Context* (Stockholm: Almqvist och Wiksell, 1995). Various scholars have taken issue with Mettinger; see essays by Herbert Niehr, Christoph Uehlinger, and Bob Becking in Karel van der Toorn, ed., *The Image and the Book: Iconic Cults, Aniconism, and the Rise of Book Religion in Israel and the Ancient Near East* (Leuven: Peeters, 1997). But see the convincing defense of Mettinger's thesis in that volume by Mettinger himself as well as the essay there by Ronald Hendel. See further Tryggve Mettinger, "A Conversation with My Critics," in Yairah Amit, Ehud Ben-Zvi, Israel Finkelstein, and Oded Lipschits, eds., *Essays on Ancient Israel in Its Near Eastern Context. A Tribute to Nadav Na'aman* (Winona Lake, Ind.: Eisenbrauns, 2006), pp. 273–96; as well as the balanced review of the issue in Miller, *Religion of Ancient Israel*, pp. 16–23.

An influential discussion of the development of monotheism is Mark Smith, *The Origins of Biblical Monotheism: Israel's Polytheistic Background and the Ugaritic Texts* (New York: Oxford University Press, 2001). An insightful essay on the origins of monotheism that presents a subtle, revealing, and convincing approach is William Propp, "Monotheism and 'Moses': The Problem of Early Israelite Religion," *Ugarit-Forschungen* 31 (1999): pp. 537–75.

Excellent essays on types of monotheism and polytheism in the ancient Near East and connections among them are found in Barbara Nevling Porter, ed., *One God or Many? Conceptions of Divinity in the Ancient World* (Chebeague Island, Maine: Casco Bay Assyriological Institute, 2000); and Beate Pongratz-Leisten, ed., *Reconsidering the Concept of Revolutionary Monotheism* (Winona Lake, Ind.: Eisenbrauns, 2011). A readable yet deeply learned discussion of the ancient Near Eastern background of Israel's monotheistic revolution, with special attention to questions of gender, is Tikva Frymer-Kensky, *In the Wake of the Goddesses: Women, Culture, and the Biblical Transformation of Pagan Myth* (New York: Free Press, 1992).

Additional collections of essays relevant to the topic are found in Ernst Haag, ed., *Gott, der Einzige: Zur Entstehung des Monotheismus in Israel* (Freiburg: Herder, 1985); and Manfred Oeming and Konrad Schmid, eds., *Der eine Gott und die Götter: Polytheismus und Monotheismus im Antiken Israel* (Zurich: Theologischer Verlag Zürich, 2003). Three especially important recent studies are Othmar Keel, *Die Geschichte Jerusalems und die Entstehung des Monotheismus*, 2 vols. (Göttingen: Vandenhoeck & Ruprecht, 2007), esp. 2:1270–82; Israel Knohl, *Biblical Beliefs* [in Hebrew] (Jerusalem: Magnes Press, 2007); and Alexander Rofé, *Angels in the Bible: Israelite Belief as Evidenced by Biblical Tradition* [in Hebrew] (Jerusalem: Carmel Publishing House, 2012).

11

❀

Creation

God and World

Hermann Spieckermann

1. ACCIDENT OR WILL?

The idea of a world created by God, on the one hand, and the knowledge of natural science about the evolution of the world and of humanity, on the other, are by no means contradictory.[1] Rather, these two views are but different perspectives on the selfsame issue. When both theology and natural science recognize their capacities and limitations, they complement one another with their different epistemological potentials, thus making creation*ism* superfluous. With its own specific competencies, natural science seeks to reconstruct the emergence and development of universe, world, and humanity all as precisely as possible—an undertaking that can be achieved only by bracketing out any idea of God, pursuant to the empirical method. Theology, by contrast, aims to fathom the meaning of why a hospitable earth exists in the midst of an inhospitable universe or why humanity experiences life not merely as the sum of vital processes but as a gift and a successful coexistence. Anyone who plumbs the depths of this connection between experience of self and world cannot help but speak of God. Such questions place the individual in an ancient community of inquirers that stretches back millennia. Recording its experiences and insights, this community has been deemed a credible witness by innumerable generations. Through a critical interrogation of the Bible's testimony to the genesis of world and humanity alike, natural science has developed its own methods and areas of inquiry, but its inevitable emancipation from theology does not demand an inevitable rivalry between the two realms. Natural science does not, and cannot, respond to questions of meaning and significance: here, a conversation between theology and natural science is urgently required. Where the contemplative individual poses those inescapable questions about the understanding of self and world, these epistemological spheres complement each other.

Indeed, theology and natural science can prove mutually beneficial where their convictions and observations converge. Both accept the finitude of earth and humankind. Moreover, each considers our planet almost certainly unique within the universe at large—this is most evident in the fact that life in all its diversity has become possible here. Such life depends on space and time. Though threats abound, this great diversity of life arises in an environment where hospitality prevails. Whether one counts the time of the world in eons or billions of years does not result in any greatly significant difference between theology and natural science. The difference between these perspectives can indeed lead to a fundamental opposition: either a divine will or the play of chance lies behind this temporally limited but nonetheless good order that lies amid a universe both inhospitable and chaotic. Yet such an alternative does not necessarily or unambiguously demarcate an absolute divide between theology and natural science. Just as a skeptical theology can recognize in coincidence and destiny the bad counterpart of a good creation (Qoh. 2:12–23, 3:18–22, 9:11–12), so natural science has no compulsion to grant sheer coincidence alone all probability as the reason for what it observes about the genesis of the world and of the human race. Theology stems from wonder at the miracle of life and combines such marvel—in accord with the credible witness of Scripture—with a God who desires a relationship with the world and therefore becomes its creator. Whether the world is plausibly seen as God's good creation, and humanity as chosen by God within it to bear God's likeness and to preserve the creation's hospitality for life, or whether, on the other hand, life arose amid a threatening chaos from sheer coincidence—these questions can be answered differently. For theology, life and the connectivity of the living are a wonder that a believing reason can only understand as a reality desired by the Creator-God. The central texts of the Jewish and Christian religions that witness to such understanding will be examined in their origins and intentions.

2. CHAOS AND CREATION

The canonized Jewish and Christian Scriptures seek to know nothing about God except in his relationship to the world.[2] Indeed, even the first page of the Bible depicts an active and dynamic God, a God who creates himself a counterpart (Gen. 1:1–2:4a; hereafter Gen. 1). Crafting his creation—from light and firmament to sea and land to sun, moon, and stars to fish, birds, and land animals (Gen. 1:3–25)—God ultimately forms a creature of particular nearness to himself, humanity (Gen. 1:26–28). God creates humanity "*as* his image" (*běṣelem*, Gen. 1:26–27). This divine likeness consists in God allowing human beings participation in himself and includes a blessed commission to rule over all fellow creatures (Gen. 1:28). Such a mandate, however, expressly precludes the consumption of animals (Gen. 1:29). On almost each day of creation, God himself declares his work to be "good" (*ṭôb*, Gen. 1:4, 12, 18, 21, 25, 31): humanity's dominion over its fellow creatures can only have the aim of helping to preserve God's own creation.

Even the choice of eight works, allotted to six days, is meant to reflect the good order God has established. Rather than list God's creation in all its entirety, Gen. 1 provides a careful selection of works. Comparison with Psalm 104 and Job 38–41 proves instructive: diverse intentions determine different collections. While God constructs a place for creation through the works recorded in Gen. 1, he also builds a concrete time frame through the chosen number of seven days. Time and space are shaped and filled by the presence of the Creator. Creating light first (Gen. 1:3–5), God precipitates a certain conflict with the heavenly bodies of day four, which themselves are also intended to give light (Gen. 1:14–19). But this functional overlap is allowed for because light as the first creation signals the presence of God from the start, for light in the ancient Near East, and in classical antiquity as well, reveals the divine presence, be it of gods or of God. Wrought by God himself, the space for creation comes from his presence, a presence that likewise displays the desire for a relationship with the world he thus creates.

The end of creation on the seventh day does not culminate in a final work. Ostensibly the crown of creation, humankind must share day six with other land animals (Gen. 1:24–31). Such a close connection between the two is intentional, for humanity bears the burden of preserving its

fellow creatures and thus God's good creation; steward rather than auto-
crat, humanity retains responsibility for all creation. As the image of
God, it represents God in and to the world. For this divine image to
destroy or even endanger the goodness of God's creation would directly
contradict God's will for his created order.

The goal of God's creation lies not in the formation of humanity but
in divine rest on the seventh day (Gen. 2:1–3). The Hebrew *mĕlā'kâ*
thrice occurs to mark the work of God (Gen. 2:2–3). Though first attested in this particular context, the lexeme describes all sorts of human
endeavors, an observation that then illuminates the rest of God upon
the seventh day. Indeed, God needs no rest; his labors do not exhaust
him. Instead, humanity requires rest from its work; God allows humankind to take part in his own repose. Like light at the start of creation,
divine rest at its end stresses divine presence throughout the entire process. Such tranquility proves so important to God that he not only blesses
but even hallows the seventh day (Gen. 2:3). Accordingly, this theological rationale precedes all pragmatic justification for human rest from
work: God permits all creation to participate in his divine reality. Through
the word *mĕlā'kâ*, God not only relates his own creative activity to that
of humankind but incorporates his own creatures in the rhythm of work
and rest as well. Stemming from the exilic/postexilic Priestly writer, this
text (Gen. 1:1–2:4a) cannot yet designate the seventh day as *šabbāt* (i.e.,
Sabbath), since the Priestly work attributes all of Israel's regulations to
the laws received by Moses at Sinai. Still, the verb *šābat* twice depicts the
rest of God (Gen. 2:2–3), unmistakably evoking the Sabbath. God's repose reveals his will that the good creation should remain good for all
creatures in toto, including those that bear his image. In the end, God
fashions his creation as himself: good (Ps. 136:1–9). In accordance with
the will of God, Creator and created remain closely tied yet strictly distinct. It will soon become evident that this contains a potential problem.

The creation of God has beginning and end alike, the latter implied
but not explicit. No text suggests that God created any of his works to
last forever; otherwise, the distinction between created and Creator
would disappear, as creation belongs to the finite. Formed by God himself, creation's time and place entail a certain limit. Consequently the
space for things to exist in is at the same time linked with the week of
creation—a conception of time that itself implies limitation. But the lim-

itation of creation emerges, too, in Gen. 1:1–2:4a, but from a different angle[3]: God's creation as described at the beginning of the Bible is not a creative act out of nothing. The conception of *creatio ex nihilo* first came to the fore in Hellenistic Judaism (2 Macc. 7:28). After the heading of Gen. 1:1 comes a description of the world before God's first deed, the generation of light. Three elements characterize the world at this time: *tōhû wābōhû* (formless and void), *ḥōšek* (darkness), and *tĕhôm* (the deep). Present in Mesopotamian myths and even Old Testament texts, this triad alludes to Chaos. The term *tĕhôm* betrays an inherent conception of Chaos, the philological equivalent of the goddess Tiamat.

Excursus: Divine Rest in Mesopotamia

Composed around the transition between the second and first millennia BCE, the Babylonian Epic of Creation—also called *Enuma Elish*— identifies the goddess Tiamat and the god Apsu as the first divine pair.[4] The first represents salt water, and the latter, freshwater, and from their union spring forth other deities whose power and number increase from generation to generation. Theogony turns to theomachy as younger gods turn on their progenitors, that is, Apsu and Tiamat. His rest disturbed, Apsu is ready to destroy the younger gods, but Tiamat rejects his plan categorically. Ea, God of Wisdom, foils Apsu's scheme by murdering him altogether, whereupon he seizes Apsu's insignia (belt, crown, and coat of light) and founds his temple upon the Apsu, the freshwater, which he continues to rule thereafter. Yet a greater threat to the divine world is still to come. Tiamat, who once protected the younger generation of gods, has her peace disturbed by their clamor. Consequently, she hatches a plot to wipe out the troublemakers, a maneuver she organizes with other divine or numinous helpers, especially her lover Qingu. Though one may dispute the legitimacy of an annihilation based on the mere disturbance of peace, ancient Near Eastern cultures deemed divine rest the highest good. This conceptual context proves essential for a proper theological assessment of God's magnanimous rest in the Genesis account of creation. Divine repose in the ancient world was also proof of power, for gods who enjoy the luxury of rest belong to the highest class of divinity, obliging the inferior classes of gods to undertake sundry labors. In this way, a divine struggle for power lies behind Tiamat's plan of destruction—a theme that comes to the fore as those gods now under threat begin to formulate countermeasures. Alongside other divinities, Ea, victor of Apsu, shies back from battle with Tiamat. Despondent and afflicted, the gods choose Marduk, son of Ea, as their champion, appointing him their king and thereby affirming his privileged status even before the battle begins. Having slain the mighty Tiamat, he takes captive her champion, Qingu. If the theogonic phase generated the cosmos's fundamental elements in the form of the various deities (sky, earth, freshwater, salt water), Marduk forms the world into its tangible dimension with the components of Tiamat's corpse, all through the guidance of his wise father, Ea/Nudimmud. His creation transforms the rebellious goddess of Chaos into a world suitable for cultivation and habitation, the latter through the temples of the gods. With the investiture with kingship as thanks for his deed, Marduk rules the gods from Babylon, which also becomes the privileged resting place of the gods (even though they have temples in other locations as well).

If divine repose remains the highest good in Mesopotamia, the question arises as to how the gods and their temples could be cared for appropriately. This demand prompts the creation of the prototypical human, again effected by Marduk with the counsel of Ea. Made from the blood of Tiamat's warrior Qingu, humanity must now assume responsibility for serving the great deities, a task once executed by the inferior divine classes. Caring for the gods is humanity's foremost duty.

Enuma Elish not only gathers but also transforms any number of themes from older Mesopotamian myth, especially that of Atrahasis.[5] Though intentionally omitted from the Babylonian Creation Epic, one episode from the latter bears directly upon the Bible's primordial history (Gen. 1–11). As in *Enuma Elish*, *Atrahasis* features a humanity created to care for the gods, under the guidance of Enki/Ea in this case. The humans make so much noise, however, that they disturb the rest of the gods, who then decide—with Ellil/Enlil leading the way—to destroy the humans by flood. Avoiding total destruction, the creator of humankind, Enki/Ea, commands Atrahasis and his family to build an ark to survive the flood. This myth of Atrahasis shows just how much the themes of threat and creation—and even the extermination of creation— correspond in Mesopotamian tradition. Such correspondence surfaces in biblical tradition as well, emerging, even earlier than the flood narrative of Gen. 6–9, in the first account of creation.

In light of *Enuma Elish*, the three components of *tōhû wābōhû*, *ḥōšek*, and *tĕhôm* betray a clear conception of Chaos, a reality that rumbles beneath the apparently peaceful surface at the beginning of God's creation in the account of Gen. 1. Indeed, Gen. 1:2 consciously and purposefully portrays this potential menace as merely a sort of stagnation, thereby incapacitating Chaos. The spirit of God (*rûaḥ*) hovers above the waters (*mayim*), not the Deep (*tĕhôm*)—spirit in the Priestly source being no longer the wind or a storm but, rather, a patent reference to the presence of God. Encountering God's presence, the waters immediately lose their threatening power.

To accomplish his creation, God need not *battle* Chaos; but the triad evinces God's will to act as Creator as itself an act against Chaos, which cannot countenance life. Consequently, the Priestly source selects the verb *bārā'* (to create) as a central concept in Gen. 1 to designate the creative action of God. A verb that only ever has God as its subject and which is a technical term for the specific type of creative activity that God prefers, *bārā'* indicates neither the matter nor the means of creation; rather, it serves as the most comprehensive term for God's creative actions in primeval times and the eschaton as well as each day of creation. Beneath this principal term fall other, more concrete conceptions of creation throughout the text of Gen. 1.

A proper exposition of God's creation in Gen. 1 requires due attention to two distinct dimensions: a feat against Chaos and a sovereign act. With this duality, God pursues a single goal: a good creation made to sustain a good life—in terms of time and space alike—not only for his "likeness," humanity, but also for all creatures, which he entrusts to that very "likeness." The various motifs woven throughout the Gen. 1 narrative largely come from Mesopotamian mythology, particularly *Enuma Elish*, though these texts do not, and cannot, serve as a final point of reference. In fact, *Enuma Elish* functions as such a good conceptual model precisely because it absorbs and commingles a host of mythic components from Mesopotamia, Anatolia, and Syria. A comparable compound almost certainly formed the basis of the Gen. 1 composition. As a result, works such as *Enuma Elish* provide a matrix for viewing the theological contours specific to Gen. 1. Creation springs from a genuine desire of the one God to fashion a counterpart to himself from his own good work, that counterpart being a means of enabling life in general, and toward which he acts in blessing and protection. Humanity receives such privileged status not for the benefit of God alone but for the sake of all creatures and creation. Moreover, God actively desires a specific kind of relationship with humanity, his likeness. God entrusts it with a dominion that deliberately lacks the trappings of kingly power, for God himself shows in the account of Gen. 1 that he ascribes no importance to royal power. Instead, human mastery must concentrate entirely on preserving the good creation. Even God displays care for his creation, deviating from standard Near Eastern convention. Rather than claim all rest for himself, God founds and commands rest for all his creatures on the seventh day. Whereas the creation of the world in *Enuma Elish* centers primarily upon space for divine repose, an occasion for Marduk's kingship, and the creation of human beings to relieve the gods of work and to serve them, the God of Gen. 1 decides to create for the sake of relationship with all his many creatures. Even further, this Creator seeks to realize his own goodness through creation itself: against a hostile chaos and for a wholesome life, God fashions a space to foster relationship among God, world, and humankind. But if such an account of creation places the goodness of creation at its core, the question inevitably arises how evil could have come to be so successful.

3. GOOD AND EVIL

The story of creation and fall in Gen. 2:4b–3:24 (hereafter Gen. 2–3) seeks to answer this very question. Closely tied to the Priestly creation account through Gen. 2:4b–7, the narrative expounds the first human pair's formation. In its current form, Gen. 2–3 hails from the postexilic period, though a preexilic etiology may well lie at its base (2:5–9a, 18–24; 3:20–21, 23). This rather straightforward etiology, like the rest of the story in its current construction, calls God by his personal name, Yahweh. He shapes the 'ādām (earthling, human) from the 'ădāmâ (soil, earth) and plants the Garden of Eden as a protective realm to pursue his creative interests. Having formed the 'ādām and founded the garden,

Yahweh turns his creative efforts to molding a proper partner, as "it is not good that the 'ādām should be alone" (Gen. 2:18). The animals owe their existence to this search for an adequate mate, though 'ādām accepts none of them as an appropriate counterpart. Only a new creature formed from part of him will finally suffice. Styling this new being 'iššâ (woman), the 'ādām quickly succumbs to an intuitive love for her. In relation to 'iššâ (woman), the 'ādām becomes 'iš (man) (Gen. 2:23); as a result, the 'ādām of Gen. 3:20 transitions from generic term (*human*) to proper name (Adam). While such an appellation names him for his origin in 'ădāmâ (soil, earth), it also evokes his mission: to work the 'ădāmâ as a fundamental necessity for the conservation of life (Gen. 3:23). The woman receives a personal name as well, ḥawwâ (Eve), expressing her commission to preserve and proliferate "all that lives" (*kol-ḥay*) (Gen. 3:20). As for their endeavors, God commissions the first human pair to procreate and cultivate, not in the Garden of Eden itself or as an immediate consequence of their expulsion from it. According to Gen. 3:23, Adam and Eve are sent from the garden to act in the world so that all humankind might spring from the first human pair.[6]

This etiology underlies the narrative of creation and fall, curse and eviction, recounted in Gen. 2–3. Even further, the story of evil enjoying such massive success in God's good creation (Gen. 2–3) significantly expands that original tale of a prosperous human creation and the distribution of duties, not to mention the overt declaration of creation's fundamental goodness (Gen. 1). A product of the postexilic period, this final version undertakes the connection of good and evil, an inquiry absent from the creation narrative of Gen. 1. The origin of evil in the good creation, however, even this later, completely composite account ignores, though it strictly precludes God as evil's author. In the middle of God's garden lies the potentiality of evil, as Chaos precedes creation in Gen. 1:2. Chaos may therefore have something to do with evil.

This, however, is not the issue: the issue is humanity's relation to evil. Indeed, humanity possesses the power to awaken the slumbering force of evil into a reality to be reckoned with. The gift of will and ability to choose act as evil's gateway, these capacities being divine endowments to humankind—to the "image" of God himself. The created can turn such faculties even against their creator. In fact, this course of action occurs when the primal humans defy the divine prohibition of eating from the tree of knowledge of good and evil (Gen. 2:17). Theologically, the ability to choose entails a judgment as to life's foundation, meaning, and goal: a grateful bond to God as Creator of life or an autonomy that brooks neither command nor interdiction in an attempt to determine, discern, and decide all things independently and—driven by a lust for power—to remain no longer created but to become instead the Creator oneself. This choice between a bestowed freedom in obedience to the Creator and a sovereign freedom without any connection to the Creator is an unavoidable crossroads. With reference to Gen. 1, God's charge for his "likeness" to rule transforms into a human pretension to rule, freed from connection to God. The story in Gen. 2–3 admits the success of evil in seducing the humans to disobey God. Such a breach is no mere trifle but raises a fundamental question: whether the "opened eyes" the serpent enticingly promises in Gen. 3:5 will indeed bestow that godly power so coveted by humanity.

Invested by God with the freedom to choose, the created being hopes to abandon its bond to him and even itself become God. This aspiration is, in essence, a rejection of creation and thus a triumph of Chaos, the sinister partner of evil. Chaos and evil, working together, build on the groundwork of a rebellious humanity's pursuit of an inflated status. Consequently, those who rebuff the Creator inevitably spurn the proper order of life. The voices of Gen. 1–3 may not know the origin of evil or Chaos, but they know full well the object of evil's seduction: humanity—the image of God, destined for knowledge, yet both willing and able to defy the will of its maker. Loath to be a God without relationship to the world and to the human race he himself created, this God must engage with a creation that would rather be an image of itself than an image of him. God's good creation, opposed to the hostile chaos, is eminently vulnerable, vulnerable to that human creature that seeks not only to deify itself but also to abuse its charge to safeguard God's good creation.

Although the divine curses of Gen. 3:14–19 punish those parties responsible for aiding and abetting evil's triumph in creation, they by no means abrogate the blessings awarded to that creation in Gen. 1:22, 28, and 2:3. Instead, they create a tension between curse and blessing in the world, which then reflects the tension in God's engagement with the world, especially the creature of his foremost devotion, humankind. These curses have serious implications for creation. His hand then forced to punish, God himself suffers in the subsequent spiral of violence and ret-ribution (Gen. 4), up to his final decision to annihilate his creation so tainted by evil (Gen. 6–9). Yet the same God rescinds his decision to wipe out creation at the end of its near-destruction by flood (Gen. 8:21; 9:11, 15), renewing his blessing upon it (Gen. 9:1). Such antagonism between blessing and curse, as well as divine discipline, remains a source of conflict throughout the primeval history (Gen. 9:26, 11:1–9), for evil remains in the world. Nevertheless, God holds to his creation and all its many creatures. He wants to see himself within his likeness and main-tain a bond between likeness and maker (Gen. 9:6).

4. CREATION AS PRESERVATION

Though enjoying pride of place at the beginning of the Jewish and Chris-tian Bibles, the initial constitution of the creation is not the earliest ver-sion of creation present within the Old Testament. In fact, the oldest concept of creation appears not in Genesis but in the Psalms. There, the kingship of Yahweh, which stands among the earliest theological con-ceptions of the Hebrew Bible, has a direct relationship with his ability to defend his earthly domain from the pretensions of other numinous powers. Already apparent in *Enuma Elish*, stories of theomachy feature in preexilic psalms concerning Yahweh's royal rule and even earlier ar-rangements from Syria in general and Ugarit in particular.[7] Ugaritic texts depict the god of chaos and sea, Yammu, and the chthonic deity, Motu, as the greatest opponents of Baʿlu, a weather and vegetation di-vinity who stars not as an adversary but as the prototype of Yahweh in various Old Testament psalms. In this context, the earth and at times even the heavens need not be created at all. Instead of the *origin* of earth, such texts concern its *ruler*: that is, who preserves (Baʿlu) and who im-perils (Yammu, Motu) it. The Ugaritic Baʿlu myth tells the tale of a king-dom recurrently threatened. Temporary losses notwithstanding, Baʿlu proves victorious in his dominion over the earth, both granting and pre-serving life for all.

The psalmic conception of a creation constantly threatened by numi-nous forces but consistently preserved by the divine king Yahweh would, in fact, be incomprehensible without this religious backdrop from ancient

Syria. If the god-king Yahweh must protect the earth from otherworldly threats in the preexilic period (Pss. 24, 29, 93), in the postexilic period he must defend his own people in a world of hostile others (Pss. 2, 46, 48, 68, 76, 98, 99). In the context of the former, earth stands not as Yahweh's primal creation (*prima creatio*) but as his possession and domain, whose persistent need of care continues to challenge his power. Psalm 93 exhibits such views of creation:

> Yahweh is king,
> Clothed in majesty,
>> clothed is Yahweh,
>>> girded in might.
> Indeed, the world is established, it does not waver,
>> established is your throne of old
>>> from eternity so also are you.
> Streams raised up, O Yahweh,
>> streams raised up their voice,
>>> streams raised up their crashing.
> More than the roar of great waters,
>> more lofty than waves of the sea,
>>> is Yahweh, lofty on high.
> Your witnesses utterly fixed,
>> your house a beautiful holiness,
>>> Yahweh for evermore.

Centered on the god-king Yahweh, this psalm was probably sung already in the Temple of Solomon, persisting into the Second Temple, albeit slightly modified. While his persona appears as divine warrior—a role he adopted from Ba'lu—the power of Yahweh features in universal kingship. Accordingly, the world is his throne's pedestal, a throne of all earthly dimensions upon which he himself sits, exceeding all earthly dimensions.

Nonetheless, Yahweh's kingdom comes under threat, with currents and masses of water surging up against it. Only through Syrian myth does this vignette become fully intelligible. Behind these waters stands a rival to Ba'lu's kingship, Yammu, god of chaos and sea. Present in Psalm 93 by the mention of water (*yām*, 93:4) and streams (*něhārôt*, 93:3), this same figure arises as the enemy of Yahweh, with the epithets *zbl ym*

(Prince [of the] Sea) and *ṭpṭ nhr* (Ruler [of the] Stream) well attested in the Ugaritic texts.

In Psalm 93, however, no combat comes into question. Yahweh rules forever (Ps. 93:2, 5). His name in each line of the psalm, his presence ends any dispute, with this presence further manifest in 93:5 as well. The "witnesses" (*'ēdōt*) may stem from later theological revision, but the ensemble of eternal name, royal-divine power, and holy temple all trace back to earlier times. Though the text assumes a universality for the power of God, such an idea is not in tension with the factual particularity. Mythologically, the god Yahweh rules the world in its entirety from the Temple in Jerusalem, just as Ba'lu from Mount Zaphon and other weather and vegetation deities from other mountains in Syria and Anatolia do. Divine power is always contested power: the struggle for power must always be fought for the survival of the world. In Psalm 93, however, the question of power among the divinity's rivals is already settled. Nonetheless, Yahweh must still be on guard so that his kingdom and his right to rule and preserve the earth do not succumb to all the threats surrounding him.

Other texts with roots in the preexilic period show that the divine king's formation and preservation of the earth was of central importance. For instance, Psalm 29 stresses the threat posed to Yahweh's power by other numinous beings. With the creation of the earth comes the foundation of the temple upon the quieted waters of chaos, which stresses Yahweh's lasting claim of ownership on the earth (Ps. 24:1–2; see Exod. 15:17; Pss. 50:10–12, 78:69). Creation's beauty and purpose then move to the center when Yahweh founds his heavenly-earthly temple-palace, which, in turn, serves as the indispensable prerequisite for the space and time of creation (Ps. 104). This good order is that participation in God's glory (Ps. 19) or reflection of his presence's fullness with which cosmos and creatures are endowed (Ps. 148). Humanity's distinction lies not in its mere creation but in its incomparable closeness to God, an exaltation not only in heaven but also on earth (Ps. 8). With regard to the motif of birth, human formation lies on the periphery; it is the significance of nearness to God that stands at the center, a relationship that justifies trust (Pss. 2:7, 22:10–11, 71:6, 139:13–16; cf. 94:9).

In terms of strengthening trust, the people's lament of the exilic Psalm 74:12–17 (cf. 89:10–15) proceeds from proclamations about the divine king to his battle with chaos at the Exodus, culminating in 74:16–17 with the association of Yahweh's creative acts with declarations of ownership, a theme also present in earlier psalms. Yahweh's portrayal as "Creator of Heaven and Earth" prevails through all literary divisions in the Persian period (Gen. 14:19; Pss. 115:15, 121:2, 124:8, 134:3, 146:6), often connected to other aspects of his activity (Pss. 33:6–7, 90:2, 102:26, 115:3, 119:89–90, 135:6, and 136) such as the creation of Israel and other nations (86:9, 95:4–7, 100:3, 149:2 [LXX]). Originally separate, the creation of heaven and earth as divine constitution and the creation of heaven and earth as divine preservation against all threats form a composite whole.

5. A CREATIVE NEWNESS AND A SAVING CREATION

Through the concept that God's creation is a constant, conservational activity (more: that God renews his creation each and every morning [Ps. 104:27–30], a theme attested in Egyptian religion as well), the idea arose that God not only renews the existent creation but even fashions new things that have never before existed.[8] While the postulate appears only sporadically in the Psalms as the re-creation of heart and spirit (Ps. 51:12–14), such an assertion arises in the context of exilic and postexilic prophecy, most clearly in Isaiah and Ezekiel, which promise new divine dealings and include the gift of a new heart and divine spirit in either the present or the future (Isa. 11:1–5, 42:1–4, 61:1–3; Ezek. 11:19–20 [contra 18:31], 36:26–27, 37:1–14; Joel 3:1–5). In this conceptual context, new divine activities can even bring together the dimensions of primordial fabrication and anticipated eschaton into a unified sketch of creation. If God's work at the beginning is a creative triumph against not only the power of chaos but also that of the Egyptians (through the Exodus), his work at the end is not just the *end* but the *ultimate*: the newly created that is also a fight against chaos and powerful peoples, a renewed deliverance that surpasses all previous experience of rescue.

For this hope, texts from the second half of Isaiah, that is, after chapter 40, prove paradigmatic. Crafted over a long process from the sixth to the fourth century BCE, these texts depict God as both creator and redeemer, casting a unity of will and deed alike throughout the past, present, and future (Isa. 43:1, 44:24). His word says what he does. All things past and present he does in a unity of purpose. Whether championing his servant Jacob/Israel, drying up the chaotic waters of the Deep at the Reed Sea, or harnessing the king of Persia to rebuild and populate Jerusalem and Judah alike (Isa. 44:24–28a), God has the world's entirety within the plans he makes. And this plan has always been rescue. Consequently, the notion of God as creator of Chaos and addressor of darkness is deceptive (Isa. 45:18–19, consciously contra 45:7); rather, "light to the nations" and guarantor of salvation and justice, his servant Jacob/Israel advocates his will in the world (49:1–6). Salvation of the world hinges on the promise to this servant—the figure of Jacob/Israel and the corporate personality of a reformed Israel—and Zion alike: Yahweh returns, to the acclamation and amazement of the nations (Isa. 46:9–13, 51:9–11, 52:7–10). The word of God—the promise of salvation—is therefore fulfilled in times past, present, or future.

The expectation of imminent fulfillment weighs heavy for these texts of Isaiah, of course, and that unsatisfied anticipation continued to grow over time. By the end of the book of Isaiah, the uncertain things once promised (Isa. 42:9) become the concrete hope of a new heaven and earth (Isa. 65:17, 66:22) with its center in Jerusalem, a city without weeping or clamor, home to evil no more (Isa. 65:18–25; cf. 11:6–9). The primeval age provides a template for the end of days; the future is becoming hope, set free from the past. In this account, the work of God is always new creation, God's fundamental yes to world and humankind against all of evil's successes. Creation in the primordial era and the eschaton is the master narrative of God's desire for relationship, whose origin lies in his desire to love. Not every ancient story may have seen things in this way, but Isaiah 54:7–10 certainly sets things in this light.

6. WISDOM AND CREATION

Wisdom theology is, at core, a creation theology.[9] From the world's good order, sages discover the ways that lead to a knowledge of God, for he himself created the heavens and the earth by wisdom and knowledge (Prov. 3:19–20; cf. Ps. 104:24). Playing before God as his "darling" (ʾāmôn, not "master workman"), personified Wisdom even boasts of spurring the Creator to his work. Creation is thus a success (Prov. 8:22–31). While God amuses himself with Leviathan—really a vile servant of the chaotic Sea (Ps. 104:26)—Wisdom takes pleasure in humanity, as God does in Wisdom itself (Prov. 8:30–31). As love and desire dominate creation (Prov. 8:17), neither God nor Wisdom can fathom the inhumanity of humanity: "The rich and poor meet together: Yahweh is the maker of them all" (Prov. 22:2; cf. 29:13). Though it contains neither warning nor threat, such a statement suggests that the dynamic of rich and poor should correspond to the proper world order, which God bestowed on his creatures. Reference to the Creator seems to enter here for those cases of abuse that endanger or even afflict the order ordained by God. Accordingly, oppression of the weak (Prov. 14:31, 17:5) and deception in trade (Prov. 16:11) summon a Creator who safeguards his order. God as fashioner of eye and ear (Prov. 20:12; see 20:27) implicitly appeals to a rightful use of gifts, but this divine capacity receives particular emphasis wherever the social structure threatens to unravel. Based on their knowledge of the parts, the sages venture to pronounce the wholeness of this order as willed by God. Accordingly, God himself made the order's greatest foe, the wicked, whom he crafted for the day of evil (Prov. 16:4). This declaration of boundaries or limitations converges with that of Yahweh's engagement with Leviathan in Psalm 104:26: with statements such as these, the sages reflect their hope that God will protect his order in the most vulnerable of spheres.

Throughout the Wisdom literature, positive and negative perspectives on creation are almost always juxtaposed, with skeptical voices increasing from the sixth century BCE. Formed in a lengthy process from the sixth to the fourth century BCE, the book of Job and that of Qohelet, which was written in at least the fourth but probably the third century BCE, display an irritation with and resignation from God's dealings with the world. The God who makes all things—even the wicked for an evil day (Prov. 16:4)—and gives all knowledge to those who seek it (Prov. 28:5) becomes unrecognizable when calamity strikes a paragon of righteousness "without cause" (ḥinnām, Job 2:3, 9:17; cf. 1:9), as in the case of Job. Here, the entirety of creation becomes ordained by God, inscrutable and perilous (Qoh. 3:11).

If the Job novella avails itself of few creation concepts, the poetry of the book sets such conceptions center stage. In the first speech cycle especially (Job 3–14), an ambivalent sense of creation emerges on both sides in various forms. Whereas justice and creatureliness do not at all converge for Job's friend Eliphaz (Job 4:17–21), Job proves himself well versed in praise for the Creator, a praise he turns into an acid text of hymn and indictment alike (Job 9:5–10; 10:3, 8–13; 12:7–25; with a gloomy affinity to Zophar's praise of God's inscrutability in 11:7–10). For the character of Job, justness and creatureliness fundamentally diverge since God cannot tolerate any human righteousness (Job 9:2–4, 20, 28–31). The challenge of Job's final speech (Job 29–31) once again places the question of law and justice at its center, yet the divine speeches and answers in Job 38:1–42:6 hardly even attempt a response. Parading his creation before Job—a presentation unique in the Old Testament for its systematization and completeness—God utterly rejects Job's demand for justice. In fact, God never claims justice as a meaningful category for his creation. Creation, presented with a sovereign gesture, is no longer self-evident, since God is obliged to promote it with a speech of his own—a rare genre for Wisdom literature. Importantly, such self-praise shows no interest of the Creator in his work, least of all in humanity. No longer a mere toying (Ps. 104:26), God's encounter with Leviathan (Job 40:25–41:26) is now a terrifying showdown with the "king over all who are proud" (41:34). Job's immediate answer shows that he has understood God: "I know that you can do all things and that no purpose of yours can be thwarted.... Therefore I despise (myself) and repent in dust and ashes" (Job 42:2, 6).

In the context of Qohelet, the paradigmatic problem is much less existential than in Job. God as Creator belongs to the fundamental thought of Qohelet, and yet he is unknowably distant, with totality—a frequent designation for creation—denied to human knowledge as well. This detachment proves all the more painful and frustrating as God has placed eternity in the heart of humankind, which, for Qohelet, is nothing less than the image of God. Although God and totality certainly belong together, totality and the good no longer coincide (Qoh. 3:10–11). An assertion of totality as the beautiful (*yāpeh*) likely functions as a denial of its goodness (*ṭôb*), a conscious critique of Gen. 1. Instead, the good can be experienced only as a contingent gift of God in the commonplace of toil (Qoh. 3:12–13; cf. 2:24, 5:17–19, 7:13–14, 9:7–10). The wholeness of creation betrays an eternal determination, one that inspires more fear than reverence, and leaves in suspense whether God pursues an end both with and through world and humankind alike or whether God himself searches for what is lost (*nirdāp*, Qoh. 3:14–15), as Qohelet does.

Composed in the first quarter of the second century BCE and translated into Greek at the end of the same, Ben Sira knows well Qohelet's skepticism toward creation. Rather than share or even restate such a view, however, Ben Sira consciously contrasts this perspective with a synthesis of authoritative traditions from the Torah, Prophets, and Writings (Sir. 16:26–17:32).[10] The connection of Wisdom and creation assumes a formative function thereby. In Sir. 24:1–22, Wisdom, the firstborn of creation, abandons her heavenly throne to find a place of rest within God's wider world, with God finally assigning her to his most beloved stake upon the earth: Jacob/Zion/Jerusalem (Sir. 24:8–12). There Wisdom dwells in the law that contains her completely (Sir. 24:23–34). The characterization of God as "Creator of All" (Sir. 24:8; see 18:1, 50:22 [LXX]) reinforces Wisdom's universal worth, which suffers no restriction from her particular connection to Zion and the law. Two compositions may constitute the end of the book, but they correspond to one another with thematic importance: Sir. 42:15–43:33 begins with the praise of God's abundant glory in creation, while Sir. 44–49 follows with the praise of God's glory in its form as Israel's ancestors, from Enoch to the time of Ben Sira. Both parts together constitute a hymnic history of world and salvation, which shows how God formed creation and history with a conspicuous purpose that rebuffs any challenge from Qohelet. Furthermore, God himself is "the all," not in the sense that he is identical with it but in the sense of the transparence of God in the world. God is therefore greater than all his works (Sir. 43:27–28).

The Creator's all-embracing presence together with his wisdom culminate in teleology. With an apparent though implicit critique of Qohelet, Ben Sira expands the goodness of creation to the point that all things have purpose and meaning. As for the gifts of creation, they turn to good for the good and evil for the evil (Sir. 39:16–35). Ben Sira thus counters Qohelet's determinism with predestination. Yet the author's theological aim lies not on this horizon but on that of praise for creation and the forefathers: their loyalty to God reveals the integrity of creation. Consequently, the service of the high priest Simeon II at the altar of the Jerusalem Temple stands at the zenith of the praise of the ancestors (Sir.

50). The grandson of Ben Sira poignantly translated Simeon's service at the altar with *kosmos kuriou* (Sir. 50:19). "Order of the Lord" may designate the rite, but the term *kosmos* indicates the world more broadly as well. As a result, service to God is "the world of the Lord," the true world, the true totality.

Written in Greek during the first century BCE, the Wisdom of Solomon (Sapientia Salomonis) seeks to fathom even further the purpose of creation.[11] God as being appears visible as Creator through his own creatures' beauty and greatness (Sap. 13:5)—so long as humanity employs its cognitive faculties to perceive him in the first place (Sap. 13:1–9). In addition, creation itself suggests that God has neither created evil nor rejoiced at the fall of the living (Sap. 1:13); on the contrary, "the creations of the world are salvific" (*soteriai hai geneseis tou kosmou*), for God exercises immortal justice in all (Sap. 1:14–15). The soteriological potential of all the divine creations cannot be reduced to an initial act: it is documented in the history of a chosen people and constantly present in Wisdom, the one saving, the other chastising (Sap. 10:1–19:22). Even so, such a history of deliverance is not restricted to a single group but is paradigmatic for the way God governs history, to enforce justice for the sake of the just (Sap. 12:15–27). Although God turns *ktisis* (creation) into a weapon against his enemies (Sap. 5:17), creation can also deploy its powers to comply with the deity's will for punishment or deliverance (Sap. 16:24, 19:6; cf. 16:17). As if the author had sensed the danger of an autonomous creation, he inserts an interpretation of Deut. 8:3 (LXX) here so that the sons—who should understand the wonderful gift of manna—are nourished not by "the creations of fruits" (*hai geneseis ton karpon*) but by "your word, which preserves all who believe" (*to rhema sou tous soi pisteuontas diaterei*) (Sap. 16:26). Wisdom may teach how to see the evidence of God in creation, but it also instructs in the art of interpreting God's word, whether the Torah, as in this particular case; the second half of Isaiah, where creation becomes soteriology; or Ben Sira, without whose connection of creation and predestination the Wisdom of Solomon could never have refined its teleology.

Second Maccabees interprets creation in a soteriological manner not all too distant from Sapientia Salomonis, especially in the story of the seven brothers' martyrdom (2 Macc. 7). With persecution under

Antiochus IV Epiphanes as its background, the legend portrays a tyrant sequentially executing seven brothers who have refused to eat pork. Their mother comforts her dying sons by referring to the power of the Creator, which gives confidence in life after death: "Therefore, the Creator of the world, who forms humanity and conceives the being of all things, will once again grant you spirit [*pneuma*] and life in his mercy, since you have not dishonored yourselves for his laws' sake" (2 Macc. 7:23). Most notable is the mother's speech to the last son, which articulates a conception of creation from nothing for the first time and thus derives a certainty that death will not have the final word:

> I beg you, my child, look at the heaven and earth,
> see everything that is in them;
> thus you will realize that God did not make them from things that
>   (already) exist [οὐκ ἐξ ὄντων],
> and humanity came about likewise.
> Do not fear this execution;
> rather, take this death upon you in a manner worthy of your brothers,
> so that I might receive you, together with your brothers, again in the time
>   of compassion. (2 Macc. 7:28–29)

In his unintuitive power to create new life in precisely that place where evil ostensibly wins the ultimate victory—that is, death—God's creation from nothing belongs to the realm of soteriology. Such creation grounds a hope that only recourse to the initial good creation could possibly have borne. Indeed, creation's only hope lies in a God whose life-creating will can break the power of death. God's yes to life at the beginning becomes, reinterpreted, a reason for hope in his yes to life at the eschaton.

NOTES

I am deeply indebted to Paul Michael Kurtz (Göttingen) and John Barton for transforming my complicated German into fluent English.

1. Further reading on the relation of theology and science, creation and evolution: E. J. Larson, *Evolution: The Remarkable History of a Scientific Theory* (New York: Modern Library, 2004); E. C. Scott, *Evolution vs. Creationism: An Introduction* (Berkeley: University of California Press, 2005); M. Welker, *Creation and Reality* (Minneapolis: Fortress Press, 2000).

2. Further reading on Gen. 1: M. Bauks, *Die Welt am Anfang: Zum Verhältnis von Vorwelt und Weltentstehung in Gen 1 und in der altorientalischen Literatur*, Wissenschaftliche Monographien zum Alten und Neuen Testament 74 (Neukirchen-Vluyn, Germany: Neukirchener Verlag, 1997).

3. Further reading on chaos and creation: S. Niditch, *Chaos to Cosmos: Studies in Biblical Patterns of Creation* (Durham, N.C.: Duke University Press Books, 1985).

4. All pertinent myths from Mesopotamia in translation: S. Dalley, ed. and trans., "The Epic of Creation," in *Myths from Mesopotamia: Creation, the Flood, Gilgamesh, and Others*, World's Classics (Oxford: Oxford University Press, 1991), pp. 228–77.

5. Ibid., pp. 1–38.

6. T. Stordalen, *Echoes of Eden: Genesis 2–3 and Symbolism of the Eden Garden in Biblical Hebrew Literature*, Contributions to Biblical Exegesis and Theology 25 (Leuven: Peeters, 2000); K. Schmid and C. Riedweg, eds., *Beyond Eden: The Biblical Story of Paradise (Genesis 2–3) and Its Reception History*, Forschungen zum Alten Testament 2, Reihe 34 (Tübingen: Mohr Siebeck, 2008).

7. The Ba'lu cycle from Ugarit in translation: M. S. Smith, *The Ugaritic Baal Cycle I*, Supplements to Vetus Testamentum 55 (Leiden: Brill, 1994); M. S. Smith and W. T. Pitard, *The Ugaritic Baal Cycle II*, Supplements to Vetus Testamentum 114 (Leiden: Brill, 2009); D. Pardee, "The Ba'lu Myth," in William W. Hallo and K. Lawson Younger, eds., *The Context of Scripture*, vol. I (Leiden: Brill, 1997), pp. 241–74. Further reading: H. Spieckermann, *Heilsgegenwart. Eine Theologie der Psalmen*, Forschungen zur Religion und Literatur des Alten und Neuen Testaments 148 (Göttingen: Vandenhoeck & Ruprecht, 1989); M. S. Smith, *The Early History of God: Yahweh and the Other Deities in Ancient Israel*, 2nd ed. (Grand Rapids, Mich.: William B. Eerdmans, 2002).

8. Further reading: C. Stuhlmueller, *Creative Redemption in Deutero-Isaiah*, Analecta Biblica 43 (Rome: Biblical Institute Press, 1970); U. Berges, *The Book of Isaiah: Its Composition and Final Form*, Hebrew Bible Monographs 46 (Sheffield: Sheffield Phoenix Press Ltd., 2012).

9. Foundational work: G. von Rad, *Weisheit in Israel* (Neukirchen-Vluyn, Germany: Neukirchener Verlag, 1970); English translation: *Wisdom in Israel*, James D. Martin, trans., 4th ed. (Nashville, Tenn.: Abingdon Press, 1978).

10. The Hebrew version of Ben Sira: P. C. Beentjes, *The Book of Ben Sira in Hebrew*, Supplements to Vetus Testamentum 68 (Leiden: Brill, 1997; republished, Atlanta: Society of Biblical Literature, 2006). Further reading: P. W. Skehan and A. A. di Lella, *The Wisdom of Ben Sira*, Anchor Bible 39 (New York: Doubleday, 1987).

11. Further reading: D. Winston, *The Wisdom of Solomon*, Anchor Bible 43 (New York: Doubleday, 1979).

FURTHER READING

Foundational Works

H. Gunkel, *Schöpfung und Chaos in Urzeit und Endzeit: Eine religionsgeschichtliche Untersuchung über Gen 1 und Ap Joh 12* (Göttingen: Vandenhoeck & Ruprecht, 1895; 2nd ed., 1921); H. Gunkel, *Genesis*, 3rd ed.

(Göttingen: Vandenhoeck & Ruprecht, 1910); English translation: *Genesis*, Mark E. Biddle, trans. (Macon, Ga.: Mercer University Press, 1997).

Present State of Research

B. Anderson, ed., *Creation in the Old Testament* (Minneapolis: Fortress Press, 1985); J. D. Levenson, *Creation and the Persistence of Evil: The Jewish Drama of Divine Omnipotence* (Princeton, N.J.: Princeton University Press, 1988); A. Schüle, *Der Prolog der Hebräischen Bibel: Der literar- und theologiegeschichtliche Diskurs der Urgeschichte (Genesis 1–11)*, Abhandlungen zur Theologie des Alten und Neuen Testaments 86 (Zurich: TVZ, 2006); B. Pongratz-Leisten, A. v. Lieven, A. K. Schuele, G. H. van Kooten, H. Görgemanns, L. DiTommaso, and N. Samuelson, "Creation and Cosmogony," *Encyclopedia of the Bible and Its Reception* 5 (2012): pp. 963–1012.

Creation Theology

T. Fretheim, *God and World in the Old Testament: A Relational Theology of Creation* (Nashville, Tenn.: Abingdon Press, 2005); R. Feldmeier and H. Spieckermann, *Der Gott der Lebendigen. Eine biblische Gotteslehre*, Topoi Biblischer Theologie/Topics of Biblical Theology 1 (Tübingen: Mohr Siebeck, 2011); English translation: *God of the Living. A Biblical Theology*, Mark E. Biddle, trans. (Waco, Tex.: Baylor University Press, 2011; rev. ed., 2013).

12

❀

The Human Condition

Hilary Marlow

"Who is man? Where can we find him in the thicket of clever plans and misguided impulses, on the way from youthful ardour to frigid old age, between the lust for aggression and the suffering of the oppressed? What does he know about his condition, his time and his place in the world? In all the abundance of his knowledge, has man's most fundamental being become for him in the end the most alien of all?"[1] These eloquent but old-fashioned words come from the opening page of Old Testament scholar Hans Walter Wolff's monograph *Anthropology of the Old Testament*, first published in Germany (as *Anthropologie des Alten Testaments*) in 1973. Wolff's ambitious aim was to produce a scholarly work on the anthropology of the Old Testament that combined textual exegesis with theological understanding in such a way that the scholar might have "the chance of entering into dialogue with the other, a dialogue through which he begins to understand his being as man."[2] His concern reflects the emphasis on biblical theology that characterized much Old Testament scholarship during the first half of the twentieth century, particularly in Germany and the United States.[3]

The aim of this essay (and, more generally, of biblical studies in the twenty-first century) is more modest. It will explore the diverse ways in which the Old Testament writers depict human beings and their relationship to God and to one another. It will look at ancient views on human purpose and the "meaning of life," including suffering, death, and the possibility of an afterlife. Finally it will consider the human relationship with nonhuman life and the question of ecology and the Old Testament.

As we set out to examine "the human condition" in the Old Testament, it is important to bear in mind some key ways in which the worldview(s) of the Old Testament differs from that of modern Western society. First, the Old Testament has a theocentric perspective; that is to say, one of its primary concerns is God's interaction with the world and human life lived in harmony with God. For the writers of the Old Testament, the existence of God is not in doubt; it is an assumption underlying all their writing. Moreover they are not much given to philosophical or ontological speculation about the being or nature of God (unlike the Greek philosophers). God is portrayed, using a variety of anthropomorphic and natural imagery, as a deterministic and active presence in the world.

Second, in the biblical world, in contrast to today's individualistic society, the focus is on human community rather than on the individual conception of self. Relationships and roles within the family and clan play an important part in the formation of identity, and meaning derives from a person's purposeful interactions with others in society. Third, the Old Testament writers seem acutely aware, in a way that we no longer are, of the close and sometimes precarious relationship between human communities and the natural world, in particular their dependence on the land and its resources of food and fuel. Each of these three areas of relationship—with God, with fellow human beings, and with nature—is important for understanding the human condition in the Old Testament.

TERMINOLOGY AND SOCIAL GROUPINGS

A number of Hebrew words are used in the Old Testament to refer to human beings, the most common being *'iyš* and *'ādām*. The masculine noun *'iyš* (man/husband) occurs nearly 2,200 times, and its feminine counterpart *'iššâ* (woman/wife), more than 780 times. *'iyš* is used in a wide range of senses, from denoting a specific individual or group of people to a generic distributive "each person." It is often found in the construct form to describe a particular characteristic (e.g., *'iyš yiśrā'ēl*, "man of Israel"; *'iyš milḥāmâ*, "man of war/warrior").

The noun *'ādām* (from which we get the name Adam) is a generic term used to denote both an individual—"a human"—and the human race—"humankind." It is found in nearly every book of the Old Testament, more than six hundred times in total, with a particular concentration in Genesis 1–11 and the books of Ezekiel and Ecclesiastes.

The use of *'ādām* in the early chapters of Genesis is particularly flexible. In the Priestly creation narrative of Genesis 1, God creates humankind (*'ādām*) in his own image as male and female (v. 27). In the Yahwist account (Genesis 2–3), *'ādām* is almost always written with the definite article, "the human" (*hā 'ādām*), and refers to a specific human being, formed by God from the ground (*hā 'adāmâ*). To complicate matters, the *'ādām* figure in Genesis 2 only seems to take on a specific male identity from verse 18, when the woman is created as his counterpart. From Gen. 4:25, when a particular individual is clearly in view, the noun *'ādām* no longer bears the definite article, and this is indicated by the NRSV translation's use of the proper noun *Adam* at this point in the narrative.[4]

In the prophetic book Ezekiel, *'ādām* occurs 133 times, ninety-four of which are when God addresses the prophet as *ben- 'ādām* (literally, "son of man"). Commentators tell us that the expression may be used to stress the prophet's human status before God; alternatively, it may suggest that he has been singled out to receive God's word. In later Jewish traditions, the "son of man" becomes an anointed, transcendent figure, who will execute justice and judgment on the earth. This tradition begins with a single reference to "son of man" (in Aramaic) in Daniel 7 and continues in the pseudepigraphic work *1 Enoch* and on into the New Testament, where it is found primarily in the gospels and usually as a self-designation on the lips of Jesus.[5]

A third term, *'ĕnôš*, only occurs just over forty times, particularly in the Psalms (thirteen times) and the book of Job (eighteen times). It is often found in parallel with *'ādām* (twenty times).[6]

WHO AM I?

The Old Testament writers sometimes reflect specifically on the meaning of life and what it is to be human. The clearest examples of this can be found in the Psalms (especially Psalms 8 and 139) and the books of Job and Ecclesiastes. Psalm 139 is a poetic reflection on the psalmist's experience of being known by God, his creator. In it he describes God as the one who "knit me together in my mother's womb" (v. 13) and concludes that "I am fearfully and wonderfully made" (v. 14). Since God has seen him from conception (vv. 15–16) there is now nowhere he can go to hide from God (vv. 7–12)—a positive idea in this psalm, in contrast to Amos 9:2–4, which is concerned with the human inability to hide from God's judgment. Psalm 139 as a whole eloquently conveys the theological mystery of God's dealings with an individual human being, as well as wonder at the biological mystery of conception and birth.

In Psalm 8 the psalmist questions God directly: "What are human beings that you are mindful of them, mortals that you care for them?" (Ps. 8:4 [5]).[7] The context of his question is a reflection on his own smallness and insignificance compared with the size and splendor of the night sky (vv. 1–3 [2–4]); the answer he gives to his own question (vv. 5–8 [6–9], echoing Gen. 1:28) reflects his positive observations on the role of human beings with regard to the natural world.

The book of Job asks a similar question (Job 7:17), but within the more negative framework of Job's complaint to God about the injustice of his suffering.[8] Job's plight (the loss of his livestock and death of his children, as well as his own physical afflictions) and the "comfort" of his well-meaning but insensitive friends provoke a series of anguished speeches.[9] In chapter 7 Job's questioning of God is a bitter one (vv. 17–19), and he concludes that he is a burden to God (v. 20) and that, anyway, life is not worth living (v. 16).

The book of Ecclesiastes is unique in the Old Testament: a collection of pessimistic and melancholy discourses on the meaning of life from someone nearing its end (known as Qohelet, the Teacher), in which God seems a distant and disinterested figure.[10] The opening words of the Teacher sum up his attitude to life: "Vanity of vanities! All is vanity. What do people gain from all the toil at which they toil under the sun?" (1:2–3). Yet there is also a thread running through the book of a pragmatic approach to human existence, as the Teacher's musings are interspersed with proverbs and practical advice, some of which seems self-directed at King Solomon, the supposed author (e.g., 4:13).

These various examples of questioning and reflection remind us that there is no single perspective on the meaning of life in the Old Testament. Different texts offer different, often partial, answers to the question "What does it mean to be human?" This is not surprising, since the Old Testament is not a single book but a library that has been collected and edited over a long period. Its diversity, on this issue as on many others, reflects a variety of genres, contexts, authors, and emphases.

IMAGE OF GOD

For many interpreters, the Old Testament's view on what it means to be human can be summed up in the idea that human beings are made "in the image of God." This enigmatic phrase is found in the Genesis 1 account of the creation of human beings—"Let us make humankind [ʾādām] in our image [ṣelem], according to our likeness [demût]" (v. 26)—and has been very influential in the history of Western thought. For example, reflecting on this Bible verse helped convince William Wilberforce, the great nineteenth-century reformer, that slavery was an affront to human dignity as "the image of God" and thus motivated his campaign to abolish the slave trade.[11] The precise meaning of the phrase has been the subject of endless debate in different theological and social contexts, by both Jewish and Christian scholars, most of which is beyond the scope of this chapter.[12] However, there are some interesting points to note about how the "image of God" concept is used in the Bible. First, from a semantic point of view, like the proper noun *Adam*, the phrase is rare in the Old Testament—in fact Genesis 1:26–27, 5:3, and 9:6 are the only places that speak of human beings as "in the image of God," and the nouns *image* (ṣelem) and *likeness* (demût) only occur together twice (Gen. 1:26 and 5:3).[13] This makes it extremely difficult to draw conclusions on meaning from the word use alone.[14]

Second, and this might be a more fruitful line of inquiry, there are a number of parallels to the biblical idea of the image of God in other ancient Near Eastern literatures.[15] Two aspects of this are particularly relevant. The first is the well-attested practice by ancient Near Eastern kings of setting up statues or images of themselves in places where they were physically absent as a symbol of their authority over those places. The second, related facet is the existence of numerous texts, particularly Egyptian ones, that describe various kings (and occasionally priests) as the image of a god. Both aspects draw on ideas of kingship or ruling to suggest the notion of representative or delegated authority. Although drawing parallels with other ancient texts can be very instructive, conclusions must be treated with caution, since exact translations and interpretations of texts are often ambiguous.[16] Nevertheless, there seems to be sufficient evidence, in both Egyptian and Mesopotamian sources, to suggest that ancient Near Eastern royal ideology lies behind the "image of God" language of Genesis 1. In Genesis the concept is democratized to include all humanity, not just the king, as the representatives and intermediaries of God on earth.

HUMAN ABUNDANCE AND TRANSIENCE

It is strange that there is so much emphasis by interpreters of the Bible on the idea of humans being made "in the image of God," despite the infrequent use of this concept in the Old Testament.[17] In fact, the Old Testament uses a rich diversity of other terms, metaphors, and similes to explore what it means to be human. Some of these are concerned with human weakness, frailty, and finitude; others, with flourishing and fertility. Some bear multiple meanings and are used with different senses in different texts. In this section we shall explore some of these key ideas and metaphors.

Far more prevalent in the Old Testament than "image of God" language is the notion that human beings are formed by God from the soil or dust. This idea, which is common to other ancient Near Eastern literature, imagines God as a master craftsman molding the human form from the earth, much as a potter crafts a pot from clay. The analogy with a potter's work is made explicit in Isaiah, where Israel is chided for questioning God's authority (29:16, 45:9; see also 64:8), as well as in the extended metaphor of Jer. 18:2–6, which emphasizes God's supreme power over his creation. The Old Testament's portrayal of the "earthy" origin of humanity, made from dust and returning to it, serves to stress the transience and frailty of human life, as well as human dependence upon God.

Genesis 2–3 makes this point particularly clearly and presents a different perspective on human origins from that of Genesis 1 (see above). Whatever the process by which these two creation stories emerged, their juxtaposition here at the start of the Old Testament is a deliberate one, intended to convey the breadth and complexity of what it means to be human. Although modern biblical scholars tend to read these as two separate and contrasting accounts, early theological reflections on Genesis do not draw such a sharp distinction between them. A good example of this is the second-century BCE book of Ben Sira (Ecclesiasticus), now part of the Apocrypha, in which the sage weaves together phrases from the early chapters of Genesis to describe the creation of human-kind (Sir. 17:1–4).[18]

In Genesis 2–3, as in Genesis 1, God is the agent, but here he crafts the first human (*hā 'ādām*) from the dust of the ground (*hā 'adāmâ*, 2:7). The Hebrew wordplay is deliberate: *'ādām* from the *'adāmâ*, perhaps best conveyed by the English translation "human from the humus." Notice, however, that the human form only becomes animate when God breathes life into it (Gen. 2:7; see also Job 33:4; Isa. 42:5). This is not distinctive of human life, as the same is true of the animals—later in the same chapter they, too, are formed from the ground (Gen. 2:19) and, like human beings, are dependent for life on the breath that God gives (Gen. 7:15; Eccles. 3:19). When God withdraws his breath, life comes to an end, and human beings return to the dust from which they were formed (Gen. 3:19; see also Job 34:14–15; Pss. 104:29, 146:4).

The notion of becoming or returning to dust is frequently used in the Old Testament, particularly in the Psalms and Job, to refer to human death, either as part of a natural and inevitable biological process (e.g., Job 21:26; Ps. 22:29) or in the context of fear and distress (e.g., Job 17:16; Pss. 7:5, 44:24–25). This association of death with dust or soil is an important one in the Old Testament. It surfaces in descriptions of people adorning themselves with dust and/or ashes as a sign of mourning (Job 2:8, 12; 30:19; Lam. 2:10; Ezek. 27:30) or of repentance and humility (e.g., Josh. 7:6; Esther 4:1; Job 42:6). At its fundamental level, it indicates an awareness that life is fragile and temporary and is a reminder of the biological processes of decay whereby organic matter decomposes and eventually turns into soil.

Other biblical metaphors that depict the transience and fragility of life are those that liken human beings to a flower or grass that quickly fades and dies (e.g., Pss. 37:2, 102:11, 103:15; Isa. 28:1, 40:6–8), or to a shadow that is here one moment and gone the next (e.g., Job 8:9; Pss. 102:11, 144:4), or to both (Job 14:2). Interestingly, these references to grass or flowers wilting as a metaphor to convey transience are balanced by those that refer to vegetation sprouting and blossoming to suggest restoration of life and abundance (e.g., Job 5:25; Ps. 72:16; Isa. 27:6, 66:14). Similarly, dust does not only symbolize human fragility or death; it can sometimes convey the idea of immense human population size (e.g., the Abrahamic covenant in Gen. 13:16 and 28:14; Num. 23:6).

Likewise, a shadow may be a sign of insubstantiality, but it can also indicate a place of shelter and protection, especially when it is God's shadow in view (e.g., Pss. 36:7, 91:1, 121:5; Hosea 14:7).

In contrast to this multivalent use of figurative language, two metaphors for humanity in the Old Testament only occur with a positive meaning to denote human flourishing and abundance, namely, that human beings will become as numerous as the grains of sand on the shore and the stars in the sky. These descriptors are particularly associated with the promises to Abraham in Genesis (Gen. 15:5, 22:17, 26:4) but recur in a number of other texts as the promise is reiterated, both positively (e.g., Exod. 32:15; Deut. 10:22; 1 Kings 4:20; Neh. 9:23) and negatively (e.g., Isa. 10:22, 48:19; Deut. 28:62).

There are two general points to note about these examples of the way that figurative language is used to describe humanity. First, nearly all the examples come from prophetic or poetic books of the Bible. This is unsurprising, since the nature of these types of literature is to use rich symbolism and fluidity of language to paint vivid word pictures. Hence the same metaphor can be used to express dynamically opposed ideas such as transience and flourishing. We will see that a different picture emerges in the narrative texts of the Old Testament. The second point to note is how much this picture language draws on the natural world—human life is so often seen as analogous to the way nature functions. This is an important observation and one that we shall return to later.

THE BEGINNING AND END OF LIFE

The narrative and legal texts of the Old Testament generally have a much more pragmatic and down-to-earth approach to life than do the poetic texts. In the stories of the Pentateuch and the Deuteronomistic History, birth and death are regarded as everyday events forming part of the cycle of life. There are, however, several important aspects to the way the beginning and end of life are regarded in these texts.

Marriage, Sex, Conception, and Birth

Although the process of finding a wife is described in some detail in Genesis with regard to Isaac (Gen. 24) and Jacob (Gen. 29), there is little in the Old Testament about actual wedding ceremonies, the Hebrew preferring simply to convey marriage by the expression "to take a wife" (*lāqaḥ 'iššâ*). This is usually the prerogative of the man himself (Gen. 28:2; Judg. 14:3) but sometimes the choice of his father (Gen. 38:6) or even the action of his first wife (Gen. 30:9). In the Old Testament, polygamy is a normal part of life, and many biblical characters have multiple wives, with stories of jealous rivalry between wives or concubines enlivening tales of the patriarchs, for example, Abraham's wife Sarah and her servant Hagar (Gen. 16 and 21) and Jacob's wives Rachel and Leah (Gen. 30).[19] The legal material of Exodus includes stipulations safeguarding the rights of one wife if a man takes a second one (Exod. 21:10). Although examples of marriage contracts can be found in other ancient Near Eastern texts, particularly from the postexilic period,[20] the Old Testament does not give specific details. However, the formal sealing of a marriage agreement and the paying of a dowry or bride-price are implicit in various texts (e.g., Ruth 4:7–10; Gen. 34:12), and laws relating to marital issues such as who may marry whom, grounds for dissolving a marriage, and provision for childless widows are interspersed with other laws, primarily in the books of Exodus and Leviticus.[21]

Although there are plenty of stories involving sexual encounters in the Old Testament, and indeed erotic love is celebrated in the Song of Songs, biblical Hebrew is rather coy when it comes to speaking of sexual intercourse. The sexual act is referred to using a number of euphemistic expressions, of which the most frequently occurring in both narrative and legal texts is the verb *šākab* (to lie with). So, for example, we read, "Reuben went and lay with Bilhah his father's concubine" (Gen. 35:22), and, "If a man lies with a woman …" (Lev. 15:18). Other verbs used to denote sexual intercourse include *yāda'* (to know, Gen. 4:1) and *bô'* (to come together, Ruth 4:13), but each of these terms can have a much wider meaning than the sexual act.

For the most part the process of conception, pregnancy, and childbirth in the Old Testament passes without drama. This does not mean that children are unimportant—quite the opposite. As we shall see in the section on death below, the Old Testament depicts no particularly strong belief by the ancient Israelites in the afterlife. This means that the continuity of life after death is by means of one's descendants—from generation to generation. This is why various genealogies and lists of descendants, which seem rather inconsequential to modern readers, occur at key moments in the narratives (e.g., Gen. 5, Gen. 10, Gen. 25). Remembering and reciting the names of ancestors gives a continuity and stability to what is otherwise a precarious existence. The inability to conceive (always regarded as the woman's fault) is thus a major problem in the Old Testament, and this theme recurs in a number of stories that highlight God's ability to overturn the physical problems caused by age or infertility. In Genesis, the story of Abraham's wife Sarah miraculously conceiving even when she is past childbearing age (Gen. 16–17) highlights God's part in the covenant with Abraham. Later in Genesis, Rebekah (Gen. 25:21) and Rachel (Gen. 30) both struggle to conceive, as does the mother of Samson in Judges 13 and Hannah, Samuel's mother, in 1 Samuel 1. In each case, it is divine intervention, often in answer to prayer, that results in the birth of a child (always male).

Childbirth is rarely described in any detail in the Old Testament, although the assistance of midwives is assumed on occasions, the most detailed and engaging story being that of the Egyptian midwives in Exodus 1. The few exceptions are where labor is difficult or even fatal, as in the story of the birth of Esau and Jacob to Rebekah (Gen. 25:19–26); the story of Rachel's last son, Benjamin (Gen. 35:16–20); and the story of the (unnamed) daughter-in-law of Eli the priest and the wife of Phinehas (in 1 Sam. 4:19–22). In each text, particularly those concerning Rebekah and Phinehas's wife, the difficult birth is given a great symbolic significance by the author.

Suffering, Death, and the Afterlife

The Old Testament is full of death and dying. Indeed the Hebrew stem *mût* (to die) and its derivations occur more than one thousand times, often in stereotypical formulas or formulaic phrases.[22] A number of poetic and prophetic texts use rich metaphors to portray death (e.g., 2 Sam. 22:5–6; Ps. 107:18) and occasionally personify it (e.g., Job 18:13; Jer. 9:21). However, most references to dying are matter-of-fact descriptions of biological death, whether the natural end of life due to old age and sickness, the murder of another person or people, or the death of the wicked as punishment from God.

The most evocative description of natural death is that of Abraham in Gen. 25:8, which uses several different phrases to portray the peaceful and timely death of an elderly leader: "Abraham breathed his last and died in a good old age, old and full of years and was gathered to his people." These phrases, or some combination of them, are also used to describe the deaths of various other characters: Ishmael (Gen. 15:15), Isaac (Gen. 35:29), Jacob (Gen. 49:33), Aaron (Num. 20:26), Moses (Num. 31:2), David (1 Chron. 29:28), and Job (Job 42:17). The fact that the death of these people represents the end of fruitful lives does not mean that their loss is not keenly felt by those nearest to them. The rituals of mourning for the dead, including anointing oneself with dust or ashes (as noted above), form an important part of Israelite culture, and the length of periods of mourning is hinted at in the legal material (Deut. 21:13).[23] In the narrative texts, Abraham mourns for his wife Sarah (Gen. 23:2), all Israel mourns for thirty days after the deaths of Aaron (Num. 20:29) and Moses (Deut. 34:8), and Samuel grieves for Saul (1 Sam. 15:35; see also 2 Sam. 1:12).

A different perspective on death is found in the story of King Hezekiah (Isa. 38:1–21; 2 Kings 20:1–7). Here it seems that premature or untimely death is regarded as something to be feared and fought against. When Hezekiah becomes seriously ill he prays earnestly to God, who responds by sending a supernatural sign through the prophet Isaiah that Hezekiah will recover and live for a further fifteen years. Likewise, when King David's young son is taken ill, David fasts and prays for the child's life for seven days. Only when the child dies and all hope is gone does he compose himself again (2 Sam. 12:10–23).

The majority of references to dying in the Old Testament concern premature death as a punishment or as the result of violence. In narrative texts, legal material, and poetry and prophecy, wickedness and disobedience to the law are punishable by death, as is graphically portrayed in the stories of the golden calf (Exod. 32) and Achan's sin (Josh. 7). The violent and seemingly excessive punishment in these and other stories is very disturbing to modern readers and has led atheists such as Richard Dawkins to dismiss the Old Testament as a "cruel ogre."[24] Despite the real ethical concerns raised by the God of the Old Testament's harsh treatment of individuals and groups, it is important to remember that the cultural world out of which these texts emerged was one of raw, often vindictive brutality. It is hardly surprising that the authors' portrayal of God's actions also jars with us. Interestingly, there is a pragmatic acceptance of the cruelty (e.g., Judg. 1:4–7) as well as a sense that there are ethical limits binding on all nations that should not be transgressed (Amos 1:3–2:3).[25]

What happens to people when they die? Unlike later Christian and Jewish thought, the Old Testament places little emphasis on life after death or bodily resurrection. The place where people go at death is often known by the Hebrew name *še'ôl* (Sheol), especially in poetic and prophetic texts. The origin of the name is unknown, and it has different connotations according to context.[26] Sheol is regarded as the region under the earth, the "underworld," and contrasted with the earth and the heavens (Deut. 32:22; Job 11:8). It is a shadowy realm, a place without hope where God is not praised (Ps. 6:5; Isa. 38:18) and from which none can escape (Ps. 89:48). Descending into Sheol is sometimes a metaphor for dying (e.g., Gen. 37:35; 1 Sam. 2:6; Job 7:9) or for being in intense danger or trouble (2 Sam. 22:6; Ps. 16:10; Jon. 2:2). More often than not, however, Sheol is portrayed as the destination of the wicked, in contrast to those who are righteous or wise (e.g., Pss. 9:16, 31:17; Prov. 15:24). God is portrayed as the one who delivers his people by bringing them up from Sheol (Ps. 30:3) and ransoming them or delivering them from its power (Pss. 49:15, 86:13). This rich and diverse tradition surrounding the name Sheol highlights the fact that the Old Testament is more concerned with life well lived and preservation from death than with life *after* death. Only a few texts, regarded as postexilic by many biblical scholars, suggest the possibility of final resurrection and the defeat of death. These include the notion of an eschatological banquet and the end of death (Isa. 25:6–8) and a vision of new heavens and a new earth, free from suffering and hardship (Isa. 65:17–25).

HUMAN AND NONHUMAN CREATION

As well as the relationship between God and his people, the Old Testament pays significant attention to the connection between human beings and the physical world. This interest plays out at a number of different yet overlapping levels—economic, sociopolitical, and theological.

In practical terms, the ancient Israelites, like their neighbors in the ancient Near East, were economically dependent on herding and farming, and therefore the Old Testament pays great interest to livestock and crops. The early chapters of Genesis record the transition from hunter-gatherers (Cain and Abel, Genesis 4) to nomadic herdsmen (e.g., Abraham and Lot, Genesis 12–13) to settled agriculturalists and pastoralists (e.g., Jacob, Gen. 37:1). In the arid conditions of the Near East, water is a precious commodity, so the provision of clean, safe water for people and animals is a practical necessity (Josh. 15:19) as well as a major theological theme (Exod. 17:1–7; Deut. 8:7). In addition, the text records numerous instances of conflict over water sources, whether natural springs or constructed wells (e.g., Gen. 26:19–22; 2 Kings 3:25).

The dependence of Israelite subsistence farmers on the earth's productivity is highlighted by the attention given in the Old Testament to seasons and weather cycles, ranging from promises of regularity in the daily and annual rhythms (e.g., Gen. 8:22; Jer. 31:35–36) to reminders that Israel's God is the guarantor of rains and harvests (e.g., Lev. 26:4; Deut. 11:14; Jer. 5:24). The book of Proverbs and other proverbial material include careful instructions on farming wisely and well (Prov. 27:23; Isa. 28:23–28) as well as warnings against poor practice (Prov. 20:4). Likewise, various instructions on sustainable farming practice as well as care for animals are found in the legal material in the Old Testament (e.g., Lev. 25:1–5; Deut. 20:19; 22:1–4, 6).

The relationship between people and the natural world is by no means always a positive one, for both pragmatic and theological reasons. In practical terms, the struggle to farm in often-inhospitable terrain with the ever-present threat of wild animals produces both an awareness of the dangers especially to livestock, as the young King David makes clear (1 Sam. 17:34–37), and a longing for an alternative idyllic reality where wild animals live at peace with humans and their livestock (Isa. 11:6–9, 35:1–2, 65:25). The wilderness (*midbār*) in the Old Testament is often portrayed by commentators either as a primitive idyll where Israel is totally dependent on her God or as a hostile and unforgiving desert.[27] The reality is more nuanced than either of these extremes. The wilderness can be a harsh place associated with danger and privation (Exod. 14:11–12, 16:2–3), but it is also the place of Moses's encounter with God (Exod. 3) and of God's covenant with Israel (Exod. 19). Indeed, the portrayal of wilderness is often deliberately ambiguous, since God is present there despite the difficulties encountered (e.g., Gen. 21:14–19; Hosea 13:4–6).

The biblical authors' interest in nature can be seen in their care in observing and cataloging species (e.g., the detailed food laws in Leviticus 11, King Solomon in 1 Kings 4:33) and the frequent use of metaphors of nature to describe God (e.g., Ps. 18:2; Hosea 5:13, 13:7–8) or humanity (e.g., Ps. 32:9; Prov. 6:5; Song of Sol. 6:5–6). In addition, numerous extended metaphors of nature in the prophetic and poetic books of the Old Testament testify to the importance of the natural world in the biblical authors' thinking and imagination. First Isaiah is particularly rich in imagery of vines and vineyards (e.g., the parables of the vineyard in 5:1–7 and 27:2–5), and the books of Ezekiel and Joel include extended metaphors featuring nature (trees in Ezek. 31:1–18, locusts in Joel 1:4, 2:1–11). In several instances, the animal kingdom is held up as a model against which human diligence and understanding can be judged (Prov. 6:6–11; Isa. 1:2–3; Jer. 8:7).

In addition to providing resources for human consumption, the whole of the natural world has intrinsic value in the Old Testament as part of God's creation. This is exemplified in the book of Job, in which God's response to Job's complaint is to urge him to humbly consider his (Job's) own limited understanding of the world and its creatures (Job 38–41). The natural world is a source of awe and wonder for the psalmists, reminding human beings of God's transcendent majesty and evoking praise and worship (Pss. 8:1–4, 19:1–6). In numerous other psalms, the whole of creation is called to praise God alongside human beings (e.g., Pss. 96:11–13, 148:3–10, 150:6).

Psalm 104 offers a detailed description of the world and its contents that demonstrates the intrinsic value of all living things, while maintaining a robust understanding of the food chain and "Nature, red in tooth and claw." Based on the stages of creation in Genesis 1, this psalm graphically and poetically portrays the formation of the cosmos (vv. 2–9), before paying great attention to the way that God provides for various species of animals and their young, describing what we would call habitats and ecosystems (vv. 10–23). In this, human beings are just one species among many that have been created through God's wisdom (v. 24) and are dependent on God for food "in due season" (vv. 27–28) and for life itself (vv. 29–30).

As is discussed elsewhere in this book, the story of the promised land and its possession and subsequent loss by the Israelites is a key theme running throughout the Old Testament, and the political and military maneuverings of Israel and the surrounding nations are invested with great theological significance by the biblical authors. It is at this theological level that the relationship between the land (or the earth—the Hebrew term *hā'āreṣ* covers a wide range of meaning)[28] and its human population is most striking. For many of the biblical authors, nature, whether the cosmos, the land/earth, or some part of it, acts as a barometer of the relationship between God and God's people.

The Old Testament prophetic books express this graphically through the notion of the earth "mourning" or "drying up" (the same Hebrew root, *'ābal*, carries both senses) as a result of human wickedness (e.g., Jer. 12:10–11) or divine judgment (e.g., Jer. 4:27–28). In agricultural terms, this may refer to the effect of drought or warfare—the texts often do not make this clear. At a theological level, the expression serves to highlight the close interconnection among Israel's God, the people, and the earth. Hosea 4:1–3 is a particularly clear example of this: the prophet first castigates the people for failing to fulfill their responsibilities—both toward God and toward their fellow human beings (v. 1). This failure results in societal breakdown, depicted in verse 2 as the neglect of the commandments and an increase in violence. By means of a strong Hebrew conjunction (*'al-kēn*), Hosea links the collapse of human society with dramatic and devastating effects in the natural world (v. 3).

A similar interplay between the wickedness of human beings and the degradation of the land is found in Isaiah 24:4–6. Here the earth mourns and withers (v. 4) and is polluted by its inhabitants because they have neglected the "everlasting covenant" (*bᵉrît 'ôlām*, v. 5). The reference to broken laws and statutes in Isaiah 24:5 suggests that it is the covenant between God and Israel at Mount Sinai that is in view. However, the phrase "everlasting covenant" is also used of the covenant with Noah and all living creatures (Gen. 9:16) and may, according to some commentators, indicate the existence of a primitive covenantal tradition between YHWH and creation.[29] The notion that the wrongdoing of human beings pollutes or defiles the land is also found in the legal material of the Old Testament (Lev. 18:27–28; Num. 35:53). According to Leviticus, the result of this defilement is that the land will "vomit out" its inhabitants, a graphic reference to the Babylonian exile (Lev. 18:25, 28). Deuteronomy portrays it in terms of a series of curses—on people, land, crops, and livestock (Deut. 28:15–19).

One form of wrongdoing on which the prophet Amos is particularly outspoken is the exploitation of the poor and weak by the rich and powerful in society (Amos 4:1, 8:4–6; see also Mic. 6:10–12). This neglect of "justice and righteousness" (the phrase that he and other prophets use to characterize the ideal Israelite sociality) has serious implications, not just for the human perpetrators of injustice but for the land too. The sequence of cause and effect that I have noted in Hosea whereby actions in one sphere have consequences in another is true here in Amos too: when the poor are oppressed and God is neglected, the rains fail and the harvest is destroyed by locusts (Amos 4:7–9), and the whole earth is subject to flood and earthquake (Amos 8:7–9).

So, the Old Testament is concerned not only with the relationship between God and his people but also with the interaction between people and nature at an economic and social level and, more profoundly, in theological terms. If, as we have seen, the natural world is adversely affected by human wrongdoings against God and against other people, what happens when the relationship between God and his people flourishes? Unsurprisingly, many Old Testament texts that speak of a hopeful future for humanity include nature in their portrayal of flourishing. At the level of economic well-being, the restoration of Israel's relationship with God results in increased fertility for the land (e.g., Deut. 28:1–6; Isa. 30:23–24; Amos 9:13–14). More dramatically, the vision of Isaiah 35 is of the restoration and flourishing of the whole natural world (vv. 1–2) alongside the healing of people from sickness and disability (vv. 5–6) and the return from exile (vv. 8–10). This exuberant and dramatic picture is one of several that inextricably link the restoration of barren and potentially hostile natural environments with the remaking of human society and of the human relationship with God (see also Isa. 29:17–21, 31:16–20; Hosea 2:16–23 [18–25]).

THE OLD TESTAMENT AND CONTEMPORARY ENVIRONMENTALISM

What implications, if any, does the Old Testament's emphasis on the transience of human life and the importance of the natural world have for contemporary ecological thinking? Some contemporary scholars, both theologians and ecologists, maintain that the Old Testament's strongly anthropocentric focus and utilitarian attitude toward nature are a problem for environmental ethics. Some even go as far as to claim that the Judeo-Christian tradition is to blame for the current environmental crisis and the alienation of human beings from nature.[30] Many commentators who are critical of the biblical text from an environmental perspective direct their attention to the creation of human beings in Genesis 1 and suggest that God's blessing of human beings in verse 28 is a divine directive to rule creation that legitimizes the current destruction and exploitation of the earth's resources. Although the Hebrew words used for subduing the earth and having dominion over other creatures, *rādâ* and *kābaš*, are strong, they are not always used in the Old Testament in a harsh and exploitative sense, as critics suggest. Indeed, ruling harshly is expressly prohibited in Leviticus (Lev. 25:43, 46), and the biblical ideal of kingly rule is far from that of a despotic tyrant (see Psalm 72; Isa. 11:1–10; Jer. 23:5–6). Moreover, Genesis 1:28 can be balanced by the role given to Adam in Genesis 2: he is to serve (*'ābad*) and watch over (*šāmar*) the garden into which he is placed by God, tasks that suggest careful husbandry, rather than domination.

Space prevents delving any further into the many issues surrounding environmental ethics and the Bible.[31] However, the Old Testament's stress on the importance of all creation and its portrayal of the complex relationship among God, people, and the natural world certainly provides plenty of food for thought on how human beings might live sensitively and sustainably on this fragile earth.

NOTES

1. Hans Walter Wolff, *Anthropology of the Old Testament* (London: SCM, 1974), p. 1.
2. Ibid., p. 3. Wolff was strongly influenced by the theology of his fellow German speaker the Swiss systematic theologian Karl Barth.

3. See Leo G. Perdue, *Reconstructing Old Testament Theology: After the Collapse of History* (Minneapolis: Fortress Press, 2005).

4. Beyond the few references to Adam in the genealogies of Genesis 5 and 1 Chronicles 1, the proper noun *Adam* does not recur in the Old Testament, and the "adamic" tradition is a development of later Jewish and Christian thought. See John R. Levison, *Portraits of Adam in Early Judaism: From Sirach to 2 Baruch* (Sheffield: JSOT, 1987); Eric Noffke, "Man of Glory or First Sinner? Adam in the Book of Sirach," *Zeitschrift für die alttestamentliche Wissenschaft* 119, no. 4 (2007): pp. 618–24. And on the development of Adam theology in the New Testament, J.D.G. Dunn, *Christology in the Making: An Enquiry into the Origin of the Doctrine of the Incarnation* (London: SCM, 1980); N. T. Wright, "Adam in Pauline Christology," in K. H. Richards, ed., *SBL 1983 Seminar Papers* (Chico, Calif.: Scholars Press, 1983), pp. 366–67.

5. See George W. E. Nickelsburg, "Son of Man," in D. N. Freedman, D. F. Graf, G. A. Herion, and J. D. Pleins, eds., *Anchor Bible Dictionary,* vol. 6 (New York: Doubleday, 1992), pp. 137–50.

6. Parallelism is a stylistic device in Hebrew poetry whereby one phrase repeats or elaborates the ideas of the preceding one. See Adele Berlin, "Parallelism," in D. N. Freedman, D. F. Graf, G. A. Herion, and J. D. Pleins, eds., *Anchor Bible Dictionary,* vol. 5 (New York: Doubleday, 1992), pp. 155–62; also George B. Gray, *The Forms of Hebrew Poetry* (New York: Ktav Publishing House, 1972).

7. All biblical references are taken from the NRSV. Hebrew versification, where different, is given in square brackets.

8. For discussion on the literary and linguistic relationship between Psalm 8 and Job 7, see Will Kynes, *My Psalm Has Turned into Weeping: Job's Dialogue with the Psalms* (Berlin: De Gruyter, 2012), pp. 63–79.

9. Chapters 3, 6–7, 9–10, 12–14, 16–17, 19, 21, 23–24, and 26–31 in the book of Job.

10. Although Ecclesiastes is attributed to King Solomon (1:1), like the book of Job it probably dates from the Persian period, when the traditional wisdom of previous centuries was being questioned.

11. See Adam Hochschild, *Bury the Chains: The British Struggle to Abolish Slavery* (London: Macmillan, 2005).

12. See, for example, the discussion in the commentaries on Genesis by Wenham and Westermann: Gordon Wenham, *Genesis 1–15*, Word Biblical Commentary (Nashville, Tenn.: Thomas Nelson Publishers, 1987); Claus Westermann, *Genesis 1–11: A Commentary*, J. Scullion, trans. (London: SPCK, 1984 [Ger., 1974]).

13. The terms are picked up in the New Testament epistles, where two texts refer to Christ as the "image of God" (2 Cor. 4:4; Col. 1:15) and in one text a man (husband) is so described (1 Cor. 11:7).

14. J. Richard Middleton, *The Liberating Image: The Imago Dei in Genesis 1* (Grand Rapids, Mich.: Brazos Press, 2005), pp. 45–48.

15. For an overview of the ancient Near Eastern background to the concept, see David Clines, "Humanity as the Image of God," *Tyndale Bulletin* 19 (1968): pp. 53–103; reprinted in *On the Way to the Postmodern: Old Testament Essays 1967–1998* (Sheffield: JSOT Press, 1998), pp. 447–97.

16. See Middleton, *Liberating Image*, pp. 93–122; Clines, "Humanity as the Image of God."

17. This is perhaps because of the theological desire throughout the ages to assert human dignity and significance and to make a clear separation between human beings

and "mere" animals. This is particularly true of the period between the sixteenth and nineteenth centuries, a time of revolutionary scientific discoveries and great intellectual and philosophical questioning. See Hilary Marlow, *Biblical Prophets and Contemporary Environmental Ethics: Re-reading Amos, Hosea and First Isaiah* (Oxford: Oxford University Press, 2009), pp. 52–56.

18. See Hilary Marlow, "'What Am I in a Boundless Creation?' An Ecological Reading of Sirach 16 & 17," *Biblical Interpretation* 22, no. 1 (2014): pp. 34–50.

19. Polygamy was not explicitly discouraged in Judaism until well after the post-exilic period.

20. See, for example, the "Document of Wifehood" from Elephantine, dating to the mid-fifth century BCE: B28, in Bezalel Porten, *The Elephantine Papyri in English: Three Millennia of Cross-Cultural Continuity and Change* (Leiden: Brill, 1996), p. 177 [TAD B2.6].

21. This is in contrast to older law collections such as the Code of Hammurabi (James B. Pritchard, *Ancient Near Eastern Texts Relating to the Old Testament* [Princeton, N.J.: Princeton University Press, 1969], pp. 171–74) or the Middle Assyrian Laws (pp. 182–83), where the marital laws are collected in a sequence of material.

22. An extensive study of these can be found in Karl-Johan Illman, *Old Testament Formulas about Death* (Turku: Åbo Akademi, 1979).

23. See Philip S. Johnston, *Shades of Sheol: Death and Afterlife in the Old Testament* (Leicester: Apollos; and Downers Grove: InterVarsity Press, 2002), pp. 47–64.

24. Richard Dawkins, *The God Delusion* (London: Random House, 2006), p. 250.

25. See John Barton, *Amos' Oracles against the Nations: A Study of Amos 1.3–2.5* (Cambridge: Cambridge University Press, 1980); reprinted in *Understanding Old Testament Ethics* (Louisville, Ky.: Westminster John Knox Press, 2002), pp. 77–129.

26. Johnston, *Shades of Sheol*, pp. 79–83.

27. E.g., Robert B. Leal, *Wilderness in the Bible: Towards a Theology of Wilderness* (New York: Peter Lang, 2004); Shemaryahu Talmon, "The 'Desert Motif' in the Bible and in Qumran Literature," in A. Altmann, ed., *Biblical Motifs: Origins and Transformations* (Cambridge, Mass.: Harvard University Press, 1966), pp. 31–63.

28. Hilary Marlow, "Land," in Mark J. Boda and J. Gordon McConville, eds., *Dictionary of the Old Testament Prophets* (Downers Grove: InterVarsity Press, 2012), p. 489.

29. Robert Murray, *The Cosmic Covenant: Biblical Themes of Justice, Peace and the Integrity of Creation* (London: Sheed and Ward, 1992).

30. This idea was first suggested by historian of science Lynn White Jr. in 1967 and has been taken up by other scholars since. Lynn White Jr., "The Historical Roots of Our Ecologic Crisis," *Science* 155, no. 3767 (1967): pp. 1203–7; see also David Attenborough, "I'd Show George Bush a Few Graphs," *Natural World*, 2005.

31. For a more extensive treatment, see Marlow, *Biblical Prophets and Contemporary Environmental Ethics*.

FURTHER READING

Clines, David. "Humanity as the Image of God." *Tyndale Bulletin* 19 (1968): pp. 53–103; reprinted in *On the Way to the Postmodern: Old Testament Essays 1967–1998* (Sheffield: JSOT Press, 1998), pp. 447–97.

Johnston, Philip S. *Shades of Sheol: Death and Afterlife in the Old Testament*. Leicester: Apollos; and Downers Grove: InterVarsity Press, 2002.

Marlow, Hilary. *Biblical Prophets and Contemporary Environmental Ethics: Re-reading Amos, Hosea and First Isaiah*. Oxford: Oxford University Press, 2009.

Middleton, J. Richard. *The Liberating Image: The* Imago Dei *in Genesis 1*. Grand Rapids, Mich.: Brazos Press, 2005.

Murray, Robert. *The Cosmic Covenant: Biblical Themes of Justice, Peace and the Integrity of Creation*. London: Sheed and Ward, 1992.

Wolff, Hans Walter. *Anthropology of the Old Testament*. London: SCM, 1974.

13

God's Covenants with Humanity and Israel

Dominik Markl

God's covenant with Israel and even with all humanity is one of the most striking and complex theological concepts in the Hebrew Bible. It is unfolded most prominently in the Pentateuch: God's covenants with Noah, with Abraham and his descendants, and with Israel. The idea is actively taken up and transformed in the later prophets. The following presentation of some key aspects of the divine covenant in the Hebrew Bible and its early reception will roughly follow a canonical order, while questions of their historical development will be discussed along the way. Since the biblical covenant forms part of the general culture of treaties in the ancient Near East and since the idea of the divine covenant is based on the institution of covenants among humans, these two aspects need to be addressed at the very outset.

1. ANCIENT NEAR EASTERN TREATIES

Ancient Near Eastern cultures developed a tradition of elaborate treaties from the second half of the third millennium BCE. Biblical covenants are clearly part of this tradition, which has inspired much comparative research, especially since George Mendenhall's study *Law and Covenant in Israel and the Ancient Near East*.[1] Mendenhall described the form of Hittite vassal treaties, which often contain the following elements: a preamble, a historical prologue, stipulations, a provision for deposit in the temple and periodic public reading, and a list of gods as witnesses as well as curses and blessings. Although comparable elements are found in biblical covenants, it is highly unlikely that these Hittite examples, which date from between the fifteenth and the thirteenth century BCE, had *direct* influence on biblical texts, since the emergence of major literary activity in Israel can be assumed only starting from the middle of the ninth century BCE.[2]

In contrast, it is most likely that Neo-Assyrian treaties did indeed have direct influence on scribes during the late monarchy of Judah. We shall here concentrate on the most prominent example—Esarhaddon's Succession Treaties[3]—which may illustrate how such influence could have happened. Having conquered and largely destroyed the northern kingdom of Israel (ca. 722–720 BCE), the Assyrians continued to threaten and partly destroy Judah, especially in Sennacherib's campaign in 701 BCE. Under Manasseh's rule (ca. 697–643 BCE), Judah was a client state of Assyria, obliged to pay tribute, perform labor duties, and support Assyrian military campaigns.[4]

In 672 BCE, King Esarhaddon made vassals (as well as his own officials) swear an oath of loyalty accepting his designated successors. In 1955, fragments of at least eight such tablets were discovered in the sanctuary of Nabu in Nimrud (ancient Calah), which addressed Median city lords. Only in 2009, a copy of the same set of texts was discovered at Tell Tayinat,[5] which is located at the Orontes River some 500 kilometers north of Jerusalem. The tablet was found in situ in a temple on the citadel mound. All these recent archaeological data allow for the assumption that a similar treaty may have been imposed on King Manasseh of Judah and a similar tablet may have been publicly displayed in the Temple of Jerusalem. This scenario may help explain the striking parallels between the curse section of Esarhaddon's Succession Treaties and a sequence of curses in Deut. 28, which are shown in the table on p. 315.[6]

The sequence of six curse motifs in Esarhaddon's Succession Treaties 418–30 (disease, blindness, corpses eaten by birds, wife taken by another, loss of the house, goods taken by strangers) is nearly identical in Deut. 28:26–31, except that the third element is moved to the beginning of the sequence. Instead of the Neo-Assyrian deities we find Yhwh as agent. On the grounds of this evidence, it seems quite probable that scribes in Jerusalem used the oppressive Assyrian imperial document to compose a subversive countercovenant, to declare Israel the people of Yhwh alone. Moreover, they may have transformed the idea of a covenant between Assyrian deities and the Assyrian king.[7] It is most likely that this happened prior to the sack of Nineveh in 612 BCE, after which the influence of the Neo-Assyrian Empire collapsed.

Esarhaddon's Succession Treaties §§38A–42 (418–30)	Deut. 28:26–31
[cf. below, 427]	[26] **Your corpses** shall be **food for every bird of the air** and animal of the earth....
[418] May Anu, king of the gods, let **disease, exhaustion, malaria**, sleeplessness, worries and ill health rain upon all your houses. [419] May Sin, the brightness of heaven and earth, [420] clothe you with **leprosy**	[27] Yhwh will afflict you with the **boils of Egypt, with ulcers, scurvy, and itch, of which you cannot be healed.**
[422] May Šamaš, the light of heaven and earth, [423] not judge you justly. May he **remove your eyesight.** [424] **Walk about in darkness!**	[28] Yhwh will afflict you with madness, **blind**ness, and confusion of mind; [29] you shall **grope about** at noon as **blind** people grope in **darkness**, but you shall be unable to find your way....
[425] May Ninurta, the foremost among the gods, fell you with his fierce arrow; [426] may he fill the plain with your blood [427] and feed **your flesh to the eagle and the vulture.**	[cf. above, v. 26]
[428] May Venus, the brightest of the stars, **before your eyes make your wives** [429] **lie in the lap of your enemy;**	[30] **You shall become engaged to a woman, but another man shall lie with her.**
may your sons [430] not take possession of **your house,**	You shall build **a house**, but not live in it. You shall plant a vineyard, but not enjoy its fruit.
but a **strange enemy** divide your goods.	[31] ... Your sheep shall be given to your **enemies** ....

2. "COVENANT" IN THE HEBREW BIBLE

While extrabiblical ancient Near Eastern treaties probably were used to shape the literary form of biblical texts on God's covenants, their most definite conceptual basis may be found in the institution of the *berīt* (usually translated "covenant") among humans described in the narratives of the Hebrew Bible. A few examples will suffice to shed light on both their diversity and their essential common meaning.

Abraham makes a covenant with Abimelech (Gen. 21:27, 32), swearing loyalty (*hsd*) to him and his offspring (Gen. 21:23–24). Abraham underlines his goodwill, giving animals as a present (v. 27), and expresses his intention to avoid future conflicts over a well (vv. 28–30). Jonathan makes a covenant with David, loving him "like his soul" (1 Sam. 18:3). David claims Jonathan's loyalty (*hesed*) when his life is threatened by Saul (20:8), and they renew their covenant "before Yhwh" (23:18). Just as friendship may be reinforced by a *berīt*, the expression "wife of your *berīt*" (Mal. 2:14) suggests that marriage as well could be understood as a form of covenant.[8]

The same term *berīt* may also refer to political pacts at the level of diplomacy and international law. The kings Solomon of Israel and Hiram of Tyre make a covenant that consolidates their "peace" (*šalōm*, 1 Kings 5:26).[9] King Asa of Judah convinces Ben-hadad, king of Aram, with a substantial gift to make an alliance and to break his *berīt* with Baasha of Israel (1 Kings 15:17–21). An international *berīt* agreement between Israel (Ephraim) and Assyria is mentioned in Hosea 12:1. Ezekiel describes how Nebuchadnezzar installs his puppet king Zedekiah by making him swear loyalty in a *berīt* (Ezek. 17:13–14).

Covenants may redefine the social status of the parties involved. The Gibeonites offer to become "servants" to convince the Israelites to make a berīt with them (Josh. 9:11). Ahab of Israel calls Ben-hadad of Aram, whom he has defeated, "my brother" to reestablish their equality (1 Kings 20:32) and makes a covenant with him (v. 34).[10] A covenant between David and the elders of Israel precedes his anointment as king of Israel (2 Sam. 5:3 // 1 Chron. 11:3). The priest Jehoiada is said to have made a *berīt* "between Yhwh and the king and the people to become a people belonging to Yhwh" (2 Kings 11:17).

While the social contexts and the character of relationships involved in covenants made between humans in the Hebrew Bible are extremely diverse, ranging from individual friendship to political loyalty to international alliances, there are basic features shared by all covenants. A *berīt* is a treaty between two (or more) parties that establishes a relationship of mutual loyalty (frequently referred to as *hesed*). Covenants are established by speech acts (frequently referred to as "swearing"). They may involve rituals such as gift-giving (e.g., Gen. 21:27), the erection of monuments (Gen. 31:45–46), or a meal shared by the parties (Gen. 26:28–30), which may include a sacrifice ritual (Gen. 31:54) or the cutting apart of animals (Gen. 15:9; Jer. 34:18), which probably is the origin of the most frequent expression for making a covenant (literally "to cut," *krt*, a covenant).

Covenants are usually established through declarations; they may involve obligations on oneself (promises) or express norms to be kept by the other party. Thus, covenants often include conditions that require obedience, which led to the metonymical use of *berīt* as referring to the norms of the *berīt* (e.g., Deut. 4:13). The opinion, however, that "obligation" might be the original and basic meaning of *berīt* cannot be sustained.[11] The probable etymological connection of *berīt* with the Akkadian *birtu/bertu*, "fetter," suggests that the word refers to the bond of the relationship (cf., similarly, the German *Bund*).

3. THE NOAHITE COVENANT (GEN. 9)

In the grand biblical narrative, the term *berīt* occurs for the first time in the story of the great flood (Gen. 6:5–9:17).[12] When God commands Noah to enter the ark (6:18), he announces making a covenant with him, which is fulfilled after Noah leaves the ark (seven occurrences of *berīt* in 9:9–17). God's covenant includes not only Noah and his descendants, and thus postdiluvial humanity, but even all animals—"the birds, the domestic animals, and every animal of the earth with you, as many as came out of the ark" (9:10; cf. vv. 15–17). The object of the covenant is God's promise never to bring a flood again over the earth (9:11, 15); its sign is the rainbow (9:12–17). While the bows of deities in the ancient Near East and also Yhwh's bow are presented as destructive weapons (cf. Hab. 3:9), the rainbow becomes the symbol of divine preservation of life.

God's promise never again to destroy the earth with a flood (Gen. 9:11, 15) is a thematic continuation of his blessing and command to multiply (9:1, 7), through which Noah is portrayed as a second Adam (compare 1:28). In the same thematic line, God emphasizes the gravity of murder (9:5–6), but the covenant following is unconditional and called "everlasting" (9:16; cf. "for generations everlasting," v. 12). Yhwh's inner thoughts reveal that he intends not to destroy humanity in future despite the evil intentions of the human heart (8:21).

A comparison with the ancient Babylonian flood tradition of the Atrahasis epic (seventeenth century BCE) shows the specific emphasis of our story. According to the epic, the god Enlil inflicts the flood on humanity because of its multiplication and the "noise" of human activity. Enki, another deity, warns the human Atrahasis and tells him to build a ship. After the flood, Enlil has to accept the survival of humanity but sets limits to its multiplication, through infertility and demons that cause infant death. While the epic provides an etiology of infertility and infant mortality as caused by divine resentment against humanity, the biblical account emphasizes God's appreciation of human life: "Viewed in this light, Gn 9,1 ff. looks like a conscious rejection of the Atrahasis Epic."[13]

Although God's covenants in several prominent texts of the Hebrew Bible describe Israel's special relationship with Yhwh, the authors or redactors of Gen. 6:18, 9:1–17—classically identified as "P"[14]—used the term *berīt* at a late stage of the formation of the covenant idea to integrate it into their account of the origins of humanity. They thus opened the concept toward a universalist perspective: not only Israel but humanity and all living things are embraced by God in a covenant relationship that becomes mysteriously visible in the sign of the rainbow.

4. THE ABRAHAMIC COVENANT (GEN. 15, 17)

If the Noahite covenant was a result of a crisis of cosmic dimensions, the next divine covenant is Yhwh's response to the crisis of an individual—Abraham's childlessness. It is unfolded in two appearances of Yhwh (Gen. 15:1, 17:1). First, before the birth of Ishmael, Yhwh promises Abraham in his *berīt* to give "this land, from the river of Egypt to the great river, the river Euphrates," to his descendants (15:18; cf. 12:1–7). The second vision happens when Ishmael is already thirteen and Abraham is ninety-nine years old (17:1, 24–25). Here, the covenant theme is much more elaborately unfolded (no fewer than thirteen occurrences of *berīt* in 17:2–21; "eternal covenant" in 17:7, 13, 19).[15] God promises abounding posterity (vv. 2, 4–6), including a son of Sarah to be named Isaac (vv. 15–16, 19), and repeats the promise of the land (v. 8).

The words "I will establish my covenant ... for an everlasting covenant, to be God to you and to your offspring after you" (Gen. 17:7) programmatically introduce an expression of the covenant relationship, which is frequently used as a formula in the Pentateuch and especially in Jeremiah and Ezekiel, as Rolf Rendtorff has shown in his analysis of the "covenant formula."[16] Its first reciprocal wording occurs in Exod. 6:7: "I will take you as my people, and I will be your God" (cf. also Lev. 26:12; Jer. 11:4, 31:33). The formulation that emphasizes the people's role is found several times in Deuteronomy (e.g., 4:20, 7:6, 14:2, 26:17–19; compare Exod. 19:5).

Another new element of the covenant in Gen. 17—framed by God's promises—is his demand to "keep" (*šmr*) the covenant by performing male circumcision as a sign (vv. 9–14). This prepares a theme central to covenants that include obedience to commandments (see esp. Exod. 19:5; Deut. 29:8; compare Pss. 78:10, 103:18). Similarly, the motif of "breaking" the covenant is introduced here (Gen. 17:14).

Already when appearing to Abraham, God announces that he will continue his covenant relationship with Isaac (Gen. 17:21).[17] Although he repeats his promise to both Isaac and Jacob (Gen. 26:3–4, 28:13–14, 35:11–12), the term *berīt* is not used anymore for them (but see Exod. 2:24; Lev. 26:42; 2 Kings 13:23; Sir. 44:22–23). The covenant with the patriarchs provides (probably only at a relatively late stage of the formation of the Pentateuch) a strong narrative link between the books of Genesis and Exodus. Perceiving Israel's suffering in Egypt, "Yhwh remembered his covenant with Abraham, Isaac and Jacob" (Exod. 2:24; compare 6:4–5), which is the reason why God calls Moses to lead Israel out of Egypt (Exod. 3:1–4:17).

5. THE SINAI COVENANT (EXOD. 19–24)

Already at the burning bush God announces that the people will worship him "at this mountain" (Exod. 3:12), a first allusion to Israel's encounter with God at Sinai. As soon as the people have arrived there (19:1–2), Yhwh establishes his covenant with them in a complex dialogic process, in which Moses serves as the mediator. The whole process of the making of the covenant spans five chapters (Exod. 19–24).[18] Those speeches immediately relevant to the covenant are shown in the following scheme:

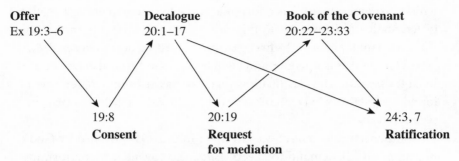

Figure 13.1. The speeches relevant to the making of the covenant (Exod. 19–24).

When God offers Israel the covenant (Exod. 19:3–6, esp. v. 5), proclaims the Decalogue (20:1–17), and conveys the "Book of the Covenant" to Moses (20:22–23:33), the people respond to each of these major speeches with a declaration of consent: the elders accept the offer (19:8); ask Moses for mediation, promising obedience to him (20:19); and ratify the content of the Book of the Covenant both after Moses presents it to them orally (24:3) and after he proclaims the written version the next day (24:4–7). This fourfold declaration of consent shows that the people of Israel play an active role and that their declarations are an essential element in the making of the covenant.

In modern political terms, the Sinai covenant is a constitutional process through which God's law becomes binding for Israel. It establishes a theocracy in the sense of God's "kingdom" over a priestly people (Exod. 19:6),[19] but it contains the democratic element of the "constitutional consensus." Theologically, this is of great significance, since God's law is seen not as imposed upon Israel by force but as freely accepted by the people. God respects his people as a partner in dialogue and mutual loyalty.

In an impressive theophany (Exod. 19:16–20:18), God proclaims the Decalogue (20:1–17), which is at the same time a climax of the making of the covenant. Yhwh's introductory words (20:2) can be translated "I, Yhwh, am your God," which can be seen as God's declaration of the covenant relationship. The following phrase, "who have brought you out of the land of Egypt, out of the house of slavery," inseparably connects the establishment of the covenant and Israel's legal constitution with the narrative of the deliverance from Egypt. This provides a fundamental perspective for the hermeneutics of law in the Pentateuch: the gift of the law is grounded in the experience of deliverance, and thus the meaning of the law is to preserve freedom.

The Sinai covenant contains both obligation and promise. It is based on the condition of Israel's obedience to God's voice (Exod. 19:5), and God promises Israel that they will become "a jewel out of all the peoples … ; and you shall be for me a kingdom of priests and a holy nation" (19:5–6). This is expounded in the instructions concerning the sanctuary (Exod. 25–31) and the commandments in the book of Leviticus, which aim at Israel's sanctification (e.g., Lev. 19:2, 20:26).

The Sinai covenant includes several rituals. Moses erects twelve stelae as a commemorative monument (Exod. 24:4), young men offer sacrifices (v. 5), and Moses performs a blood ritual applying the blood to both the altar and the people, thus connecting Israel with the divine sphere through the symbol of life (vv. 6, 8). Moses declares the successful completion of the covenant: "See the blood of the covenant that Yhwh has made with you in accordance with all these words" (v. 8). Finally, Moses, Aaron, his sons, and seventy elders participate in a festive meal as a covenant celebration at the mountain (vv. 9–11). Despite the frequently emphasized danger in perceiving God too closely (e.g., Exod. 19:10–13, 21–24; 33:20), they are said to "see the God of Israel" (Exod. 24:10). After Moses's subsequent ascent to the mountain for forty days (Exod. 24:12–18), the making of the golden calf (Exod. 32) is shown as a paradigmatic breaking of the covenant, which is only renewed following a process of reconciliation (esp. Exod. 34:10, 27–28; compare Deut. 9:7–10:11).

Historically, the conception of the Sinai covenant developed in a complex process. It is generally held that the Book of the Covenant contains the most ancient preexilic legal material of the Hebrew Bible. Yet it was clearly reworked to fit the narrative framework of the Sinai covenant (e.g., Exod. 23:20–33). This framework was most probably created after 587 BCE, when the monarchy of Judah had been dethroned and its people had to redefine their political and religious identity. Sophisticated priestly scribes projected Mount Sinai as a "utopian" setting for the idea of Israel's formation as a theocracy in the remote past.

6. THE MOAB COVENANT (DEUTERONOMY)

Israel's covenant with God as presented in the canonical form of the book of Deuteronomy is highly complex. Its basic vision, however, is twofold. On the one hand, Moses reenacts the covenant at Horeb (Deuteronomy's expression for "Sinai") for the second generation, because the generation of the Horeb covenant had to die during the forty years in the desert (Deut. 2:16; cf. Num. 14:35, 26:65): "Yhwh our God made a covenant with us at Horeb. Not with our ancestors did Yhwh make this covenant, but with us, who are all of us here alive today" (Deut. 5:2–3). This statement, which—on the surface—seems to be a blatant lie, rhetorically invites the Moab generation to consider themselves included in the Horeb covenant. At the same time, Moses's invitation is shaped in a wording that future generations—and thus even the audience of Deuteronomy—can apply to themselves, whether in their private meditation of "these words" (Deut. 6:6–7) or in their public teaching (as envisioned in Deut. 31:9–13).

The second major conception of Yhwh's covenant with Israel in Deuteronomy is introduced toward the end of Moses's speeches, when the narrator informs us that Moses made another covenant "in the land of Moab, in addition to the covenant that he had made with them at Horeb" (Deut. 29:1), which serves as a rubric for Moses's speech in Deut. 29–30.[20] The speech contains several elements that resemble ancient Near Eastern treaties, such as a "historical prologue" (29:2–9) and a reference to "blessings and curses" (30:1). Yet the rhetorical force of this speech lies in its free deviations from any ancient Near Eastern pattern. Moses not only warns his audience that a false covenant oath would have destructive consequences and finally lead to exile (29:18–27), but he also announces the possible return to the Promised Land from exile and new prosperity (30:1–10). Moreover, he emphasizes that "the word" (i.e., the content of his speeches) is close to Israel's heart (30:11–14). Finally, Moses urges Israel in the ultimate rhetorical climax of his addresses in Deuteronomy to make a choice between life and death (30:15–20)—"Choose life so that you may live!" (30:19).

In Deuteronomy, we do not find any explicit response by Israel to this urgent appeal. One should note that this is in stark contrast with both the Sinai covenant and the covenant that Joshua made "for the people" in Shechem (Josh. 24:25): his demand for a decision (24:15) is followed by a series of assertions, culminating in "Yhwh our God we will obey and his voice we will obey!" (24:24). Why does Israel not make any response in Deuteronomy? Is their consent simply presupposed? Or is an explicit response avoided because the people's consent in the Sinai covenant had quickly been followed by faithlessness and disobedience? While Deuteronomy does seem to provide an indirect response by reporting Israel's actual obedience to Moses's commands after his death (Deut. 34:9),[21] it remains a glaring lacuna that we do not hear any verbal response to Moses's powerful covenant speech.

The solution to our question may be found in Deuteronomy's strategies of reader communication. As with the reenactment of the Horeb covenant, the Moab covenant speech needs to be read on two levels: the narrated world, on the one hand, and the perception of the audience, on the other. Moses's speech seems to engage an implied audience of readers who are actually experiencing or have experienced a situation of exile: "Because they abandoned the covenant ... the anger of Yhwh was kindled against that land, bringing on it every curse written in this book. Yhwh uprooted them from their land in anger, fury, and great wrath, and cast them into another land, as is the case today" (29:25–27). Readers are directly reminded not only of the experience of exile (note the final word *today* as the rhetorical climax!) but also of the terrifyingly powerful reality of "this book" that they are reading with its curses (Deut. 28:15–68).

Furthermore, Moses continues to address a future Israel who are to return to Yhwh in exile ("you and your children," Deut. 30:2). Viewed in this light, "your fathers" is unlikely to refer to the Exodus generation (as in 5:3) or to the patriarchs, to whom God had promised the land (as in 6:10); rather, the "fathers" are most easily seen in the Moab generation, who "had taken [the land] into possession" (30:5; as Moses had constantly reminded them to do, e.g., 9:1). In the ears of readers, the voice of Moses sublimely transcends the threshold of the narrated world. His speech is meant to speak to the heart of those who know exile.

It is they who are promised that God will circumcise their hearts (Deut. 30:6)[22] so that they will be able to love God and keep his commandments (30:6, 8, 10). It is they who are reassured that Moses's word is "in their heart and in their mouth" (30:14). Finally, it is they who are commanded to choose life (30:15–20). They are expected to give their consent to the Mosaic Torah, which allows them to reestablish the Moab covenant (which certainly had been broken, as announced by Yhwh himself in 31:16–21).[23] The very words with which these future generations should express their consent could be suggested in the enigmatic verse Deut. 29:29, which strangely interrupts Moses's discourse at its most dramatic point with a statement of an unidentified "we-group": "The secret things belong to Yhwh our God, but the revealed things belong to us and to our children forever, to observe all the words of this *torah*."

The Moab covenant speech as a whole redefines Moses's preceding discourses in Deuteronomy. It aims at Israel's commitment to Moses's "commandments, decrees, and ordinances" (Deut. 30:16), which is a general reference to Deut. 5–26. It also refers to the "blessing and the curse" (30:1, 19) that Moses had unfolded in Deut. 28. Therefore, all the central discourses of Deuteronomy are seen to serve the making of the Moab covenant.

On the same line, the structure of Deuteronomy can be seen in a rough analogy to ancient Near Eastern treaties: Moses's introductory discourse (Deut. 1–3) can be compared with the "historical prologue"; the Deuteronomic laws (Deut. 12–26), with the "covenant stipulations"; and the subsequent speeches (Deut. 27:12–26; 28), with the "blessing and curse." However, such comparisons should not be overemphasized. While Deuteronomy clearly shares these basic elements of the general rationale of ancient Near Eastern treaties and deliberately engages with Assyrian patterns, it should not be overlooked that its literary shape is much more complex and elaborate than any comparable text of the ancient Near East. Similarly, although William L. Moran correctly pointed out that the demand to "love" God in Deuteronomy (e.g., 6:5) is related to the demand to love the monarch in Assyrian treaties, Jacqueline E. Lapsley has justly argued that the love of God in Deuteronomy has different qualities and involves not just obedience but also emotional affection.[24]

The historical development of the texts related to the covenant in Deuteronomy seems to be most intricate. While some of the curses of Deut. 28 are likely to be an expression of anti-Assyrian subversive theology in the seventh century BCE (see above), the final form of Deut. 29–30 clearly suggests an address to the people of Judah, who have suffered exile and have a prospect of rebuilding their collective identity in the land, which can hardly be imagined before the second half of the sixth century BCE.

Both historically and theologically it is most relevant that the final section of the Pentateuch (esp. Deut. 28–32) emphatically announces a future disaster for Israel and at the same time opens a new perspective after the return to the land (Deut. 30). The "finding" of the "book of the *torah*" under King Josiah (2 Kings 22:8) clearly refers to Deuteronomy, and the obvious fulfillment of its threats (2 Kings 22–25) strengthens the authority of this very book.[25] These ingenious literary conceptions largely contributed to the Pentateuch's "canonical success" from Persian times onward. A problematic witness of this can be seen in the reception of Deuteronomy's resentment against intermarriage in Ezra's prayer (Ezra 9:2, 12, 14; cf. Deut. 7:3),[26] which prepares for the separation from foreign women and children in a "covenant for our God" (Ezra 10:5).

7. THE DAVIDIC COVENANT

The tradition of God's covenant with David is somewhat elusive,[27] since we do not find it where we should expect it most—in Nathan's oracle (2 Sam. 7:4–16 // 1 Chron. 17:3–15). Although God promises David the eternal establishment of his throne with great emphasis, the term *berit* and covenant-related expressions such as "swear" and "oath" are conspicuously missing here. In the "Deuteronomistic History" (DtrH), God's response to Solomon's prayer adds that God's promise depends on Solomon's obedience (1 Kings 9:5), which is soon seen to fail, so that God announces the reduction of the Davidic kingdom to a single tribe (1 Kings 11:1–13). Whether the kingship of the Davidic line should have a future after the destruction of Jerusalem to confirm Nathan's oracle is one of the questions mysteriously left open by DtrH (2 Kings 25).[28]

In DtrH, only David's poetic "last words" (2 Sam. 23:1–7) speak about the "eternal covenant" that God had made with him (v. 5), and the immediately preceding reference to "my house" may well allude to Nathan's oracle. Outside DtrH, a covenant with David is referred to several times, mostly in texts that are clearly late. In Chronicles, the idea is introduced at least twice (2 Chron. 13:5, 21:7; cf. also the verb *krt*, "to cut," in 2 Chron. 7:18).[29]

Most prominently, Psalm 89 refers to God's covenant with David. It solemnly quotes it in the voice of God (vv. 3, 28, 34), finally accusing God of having broken it (v. 39) and imploring him to restore "your steadfast love of old" (v. 49; cf. v. 1). Less clear is the reference to the divine *berīt* in Ps. 132. Although the psalm claims that Yhwh had "sworn" to David to put his descendants on his throne (v. 11), the further succession of their sons depends on the condition that they "keep my covenant and my decrees that I shall teach them" (v. 12). Thus, this covenant does not seem to be identical with the promise made to David.

David is also mentioned in prophetic covenant texts in the context of postexilic restoration. Jeremiah's oracles during his captivity in the court of the guard under Zedekiah (Jer. 32, 33) speak twice about a covenant that is to be realized after the return from exile. The first says that God will enable the people to fear him (32:37–40; compare the new covenant, below); the second is called a covenant with David that secures the stability of the succession to his throne as securely as the succession of day and night (33:20–21). Here, the covenant with David is paralleled with the Levitic covenant (see also Neh. 13:29; Mal. 2:4–5, 8; Sir. 45:25; cf. with Pinhas: Num. 25:12–13).[30]

In Isaiah 55:3, God offers to a group of addressees an "eternal covenant," which is equated with the "mercies" (*hsdy*) of David (or for David, perhaps influenced by Ps. 89:1–3?). This covenant, which may well be offered to the "servants" of 54:17, gains a universal significance, since the Davidic reign extends to other peoples (55:4) and attracts unknown nations (55:5). It seems, thus, that the Davidic monarchy, which has been dethroned by Nebuchadnezzar, is here transformed and universalized in postexilic times.

8. THE "NEW COVENANT" (JER. 31) AND OTHER PROPHETIC TRANSFORMATIONS

Lothar Perlitt observed that earlier prophets rarely mention the covenant, which he called the "covenant silence" of the prophets, supporting his argument that covenant theology did not emerge before the seventh century BCE.[31] The covenant theme, however, becomes quite vigorous in later prophecy.[32]

Jeremiah emphatically accuses Israel and Judah of having broken the Sinai covenant (11:1–10; compare also 34:12–16 with reference to Deut. 15:12). He exhorts God not to break his covenant (Jer. 14:21, probably twisting Deut. 31:20). And he quotes the nations' accusation of Israel's abandonment of Yhwh from the Moab covenant (Jer. 22:9; cf. Deut. 29:24; 1 Kings 9:9). Against this backdrop, and explicitly contrasted with the Sinai covenant, Jeremiah announces—uniquely in the Hebrew Bible—a "new covenant" (31:31–33).[33] It is unfolded in active dialogue with Deuteronomy. While according to the Moab covenant God will circumcise Israel's hearts to enable them to love God and obey (Deut. 30:6–10) the written Torah of Moses (31:9), which is to be taught and learned (e.g., 5:1, 31; 31:12) and is thus in Israel's hearts (30:14), Jeremiah's new covenant announces that God's Torah will be written on Israel's hearts (Jer. 31:33) and they will no longer teach one another (31:34). The "new covenant" may be identical with the "eternal covenant" announced for those who return from exile (32:40, see above; cf. 50:5). From Jeremiah's new covenant, the "New Testament" derives its name (see below).

Another specific transformation of the covenant idea is found in the book of Isaiah (42–59). Twice, God announces that he will install his servant as a "covenant of/with the people" (Isa. 42:6, 49:8). Although "people" seems to refer to humanity in 42:5, the "covenant of/with the people" most probably portrays the servant as a symbol of God's covenant with Israel (compare its context in 49:8).[34] In the first occurrence, this is immediately followed by the title "a light for the nations" (cf. also 49:6), reminiscent of the pilgrimage of the nations to Zion and their quest for "Torah" (2:3, 5; 42:4). Despite these universalistic tendencies, God's berīt seems to remain reserved for Israel in Isaiah. In contrast to the "eternal covenant" broken according to Isaiah 24:5, God announces another "eternal covenant" in Isaiah 55:3 (see above) and 61:8. Yhwh's consolation of the barren lady Zion contains an announcement of a "covenant of my peace/welfare [šalōm]" (54:10, compared with the Noahite covenant in 54:9). The widest opening for strangers is found in the covenant offered to eunuchs and strangers (56:4, 6), who are mainly meant to keep the Sabbath (as a berīt; cf. Exod. 31:16), through which they become integrated into Israel. Finally, the covenant is closely linked with the gift of "my spirit that is upon you, and my words that I have put in your mouth" (59:21; for "spirit," see 42:1, 44:3, 61:1; for "word," 51:16).

Ezekiel introduces the theme of the divine covenant in the metaphorical account of Jerusalem's history as the biography of a woman (Ezek. 16). Yhwh takes her into a marriage covenant (v. 8).[35] The theme is unfolded at the end of the chapter (vv. 59–62). Remembering the covenant of her past, God will establish an "eternal covenant" in the future (v. 60). The second major historical reflection (Ezek. 20) mentions the giving of the law (vv. 11–12), but the term *berīt* occurs only in the context of Israel's judgment during their return from exile (vv. 34–37). Twice, the future covenant is called a "covenant of peace" (34:25, 37:26; cf. Isa. 54:10),[36] both times immediately following the motif of the Davidic reign. The breaking of the divine covenant is mentioned as committed by Zedekiah (Ezek. 17:19) and by Israel through allowing foreigners to profane the Temple (44:7).

Among the Twelve Minor Prophets, specific aspects in the writings of Hosea, Zechariah, and Malachi should be pointed out. Hosea refers to a divine covenant with the wild animals (Hosea 2:18),[37] together with the breaking of "bow, sword and war," which is made for the sake of Israel (on their breaking of the covenant, see 6:7, 8:1). Zechariah announces a king reigning in Jerusalem to bring universal peace (Zech. 9:9–10), adding that prisoners will be freed "because of the blood of your covenant" (Zech. 9:11, alluding to Exod. 24:8?). Zech. 11:10 surprisingly mentions God's breaking of a covenant "that I had made with all the peoples." Although it cannot be ruled out that this plural refers to Israel, the context seems to speak of humanity in general (vv. 6–11). Finally, in Malachi God's voice announces a "messenger of the covenant" (Mal. 3:1; cf. Exod. 23:20), whose identity is highly disputed.[38]

9. THE DIVINE COVENANT IN PSALMS AND WRITINGS

Psalms encourage humans to keep God's covenant by observing his commandments (Pss. 25:10, 103:18), and they praise God for remembering his covenant forever (105:8, 111:5). References to the covenant are relatively frequent in history psalms (Pss. 78, 105–6; on Pss. 89 and 132, see above). Psalm 78 emphasizes Israel's unfaithfulness to the covenant and the Torah (vv. 10, 37), while Ps. 44:18 denies such guilt. The contrasting reflections on history in Psalms 105 and 106 are framed by the covenant motif. Psalm 105 recalls the covenantal promise of the land for the patriarchs (vv. 8, 10–11 // 1 Chron. 16:15, 17), which God remembers, according to the end of Psalm 106, to be merciful to those in exile (vv. 45–46). From a similar perspective, the end of Psalm 74 asks God to "have regard for your covenant" in view of the destruction caused by enemies (v. 20). The Asaph Psalm 50 speaks about the covenant to be made in the context of cultic sacrifice (v. 5) and of the demand to keep commandments (v. 16).

Norbert Lohfink has suggested reading Psalm 25 against the background of Psalm 24 as a prayer of the nations at Zion, which would provide the only text to include the nations in the divine covenant with Israel (Ps. 25:10, 14). Lohfink also discovered tendencies to universalize the covenant formula in Psalm 33 (v. 12) and Psalm 100 (v. 3).[39] Indeed, the conception of God's universal kingship and the call for all nations to worship him in the Temple (Pss. 95–100) may justify an understanding of "his people" (Ps. 100:3) as referring to humanity.

The divine covenant generally plays little role in wisdom literature. It is missing in Job and Qohelet, and there are only single references to it in Proverbs (2:17) and in the Wisdom of Solomon (18:22). Sirach, however, exceptionally portrays the history of Israel as a history of covenants (esp. Sir. 44:12–45:25), with strong emphasis on the priestly covenants, representing the interests of the Temple community of the second century BCE. Moreover, Ben Sira emphasizes the importance of the "book of the covenant of the most high God," which is the Torah of Moses (Sir. 24:23; cf. 1 Macc. 1:57) and develops a universalizing idea of the covenant for humanity (Sir. 17:11–12).[40] The great importance of the covenant idea in the second century BCE is also attested in its overarching significance in the *Book of Jubilees* and the use of "(holy) covenant" as a metonymic reference to Jewish religion in Daniel (11:28, 30, 32) and Maccabees (1 Macc. 1:15, 63; 2:20, 27, 50).[41]

10. RECEPTION IN QUMRAN AND THE NEW TESTAMENT

In the Qumran writings "covenant" is a dominant category (257 occurrences, virtually all of them theological). They adduce many covenant conceptions from the Hebrew Bible, including Jeremiah's "new covenant"

(CD 6,19; 8,21; 19,33–34; 20,12). Members of the Qumran community committed themselves to religious obligations in a covenant ritual that was annually renewed. The sectarian movement understood itself as a "community of the covenant" (*yahad berīt*; 1QS 5,5; 8,16).

Compared with the notion of the covenant's importance in the Qumran texts, it is of much less significance in the New Testament (no more than thirty-three occurrences of *diatheke*). Nevertheless, it acquired great prominence, especially because of its use in Jesus's words during the Last Supper, "This cup is the new covenant in my blood" (1 Cor. 11:25 // Luke 22:20) or "This is my blood of the covenant" (Mark 14:24 // Matt. 26:28; cf. in the background Exod. 24:8; Zech. 9:11), which was received as the institution of the Eucharist or the Lord's Supper, the central liturgy of Christianity. Another indication of the importance of the motif of the "new covenant" is the quotation of Jer. 31:31–34 in Heb. 8:8–12—the longest quotation of an Old Testament text in the New Testament. The most elaborate theology of the covenant in the New Testament is found in the Pauline letters.[42] Since Clement of Alexandria and Origen (second/third century CE), Christians have referred to the writings of the Bible as the "old" and the "new testaments."[43]

11. HISTORICAL AND THEOLOGICAL EVALUATION

In the history of ancient Near Eastern religions, the idea of a covenant between a deity and humans is not unique to Israel. Certainly unique, though, is its elaborate and multifaceted unfolding in the Hebrew Bible. While making covenants "before" a deity had most likely been an old custom in ancient Israel, the idea of a covenant *with* Yhwh seems to have developed in a theological reaction against Assyrian rhetorics of power. Yet only the catastrophe of the Babylonian exile led to the climax of covenant theology. Israel's breaking of the covenant served as an explanation of the disaster (e.g., Lev. 26:14–39; Deut. 29:18–27; Josh. 23:15–16; 2 Kings 17:15, 35, 38; Jer. 11:1–10, 31:32; Ezek. 16:59), ancient covenant promises were invoked to inspire hope (Lev. 26:42, 44–45), and the idea of God's renewed or new "eternal" covenant became a crucial category to express the perspective of restoration (Deut. 29–30; Isa. 55:3, 54:10, 59:21, 61:8; Jer. 31:31–33, 32:40, 50:5; Ezek. 16:60, 20:37, 34:25, 37:26;

Zech. 9:11; Mal. 3:1; Ps. 106:45–46; Bar. 2:35).[44] Postexilic readers could "be addressed by diverse covenant theologies at the same time; the deuteronomic, because it convicts of guilt and offers that torah that will be in force also at the end; the prophetic, stepping out into the universal, because it contains hope; the priestly, because it offers the ultimate ground for hope: God's eternal faithfulness that no human unfaithfulness can destroy."[45]

Theologically, the divine covenant portrays God as caring for all living creatures (Gen. 9); as a loyal partner, committing himself to generous gifts (Gen. 15, 17); and as a lawgiver with kingly authority who, nevertheless, engages with Israel in a constitutional process (Exod. 19–24; Deut. 29–30). Moreover, divine covenants typically follow crises: human sinfulness and the great flood, Abraham and Sarah's childlessness, Israel's oppression in Egypt and their dramatic exodus, their rebellion and forty years of wandering in the wilderness, and, not least, the Babylonian exile. God's covenants are always a means of reestablishing human confidence in personal or communal life through strengthening the relationship, often even despite human failure. God is therefore praised as "keeping the covenant and loyalty" (Deut. 7:9; 1 Kings 8:23 // 2 Chron. 6:14; Dan. 9:4; Neh. 1:5, 9:32). These foundational ideas and their intensive reception during the Second Temple period led to the covenant's central importance in both Judaism and Christianity.

For Christian theology, it is fundamental to acknowledge that the New Testament's notion of the covenant is grounded in, and dependent on, its manifold conceptions in the Hebrew Bible and that a simplified juxtaposition of "the old" and "the new covenants" does not do justice to its biblical conception. From a canonical perspective, any covenant theology can only be considered as grounded in God's covenant with humanity (Gen. 9)—which gains new shades of meaning when humanity may become able to cause or avoid climate catastrophes.

NOTES

I am indebted to Norbert Lohfink, Eckart Otto, and Georg Fischer for commenting on a draft of this chapter.

1. George Mendenhall, *Law and Covenant in Israel and the Ancient Near East* (Pittsburgh: Biblical Colloquium, 1955) = *Biblical Archaeologist* 17 (1954): pp. 26–46, 49–76.

Another important early contribution is Klaus Baltzer, *Das Bundesformular*, Wissenschaftliche Monographien zum Alten und Neuen Testament 4 (Neukirchen, Germany: Neukirchener Verlag, 1960; 2nd ed., 1964); Klaus Baltzer, *The Covenant Formulary in Old Testament, Jewish, and Early Christian Writings*, David E. Green, trans. (Philadelphia: Fortress Press, 1971). A much more elaborate study is provided in Dennis J. McCarthy, *Treaty and Covenant: Study in Form in the Ancient Oriental Documents and in the Old Testament*, Analecta Biblica 21 (Rome: Pontifical Biblical Institute, 1963; new ed., 1978).

2. Konrad Schmid, *The Old Testament: A Literary History*, Linda M. Maloney, trans. (Minneapolis: Fortress Press, 2012), pp. 32–33; David W. Jamieson-Drake, *Scribes and Schools in Monarchic Judah: A Socio-archaeological Approach*, Journal for the Study of the Old Testament Supplement Series 109 (Sheffield: Almond Press, 1991). However, George E. Mendenhall and Gary A. Herion, "Covenant," *Anchor Bible Dictionary* 1 (1992): pp. 1179–1202, still struggles to defend the idea of direct influence of Hittite treaties on the Hebrew Bible.

3. These same texts have, according to a different interpretation of their function, also been called Vassal Treaties of Esarhaddon; some refer to them by the Akkadian term *adê*. For the text, see esp. the edition Simo Parpola and Kazuko Watanabe, *Neo-Assyrian Treaties and Loyalty Oaths*, State Archives of Assyria 2 (Helsinki: University Press, 1988); transcriptions and translations are available online: http://oracc.museum.upenn.edu/saao/saa02/corpus (accessed November 30, 2015).

4. On Sennacherib's campaign, see Isaac Kalimi and Seth Richardson, eds., *Sennacherib at the Gates of Jerusalem: Story, History and Historiography*, Culture and History of the Ancient Near East 71 (Leiden: Brill, 2014); on Judah under Manasseh, see Gunnar Lehmann, "Survival and Reconstruction of Judah in the Time of Manasseh," in A. Berlejung, ed., *Disaster and Relief Management: Katastrophen und ihre Bewältigung*, Forschungen zum Alten Testament 81 (Tübingen: Mohr Siebeck, 2012), pp. 289–309, esp. p. 303.

5. See Timothy P. Harrison and James F. Osborne, "Building XVI and the Neo-Assyrian Sacred Precinct at Tell Tayinat," *Journal of Cuneiform Studies* 64 (2012): pp. 125–43; Jacob Lauinger, "Esarhaddon's Succession Treaty at Tell Tayinat: Text and Commentary," *Journal of Cuneiform Studies* 64 (2012): pp. 87–123.

6. Translations of Esarhaddon's Succession Treaties from http://oracc.museum.upenn.edu/saao/saa02/corpus. For this and other comparisons, see Hans U. Steymans, "Deuteronomy 28 and Tell Tayinat," *Verbum et Ecclesia* 34 (2013), art. #870, http://www.ve.org.za/index.php/VE/article/view/870/1867; Hans U. Steymans, *Deuteronomium 28 und die* adê *zur Thronfolgeregelung Asarhaddons: Segen und Fluch im Alten Orient und in Israel*, Orbis biblicus et orientalis 145 (Freiburg: Universitätsverlag, 1995).

7. Simo Parpola, *Assyrian Prophecies*, State Archives of Assyria 9 (Helsinki: University Press, 1997), pp. 22–27; Eckart Otto, *Das Deuteronomium: Politische Theologie und Rechtsreform in Juda und Assyrien*, Beihefte zur Zeitschrift für die alttestamentliche Wissenschaft 284 (Berlin: de Gruyter, 1999), pp. 79–84.

8. Gordon Paul Hugenberger, *Marriage as a Covenant: A Study of Biblical Law and Ethics Governing Marriage Developed from the Perspective of Malachi*, Supplements to Vetus Testamentum 52 (Leiden: Brill, 1994).

9. For the sake of precision, it should be noted that 1 Kings 5:26 does not speak about a "treaty of brotherhood," as claimed in Frank Moore Cross, "Kinship and Cove-

nant in Ancient Israel," in *From Epic to Canon: History and Literature in Ancient Israel* (Baltimore: Johns Hopkins University Press, 1988), pp. 3–21, here p. 10. Only in Amos 1:9 does there occur "*berīt* of brothers," which may be adduced to support Cross's thesis that covenant language is grounded in the language of kinship.

10. Cf. Paul Kalluveettil, *Declaration and Covenant: A Comprehensive Review of Covenant Formulae from the Old Testament and the Ancient Near East*, Analecta Biblica 88 (Rome: Pontifical Biblical Institute, 1982), pp. 198–209.

11. This opinion had been most elaborately presented by Ernst Kutsch; see, e.g., his entries on *bryt* in *Theological Lexicon of the Old Testament* 1 (1997): pp. 256–66, and on *Bund* in *TRE* 7 (1980): pp. 397–403. It was supported by Lothar Perlitt's influential study *Bundestheologie im Alten Testament*, Wissenschaftliche Monographien zum Alten und Neuen Testament 36 (Neukirchen-Vluyn, Germany: Neukirchener Verlag, 1969); see also his entry "Covenant," *Encyclopedia of Christianity* 1 (1999): pp. 709–11. For criticism of this position, see, most prominently, James Barr, "Some Semantic Notes on the Covenant," in Herbert Donner, Robert Hanhart, and Rudolf Smend, eds., *Beiträge zur Alttestamentlichen Theologie: FS W. Zimmerli* (Göttingen: Vandenhoeck & Ruprecht, 1977), pp. 23–38; Erich Zenger, *Der Neue Bund im Alten: Zur Bundestheologie der beiden Testamente*, Quaestiones disputatae 146 (Freiburg i.Br.: Herder, 1993), pp. 26–27; and Eckart Otto, "Die Ursprünge der Bundestheologie," *Zeitschrift für Altorientalische und Biblische Rechtsgeschichte* 4 (1998): pp. 1–84, esp. pp. 26–27.

12. For a concise interpretation of the flood narrative, see Victor P. Hamilton, *The Book of Genesis: Chapters 1–17*, New International Commentary on the Old Testament (Grand Rapids, Mich.: Eerdmans, 1990), pp. 272–319.

13. William L. Moran, "Atrahasis: The Babylonian Story of the Flood," *Biblica* 52 (1971): pp. 51–61, here p. 61.

14. Cf., e.g., Claus Westermann, *Genesis 12–26: A Commentary*, J. J. Scullion S.J., trans. (Minneapolis: Augsburg Publishing House, 1984), esp. pp. 459–480. On the concept of the covenant in P, see Christophe Nihan, "The Priestly Covenant, Its Reinterpretations, and the Composition of 'P,'" in Sarah Shectman and Joel S. Baden, eds., *The Strata of the Priestly Writings: Contemporary Debate and Future Directions*, Abhandlungen zur Theologie des Alten und Neuen Testaments 95 (Zurich: Theologischer Verlag Zürich, 2009), pp. 87–134.

15. On its function as a *Leitwort* and its planned distribution, see Westermann, *Genesis 12–26*, p. 256.

16. Rolf Rendtorff, *The Covenant Formula: An Exegetical and Theological Investigation*, M. Kohl, trans., Old Testament Studies (Edinburgh: T&T Clark, 1998), here esp. pp. 13–15.

17. The question whether Ishmael is to be considered as integrated into or excluded from the covenant with Abraham is controversial. Cf. Konrad Schmid, "Gibt es eine 'abrahamitische Ökumene' im Alten Testament? Überlegungen zur religionspolitischen Theologie der Priesterschrift in Genesis 17," in Anselm C. Hagedorn and Henrik Pfeiffer, eds., *Die Erzväger in der biblischen Tradition: Festschrift für Matthias Köckert*, Beihefte zur Zeitschrift für die alttestamentliche Wissenschaft 400 (Berlin: de Gruyter, 2009), pp. 67–92; and Matthias Köckert, "Gottes 'Bund' mit Abraham und die 'Erwählung' Israels in Genesis 17," in Nathan MacDonald, ed., *Covenant and Election in Exilic and Postexilic Judaism*, Forschungen zum Alten Testament 2, Reihe 79 (Tübingen: Mohr Siebeck, 2015), pp. 1–28.

18. For a detailed interpretation, see Dominik Markl, *Der Dekalog als Verfassung des Gottesvolkes: Die Brennpunkte einer Rechtshermeneutik des Pentateuch in Exodus 19–24 und Deuteronomium 5*, Herders Biblische Studien 49 (Freiburg i.Br.: Herder, 2007), esp. pp. 33–173.

19. See Jean Louis Ska, "Exodus 19:3–6 and the Identity of Post-exilic Israel," in *The Exegesis of the Pentateuch*, Forschungen zum Alten Testament 66 (Tübingen: Mohr Siebeck, 2009), pp. 139–64, esp. pp. 147–53.

20. In standard editions of the Hebrew Bible, this verse is counted as 28:69. Here, verses are quoted according to the count generally used in English Bible translations. On the issue of the function of this verse as a colophon or a superscript, which has been discussed by Herrie F. van Rooy and Norbert Lohfink, see Dominik Markl, *Gottes Volk im Deuteronomium*, Beihefte zur Zeitschrift für biblische und altorientalische Rechtsgeschichte 18 (Wiesbaden: Harrassowitz, 2012), pp. 90–91, and more elaborately on the interpretation of the Moab covenant as presented above, pp. 88–125.

21. This aspect has been emphasized in Jean-Pierre Sonnet, "Redefining the Plot of Deuteronomy—from End to Beginning. The Import of Deut 34:9," in G. Fischer, D. Markl, and S. Paganini, eds., *Deuteronomium—Tora für eine neue Generation*, Beihefte zur Zeitschrift für biblische und altorientalische Rechtsgeschichte 17 (Wiesbaden: Harrassowitz, 2011), pp. 37–49.

22. The import of the motif of the circumcision of the heart as the internalized sign of the covenant with Abraham was recently analyzed in Ernst Ehrenreich, *Wähle das Leben! Deuteronomium 30 als hermeneutischer Schlüssel zur Tora*, Beihefte zur Zeitschrift für biblische und altorientalische Rechtsgeschichte 14 (Wiesbaden: Harrassowitz, 2011), pp. 156–200.

23. An alternative theological view for overcoming the crisis of exile seems to be presented in the high point of priestly covenant theology in Lev. 26: God will not break his covenant even in exile (v. 44) but will remember his covenant with the patriarchs (vv. 42 and 45). Cf. Thomas Hieke, "The Covenant in Leviticus 26: A Concept of Admonition and Redemption," in Richard J. Bautch and Gary N. Knoppers, eds., *Covenant in the Persian Period: From Genesis to Chronicles* (Winona Lake, Ind.: Eisenbrauns, 2015), pp. 75–89.

24. William L. Moran, "The Ancient Near Eastern Background of the Love of God in Deuteronomy," *Catholic Biblical Quarterly* 25 (1963): pp. 77–87; Jacqueline E. Lapsley, "Feeling Our Way: Love for God in Deuteronomy," *Catholic Biblical Quarterly* 65 (2003): pp. 350–69.

25. Dominik Markl, "No Future without Moses: The Disastrous End of 2 Kings 22–25 and the Chance of the Moab Covenant (Deuteronomy 29–30)," *Journal of Biblical Literature* 133 (2014): pp. 711–28.

26. Juha Pakkala, *Ezra the Scribe: The Development of Ezra 7–10 and Nehemiah 8*, Beihefte zur Zeitschrift für die alttestamentliche Wissenschaft 347 (Berlin: de Gruyter, 2004), esp. pp. 108–9.

27. For the history of research and the discussed texts, see Griphus Gakuru, *An Inner-Biblical Exegetical Study of the Davidic Covenant and the Dynastic Oracle* (Lewiston, N.Y.: Mellen Press, 2000); Steven L. McKenzie, "The Typology of the Davidic Covenant," in J. Andrew Dearman and M. Patrick Graham, eds., *The Land that I Will Show You: Essays on the History and Archaeology of the Ancient Near East in Honour of J. Maxwell Miller*, Journal for the Study of the Old Testament Supplement Series 343 (Sheffield:

Academic Press, 2001), pp. 152–78; Hans U. Steymans, *Psalm 89 und der Davidbund: Eine strukturale und redaktionsgeschichtliche Untersuchung*, Österreichische biblische Studien 27 (Frankfurt a.M.: Lang, 2005), esp. pp. 367–443.

28. David Janzen, "An Ambiguous Ending: Dynastic Punishment in Kings and the Fate of the Davidides in 2 Kings 25.27–30," *Journal for the Study of the Old Testament* 33 (2008): pp. 39–58.

29. On the meaning of covenant in Chronicles, see Gary N. Knoppers, "Judah, Levi, David, Solomon, Jerusalem, and the Temple: Election and Covenant in Chronicles," in MacDonald, *Covenant and Election in Exilic and Post-exilic Judaism*, pp. 139–68; and the chapters by Mark J. Boda and Louis C. Jonker in Bautch and Knoppers, *Covenant in the Persian Period*, pp. 391–407 and 409–29.

30. On the covenant with the Levites, see Filippo Serafini, *L'alleanza levitica. Studio della berît di Dio con i sacerdoti leviti nell'Antico Testamento* (Assisi: Cittadella, 2006).

31. Perlitt, *Bundestheologie*, pp. 129–55.

32. For an analysis of the relevant texts, see Bernard Renaud, *Nouvelle ou éternelle Alliance? Le message des prophètes* (Paris: Cerf, 2002).

33. See esp. Georg Fischer, *Jeremia 26–52*, Herders Theologischer Kommentar zum Alten Testament (Freiburg i.Br.: Herder, 2005), pp. 171–76. LXX presents a markedly different view of the history of covenants, esp. in Jer. 32:32–33; for a discussion, see Adrian Schenker, *Das Neue am neuen Bund und das Alte am alten: Jer 31 in der hebräischen und griechischen Bibel*, Forschungen zur Religion und Literatur des Alten und Neuen Testaments 212 (Göttingen: Vandenhoeck & Ruprecht, 2006). The theme of the new covenant forms part of several theological transformations, as observed in Moshe Weinfeld, "Jeremiah and the Spiritual Metamorphosis of Israel," *Zeitschrift für die Alttestamentliche Wissenschaft* 88 (1976): pp. 17–56.

34. See Jan L. Koole, *Isaiah III*, vol. 1, *Isaiah 40–48*, Historical Commentary on the Old Testament (Kampen, the Netherlands: Kok Pharos, 1997), pp. 230–33. For a discussion of the covenant theme in Isaiah, see Norbert Lohfink, "Covenant and Torah in the Pilgrimage of the Nations (the Book of Isaiah and Psalm 25)," in Norbert Lohfink and E. Zenger, *The God of Israel and the Nations*, E. R. Kalin, trans. (Collegeville, Minn.: Liturgical Press, 2000), pp. 33–84, esp. 42–57; on Torah, Marvin A. Sweeney, "The Book of Isaiah as Prophetic Torah," in R. F. Melugin and M. A. Sweeney, eds., *New Visions of Isaiah*, Journal for the Study of the Old Testament Supplement Series 214 (Sheffield: Academic Press, 1996), pp. 50–67.

35. Hugenberger, *Marriage as a Covenant*, pp. 302–9.

36. On its explication in cosmological terms and in relation with Lev. 26:4–13, see Daniel I. Block, *The Book of Ezekiel: Chapters 25–48*, New International Commentary on the Old Testament (Grand Rapids, Mich.: Eerdmans, 1998), pp. 301–7.

37. On the relationship of Hosea 2:18 and other relevant texts with the Noahite covenant, see Katharine J. Dell, "Covenant and Creation in Relationship," in A.D.H. Mayes and R. B. Salters, eds., *Covenant as Context: Essays in Honour of E. W. Nicholson* (Oxford: Oxford University Press, 2003), pp. 111–33.

38. See Andrew E. Hill, *Malachi: A New Translation with Introduction and Commentary*, Anchor Bible (New York: Doubleday, 1998), pp. 286–89.

39. Lohfink and Zenger, *God of Israel and the Nations*, pp. 57–122; Norbert Lohfink, "Die Universalisierung der Bundesformel in Ps 100,3," *Theologie und Philosophie* 65 (1990): pp. 172–83.

40. See Otto Kaiser, "Covenant and Law in Ben Sira," in A.D.H. Mayes and R. B. Salters, eds., *Covenant as Context: Essays in Honour of E. W. Nicholson* (Oxford: Oxford University Press, 2003), pp. 235–60; Luis Alonso Schökel, "The Vision of Man in Sirach 16:24–17:14," in John G. Gammie, Walter A. Brueggemann, W. Lee Humphreys, and James M. Ward, eds., *Israelite Wisdom: Theological and Literary Essays in Honor of Samuel Terrien* (Missoula, Mont.: Scholars' Press for Union Theological Seminary, 1978), pp. 235–45.

41. See James C. VanderKam, "Covenant," *Encyclopedia of the Dead Sea Scrolls* 1 (2000): pp. 151–54, at pp. 151–52.

42. Nicholas T. Wright, *The Climax of the Covenant* (London: T&T Clark, 1991).

43. LXX usually renders *berīt* with διαθήκη, with Latin translations usually of *testamentum* or *pactum*. These are, of course, not close semantic equivalents of the Hebrew term.

44. On the expression "eternal covenant" (sixteen occurrences in the Hebrew Bible; in the New Testament, only Heb. 13:20), see Stephen D. Mason, *"Eternal Covenant" in the Pentateuch: The Contours of an Elusive Phrase*, Library of Hebrew Bible/Old Testament Studies 494 (New York: T&T Clark International, 2008).

45. Norbert Lohfink, "The Concept of 'Covenant' in Biblical Theology," in Lohfink and Zenger, *God of Israel and the Nations*, pp. 11–31, here p. 29.

FURTHER READING

The most recent and substantial dictionary entry on *covenant* was written by Christoph Koch, in *EBR* 5 (2012): pp. 897–908. Moshe Weinfeld's article on *berit* in *TDOT* 2 (1977): pp. 253–79, is still valuable, especially regarding the biblical covenant's relationship with other treaty cultures of the ancient world. For comparative study, Kenneth A. Kitchen and Paul J. N. Lawrence have recently provided a vast collection of material in their *Treaty, Law and Covenant in the Ancient Near East*, 3 vols. (Wiesbaden: Harrassowitz, 2012); opinions on dating and interpretation expressed in these volumes, however, should be considered critically.

Significant contributions on exegetical and theological issues include Richard J. Bautch and Gary N. Knoppers, eds., *Covenant in the Persian Period: From Genesis to Chronicles* (Winona Lake, Ind.: Eisenbrauns, 2015); Nathan MacDonald, ed., *Covenant and Election in Exilic and Postexilic Judaism*, Forschungen zum Alten Testament 2, Reihe 79 (Tübingen: Mohr Siebeck, 2015); A.D.H. Mayes and R. B. Salters, eds., *Covenant as Context: Essays in Honour of E. W. Nicholson* (Oxford: Oxford University Press, 2003); Christoph Dohmen and Christian Frevel, eds., *Für immer verbündet: Studien zur Bundestheologie der Bibel* (Stuttgart:

Katholisches Bibelwerk, 2007); Walter Groß, *Zukunft für Israel: Alttesta-mentliche Bundeskonzepte und die aktuelle Debatte um den Neuen Bund* (Stuttgart: Katholisches Bibelwerk, 1998); and Erich Zenger, ed., *Der Neue Bund im Alten: Zur Bundestheologie der beiden Testamente* (Freiburg i. Br.: Herder, 1993). On the history of research from Wellhausen to Perlitt, see Ernest W. Nicholson, *God and His People: Covenant and Theology in the Old Testament* (Oxford: Clarendon, 1986), pp. 1–117.

On the Qumran texts, see esp. the article on *bryt* by Brent A. Strawn in *ThWQ* 1 (2011): pp. 508–21 (the English version is in preparation: *Theological Dictionary of the Qumran Texts*, to be published by Eerd-mans); and the collection edited by Stanley E. Porter and Jacqueline C. R. de Roo, *The Concept of the Covenant in the Second Temple Period* (Leiden: Brill, 2003).

For the New Testament and early Judaism, see—besides Johannes Behm's entry "The Greek Term διαθήκη" in *TDNT* 2 (1964): pp. 124–34—esp. Ellen J. Christiansen, *The Covenant in Judaism and Paul* (Leiden: Brill, 1995); and Friedrich Avemarie and Hermann Lichtenberger, eds., *Bund und Tora: Zur theologischen Begriffsgeschichte in alttestamentlicher, früh-jüdischer und urchristlicher Tradition* (Tübingen: Mohr Siebeck, 1996).

14

Ethics

C. L. Crouch

Over the last century or so there have been a number of attempts to address the nature of the ethical content of the Old Testament/ Hebrew Bible. The majority of these are appropriately described as investigations into "the ethics of the Old Testament," by which we mean investigations into the ethical instruction and moral logic of these texts as Christian scripture (hence: "Old Testament"). The motivation behind studies of this kind lies in the fact that these biblical books form a (large) part of the Christian canon and, as such, are considered normative texts for contemporary Christian communities. Their instructions and insights on moral and ethical matters are therefore relevant to Christians today. With the modern application of these biblical insights in mind, this kind of investigation tends to be interested in the ethics of the texts as a canonical whole, often seeking to elicit overarching moral principles or ethical paradigms. While differences of opinion within and among the texts may be acknowledged, the ultimate interest in practical application of the results tends to favor an emphasis on unity and coherence.

A much smaller number of investigations into ethics and the biblical texts, most of them relatively recent, have been interested in the ethical and moral thinking of these texts from a historical point of view. In these studies the texts are used as a window into the moral world of ancient Israel and its people. This kind of investigation is thus sometimes referred to as the study of "ethics in ancient Israel." Because they are interested in the specific historical contexts of the biblical texts, these investigations tend to focus on individual texts (or groups of texts): ethics in the book of Ezekiel, for example, or ethics as reflected in the narratives about David in the books of Samuel.

As with other historical investigations, this kind of study may be undertaken for the purpose of better understanding the biblical text, so that the text may be better elucidated for contemporary audiences—and, sometimes, so that they may be used to inform contemporary moral thinking and practice. These two kinds of investigations into ethics and the biblical texts are therefore not unrelated to each other, though they have different objectives and their methods are important to distinguish. The kinds of questions and methods used to investigate how ancient Israelites fought and justified war, for example, will be different from those employed in a discussion of how the depictions of kings as divinely sanctioned warriors in pursuit of justice and righteousness might inform our own thinking about modern warfare—though we might want to use the answers to the former to inform our discussion of the latter.

A related point is that the ethical interests and concerns of a modern audience may not overlap with those of the ancient authors; there are many matters of contemporary moral concern that have no direct counterparts in the biblical texts. Likewise, actions and principles that were quite ordinary in the ancient world may not be so today (and vice versa). This might seem obvious, but especially when thinking about ethics, which are part of how we see and approach the world, it can be easy to conflate our own moral concerns with those of the authors and audiences of the texts, forgetting that the world we live in is very different from the world inhabited by these texts' authors. On the one hand, this can cause an anachronistic kind of moral quandary (*How could the Israelites slaughter the Canaanites when genocide is morally reprehensible?*), and on the other, it can preclude further investigations into the moral logic and moral priorities of the biblical texts—the kinds of investigations that might help bridge the gap between ancient and modern moral concerns.

One of the reasons to investigate the biblical texts from a historical perspective, then, is that no single moral imperative exists in a vacuum. Ethics are connected to other ideas about right and wrong behavior as well as to more general ideas about the structure of society, the relationship between this society and the individual, and even the way that the world is organized and operates. This means that knowing more about the context of a biblical text can result in a better understanding of its moral logic. More specifically, we might think about the political context, social context, or theological context of an ethical idea or imperative, asking how a particular idea responds or relates to its particular circumstances. Ezekiel, for example, is presented as having been a priest in Jerusalem, with certain moral and cultic obligations arising from that fact. These obligations would have been profoundly affected by deportation and exile, requiring adaptation and modification in order to have meaning in a new context. The account of the simultaneous creation of male and female in Genesis 1 was written in a context of male social dominance; it would be easy to miss how radical this depiction is if this context is ignored or forgotten. Both Ruth and Tamar are faced with a choice of moral priorities, in the context of the conflicting imperatives of family survival and sexual reserve. One contribution of studies on "the ethics of ancient Israel" to "the ethics of the Old Testament," then, has been the recognition of the usefulness of historical context for understanding the moral logic and intentions of the biblical texts, insofar as knowing more about the ancient context that provoked a particular text can help the modern reader to recognize and engage with the text's moral complexity. If we want to think about the modern relevance of these texts—for Christians, for Jews, for nonbelievers, and so on—knowing something about context enables a more informed judgment about whether a particular text might be meaningful in the modern world as well as a richer statement of how and why it might be so.

We might also think about *literary* context, and to this we now turn in greater detail.

GENRE

Given that our ethical investigations are focused on the biblical texts themselves, one important component of the context of these texts is their *genre*, or the *kind of text* that they are. Different kinds of texts develop for different kinds of purposes; as a result they often have different ways of revealing moral norms and opinions. Some texts are quite overtly trying to make a moral point, for example, while others' moral logic is revealed accidentally, while they are busy doing something else. Legal and proverbial material, for instance, tends to be explicit (at least about the imperative, if not always about its logic): "You shall not kill." Often, however, ethical norms are less obvious: a psalm might praise the king for being "just" and "righteous," without saying directly what that justice and righteousness involves. A story might reward its hero at the end of the tale, but we might have to examine the story carefully to figure out which of the hero's actions merited the reward.

Law

Legal texts are often what people think of first when they think of ethics and the biblical texts. These texts have an obviously instructive format, with explicit instructions about what people should or should not do. For this reason they have been the focus of many scholarly discussions of ethics as well as serving as a go-to source for contemporary ethics. Conversations about Christian attitudes to same-sex marriage, for example, often refer to Leviticus 18:22 ("You shall not lie with a male as with a woman; it is an abomination") and 20:13 ("If a man lies with a male as with a woman, both of them have committed an abomination; they shall be put to death; their blood is upon them"), while, in positive terms, the injunction in Leviticus 19:18 to "love your neighbor as yourself" appears in the New Testament and is often cited as a key principle for Christian ethics. Besides their obvious instructive intent, one advantage of legal texts for thinking about ethics is that they often include an explanation of their rationale. Deuteronomy 22:8, for example, is clear that its roof-building instructions relate to the importance of making sure that no one is injured falling off it, while the Leviticus texts just mentioned explicitly base their objections in statements that the same-sex activities they describe are an "abomination."

Keeping in mind the two kinds of investigations into ethics, there are at least two different kinds of questions with which we might further probe these texts. We might, first, inquire as to the historical circumstances that prompted a particular law and its rationale: Why is Deuteronomy so worried about people falling off roofs that it includes a law mandating parapets? If we know that most ancient houses were built with flat roofs that doubled as terraces, the law makes more sense: if people are on the roof frequently, there is a high risk of falling and a need for parapets in order to prevent tragic accidents. Still thinking historically, we might also ask what the rationale suggests about the moral principles underlying the legislation. Thus we might ask: Why is it so important to keep people from falling off the roof? In this case, the underlying issue is obvious: when people fall off a roof they are liable to die or at least suffer significant injury. Developing this line of questioning toward more general principles, we might observe that the very fact of legislation designed to prevent fatal or injurious consequences suggests that the author values human life and sees it as something that ought to be protected. The warning that the owner of the roof might incur guilt if someone does fall also suggests that the author views his audience as morally responsible for the consequences of their actions.

For an "ethics of the Old Testament," the key question is, *What relevance does this have for today?* At first glance, the answer might be: *Not a lot!* (Certainly there are not very many houses built with parapets these days.) On closer inspection, however, the historical investigation can push this application question in a more productive direction. Thus, having worked out the law's motives, we might still conclude that a house with a slanted roof and no roof terrace has no need of a parapet—but by recognizing the underlying emphases on the value of human life and on moral responsibility we might argue that a modern application of the text means ensuring that buildings are safe for their inhabitants and visitors. Depending on the modern context, that might mean the installation of reliable electrical wiring or designing a house to be earthquake resistant.

Unfortunately for both kinds of investigations, the reasoning behind a law is not always so clear. The laws in Leviticus, for example, base their prohibitions on the idea of an act being "abominable"—but what does that mean, and what might it tell us about the underlying principles at work? Elsewhere, Deuteronomy 22:5 prohibits transvestitism, again using the language of abomination. Here matters are complicated even further by the laconic phrasing: Does the law apply to all garments or only certain specific kinds? Most ancient clothing was more or less unisex: Is the law referring only to items of clothing worn only by men or only by women, or does it mean to include all clothes based on who owns them? The answers to these and other questions will affect our interpretation of the law and, in turn, interpretations of whether or how it might inform modern life. If we conclude that transvestitism was linked to the worship of other gods, then we might interpret the law as reflecting religious concerns and its current relevance to be in the liturgical domain. Knowing that the word *abomination* often appears in contexts concerned about certain kinds of boundaries (ethnic boundaries, social boundaries, religious boundaries) might suggest that the law is trying to preserve what it sees as a categorical distinction between men and women—which, in turn, might prompt questions about ancient ideas about human biology and male-female social relations. Eventually we might want to bring this into dialogue with developments in the field of human biology—and perhaps also with the aforementioned depiction of male-female relations in Genesis 1.

Even if we were always clear on the intentions and principles of the laws, however, they would still pose another challenge, directly related to the diversity of moral opinions that they preserve. Instead of all reflecting a single underlying principle and being directed toward a single overarching goal, different laws prioritize different moral principles or even instruct different things. The biblical text includes not just one but several legal collections: the Covenant Code (Exodus 20–23), the Decalogue (Exodus 20 and Deuteronomy 5), the Holiness Code (Leviticus 17–26), the priestly legislation (parts of Leviticus and Numbers), and the Deuteronomic Code (Deuteronomy 12–26). Each of these has its own unique history and its own particular interests, reflected in the laws each collection contains and the explanations it provides. The Holiness Code and the priestly laws, for example, are concerned with the priesthood and with applying priestly values to the people as a whole. Deuteronomy is focused on what it means to be an Israelite and a faithful worshipper of Israel's one God; although it draws on many of the laws contained in the Covenant Code, it excludes some, alters others, and adds its own, reflecting its own special interests. We can see a similar phenomenon in the two versions of the Decalogue: though both include the commandment to keep the Sabbath, Deuteronomy connects it to the Israelites' experience as slaves in Egypt, while Exodus connects it to God's rest on the seventh day of creation. Elsewhere, some laws about debt slavery command the release of the debt slave in the sabbatical year (the seventh year) (Exodus 15:2–6 and Deuteronomy 15:12–18), while a third version legislates release only in the Jubilee year (the forty-ninth or fiftieth year) (Leviticus 25:39–46).

Such differences raise questions about the origins and intentions of individual texts—Why do different texts instruct different things?—as well as the intentions and principles of those who brought the texts

together—Why not make sure that instructions were consistent throughout the whole collection? (Perhaps relevant is that no one knows whether
these laws were written to be used in everyday life or, if so, how. Even all
together they contain only a small number of laws; many topics are not
covered or are only covered to a limited extent. The evidence of other
ancient Near Eastern law codes, such as the Laws of Hammurabi, also
suggests that law codes could be used as school exercises or as a formalized way of asserting a king's commitment to justice and righteousness,
without necessarily meaning that the individual laws were put into practice.) If we are interested in the use of these texts today, we also need to
think about how we might deal with this diversity; since this is a question applicable to all genres of biblical text, we will return to this question
at the end.

Narrative

The canonical location of these legal texts might also have an effect on
our understanding of their ethical content: What is the significance—or
is it significant at all—that these law codes are now embedded in narratives? Although narrative might not be the first thing to come to mind
when thinking about sources for thinking about ethics, there is a very
long tradition of using stories to convey moral ideas, promoting values
such as honesty and loyalty over the pursuit of power and material success. Including narrative texts in investigations into biblical ethics also
has a significant practical advantage insofar as it dramatically expands
the corpus of relevant texts. These include the stories of Noah and the
other antediluvians, the travels and encounters of the patriarchs and
their families, and the adventures (and misadventures) that form the
many episodes in the long narrative of Israel—from Moses and Miriam
in Egypt to David, Solomon, and their fellow kings in the land to the
stories of Daniel and Esther and so on, not to mention the many minor
and sometimes nameless characters who come and go throughout.

Like the laws, these stories present both opportunities and challenges.
First and foremost, the ethical aspects of biblical narratives are rarely
offered up to the reader in a neat, clear assessment. The "moral of the
story" is often ambiguous or at least open to interpretation; though the
narratives often exhibit an interest in the behavior of their various char-

acters, they rarely pronounce their judgment explicitly. It can therefore be difficult to discern who gains or loses the text's moral approbation and why. Indeed, the activities of many of the most famous players are often exceedingly suspect: Jacob steals his brother's birthright (Genesis 25) and conspires with his mother, Rachel, to steal his father's blessing (Genesis 27); both Abraham and Isaac deceive foreign kings by pretending that their wives are their sisters (Genesis 12, 20, and 26); David is an adulterous murderer (2 Samuel 11). One is left wondering whether, or to what extent, these heroes are intended to serve as moral paragons—while at the same time asking after the principles and values that might enable the recognition of these morally complicated characters as worthy nonetheless. At other times it is not at all clear that the text is even interested in ethics. While Nathan's condemnation of David for his behavior with Bathsheba and his treatment of Uriah the Hittite is explicit ("You are the man," 1 Samuel 12:7), whether the authors of the stories about the patriarchs are even interested in the morality of their various activities is a matter for debate. This in turn raises a question for the interpreter: Is it a legitimate interpretive move to investigate the moral logic of a text whose interests are elsewhere?

Even if there is reason to think that the text has an interest in the moral lives of its characters, discerning ethical information from texts that address those concerns only in a roundabout, indirect way remains a challenge. An added layer of complexity derives from the fact that the moral values discerned in a narrative may belong to the author, or they might reflect the norms of the audience—or they might belong to the moral world of the characters, without a clear connection to either the author or the audience. Yet this moral complexity, the ability to explore ethical gray areas, is also one of the great strengths of the narrative form. Narratives are not obliged to make the kinds of absolute statements that laws do; as a result, they are able to bring into the picture a greater degree of nuance and complexity. Given the potentially hostile situations with which they are faced, are Abraham and Isaac right to pass off their wives as their sisters? Is Jacob's craftiness praiseworthy, or does it go too far? Is David a hero because or in spite of his willingness to make controversial moral decisions—or is he a hero in a moral sense at all? Though the indirectness of this kind of ethical contemplation can be frustrating, because it is not always clear whether a narrator approves of a character's acts (or which ones), the narratives offer a way of thinking morally about the complexity of actual human life. The unnamed messenger of 1 Samuel 11 disobeys his senior officer's order when he tells David immediately of Uriah's death, apparently in order to preempt a royal rage; Ruth risks shame and humiliation in the pursuit of economic and social security; Abigail, faced with David on the warpath, belittles her husband to save their skins (1 Samuel 25). By avoiding explicit evaluations, these narratives invite readers to reflect on the difficult choices made by their characters.

Prophecy

The prophetic books contain some of the most powerful ethical statements of any biblical texts. These books are strong proponents of social justice, condemning the neglect and abuse of weaker members of society and adjuring the pursuit of justice and righteousness. The book of Micah implores its audience "to do justice, and to love kindness, and to walk humbly with your God" (Micah 4:3), while Amos's injunction to "let justice roll down like waters, and righteousness like an ever-flowing stream" (Amos 5:24) inspired Martin Luther King Jr. in his "Letter from a Birmingham Jail." Micah and Amos speak against judicial corruption and those who would take advantage of the poor; both Isaiah and Micah preserve a desire to see the end of war and a future full of peace; and Isaiah berates his audience for their failures to live up to YHWH's standards of justice and righteousness.

From the interpreter's perspective the prophetic texts fall somewhere between law and narrative, albeit with their own particular challenges as well. Many of the ethical issues in the prophets are obviously so: there are passages dealing with the (mis)use of wealth, the treatment of the poor, the behavior of Israel's leaders vis-à-vis the people, and so on. Thus when Amos condemns those "who afflict the righteous, who take a bribe, and push aside the needy in the gate" (Amos 5:12), the moral issue is one that is recognizable to a modern reader. It helps flesh out the picture to know that the city gate was the locus of an ancient town's justice system, and thus "to push aside the needy" means not only to ignore those in need but to subvert their access to the means of justice, but the abuse of weak and marginal members of society by the powerful is one that is as much an issue in the modern world as it was in the ancient one and is easily recognizable as a moral concern.

Other parts of the prophetic material, however, are concerned with issues that are less obviously ethical. Prophetic tirades about Israel's cultic practices, for example, at first might not seem relevant to discussions of ethical behavior, either ancient or modern. Thus when Amos, speaking for YHWH, declares that "I hate, I despise your festivals, and I take no delight in your solemn assemblies; even though you offer me your burnt-offerings and grain-offerings, I will not accept them" (Amos 5:21–22), this looks like a rejection of sacrifice—a matter perhaps of liturgical interest but not obviously an ethical issue. Yet, though it might take a different form, this prophetic condemnation contains an implicit imperative, akin to the explicit instructions contained in the legal material: the sacrifices offered are unacceptable. The implied imperative: "You must not make these sacrifices (at all)" or "You must not make these sacrifices (like this)." This suggests that there is either something wrong with making sacrifices or something wrong with the way that the sacrifices are being made. As with the laws, then, it is instructive to ask after the underlying rationale: Why does Amos condemn these sacrifices? Once we start to investigate, we realize that this is the immediate context of the famous summons to "let justice roll down like waters, and righteousness like an ever-flowing stream." This suggests that the problem is not the sacrifices themselves but their relationship, or lack thereof, to justice and righteousness. What initially appeared to be a cultic matter turns out to be also an ethical issue. Further investigation might flesh out the details of what this justice and righteousness entails, but already at this stage the inquiry has implications for both historical and contemporary ethical investigations. First, it is significant that the ethical principle at work here is intimately connected to Amos's understanding of God. This is also the case for Isaiah and Ezekiel, for whom YHWH's supreme holiness correlates to an expectation that YHWH's people act in a holy fashion. (Further investigation might reveal how these prophets' different ideas about YHWH's character, or different emphases, affect their expectations for human behavior.) Second, we might consider how the principle underlying Amos's condemnation—that the rightness or wrongness of a certain action is related both to the attitude of the actor and to other acts—might reflect a wider moral system, beyond the morality or immorality of isolated acts. Third, we might ask how the principles of this ancient system might influence a modern moral system.

Poetry

An added complication inherent to much of the prophetic literature is shared with other, nonprophetic poetic texts. The majority of this comprises the poetry of the psalter, but it also includes the Song of Songs and several hymns that have been set into narrative texts elsewhere (such as Deuteronomy 32 and Exodus 15), in addition to the poetic material from the prophets. This poetry includes a diversity of form and subject, ranging from royal psalms and meditations on wisdom to victory hymns to love poetry to hymns of praise to Yhwh for his activities and attributes. Like the narrative and prophetic material, poetry can be difficult to deal with but also rewarding. Its major challenge for the student of ethics is that much of its contents are couched in metaphorical language and artistic imagery—a far cry from the direct statements of the legal material!

Wisdom

The final genre to note is the wisdom literature. This contains many elements of the genres already discussed: explicit instruction, akin to the legal material, in Proverbs; poetry, including both the poems about Woman Wisdom in Proverbs 1–9 and the arguments among Job and his friends in the book of Job; and narrative texts, in the form of the introduction and conclusion to Job and some of the musings of Ecclesiastes. While none of the "wisdom" books contain prophecy as such, many parts of the prophetic books also reflect this tradition.

Summary

Each of these different genres raises its own particular methodological issues for the study of ethics. Common to most of them are issues about whether, or to what extent, we are able to extract ethical information from texts that may not have been written with ethical instructions in mind. I have also noted that there can be, and often are, issues of consistency among different texts. Depending on what we are trying to achieve with our ethical investigations, the implications of these points may vary: if we are interested in the historical relationships among these texts, we may approach such variations one way, while if we are interested in the contemporary application of these texts' ethical ideas, we may approach them in another.

ORIGINS

At the beginning of this essay I mentioned that specific ethical instructions always exist in the midst of a wider collection of ideas about the world and society. One element of this wider context that is particularly important in thinking about ethics has to do with the perceived source of ethics. That is to ask, Where do these moral norms come from? Related to this is the question of how human beings are supposed to know whether something is (or is not) morally commendable.

The first and perhaps the most obvious answer to the first question, at least in the biblical context, is that ethics come from God and, to the second, that human beings know about these moral norms because God has told humans about them. That is, human beings are able to distinguish between right and wrong behavior on the basis of explicit moral statements that are attributed to the deity. In their current narrative context, many of the laws in the Torah are presented this way: Moses is said to have gone up onto the holy mountain in order to receive the commandments, whereupon he wrote them down on stone tablets for Israel's future reference (Deuteronomy 5 and elsewhere). Israel's moral imperatives are thus presented as deriving directly from God, and the Israelites know about these imperatives as a result of direct divine revelation.

It is important to notice that this explanation requires the God who gives these instructions and the people who are expected to follow them to have some kind of relationship, so that the people pay attention to the instructions and so that God is able to communicate them. As far as Israel is concerned, this works just fine. YHWH is Israel's god and is clearly able to communicate information to Israel, first through Moses and later through other prophets and priests.

Yet numerous other biblical texts assume that other, non-Israelite peoples also have moral responsibilities. The punishments that Amos calls down on the nations for their war crimes, for example, imply that these nations ought to have known that such deeds were reprehensible. Other texts also presuppose moral norms valid for all humanity—regardless of whether a person is privy to the more specific instructions revealed to Israel. In Genesis 9:6, for example, we read that "whoever sheds the blood of a human, by a human shall that person's blood be shed; for in his own image God made humankind." This is presented not as an imperative revealed to and only applicable to Israelites ("You, an Israelite, will not kill another human being") but as a moral norm based on the very nature of all human beings and which all human beings are expected to reflect in their actions.

This suggests that the question of how humans are supposed to know about moral norms is more than just a matter of divine revelation, because YHWH does not have a relationship with other peoples and there is no indication that other peoples are expected to know the laws given directly to Israel. How, then, are these other peoples supposed to know what constitutes right and wrong behavior? The most convincing explanation is that human beings are expected to be able to figure out certain basic ethical norms for themselves. But how?

The lack of any sustained discussion of the nature and origins of ethics—something akin to a Greek philosophical treatise—makes this a difficult question. One possibility is that these universal norms are perceived to be innate: simply part of the makeup of a human being. Perhaps suggesting this kind of thinking is that some of the prophets' exasperated exhortations, for example, imply an expectation that their audiences (even the Israelites) ought to know certain things without needing to be told them explicitly. Thus Isaiah 1:3 announces that Israel is acting even less intelligently than the animals ("The ox knows its owner and the donkey its master's crib, but Israel does not know; my people do not understand"), in the process implying that humans ought to be able to work out certain of the divine expectations even if they were, like the animals, completely deprived of revelation. There are certain things that are just "obviously" wrong, for which an explicit divine statement is unnecessary, and which may be supposed somehow to be built into the human moral compass. Perhaps the condemnations of Amos 1 also fall into this category.

This idea that moral norms might be built into the very fabric of things—human or otherwise—is closely related to another possible explanation. This is the idea that it might be possible to work out certain general ethical principles through observation of and knowledge about the world. This kind of inductive moral reasoning is sometimes referred to as "natural law," reflecting the idea that this is a kind of moral "law" that is inbuilt and therefore observable in the "natural" world (differing ideas about what is "natural" can make this more of a challenge in practice than it might seem in principle). In the biblical context we might point to the passage in Genesis already mentioned, in which the prohibition of murder is grounded in an idea about the nature of a human being. Human beings are *like this*, and this implies that moral action in relation to them should be *like that*. This particular example, however, draws attention to another feature of natural law, at least in the context of a theistic worldview: insofar as creation reflects its creator, any moral norms derived from the natural world may be supposed, ultimately, to derive from God.

This suggests another way in which human beings might work out what constitutes ethical behavior: by asking, What would God do? This is the principle of *imitatio dei*, the imitation of God. The underlying premise is that human beings ought to aspire to be as like God as they can. In the biblical tradition this is ultimately based on the idea that human beings are made in the image of God (Genesis 1:26–27). Ideas about what God is like can therefore serve as a guide to what human beings should be like. Imperatives and adjurations reflecting this principle appear often and across a range of texts. Yhwh's own holiness, for example, requires a certain level of holiness from anyone in proximity to him (much of Leviticus and Ezekiel), while many of the prophetic exhortations to justice and righteousness are implicitly or explicitly based in the attribution of these characteristics to God (Amos 5, Isaiah 56, and so on). *Imitatio dei* is a middle ground between divinely revealed commands and natural law, because reasoning out human behavior on the basis of the divine behavior or essence implies some kind of knowledge of the divine—and knowledge of the divine, it can be argued, also has to be revealed. It might also be argued, however, that the values and attributes of the deity might be reasoned out from observations about the natural world and the human condition, if those are things that the deity is supposed to have created.

This, finally, brings us back to the second question: Where do moral norms come from? The ultimate issue here concerns the relationship between ethics and God. Is an act considered morally commendable because God commanded it (that is, anything divinely commanded is, simply by virtue of being divinely commanded, morally sound)? Or does God command certain acts because they are morally commendable according to some kind of overarching (and divinely recognized) moral principles? This question also relates to how humans discern moral norms. The first option might suggest that the only way of knowing what constitutes right behavior is revelation, insofar as it implies that moral norms are arbitrarily determined by God. The second option suggests a moral system according to which the deity issues instructions—and perhaps therefore implies that an observant human might be able to work out the general principles of this system even in the absence of direct revelation. Another way of putting this question is: Is God *in* the moral system, or did God *create* the moral system?

One text often thought to shed light on this issue is Genesis 18, in which Abraham negotiates to spare the city of Sodom. The entire passage is a theoretical exercise, but its premise is that both Abraham and God agree on punishing the righteous being objectionable—and thus suggests both that God's actions are not arbitrary and that there are moral principles recognizable by both humans and God. It might also be taken to imply that God is bound by certain moral norms. A similar kind of thinking might be suggested by the hints in Proverbs and other texts that God is expected to serve as the guarantor of justice, ensuring that the right consequences are meted out for any given crime—and thus, again, that there are standards of right and wrong that are mutually agreed on by, and recognizable to, both God and humans. The book of Job, on the other hand, appears to emphasize just the opposite: while Job succeeds, to a degree, in calling God to account for his apparently unjustified suffering, God's ultimate response points to the unfathomable nature of the deity. God is not bound by or restricted to a moral system that is comprehensible to human beings and is not obliged to counteract instances of what appear, from a human perspective, to be injustice. (Nevertheless, Job is restored.)

None of these texts are systematic treatments of the origins of moral norms or the moral relationship between God and his human interlocutors. They reflect a variety of viewpoints and approaches: in some cases ethical expectations are articulated as divine command, while in others they seem to be derived from the nature of the world or beliefs about God. Ultimately, however, the question of whether God is inside and bound by or creates and is outside the moral system is probably a false dichotomy, at least as far as the biblical authors are concerned. It would be more accurate to suggest that God *is* the moral system—and because God is creator of the universe, the moral laws of the universe reflect the nature of God. Like God, these moral laws may not be fully comprehensible to human beings in all their details—and this perhaps is where revelation plays a role—but there is an underlying and unifying principle at work that, at least in its broad strokes, may be discerned from observation of the natural world.

FINAL REMARKS

The biblical texts preserve a remarkable diversity of opinions on matters ethical. For those with historical interests, this diversity offers a delightful variety of points of access to the moral world(s) of ancient Israel. For those for whom these texts are in some way authoritative, it raises questions about the nature of the texts themselves and, in particular, their role and relevance in modern moral philosophies.

The complexity of current arguments over the appropriate use of the biblical traditions in contemporary ethics reflects the complexity of the biblical texts themselves. Such debates are not merely an argument between those for whom these texts are authoritative and those for whom they are not—an argument over whether the contents of these texts are relevant to a contemporary conversation at all. Rather, the cacophony of modern voices reflects the cacophony of the ancient voices with whom they are in conversation. It is possible to point to different texts, to different interpretations, in connection with current moral challenges precisely because the texts themselves preserve multiple and divergent opinions on the subjects they address.

The biblical texts represent a diversity of ancient opinions on what it means to be human, on what it means to be a human being in relation with the divine, and on the appropriate manifestations of these in ordinary (and extraordinary) human lives. In their diversity, these texts preserve a dialectic—a dialogue—a conversation—about some of the most profound questions human beings face. The mere fact that the canonical collection(s) of scripture preserves this dialectic demands the attention of those interested in the ongoing relevance of these texts. It suggests that the forces behind this agglomeration of texts were less interested in the production and dictation of absolute moral norms than they were in the process of trying to discern them—more interested in the lived experience of human beings, trying to work out what it means to live in a world created by God, than in preempting that process by fiat.

It also suggests that these texts recognize the contingent nature of their interim conclusions and preserve them not as the final word on the subjects they pursue so much as a witness and an invitation to the process in which they are deeply engaged and to which they are deeply committed. A faithful engagement of these texts in the context of modern dilemmas, then, is to accept an invitation to join their conversation. Rather than declaring, *This is what it means to be human*, these texts invite their audience to ask, *How does the Bible acknowledge and engage with both the diversity of human experience and the diversity of interpretations of that experience—and how might I join that conversation?*

FURTHER READING

The most well-known methodological musings on ethics in and of the Old Testament/Hebrew Bible have been by John Barton, including *Ethics and the Old Testament* (London: SCM, 1998), *Understanding Old Testament Ethics: Approaches and Explorations* (Louisville, Ky.: Westminster John Knox, 2003), and *Ethics in Ancient Israel* (Oxford: Oxford University Press, 2014). Another accessible introduction is Eryl W. Davies's *The Immoral Bible: Approaches to Biblical Ethics* (London: T&T Clark,

2010). Prominent studies of Old Testament ethics from a Christian perspective include B. C. Birch's *Let Justice Roll Down: The Old Testament, Ethics, and Christian Life* (Louisville, Ky.: Westminster John Knox, 1988) and C.J.H. Wright's *Old Testament Ethics for the People of God* (Downers Grove: InterVarsity, 2004). Recent studies of specific texts include Andrew Davies's *Double Standards in Isaiah: Re-evaluating Prophetic Ethics and Divine Justice* (Leiden: Brill, 2000), Andrew Mein's *Ezekiel and the Ethics of Exile* (Oxford: Oxford University Press, 2001), J. Gary Millar's *Now Choose Life: Theology and Ethics in Deuteronomy* (Grand Rapids, Mich.: Eerdmans, 1999), my *War and Ethics in the Ancient Near East: Military Violence in Light of Cosmology and History* (Berlin: de Gruyter, 2009), Richard G. Smith's *The Fate of Justice and Righteousness during David's Reign: Narrative Ethics and Rereading the Court History according to 2 Samuel 8:15–20:26* (London: T&T Clark, 2009), and two volumes by Gordon J. Wenham: *Psalms as Torah: Reading Biblical Song Ethically* (Grand Rapids, Mich.: Baker Academic, 2012) and *Story as Torah: Reading the Old Testament Ethically* (Edinburgh: T&T Clark, 2000). There are now also several collections of shorter studies of various texts and topics, including John W. Rogerson, Margaret Davies, and M. Daniel Carroll R., eds., *The Bible in Ethics: The Second Sheffield Colloquium* (Sheffield: Sheffield Academic Press, 1995); M. Daniel Carroll R. and Jacqueline E. Lapsley, eds., *Character Ethics and the Old Testament: Moral Dimensions of Scripture* (Louisville, Ky.: Westminster John Knox, 2007); and Katharine Dell, ed., *Ethical and Unethical in the Old Testament: God and Humans in Dialogue* (London: T&T Clark, 2010).

15

Religious Space and Structures

Stephen C. Russell

A variety of spaces and structures served religious functions in ancient Israel and Judah, as witnessed in the Hebrew Bible and the Levantine archaeological record. Such spaces are differentiated from other kinds of space because they served as a venue for the performance of religious rituals.[1] I organize this survey of religious space according to ritual performers. The principal social unit in ancient Israel and Judah was the individual patriarchal household, known as "the house of the father."[2] Such households were grouped together either in small hamlets and villages or in towns, and they were held together by an ideology of kinship as belonging to the same clan and tribe. Larger social structures also existed. Israel, in the north, was a tribal collective that had an active tradition of distributed governance even as it also had a monarchy. Judah, in the south, was much more highly centralized and controlled by its monarchy, the House of David. This survey treats religious space at these three nested layers of society—the household; the clan, the town, and the tribe; and the tribal collective and the monarchies. It concludes with an examination of certain spaces that had no existence in the material world but were the product of religious imagination.[3]

THE HOUSEHOLD

The family dwelling and family tomb were loci for the performance of family rituals. During the Iron Age a distinctive form of Israelite dwelling emerged.[4] The typical Israelite house was rectilinear and consisted of four rooms, sometimes fewer. Typically, two rows of stone pillars demarcated a central room from two side rooms. A stone wall separated these from a fourth room at the back of the house. In light of its distinctive architectural form, the house is known as the "four-room" or "pillared" house. Animals were kept on the ground floor in the front rooms, while the back room was used for storage. Pillared houses were completely roofed and may have included an open room on a second floor, where the family would have slept (cf. 1 Sam. 9:25–26; 2 Sam. 11:2; 1 Kings 17:19; 2 Kings 23:12; Jer. 19:13). The house often opened onto a courtyard shared by a handful of other dwellings. These structures were occupied by multiple generations of an extended household. In addition to rearing animals, the family cultivated nearby agricultural land.

Although the Israelite dwelling was by and large a profane space, filled with the smell of animals and the activities of everyday life, much of Israelite religious practice centered on the household. Important life events and some festivals of national importance were accompanied by rituals performed in the context of family: birth and circumcision, Passover and Sukkoth, and death and burial. As such, the Israelite dwelling acquired religious significance on special occasions.

Conception, birth, and child rearing had their hazards for the household and required special rituals. About a thousand roughly six-inch-tall Iron Age II statues of an abstracted female form have been unearthed, largely in domestic contexts.[5] The precise function of these so-called Judahite pillar figurines remains unknown—perhaps they represent a particular female deity or functioned in a more general way as a talisman. Nevertheless, because of their exaggerated breasts, they are generally assumed to have played some ritual domestic role in relation to fertility or the lactation required for child rearing.[6] Birth, even more dangerous for mother and infant before the advent of modern medicine, was no doubt accompanied by rituals to safeguard those involved (cf. the poetic metaphor in Ezek. 16:4). According to the priestly prescriptions in the book of Leviticus, birth initiated the mother into a period of ritual impurity that ended after a prescribed period via the performance of rituals at a central sanctuary (Lev. 12:1–8). Before the late monarchic period, however, it is doubtful that the central sanctuary in Jerusalem played a major role in rituals accompanying birth for the vast majority of Israelites. Such activities were centered upon the family home.

According to the biblical text, Israelite sons were circumcised on the eighth day after their birth (Gen. 17:12, 21:4; Lev. 12:3).[7] Evidently, circumcision was performed by the father, at home, rather than by a priest at a sanctuary (Gen. 21:4; compare the case of circumcision by a mother in Exod. 4:24–26). It served as a sign of the covenant between Israel and Yahweh (Gen. 17:10–14) and thus marked insiders from outsiders (Exod. 12:48–49). Although the details of the circumcision ritual are not described in the Hebrew Bible (though again, compare Exod. 4:24–26), the event must have held religious significance in a family's life. According to the book of Deuteronomy, children were to be brought up with constant exposure to the teachings of Yahweh in the context of family, so that even the mundane Israelite dwelling was understood to be a space for sacred instruction (Deut. 6:6–9).

Certain annual religious feasts of national importance may have had their roots in familial contexts.[8] Passover, which celebrated the deliverance of Israel from bondage in Egypt, was in the late monarchic period understood to be a pilgrimage feast to Jerusalem (Deut. 16:1–8; 2 Kings 23:23; cf. 1 Kings 12:25–33). Reading between the lines of Exodus 12:1–13, 21–23, however, this pilgrimage feast seems to overlay an older festival that was celebrated in a family context. Likewise, although Sukkoth was perceived in a later period as a pilgrimage feast (Deut. 16:13–15), it was rooted in the rhythms of the agricultural year and may therefore also have been celebrated originally in a family context at harvest time.

The book of Judges also imagines that shrines could be set up in household contexts. According to Judges 17, a wealthy Ephraimite family commissioned a silver cult image and erected it in their house. They hired a Levite to permanently serve as priest in this household shrine. The narrative may date from several hundred years after the events it portrays purportedly occurred, and it is therefore difficult to take it as a reliable record of this particular family's religious practice.[9] In its current form, the story is meant to illustrate the supposed religious chaos that existed before the time of kings. Even so, however, the house shrine and image were conceived as Yahwistic (Judg. 17:13). For the story's didactic purpose to be fulfilled, its ancient audience must have deemed it plausible that a wealthy family could have established a Yahwistic shrine in their home. Two cult stands discovered at Taanach in what some scholars regard as a domestic context may confirm this impression gained from Judges 17 that wealthy families could have set up cultic spaces within their domiciles.[10]

Rituals associated with death and burial took place in the family home and family tomb. Mourning for the deceased included a wide variety of gestures that were part of a cultural vocabulary of grief and that served to separate mourners from normal life (e.g., Gen. 37:34; Deut. 34:8; 2 Sam. 1:11–12, 3:35, 13:9, 14:2, 15:30; Jer. 6:26, 16:17; Ezek. 24:17, 22; Joel 1:8; Mic. 1:8; Job 42:11). Rites associated with burial itself could begin in a domestic context (Num. 19:14; Amos 6:10). Afterward, the body was removed to the family tomb (e.g., 2 Sam. 3:31–37).

A distinctive form of Judahite burial emerged in the Iron Age II.[11] The deceased was interred in a communal, hewn-out cave. Typically, a rectilinear entrance led down into a chamber containing several elevated benches along its walls. The dead were laid on these benches. After some months or years, when space was required for new burials, the defleshed bones of the deceased were removed from the bench and added to an accumulating pile of old bones at the rear of the cave. Iron Age I burials are attested in three locations: on the slopes of tells, on cliffs or hills facing tells and within view of them, and in the three-kilometer-long necropolis framed by Dhahr Mirzbaneh in the south and 'Ein es-Samiya in the north.[12] The practice of burial adjacent to a town is reflected in the Hebrew Bible: Gideon was interred in his family tomb at Ophrah (Judg. 6:11, 8:32); Asahel, in his family tomb in Bethlehem (2 Sam. 2:32); Tola, in Shamir, where he had lived (Judg. 10:1–2); Jair, in Kamon (Judg. 10:5); Jephthah, in an unspecified town in Gilead (Judg. 12:7); Ibzan, in his hometown of Bethlehem (Judg. 12:8, 10); Elon, in Aijalon (Judg. 12:12); Abdon, in his hometown of Pirathon (Judg. 12:15); and Samuel, according to one strand of tradition, in Ramah (1 Sam. 28:3; but cf. 25:1). The proximity of family tombs to residential towns may suggest that convenient access to the tomb was one factor in determining its location.

A number of biblical texts reflect rituals associated with death and burial. The descriptions of mourning carried out by Jacob and David may draw on the language of ritual descent into the underworld (Gen. 37:35; 2 Sam. 12:15–24). According to Psalm 106:28, the evils committed by the Israelites included eating the sacrifices of the dead. Ritual eating and drinking for the deceased, as well as mourning lacerations and shaving, are assumed by Jeremiah 16:5–8. By prohibiting such activities, the Holiness Code and the book of Deuteronomy acknowledge their existence (Lev. 19:28; Deut. 14:1, 26:14). Ritual care for the corpse may also be implied in 2 Kings 9:34. An ancestral stela could be located at the tomb it-self (Gen. 35:20). Texts from a later period also connect the feeding of the dead with the ancestral tomb (Tob. 4:17; Sir. 30:18). Taken together, the biblical evidence suggests a belief in the ongoing existence of the dead and in the mutually beneficial relationship between the living and the dead.[13]

In sum, although the family domicile was largely concerned with the mundane affairs of everyday life, on special occasions related to the agri-cultural cycle or to the family's life cycle both it and the family tomb could serve as loci for the performance of religious rituals of various kinds. For most of the Israelite and Judahite populations, the family was the primary sphere within which religion was practiced.[14]

THE CLAN, THE TOWN, AND THE TRIBE

Whether in rural hamlets and villages or in larger, walled towns, Israelite households were clustered together into larger social units. These units were based on shared locality and on an ideology of shared kinship. Several spaces held religious significance for these larger social units, either permanently or at significant times of the year.

The biblical stories linking David, son of Jesse, with Bethlehem serve as an example of an extended family's connection to a town and its cult. According to 1 Samuel 16, the prophet Samuel was commanded by Yah-weh to go to Bethlehem and anoint David king. In order to avoid the wrath of the incumbent king, Samuel hid the purpose of his visit by bringing a heifer to offer as a sacrifice to Yahweh. He invited the town elders and Jesse and his family to the feast, where, eventually, David was revealed to be Yahweh's chosen king. Although the story may have been written many centuries after the events it purports to portray, and thus must be used cautiously as historical evidence for the rise of the House of David, its ancient audience evidently found its main plot lines plau-sible.[15] The story thus suggests that a leading religious figure could go to a small town such as Bethlehem to offer a Yahwistic sacrificial feast that was attended by the leading families of the town. Evidently, even a rela-tively small town such as Bethlehem would have had a sacrificial altar either within its boundaries or in close proximity. Later in the narrative, after David had become friends with Saul's son Jonathan, they test Saul's intentions toward David. Their ruse rests on the assumption that David would be expected to attend an annual sacrifice for his extended clan in his city, Bethlehem (1 Sam. 20:6). Again, although the incident may never have occurred, the narrative logic of the text rests on the assumption that the audience, and the character Saul, would have perceived attendance at an annual clan festival in one's hometown as mandatory. No religious architecture is described in these narratives, but they imply that rituals were performed in some religious space associated with the town. Indeed, a variety of spaces with local religious significance are well attested in the archaeological record.

Cultic rooms that were not part of a larger sacred precinct or complex have been found at Lachish, Megiddo, and Ai. I classify these as religious space because they contained various objects that would have been used for religious rituals, such as altars or incense stands. The scale of these rooms suggests that they were of local significance only. For example, cult room 49 at Lachish, dated by the excavators to the tenth century BCE, is a small, broad room lined with plaster-covered stone benches. It contained a horned limestone altar, four clay stands, eight chalices, two stand bowls, three lamps, and other pottery.[16] The altar in particular points to ritual use of the room. At only 7.5 feet wide by 11 feet long, the room could not have accommodated more than two or three ritual actors. Nor does its simple layout permit the successive layers of sanctity found at larger temple complexes. As such, this religious space must have served the needs of the local population only. Similarly scaled religious structures include Megiddo locus 2081,[17] Megiddo room 340 in building 338,[18] and a partially excavated cult room from Iron Age I Ai.[19]

Even larger structures may have served primarily a local population. Iron Age I Hazor evidently had a temple area in its northwest corner.[20] The main sanctuary included an elevated podium with a standing stone. The shrine proper was surrounded by courtyards that, to judge by the presence of incense stands and other cultic objects, also served as spaces for the performance of religious rituals. The elaborated architecture of the sacred precinct suggests that it was conceived of as containing differentiated levels of holiness. The structure was large enough to accommodate a number of ritual actors. Its size suggests that it was a relatively important shrine. At the same time, no mention is made in the Hebrew Bible of Israelite pilgrimage to Hazor. Despite its complex structure, then, the temple at Hazor may have been primarily of local, rather than national, importance.

City gates, though associated mostly with the affairs of profane, everyday life, were also venues for religious rituals. Iron Age Israelite city gates were very large structures that served much more than defensive functions. Typically, a central walkway was flanked by one or more pairs of open chambers, sometimes lined with stone benches.[21] There, legal cases were brought before town elders, and the commerce of city life was conducted. At a limited number of sites, there is also some evidence of a cultic function for city gates.[22] At Bethsaida, for example, a stepped, open-air altar was located at the niche of the northern tower that flanks the city gate.[23] A broken stela depicting a deity in the form of a bull with crescent-like horns was found on top of the altar. Other altars and cultic stelae were found in the vicinity of the gate. Elevated podiums with standing stones were found in the Iron Age II gate complexes at Dan.[24] Such cultic paraphernalia are not always found in Iron Age Israelite gates, but they make clear that city gates could function as religious space in ancient Israel. Unlike the inner sanctums of temple complexes, which would have been accessible, for the most part, only to professional priests, altars at city gates were openly accessible in the busiest area of a town.

Among the open-air altars attested in the archaeological record, the Iron Age cult complex on Mount Ebal deserves special mention.[25] No other Iron Age settlements have been found in the vicinity. A low wall surrounds a roughly 3.5-acre elliptical area. In the northwest area of this enclosure is a smaller enclosure that contains a very large elevated podium constructed largely of fieldstones. Its core was composed of alternate layers of fieldstone, earth, and ash. In the ash layers were found the bones of bulls, sheep, and deer that had evidently been burned at low temperatures. The site's pottery suggests that it was used only during Iron Age I. The excavator has interpreted the large structure as an altar, though this interpretation has not been universally accepted since the structure is unique. If it is a cult complex, the successive enclosures may have marked out successive levels of sanctity. Since no settlement is located nearby, and since the pottery found at the site does not reflect any known typical domestic assemblage, it is perhaps best to regard the cult complex as a pilgrimage site.

The so-called high places, mentioned especially in the books of Samuel and Kings, are generally identified with open-air altars, whether rural or urban.[26] Evidently, the term used could refer to a naturally elevated sacred site or to a built platform. The elevated nature of such religious space is emphasized by the use of verbs of ascent and descent in the narrative of Saul's search for his father's donkeys (1 Sam. 9:13, 14, 19, 25). At the "high place" mentioned in this text, sacrifices were offered, with prominent local residents and their guests invited to the resulting feast (1 Sam. 9:13, 19). This high place was associated with Samuel's town but was apparently located outside it (1 Sam. 9:14). An association between high places and the outdoors is also evident in Jeremiah 17:1–4, 26:18, and in Micah 3:12. Although the precise referent of the biblical term remains debated, high places are perhaps distinguished by the absence of walls separating them from profane space.[27] If so, they may have been more accessible to the general public than the inner rooms of an enclosed temple. At the same time, to judge from the biblical evidence, the vast majority of high places were sacred sites of local, rather than national, importance (e.g., 2 Chron. 28:25). The editorial framework of the book of Kings, which was written largely in the late monarchic period, condemns prior generations for their failure to abolish the many high places scattered throughout Israel and Judah (e.g., 1 Kings 15:14, 22:44; 2 Kings 12:4; 14:4; 15:4, 35; 16:4; 17:9; cf. Jer. 17:1–4; Ezek. 6:3–6).[28] In these texts, the term refers to shrines that are, in the editor's view, illegitimate, wherever and however they were constructed. The book of Kings considers Jerusalem the only legitimate site of sacrificial worship. Such an exclusively centralized view of religious space, however, was no doubt limited to certain Hezekian and Josianic circles in the late monarchic period (2 Kings 18:4, 23:8). Solomon purportedly built high places for the worship of foreign deities on the hills surrounding Jerusalem (1 Kings 11:7). For the majority of Israelites and Judahites during most of the monarchic period, however, worship at local open-air sanctuaries was a legitimate expression of religious devotion to Yahweh. The narrative in 1 Samuel 9, even if it is historical fiction, assumes as much.

It has also been suggested that threshing floors, on which grain was winnowed, held religious significance, particularly because of their association with the harvest and its accompanying celebration.[29] In my assessment, though threshing floors may have been used on rare occasions for religious purposes, there is no compelling biblical evidence to suggest that they had any regular, normal sacred function. According to 2 Samuel 24, the prophet Gad instructs David to build an altar to Yahweh on the threshing floor of Araunah the Jebusite. The location, however, is determined not by the sanctity of the threshing floor itself but, coincidentally, by the fact that a destroying angel from Yahweh had reached as far as Araunah's threshing floor in his march of destruction throughout the land. Furthermore, in purchasing the site David specifies the new use to which it will be put: he intends to build an altar there. The site ceases to be used as a threshing floor. To my mind, the incident in which Uzzah is struck dead as the Ark procession passes the threshing floor of Nacon is also coincidental. According to 1 Kings 22:10, the kings of Israel and Judah sat on the threshing floor by the entrance to Samaria with prophets divining for them. This text suggests that at least some threshing floors were large open spaces associated with the community or town rather than with a private individual. Such large, public spaces might have on occasion been the site of religious events. But there is little evidence that threshing floors were regularly used for religious ceremonies.

THE TRIBAL COLLECTIVE AND THE MONARCHIES

Both Israel and Judah had religious sites of national importance to which the devoted would undertake pilgrimage.[30] In the north, the Israelite tribal collective maintained a political identity that was distinct from its successive monarchies.[31] For this reason, the centers of Israelite tribal pilgrimage—Carmel (1 Kings 18:30–32), Bethel (Gen. 28:10–19, 35:1; Judg. 20:18; 1 Sam. 10:3; 1 Kings 12:25–33; Hosea 12:5; Amos 3:14, 4:4, 5:5, 7:9–17), Shiloh (Josh. 18:1, 8; 21:19; 1 Sam. 1:3, 4:4; Jer. 7:12; Ps. 78:60), Dan (Judg. 18:29–31; 1 Kings 12:25–33), Gilgal (1 Sam. 7:16; Amos 4:4, 5:5), and perhaps also Mizpah (Judg. 20:1; 1 Sam. 7:5–6) and Ebal (Deut. 27:4–8)—never coincided with the centers of Israelite monarchic power—Shechem, Tirzah, and Samaria.[32] Among these, Bethel and Dan were perceived by Judahite scribes in the late monarchic period as the chief rivals to the Temple in Jerusalem (cf. 1 Kings 12:25–33).

Two of the most famous biblical depictions of Bethel are found in Amos 7:9–17 and 1 Kings 12:25–33.[33] Amos 7:9–17 recounts a confrontation between Amaziah, the priest of Bethel, and the prophet Amos. According to 1 Kings 12:25–33, Jeroboam, king of Israel, set up an image of a calf at Bethel and established a priesthood there. Both texts imagine Bethel as a sanctuary under the jurisdiction of the kings of Israel, with a priesthood that had a special relationship to the Israelite monarchy. The texts, however, are demonstrably from the hands of Judahite scribes, who appear to have assumed that Bethel's relationship to the Israelite monarchy was just like the Jerusalem Temple's relationship to the Judahite monarchy.[34] Outside of these Judahite depictions of Bethel, a different picture of Israelite Bethel's social space emerges in the Book of the Twelve. Rather than being a royal sanctuary under the patronage and jurisdiction of the Israelite king, Bethel appears to have been a site of pilgrimage for the Israelite tribal collective (Amos 4:4–5; cf. Amos 5:5; Hosea 4:15). It functioned as a preserver and disseminator of the exodus formulary (Amos 9:7; Hosea 12:14; cf. Hosea 12:10, 13:4). The exodus tradition has no inherent connection to the monarchy and instead emphasizes the relationship between Yahweh and the Israelite tribal collective. The Bethel exodus formula thus suggests that Bethel's sanctuary served to assert Israelite tribal collective identity, rather than the kind of royal ideology associated with the House of David and the Jerusalem sanctuary.

Dan, although not quite as prominent in the biblical record as Bethel, also held significance for Israel as a whole.[35] The sanctuary at Bethel was located toward Israel's southern border, in relatively close proximity to Jerusalem. Dan, on the other hand, was situated to the north. A story about its foundation is now preserved in Judges 18, as noted above. That narrative claims an association between the sanctuary and a particular priestly family, the Mushites, and it describes various cultic paraphernalia associated with the sanctuary—a silver image, an ephod, teraphim. Tel Dan has been extensively excavated. A large sacred precinct is found in the northwest quarter of Dan.[36] Remarkably, this sacred complex was in continuous use for almost a millennium, from the tenth century BCE down to the Roman period. In the early monarchic period, it was separated from the surrounding city by a wall that marked off the precinct from the rest of the city. The complex included a massive podium of ashlar masonry accessible via a monumental stairway. The podium was enlarged in several phases and at its largest was approximately sixty feet square by nine feet high. The stairway was an additional twenty-seven feet long. The excavator identifies the podium as a "high place" (cf. 1 Kings 12:31). To judge by socles on the podium, a temple may have stood on its top. Other buildings were located within the sacred precinct. The size and complexity of this sacred precinct suggest that it held much more than local importance. This impression gained from the archaeological record corroborates the biblical portrait of Dan as a pilgrimage site for the Israelite tribal collective (1 Kings 12:30).

In the south, Judah was sufficiently controlled by the House of David for Jerusalem to serve as both the political and religious capital of the nation. According to 1 Kings 5–8, David's son Solomon constructed the Jerusalem Temple as a royal chapel, adjacent to the palace. The biblical account shows signs of multiple stages of editorial development and was probably written, by and large, in the late monarchic period. The portrayal of Jerusalem as a pilgrimage center for the whole nation in 1 Kings 8, for example, probably reflects the situation in the late monarchic period rather than Israelite religious practice in the time of Solomon himself. The narrative of the Temple's construction conforms to a literary pattern known from several other ancient Near Eastern texts, for example, the Cylinders of Gudea.[37] The description includes the divine commissioning of the Temple, preparations for building, a description of the Temple, an account of its dedication, and blessings for the builder and his descendants. According to the narrative, the Temple was built in a foreign architectural style (1 Kings 5:21–28, 32; 7:13–45). This utilization of foreign architecture is consistent with the portrayal of Solomon as establishing his power by making himself central to a network of international connections. According to First Kings, he strengthened ties with international allies through marriage (3:1, 11:1–8), he spearheaded international maritime trade (5:15–28; 9:26–28; 10:15, 22, 28), he hosted foreign dignitaries in Jerusalem (5:14; 10:1–13, 24), and he commanded tribute from neighboring kingdoms (5:1, 4; 10:10, 15, 25). The Temple's foreign architecture fits this pattern of prestige-based power.[38]

As it is described in Kings, the Jerusalem Temple finds its closest parallels in temple designs known from the archaeological record up the

Levantine coast, at 'Ain Dara temple and Tell Tainat.[39] This long-room temple form consisted of three consecutive rooms with the shrine proper, containing the image of the deity or its equivalent, located in line with and on the opposite side from the entrance to the temple. The entrance was flanked by a pair of columns that were primarily decorative and symbolic, rather than structural. The temple precinct extended beyond the walls of the temple itself to include various courtyards and storage rooms. The overall effect at the Jerusalem Temple was to create an increasingly exclusive set of holy spaces, with each space accessible only to certain sectors of society and at certain times.

According to the book of Kings, Hezekiah (2 Kings 18–20) and especially Josiah (2 Kings 22–23) undertook programs of religious reform and attempted to make Jerusalem and its Temple the only legitimate site for sacrificial worship. In the time of Josiah, a Scroll of the Law was purportedly discovered in the Temple, and it formed the basis of Josiah's reform program. He tore down the open-air sanctuaries and defiled the sanctuary at Bethel. Since several aspects of his reform reflect themes found especially in the book of Deuteronomy, and since Deuteronomy is the only Pentateuchal book to call itself the Scroll of the Law (Deut. 28:61, 29:20, 30:10, 31:26), scholars have long identified the scroll mentioned in the narrative about Josiah's reform with some version of the book of Deuteronomy.[40] Despite the strong Deuteronomistic conception of Jerusalem as the only sacred site for legitimate sacrificial worship to Yahweh, the archaeological record suggests that many sanctuaries, including the Bethel temple, continued to function as centers of worship after the reigns of Hezekiah and Josiah.[41] In fact, it has recently been argued that the account of Josiah's reform in 2 Kings 22–23 contains an older core written by the so-called Holiness School—a group of scribes responsible for the Holiness Code in Leviticus 17–26 who were closely related to, if not a subset of, the group responsible for the Priestly work—and only later expanded by Deuteronomistic scribes to reflect their concern with centralized worship.[42]

It has been argued that the temple at Tell Arad provides some archaeological evidence for cult centralization on a limited scale in the late monarchic period.[43] The Iron Age settlement at Arad was excavated in the 1960s.[44] At its center was a paved enclosure with a raised platform and square altar. A temple was erected on the site in the tenth century BCE, when the previously open settlement was also converted into a fortified citadel. It consisted of one main room with a raised shrine to its west. The shrine contained a rounded cult stela, a stone slab for making offerings, and two stone altars for burning incense. Marking the entrance to the building from the courtyard to the east are two stone slabs, on which columns may have stood. The outer courtyard contained a fieldstone altar, which was used through the middle of the eighth century. The temple was no longer in existence by the late seventh century. The presence of this temple in an official, state-run citadel suggests that for much of the monarchic period Jerusalem was not viewed as the exclusive center of Judahite worship. Its discontinuation from the seventh century may point to increasing cult centralization in the late monarchic period. The stratigraphy of the site, however, has been debated, and the destruction of the temple by fire may have occurred at the same time as the destruction of the fortress itself.[45]

Although Israelite and Judahite religious space possessed some inertia—sites tended to preserve their existing sanctity through time—it was also possible to commission or decommission religious structures. David, as I have noted, built an altar on a previously profane threshing floor. In biblical tradition, this location went on to become the site for the Temple of Yahweh built by Solomon (2 Chron. 3:1). As Eliade observed, sanctuaries often preserved one or more narratives about their founding event, in this case, the appearance of a destroying angel near Jerusalem (2 Sam. 24:16–25). Sacred sites could also be deconsecrated. Invading armies might burn a temple, demolish its architecture, and destroy, bury, or take as the spoils of war cult images or other cultic paraphernalia (e.g., Exod. 34:13; Deut. 7:5, 12:3; 1 Sam. 5:1–2; 2 Kings 25:9; Mesha Stele 12–13). Such acts asserted the superiority of the invading army and its deity. They bolstered the legitimacy of the conquering army's leader at home while also curtailing the power of institutions around which the conquered might rally. Internal religious reforms, closely related to issues of power and legitimacy, could also lead to the desacralization of particular sanctuaries. Josiah, whom I have already mentioned, purportedly defiled the sanctuary at Bethel by burning human bones on its altar (2 Kings 23:15–16). Jehu reportedly destroyed the temple of Baal in Samaria by converting it into a latrine (2 Kings 10:27). Desacralization in these narratives involved the physical destruction of the architecture that marked the site as sacred and also a variety of acts designed to render the location ritually impure in perpetuity.

SPACE IN THE RELIGIOUS IMAGINATION

The opening chapter of the Hebrew Bible contains an account of creation that is considered part of the "Priestly" work—a literarily distinct layer running at least through the first five books of the Bible and characterized by priestly and Levitical concern with purity and sanctity, by a penchant for lists of various kinds, and by a desire to classify and structure the world.[46] Creation, according to the Priestly account, consists in ordering an undifferentiated watery chaos into the world as we know it (Gen. 1:2). The sky is separated from the land, which is separated from the seas (Gen. 1:6–10). No mention is made of an ethereal realm in which the beatific dead or angels or God himself reside, nor is any mention made of a fiery hell for the forces of evil. Those representations of space do not belong to the Priestly conception of the created order. At the same time, the larger Priestly work treats the material world as distinct from the divine world.[47] And the Priestly work will go on to show great concern for layers of purity and sanctity associated with an official class of priests and with a portable sacred tent, discussed below. But here, at the start, there is no hint that space itself could be differentiated into the sacred and the profane. Spatial sanctity is not understood to be part of the fabric of the cosmos. Rather, the cosmos is primarily structured according to sacred time. God rested on the seventh day of creation, and every seventh day is to be consecrated to God as a day of rest (Gen. 2:1–3).

The Priestly work imagines a distinct period in Israelite history between the Exodus and the settlement in the land during which Israel's tribes wandered in the desert. They moved about under Yahweh's guidance and would set up camp around a portable shrine, the Tabernacle.[48] The notion of a ceremonial tent predates biblical literature, but the detailed Priestly description of the Tabernacle from the postmonarchic period is not generally considered a reliable source of information about

Israelite religious space in the premonarchic period.[49] It may even be a literary fiction. The Tabernacle's dimensions, layout, and furniture parallel those of the Solomonic Temple. The use of exotic construction materials added to a sense of its sanctity. The craftsmen who built it were said to be endowed with special divine ability, suggesting that it was perceived as being much more ornate than the average structure. Detailed plans for its construction and a description of the carrying out of those plans can be found in Exodus 25–27, 35–40. The Priestly literature gives a more detailed description of the rituals associated with the Tabernacle than the Deuteronomistic Historian does of rituals conducted in Solomon's Temple. For example, according to the Priestly account, only the Aaronic high priest was permitted to enter the Holy of Holies at the sacred center of the Tabernacle and only once per year on the Day of Atonement (Lev. 16:1–34). The Priestly tradition of the Ark, which contained stone tablets inscribed by God, may draw on the Mesopotamian tradition of foundation deposits for Mesopotamian temples. Yet the notion of the Tabernacle as developed by the Priestly school was radically different from the Mesopotamian concept of the temple. The latter was fixed, being built on a site that had acquired special status. The Tabernacle, in contrast, is always located at the center of Yahweh's people, wherever they may be.[50]

In addition to the Tabernacle, the Priestly work attaches great importance to Mount Sinai. The tradition of a mountain of god is known already from the Ugaritic literature of the fourteenth century BCE (e.g., Baal's association with Mount Zaphon) and can be found in some of the earliest biblical poems (Exod. 15:13, 17; Hab. 3:3). The association of Yahweh with Sinai is also quite old (e.g., Deut. 33:2; Judg. 5:5; Ps. 68:9). The Priestly work develops the Sinai and mountain of god traditions by making Mount Sinai the location for the theophany in which Yahweh reveals his instructions to Moses and the people of Israel and makes a covenant with them.[51] Mount Sinai has not definitively been identified, but in the biblical imagination it lies in the desert south of Judah, perhaps on the Sinai Peninsula. Remarkably, the Priestly work has chosen a location outside the land of Israel to be one of Israel's most holy sites. By choosing such a location, the work may intend to portray the revelation at Sinai as belonging to a mythological time of origins and to a mode of divine communication no longer accessible. In the Priestly work, the Holy of Holies in the Tabernacle and Mount Sinai constitute sacred centers in the world. Neither, in my assessment, ever existed in material space in anything like the Priestly description of them. They were, rather, the product of religious imagination.

Yahweh's increasing prestige within Israelite religion led to a fundamental problem in the spatial conception of the divine. How could Yahweh be God of the whole world and also be very strongly associated with a particular place and people? In an earlier period, when Yahweh had been understood as one of the divine sons under the Most High (see Deut. 32:8–9 in LXX and 4QDeut[j]), it made perfect sense for him to be attached to one people and one place. But when he came to be understood as the head of the pantheon, with no other deities as such competing with him, a new spatial conception of his location was required. Apocalyptic literature resolved the paradox by drawing both on the old tradition of Yahweh's mountain abode and on a newly emergent conception of the structure of space that was shaped by the experience of the Persian Empire. Isaiah 66:18–23 and Zechariah 14:16 imagine a future in which Jerusalem will be recognized as the center of the world, with all the nations of the world making an annual trip to pay tribute to Yahweh in Jerusalem. The cyclical nature of this annual journey restructures space, and the whole world comes to be represented in microcosm in Jerusalem, its sacred center.

CONCLUSION

Two characteristics of religious space emerge from this survey of the biblical and archaeological evidence. First, space was conceived of as falling along a spectrum of sanctity. The domicile, normally devoted to the activities of everyday life, might at certain times host religious activities. Local shrines or open-air altars held significance for clans and tribes and were more exclusively devoted to religious activity than the family home. A few great sanctuaries were of national importance. The architecture of large shrines also operated on the principle of gradated sanctity. Outer courtyards were open to pilgrims, while access to inner, holier rooms may have been rather more restricted. Second, religious space was understood to be inherently linked to religious time. At certain times, a particular place might acquire greater sanctity than it held at other times. Sacred sites could be founded or destroyed. And narratives could tie real and imagined spaces to a mythic time of origins.

NOTES

1. Here, I set aside the concept of sacred space as it was developed by the great historian of religion M. Eliade. His concept of sacred space is developed in M. Eliade, *Patterns in Comparative Religion*, R. Sheed, trans. (London: Sheed and Ward, 1958), pp. 367–87; M. Eliade, *The Sacred and the Profane: The Nature of Religion*, W. R. Trask, trans. (New York: Harcourt, 1959), pp. 20–67. On ritual in relation to space, see J. Z. Smith, "The Wobbling Pivot," *Journal of Religion* 52 (1972): pp. 134–49; J. Z. Smith, "Map Is Not Territory," in *Map Is Not Territory: Studies in the History of Religions* (Leiden: Brill, 1978), pp. 289–310. See also J. Z. Smith, *To Take Place: Toward Theory in Ritual* (Chicago: University of Chicago, 1992).

2. J. D. Schloen, *The House of the Father as Fact and Symbol: Patrimonialism in Ugarit and the Ancient Near East* (Winona Lake, Ind.: Eisenbrauns, 2001), esp. pp. 135–83.

3. H. Lefebvre developed a triad for conceiving of space that allowed him to expand the definition of space beyond its purely material dimensions. See H. Lefebvre, *The Production of Space* (Oxford: Blackwell, 1991), esp. pp. 32–50.

4. L. E. Stager, "The Archaeology of the Family in Ancient Israel," *Bulletin of the American Schools of Oriental Research* 260 (1985): pp. 1–35.

5. J. B. Pritchard, *Palestinian Figurines in Relation to Certain Goddesses Known through Literature* (New Haven, Conn.: American Oriental Society, 1943); Z. Zevit, *The Religions of Ancient Israel: A Synthesis of Parallactic Approaches* (London: Continuum, 2001), pp. 267–76.

6. S. Ackerman, "At Home with the Goddess," in W. Dever and S. Gitin, eds., *Symbiosis, Symbolism, and the Power of the Past: Canaan, Ancient Israel, and Their Neighbors from the Late Bronze Age through Roman Palaestina* (Winona Lake, Ind.: Eisenbrauns, 2003), pp. 455–68.

7. M. Thiessen, *Contesting Conversion: Genealogy, Circumcision, and Identity in Ancient Judaism and Christianity* (Oxford: Oxford University Press, 2011), pp. 17–65.

8. J. A. Soggin, *Israel in the Biblical Period: Institutions, Festivals, Ceremonies, Rituals* (Edinburgh: T&T Clark, 2002), pp. 87–100, 111–28.

9. On the redactional history of Judges 17–18, see Y. Amit, *The Book of Judges: The Art of Editing*, J. Chipman, trans., Biblical Interpretation Series 38 (Leiden: Brill, 1998), pp. 317–36; J. S. Bray, *Sacred Dan: Religious Tradition and Cultic Practice in Judges 17–18*, Library of Hebrew Bible/Old Testament Studies 449 (New York: T&T Clark, 2006), pp. 16–29.

10. P. Lapp, "Taanach by the Waters of Megiddo," *Biblical Archaeologist* 30 (1967): pp. 2–27.

11. E. Bloch-Smith, *Judahite Burial Practices and Beliefs about the Dead* (Sheffield: JSOT Press, 1992).

12. E. Bloch-Smith, "Resurrecting the Iron I Dead," *Israel Exploration Journal* 54 (2004): pp. 77–91.

13. For further discussion of the textual evidence, see especially Klaas Spronk, *Beatific Afterlife in Ancient Israel and in the Ancient Near East*, Alter Orient und Altes Testament 219 (Neukirchen-Vluyn, Germany: Neukirchener, 1986); T. J. Lewis, *Cults of the Dead in Ancient Israel and Ugarit*, Harvard Semitic Monographs 39 (Atlanta: Scholars' Press, 1989).

14. On family religion, see K. van der Toorn, *Family Religion in Babylonia, Syria and Israel: Continuity and Change in the Forms of Religious Life*, Studies in the History and Culture of the Ancient Near East 7 (Leiden: Brill, 1996); Rainer Albertz, "Family Religion in Ancient Israel and Its Surroundings," in J. Bodel and S. M. Olyan, eds., *Household and Family Religion in Antiquity* (Malden, Mass.: Blackwell, 2008), pp. 89–112; S. Ackerman, "Household Religion, Family Religion, and Women's Religion in Ancient Israel," in J. Bodel and S. M. Olyan, eds., *Household and Family Religion in Antiquity* (Malden, Mass.: Blackwell, 2008), pp. 127–58; C. Meyers, "Household Religion," in F. Stavrakopoulou and J. Barton, eds., *Religious Diversity in Ancient Israel and Judah* (London: T&T Clark, 2010), pp. 118–34.

15. On the redactional history of 1 Samuel 16–18, see E. Tov, "The Composition of 1 Samuel 16–18 in the Light of the Septuagint Version," in J. H. Tigay, ed., *Empirical Models for Biblical Criticism* (Philadelphia: University of Pennsylvania Press, 1985), pp. 97–130; T. Seidl, "David statt Saul: Göttliche Legitimation und menschliche Kompetenz des Königs als Motive der Redaktion von I Sam 16–18," *Zeitschrift für die alttestamentliche Wissenschaft* 98 (1986): pp. 39–55.

16. Y. Aharoni, *Investigations at Lachish: The Sanctuary and the Residency*, Lachish V (Tel Aviv: Tel Aviv University Institute of Archaeology, 1975), pp. 28–31.

17. G. A. Loud, *Megiddo II: Seasons of 1935–39* (Chicago: University of Chicago Press, 1948), pp. 44–46.

18. D. Ussishkin, "Schumacher's Shrine in Building 338 at Megiddo," *Israel Exploration Journal* 39 (1989): pp. 149–72.

19. Zevit, *Religions of Ancient Israel*, pp. 153–56.

20. R. Amiran, "Area B," in A. Ben-Tor, ed., *Hazor III–IV: An Account of the Third and Fourth Seasons of Excavations, 1957–58* (Jerusalem: Israel Exploration Society, 1989), pp. 70–134.

21. Z. Herzog, *Das Stadttor in Israels und in den Nachbarländern* (Mainz: P. von Zabern, 1986); Z. Herzog, "Settlement and Fortification Planning in the Iron Age," in A. Kempinski and R. Reich, eds., *The Architecture of Ancient Israel: From the Prehistoric to the Persian Periods* (Jerusalem: Israel Exploration Society, 1992), pp. 231–74.

22. T. H. Blomquist, *Gates and Gods: Cults in the City Gates of Iron Age Palestine. An Investigation of the Archaeological and Biblical Sources* (Stockholm: Almqvist och Wiksell International, 1999).

23. R. Arav and R. A. Freund, *Bethsaida, a City by the North Shore of the Sea of Galilee*, vol. 3: *Bethsaida Excavations Project* (Kirksville, Mo.: Truman State University Press, 2004); M. Bernett and O. Keel, *Mond, Stier und Kult am Stadttor: Die Stele von Betsaida (et-Tell)*, Orbis biblicus et orientalis 161 (Göttingen: Vandenhoeck & Ruprecht, 1998).

24. A. Biran, "High Places at the Gates of Dan?" [in Hebrew], *Eretz Israel* 25 (1996): pp. 55–58; A. Biran and J. Naveh, "The Dan Inscription, the Mazzebot, and the Market

Places" [in Hebrew], *Quadmoniot* 28 (1995): p. 40; A. Biran, "The High Places of Biblical Dan," in A. Mazar, ed., *Studies in the Archaeology of the Iron Age in Israel and Jordan,* Journal for the Study of the Old Testament Supplement 331 (Sheffield: Sheffield Academic Press, 2001), pp. 148–55.

25. A. Zertal, "An Early Iron Age Cultic Site on Mount Ebal: Excavation Seasons 1982–87. Preliminary Report," *Tel Aviv* 13–14 (1986–87): pp. 105–65. Cf. the cult complex known as the bull site, near which a small bronze image of a bull was discovered. See A. Mazar, "The 'Bull Site': An Iron Age I Open Cult Place," *Bulletin of the American Schools of Oriental Research* 247 (1982): pp. 27–42.

26. W. B. Barrick, "On the Meaning of *byt-h/bmwt* and *bty-hbmwt* and the Composition of the Kings History," *Journal of Biblical Literature* 115 (1996): pp. 621–42; M. Gleis, *Die Bamah,* Beihefte zur Zeitschrift für die alttestamentliche Wissenschaft 251 (Berlin: De Gruyter, 1997), pp. 1–26. For an alternative view, see L. S. Fried, "The High Places (*Bāmôt*) and the Reforms of Hezekiah and Josiah: An Archaeological Investigation," *Journal of the American Oriental Society* 122 (2002): pp. 437–65. Fried understands the biblical term to refer to a sanctuary complex.

27. Zevit, *Religions of Ancient Israel,* p. 195.

28. On much of the book of Kings being edited in the late monarchic period, see F. M. Cross, *Canaanite Myth and Hebrew Epic: Essays in the History of the Religion of Israel* (Cambridge, Mass.: Harvard University Press, 1973), pp. 274–89; B. Halpern and D. S. Vanderhooft, "The Editions of Kings in the 7th–6th Centuries B.C.E.," *Hebrew Union College Annual* 62 (1991): pp. 179–244.

29. For example, G. H. Jones, *The Nathan Narratives,* Journal for the Study of the Old Testament Supplement 80 (Sheffield: JSOT Press, 1990), p. 129.

30. On the practice of pilgrimage in Israel and Judah, see M. S. Smith, *The Pilgrimage Pattern in Exodus,* Journal for the Study of the Old Testament Supplement 239 (Sheffield: Sheffield Academic Press, 1997), pp. 52–80, 127–42.

31. D. E. Fleming, *The Legacy of Israel in Judah's Bible: History, Politics, and the Reinscribing of Tradition* (Cambridge: Cambridge University Press, 2012), pp. 18–28, 91–97.

32. On Shiloh, see D. G. Schley, *Shiloh: A Biblical City in Tradition and History,* Journal for the Study of the Old Testament Supplement 63 (Sheffield: JSOT Press, 1989); I. Finkelstein, *Shiloh: The Archaeology of a Biblical Site* (Tel Aviv: Institute of Archaeology of Tel Aviv University, 1993). On Gilgal, see H.-J. Kraus, "Gilgal: Ein Beitrag zur Kultusgeschichte Israels," *Vetus Testamentum* 1 (1951): pp. 181–99. On Mizpah, see J. R. Zorn, "Nasbeh, Tell en-," in E. Stern, ed., *The New Encyclopedia of Archaeological Excavations in the Holy Land* (Jerusalem: Carta, 1993), 3:1098–1102.

33. On Bethel, see H. Pfeiffer, *Das Heiligtum von Bethel im Spiegel des Hoseabuches* (Göttingen: Vandenhoeck & Ruprecht, 1999); K. Koenen, *Bethel: Geschichte, Kult und Theologie* (Göttingen: Vandenhoeck & Ruprecht, 2003); J. F. Gomes, *The Sanctuary of Bethel and the Configuration of Israelite Identity,* Beihefte zur Zeitschrift für die alttestamentliche Wissenschaft 368 (Berlin: De Gruyter, 2006).

34. On the Judahite provenance of 1 Kings 12:25–33, see S. C. Russell, *Images of Egypt in Early Biblical Literature: Cisjordan-Israelite, Transjordan-Israelite, and Judahite Portrayals,* Beihefte zur Zeitschrift für die alttestamentliche Wissenschaft 403 (Berlin: De Gruyter, 2009), pp. 27–47. On the late date of Amos 7:9–17, see H.G.M. Williamson,

"The Prophet and the Plumb-Line: A Redactional-Critical Study of Amos vii," in A. S. van der Woude, ed., *In Quest of the Past: Studies on Israelite Religion, Literature and Prophetism: Papers Read at the Joint British-Dutch Old Testament Conference, Held at Elspeet, 1988*, Oudtestamentische Studiën 26 (Leiden: Brill, 1990), pp. 101–21.

35. On the biblical portrayal of Dan as an eponymous ancestor, tribe, and city, see M. Bartusch, *Understanding Dan: An Exegetical Study of a Biblical City, Tribe and Ancestor*, Journal for the Study of the Old Testament Supplement 379 (Sheffield: Sheffield Academic Press, 2003).

36. A. Biran, *Biblical Dan* (Jerusalem: Israel Exploration Society, 1994), pp. 159–233.

37. V. Hurowitz, *I Have Built You an Exalted House: Temple Building in the Bible in the Light of Mesopotamian and North-West Semitic Writings* (Sheffield: JSOT Press, 1992), pp. 311–20.

38. On an exclusionary strategy of power, which depends on prestige gained through international connections, see Richard E. Blanton, Gary M. Feinman, Stephen A. Kowalewski, and Peter N. Peregrine, "A Dual-Processual Theory for the Evolution of Mesoamerican Civilization," *Current Anthropology* 37 (1996): pp. 1–14.

39. C. J. Davey, "Temples of the Levant and the Buildings of Solomon," *Tyndale Bulletin* 31 (1980): pp. 107–46, esp. 142–43; V. Fritz, "Temple Architecture: What Can Archaeology Tell Us about Solomon's Temple?" in F. E. Greenspahn, ed., *Essential Papers on Israel and the Ancient Near East* (New York: New York University Press, 1991), pp. 116–28. On the temple at Tell Tainat, see R. C. Haines, *Excavations in the Plain of Antioch II* (Chicago: University of Chicago Press, 1971), pp. 53–55, pl. 103. On the temple at 'Ain Dara, see F. Seirafi, A. Kirichian, and M. Dunand, "Recherches archéologiques à Ayin Dara au nord-ouest d'Alep," *Annales archéologiques arabes de Syrie* 15, no. 2 (1965): pp. 3–20.

40. The identification of the Scroll of the Law found in the Temple with the book of Deuteronomy was made in a footnote to an 1805 dissertation by M. de Wette. See T. C. Römer, *The So-Called Deuteronomistic History: A Sociological, Historical and Literary Introduction* (London: Continuum, 2005), pp. 16–17.

41. Fried, "The High Places (*Bāmôt*) and the Reforms of Hezekiah and Josiah."

42. L.A.S. Monroe, *Josiah's Reform and the Dynamics of Defilement: Israelite Rites of Violence and the Making of a Biblical Text* (Oxford: Oxford University Press, 2011), pp. 121–38.

43. Y. Aharoni, "Arad: Its Inscriptions and Temple," *Biblical Archaeologist* 31 (1968): pp. 26–37; A. Mazar, *Archaeology of the Land of the Bible, 10,000–586 B.C.E.*, Anchor Bible Reference Library (New York: Doubleday, 1990), pp. 496–98. Note also the decommissioned altar at Tel Beersheba in the northern Negev. See Z. Herzog, "Perspectives on Southern Israel's Cult Centralization: Arad and Beer-sheba," in R. G. Kratz and H. Spieckermann, eds., *One God—One Cult—One Nation: Archaeological and Biblical Perspectives* (Berlin: Walter de Gruyter, 2010), pp. 169–200.

44. R. Amiran and Y. Aharoni, *Ancient Arad: Introductory Guide to the Exhibition Held at the Israel Museum, January–April, 1967* (Jerusalem: Israel Museum, 1967).

45. D. Ussishkin, "The Date of the Judaean Shrine at Arad," *Israel Exploration Journal* 38 (1988): pp. 142–57.

46. For an introduction to Priestly literature in the context of other biblical literature written in the same period, see D. M. Carr, *An Introduction to the Old Testament: Sacred*

Texts and Imperial Contexts of the Hebrew Bible (Malden, Mass.: Wiley-Blackwell, 2010), pp. 187–206; K. Schmid, *The Old Testament: A Literary History*, L. M. Maloney, trans. (Minneapolis: Fortress Press, 2012), pp. 147–52. On Genesis 1, see M. S. Smith, *The Priestly Vision of Genesis 1* (Minneapolis: Fortress Press, 2010).

47. R. S. Kawashima, "The Priestly Tent of Meeting and the Problem of Divine Transcendence: An 'Archaeology' of the Sacred," *Journal of Religion* 86 (2006): pp. 226–57.

48. For a reading of the Tabernacle narratives influenced by the work of H. Lefebvre, see M. K. George, *Israel's Tabernacle as Social Space* (Atlanta: Society of Biblical Literature, 2009).

49. On a large ceremonial tent at Mari, see D. E. Fleming, "Mari's Large Public Tent and the Priestly Tent Sanctuary," *Vetus Testamentum* 50 (2000): pp. 484–98. On El's tent in the Ugaritic literature, see M. S. Smith and W. E. Pitart, *The Baal Cycle*, vol. II, *Introduction with Text, Translation and Commentary of KTU/CAT 1.3–1.4*, Supplements to Vetus Testamentum 114 (Leiden: Brill, 2009), pp. 337–39.

50. In dialogue with the work of M. Douglas, R. S. Kawashima argues that the Priestly work conceives of Israel as a whole as a spatialized kinship structure and tries to maintain the spatial purity of the nation as a whole. See R. S. Kawashima, "The Jubilee Year and the Return of Cosmic Purity," *Catholic Biblical Quarterly* 65 (2003): pp. 370–89.

51. F. Crüsemann, *The Torah: Theology and Social History of Old Testament Law*, A. W. Mahnke, trans. (Minneapolis: Fortress Press, 1996), pp. 27–58. On the lateness of the incorporation of the Sinai material into the Pentateuch, see already G. von Rad, "The Form-Critical Problem of the Hexateuch," in *The Problem of the Hexateuch and Other Essays*, E. W. Trueman Dicken, trans. (Edinburgh: Oliver and Boyd, 1966), pp. 1–78.

FURTHER READING

A clear and well-illustrated reconstruction of life in ancient Israel and Judah, focusing particularly on the household and on archaeological evidence, is P. J. King and L. E. Stager, *Life in Biblical Israel* (Louisville, Ky.: Westminster John Knox, 2001). Z. Zevit surveys Israelite and Judahite cultic sites and architecture in *The Religions of Ancient Israel: A Synthesis of Parallactic Approaches* (London: Continuum, 2001), pp. 81–266. The archaeology of Iron Age Israelite and Judahite religious space is set in greater historical perspective in B. Alpert Nakhai, *Archaeology and the Religions of Canaan and Israel* (Boston: American Schools of Oriental Research, 2001). W. Zwickel surveys the archaeology of temples and their cults and correlates these with biblical evidence in *Der Tempelkult in Kanaan und Israel: Studien zur Kultgeschichte Palästinas von der Mittelbronzezeit bis zum Untergang Judas*, Forschungen zum Alten Testament 10 (Tübingen: Mohr Siebeck, 1994). Several essays related to Israelite and Judahite temples and rituals are collected in J. Day, ed., *Temple and Worship in Biblical Israel* (London: T&T Clark, 2005). An older survey of temples in ancient Israel and the personnel and rituals associated with them is provided in M. Haran, *Temples and Temple-Service in Ancient Israel: An Inquiry into the Character of Cult Phenomena and the Historical Setting of the Priestly School* (Oxford: Clarendon Press, 1977).

16

※

Ritual

Diet, Purity, and Sacrifice

Seth D. Kunin

Biblical ritual, as depicted in the Hebrew Bible, is both highly complex and pervasive in Israelite culture. It ranges from quotidian practices relating to food and ritual purity to the large set pieces associated with the Temple. The rituals move well beyond the narrow understanding of religion as seen in many modern societies, encompassing most if not all aspects of Israelite cultural action and experience. While it is possible to see these rituals as arising from a complex process of historical development and transition, they can also be seen as arising from a common cultural matrix or underlying structure. This chapter focuses on this second approach; it seeks to demonstrate that while the rituals utilize a wide range of symbolic elements and forms, and mobilize many different aspects of experience, they are all shaped by a common structure and ultimately can be understood as part of a cohesive and meaningful structural system.

It should be noted from the outset that my general approach focuses on the editorial present of the text. While I am clearly aware of the complex nature and development of the biblical text, arising from a long process of editing and redaction, an analysis of the rituals or aspects of rituals that might be assigned to different strata is well beyond the scope of this chapter. The editorial present, that is, the final edited/redacted version of the text as existing in both manuscript and printed editions, is taken as the ethnographic source. This approach is justified on three related bases. First, the final text is in itself a structured cultural creation, in which the editors/redactors have reshaped earlier material, by both emendation and combination, to fit their own structural needs—thus it can be viewed as an object in itself. Second, even if we break the text down into the units proposed by textual scholars, these smaller units can be shown to have a very similar structural form both to the units from other sources and to the structure of the final composite text.[1] Finally, the text in its final version presents rituals and practices, albeit as a composite, in a way that fits in with the editors'/redactors' own cultural context. While it maintains explanations and sometimes contradictions from past understandings, these were acceptable to the editors and provide additional material to deepen our analysis.

The approach to ritual taken in this chapter derives from structuralist analysis as developed by Claude Lévi-Strauss.[2] It argues that objects created by cultures, for example, myths or rituals, are shaped by an underlying structure or pattern. This structure determines how elements of the ritual relate to one another and ultimately allows them to communicate in a culturally meaningful or understandable way. The argument presented here works on two related levels: it demonstrates how the underlying structure allows us to understand how individual practices or sets of related practices work and how the same underlying structure is the basis for all of the rituals found in the biblical text. Rather than spending time explicating the theory in an abstract way, I give an extended discussion of the Israelite food rules as both an exemplar of the theory and a basis for the analysis of the remaining ritual practices.

Before moving to the analysis and discussion, it is important to touch on one further theoretical aspect, the interrelationship of meaning and affect. Most structuralist and nonstructuralist discussions of biblical ritual have tended to focus on the meaning or information communicated by the practices.[3] They look on rituals as a way of manipulating symbols, with the primary role of conveying cognitive information—rituals are thus seen as myths in action. While my argument also focuses on cognitive aspects, I view rituals as being particularly associated with affect. Thus, rituals that engage a wide range of bodily practices and evoke a wide range of emotional responses should not be seen as merely conveyers of information but, rather, first and foremost, as creating affective experience. The argument developed here suggests that affect and embodiment play a key role in relation to underlying structure and are fundamental to Israelite (and all) religious practice and culture.

This chapter primarily focuses on the interrelated complexes of food rules, purity, and sacrifice. While these three areas overlap, they need to be examined singly before moving to an integrated analysis. It also touches on a second ritual complex, which brings together pilgrimages, festivals, and celebrations associated with particular times or occasions. While this complex, particularly in its biblical forms, utilizes food, purity, and sacrifice, the nature of the festivals and their meanings allows us to explore the relationship among narrative, identity, and ritual. One of the interesting features of both sets of rituals is their broad cultural span. In both cases they bridge rituals based in the home or locality and those bringing together Israelite society as a whole.

THE FOOD RULES COMPLEX

The "food rules" complex brings together three closely related areas[4]: food rules, purity, and sacrifice. Groundbreaking work examining this complex is found in various publications by Mary Douglas.[5] Her work examines all three areas as part of a single larger system. While we ultimately will move to a single structure uniting the three areas, it is initially necessary to examine them individually—determining the specific way in which each of the areas works and the ways in which they utilize the different symbolic elements out of which they are composed. This distinction is necessary due to the possibility that while the three areas may be similarly structured and indeed part of a larger structural system, they may use particular elements in different ways, and thus examining them together from the start might lead to confusion. On this basis we initially examine the food rules, which are the quotidian building block of biblical cultural experience, and then move to purity and sacrifice. Ultimately sacrifice will allow us to begin to explore the large ritual set pieces that unite biblical society as a whole.

Biblical food rules can largely be divided into two main categories. The first is composed of a distinction between types of animals, that is, those animals that can be eaten and those that are forbidden (see Leviticus 11 and Deuteronomy 14). The second relates to mixtures. In relation to food, this is exclusively found respecting milk and meat (see Exodus 23:19 and Deuteronomy 14:21). While these two categories deal with different levels of prohibition, the first based on intrinsic aspects of the animals and the second based on the mixture of otherwise permitted foods, they are closely interrelated, and each provides keys to understanding the system as a whole.

In order to understand the basis of the categorization of animals as permitted or forbidden (for food) it is helpful to divide them into three groupings based on the geographic space they primarily occupy: water, air, and land. The distinctions between animals are related to other animals in these spaces rather than to animals as a whole. In each case those animals that are permitted must have specific physical characteristics, with animals lacking those characteristics being forbidden.

Land animals include all those creatures that primarily live on land. Edible land animals must chew their cud and have cloven hooves. If an animal lacks one or both of these elements, it is not permitted. Based on this definition, edible animals include cows, sheep, goats, and deer, as all of these both chew their cud and have cloven hooves. It should be noted that the requirement that the animal chew its cud means that it will also be a herbivore, intrinsically not an eater of meat. Animals such as horses and pigs are forbidden as they, despite having cloven hooves, do not chew their cud, and the camel is similarly forbidden as it chews its cud but does not have cloven hooves. Animals that have neither element, such as bears, dogs, and all land insects, are clearly forbidden. Thus land animals are clearly divided into two distinct categories defined by elements intrinsic to the particular species. Category A chews its cud and has cloven hooves; category B includes all animals that lack one or both elements. As the defining elements are intrinsic, animals are clearly and permanently in a single defined category.

One interesting aspect of the categorization of land animals is the particular emphasis placed on the pig. In many depictions of the food rules the pig becomes almost paradigmatic for the system as a whole. The pig appears on the surface to be a mediating animal; it contains elements belonging to both categories—that is, it has cloven hooves but does not chew its cud. It appears to suggest that there is a potential connection between permitted and forbidden, and evidence suggests that it was eaten in Canaan (see, for example, the discussion in Macdonald 2008:32). The Israelite system, however, rather than allowing this weakening of boundaries, makes the pig the most negative animal—thereby emphasizing that despite having one element, the pig and any other similar animal are just as forbidden, or indeed symbolically even more forbidden, than any other animal that has none of the required elements. This symbolic emphasis denies mediation and structurally emphasizes the unbridgeable nature of the boundary between categories.

Water animals include all animals and insects that primarily dwell in water, be it fresh or sea. Edible water animals must have fins and scales. All animals that lack either one or both of these elements are forbidden as food. Thus most fish are edible, for example, bass, cod, and tuna. All of these have the two required elements. Animals such as sharks and dolphins are forbidden as they lack scales, despite having fins. Eels likewise are forbidden due to the lack of fins, although they do have scales. In addition, all animals that have neither of these, for example, shellfish and shrimp, are also forbidden. In relation to food, water animals can thus be divided into two clear categories based on the animals' intrinsic characteristics. Category A includes those animals that have both fins and scales, and category B includes those that do not fulfill that requirement. Within the food rules system there is no need for any other categories. As the characteristics are intrinsic, there can be no movement between the two categories.

Air animals include all animals that can (or potentially can) fly—thus including, for example, all birds (including flightless birds), bats, and insects with wings. Although there is no clear statement of the characteristics required of air animals, several required elements can be discerned. The general rule is that they are fowl or other game birds that do not eat meat or carrion. In general they must in principle be able to fly, even if the domesticated version no longer has that ability. In most cases there seems to be a distinction between bird and nonbird, thus excluding the bat, although this distinction is not present in the case of the locust. The text from the Bible on the locust, Leviticus 11:20–23, adds in a requirement that the flying animals need to be able to hop.[6] Despite the lack of the absolute clarity found in a general rule, the text creates clear categories by enumerating the forbidden birds and including some general statements. An abbreviated definition of the permitted category is that they must fly, hop, and not eat meat or carrion. The permitted animals are in category A, and the forbidden are in category B—while there may be discussion of where animals fit, in principle they belong intrinsically in one category and can never move between the two.

One interesting question that arises from the categorization of birds is the placement of those birds that eat fish, for example, ducks. Despite the fact of eating other animals, ducks are permitted for human consumption. This creates a potential structural problem, which can only be resolved by a proper understanding of how the Israelites characterized fish as a whole. We will return to this question in the discussion of milk and meat, in which I demonstrate a categorical distinction between fish and other living animals.

If we examine all three of these groups of animals together it becomes apparent that there is a common underlying structure. In all three cases animals are divided into two clear and distinct categories: (a) animals that can be eaten and (b) those that cannot be eaten. Each category is defined by clear and intrinsic characteristics that determine into which category the animal can be placed. Animals can only be in one category or the other; even if they have one aspect of the permitted category, if they lack other necessary elements, then they are in the forbidden category. There is no ambiguity or movement possible between the categories. With the exception of fish eaters, the permitted category is composed of herbivores. In general insects and other swarming animals are forbidden, with the exception of the locust and related grasshoppers, but even in these cases, the distinction between permitted and forbidden is clearly maintained.

The final category of food rules relates to the mixing of milk and meat. This prohibition is found in Exodus 34:26 and in Deuteronomy 14:21. In both cases it is a general rule arising from a particular case, that is, do not cook a kid in its mother's milk. In postbiblical times this was extended to encompass the eating of milk products together with both land and air animals, but excluding fish. The prohibition also fits into the context of other prohibited mixtures, for example, mixing linen and wool or yoking together an ox and an ass. While the prohibition is framed in a moral context, it can also be understood as being structured in a similar way to the forbidden foods discussed above, as well as providing important additional data allowing us to understand why duck are permitted to be eaten despite eating living animals, that is, fish.

The specific texts presenting the prohibition give little obvious help in understanding the nature of the prohibition. If, however, we look at the two categories separately, the qualities that define them, and place them in opposition, can be clarified. The first category, milk, has certain clear characteristics, particularly if understood in the context of mother and child (the form presented in the text). Milk is a white liquid that, when emerging from the mother's body, gives life to the child. If we consider meat in this context, then the aspect of meat that stands in opposition to milk is blood, which is intrinsically part of slaughtered meat. The identification of blood as the structurally operative element gains support from the importance of blood within both purity and the sacrificial cult; blood was a key aspect in defining the main objects of sacrifice (and equally defining fish as nonsacrificable). Blood is opposite in quality to milk. While blood is called "the life," it fulfills this role in the opposite location from milk. If blood comes forth from the body, this is both negative and polluting (see Leviticus 3:17 and 17:11). Blood is only the life when it is in its proper place, inside the body. It is forbidden for it to be consumed, in direct contradistinction to milk. The structure of these elements places them into opposite and unbridgeable categories.

On one level the structure of forbidden combinations seems different from the categories described above. In the animal categories one category is positive and permitted, while the second category is negative and forbidden. The key aspect of the structure, however, is not the positive or negative categorization but, rather, that the two categories be set in opposition to each other and be unbridgeable. Thus, the milk and meat/blood category is structurally consistent. Despite the fact that neither milk nor meat/blood (in their proper places) is intrinsically negative, in relation to each other they are oppositional and unbridgeable categories: milk is intrinsically milk, and blood is intrinsically blood.

It is important to note that meat can be considered to be bloody, and it is this feature that renders it unmixable with milk. Although in later practice blood is significantly removed from meat through a process of salting, meat retains an aspect of blood. While this remnant of blood within the meat is consumable, blood as blood is forbidden. On the surface this prohibition of blood is similar to that of other foods, but examination of the sacrificial practices suggests that while animals are forbidden due to their negativity, blood may be forbidden due to its extreme positivity, as food for God and no one else—in this sense it is similar to other parts of permitted animals that are reserved for burning on the altar but forbidden for human consumption.

If this analysis is correct, then blood fits into a category of objects that become structurally relevant at lower levels of opposition, that is, opposition within the wider categories defined by the more general food rule system. These levels progressively designate particular elements, be they specific animals (firstborn animals, for example) or parts of animals (such as blood), to be increasingly holy and permitted either to a subclass of Israelites, for example, the priests, or only to God. These elements are forbidden or even create a type of impurity, not because they are negative but more precisely because they are too positive. We will return to this aspect of the progressive recapitulation of structure in the discussion of sacrifice.

This analysis of blood as an opposing liquid to milk argues that the prohibition on milk and meat is due to the presence of blood in the meat. The argument also suggests that one reason for the prohibition on eating meat-eating animals is that they are eaters of blood and therefore forbidden for human consumption as they infringe on the domain of food restricted to God. How, then, can some birds that eat fish be permitted as human food? At least from our perspective, they, too, have blood and thus should be forbidden.

This question can be resolved by examining the rejection of fish within the sacrificial cult and, at least suggestively, by the postbiblical rules permitting the eating of fish with dairy products. Unlike land animals and birds, fish are not permitted to be sacrificed. While this in part may relate to issues of domesticity (see below), within the context of the discussion here it may also relate to the issue of blood. Blood plays a major role in the sacrifice of animals, being scattered on the altar and on the lintels of the Temple during the process; this centrality suggests that blood may be one of the defining characteristics of animals that are suitable for sacrifice. The rejection of fish may be due to the perception that their flesh is bloodless. Although ancient Israelites would clearly have been aware that fish do have blood, the flesh of fish seems in itself to be without blood, hence its possible rejection.

This analysis is supported by the rabbinic extension of biblical rules concerning milk and meat. The specific biblical prohibition is extended to permitted animals that have mammary glands, for example, cows, sheep, and deer. After extended discussion it is also extended to permitted birds, for example, chicken—the logic of this extension is in part that both mammals and birds have bloody flesh. The prohibition, however, is not extended to fish, as fish do not have bloody flesh. Based on this argument, ducks and other fish eaters are permitted for consumption as, despite eating living animals, they eat flesh without blood and hence do not infringe on the divine.

THE PURITY COMPLEX

Alongside the food rules, purity rules are both equally quotidian and pervasive (see Leviticus 11).[7] Rules about purity shaped everyday Israelite activities in the home and extended to the actions of the high priest sacrificing on the holiest days of the year. Although in relation to animals there is some overlap between food and purity rules, there is no direct or necessary association between animals that are forbidden as food and those that are carriers of impurity—the only clear relation is that any animal that is intrinsically impure will also be forbidden, but the equation does not work in the other direction.

The purity rules are perhaps some of the most complex of those found in the biblical text; the details of this system would require more space than is possible in this chapter. Thus, I examine some pervasive aspects in order to provide a basis for explaining the system as a whole. I focus on three interrelated areas: the structural opposition between pure and impure, and the defining characteristics of the structure; the issue of contagion, with humans and objects having the capacity to become impure, that is, move from a state of purity to impurity, and through ritual processes return to a state of purity; and finally, the ritual of the red heifer as a ritual of inversion and the primary means of resolving the crisis of ritual impurity. The ritual of the scapegoat will also be discussed, a ritual inversion dealing with the problem of sin or moral impurity.

On a broad structural level the distinction between pure and impure is clear; the text defines these categories, with animals or objects being in one category or the other. Its definition of whether an animal is pure or impure is more complex than the above definitions relating to consumption. With a small number of exceptions, no living animal is impure. This includes even such animals as pigs, which are emblematic of the system of food rules. This also includes all forms of insects—which, living or dead, do not cause impurity. The animals that do carry impurity are specifically named and come under the general designation of "creeping." They are small animals, for example, rodents, that would have been found in some houses and would cause impurity to the food or objects with which they were found.

The primary distinction, however, seems to be related to death.[8] Dead animals, whether consumable or nonconsumable, could be bearers of impurity. Animals permitted as food were generally pure, living or dead. If, however, they died a natural death, they were carriers of impurity. Forbidden land animals upon death were impure whether their death was natural or purposive. Interestingly, air and sea animals were never impure, whether living or dead. It is clear from this analysis that while the status of the animal in relation to food plays a role in defining the nature of impurity, the primary defining aspect of the model is the presence or absence of life. Thus, in respect to animals, the relation between the categories is clear (with the exception of the creeping animals mentioned). Pure is defined primarily by life, and impure, by death.

Humans were also causes of several different forms of impurity (see Leviticus 15). Impurity was caused by a number of forms of emission. Thus, menstruation and the emission of blood at other times were sources of impurity (Leviticus 15:19). Impurity was also caused by the emission of semen. Birth was a cause of impurity as well (Leviticus 12). The most significant cause of impurity was a corpse.

While the impurity associated with a corpse (Numbers 19) is of a similar kind to that associated with dead animals, the other forms of human impurity are based on a different logic. They may be in part explained by the logic discussed above in relation to milk and blood, that is, bodily fluids found in the wrong place—a classic definition of the impure and a source of danger. Menstrual blood, and other blood in nonmenstrual emissions, fits the above discussion of blood, which, while being "the life," is only so while within the body; outside the body is not its proper place, and it is therefore both impure and dangerous. Similarly, to be the source of life, semen must be within the woman's body, while particularly a nocturnal emission is out of place and thus impure.

While most of the examples discussed above fit in with the intrinsic aspect of categorization found in respect to the food rules, impurity has a key characteristic of contagion that distinguishes it. Objects are not only impure in themselves; they are also the cause of other objects becoming impure. While most of this contagion is based on direct contact, it can also occur through being in the same tent as the impure object (see Leviticus 11:31 and following). Similarly, a man is rendered impure by having a nocturnal emission, and a woman, through menstrual blood and birth.

Contagion suggests transformation and therefore the potential movement of objects between categories. Transformation and movement would suggest a structure that is almost the opposite of that found in the food rules and in other aspects of Israelite narrative and practice. The apparent discrepancy, however, upon closer analysis is significantly minimized or indeed removed.

The most significant point is that the intrinsic nature of the object, as in the oppositional structure identified above, remains significant and the definitional element in relation to categorization. If the object is intrinsically impure, then it can never move into the pure category. Neither transformation nor movement is possible. If the object is intrinsically pure, then it is subject to potential impurity. In most cases, however, provided the impurity can be removed (through different forms of cleansing), it can be returned to a state of purity. The significant point is that the impurity does not impact on the intrinsic nature of the object; it is a temporary imposition, which can be removed through cleansing or time.

It is important to emphasize in this context the technical usage of the term *intrinsic*. *Intrinsic* refers specifically to essential or definitional aspects of an object or category. These elements are, by definition, unchangeable and thus establish, within Israelite structure, the basis for the categorical distinctions.

The temporary nature of impurity and the apparent transformation associated with it can be explained on the basis of a higher-level structural opposition within the purity system. The purity complex is closely associated with that of sacred space, as well as the categorization of people who act within those sacred places. In the cases of space and people there is a system of recapitulation in which increasingly narrower definitions of holiness are applied—at each level both space and access to that space are restricted (as well as the rules applying to the people who live and act within those spaces). The logical extension of the model creates a final set of oppositions: God/world and God/man. If this is extended to purity, then the final opposition places God alone in the pure category and everything else into the impure category (that is, relative to God they are impure, whereas at other structural levels they may be defined as pure, even intrinsically pure).

The nature of this structure is further clarified by returning to life and death as key defining characteristics of the system. At the level of God/everything else, God is intrinsically alive or intrinsic being, while everything else is not and indeed is ultimately subject to death. On this basis, the purification system is an inversion of the natural process in the material world that leads to death. The purification system through the removal of impurity (death) allows for a temporary move from pure to impure and back to pure, creating a logic that in part is a denial of death. In relation to God, material objects can be seen as moving from impure (prior to life) to pure and ultimately back to impure. The temporary impurity is a structurally associated inversion of the temporary possession of life. Through the logic of the ritual system, and the possibility of purification, the second logic is obscured in favor of the first.

Due to the structurally necessary temporary quality of impurity, Israelite culture required ritual processes that enabled the individual or object rendered impure to return to its original pure state. These rituals were more or less complex and time-consuming depending on the level of impurity. Most forms of (temporary) impurity required a period of time outside of the camp followed by immersion in clean flowing water. The period of exclusion could be of one day's duration or extend to seven days. Thus, for example, the menstruant would be unclean for seven days, while a person who came into contact with her was unclean for one.

The most complex rituals associated with impurity are found relating to the most significant form of impurity, that imparted by a corpse (which interestingly is symbolically the inversion of the purity system, in which impure moves to pure, whereas a corpse in its move from life to death moves from pure to a permanent and final state of impurity). Corpse impurity required a complex and contradictory ritual to return a person who had come in contact with the corpse from impure to pure.

The basis of this ritual is found in Numbers 19, the ritual of the red heifer. The red heifer, a particularly rare animal, becomes the basis of a substance that is used to purify those who are subject to corpse impurity. The heifer is removed from the camp and slaughtered. Although the form has similarities to other sacrifices, including the splashing of blood toward the Tent of Meeting, it is not done by the altar outside the tent. The heifer is entirely burned to ashes, with other ritual substances. The ambiguity of the process is emphasized by the fact that both the priest performing this part of the ritual and the person doing the burning are rendered impure and must be cleansed in water and remain outside of the camp until the evening. The ashes are gathered by a third man (who is also rendered impure) and placed in a clean place outside of the camp until needed for the purification ceremony. The ceremony itself utilizes the ashes mixed with running water in a seven-day cleansing process.

The rituals associated with the red heifer seem contradictory; they utilize a substance, the ashes of a burned sacrificial animal, that is usually a source of impurity. The process of burning and dealing with the ashes renders the actors impure, and the ashes themselves are kept outside of the camp, that is, in the wilderness, often a place of impurity (as seen by the expulsion of those who are impure into the wilderness outside of camp); yet, when mixed with running water, the ashes become a source of cleansing.

At one level the ritual may be seen as one of inversion. Temporary impurity of all kinds and especially corpse impurity challenge the structural coherence of the system. They suggest that an element that is in one category can move to the other category, thus undermining the unbridgeable nature of Israelite structure. In the case of the pig discussed above in relation to food, this type of challenge is met by making the ambiguous element even more negative, thus preserving the integrity of the system. This solution, however, was not possible in the case of purity, as ultimately all Israelites would potentially be rendered impure. The system thus matches the transformation implied by the move from pure to impure with an inverted ritual that mirrors this with a move from impure to pure. This inversion obviates the original transformation and thus preserves structural coherence.

The red heifer itself may also further symbolize this process. Unlike in many other forms of sacrifice, the red heifer is female. In association with her color, red, this suggests, as argued by Maccoby (1999:105–17), that the heifer may symbolize menstrual blood. If this is so, then the impurity created by menstrual blood and the red heifer herself may be due to an excess of purity (which is impure to humans) rather than negative impurity. This argument relies on the understanding of blood in both the food and sacrificial systems as pertaining to God but not humans. God has the right to eat "life"; created animals, including humans, do not and are forbidden from doing so. If this is correct, then the red heifer ritual works on two interrelated levels, through the ritual of inversion indicated above and through the use of excessive purity to return the impure to a state of purity.

THE SACRIFICIAL COMPLEX

Perhaps the most complex and elaborated form of Israelite ritual practice was associated with the sacrificial cult.[9] While sacrifices were most likely practiced locally, the cult was particularly located in the main religious centers and ultimately within the Temple in Jerusalem. Sacrifice has significant associations with purity, as already indicated in the discussion of the red heifer, and in many respects can be seen as an extension of the food rule system. Its categorization of animals fit for sacrifice depends on the food rule complex, and consumption is a key to understanding many aspects of the cult of the sacrifice.

The sacrificial cult, as perhaps the most dramatic and public representation of Israelite ritual, also allows me to introduce an additional aspect to the structuralist analysis of ritual not hitherto discussed here: the somatic and affective impact. While this aspect plays a part in both the food rules and purity complexes, as both include embodied elements, it comes to the fore in the bloody, large-scale sacrifices that are emblematic of the sacrificial complex.

In the discussion of food rules animals as a whole were divided into three types: land, air, and water. Of these types only land and air were suitable for sacrifice. We return to the exclusion of water animals below.

Land and air animals were each divided into two categories, edible and not edible, following the food rules system. Sacrificable animals are a subcategory of the edible categories.

Thus, for example, in the case of land animals, animals that chew their cud and have cloven hooves are divided into two unbridgeable categories, domesticated and nondomesticated animals. Animals in the nondomesticated category are never suitable for sacrifice, while animals in the domesticated category are suitable. The categorization found here recapitulates the structure found in relation to edibility and nonedibility. Among the domesticated animals there are additional levels also based on intrinsic characteristics, for example, firstborn animals. At each level the structure of oppositional categories based on intrinsic qualities is repeated. The structural level is directly related to the significance of the sacrifice.

Before moving to the different sacrifices and the rituals surrounding them, it is necessary to briefly discuss the structure of Israelite society, culminating in the main ritual actors, and the idealized organization of Israelite geography, which culminates in the Temple and the Holy of Holies. Both the actors and the space of sacrifice are essential in understanding the ritual system.

Israelite society and space are structured in the same way as are animals. At the highest level, Israel is set in structural opposition to the nations. As in the case of the animal world this is based on intrinsic qualities; Israel is descended from the sons of Jacob, while the nations are not—at least structurally there is an unbridgeable relation between these two categories. Within Israel this structure is recapitulated. The members of eleven tribes are set in opposition to the Levites—based again on genealogical descent. The Levites are subject to specific laws and are the primary functionaries who act within the Tabernacle. The Levite category is similarly subdivided into the Levitical families set in opposition to the descendants of Aaron, the Cohanim or priests. As in the above levels this is based on genealogical, hence intrinsic qualities. The Cohanim, particularly the high priest, are the main functionaries in the Temple and, as in the case of the Levites, are distinguished by laws.

As already indicated in the discussion of Israelite society, space is divided into a set of increasingly holy places, which are set in similar oppositional categories. Thus at the highest level the land of Israel or the camp is set in opposition to the rest of the world, or the wilderness—with the first being the abode of Israel and the second that of the nations. Within the land/camp there are progressively more sacred places, which culminate in the Temple and the Holy of Holies. While this can be seen as a set of concentric circles, given the oppositional nature of the rest of Israelite culture, it is likely that it works in a similar oppositional structure.

A key aspect in understanding all of the examples of recapitulated structure is the operational level of oppositional structure that is being used. If the structure is setting something in opposition to the nations, then the same level of structure will be utilized, hence Israel as a whole; this is similarly the case whether discussing society, geography, or the animal world. This observation explains the often misunderstood statement of Israel being a kingdom of priests. It is assumed that this suggests that Israel will become priests, that is, be transformed into the priest category. If, however, the level of operational opposition is maintained, then this structurally impossible transformation is unnecessary. Structurally Israel is in the role of priest in relation to the nations, whereas at lower levels of structure it clearly is not.

SIGNIFICANT BIBLICAL SACRIFICES

The most significant biblical sacrifices can be divided into five general types: the burnt offering (Lev. 1), the "meal offering" (Lev. 2), the peace offering (Lev. 3 and 7:11–34), the sin offering (Lev. 4), and the guilt or trespass offering (Lev. 5). Each of these types is distinguished by the reason for the sacrifice, the types of animals offered, and the actor who consumes the sacrifice:

1. The burnt offering was either a male without blemish, taken from the herd, or a fowl. In either case, the animal was completely burned, with God being the only consumer (as highlighted in Lev. 1, both verses 13 and 17). The sacrifice serves as a means of atonement, between the offered and God (verse 4).[10]

2. The meal offering was the main sacrifice that did not involve animals; it was composed of grain or other agricultural produce. A memorial portion of it was burned, with the remainder being eaten by the priests. This

offering does not appear to be associated with individual or communal sins and is specifically associated with the concept of tithing.

3. The peace offering could be a male or female animal that was without blemish. Specific parts reserved for God were burned on the altar, with the remainder being eaten by both the priests and the donor and, it is usually assumed, the donor's family. The name indicates that the sacrifice was related to communal harmony.

4. The sin offering was a male bullock that was without blemish. The whole animal was burned. The sin offering was made for transgressions of negative commandments. This could be either an individual or a corporate sin.

5. The guilt offering was a female from the flock or two turtledoves or pigeons. The offering was partially burned (those parts reserved for God), with the remainder eaten by the priests. The reasons for the offering include infringements against the rights of priests as well as a range of infringements particularly against other Israelites.

The aspect of consumption provides an essential avenue to understanding Israelite sacrifice. In a sense it harks back to the concept of covenantal meal first suggested by Roberson Smith and taken up by subsequent scholars.[11] This aspect is also highlighted by the fact that even more than the purity system, the sacrificial complex is a subset of the food complex—focusing on the fact that the food that God eats is a subset of the food that Israelites eat.

As indicated in the outline of the various forms of sacrifice, different actors are involved in consumption. In each case God is one such actor, with the priests and the community as a whole coming into play in different sacrifices. In light of the concept of covenantal meal, the act of consumption becomes one of covenant, that is, establishing or reestablishing the proper covenantal relations.[12] Given that sin is a key aspect of the system, and the rationale for many of the offerings, it is likely that the issue at stake is covenantal tension or disruption.

On this basis it is possible to see each of the sacrifices as serving to resolve a different level of disruption. Thus in the sin offering, with its association with infringement of negative commandments, which are inadvertent sins directly against God, the level of covenantal restoration is between the sinner (individual or corporate) and God. In this context, the entire animal is burned; hence God alone consumes it, reflecting the fact that God is the injured party. The peace offering, on the other hand, is consumed by God, the priests, the donor, and perhaps a wider kin group, reflecting an arena of covenantal tension.

The Paschal sacrifice, touched on below in relation to pilgrimage festivals, highlights the role of consumption. This sacrifice was performed on the festival of Passover by each family. The significant issue for our discussion is that the lamb had to be entirely eaten by the family, in what was in effect a covenantal meal. Those who were able to participate in the meal are instructive: only those who were included within the covenant were allowed to partake. It is particularly noteworthy that anyone who was uncircumcised (even an Israelite man) was not allowed to participate—being uncircumcised is symbolically equivalent to being one of the nations, that is, outside the covenant (Exodus 12:43–45). The ritual itself, rather than being a resolution of covenantal tensions, is a communal restatement and reaffirmation of the covenant. As in the sacrifices above, this covenantal meal, which includes God and all of Israel, serves an essential covenantal purpose.

The aspect of consumption makes sacrifice a particularly salient ritual through highlighting its somatic/affective engagement. These aspects, through their association with the underlying structure, make that structure equally salient. The rituals focus on the killing and burning of animals, as well as the liberal splashing of blood both on the altar and on the lintels of the Temple. Although ancient Israel had agrarian roots, the killing and consumption of animals in such societies was rare, as animals were a source of wealth, and was often done in a sacrificial context. Thus, even the local forms of the ritual would be dramatic and have emotional impact. This would be significantly enhanced in the large public rituals, at which, at least notionally, large numbers of animals would be sacrificed. The impact of such an event would be significant, with the sounds of dying animals, the smell of burning, and the sight and smell of flowing blood, not to mention the crowds of people engaged in the ritual.

Alongside the killing and burning, the use of blood in the rituals would have had particular emotional impact. Blood in the food and purity system was particularly abhorrent. For humans it was both forbidden as food and a source of impurity. Its use in the Temple, however, emphasizes its connection with the divine—it was splashed on the altar and the Temple itself. This double-edged response to this symbol would have heightened the tension and ambiguity in the ritual, as well as emphasizing the gulf between human and divine.

The final aspect, which has been the heart of our discussion, is the consumption of the sacrifice at the conclusion of the ceremony. The act of eating or not eating engages the body in a way that almost no other ritual process can. As indicated above, different sacrifices bring different actors into the process of consumption; ultimately, however, this ends at the boundary between Israel and the nations: only those within the covenant can share this meal with God. Thus, at its heart, sacrifice as an act of consumption is the embodiment of the covenant, defining its boundaries—it focuses on who eats and with whom one is allowed to eat.[13]

Perhaps as the inversion of covenant, and indeed the primary feature endangering covenantal relations, sin is one of the operative issues in most of the forms of sacrifice and becomes particularly significant in the rituals associated with the Day of Atonement, one of the major ritual set pieces of the biblical ritual calendar. Sin in many respects is analogous to the impurity discussed above—being moral impurity rather than ritual impurity. The structural problem created by sin is the same as that created by impurity: sin temporarily (in principle) moves the individual or community from a (relatively) morally pure status into a morally impure status. This apparent movement between categories suggests that the categories are not unbridgeable.

The sacrificial system provides a resolution to this problem that is analogous to the role of the red heifer in the purity complex. While individual sins and some corporate sins could be atoned for by the individual sacrifices discussed above, the scapegoat ritual, performed on the Day of Atonement, provided a way of resolving the moral impurity of the community as a whole (Leviticus 16:1–34). Two goats were brought before the Temple, and one was chosen as the "Lord's goat," which was sacrificed in front of the Temple. It was, however, upon the second goat, "for Azazel," that Israel's sins were placed. This goat was taken into the desert and, in rabbinic texts, killed by being thrown off a cliff.[14]

This ritual, like that of the red heifer, is one of inversion. The goat that is sacrificed does not atone for sin, as it would normally do. The goat that is not sacrificed, that moves from sacred space into profane space, that is, the wilderness (this impurity is reflected in the fact that the individual taking the goat into the wilderness is rendered impure by doing so), carries away Israel's sin. This ritual is the opposite of the other rituals of atonement. The inversion is emphasized in the rabbinic version, in which the goat is killed by being thrown off the cliff, an act of inverted sacrifice. Within this ritual the goat moves from being pure (it was randomly selected and could have been either "for God" or "for Azazel") to being impure, symbolized by carrying the sins and being sent into the wilderness, the realm of the impure. The ritual inverts the process of sin, in which a pure nation is rendered impure through sin. The performance of the ritual, mirroring the original transformation, through its inversion of it obviates the transformation and allows Israel to return to its original morally pure state.

THE PILGRIMAGE FESTIVAL CYCLE

The Israelite ritual calendar was built up from the quotidian daily sacrifices, the cycle of weekly Sabbaths, every seven days, to the major pilgrimage festivals of Sukkoth, Passover, and Shavuot.[15] In addition there was the new year's atonement cycle of the New Year and the Day of Atonement. All of these festivals included sacrificial rituals, ideally occurring in the Temple in Jerusalem. While each of these festivals and events had elements of unique ritual practice, they are constructed of the same ritual elements and shaped by the same underlying structure. This is best touched upon through a brief excursus examining some aspects of the pilgrimage festivals.

The biblical text suggests that the three pilgrimage festivals were the most important, and indeed they can be seen as significantly constructive of Israelite identity. Originally the three festivals were associated with the agricultural cycle, and some aspects of their ritual performance retain agricultural motifs. These are seen in the sukkah, or booth utilized during Sukkoth, and the matzo and lamb, which were key symbols of the Passover celebration. More significantly, however, for our purposes, each of the festivals was reinterpreted to memorialize an aspect of Israel's journey from Egypt to the land of Canaan, the journey in which

Israel became a covenantal people. Thus, Sukkoth is taken to represent the forty-year journey in the wilderness; Passover, the Exodus from Egypt; and Shavuot, the receiving of the Ten Commandments. Thus, the celebration of these festivals, as major ritual processes, becomes a means of reaffirming the origins of the nation and its covenant with God.

The three festivals were most significantly pilgrimage festivals—in which all Israelites were commanded to participate. The pilgrimage culminated (in the ideal editorial present) in Jerusalem, with the major ritual performances occurring in the Temple. The nature of these pilgrimages focused on the creation of national corporate identity, as opposed to the individual antistructural identity found in the analysis of pilgrimage by Victor Turner. The Israelite pilgrimage was meant to be performed three times yearly, by all Israelites. Thus, the pilgrimage, rather than emphasizing the individual or the individual spiritual journey, emphasizes the people as a whole—creating a sense of corporate spiritual identity. The location is also significant; rather than being on the periphery of Israelite society, it was in its political and spiritual center. Hence, the pilgrimage affirmed and emphasized societal structures rather than challenging them.

In these and other senses, the role of pilgrimage was structurally coherent. It denied the possibility of individual transformation, emphasizing the corporate rather than the individual. The annual and repeated nature of the process also minimized the possibility of significant transformation. The ritual as a whole, in terms of both its narrativization and the definition of participation, a commandment to all Israelites, emphasized both the covenant and its boundaries.

The role of sacrifices within this process, while differing in each of the three festivals, enhanced this process of structural identification and differentiation. The somatic impact of the sacrifices, the blood, the noise, and most importantly the crowds would create an experience of *communitas*, which in the context of Israelite structure emphasizes connectedness within the community, again building up from local communities to (at least symbolically) Israel as a whole. Again, this aspect is shaped by inclusion and exclusion, which are closely connected with underlying structural categories.

The Passover ritual process helpfully brings together many of the arguments presented here. The Paschal sacrifice, discussed above, provides an example of the paradigmatic covenantal meal, a meal shared with God and the people as a whole. Thus both the sacrificial process and the shared commensality provide a strong basis for a shared experience of communitas. This feeling is given narrative form through the association with the Exodus and the eating of other ritual foods, that is, the matzo and the bitter herb. Each of these foods is given a narrative explanation and through its consumption allows for the embodiment of both the narrative and the structure that underlies it.

LAST WORDS

This chapter briefly touched on the basic elements out of which Israelite ritual was constructed. The food, purity, and sacrificial complexes were focused on as they allow for a clear explication of the underlying structure of Israelite culture, that is, a system built upon two categories that have an oppositional relation. The purity and sacrificial complexes also allowed us to explore the means by which the system maintained its integrity despite the possibility and danger posed by ritual impurity and moral impurity or sin.

The discussion of sacrifice also introduced a somatic or affective element to the analysis. This aspect is perhaps one of the most salient features of ritual as opposed to myth—rituals engage the body and must be understood somatically rather than merely being a set of symbols presented in material rather than verbal (or written) forms. Rituals are symbolic and structured, but they gain their power through engagement with the body. Although I did not discuss the somatic aspects of the food and purity complexes, it is clear that they, too, are primarily embodied—engaging appetite, consumption, abstention, and perhaps most importantly for the system, abhorrence.

The final section, touching on the pilgrimage festivals, brings my argument together. While the pilgrimage festivals have all been reinterpreted to fit in with the Israelite understanding of self, history, and covenant, the key aspects of the performance from the pilgrimage itself to the events taking place in Jerusalem were most significantly somatic experiences—culminating in a strong sense of communitas, through which Israel is defined in structural opposition to the nations.

NOTES

1. For example, the structural similarity/identity of the four strata out of which the biblical text is often assumed to be composed and their structural relation to the final redacted version are demonstrated in Kunin 1995:269–70.

2. The most accessible account of Claude Lévi-Strauss's structuralism is found in *Structural Anthropology* (1963).

3. While many texts explore different aspects of biblical ritual, two texts that approach it specifically through the lens of ritual theory are noteworthy: Gruenwald 2003 and Klingbeil 2007.

4. This discussion is based on research first published in Kunin 2004. Particularly useful wider discussions of food in the biblical context can be found in Macdonald 2008 and Feeley-Harnik 1981.

5. Mary Douglas's work on biblical ritual, particularly purity, went through two stages. The first, characterized by *Purity and Danger* (1966), takes a more tradition structuralist approach as its starting point and focuses on structural relations. Her second phase, characterized by *Leviticus as Literature* (1999), moves to a more literary structuralist approach and has a stronger emphasis on moral arguments than found in her earlier work. I draw primarily on the early work, which can be found in Douglas 1975, 1993.

6. Talmudic texts that in part seem to redefine these insects as birds are found in Culin 59a, 65a–66b; and Avodah Zarah 37a.

7. Some of the most important work on purity is found in Milgrom 1991. His approach is noteworthy as it is influenced by structuralist analysis, though, as his analysis includes transformation, it moves in a significantly different direction than taken here. Maccoby 1999 also presents a useful, if at times idiosyncratic, analysis of biblical purity, with a critique of the work of both Milgrom and Neusner.

8. My argument here is related to that developed in Milgrom 1991:767.

9. Jonathan Klawans (1996) provides a useful overview of issues relating to both sacrifice and purity. Gruenwald's (2003:180–230) discussion presents an alternative approach to sacrifice drawing on recent anthropological discussions. Gruenwald's approach, perhaps echoing Girard (1977), emphasizes the violent aspect of sacrifice, associating it with a rupture in existence or reality. The sacrifice mimics or echoes this rupture and through doing so allows for it to be resolved. In effect Gruenwald is focusing on the opposite end of the sacrificial ritual, the act of killing, whereas my argument building on the close relation between sacrifice and the food complex focuses on the act of consumption whereby covenant is restored.

10. The burnt offering is also described in Numbers 28 in the context of a daily offering of two lambs. Many texts, however, use it as a sin offering for specific sins, and the animal is completely burned in a similar way as the sin offering.

11. See, for example, Smith 1927:224. The concept is also taken up in differing ways in Feeley-Harnik 1981 and Davies 1985. The unifying idea in each of these discussions is that commensality between the divine and human and between different human groups creates and reflects different forms of covenantal relation.

12. Douglas Davies provides an interesting insight into the relationship between sacrifice and covenant. Davies's (1985) argument draws on that of Mary Douglas in her discussion of Israeli purity and food rules. His overall argument focuses on the use of

various sacrifices as a means of restoring social/religious order within a covenantal context. The covenantal context is based on a number of significant relations: God:nation, God:priesthood, God:Israelite, Israelite:nation (Davies 1985:156). The critical factor in these relations, and Davies's argument as a whole, is that both sides of the relation are significant participants—although he does not discuss the consumption of the sacrifice as such, his argument provides a basis for seeing God as well as humans as being consumers in the process of rebalancing or restoring appropriate covenantal relations. Although Davies sees these elements as parts of continua, if we reinterpret continuum into oppositional categories, then his argument provides an important basis for that developed here.

13. A similar embodied element is also found in the Israelite food rules, in which the focus is on what one eats rather than with whom one eats; in either case the very act of eating allows for the instantiation of the underlying structure.

14. Gruenwald provides a description of this ritual, highlighting that the biblical fate of the goat is different from the rabbinic. Although he does suggest that the two goats "epitomise two aspects of destruction" (2003:214), it is not at all clear in his analysis why the second goat, "for Azazel," which in his analysis was left alive, is a symbol of destruction or why it should carry the sins as opposed to the goat that was sacrificed in the normal way.

15. Klingbeil (2007:127–46, particularly 136–40) presents an interesting discussion that touches on the annual ritual cycle. His analysis explores the events or contexts that trigger ritual performances.

BIBLIOGRAPHY

Davies, Douglas. 1985. "An Interpretation of Sacrifice in Leviticus." In B. Lang, ed., *Anthropological Approaches to the Old Testament*, pp. 151–62. London: SPCK.

Douglas, Mary. 1966. *Purity and Danger*. London: Routledge.

Douglas, Mary. 1975. *Implicit Meanings*. London: Routledge.

Douglas, Mary. 1993. "The Forbidden Animals in Leviticus." *Journal for the Study of the Old Testament* 59: pp. 3–23.

Douglas, Mary. 1999. *Leviticus as Literature*. Oxford: Oxford University Press.

Feeley-Harnik, Gillian. 1981. *The Lord's Table*. Washington, D.C.: Smithsonian Institution Press.

Girard, René. 1977. *Violence and the Sacred*. Baltimore: Johns Hopkins University Press.

Gruenwald, Ithamar. 2003. *Rituals and Ritual Theory in Ancient Israel*. Atlanta: Society of Biblical Literature.

Klingbeil, Gerald. 2007. *Bridging the Gap*. Winona Lake, Ind.: Eisenbrauns.

Kunin, Seth. 1995. *We Think What We Eat*. London: T&T Clark.

Lévi-Strauss, Claude. 1963. *Structural Anthropology*. New York: Basic Books.

Maccoby, Hyam. 1999. *Ritual and Morality*. Cambridge: Cambridge University Press.

Macdonald, Nathan. 2008. *Not Bread Alone*. Oxford: Oxford University Press.

Milgrom, Jacob. 1991. *Leviticus, 1–16*. New York: Doubleday.

Part IV

The Study and Reception of the Hebrew Bible

17

❁

Reception of the Old Testament

Alison Gray

Interpretation today is beginning to discover its own history—
not only the limitations of its respective norms but also those
factors that could not come to light as long as traditional
norms held sway.
—Wolfgang Iser, *The Act of Reading: A Theory of Aesthetic Response*

"Reception" of the Hebrew Bible (HB)/Old Testament (OT) is currently the subject of one of the fastest-growing, and still evolving, areas of biblical studies. It pertains to the ways in which the texts and *all* that is related to them—their beliefs, characters, ideas, motifs, stories, underlying traditions—have been understood, used, transmitted, translated, interpreted, expressed, and retold within any medium since their conception. How the HB/OT has been "received"—that is, understood or interpreted, in different cultures and at different times—can be seen in the Dead Sea Scrolls; the New Testament; rabbinic exegesis; or in works of art, literature, or musical compositions throughout history, or on the political stage, or in cinemas. The dizzying array of subjects that may be considered under its umbrella can thus include such diverse topics as William Blake's *Illustrations of the Book of Job*, the use of the "curse of Ham" in Genesis 9 to justify slavery, and the figures of Adam and Eve in contemporary advertising.[1]

We are, it seems, unable to avoid living a *zitathaftes Leben*—a life in quotation.[2] Western culture is shot through with streaks of biblical "reception": the consumer cannot escape biblical verses on T-shirts, fridge magnets, or even car bumper stickers, let alone the steady stream of movies that retell, and play with, biblical stories, such as the 2014 American film *Noah*, directed by Darren Aronofsky. But so what? And why is it worthy of intellectual inquiry? Primarily because biblical "reception" involves anthropology, sociology, and hermeneutics and the attempt to bring these three vast disciplines into dialogue with one another.

The study of biblical reception is fundamentally *anthropological*—it tells us about humans and about how texts can impact, and be used to influence, human history and culture. It also draws on *sociology*, shedding light on the history of how biblical texts have functioned, and still function, in different societies, with positive and negative effects. Finally, it is about *hermeneutics*—it explores the meanings of a text and how humans interpret texts. It reminds us how much our situatedness in a particular time and place conditions our readings of texts and how we "receive" certain ideas or respond to certain characters. We are driven, it seems, to constantly make use of what has gone before in order to make sense of the present, to constantly tell and retell old stories so that they speak afresh to new audiences. How and why we do this is not only intriguing in itself but also has the potential to inform and enrich our knowledge and understanding of the biblical texts themselves and to highlight the kinds of things that influence our "retellings."

This chapter aims first to introduce and explore some of the terminological and methodological questions surrounding the endeavor of HB/OT reception studies and to identify some of the branches or movements within it. Second, it will turn to the question "Reception of what?" to illustrate the complex relationships that exist between oral traditions and texts and between different texts within Scripture. This will lead into a very brief overview of the reception of the Hebrew Bible/Old Testament in early Jewish and Christian literature. The chapter will conclude with a summary of some helpful vocabulary that has been suggested by Lesleigh Cushing Stahlberg for making sense of different "retellings" of Scripture.

TERMINOLOGY AND DIFFERENT APPROACHES TO BIBLICAL RECEPTION STUDIES

The current flood of biblical reception studies seems so unwieldy in part because there is a fluidity or inconsistency in how particular terms are used and understood. A variety of labels are used in relation to academic studies that engage with the abundance of reception "material" in the HB/OT, including "reception history," "reader-response criticism," "reception criticism," "cultural history," "history of biblical interpretation," and "reception exegesis." The disagreement over the assumptions and ultimate aims of these areas of study leads to tensions between different approaches, and so some attempt at terminological detangling is in order.

The academic study of how a text (and related material) has been read and interpreted is usually referred to as *reception history*, or *Rezeptionsgeschichte*. This idea was developed by Hans Robert Jauss (1921–97) as part of a methodological framework for interpreting literature, which he outlined in *Toward an Aesthetic of Reception* (1982).[3] Jauss's work is rooted in the philosophical hermeneutics of his mentor Hans-Georg Gadamer (1900–2002). Central to Gadamer's explorations into the nature of interpretation is the principle of *Wirkungsgeschichte*, usually translated as "history of effects" or "history of influence" (although this has been used and understood in a variety of ways, as we shall see below).

Gadamer drew attention to the extent to which one's interpretation is affected by one's historical location and linguistic context, and he sought to revive tradition as a dialogue partner.[4] For Gadamer and for Jauss, the meaning of a text is therefore to be found in the fusion that results from the dialogue between a reader and the text—a fusion of two historical and cultural interpretative "horizons."[5] Consequently there can be no single meaning of a text, since it has the potential for as many different readings as there are readers.

This view that the meaning of a text is to be found in the interaction between text and reader is shared by the literary-critical approach named *reader-response criticism*. The work of Wolfgang Iser, one of Jauss's colleagues in the Constance literary school, was particularly influential on literary theorists in the United Kingdom and the United States (e.g., Stanley Fish) who were less concerned with the historical dimension of reception and more interested in the indeterminacy of a text's meaning. Although reception history is sometimes treated as a subset of reader-response theories, it is helpful to bear in mind an underlying distinction between the philosophical theory of "aesthetic response" that undergirds reader-response approaches and the more historically inclined "aesthetics of reception," which motivates reception-historical studies.[6] To put it another way, whereas reader-response criticism is primarily concerned with the meaning of a text for the modern reader, reception-historical studies are interested in the creation of meaning from the text in a variety of media (such as the arts) throughout history. The Blackwell Bible Commentaries, for example, offer a unique approach to biblical texts, with a focus on their reception in art, music, literature, politics, and religion: "The volumes explore the fascinating reception history of the Bible, since what people believe a sacred text like the Bible means is often as interesting and historically important—theologically, politically, morally, and aesthetically—as what it originally meant."[7]

How, then, does reception history differ from the *history of biblical interpretation*, which is already evident in some of the earliest Jewish and Christian commentaries? The answer depends on the flexibility of one's understanding of "interpretation" and on what one considers to be the appropriate subject matter of reception history. Ulrich Luz, known for his attention to reception in his commentaries on the Gospel of Matthew, tries to distinguish between reception history and the history of interpretation on the basis of genre: the latter being concerned with commentaries and theological writings, and the former, with media of all types. Such a distinction certainly makes sense in terms of the respective aims of the two genres: one has the explicit aim of expounding the meaning of a text, and the other appears to do so only implicitly.

However, making this distinction creates a dichotomy between the scholarly and nonscholarly, which, while understandable, is problematic. It fails to highlight that the history of biblical interpretation has traditionally been concerned with how a particular *text* has been understood, whereas reception history is interested in *everything* associated with the texts: their characters, stories, motifs, and so on. It also serves to underpin a negative evaluation of reception history as outside the bounds of "proper" academic study. As Choon-Leong Seow has pointed out, broader understandings of "interpretation" were in existence even before the advent of reception history. In 1947, for example, Gerhard Ebeling explored the issue of the interpretation of Scripture in Christian ritual, church history, and politics, including how Scripture was used as a justification for war or as motivation for witch hunts in the past.[8]

One possible solution to the relationship between reception history and the history of biblical interpretation is to subsume the history of biblical interpretation into the long narrative of reception history. Such an approach is exemplified by Paul Joyce and Diana Lipton in their reception-historical commentary on Lamentations. If one was to plot a narrative history of responses to the biblical text, historical criticism could be seen as "a relatively recent phase" in the history of responses to the text.[9] Reception history therefore goes beyond, but may also include, the traditional remit of the history of biblical interpretation.

What is intriguing about the discourse of reception studies is that it provokes dialogue between those who are committed to the "original" sense(s) of a text and those who eschew any kind of hermeneutical positivism. The question of whether or not reception history can comfortably accommodate the concerns of traditional historical criticism is a moot point and depends upon the hermeneutical orientation of the study. Studies in reception history often select and reflect upon certain aspects of historical or contemporary responses to the HB/OT, offering an alternative paradigm for biblical studies—one that relinquishes questions of a text's "original" meaning and authorial intent. This marks a shift from questions of meaning *in the texts* to how meaning has been created *from the texts*, and from questions about what influenced the formation of the Bible to what the Bible has influenced and shaped: "The first point, then, is to see the Bible not merely as a set of ancient documents or even as a first- and second-century product but as a third-century and twelfth-century and nineteenth-century and contemporary agent.... The dominant point in this case is to understand the potential and the actual roles of such a Scripture in the life of the imagination, its role as an organizer of ideas, images, and emotions, as an activating symbol."[10]

This call for a redirection of biblical studies by the Canadian Qur'anic scholar Wilfred Cantwell Smith in the 1970s has been answered by numerous diachronic studies of the interpretation and use of particular biblical books, stories, characters, or motifs in different historical and cultural contexts. Texts are described as having a "career" or an "afterlife," which can be traced and analyzed.[11] It is in this context that the term *reception criticism* is sometimes preferred, since it highlights the aspect of critical analysis involved in the enterprise of reception history. Others focus on the sociopolitical use or function of a particular text or belief in a specific historical situation.

However, for those with a more irenic disposition toward what might otherwise be seen as "competing" hermeneutical branches of biblical studies, the analyses of some reception-historical interpretations also have the potential to shed light on the traditional (historical-critical) task of biblical exegesis. Cheryl Exum, for example, reflecting on a painting by Gustave Moreau, *Scene from the Song of Songs*, notes that it led her to consider an alternative interpretation of a particularly difficult verse (Song of Sol. 5:7) because of his representation of the scene as a sexual attack. She asks, "And is that not what we, as scholars, want: to be challenged to look at our material from new angles, though we may remain persuaded by one?"[12] It is this recognition of the potential for artistic representations in all forms to help biblical scholars in their exegetical studies that has led to the recently coined expression *reception exegesis*, by Paul Joyce and Diana Lipton: "Reception exegesis can shine a spotlight on biblical verses that have been dulled by familiarity; it can foreground biblical concepts and concerns that have faded over time into the background; and it can even give rise to radical new readings of difficult Hebrew terms and texts."[13]

Joyce and Lipton clarify that the identification of this dimension is not intended to devalue other aspects of reception history that do not "yield exegetical fruit," but it acknowledges the potential contributions to be made from the field of reception history for those biblical scholars who are concerned to better understand the biblical text. This illustrates the declaration in the introduction to *The Oxford Handbook of the Reception History of the Bible* that "no individual, school, or group does or can own biblical reception."[14] It also advocates a certain humility, characteristically lacking in historical-critical endeavors, to acknowledge one's presuppositions and prejudices, which then facilitates "two-way interdisciplinary interaction in which biblical scholars do not merely give but also receive."[15] This echoes Gadamer's own reflections on dialogue in hermeneutics: "To conduct a conversation means to allow oneself to be conducted by the subject matter to which the partners in the dialogue are oriented. It requires that one does not try to argue the other person down but that one really considers the weight of the other's opinion."[16]

A different "solution" to the relationship between the history of biblical interpretation and reception history is to distinguish more carefully between those studies that have a theological/exegetical focus and those that have a historical/cultural one. Mary Callaway, writing in response to the challenge raised by the Blackwell series on the reception history of the Bible, offers the following conclusion:

The term History of Interpretation is used in general for studies that take an exegetical approach and have a theological interest. The object of study may be a work of art or a piece of music, so long as the approach is exegetical and explores the hermeneutic by which the biblical text was interpreted. The term Reception History, as its origins in *Wirkungsgeschichte* imply, should describe studies that employ a mixture of historical, sociological and anthropological approaches to illuminate the mutual interplay of *effects* that a biblical text has had on a given culture and that a culture manages to encode in a biblical text.[17]

However, as Callaway herself points out, it is possible for the borderline between the two to become blurred. As we shall see further on, the exploration of one to some extent entails an exploration of the other, precisely because of the relationship between the "text" and how it is "retold." Texts can be both transformed and transforming. This relates to an area of dialogue that is opening up more widely between reception history and *cultural history*.

Reception history draws on cultural history in its analyses of interpretations of Scripture. Timothy Beal has recently drawn attention to the limitations of reception history and calls for a shift in focus toward cultural history, which, in his view, would facilitate more fruitful dialogue between biblical studies and comparative religious studies.[18] For Beal, reception history pays too much attention to the "word" of Scripture at the expense of its "materiality" and cultural production: "Scriptural culture is always material as well as symbolic, sensual as well as semantic."[19] This is an important dimension of biblical reception, which is often overlooked. It is worth considering, for example, how much artistic and musical representations of biblical texts have influenced readers' understandings and recollections of characters and stories. As Cheryl Exum observes, "What many people know or think they know about the Bible often comes more from familiar representations of biblical texts and themes in the arts than from study of the ancient text itself."[20] What people "think they know" about the Bible, gathered from paintings or movies, can have an enormous impact on their religious and political views.

This brings us to a discussion of the aims and subject matter of reception history and to the main questions that are being asked. Reception-historical studies, in all their diversity, are usually united by a consideration of one or more of the following three interrelated questions, often with a particular orientation toward a more hermeneutical, anthropological, or sociological approach:

- What is the effect of the text on the reader? What meanings does the text have for the reader?
- What is the effect of the reader's historical, cultural, geographic, and linguistic context on his or her interpretation of the text?
- How does the text, through its "retellings" or cultural production, influence the language, culture, and history of a particular group or society?

Text in each case is an umbrella term for all that relates to the text, for example, characters, stories, and so on.

One way of understanding the differences in approach or focus between different reception-historical studies might be to look at the relative weight given to each of these questions. Despite the tensions, the questions and approaches have more overlap than is often acknowledged. The questions have a slightly different emphasis than those being asked by what was traditionally considered under the remit of the history of biblical interpretation, but they naturally fall under the broader question, "What is the history of responses to, or interpretations of, the text?"

RECEPTION OF WHAT?

So, where to begin? Biblical reception history raises fundamental questions about what "the Bible" or, as is the focus of this chapter, the "Hebrew Bible" or "Old Testament" actually *is*. There are two main aspects to this problem: the materiality of the Bible and the imposition of boundaries between the "original" text and the "received" text. Timothy Beal draws attention to the fact that "reception" implies origination, yet "there is no original, singular, 'the Bible' to be received through history."[21] This is stark in its presentation, but the materiality of the Bible does need to be taken into account, since bibles are "generated and generative in different scriptural cultures."[22] Or, if we go back a few centuries, how did the Authorized Version of the Bible, the King James translation of 1611, impact the English language, European culture, church and political history, and biblical scholarship of the seventeenth century and beyond? Along with the works of Shakespeare, it remains one of the most influential books in English and for English-speaking cultures.

A study of the "world behind the text" or the "world in the text" is therefore necessarily mediated by the "world in front of the text"—What kind of translation or mediation of the biblical text is being used? For example, the most widely used critical edition of the Hebrew Bible, the *Biblia Hebraica Stuttgartensia*, is a twentieth-century edition of a medieval manuscript. How does the presentation and edition of this text affect its interpretation? Brennan Breed focuses on this question in his introduction to *Nomadic Text: A Theory of Biblical Reception History*,[23] in which he raises the related question of where interpretation or "reception" starts. Breed criticizes the artificial boundary that is drawn between the "original" text and the "received" text, which rests on a static view of the biblical text. The language used in reception studies is significant here: the *Nachleben*, or "afterlife," of a biblical story or text implies that its former life has come to a discrete end, whereas others use the term *Überleben*, or "survival," which softens the boundary a little.

The question "Reception of what?" also probes further questions of oral tradition, inner-biblical exegesis, and textual redaction. For example, biblical stories may originally have been independent in oral form or already part of a cycle in oral tradition. Some of these stories themselves incorporate "receptions" of stories, myths, or motifs borrowed from the writers' neighboring nations, and so biblical reception studies may find itself reaching back even further into the past, beyond the Bible's own history. The first tangible examples of "reception" of biblical material are therefore within the texts themselves, composed from elements of oral tradition by authors who committed characters, stories, laws, and history to paper for their own particular purposes.

Another layer of reception can be detected by looking at the relationship between texts, usually termed "inner-biblical exegesis." Biblical texts are often quoted verbatim, paraphrased, or embedded more covertly in other biblical texts. In the book of Job, for example, there are numerous examples of biblical texts that have been quoted or parodied, perhaps to offer a theological reflection or to challenge a particular interpretation or view.[24] Inner-biblical interpretation can even be identified within a single text. Zakovitch uses the example of the portrait of Jacob in Genesis 27. The narrative holds a tension between presenting Jacob as the "archetypal trickster," deceiving his brother Isaac (Gen. 27:1–45, ascribed to the "J" source), and attempting to explain or justify his actions (e.g., by discrediting Esau in Gen. 26:34–35 and 27:46–28:9, ascribed to "P"). Subsequent reception—translations, retellings, and reflections on the story—similarly sought to clear Jacob's name and present him as a perfect example to follow. We can therefore identify different stages in the history of biblical reception if we look at inner-biblical interpretation and at the very process of editing the biblical texts and the formation of the canon.[25]

The magnificent sculpture of Moses by the Renaissance artist Michelangelo (ca. 1515) provides an intriguing example of the reception of different biblical translations and of the reception of texts through art. This Moses, with the Ten Commandments under one arm, has two horns protruding from his head, consistent with other (but by no means all) representations of Moses from the Middle Ages. Explanations for this range from the suggestion that Michelangelo was following the Vulgate's translation of the Hebrew *qāran* (shine/send out rays) with the Latin *cornuta* (horn; Exod. 34:29, 30, 35) to speculation that the horns were intended not to be seen but merely to reflect light on the sculpture or that they were in fact designed to represent shining rays. Other, more negative interpretations draw attention to demonic representations of Jewish figures in the Middle Ages and "read" the horns on Moses as a similarly defamatory image.

However, *horn/horned* in the Hebrew Bible carries associations of strength and honor, making the connection between horn and radiance or glory more comprehensible (note the Greek verb *doxazo* in the LXX rendering of these verses). As Ruth Mellinkoff has persuasively argued, this could well account for Jerome's choice of *cornuta* as a translation. In terms of the impact of these literal depictions of horns, Mellinkoff notes that it is only in the Latin Church that there were horned bishop's miters, "symbols of honour, station, and power."[26] Without an informed study of the semantic range of a particular word in any given language, or of the changing cultural contexts in which biblical texts have been interpreted, there is room for huge misunderstandings, which biblical reception studies can hopefully challenge.

THE HEBREW BIBLE/OLD TESTAMENT IN JEWISH AND
CHRISTIAN LITERATURE

What is intriguing about a closer look at inner-biblical interpretation is the extent to which the direction of the exegetical trajectory of post-biblical Judaism can be detected within the Hebrew Bible itself. Michael Fishbane offers a systematic review of exegesis within the Hebrew Bible in order to address this issue of continuity between the text and postbiblical Judaism. Fishbane identifies four main categories of inner-biblical interpretation: (i) scribal comments and corrections, (ii) legal exegesis (clarification and interpretation of laws), (iii) aggadic exegesis (all non-halakhic exegesis, e.g., narrative [re]use of motifs, types, theological reflection, etc.), and (iv) mantological exegesis (interpretation of dreams, oracles, and omens).[27] He also pays attention to the sociohistorical contexts from which these interpretations emerged and the ideologies governing their expression.

The first category, scribal comments, brings us back to the question "Reception of what?" The texts were copied with mistakes and corrections and were annotated with explanations or emendations. Even these sometimes show examples of interpretation and therefore of reception. The third category, aggadic exegesis, is the biggest category conceptually and is perhaps the most fruitful in terms of offering analogues for a variety of postbiblical forms of biblical reception. Its goal, according to Fishbane, is "to envisage the future in the light of the past, and thereby affirm continuity between past and present as the sure link between memory and hope."[28] Traditions were thus reused and recontextualized to speak to a new generation, such as Moses typology in Joshua (e.g., Josh. 4:23; 5:2–9, 10–12), or Exodus typology in Deutero-Isaiah (e.g., Isa. 43:16–21), or reinterpretation of Jeremiah's prophecy in Daniel (Dan. 9:2).

The Hebrew Bible and the Dead Sea Scrolls

Such recontextualization is found in abundance in the Qumran texts, composed between the mid-second century BCE and the first century CE and saturated with scriptural citations and allusions. The Qumran community, an ascetic, millenarian Jewish sect, believed that they had a privileged relationship with God such that they saw themselves as the faithful remnant of Israel, the true inheritors of the divine promises, and thus God's agent in eschatological renewal. Reading Scripture, particularly prophecies, according to this interpretive horizon of living in the last days, they believed that it was their interpretation that revealed the hidden, true meaning of Scripture:

> It is precisely because the community sees itself as living in the last days, and itself as the only true remnant of Israel and inheritor of the covenant, that it can interpret Scripture ... as being fulfilled in this very community, and as applying directly to it and to the age in which it finds itself living. It is this perspective also that allows it to hold that the true meaning and hidden secrets of Scripture are now finally and uniquely made known to it through direct revelation and inspired interpretation.[29]

A variety of exegetical techniques are demonstrated in the different genres, particularly in the *pesharim* (interpretive commentaries on scriptural texts) but also in the Community Rule (1QS), the Hodayot (1QH, the thanksgiving hymn), the Damascus Document (CD), the Temple Scroll (11Q), and the War Scroll (1QM). Many of these techniques are also found in later rabbinic exegesis, such as verbal analogy (reading the meaning of a particular word in one text into another), providing scriptural support for a particular interpretation, paronomasia (play on words), allusion, and anthology (e.g., 1QH 8.4ff.; 1QM 10.1–8). Sometimes texts are cited and understood in a similar way to their original literary context, for example, Deut. 5:12 is cited in CD 10.16–17 and then elaborated with further rules and regulations for the community. In other cases, several texts are used in dialogue with one another to shed light on a contemporary situation, for example, CD 7.9–8.2, which draws on Isaiah 7:17; Amos 5:26–27, 9:11; and Numbers 24:17. The Hebrew Bible was therefore used both to interpret events in the past and to provide hope for the future, making sense of the community's experiences, strengthening its eschatological identity, and shaping its way of life.

Rewritten Scripture

Further significant examples of reuse and recontextualization are found in literature commonly known as "Rewritten Bible," a term first used by Geza Vermes in 1961. It describes the rewriting of biblical narratives and laws in the intertestamental period, including some found in the caves at Qumran, which were shaped by the writers' own methods of exegesis and theological outlooks. One might consider the books of Chronicles as the biblical forerunner to this genre.[30] They are largely historical narratives, seamlessly weaving together biblical and nonbiblical traditions. The various methods of reworking biblical material range from slight modification of the text, such as using different word forms or phrases, to major interpretive changes. 4QReworked Pentateuch, for example, has only minor changes, whereas Jubilees appears to be a substantial reworking of material from Genesis 1:1–Exodus 16:1. As a result, there is much debate about which texts should be included within this genre.

One of the intriguing aspects of some of these early "rewritten" texts, particularly those from Qumran, is that it is possible that they preserve earlier readings than the Masoretic Text. Apocrypha and pseudepigrapha are significantly different, quantitatively and qualitatively, from the books that they "rework." Compositional techniques include the addition of new text or material from another text to the existing text, rearranging the material, and paraphrasing. Each of these presents the text in a new way, its interpretation lying in its reformulation.[31]

Old Testament in the New Testament

Material from the Hebrew Bible, often via the Septuagint (but sometimes also via different text forms), is reused and reinterpreted in a variety of ways in the New Testament, sometimes (as at Qumran) by direct citation in a new context (e.g., Mark 1:44 cf. Lev. 14:2ff.; Luke 4:12 cf. Deut. 6:16) and at other times by indirect citation or allusion (e.g., Mark 12:40 cf. Exod. 22:22). It is often difficult to determine if and when a New Testament writer has used the Scriptures intentionally or unconsciously.

One of the interpretive "horizons" of the New Testament writers was that Jesus was the long-awaited Messiah, God's chosen one, who had died for their sins. The early Christians therefore used the Hebrew Scriptures to understand the person of Jesus, his teaching and his actions, and certain texts, particularly prophecies, to shed light on the meaning of his life, death, and resurrection (cf. Luke 24:27; 1 Cor. 15:3–4): "As the early Christians began to think and preach about the significance of Jesus' death, they must have utilised categories provided by the OT—

sacrifices, the atoning death of the Servant, the innocent sufferer."[32] They also then turned to Scripture for apologetic reasons, to address doubts about Jesus's messiahship and resurrection (e.g., Luke 22:37; Acts 2:25–28 cf. Ps. 16:8–11; John 1:45).

A second "horizon" of interpretation is an eschatological one. Some of the New Testament writers, like the Qumran community, believed that they were living in the last days, which led them to see their own situation in the light of Scripture and vice versa. The ways in which the Scriptures were used in the New Testament share some similarities with their use in the Qumran texts: Scripture is sometimes used in a literal, straightforward way, to refer to something described in the texts or when citing a law whose validity is being affirmed in a particular situation (e.g., Mark 2:23–3:6); at other times a text is used to identify the fulfillment of a prophecy (e.g., Matt. 8:17, 13:35; Acts 8:34–35); some texts are used typologically, in a *peshat* style, to establish a correspondence between a past and present situation in order to understand their significance more fully; other texts are used allegorically, "to draw parallels between an OT story and a contemporary situation or piece of teaching."[33] For example, redemption through Christ was understood through the paradigm of Israel's deliverance from Egypt—the OT event could be seen as an anticipation of, and a hermeneutical key to, the current situation: just as the Israelites were slaves in Egypt, so now people were slaves to sin.

This reading of the Old Testament in the light of the New Testament has shaped centuries of Christian interpretation of Scripture, also evident in Christian art, music, and literature. Tragically, it has also shaped centuries of an insidious, and frequently anti-Semitic, relationship to Judaism. Christological and Christocentric readings of the Old Testament became, for some Christians, the *only* way of interpreting the Old Testament. The person of Jesus was understood and used as a kind of hermeneutical key to unlock the "true" meaning of the stories and characters within it. For some Christians, this meant that Judaism found its true fulfillment in Christianity.

George Frederick Handel's famous and much-loved oratorio *Messiah* provides a masterly illustration of an eighteenth-century Christological interpretation of the Bible and a musical portrait of salvation history. The text, made up exclusively of biblical texts from the Old and New

Testaments (mostly according to the Authorized Version), was compiled by the librettist Charles Jennens in 1741–42.

Musical representations of biblical texts present their own unique set of challenges for biblical reception historians, who need to be conversant in musical terminology while being able to communicate with non-musicians. Like paintings, musical settings, particularly oratorios, with their combination of words and music, speak powerfully to our imaginations and invite us to read the texts in a new light.

However, musical retellings do not emerge in a cultural or historical vacuum and are as much a product of their time and place as texts and paintings. Some recent musicological research has turned to address charges of anti-Judaism and anti-Semitism in compositions that use biblical texts in ways that seem to endorse a triumphalist Christian approach to Judaism.[34] In 2007 there was a heated debate over Handel's triumphalism in *Messiah* at the American Handel festival, which was left somewhat unresolved.[35] This perhaps signals a need for greater collaboration among musicologists, historians, biblical scholars, and theologians to look together at the unsettling question of the roots and history of anti-Semitism, beginning with the interpretation of the Old Testament in the New Testament.

Talmud and Midrash

Historically, Judaism has assumed that the fundamental task of biblical exegesis is "to demonstrate the capacity of Scripture to regulate *all* areas of life and thought."[36] Fishbane observes that different modes of exegesis have developed within Judaism: "textual exegesis"—deriving a new teaching from Scripture—and "textual justification"—using scriptural associations to legitimate certain customs and laws. These two modes of exegesis together establish the divine scriptural foundation of a community's social and religious traditions. The earliest rabbinic texts date from the third century CE. The Mishnah, a legal commentary on the Torah, preserves the oral law that was codified into tractates around 200 CE. The Gemara preserves rabbinic commentaries and discussions on the Mishnah, although the term is often used interchangeably with *Talmud*, which incorporates both the Mishnah and the Gemara. The Jerusalem Talmud was compiled in Palestine in circa 400 CE. The Babylonian

Talmud, compiled in circa 500 CE, contains several traditions, some of which are also found in the Jerusalem Talmud.

Midrash, a form of rabbinic biblical interpretation found in various collections (e.g., Midrash Rabbah) and in both Talmuds, is a creative method of exegesis that seeks to understand and unfold some of the manifold meanings of Scripture and its contemporary relevance, often by bringing biblical texts into dialogue by placing them alongside one another. The term is often associated with the Hebrew verb *darash* (to search, investigate), often contrasted with *peshat*—an explanation or interpretation conceived as the "plain" meaning of the text. Daniel Boyarin understands midrash as "a continuation of the literary activity which engendered the Scriptures themselves."[37] He writes: "If God is the implied author of the Bible, then the gaps, repetitions, contradictions, and heterogeneity of the biblical text must be *read*, as a central part of the system of meaning production of that text. In midrash the rabbis respond to this invitation and challenge."[38]

Midrash highlights the dialogical nature of the biblical text and the gaps in the text that facilitate multiple "readings" and "receptions." Midrashim contain multiple interpretations of the same text—bearing witness to a polyphony of rabbinic voices in dialogue with the text and with one another. Boyarin contends that they do not seek merely to "update" the biblical text, or only to read the text in the light of their own experience, but, rather, to open up the world of the text, allowing the "biblical past" to come alive in the "midrashic present." These insights into the nature and purpose of midrash lend themselves to our discussion of reception studies, as we contend with different approaches to the polyphony of readings, reflections, and effects of the Old Testament/Hebrew Bible over the centuries.

COMING FULL CIRCLE: MIDRASH TO RECEPTION HISTORY?

It is easy to see how midrash has appealed to scholars interested in reception studies and why the term *midrash* lends itself to a broad description of creative "retellings" (e.g., in the title of Helen Leneman's article "Ruth and Boaz Love Duets as Examples of Musical Midrash"[39]). In the 1980s, a group of literary theorists and rabbinic scholars met together for a year at the Hebrew University in Jerusalem to discuss the subject of midrash and literary theory.[40] In both, there is a shared interest in the interaction among text, reader, and audience and a marked difference from Hellenistic approaches to literature.

Boyarin describes how midrash has been "suppressed in Jewish hermeneutics" and "marginalized in the West," overshadowed by the allegorical-Aristotelian tradition.[41] It is only with the questioning of Enlightenment assumptions and values in modern literary theory that midrash has received a more generous welcome in intellectual circles, rather than being regarded merely as "poetical conceits."[42] Somewhat elliptical and puzzling, often apparently far removed from the surface meaning of the text, midrash raises the question of whether a text has only one "right" interpretation and whether it has any stable meaning. It embodies what can occur in the creative interaction between a text and its reader and thus provides a natural ally for deconstructionists and reader-response theorists.

However, as Boyarin cautions, midrash is not simply a forerunner of deconstruction. In midrash, the act of reading produces meaning through interaction among the reader, the text, and other texts. The lines between text and interpretation are often blurred so that the historical situatedness of the interpretation is ambiguous, but it offers an exegesis of the text, a way of seeing how the Bible reads itself and what it has to say to the reader. In this sense, then, the interface between midrash and reception studies would have quite a narrow appeal, restricted to those primarily interested in the hermeneutical and exegetical focus of reception history.

BACK TO TERMINOLOGY: *APPROACH, STANCE,* AND *FILTER*

One possible way of providing a broad language or set of questions that can guide and facilitate discussion between those involved in reception studies has been proposed by Lesleigh Cushing Stahlberg in her monograph entitled *Sustaining Fictions: Intertextuality, Midrash, Translation, and the Literary Afterlife of the Bible* (2008).[43] Seeking to describe the nature of the "retelling" that takes place in the reception of biblical texts, she draws on the vocabularies of literary, midrashic, and translation theories.

The language Stahlberg chooses to explore particular "retellings" focuses on three aspects of reception: "approach," "stance," and "filter," which will be outlined below. The advantage to this approach is that it provides a framework that can be employed across the breadth of perspectives in the enterprise of biblical reception studies and can be appropriated by those who are oriented toward more anthropological, sociological, or hermeneutical questions:

APPROACH: *How is the reader approaching the text?*
This includes questions such as, How is the original used? Whose point of view dominates or narrates the story? Where is the story set? Has it been transposed or reframed? For example, *The Red Tent* is a novel by Anita Diamant told in Dinah's voice, filling in gaps in the biblical narratives about women and their experiences, relationships, and emotions, connecting with contemporary female readers.

STANCE: *What is the reader doing to the text?*
This explores the "attitude" taken toward the original: Does it seek in its reading to invalidate, subvert, or replace the original? Does it embrace and affirm the original or defamiliarize it? Does it invert or misapprehend the text? Marc Chagall's *Creation of Man*, in offering an interpretation of Genesis 1:26–27, itself draws attention to the multiple possible readings of the text. It is saturated with allusions to other biblical narratives, from the Ten Commandments to the Crucifixion, such that it "rings with many of the same intertextual allusions and echoes that are often brought by interpreters to the text of Genesis."[44]

FILTER: *What does the reader bring to the text?*
This concerns the interpretive "lens" through which the retelling approaches the original. There is no normative "clear" lens—a reader with no baggage, untainted by culture, history, or politics. All interpretation is socially, culturally, and ideologically situated somewhere, and therefore all interpretation has some kind of filter. "Bullet the Blue Sky," a song by U2, from *The Joshua Tree* album, for example, makes use of the reference to Jacob wrestling with the angel (Gen. 32:24), which needs to be understood in light of the band's condemnation of American foreign policy in the 1980s.[45]

Particularly illuminating is Stahlberg's adaptation of the principles of rabbinic exegesis, the *middot*, outlined by Hillel, as a basis for discussing the relationship between texts and their "retellings": "They consist of rules by which an exegete can gain entry into a text; they offer a way of defining relationships between Urtexts and texts."[46]

To accompany a description of each of these rules, Stahlberg offers examples of postbiblical interpretations of the Akedah, the binding of Isaac (Genesis 22), from antiquity to modernity. For instance, taking the fifth principle—inference from general and particular—Stahlberg describes how a retelling sometimes zooms in on the biblical story, magnifying and expanding certain details. At other times it pans out, yielding a view of the whole in a broader context. She illustrates this with Wilfred Owen's poem "The Parable of the Old Man and the Young," composed in the aftermath of World War I:

> So Abram rose, and clave the wood, and went,
> And took the fire with him, and a knife.
> And as they sojourned both of them together,
> Isaac the first-born spake and said, My Father,
> Behold the preparations, fire and iron,
> But where the lamb for this burnt-offering?
> Then Abram bound the youth with belts and straps,
> And builded parapets and trenches there,
> And stretched forth the knife to slay his son.
> When lo! an angel called him out of heaven,
> Saying, Lay not thy hand upon the lad,
> Neither do anything to him.
> Behold, A ram, caught in a thicket by its horns;
> Offer the Ram of Pride instead of him.
> But the old man would not so, but slew his son,
> And half the seed of Europe, one by one.[47]

Here the author's *approach* to the narrative of Abraham binding Isaac is to condense it, and yet the author also adds unfamiliar details—the belts and straps, parapets and trenches. The episode is seen through the *filter* of the horror of war and the experience of betrayal of the young men of Europe, for the sake of pride, the "Ram of Pride." The ram, a gift

in the original story—a substitute sacrifice and gracious act of God—
becomes something negative, an obstacle to the deliverance of the son
that the reader is anticipating. The *stance* of the author thus both affirms the original and defamiliarizes it, giving the narrative a chilling
ending. The son is not saved but destroyed, and not just the one son but
"half the seed of Europe, one by one," magnifying and intensifying the
terror of the original command to sacrifice.

These categories have much to offer future reception studies in clarifying the nature of a particular retelling of a biblical text. They are similar
to the list of questions that Cheryl Exum proposes as the basis for dialogue between a painting and the biblical text but provide a more generic
framework that can encompass a variety of media.[48] A common criticism leveled at studies of biblical reception history is that they are too
often a collection or catalog of examples of reception rather than an exploration of the interaction between the text and a particular reader or
audience in a specific historical and cultural location. Even in the act of
cataloging examples there are presuppositions at work, consciously or
unconsciously shaping the compilation, which need to be acknowledged,
requiring a degree of self-awareness and integrity in the enterprise.

Perhaps this vocabulary of approach, stance, and filter can help to
direct (or at least supplement) questions that may be asked of receptions
of a text. They provide a focus and a platform for the questions of hermeneutics, anthropology, and sociology identified at the beginning, concerned with the nexus of relationships among texts, readers, and their
contexts. As we saw earlier, texts can be both transformed and transforming. By concentrating on the nature of the relationship between the
"text" and how it is "retold," these categories of approach, stance, and
filter can help to identify more clearly the places where reception studies, with their diverse agendas, may converge and diverge.

CONCLUDING REMARKS

This brief survey of some of the questions raised by the broad area of reception of the Old Testament has shown that much of reception history
involves an examination of our *zitathaftes Leben* and of the manifold
ways in which the Bible has been interpreted, reinterpreted, and adapted

to suit the needs or desires of particular ages and places. Research into the "reception" of the Hebrew Bible/Old Testament is bringing a heightened awareness of the significance of this collection of ancient Israelite texts as a treasure trove of characters, stories, myths, images, metaphors, and symbols that have shaped different cultures and histories, in profound, sometimes violent, and often unacknowledged ways.

ETHICS OF RECEPTION HISTORY: A POSTSCRIPT

While the discourse of reception studies has opened up huge areas of debate about the relationship between texts and their readers, and about the "situatedness" of all biblical interpretation, it also feeds into conversations about the academic and ethical parameters of *legitimate interpretation*. Are all forms of biblical reception and interpretation equally valid? Can the study of reception history ever be ethically neutral? Surely scholars should not be reticent about anti-Semitic or patriarchal or homophobic readings of Scripture, for example, and should speak out against such "reception"? If "ethos is the shared intellectual space of freely accepted obligations and traditions as well as the praxial space of discourse and action," biblical scholars should be accountable for their ethos.[49]

The enterprise of reception history foregrounds, and demands a response to, the question that Elisabeth Schüssler Fiorenza posed in 1988: "Do we ask and teach our students to ask in a disciplined way how our scholarship is conditioned by its social location and how it serves political functions?"[50] Reception historians therefore have an opportunity to sustain the challenge of liberationist hermeneutics to those engaged in biblical interpretation to take responsibility for the consequences of their research.

It is essential for all those engaged in biblical exegesis to pay close attention to those studies of biblical reception history that highlight how biblical texts have been used in the past—and continue to be used in the present—to legitimate oppressive political structures or justify humanitarian atrocities. How people interpret the Bible and how others "inherit" and "actualize" those interpretations are not just a quaint pastime for biblical scholars. Particularly in the post-Christian, postmodern cultures in the West, it may be easy for people to fall into the trap of believing that the Old Testament is irrelevant to modern society.

Stephen Haynes has written a powerful and sobering study of the history of American interpretation of Noah's curse of his son Ham in Genesis 9, examining how it came to be used to justify American slavery and segregation. He concludes:

> This book ... provides voluminous evidence that, whatever else may be said about the history and dynamics of American racism, its stubborn links with religion in general and scriptural traditions in particular should not be underestimated or approached simplistically. Given the apparent permanence of racism in the United States, the American revival of religion and spirituality, and the unlikely survival of biblical images in an otherwise secularized culture, it would be naive indeed to assume that the American mind has become resistant to racist readings of the Bible with the advent of a new millennium. If cultural expressions of these readings are subtler than in the past, the task of the scholar becomes that much more challenging—not to mention crucial.[51]

More recently, Katie Edwards, author of *Admen and Eve* (2012),[52] has pioneered studies into the role of the Bible in contemporary advertising and consumerism. She highlights the reciprocal process of how images can both reflect and direct a culture's ideals and ideas of gender roles. For example, a number of perfume advertisements for women transform the figure of Eve into an icon of female sexual and consumer power, appealing to women in the "postfeminist" era and influencing how women and men see themselves and one another. Biblical reception history is well placed to add a vital corrective to the ivory-towered enterprise of white, male, Western scholarship, to kindle awareness not only of the interpretations or readings we may have unconsciously accepted but also of the transformative potential of our own interpretations and readings.

There is currently an organization dedicated to supporting the development of contemporary interpretations of Scripture, the Institute for Contemporary Midrash in Philadelphia. Its belief in the social and cultural benefits of this enterprise was explicitly stated on its website:

> The Bible is one of the most important underpinnings of Western language and culture. It is an invisible glue that holds our diverse civilization

together, but, sadly, a glue that is fast deteriorating through disuse. At the same time, a fundamentalist grip on the religious imagination is capitalizing on ignorance of biblical text to promote regressive agendas. Conversely, the midrashic process holds the potential to re-animate biblical text for this generation, to restore ownership of religious imagination to individuals, and to provide healing and meaning in an often fragmented society.[53]

This testifies to the potential for biblical reception and interpretation to have a profoundly positive impact on society and culture, a necessary note of hope in the history of abuses of the biblical texts at the service of oppressive ideologies.

NOTES

1. E.g., Emma Mason, "Elihu's Spiritual Sensation: William Blake's *Illustrations of the Book of Job*," in M. Lieb, E. Mason, and J. Roberts, eds., *The Oxford Handbook of the Reception History of the Bible* (Oxford: Oxford University Press, 2011), pp. 460–75; David M. Goldenberg, *The Curse of Ham: Race and Slavery in Early Judaism, Christianity, and Islam* (Princeton, N.J.: Princeton University Press, 2003); Katie Edwards, *Admen and Eve: The Bible in Contemporary Advertising*, Bible in the Modern World 48 (Sheffield: Sheffield Phoenix Press, 2012).

2. Thomas Mann, "Freud und die Zukunft," in *Gesammelte Werke* (Frankfurt am Main: Fischer, 1960), p. 497, cited in Michael Fishbane, *Biblical Interpretation in Ancient Israel* (Oxford: Oxford University Press, 1985), p. 1.

3. Hans Robert Jauss, *Toward an Aesthetic of Reception, Theory and History of Literature*, vol. 2, Timothy Bahti, trans. (Minneapolis: Minnesota Press, 1982).

4. Hans-Georg Gadamer, *Truth and Method*, J. Weinsheimer and D. G. Marshall, trans. (New York: Sheed and Ward, 1989), from *Wahrheit und Methode* (Tübingen: Mohr, 1960); Hans Robert Jauss, "Literary History as a Challenge to Literary Theory," *New Literary History* 1 (1970): pp. 7–37, trans. of chaps. V–XII of *Literaturgeschichte als Provokation der Literaturwissenschaft*, Konstanzer Universitätsreden 3 (Constance: Druckerei und Verlagsanstalt Konstanz Universitätsverlag, 1967).

5. Jauss, "Literary History as a Challenge to Literary Theory."

6. Mark Knight, "*Wirkungsgeschichte*, Reception History, Reception Theory," *Journal for the Study of the New Testament* 33, no. 2 (2010): p. 141.

7. See http://eu.wiley.com/WileyCDA/Section/id-398210.html (accessed September 4, 2014).

8. Gerhard Ebeling, *Kirchengeschichte als Geschichte der Auslegung der heiligen Schrift* (Tübingen: Mohr, 1947).

9. Paul M. Joyce and Diana Lipton, *Lamentations through the Centuries*, Wiley-Blackwell Bible Commentaries (Chichester: Wiley-Blackwell, 2013), p. 11.

10. Wilfred Cantwell Smith, "The Study of Religion and the Study of the Bible," *Journal of the American Academy of Religion* 39, no. 2 (1971): pp. 131–40, at p. 134.

11. E.g., Jeremy Cohen, *"Be Fertile and Increase; Fill the Earth and Master It" (Gen 1.28). The Ancient and Medieval Career of a Biblical Text* (Ithaca, N.Y.: Cornell University Press, 1989); Yvonne Sherwood, *A Biblical Text and Its Afterlives: The Survival of Jonah in Western Culture* (Cambridge: Cambridge University Press, 2000).

12. J. Cheryl Exum, "Toward a Genuine Dialogue between the Bible and Art," in M. Nissinen, ed., *Congress Volume Helsinki 2010* (Leiden: Brill, 2012), pp. 473–503, at p. 501.

13. Joyce and Lipton, *Lamentations through the Centuries*, p. 18.

14. Jonathan Roberts, "Introduction," in M. Lieb, E. Mason, and J. Roberts, eds., *The Oxford Handbook of the Reception History of the Bible* (Oxford: Oxford University Press, 2011), pp. 7–8.

15. Joyce and Lipton, *Lamentations through the Centuries*, p. 19.

16. Gadamer, *Truth and Method*, pp. 360–61.

17. Mary Callaway, "What's the Point of Reception History?" (paper presented at the Society of Biblical Literature Annual Meeting, San Antonio, 2004).

18. Timothy Beal, "Reception History and Beyond: Toward the Cultural History of Scriptures," *Biblical Interpretation* 19 (2011): pp. 357–73.

19. Ibid., p. 370.

20. Exum, "Toward a Genuine Dialogue between the Bible and Art," p. 474.

21. Beal, "Reception History and Beyond," p. 367.

22. Ibid., p. 370.

23. Brennan Breed, *Nomadic Text: A Theory of Biblical Reception History*, Indiana Series in Biblical Literature (Bloomington: Indiana University Press, 2014).

24. See, e.g., Katharine J. Dell and Will Kynes, eds., *Reading Job Intertextually*, Library of Hebrew Bible/Old Testament Studies (New York: Bloomsbury, 2013).

25. Yair Zakovitch, "Inner-Biblical Interpretation," in Ron Hendel, ed., *Reading Genesis: Ten Methods* (Cambridge: Cambridge University Press, 2010), pp. 92–118, at p. 99.

26. Ruth Mellinkoff, *The Horned Moses in Medieval Art and Thought* (Berkeley and Los Angeles: University of California Press, 1970), p. 139.

27. Fishbane, *Biblical Interpretation in Ancient Israel*.

28. Ibid., pp. 281–82.

29. Andrew Chester, "Citing the Old Testament," in Don A. Carson and Hugh G. M. Williamson, eds., *It Is Written: Scripture Citing Scripture; Essays in Honour of Barnabas Lindars* (Cambridge: Cambridge University Press, 1988), pp. 141–69, at pp. 149–50.

30. Philip Alexander, "Retelling the Old Testament," in Carson and Williamson, *It Is Written*, pp. 99–121, at p. 100.

31. Cf. Molly Zahn, *Rethinking Rewritten Scripture: Composition and Exegesis in the 4QReworked Pentateuch Manuscripts* (Leiden: Brill, 2011).

32. Douglas J. Moo, *The Old Testament in the Gospel Passion Narratives* (Sheffield: Almond Press, 1983), p. 394.

33. I. Howard Marshall, "An Assessment of Recent Developments," in Carson and Williamson, *It Is Written*, pp. 1–21, at p. 10.

34. E.g., Jeffrey Sposato, *The Price of Assimilation: Felix Mendelssohn and the Nineteenth-Century Anti-Semitic Tradition* (Oxford: Oxford University Press, 2008).

35. James Oestreich, "Hallelujah Indeed: Debating Handel's Anti-Semitism," *New York Times*, April 23, 2007.

36. Fishbane, *Biblical Interpretation in Ancient Israel*, p. 3.

37. Daniel Boyarin, *Intertextuality and the Reading of Midrash* (Bloomington: Indiana University Press, 1990), p. 128.

38. Ibid., p. 40.

39. Helen Leneman, "Ruth and Boaz Love Duets as Examples of Musical Midrash," *Lectio Difficilior* 1 (2006), http://www.lectio.unibe.ch/06_1/leneman_love_duets.htm.

40. This culminated in a volume of essays: G. Hartman and S. Budick, eds., *Midrash and Literature* (New Haven, Conn.: Yale University Press, 1986).

41. Boyarin, *Intertextuality and the Reading of Midrash*, p. xii.

42. Maimonides, *Guide of the Perplexed*, III, 43, cited in ibid., p. 1.

43. Lesleigh Cushing Stahlberg, *Sustaining Fictions: Intertextuality, Midrash, Translation, and the Literary Afterlife of the Bible* (New York: T&T Clark, 2008).

44. Lynn R. Huber and Dan W. Clanton Jr., "Introduction: Teaching the Bible with Art," in M. Roncase and P. Gray, eds., *Teaching the Bible through Popular Culture and the Arts* (Atlanta: Society of Biblical Literature, 2007), p. 179.

45. Niall Stokes, *U2: Into the Heart: The Stories behind Every Song* (Boston: Thunder's Mouth, 2005), p. 68.

46. Stahlberg, *Sustaining Fictions*, p. 140.

47. Wilfred Owen, *The Poems of Wilfred Owen*, Jon Stallworthy, ed. (London: Chatto and Windus, 1990), p. 151.

48. Exum, "Toward a Genuine Dialogue between the Bible and Art," pp. 475–76.

49. Elisabeth Schüssler Fiorenza, "The Ethics of Biblical Interpretation," *Journal of Biblical Literature* 107, no. 1 (1988): pp. 3–17, at p. 9.

50. Ibid., p. 10.

51. Stephen Haynes, *Noah's Curse: The Justification of American Slavery* (Oxford: Oxford University Press, 2002), p. 222.

52. Edwards, *Admen and Eve*.

53. P. Campbell, *Spirituality in Young Adult Literature: The Last Taboo* (London: Rowman and Littlefield, 2015), p. 19.

ANNOTATED BIBLIOGRAPHY

For a basic introduction to the methodological questions raised by reception theory in biblical studies, see David P. Parris, *Reception Theory and Biblical Hermeneutics*, Princeton Theological Monograph Series 107 (Eugene, Ore.: Pickwick, 2009); and Emma England and William J. Lyons, eds., *Reception History and Biblical Studies: Theory and Practice*, Library of Hebrew Bible/Old Testament Studies 605 (London: Bloomsbury, 2015). For a clear and concise analysis of Gadamer's and Jauss's contributions, see Mark Knight, "*Wirkungsgeschichte*, Reception History,

Reception Theory," *Journal for the Study of the New Testament* 33, no. 2 (2010): pp. 137–46.

Dale C. Allison Jr., Christine Helmer, Choon-Leong Seow, Hermann Spieckermann, Barry Dov Walfish, and Eric Ziolkowski, eds., *Encyclopedia of the Bible and Its Reception* (Berlin: Walter de Gruyter, 2010–), a projected thirty-volume series, is a reference work on all aspects of reception of the Bible from an interreligious perspective. For the reception history of individual biblical texts, see the Blackwell Bible Commentaries series. For early biblical interpretation, see Matthias Henze, ed., *A Companion to Biblical Interpretation in Early Judaism* (Grand Rapids, Mich.: William B. Eerdmans, 2012); James L. Kugel and R. A. Grier, *Early Biblical Interpretation* (Philadelphia: Westminster Press, 1986). Some recent examples of liberationist approaches to biblical reception can be found in M. Lieb, E. Mason, and J. Roberts, eds., *The Oxford Handbook of the Reception History of the Bible* (Oxford: Oxford University Press, 2011); Katherine Low, *The Bible, Gender and Reception History: The Case of Job's Wife* (London: T&T Clark, 2013). The following collection provides an orientation through worked examples to some of the issues raised by reception in different artistic media: J. Cheryl Exum, ed., *Retellings: The Bible in Literature, Music, Art and Film* (Leiden: Brill, 2007). For recent approaches to the reception history of biblical and other sacred texts, see the online journal *Relegere: Studies in Religion and Reception* (https://relegere.org/relegere).

18

Historical-Critical Inquiry

Christoph Bultmann

W hat questions moved Robert Bellarmine (1542–1621) when, more than four hundred years ago, he set out on his career as an academic theologian in the Roman Catholic Church? Rather than presenting a comprehensive narrative of scholarly progress or introducing recent explications of historical criticism (see, e.g., Barton, Collins, Sparks), this chapter is designed to invite thoughts on the merits and deficiencies of historical-critical inquiry into the biblical tradition. Historical-critical inquiry has never dominated the reception history of the Bible in the modern, post-Wittenberg, post-Geneva, and post-Trent period but has always been just one strand of reading and exploring biblical texts that ran parallel to several other strands of liturgical, homiletic, pastoral, devotional, applicative, imaginative readings. Even today it can safely be claimed that a biblical text such as Psalm 105 informs the general understanding of the history of Israel, and the history of God's revelation in Israel, in a much more influential way than any critical textbook on the history of monarchical and postmonarchical (Israel and) Judah in its Near Eastern territorial, political, social, and cultural context, and this applies equally to readers in Judaism and in Christianity, to readers with a religious orientation and readers with a secular orientation, and to those who produce works of art and those who produce pieces of journalism. Thus while historical-critical inquiry aims at knowledge and understanding, other ways of relating to the biblical tradition aim at edification and ideology. The question of how the one should be related to the other is a matter of negotiation, and scholarly interest in historical-critical inquiry does not normally hold a particularly strong position in this controversy.

One of the questions that had moved Bellarmine at the start of his career is set out in the preface to his small book on the "Writers of the Church," *De scriptoribus ecclesiasticis*, which was published in Rome in 1613 and soon went through many further editions. Biblical authors of the Hebrew Bible (Old Testament) as well as the New Testament were perceived by Bellarmine as belonging to the same class of writers as later Christian theologians, namely, as *scriptores ecclesiastici*, and it is worth trying to see what kind of historical sense can be discovered behind his project—which effectively looks more like an annotated library catalog. In his preface, Bellarmine states:

> About 40 years ago, when I prepared myself for teaching sacred theology at university [*ad sacram theologiam in scholis explicandam*], I applied myself carefully [*non indiligenter*] to the study of the old writers in order to imbibe their teaching [*doctrina*] as well as to distinguish their authentic and genuine works from forged and spurious ones. Therefore I wrote a booklet about the Writers of the Church and added my judgment stating which of their works were certain, which were doubtful, and which were evidently spurious. (1617:a ij; all translations are mine unless otherwise noted)

About the year 1569, when he had moved to the University of Leuven, young Bellarmine's interest was clearly a historical interest: there is an awareness that in the course of history the transmission of texts is subject to developments through which—for whatever reasons—the authority of great writers of the past may be used to propound and assert teachings that originated in other contexts. The critical reader starts to "doubt" the ascription of a certain text to a particular writer and seeks to assign such texts their proper place in the tradition. There seems to be an assumption that on hermeneutical grounds a correct elucidation of the origin of a text matters for the interpretation of that text.

Bellarmine goes on to explain his differentiation between "Writers of the Church" and writers in the wider cultural context of the church. Thus he states:

> My intention in this book was not to review in a catalog all writers altogether but only those who in some way treat of ecclesiastical themes [*de rebus ecclesiasticis*]. Therefore all pagan authors [*scriptores ethnici*] and

those who treat of common things only or of most respectable, but political and human concerns [*de honestissimis quidem, sed politicis et humanis*], such as are the authors who discuss civil law, philosophers, medical doctors, orators, poets, historians, mathematicians, will find no place in this catalog. (1617:a ij^v)

Again one can recognize a kind of historical sense in this statement since Bellarmine is aware of the cultural dynamics in law and literature and philosophy and science (mathematics and medicine), which, starting from Greek and Roman antiquity, had given rise to a vast number of works that could also become the subject of critical inquiry. While matters of faith or "ecclesiastical themes" are considered a distinctive area of study, it is obvious that they belong in some interdisciplinary intellectual context. In the academic world of Bellarmine's time this context had its specific institutional location in the faculties of philosophy, of law, and of medicine, and most theologians would have had some background in the study of the liberal arts (*artes liberales*), where many of those writers who are excluded from Bellarmine's catalog of *scriptores* played their role.

For practical reasons Bellarmine limits his catalog to the time up to 1500 (generously including some writers from around 1500) since his historical bibliographical investigations did not need to include the work of contemporary scholars and also because in this way a nice symmetry can be constructed of writers before and after the time of Jesus of Nazareth: "Finally not all writers of the church whose books are available will be listed in my catalog but only those who flourished to the praise of ecclesiastical wisdom [*sapientiae ecclesiasticae laude*] from the year 1500 before the coming of Christ until the year of the Lord 1500, i.e., from Moses as the first writer of the church up to our age" (1617:a ij^v–iij). In historical terms, Bellarmine conceives of a continuous tradition of the church that, as far as literary history is concerned, started from Moses. As he will be arguing in his discussion of the book of Job, the book of Job cannot have been written by Job, because for him Job had lived prior to Moses's time and would—against all church tradition—have to be considered the first writer if he was considered the author of the book that bears his name. In Bellarmine's historical imagination Moses can confidently be regarded as the most original writer:

Moses, the most holy and most ancient prophet and the first among the writers of the church was born, according to my calculation, in the year 2403 from the beginning of the world [*ab initio mundi*]. He lived 120 years. In his 80th year, at the command of God, he took over the supremacy over the Hebrews, i.e., in the year of the world 2483. He died in the year of the world 2523. He wrote the Pentateuch.... From these books it can be discerned that Moses was a most learned man, not just in all the wisdom of the Egyptians, as is claimed by St Stephen in Acts 7, but also in the art of historiography, of poetry, of oratory, of moral philosophy and of theology. (1617:1)

While it would have been inconceivable for Bellarmine not to accept the idea in Acts 7:22 that Moses "was instructed in all the wisdom of the Egyptians," he also offers his own corroborative arguments to support this ideal image of Moses. As to historiography, he provides the following reason: "He wrote about the history, genealogies and actions of the patriarchs from the foundation of the world [*ab orbe condito*] until the exodus of the sons of Israel from Egypt, i.e., from the beginning of time [*ab initio temporum*] until the year 2483 and even until his death, i.e., until the year 2523." He adds the critical but already traditional comment: "However, what is written in the concluding chapter of Deuteronomy [about the time] after Moses himself had died, are additions either by Joshua or by Ezra or by some other prophet" (1617:1–2). As to poetry, Bellarmine refers to Exod. 15 and Deut. 32; as to oratory, he mentions the speech that Moses wrote in the name of Judah in Gen. 44, Moses's address to God in Num. 14, and generally his admonitions and reprimands of his people. Moral philosophy can be detected in the laws of the Torah, and theological mysteries are predominantly enshrined in the images of the ark of the covenant, the priestly garments, and the Tabernacle, for which reading Bellarmine refers to the allegorical interpretations of Philo of Alexandria (ca. 20 BCE–45 CE).

Bellarmine's historical project offers an imposing example of historical inquiry under the conditions of the intellectual culture of his time. The biblical tradition is regarded as the reliable key to universal history, and the narrative construct of a primeval and patriarchal period as well as a foundational period of Israel's history after the escape from some tyrannical pharaoh in Egypt is accepted as the historiographical achievement of Moses the prophet. Biblical paraphrase means the production of historical knowledge. Along this line of thinking all biblical writers are assigned their place in history according to biblical information, and the book concludes with a brief "chronology from the foundation of the world up to our time." Hermeneutically, the project builds on a concept of the "church" that takes its course from the time of the creation and the first patriarchs to the present and beyond into the future and is in some way related to surrounding cultures.

Another example of historical inquiry is the survey of universal history that was compiled by the reformed scholar Louis Cappel (1585–1658) and published in 1658 as part of the introductory volume to the London Polyglott Bible edited by Brian Walton (1600–1661). Cappel produced a "sacred chronology from the foundation of the world [*a condito mundo*] to its refoundation [*ad eundem reconditum*] through Jesus Christ the Lord, and from then to the final captivity of the Jews under the Romans." His interest is in matters of chronology only since, as he explains in his introduction, the historical events themselves are "sufficiently known and clear to everyone who is familiar with reading the sacred scriptures" (1673:1). Biblical chronology, however, can be investigated and discussed, and Cappel offers, for example, the year 2008 from the creation of the world as the year of Abraham's birth—where Bellarmine has the year 1978—and the year 3125 from the creation of the world as the year of Solomon's death—where Bellarmine has the year 2999. The year of Noah's flood—1656 from the creation of the world—is still the same in both writers.

What need to be considered even more than such questions of chronology are central aspects of the hermeneutical concept that go beyond historical ideas about universal history, the origin and history of the church, and the character of the Mosaic writings as the most ancient historical source. In Bellarmine's *De scriptoribus ecclesiasticis* an indication of basic hermeneutical assumptions can be found, for example, in his entry on Isaiah: "He was a noble man [*vir nobilis*], of the tribe of Judah, and a rhetorically brilliant man [*facundissimus*], as anyone can see from his book. He wrote about the coming of Christ, his birth by the virgin, his life, message [*praedicatio*], reign, miracles, suffering, burial, and his further mysteries, so that he seems to have been an evangelist rather than a prophet" (1617:13–14). Reference could also be made to a treatise by

Bellarmine on the Divine Word (in his *Disputationes*, vol. 1 [1587]). However, in the present context a Lutheran author will be referred to who in his turn wrote a similar treatise partly in response to Bellarmine. This is Salomon Glassius (1593–1656), who in 1623 published the first two parts of a massive *Philologia Sacra*, which remained in print for more than a hundred years.

Glassius's work is characterized not just by his impressive philological and literary-critical ambitions but also by his careful differentiation of layers of meaning that would allow a Christian theologian to consider the Hebrew Bible/Old Testament as a witness to Christ. In the introduction to his treatise on defining (*dignoscere*) and exploring (*eruere*) the meaning of the Bible, Glassius starts from the definition: "The meaning of Sacred Scripture is nothing but what God who is the author of the scriptures presents in the scriptures and through the scriptures as through a most explicit expression of the divine mind for human readers to learn [*cognoscere*] and understand [*intelligere*]" ([1623] 1743:347). This understanding of the Bible is further specified in the definition: "The meaning of Sacred Scripture is a double [*duplex*] meaning: the literal sense and the spiritual or mystical sense" (Glassius [1623] 1743:348). However, Glassius does not want to open the gates for any allegorical reading of biblical texts but, rather, to make space for the use that New Testament writers made of Old Testament texts. Thus he states:

> We are speaking of scripture in general and saying that not in all, but in some places and texts, which scripture itself identifies as if pointing with an outstretched finger, it must not only be explained literally, but in addition to the literal sense that is explored in the words also admits a mystical sense, i.e., we are saying that the Holy Spirit itself intends some mystery and spiritual idea [*res spiritualis*] in such a text—which first has to be literally understood and explained—and makes clear that this too must be explored. ([1623] 1743:349)

Wherever events in Old Testament history carry this extra layer of meaning, this is the allegorical sense; wherever individual facts or prophetic visions carry this spiritual layer, this is the typical sense; and wherever fictional narratives carry this layer, this is the figurative or metaphorical (parabolic) sense (Glassius [1623] 1743:406). To explore this spiritual layer of the texts following the guidance of the New Testament is not just about studying a form of accommodation of these texts, as Glassius ([1623] 1743:350) explains with reference, for example, to Moses's saving action in Num. 21:8–9 and the response to it in John 3:14–15.

Notwithstanding his extensive elaboration of the question of a spiritual sense, Glassius also provides straightforward rules for investigating the teachings of the biblical texts. These include the question of the speaker, his motivation, and his rhetoric as well as the questions of time and place. Thus he comments, "Of great consequence for the genuine understanding [*genuina intelligentia*] of scripture is this circumstance [of the temporal conditions]. For God dealt with human beings differently at different times and revealed himself to them sometimes in a more hidden [*obscurius*], sometimes in a more open way [*evidentius*]" ([1623] 1743:503). While so far the set of criteria refers to the circumstances under which a text emerged, two further criteria to be taken into account are the main thematic thrust of a text (*scopus*) and the question of its central or peripheral status for a certain doctrine (*sedes doctrinae*) (Glassius [1623] 1743:502–3). For a general rule in explaining biblical texts, and especially difficult texts, Glassius refers to a rabbinic saying, "There is no objection to a law of the Torah that will not find its resolution on the wings" [*Nulla est objectio in lege, quae non habeat solutionem in latere*], that is, to understand a difficult passage, the preceding and following texts must be taken into consideration ([1623] 1743:500). Glassius encourages a careful philological and historical study of the Old Testament; however, this is framed by the concept of a spiritual meaning with an absolute focus on Christ.

The authenticity and antiquity of the Mosaic writings are a topic in which also Hugo Grotius (1583–1645) showed an interest when he worked on what for more than a century became the most popular book of Christian apologetics, his *De veritate religionis christianae* (*The Truth of the Christian Religion*) of 1622/29 (expanded 1640). Since miracles play a major role in the apologetic project, Grotius addresses the reliability of the Mosaic writings (bk. 1, sec. 15–16) and asserts three main points. First, he portrays Moses as an incorruptible and, therefore, trustworthy leader; second, he defends the undeniable antiquity of his writings (*indubitata scriptorum Mosis antiquitas*); and third, he presents a view of history according to which letters and laws of ancient Greece, and traditions about primeval history throughout all cultures in the Mediterranean world (*vetustissima apud omnes gentes fama*), are derived from and therefore confirm the Mosaic tradition. A further argument in support of the truth of the Mosaic writings is the idea of a continuous line in Judaism of a firm belief in this tradition. Thus Grotius states:

> If any one should ask, whence it is that the *Jewish* Religion hath taken so deep Root in the Minds of all the *Hebrews*, as never to be plucked out; there can be no other possible Cause assigned or imagined than this; That the present *Jews* received it from their Parents, and they from theirs, and so on, till you come to the Age in which *Moses* and *Joshua* lived; they received, I say, by a certain and uninterrupted Tradition [*certa ac constanti traditione*], the Miracles which were worked as in other Places, so more especially at their coming out of *Aegypt*, in their Journey, and at their Entrance into *Canaan*; of all which, their Ancestors themselves were Witnesses. ([1640] 2012:46; bk. 1, sec. 14; see also bk. 5, sec. 2)

The Mosaic tradition is as significant for Christians as it is for Jews since, as Grotius notes, "Jesus ... taught us [the Christians] to reverence the Writings of *Moses*, and those prophets which followed him" ([1640] 2012:193; bk. 5, sec. 5). However, with Jesus originated a new religious dynamic that resulted in a different law: "Neither will it follow, that because the Law given by *Moses* was good, therefore a better could not be given" (Grotius [1640] 2012:194; bk. 5, sec. 6). On the other hand, the Mosaic law had been limited from the start since it came late in history and was promulgated in one people only:

> Now that Part of the Law, the Necessity of which was taken away by Christ, did not contain in it any thing in its own Nature virtuous; but consisted of things indifferent in themselves, and therefore not unalterable: For if there had been any thing in the Nature of those things, to inforce their Practice, God would have prescribed them to all the World, and not to one People only; and that from the very Beginning, and [not] two thousand Years and more after Mankind had been created. (Grotius [1640] 2012:196; bk. 5, sec. 7)

Thus the historically contingent character of the laws of the Torah becomes an issue for biblical exegesis.

Grotius takes his critical view of the biblical writings further when, in a controversy with the Dutch Calvinist theologian André Rivet (1572–1651) in the 1640s, he puts forward a theory of the prophetic quality of biblical writers that could only be ascribed to a certain number of them. Thus in his first contribution to the controversy he states:

> Doctor Rivet is greatly mistaken when he thinks that all the books of the Old Testament that are in the Hebrew canon were dictated by the Holy Spirit. According to all Jewish teachers Ezra was neither a prophet nor was he endowed with the Holy Spirit. However, his books [Ezra and Nehemiah] and the entire collection of older books that he brought together was approved by the "great synagogue" to which also a number of prophets belonged, although, as Jewish tradition has it, there was some hesitation about the book of Qohelet [Ecclesiastes], but the judgment of those who adopted it prevailed. To whose judgment I willingly subscribe. ([1640] 1972:647b)

Thus in addition to the concept of prophecy, tradition also plays a significant role. In his second contribution Grotius reasserts his view:

> Rightly have I said that not all the books of the Old Testament that are in the Hebrew canon were dictated by the Holy Spirit. I do not deny that they were written by a pious impulse of the mind [*cum pio animi motu*]: and this is what the "great synagogue" concluded, to whose judgment in this matter the Jewish tradition holds on. But there was no need for the historical books [*historiae*] to be dictated by the Holy Spirit: it was sufficient that a scribe had a reliable memory about the things that he had seen himself or that he took great care in transcribing the notes of earlier generations. ([1640] 1972:672b)

Grotius then refers to Maimonides for the view that the notion of "Holy Spirit" can refer either to the divine inspiration of a prophet (*adflatus divinus*) or to the pious impulse (*pius motus*) or some particular motivating force for pronouncing salutary rules of life or in matters of politics or society. In a third contribution the issue is again addressed, and Grotius states:

> That the prophets said what they said and wrote what they were told to write through divine inspiration, Grotius accepts with full heart.... Of

the historical writings and of the moral sentences of the Hebrews he thinks differently. It is sufficient that they were written with a pious mind and in full sincerity and about substantial issues. What books of this kind were approved by the Synagogue, are canonical books for the Jews. What books of this kind were approved by the Church, are canonical books for the Christians. ([1640] 1972:722b–723a)

In the context of desperate attempts to resolve the disturbing conflicts between the post-Reformation churches in Europe, Grotius thus insists on a debate about scripture and ecclesiastical traditions and emphasizes the significance of the tradition in juxtaposition to genuine prophecy.

As a philosopher of religion Grotius also includes a section on the basic principles of religion in his book on natural law, *The Rights of War and Peace* of 1625. In this context he claims that there are only four "fundamental principles" that characterize religion in general and that it is only this elementary religion that is relevant with regard to the "great society of mankind in general" ([1625] 2005:1032, 1031). Grotius distinguishes between the "true religion which has been common to all ages" ([1625] 2005:1032) and religions that, like Judaism and Christianity, are built on additional traditions. The four principles—that is, the existence and unity of God, the invisible nature of God, God's "knowledge and care of the affairs, even of the thoughts," of human beings, and the world as being created by God—are "common to all ages" and go back to a tradition that is "derived ... from the very first men in the world, and has never been solidly confuted," while at the same time they can also be "demonstrated by arguments drawn from nature" (Grotius [1625] 2005:1032–35). In the biblical tradition, these principles are enshrined, Grotius ([1625] 2005:1032) claims, in the Decalogue in Exod. 20 and Deut. 5. As has already been pointed out above, in addition to these basic notions the Torah can be seen as a law of God that was specifically "delivered to a nation" (Grotius [1625] 2005:1038). In the same manner, the "truth of the Christian religion, in those particulars which are additional to natural and primitive religion," is accessible only through some form of historical belief and cannot be "evidenced by mere natural arguments" (Grotius [1625] 2005:1041). Thus Grotius explains that this kind of religious truth "depends upon the history we have of Christ's resurrection, and the miracles performed by him and his apostles, which have been confirmed by unexceptionable testimonies, but many ages since, so that the question now is of matters of fact, and those of a very ancient date; for which reason this doctrine cannot so easily gain belief, and procure men's assent upon the first promulgation of it, without the inward assistance of God's grace" ([1625] 2005:1041). The distinction between natural and revealed religion, between a philosophical universal and a particular historical religion, also represents a challenge for biblical studies since it invites investigations of what can be considered to be expressions of natural religion in the biblical writings (in addition to the Decalogue, Grotius refers to Heb. 11:6) and what belongs to those "additional" elements that do not directly have an impact on the "universal society of mankind." Although in his *De veritate religionis christianae* Grotius attempts a full demonstration of the truth of the particular Christian religion, not least building on the miracles in the narrative tradition, it becomes clear that biblical interpretation does not have priority over the philosophy of religion.

In the same constellation of religious discourse Herbert of Cherbury (1583–1648) contributed a short treatise and wrote about the idea of some itinerant philosopher of religion who tries to make sense of the religious conflicts in Europe and the plurality of religions more generally. In Herbert's *De religione laici* of 1645, this "layperson" comes to the conclusion that there are a number of religious truths that are truly universal and which, at the same time, are also the point of convergence for the biblical tradition. Against the background of a philosophical theory about such universal truths, it is essential, Herbert claims, "to inquire very thoroughly what really sounds the pure and uncontested word of God in the sacred scriptures" or "what in the sacred books is, as it were, truly the own word of God and what is, moreover, truly necessary for salvation" ([1645] 1966:135). The universal religious truths—love and fear of God, love of one's neighbor, repentance, the hope of a future life— are "illustrated, signified, and confirmed" (Herbert of Cherbury [1645] 1966:135) by all those particular aspects that offer themselves to a historical faith (*fides circa praeterita*) in the biblical tradition. Not even the most foolish priest or preacher (*ineptissimus sacerdos*) would claim that "whatever is contained in sacred scripture is proclaimed with an equal authority" (Herbert of Cherbury [1645] 1966:135). The ultimate purpose of Scripture is the orientation of the believer toward universal religious truths.

A well-known attitude toward the Hebrew scriptures is adopted by Thomas Hobbes (1588–1679), who, on the one hand, represents the conventional view of the historical significance of the narratives while, on the other hand, is not bound to a doctrinal view of the Mosaic Torah. Thus he can expand the traditional view according to which the notices about the death of Moses were added by some writer other than Moses and point out that remarks such as in Gen. 12:6 and Num. 21:14 are post-Mosaic elements in the Torah. However, since his main interest is in the question of political authority, the text that matters most to him is Deut. 17:14–18, and for this he can refer to Deut. 31:9 and 31:24–26 as self-referential texts in the book of Deuteronomy about some collection of revealed laws that can be identified as Deut. 11–27. Thus he states: "It is ... sufficiently evident, that the five Books of *Moses* were written after his time, though how long after it be not so manifest. But though *Moses* did not compile those Books entirely, and in the form we have them; yet he wrote all that which he is there said to have written" ([1651] 1991:262). Deut. 11–27 is linked by Hobbes with Deut. 17:18, 31:25–26, and 2 Kings 22:8–10 and regarded as a text that goes directly back to Moses. Hobbes does not pursue any further questions about the literary history of the Pentateuch, and since he ([1651] 1991:293–95, 324–29) adopts a theory of the continuous succession of high priests as "supreme" prophets after the death of Moses, not much irritation could have arisen about the authoritative nature of the texts in the Pentateuch that were written at some later time by whatever scribal schools under the supervision of the high priests. For methodological guidance, Hobbes suggests the following principle:

> Who were the originall writers of the severall Books of Holy Scripture, has not been made evident by any sufficient testimony of other History, (which is the only proof of matter of fact); nor can be by any arguments of naturall Reason: for Reason serves only to convince the truth (not of fact, but) of consequence. The light therefore that must guide us in this question, must be that which is held out unto us from the Bookes themselves: And this light, though it shew us not the writer of every book, yet

it is not unusefull to give us knowledge of the time, wherein they were written. ([1651] 1991:261)

As far as the laws of the Pentateuch are concerned, Hobbes is aware of the philosophical issue of natural law and therefore differentiates between different grounds for accepting religious laws as laws. Thus he states: "As far as they differ not from the Laws of Nature, there is no doubt, but they are the Law of God, and carry their Authority with them, legible to all men that have the use of naturall reason: but this is no other Authority, then that of all other Morall Doctrine consonant to Reason; the Dictates whereof are Laws, not *made*, but *Eternall*" ([1651] 1991:268, cf. 323). This view is strengthened by the statement in the introduction to part 3 of the *Leviathan*: "We are not to renounce our Senses, and Experience; nor (that which is the undoubted Word of God) our naturall Reason" (Hobbes [1651] 1991:255). The question of the authority of particular "written laws" or "positive commandments" as well as the power "to approve, or disapprove the interpretation" of these laws is closely tied up with Hobbes's discussion of the idea of a "Christian Commonwealth" generally ([1651] 1991:268–69, 323, 326).

Methodological aspects of biblical interpretation are more distinctly discussed in the intellectual circle of Baruch Spinoza (1632–77), where Louis Meyer (1630–81) published a treatise on philosophy as the guide to and standard of understanding biblical texts (*Philosophia scripturae interpres*, 1666) and Spinoza himself published a treatise on countering self-destructive tendencies in doctrinal theology and religious politics (*Tractatus theologico-politicus*, 1670), which includes substantial reflection on biblical hermeneutics (esp. chap. 7: "De interpretatione scripturae"; see Gibert 2010:131–75). A particular strength of the treatise is Spinoza's interest in the philosophy of religion and of human liberty. With regard to the highly contested interpretation of the Bible in Judaism as well as in Christianity, Spinoza, on the one hand, aims at gaining a picture of the historical conditions under which the individual biblical texts, and especially the Pentateuch, were written (chaps. 8–10) and, on the other hand, provides an outline of the history of the "Hebrew republic" (*De republica Hebraeorum*; chaps. 17–19). In critical terms Spinoza accepts the view—which is familiar from Hobbes—that building on Deut. 31:9 only the core of the collection of laws in Deuteronomy can be considered a "book" that goes directly back to Moses (as, for him, does the song of Moses in Deut. 32). In historical terms he develops a theory about a Mosaic constitution and a somewhat problematic succession of high priests after Moses during a first "dominion" (*imperium*), which lasted until the Babylonian conquest of Jerusalem. Legitimate power was then transferred to the Babylonians, only to be retransferred to the high priests at the Second Temple during a second "dominion," which, as Spinoza claims, was merely a shadow of the first (*vix umbra fuit primi*; [1670] 1979:552).

Modern historical-critical inquiry into the Hebrew Bible/Old Testament is distinguished from historical criticism as it has been illustrated with reference to some early modern scholars by two main features. In historical-critical inquiry the biblical time frame and story line as well as the essential orientation of the Old Testament writers toward Jesus Christ (see, e.g., Luke 24:27; John 5:45–47; 2 Cor. 3:7–8) are no longer accepted. While the biblical narrative at Gen. 25:7 has Abraham die at the age of 175 years, at Gen. 50:26 has Joseph die at the age of 110 years, and at Deut. 34:7 has Moses die at the age of 120 years, the implication connected with such numbers of a full chronology from the primeval age to the constitution of Israel as a people living under a theocratic law since the time of Moses began to lose its plausibility. The idea that the biblical tradition was the key to universal history had to be abandoned, and the history of the people of Israel and consequently of the Christian church—or "salvation history"—came to lose its absolute point of origin. As long as Bellarmine's Moses could be regarded as the writer who commanded the true picture of human history, this would confirm in a kind of circular argument the authority of the Mosaic writings and the truth of the religious tradition, Jewish as well as Christian, that is built on those writings. As to the second aspect, the concept of a layer of meaning in the texts of the Hebrew Bible/Old Testament that would directly refer to Jesus Christ gradually came to be abandoned. Since most New Testament texts support the idea of such a specific layer of Christological meaning as well as the corresponding idea of an "obscuring" or "hardening" of the hermeneutical vision of Jewish readers of these texts, abandoning the traditional concept of prediction and prefiguration was at least as difficult a process as allowing history to open up toward a horizon beyond the biblical tradition. However, it needs to be remembered that debates about the relationship between a philosophy of religion and the idea of "natural religion," on the one side, and biblical interpretation and the idea of "revealed religion," on the other, had already been conducted long before the issue of history and more specifically the issue of historicity moved into the focus of interest. Yet the impact of the philosophy of religion on the study of biblical traditions is not easily assessed. Even where a new emphasis on history developed, historical criticism did not necessarily lead to an engagement with that "universality, comparability, and naturalness of religion" (Byrne 1989:53) that was put on the agenda by the philosophers. Historical criticism could simply be regarded as a way to investigate more specifically the "circumstances" of the origin of biblical texts, which would themselves be exempted from philosophical scrutiny.

Only a small selection of historical assumptions gained through historical-critical inquiry into the origin of biblical texts can be mentioned here. The question was pursued further whether Moses himself or, rather, some group or school of scribes was responsible for the complex and composite text of the Pentateuch. While Hobbes at least vaguely suggested the hypothesis that a priestly succession after Moses ought to be taken into account, the philologist and critic Richard Simon (1638–1712) explicitly introduced the concept of a class of scribes that had been established by Moses in analogy to a class of priestly scribes in Egyptian religious and political culture ([1678] 1967:15–16). Moses, for Simon, can be considered the author of the laws but not of the narratives in the Pentateuch. Across the centuries, the scribes would not only record the events of their own time but also revise the accounts of the past through "enlarging or diminishing" older texts (Simon [1678] 1967:18). Since Simon refers for this concept to Isaac Abrabanel (1437–1508), he can also speak of "Abrabanel's principle" for this model for explaining biblical texts, notably the biblical narrative tradition ([1678] 1967:18–19). In other circles the "Mosaic" Pentateuch attracted a specific scholarly interest with regard to the question of what documents Moses might have used for writing the book of Genesis. This approach pointed in the direction of pre-Mosaic texts and traditions and eventually led to the concept of mythological traditions in the Bible.

The Scottish geologist James Hutton (1726–97) is remembered for his statement about the age of the earth: "We see no vestige of a beginning, no prospect of an end" (Laudan 1990:316). Within a cultural context marked by this interpretation of the "history of the earth," it became possible in biblical studies to accept the concept of mythology, familiar from classical studies, as an explanation of biblical primeval history and apocalyptic imagery. From a historical-critical perspective, ideas about the beginning of human history in Adam and Eve's paradise and the unfolding of human civilizations from the "event" of the confusion of language at Babel and along the lines of "genealogies" that could be traced back to the three sons of Noah could no longer be considered to be ideas that offered the key to understanding the origin of humanity at a historical level. The significance of the respective biblical texts was shifted onto a mythological, symbolical level, and what remained as the substance of the tradition at a historical level was the reflection of a scribal culture through which these ideas had been shaped. Historical criticism was acknowledged as a scholarly method of investigating literary texts, while the discipline of archaeology began to develop as a field in its own right. However, the search for some kind of normative first origin or, if not origin, at least paradigmatic foundational period remained an issue in biblical studies even after the concept of historical events in primeval history had been abandoned. Thus assumptions about some patriarchal age, some Mosaic age, the age of some tribal federation in Israel, and the age of some unified royal state with its capital Jerusalem became issues mostly to be discussed from an idealizing perspective rather than on the grounds of a methodologically sound investigation of the sources. The view of Grotius, quoted above, of biblical historians whose writings were built on their recollection of events they had witnessed themselves (*memoria circa res spectatas*) or their care in transcribing older sources (*diligentia in describendis Veterum commentariis*; [1640] 1972:672b) can be said to have prevailed in biblical studies long after the idea of the historicity of the primeval history had been abandoned. No statement can be found about the Bible in tune with the cutting remark, in an essay of 1752, by David Hume (1711–76) concerning the ancient Greek historians: "The first page of Thucydides is ... the commencement of real history. All preceding narrations are so intermixed with fable, that philosophers ought to abandon them, in a great measure, to the embellishment of poets and orators" ([1777] 1985:422). Whatever ideas about sources in the Mosaic writings or a continuous succession of scribes after

Moses had been suggested, the concept of a Mosaic age as the beginning of the Israelite "republic" (in the sense of the Latin *res publica*) or "theocracy," in other words, a political entity governed by the sacred legislation of Moses as the founding figure, remained the dominant concept. Biblical scholars continued to struggle with supposedly historical traditions about periods prior to the time of the Egyptian pharaoh Shishak (Sheshonq I, ruled ca. 946–924 BCE), whose name is the first name of a pharaoh to be mentioned in the Hebrew Bible (1 Kings 11:40, 14:25).

The argument that Hobbes, as quoted above, used with regard to the Mosaic writings, namely, that Moses "wrote all that which he is there [sc., in the Pentateuch] said to have written," was no longer accepted when Wilhelm Martin Leberecht de Wette (1780–1849) suggested the historical hypothesis that the collection of ritual (and other) laws in Deuteronomy could be identified as the "book of the law" that Hilkiah, high priest at the Temple in Jerusalem during the reign of King Josiah (639–609 BCE), is reported to have sent to the king in order to inspire a cultic reform in Judah (2 Kings 22–23). For de Wette ([1806/7] 1971:265–99), this law code had indeed been written at about the time of its "discovery," since the idea of the Temple in Jerusalem as the only sanctuary in Judah and of Passover as a religious festival at the Temple (Deut. 16:1–8; 2 Kings 23:21–23—without considering the conceivably legendary character even of this tradition) could not be traced back to a period prior to Josiah. The rhetoric of Deuteronomy (as well as other parts of the Pentateuch) that makes Moses the authoritative speaker is classified by de Wette as "legal-historical fiction" and thus a literary device of the scribes ([1806/7] 1971:291). De Wette's historical hypothesis had the potential to inspire a new appreciation of the religious, and more specifically priestly, culture of Judah around 600 BCE; however, rather than adopting this critical perspective on the priesthood and moving beyond what de Wette called "the long night of uncritical trust in traditions" (1817: §164; the 1843 translation builds on the revised fifth edition of 1840), a discourse about "early" and "late" texts and traditions developed, and the collection of laws in Deuteronomy was regarded as "late." For the priesthood at the Temple in Jerusalem during the Persian and Ptolemaic periods (ca. 520–200 BCE) to be considered a major factor of the religious history of Israel, more critical analyses of the texts of the Hebrew Bible were required.

While for Hobbes the "high priests" could be seen as "successors" of Moses in a historical sense ([1651] 1991:267, 328–29), the priests at the Second Temple in Jerusalem eventually came to be understood as a priesthood that itself constructed an ideal foundational period under Moses (and Aaron)—which in turn was then linked to the creation of the world when the Sabbath was instituted by a divine command (Gen. 2:2–3; Exod. 20:8–11). The development of this change of perspective was decisively advanced by Abraham Kuenen (1828–91) and Julius Wellhausen (1844–1918). Wellhausen removed the idea of a "theocracy" from the scholarly understanding of the religious history of Israel and Judah prior to the destruction of the Temple in Jerusalem by the Babylonians in 587 BCE and applied this idea to the religious culture that had its center at the Second Temple from 515 BCE. The question of whether the word *theocracy* is itself an appropriate term for a historical-critical description and explanation of religious ritual and religious doctrine during that time remains to be discussed, especially since most of the psalms must be dated to this period as well.

A line of research that runs parallel to the investigation of priestly concepts as they are documented in the Pentateuch focuses on the prophetic traditions. The typical forms of the reception of Old Testament prophecy in the New Testament came to be analyzed as a theological discourse in their own right, so that the prophetic texts from the religious culture of (Israel and) Judah could be related more directly to the times of the prophets and their followers. Only one significant step in the historical-critical reading of the prophetic sayings and compositions in the Hebrew Bible can be mentioned in the present context. This is the claim that where the name of the Persian king and conqueror Cyrus II (ruled 559–530 BCE) is mentioned in Isa. 45:1, this is an indication that the prophetic speaker and his original audience were contemporary with (or later than) this political figure. The occurrence of the name in the poetic prophetic utterance is no less strong an argument than is the reference to King Darius I (ruled 522–486 BCE) in the superscription of Hag. 1:1. Isa. 40–55 or, rather, 40–66 were no longer attributed to the rhetorical brilliance (*facunditas*) of Isaiah of Jerusalem but, rather, to an anonymous speaker who received the designation "Deutero-Isaiah" and was claimed to have lived among a group of Judaean exiles in Babylonia. The suggestion was first promoted by Johann Gottfried Eichhorn (1752–

1827) and came to inspire further research into the composite nature of the prophetic books in accordance with the critical differentiation between what is "predicted" in a prophetic saying and what is "presupposed" in it (de Wette 1817/1843: §208a.2). While the idea of prophecy—conceptually surprising—is even anchored in the Hebrew Bible in scribal presentations of Abraham (Gen. 20:7) and of Moses (Deut. 34:10) as "prophets," the editorial decision of the scribes who turned collections of prophetic sayings into books with a superscription and placed each respective prophet in his historical context (Isa. 1:1; Jer. 1:1–3; Ezek. 1:1; etc.) made it generally less controversial to embark on a historical-critical study of the prophetic tradition than of the priestly tradition.

In terms of literary criticism the transition between "prophecy" and "poetry" seems to be rather obvious, so that critical inquiry into prophecy to a certain extent means inquiry into religious poetry. In addition, the immediately poetic books of the Hebrew Bible also became the subject of historical-critical study. Again one example only can be mentioned here: in Bellarmine's day the book of Job could be considered a pre-Mosaic or indeed an early Mosaic composition, since it contains no references or allusions to the religious rituals that are specified in the laws of the Pentateuch. This idea of the antiquity of Job still informed the appreciation of the book by Robert Lowth (1710–87) and Johann Gottfried Herder (1744–1803) in their discussions of the "sublime" and "emotive" character of its religious poetry. According to de Wette, the book of Job belongs in the "later period of Hebrew literature"; however, while in 1817 he assigned the book to the age of the "Babylonian exile," he later came to assume that Jeremiah "had probably read the book" and suggests the "age of Judah in decline" as the time of its origin (1817/1843: §291). According to Samuel R. Driver (1846–1914), the book dates from a time when "a mature stage of literary culture" had been reached and should be given a date "more or less contemporary" with Deutero-Isaiah (1894:407–8). In contemporary biblical studies the book of Job, like the book of Qohelet (Ecclesiastes), is normally attributed to some intellectual constellation at a time during the Second Temple period when Israelite wisdom schools had started to integrate skeptical views of human understanding.

In the preface to the first edition of his comprehensive critical *Introduction to the Old Testament* of 1817, de Wette states: "The highest objective which the historical criticism of the Bible strives to reach and towards which it is at least supposed to show the way is an understanding of the phenomena of the biblical literature in their authentic historical setting and characteristics [*in ihren echt geschichtlichen Verhältnissen und Eigentümlichkeiten*]" (1817:VI/1843:V). The "scholarly character" of the discipline in which this objective is pursued is explained thus: "The Bible is being considered as a historical phenomenon in one and the same series with other such phenomena and subjected to the laws of historical investigation" (de Wette 1817/1843: §4). This scholarly interest, however, could not be developed without controversy; de Wette notes that "historical criticism" was confronted with and contested by "the spirit of uncritical naivity" (*der Geist der Unkritik*; 1817/1843: §6) or by "the spirit of doctrinal reservations" (*der Geist dogmatischer Befangenheit*; 1844: §6). The same experience has continued to be characteristic of scholarly debates across the generations, since on logical grounds there is a strong tension between doctrinal dogmatism and the study of the history of religious ideas and their philosophical evaluation. In Bellarmine's statement, quoted above, two lines of interest are marked: the investigation and interpretation of the teachings of an individual author (*doctrinam haurire*) and the critical analysis of the authorship of individual texts (*opera certa/dubia/manifeste suposititia*). In a comparable manner Glassius, quoted above, defined a differentiation between the essential religious teaching (*scopus*) and doctrinal significance (*sedes doctrinae*) of any particular text, on the one hand, and the circumstances of its composition (*quis impellens, tempus, locus, modus*), on the other. The plurality of voices that can today be recognized in the biblical texts, of course, no longer fits in with the categories of an obvious, questionable, or indefensible "authenticity" of individual books or texts but has come to be understood in terms of a broader intellectual debate and refined scribal culture in antiquity. In early modern and modern biblical studies not many scholars have succeeded in striking the right balance between a hermeneutical interest in the interpretation of the teaching of a text and a historical interest in the investigation of the origin of a text; however, historical-critical inquiry has been a major factor in retaining a link between theological and philosophical, and more generally cultural, sensibilities. As far as the study of the Hebrew Bible/Old Testament is concerned, the rediscovery of the religious culture of Israel during the age of the Second Temple and its prehistory in the religious culture in Judah during the age of the royal, Davidic dynasty—and including some traces of the religious culture of the kingdom of Israel to the north of Judah, with its checkered history prior to its conquest by the Assyrians— has established a new scholarly basis for relating to that unique religious discourse of "priests, prophets, and sages" (see Blenkinsopp 1995) that is reflected in the biblical texts and invariably holds the promise of religious insight and moral inspiration beyond mere ritualism, edification, and ideology.

SOURCES

Bellarmine, R. *De scriptoribus ecclesiasticis* (1613). Paris, 1617.

Bellarmine, R. *Disputationes.* Vol. 1. Ingolstadt, 1587.

Blenkinsopp, J. *Sage, Priest, Prophet. Religious and Intellectual Leadership in Ancient Israel.* Louisville, Ky.: Westminster John Knox Press, 1995.

Byrne, P. *Natural Religion and the Nature of Religion. The Legacy of Deism.* London: Routledge, 1989.

Cappel, L. *Chronologia sacra a condito mundo [...]* (1658). In J. H. Heidegger, ed., *Apparatus chronologico-topographico-philologicus [...].* Zurich, 1673.

de Wette, W.M.L. *Beiträge zur Einleitung in das Alte Testament* (1806/7). Repr. Darmstadt: Wissenschaftliche Buchgesellschaft, 1971.

de Wette, W.M.L. *A Critical and Historical Introduction to the Canonical Scriptures of the Old Testament,* enlarged ed. T. Parker, trans. Boston, 1843.

de Wette, W.M.L. *Lehrbuch der historisch kritischen Einleitung in die kanonischen und apokryphischen Bücher des Alten Testaments.* Berlin, 1817; 6th ed., 1844.

Driver, S. R. *An Introduction to the Literature of the Old Testament,* 5th ed. Edinburgh: T&T Clark, 1894.

Gibert, P. *L'invention critique de la Bible. XVe–XVIIIe siècle.* Paris: Gallimard, 2010.

Glassius, S. *Philologia sacra, qua totius [...] scripturae tum stylus et literatura, tum sensus et genuinae interpretationis ratio et doctrina [...] expenditur [...]* (1623). Leipzig, 1743.

Grotius, H. *Opera theologica,* vol. 3, *Opuscula diversa* (in part 1640). Amsterdam, 1679; repr., Stuttgart: Frommann-Holzboog, 1972.

Grotius, H. *The Rights of War and Peace,* bks. 1–3 (1625). R. Tuck, ed. Indianapolis: Liberty Fund, 2005.

Grotius, H. *The Truth of the Christian Religion* (1640). John Clarke, trans.; M. R. Antognazza, ed. Indianapolis: Liberty Fund, 2012.

Herbert of Cherbury. *De veritate. Editio tertia [...] De religione laici.* London, 1645; repr., Stuttgart: Frommann-Holzboog, 1966.

Hobbes, T. *Leviathan* (1651). R. Tuck, ed. Cambridge: Cambridge University Press, 1991.

Hume, D. *Essays, Moral, Political, and Literary* (1777). E. F. Miller, ed. Indianapolis: Liberty Fund, 1985.

Laudan, R. "The History of Geology, 1780–1840." In R. C. Olby, G. N. Cantor, J.R.R. Christie, and M.J.S. Hodge, eds., *Companion to the History of Modern Science*, pp. 314–25. London: Routledge, 1990.

Simon, R. *Histoire critique du Vieux Testament* (1678). Rotterdam, 1685; repr., Frankfurt: Minerva, 1967.

Spinoza, B. *Tractatus theologico-politicus* (1670) [in English]. S. Shirley, trans.; B. S. Gregory, ed. Leiden: Brill, 1989.

Spinoza, B. *Tractatus theologico-politicus* (1670) [in Latin/German]. G. Gawlick and F. Niewöhner, eds. Darmstadt: Wissenschaftliche Buchgesellschaft, 1979.

FURTHER READING

A good impression of scholarly sincerity and ambition in the early nineteenth century can be gained from W.M.L. de Wette's *A Critical and Historical Introduction to the Canonical Scriptures of the Old Testament*, enlarged ed., T. Parker, trans. (Boston, 1843). A profile of this scholar has been drawn by J. Rogerson, in *W.M.L. de Wette. Founder of Modern Biblical Criticism. An Intellectual Biography* (Sheffield: Sheffield Academic Press, 1992); chapters on de Wette can also be found in R. Smend, *From Astruc to Zimmerli. Old Testament Scholarship in Three Centuries*, M. Kohl, trans. (Tübingen: Mohr Siebeck, 2007); and H. Graf Reventlow, *History of Biblical Interpretation*, vol. 4, L. G. Perdue, trans. (Atlanta: Scholars Press, 2010). Both these books as well as J. Rogerson, *Old Testament Criticism in the Nineteenth Century. England and Germany* (London: SPCK, 1984), offer accessible studies of major representatives of biblical scholarship from around 1800. The most comprehensive work on the history of scholarship from antiquity to the twentieth century is the multivolume M. Sæbø, ed., *Hebrew Bible/Old Testament. The History of Its Interpretation*, 3 vols. in 5 (Göttingen: Vandenhoeck & Ruprecht, 1996–2015); for quick reference S. E. Porter, ed., *Dictionary of Biblical Criticism and Interpretation* (London: Routledge, 2007), can be consulted.

Scholarly debates about the critical analysis of the individual biblical writings and the authors who inspired and shaped them are from time to time summarized in "introductions" to the Hebrew Bible/Old Testament, of which only two can be mentioned here: S. R. Driver, *An Intro-*

duction to the Literature of the Old Testament, 5th ed. (Edinburgh: T&T Clark, 1894); O. Eissfeldt, *The Old Testament. An Introduction. The History of the Formation of the Old Testament*, P. R. Ackroyd, trans. (Oxford: Oxford University Press, 1965). The current state of debate has been outlined in some of the preceding chapters of the present volume. Controversial issues concerning the method and meaning of historical-critical inquiry are discussed in a circumspect way by J. Barton, in "Historical-Critical Approaches," in J. Barton, ed., *The Cambridge Companion to Biblical Interpretation* (Cambridge: Cambridge University Press, 1998), pp. 9–20, as well as in his *The Nature of Biblical Criticism* (Louisville, Ky.: Westminster John Knox Press, 2007); with particular regard to certain modern trends by J. J. Collins, in *The Bible after Babel. Historical Criticism in a Postmodern Age* (Grand Rapids, Mich.: Eerdmans, 2005); and with particular regard to certain evangelical trends by K. L. Sparks, in *God's Word in Human Words. An Evangelical Appropriation of Critical Biblical Scholarship* (Grand Rapids, Mich.: Baker Academic, 2008). Significant contributions to a critical awareness of the challenges of biblical scholarship and its relation to theology as well as philosophy have been made by J. Barr, whose *Holy Scripture. Canon, Authority, Criticism* (Oxford: Oxford University Press, 1983; repr., 1998) can especially be recommended.

The issue of biblical interpretation and intellectual history can be approached through the comprehensive work edited by M. Sæbø (see above) and the biographical sketches by H. Graf Reventlow (vols. 1–4; see above). With regard to the early modern period, the following surveys and studies will offer helpful orientation: P. Gibert, *L'invention critique de la Bible. XVe–XVIIIe siècle* (Paris: Gallimard, 2010); J. Bernier, *La critique du Pentateuque de Hobbes à Calmet* (Paris: Champion, 2010); J. Sheehan, *The Enlightenment Bible. Translation, Scholarship, Culture* (Princeton, N.J.: Princeton University Press, 2005). Two conference volumes address a range of further relevant questions: J. Jarick, ed., *Sacred Conjectures. The Context and Legacy of Robert Lowth and Jean Astruc* (London: T&T Clark, 2007); and W. Johnstone, ed., *The Bible and the Enlightenment. A Case Study—Dr Alexander Geddes (1737–1802)* (London: T&T Clark, 2004). For the broader context of the development of modern science, the massive R. C. Olby, G. N. Cantor, J.R.R. Christie, and M.J.S. Hodge, eds., *Companion to the History of Modern Science*

(London: Routledge, 1990), may be consulted; while an excellent intro-
duction to developments in the philosophy of religion is the study by
P. Byrne, *Natural Religion and the Nature of Religion. The Legacy of Deism*
(London: Routledge, 1989). An intriguing attempt at tracing the intel-
lectual world of Israel in antiquity is the book by J. Blenkinsopp, *Sage,
Priest, Prophet. Religious and Intellectual Leadership in Ancient Israel*
(Louisville, Ky.: Westminster John Knox Press, 1995).

19

Literary Approaches

David Jasper

"THE BIBLE AS LITERATURE":
FROM R. G. MOULTON TO T. R. HENN

If this essay might seem to be largely historical and descriptive in nature, there is a reason for this. Not only has the science of biblical
criticism for the past two hundred years, as a branch of the complex field
of literary criticism, tended to stand apart from contemporary critical
movements through its immersion in historical issues, but the Bible itself occupies an odd, indeed unique, position *as* literature inasmuch as
it comes to us, unavoidably, in some sense as "sacred" literature. So we
find in literary critics from S. T. Coleridge (who plainly describes the
Bible as "having proceeded from the Holy Spirit"[1]) to T. S. Eliot, whom
I shall discuss later. The Bible's very oddness as literature places it in an
unusual position with regard to its cultural context and critical shifts in
the study of literature and language. But if it is prey to varieties of hermeneutical fundamentalism, the Bible does exist as a kind of shadow
both over and within critical movements in culture, a looming, uneasy,
sometimes authoritative presence in discussions of structuralist theory
(Roland Barthes on wrestling Jacob), feminist criticism (Mieke Bal on
the book of Judges), or poststructuralism (Jacques Derrida on the Tower
of Babel).[2] In an early issue of the journal *Literature and Theology* in
1987, Lyle Eslinger remarked that the contemporary study of European
and English literature had gone through three broad phases, from historical criticism to the "New Criticism" of formalism and "recently, among
other things, Reader-Response Criticism."[3] "Postmodernism" had at that
time barely entered the scene. Then there was a "but." The critical reading of the Bible cannot be entirely immune to such shifts; it stands awk-
wardly inasmuch as it "has a long history of use as Scripture—*normative*

literature."[4] The Bible stands critically apart—and thus, while the following essay will touch upon critical contexts and cultural currents, it will do so largely at a distance, recognizing, as we shall see in an essay of Peter Hawkins, the deceptively simple problem of the *and* in the phrase "the Bible as literature and sacred text."[5]

Although the phrase "the Bible as literature" first appeared in Matthew Arnold's *Isaiah of Jerusalem* (1883), twentieth-century study of the Bible as literature truly began with the work of Richard Green Moulton, professor of literary theory and interpretation at the University of Chicago.[6] Beginning with *The Literary Study of the Bible* (1896), Moulton (with others) published a collection of essays under the title *The Bible as Literature* (1899) and, more popularly, *A Short Introduction to the Literature of the Bible* (1901). His work, though idiosyncratic, remains valuable and even prophetic, with David Norton describing him as "a structuralist before his time."[7] Moulton was, above all, a literary critic with essentially no interest in theology, his interest focusing almost entirely on literary morphology and form. In his treatment of verse and the Psalms Moulton looks directly back to the eighteenth century and Robert Lowth's *Lectures on the Sacred Poetry of the Hebrews* (1753), with their "discovery" of literary parallelism, and his work, like Lowth's, following the words of the latter's translator into English,[8] George Gregory, is "more calculated for persons of taste and general reading, than for what is commonly termed the learned world."[9]

Moulton was only concerned with the English Bible, and, oddly, specifically the Revised Version (1881–85) rather than the 1611 King James Bible, yet his work contains valuable insights, not least the sense of the wholly unclear distinction between poetry and prose in Hebrew literature.[10] It was a point picked up much later by James L. Kugel in his book *The Idea of Biblical Poetry* (1981).[11] Although Moulton spawned no immediate successors in his field, the purely literary interest in the Bible continued in the earlier part of the twentieth century in such works as Sir James George Frazer's *Passages of the Bible Chosen for Their Literary Beauty and Interest*, first published in 1895 but reprinted in an enlarged form in 1909 and frequently thereafter. Frazer's interest in the English Bible as "pure literature" was aesthetic and unscholarly. He writes in his preface to the first edition:

That our English version of the Bible is one of the great classics in the language is admitted by all in theory, but few people appear to treat it as such in practice. The common man reads it for guidance and comfort in daily life and in sorrow; the scholar analyses it into its component parts and discusses their authorship and date; and the historian, the antiquary and anthropologist have recourse to it as a storehouse of facts illustrative of their special subjects. But how many read it, not for its religious, its linguistic, its historical and antiquarian interest, but simply for the sake of enjoyment which as pure literature it is fitted to afford?[12]

Frazer seeks, therefore, to render a "service to lovers of literature" and picks out the "gems" of the Bible in order to "delight, to elevate and to console."[13]

Yet some thirty years later it was a major poet, T. S. Eliot, in an influential essay entitled "Religion and Literature" (1935), who summarily dismissed all such claims for "the Bible as literature," setting it apart and *fulminating*, in his word, against such, inasmuch as, he suggests, "the Bible has had a *literary* influence upon English literature *not* because it has been considered as literature, but because it has been considered as the report of the Word of God. And the fact that men of letters now discuss it as 'literature' probably indicates the *end* of its 'literary' influence."[14] But there was also a third and middle path—that of literature as a devotional aid. A year before Eliot's essay appeared, William Ralph Inge, dean of St. Paul's, published *Every Man's Bible: An Anthology Arranged with an Introduction* (1934), a literary anthology without scholarly notes or commentary, designed for "those who wish to use the Bible as their chief devotional book."[15]

By the middle years of the twentieth century literary scholarship began to focus firmly and critically on the Hebrew Bible. Writing in German in Istanbul during the years of World War II, Erich Auerbach composed his great work, *Mimesis: The Representation of Reality in Western Literature* (1946). The first chapter of this book, "Odysseus' Scar," remains a classic of comparison between the Greek and Hebrew literary traditions, its reading of Genesis 22, the sacrifice of Isaac, still a fundamental text for students of both literature and theology on the literary qualities of the Hebrew text as a narrative that is mysterious and "fraught with background."[16] More specifically in England, as the century wore on, the preparation of the New English Bible (1970), quite different from the tradition of the King James Bible, drew on the work of both biblical and literary scholars and aroused a debate that was as much literary as it was theological. In the same year the distinguished Cambridge literary scholar T. R. Henn, more noted for his work on W. B. Yeats, published his book *The Bible as Literature*, admitting in the opening words of the introduction that "the title of this book is clearly open to many and grave objections."[17] Yet, rather oddly, Henn's sense of this difficulty has no religious element in it—rather, it is the purely *literary* challenges of the Bible that he addresses: its variety and lack of unity, its different languages and lack of a "common style," its lack of a *Textus Receptus*. His interest in the unity of the Bible, inasmuch as it has any, Henn dismisses in one undefined word—*spiritual*—and he then proceeds as a literary critic to suggest "some kind of redefinition and method of control" in the reading of the Bible.[18] Henn is perfectly prepared to be critical of the imperfections of the biblical authors—an admission that, as we shall see, very few other so-called literary critics of the Bible whom we shall be considering were prepared to make. Thus, more typically, Robert Alter, a professor of Hebrew and comparative literature, in *The Literary Guide to the Bible* (1987), writes "that elements like disjunction, interpolation, repetition, contrastive styles, which in biblical scholarship were long deemed sure signs of a defective text, may be perfectly deliberate components of a literary artwork, and recognised as such by the audience for which it is intended."[19] In Alter, the literary scholar is making new claims as a professional reader alongside, and perhaps even above, the biblical critic as such.

THE BIBLE IN LITERARY AND CULTURAL CRITICISM

Long ago it was C. S. Lewis who made the reasonable point that those who call themselves professional biblical critics may not be best qualified as literary critics.[20] He warned also in his 1950 essay "The Literary Impact of the Authorised Version" that the influence of the King James Bible on English literature should not be overestimated, and he reminds his reader, rather in the manner of T. S. Eliot, that when William Tyndale was working on his English Bible his considerations were not literary: "The matter was much too serious for that: souls were at stake. The same holds for all translators."[21] In short, literature and its study do not necessarily relate easily to the matter of the Bible and its critical readers. Perhaps, then, it might be more exact to regard the English Bible within the context of culture more broadly rather than specifically literature. A major recent work, *The Blackwell Companion to the Bible and Culture* (2006) explores the influence of the Bible on a variety of social contexts, from the ancient to the postmodern world, its final section giving attention to varieties of contemporary reading practices in the study of the Bible, from the political to the ecological and the postcolonial.[22] Other collections such as George Aichele's *Culture, Entertainment and the Bible* (2000) review the role of the Bible within popular entertainment, from the tabloid press and the films of Walt Disney to its place within modern ideologies and understandings of the nature of power.[23] On the whole, however, such cultural expeditions have not been particularly fruitful and have tended to die away.

Yet the attention of serious literary critics was not to be silenced. It was largely by Jewish critics in the early 1980s that the Bible *as* literature was taken seriously, its literary genius held as an intrinsic part of its religious message. Furthermore, the reemergence of rabbinic interpretation in the business of modern literary theory, as proposed by scholars such as Susan A. Handelman,[24] brought the study of the Bible—and in particular the Hebrew Bible—into close touch, though in a rather dominant manner, with the radical theoretical shifts in literary study associated with philosophical thinkers such as Derrida and Levinas. There was, it has to be admitted, some resistance to the blurring of the distinctions among literary study, literary theoretical study, and cultural study of the Bible, as stated by Robert Alter and Frank Kermode in their general introduction to *The Literary Guide to the Bible*, where they write somewhat dismissively, and keeping the Bible at a safe distance, that "we have not included critics who use the text as a springboard for cultural or metaphysical ruminations, nor those like the Deconstructionists and some feminist critics who seek to demonstrate that the text is necessarily divided against itself."[25] Yet it cannot be denied that some of the most brilliant contemporary readings of the texts of the Bible are found in Jacques Derrida's "glosses" on the stories of Babel and Abraham (after

Kierkegaard and Kafka), on Tobias, and in his essay "Shibboleth."[26] This latter, originally given as a lecture at a conference on the works of the poet Paul Celan, was reprinted in a volume entitled *Midrash and Literature* (1986), edited by Geoffrey H. Hartman and Sanford Budick, which examines the burgeoning interest among literary theorists at the time in midrash, or "the rabbinical exegesis of Old Testament writings," and brings together literary readings of texts as diverse as the book of Genesis, kabbalah, Milton, and Kafka. Hartman, in the opening essay on Genesis 32:1–22, the narrative of wrestling Jacob, offers a close reading of the text (with clear deference to Auerbach and Barthes) that begins with the question, "Is there a basis to the distinction between fiction and scripture?"[27] At the center of Hartman's literary analysis is the "struggle for the text," for a supreme fiction that the "accreted, promissory narrative we call Scripture" offers in common with all literature.[28] The necessary ambivalence of any answer to the question of the uniqueness of the Bible is reflected in the persistent yet uneasy tradition of poetic and fictive writing from Scripture, with its great example of John Milton's *Paradise Lost* (1667), about which one of Milton's fellow poets expressed a fear of the "ruin of sacred truths to fable and old song."[29] Yet in the twentieth century novelists continually returned to the narratives of the Old Testament for their themes, perhaps the greatest being Thomas Mann's *Joseph und seine Brüder* (1933–42), drawing on Genesis 12–50 and exploring the beginnings of religion and the emergence of the God of Israel.[30] One of the possibilities of such fictional intertexts with Scripture is the giving of voices to characters who are silent in the Bible, a fine example being the Swedish novelist Torgny Lindgren's *Bathsheba* (1984; trans., 1988), written in the rhythms and cadences of the Hebrew original and subtly developing the shadowy figure of the original biblical Bathsheba. Novelists and writers have also contributed to creative readings of the Old Testament, notably in a collection of Jewish authors entitled *Congregation* (1987), edited by David Rosenberg, in which the novelist Isaac Bashevis Singer writes movingly on the early effect of the book of Genesis on him as a writer:

> I have heard Bible critics maintain that the Book of Genesis was written not by one person but by many, who pieced various legends together. Yet I am sure it was the same master writer, who knew exactly where his pen

was leading him. I feel the same way even now, some sixty or seventy years later.... In our times, Tolstoy was a writer of such calibre, and so was Dostoevsky, and so were, to a lesser degree—such remarkable talents as Sholem Aleichem, Peretz, Knut Hamsun, Strindberg, and many others whose books I read in Yiddish or Polish translation and admired immensely.

I am still learning the art of writing from the Book of Genesis and from the Bible generally.[31]

Other contributors to *Congregation* include Elie Wiesel and the novelist Cynthia Ozick.

NARRATIVES, POETRY, AND THEATER

In his classic, and much debated, book *The Eclipse of Biblical Narrative* (1974), Hans Frei recounts the rise of historical criticism of the Bible in the eighteenth and nineteenth centuries and the critical fading of what he calls "strongly realistic" readings of biblical stories: "Most eminent among them were all those stories which together went into the making of a single storied or historical sequence."[32] In the twentieth century, with the emergence of literary readings of Scripture, a focus on biblical narrative returned both in the work of literary critics and among theologians, both influenced by the work of Erich Auerbach.[33] Thus, in an essay in the report of the Doctrine Commission of the Church of England, *Believing in the Church* (1981), John Barton and John Halliburton attempt to recover the category of "story" in the study of theology and liturgy, seeking "to show that it can be used in a positive way, to describe the way in which much of the Bible, and of other traditions and formularies of Christian faith, actually function in the life of the Church."[34] In the same year, Robert Alter's widely read book *The Art of Biblical Narrative*, building on the work of such theoreticians as Tzvetan Todorov and essays in the journal *Semeia*, suggested that it is "not presumptuous" to analyze the narratives of the preexilic literature of the Pentateuch and the early Prophets with the critical tools used on the novels of Flaubert, Virginia Woolf, Tolstoy, or Henry James. Employing a structuralist approach to examine such elements as narrative pace, the use of dialogue, and imagery, Alter defends such attention as leading "not to a more 'imaginative' reading of biblical narrative but to a more precise one; and since all these features are linked to discernible details in the Hebrew text, the literary approach is actually a good deal *less* conjectural than ... historical scholarship."[35] Thus literary critics make a strong claim to serious interpretations of the Bible read *as* literature, released from the criticisms of historical anachronisms. In the field of New Testament scholarship, Frank Kermode, whose critical work has clear structuralist tendencies, reinstated the biblical work of the Oxford theologian Austin Farrer when even Farrer himself (and theologians fearing the loss of the historical bases of Scripture) had largely abandoned his theories: "He himself altered them and then more or less gave them up, partly persuaded, no doubt, by criticisms of them as farfetched, partly disturbed by the imputation that a narrative of the kind he professed to be discussing would be more a work of fiction than an account of a crucial historical event. Neither of these judgments seems to me well founded."[36]

But it was the Hebrew Bible rather than the New Testament that yielded the richest fruits of critical attention to the structural forms of narrative and the genres of literature.[37] Furthermore, Jewish critics, their critical souls steeped in the midrashic tradition, have been preeminent in close critical readings from the perspective of biblical narrative poetics. Meir Sternberg, a professor of poetics and comparative literature at Tel Aviv University, published *The Poetics of Biblical Narrative* in 1987, which focuses on the omniscient biblical narrator who "concretizes the opposition to the human norm ... in the form of dramatic irony that no character (and, to rub it in, no reader) escapes."[38] With this (and the emphasis is deeply patriarchal) the biblical narrator has insight into the minds of his dramatis personae, including that of God himself—a tale told like no other. The telling of the biblical story is uniquely rhetorical— a narrative constructed to persuade. Like other biblical literary critics, Sternberg draws on the work of Auerbach, who compares biblical rhetoric with that of Homer—who seeks to enchant us, while the Bible claims our subjection. Sternberg is clear about the unique status of the Bible—but that uniqueness is rooted in literary and rhetorical origins, which are also universal: "Like all speakers ... the biblical storyteller is a persuader in that he wields discourse to shape response and manipulate attitude. Unlike most speakers, however, his persuasion is not only geared to an ideology but also designed to vindicate and inculcate it. Even among ideological persuaders, he has a special claim to notice, due less to the theology preached than to the rules and rhetoric of its preaching."[39]

For Sternberg, then, the Bible is unique not so much for its theological as for its literary quality, its narrator suspended, trickily, between heaven and earth—both human and divine. The literary dilemma originates in the status of the figure of God, who is both a subject of representation—a dramatic figure in the poetics of biblical narrative—and its "inspiring originator." The narrator is, then, both master and subject of his own narrative, a dilemma shared by no literature, as Sternberg observes, from Petronius to Joyce, for "the world of the Bible is hardly so literate."[40]

Thus the poetics of biblical narrative are both universal and unique, a tension described by Harold Fisch in his book *Poetry with a Purpose* (1990) as caught between the aesthetic and the nonaesthetic modes of discourse within biblical literature. Do the biblical books offer an instance of literary art—or is such art subsidiary to their real business? The answer must be both affirmative and negative—for their real business, which is beyond the literary, can only be conducted through literary means. Citing both Christian and Jewish authorities, Fisch argues that the Bible is both literature and, in his term, "anti-literature"—and it is the latter because it is the former. Appealing to Milton, Blake, and after them Northrop Frye, Fisch acknowledges the "mythopoeic power of the biblical narratives"; and yet, from Saint Augustine to the medieval Jewish philosopher Yehuda Halevi to Samuel Johnson, it has been argued that, in Johnson's words, "the intercourse between God and the human soul cannot be poetical."[41] The Bible contains poetry with a purpose—in Sternberg's term, it is an "ideological literature."

The form and structure of biblical poetics were the subject of a number of studies in the later twentieth century, notably Robert Alter's *The Art of Biblical Poetry* (1985) and James L. Kugel's *The Idea of Biblical Poetry*. Both look back (Alter more critically) to the seminal work of Robert Lowth in the eighteenth century and his *Lectures on the Sacred Poetry of the Hebrews*, which, with its "discovery" of parallelism, brought Hebrew poetry back into the mainstream of English verse, in, for example, the poetry of Christopher Smart, who praised Lowth's work for "its elegance, novelty, variety, spirit and (I had almost said) divinity,"[42] and above all in the poetic forms of William Blake, who, in the introduction to *Jerusalem*, left the "Monotonous Cadence" of English blank verse for "a variety in every line, both of cadences & number of syllables."[43] The implication is that poets could share their vocation with the psalmists and prophets and dare to articulate what Alter calls "the intricate substantive links between the poetic vehicle and the religious vision of the poets, and the crucial place of the corpus of biblical poetry in the complex growth of the Western literary tradition."[44]

While much attention has been given to the narrative and poetic qualities and forms of biblical literature, less has been said about its theatrical qualities. Certainly the impact of the Hebrew Bible on world drama has been considerable, but one recent study, Shimon Levy's *The Bible as Theatre* (2000), examines the theatricality of the texts themselves, recalling "that the Old Testament was not intended only for silent reading, but also to be read aloud in public."[45] In a series of creative readings that find in the biblical narratives the "potential" for theater, Levy explores the possibilities for biblical theater by opening up the texts and their characters to a dramatic vision that exchanges with Shakespeare's stage and the capacity of the stage to *see*, in part V, "a theatrical gaze," that which in the Bible can only be read.[46]

EMANCIPATORY AND POLITICAL READINGS OF THE BIBLE

The capacity for literary readings of the Bible to "open" the text to reveal what is hidden and therefore too often forgotten below its surface can lead to an emancipatory experience that may be either liberating or threatening. The study of literature in the twentieth century saw a shift of attention away from merely the text itself to the response of the reader[47]—and nowhere has this been more apparent than in feminist revisionary readings of the Bible. In her book *God and the Rhetoric of Sexuality* (1978), and continuing in the literary tradition of structuralist readings, Phyllis Trible opens her discussion of the book of Ruth with a search for the "deep structures" that underlie its "surface design."[48] Trible's reading of the story of Naomi and Ruth "as they struggle for survival in a patriarchal environment" begins with an observation of the power of the *grammar* of the text: "The story begins in the tension of

grammar (vv. 1–5). Third-person narrative names the characters, specifies their relationships, and describes their plight, but it does not allow
them to emerge as human beings."[49] It is precisely this hiddenness that
feminist exegesis has sought to bring to the surface in readings that do
not so much apply any critical theory to the text but bring the biblical
text into conversation with theoretical approaches that oblige it to speak
in ways hitherto rendered inaudible within the traditions of "patriarchal"
interpretation.[50] Alicia Suskin Ostriker writes of "the buried woman in
biblical narrative" who remains "out of my sight" until readings of the
text effect an emancipation and a challenge to the politics of interpretation that have for so long deliberately bred such burials.[51] Cheryl Exum
has, more recently, taken in cultural studies to the task of feminist readings in her book *Plotted, Shot, and Painted: Cultural Representations of
Biblical Women* (1996), using the lens of film and the images of the visual arts to reveal the hidden lives of such women as Bathsheba, Naomi,
and Delilah and claiming critical importance for the "cinematic power
and interpretive genius" of Cecil B. DeMille in his Oscar-winning film
Samson and Delilah (1949).[52]

The anger that is so often a characteristic of such feminist readings
of the Bible is rooted in the felt need to unpick the *coherence* of the Bible
as this is imposed by certain demands of history and theology. In short,
there are different stories to be found within the narratives of the texts,
and thus, in her study of the book of Judges, *Death and Dissymmetry*
(1988), Mieke Bal seeks to establish a *countercoherence* against the grain
of the patriarchal stories and politics that have dominated its readings
(and, indeed, its writing). This necessarily deconstructive exercise begins with a creative moment that finds a voice to address the issue of
women's anonymity in Judges (specifically Jephthah's daughter, the Levite's concubine, and Samson's bride). Bal gives them names:

> No names; no narrative power. They are subjected to the power of, mostly
> named, men. The first act that awaits us, then, is to provide the victims
> with a name. A name that makes them into subjects, that makes them
> speakable. Naming the victims is an act of insubordination to the text. Is
> it a distortion? In fact, the problem of naming is a useful way to become
> aware of the need of readerly activity. But the goal is not to embellish the
> text; only to account for its effect.[53]

The responsibility of the reader against the grain of the politics of patriarchal interpretation is clearly asserted—reading as creative as well as critical in order to rewrite those forgotten by history into history. This is a form of aggressive reading that rescues characters within the text from becoming mere textual objects. Implicit within it is the possibility that biblical texts may finally be irrecoverable (a conclusion reached, for example, by Daphne Hampson) and that the book of Hosea, for example, may finally be irredeemably a work of "prophetic pornography."[54] But this is merely to place the Bible into the context of *all* other literature, which must take its chance unprotected by the odor of sanctity that surrounds the "sacred text."

More broadly, the attention given by gender studies to the reading of the Bible has provoked conversations that are self-consciously literary in their manner and discipline and which aim to rescue biblical studies from the "ghetto" in which it has been academically, not to say religiously, in danger of consigning itself.[55] Apart from feminist criticism, less attention has been given to homoeroticism within the biblical texts, though a notable exception to this is the work of Stephen D. Moore, nothing if not a creative reader, with his essays on the "handsome Jesus," the "ugly Paul," and the "revolting Revelation" in his book *God's Beauty Parlor and Other Queer Spaces in and around the Bible* (2001), writings on Christian themes but rooted in the Old Testament literature of the Song of Songs, traditions of sacrifice, and the "bodies of Yahweh."[56]

The politics of "emancipatory" readings have not been limited to issues of feminism and gender. As novelists such as Howard Jacobson have given dramatic readings of the figure of Cain, so the critic Regina Schwartz has given detailed readings to expose the "violent legacy of monotheism" in her book *The Curse of Cain* (1997), with its focus on the city (Babel), the possession of the land, and the identity of nationhood.[57] The beautifully ironic opening paragraph of Jacobson's novel best expresses the essence also of Schwartz's concerns: "The Lord was our shepherd. We did not want. He fed us in green and fat pastures, gave us to drink from deep waters, made us to lie in a good fold. That which was lost, He sought; that which was broken, He bound up; that which was driven away, He brought again into the flock. Excellent, excellent, had we been sheep."[58]

This familiar pastoral (and patriarchal) image from Psalm 23 resonates through R. S. Sugirtharajah's work on biblical interpretation and postcolonial criticism.[59] His revisioning of biblical hermeneutics begins with the critical role played by creative literature as a precursor of current postcolonial thinking. In the Ugandan author Akiki Nyabongo's novel *Africa Answers Back* (1936), the Bible comes under critical scrutiny in a scene when the missionary Abala Stanley Mujungu reads from the Bible the story of the Israelites' crossing of the Red Sea to the king of Buganda and one of the chiefs relates immediately to the "white man's mythology," remarking: "Hm, that's just like our story, because when the Gods came from the north they reached the River Kira and the waters stopped flowing, so that they could get across. Isn't it strange that his story and ours should be the same."[60] The Bible, as a text of Western imperial authority, becomes, in the novel, a place of "hermeneutical contestation."[61]

DECONSTRUCTION AND POSTMODERNISM

The "postmodern condition" that is heralded by Jean-François Lyotard in his much-quoted *Report on Knowledge* of 1979 has, arguably, had little lasting effect on biblical criticism. Indeed, the fact that most of the books so far referred to in this essay were published some thirty years ago might suggest that, apart from a few ripples on the surface, reading of the Bible has gone on much the same way, if anything critically even more conservative, in the present century, even while "literary approaches" to Scripture have continued with little further critical impact or effect on the fading but still formidable citadel of biblical authority. In 1988, Edgar V. McKnight published his *Postmodern Use of the Bible*, a work that does not go much further than reflecting upon the shift of attention from text to reader-response criticism and the movement away from historical methods of criticism.[62] A.K.M. Adam, in *What Is Postmodern Biblical Criticism?* (1995), suggests that postmodernism is little more than a revising of earlier bad habits and that "most intellectuals and academies continue to function along typically modern lines."[63] (The practice of and reflection upon literature presumably, it would seem from this, stand outside the business of intellectuals and colleges.)

But this is to miss the point that at the heart of Lyotard's *Report* is essentially a literary observation: "Simplifying to the extreme, I define *postmodern* as incredulity towards metanarratives."[64] Linking post-modernism with poststructuralism, Stephen D. Moore focuses on the Derridean relationship of speech with writing in the biblical texts in his book *Poststructuralism and the New Testament* (1994),[65] locating the history of Western "logocentrism" in Genesis 3:8—"They heard the sound of the Lord God walking in the garden at the time of the evening breeze, and the man and his wife hid themselves from the presence of the Lord God"—and quoting the Jewish poet Edmond Jabès, *"The garden is speech."*[66] Derrida carries Jabès's comment on language beyond the Fall: "God no longer speaks to us; he has interrupted himself: we must take words upon ourselves. We must ... entrust ourselves to traces ... because we have ceased hearing the voice from within the immediate proximity of the garden.... The *difference* between speech and writing is sin, ... lost immediacy, work outside the garden."[67] Such work, then, is the work of literature, its contours in the context of readings of the Bible examined at length by Stephen Moore and other members of the so-called Bible and Culture Collective in the volume entitled *The Postmodern Bible* (1995).

The themes of the chapters in this collection of essays will already be familiar to the reader of the present essay: reader-response criticism, structuralist and narratological criticism, feminist and womanist criticism, ideological criticism. The task that the members of the Bible and Culture Collective set themselves was to "transform" readings of the Bible, which then become transforming of reading. They engage in a "politics of reading," and they regard their enterprise as one of many possible "literary approaches" to the Bible.[68] Setting themselves in direct opposition to Robert Alter and Frank Kermode in their *Literary Guide to the Bible*, the members of the collective seek to deconstruct the "institutionalizing and normative effects" of the work of Alter, Kermode, and others, finding "central and energizing" what Alter and Kermode dispatch to the margins, including the "literary criticism" of feminism, ideological readings, and psychoanalytic and Marxist approaches.[69] Like Mieke Bal, they seek to read against the grain of both biblical texts and the institution of biblical scholarship, and they, too, begin not with theory but with close and creative readings of particular texts in acts of "consciousness-raising about our own reading experiences."[70] It thus seems appropriate that when *The Postmodern Bible Reader* appeared in 2001, deliberately dedicated to "our friends and colleagues" of the Bible and Culture Collective, its focus was firmly on the writings of literary critics and writers, from Umberto Eco to Roland Barthes, Hélène Cixous, J. Hillis Miller, Mieke Bal, Terry Eagleton, and Jacques Derrida.[71]

But for one example of "postmodern" and creative biblical criticism we might turn to the joint work of a poet and a literary critic, David Rosenberg and Harold Bloom's *Book of J* (1990). Rosenberg and Bloom begin with the critical tradition that suggests that the Pentateuchal literature is a composite work from a number of different "authors" or strands—and identifying the so-called J author, they claim to have recovered a literary and religious masterpiece from some of the oldest elements of the Hebrew Bible. My own reading of Bloom's introductory essay to *The Book of J*, in Rosenberg's new translation, suggests that this is a masterpiece of postmodern irony—deconstructive, playful, oblique—and literary to the highest degree. Bloom plays the game of Old Testament criticism to perfection. Yet his tone from the outset is deliberately that of the storyteller—the maker of fictions: "In Jerusalem, nearly three thousand years ago, an unknown author composed a work that has formed the spiritual consciousness of much of the world ever since."[72] He (ironically?) assumes, of course, without comment, the proposal of the scholarly authorities who subscribe (as a clearly established fact) to the "four author" hypothesis—the strands in the narrative of the Pentateuch known as J, E, P, and D. As Gerhard von Rad confidently states (in a way, perhaps, no literary critic ever would): "The books Genesis to Joshua consist of several continuous source documents that were woven together more or less skilfully by a redactor."[73] Deliberately following the historical methods of von Rad, Bloom concludes that the author of "J" was a woman of high birth "and that she wrote for her contemporaries as a woman, in friendly competition with her only strong rival among those contemporaries, the male author of the court history narrative in 2 Samuel."[74] Building upon an understanding of irony, humor, and an analysis of literary sophistication "as knowing as Shakespeare or Jane Austen,"[75] Bloom meets biblical critics on their own turf and establishes "J" as the "ultimate ancestor of *The Canterbury Tales* as well as of Tolstoy's fictions and Kafka's parables."[76] His ultimate purpose in "scrubbing away the varnish" seems to be anything but religious: "I do not think that appreciating J will help us love God or arrive at the spiritual or historical truth of whatever Bible. I want the varnish off because it conceals a writer of the eminence of Shakespeare or Dante, and such a writer is worth more than many creeds, many churches, many scholarly certainties."[77]

Bloom's "commentary" on J is unsettling and destabilizing, serious and mocking, irreligious yet reverent. It poses the problem of the Bible *as* "pure" literature while entering the camp of biblical criticism that is concerned with the Bible as a sacred text. It also enters the Derridean world of "the adventure of the text as weed, as outlaw far from *'the fatherland of the Jews,'* which is a *'sacred text surrounded by commentaries.'"*[78] In this postmodern and Kafkaesque world writing and the Bible as the Book become the problem, the way of God being the way of detour. Derrida again quotes Jabès, both of them Jewish writers, looking back to the figure of Jacob: *"Reb Jacob, who was my first master, believed in the virtue of the lie because, he said, there is no writing without a lie and writing is the way of God."*[79]

THE BIBLE AS LITERATURE/THE BIBLE AND LITERATURE

The English Bible, as Harold Bloom notes, looks back to two literary geniuses, William Tyndale and Miles Coverdale, though their purpose as translators (contra the scholarship of Bloom himself) was certainly not to create literature but to seek the salvation of souls. Bloom regards the great King James Bible of 1611 as "essentially a correction" of Tyndale-Coverdale.[80] In their introduction to the Oxford World Classics text of what they entitle the Authorized King James Version, Robert Carroll and Stephen Prickett introduce it as a work of literary, religious, and cultural importance: "The Bible is the basic book of our civilization. It holds a unique and exclusive status not merely in terms of the religious history of the western world but also in literary history and even in what might be called our collective cultural psyche."[81] As the four hundredth anniversary of the publication of the King James Bible, 2011 saw a large number of publications, the majority of which were not by biblical scholars as such but by authors concerned with its place in Western literature and culture. One of the more scholarly of these books,

Hannibal Hamlin and Norman W. Jones's *The King James Bible after 400 Years* (2010) opens with attention given to the *language* of the King James Bible and the "literary power" of the Hebrew original. Robert Alter states in his essay in this book: "Much of the literary power of the ancient Hebrew texts derives from their terrific compactness of formulation. This quality often cannot be readily conveyed in English because English is an analytic language and biblical Hebrew is a synthetic language."[82] Gabriel Josipovici's influential conversation with the biblical text entitled *The Book of God* (1988) is rooted in his sense of the resonance, grammar, and rhythm of the biblical Hebrew as essential to our understanding of it, criticizing an authority as established as Gerhard von Rad for his neglect of "the natural syntax and grammar of the Bible" when it does not fit "in with certain religious dogmas he accepts independently of the Bible."[83] Josipovici, a professor of English literature, responds vigorously to the text of the Hebrew Bible as literature, commenting that, "though supremely authoritative for Jews and Christians," the Bible does not seem "anything like as authoritarian as the *Aeneid* or *Paradise Lost*" but, rather, much more "modern" and "much quirkier, funnier, quieter than I expected."[84]

Josipovici's book is much more "literary" and less historical than a number of textbooks on the Bible as literature to appear in recent years, including David Norton's comprehensive two-volume *A History of the Bible as Literature* (1993) and the introductory *The Bible as Literature* by John B. Gabel, Charles B. Wheeler, and Anthony D. York, originally published in 1986 and now into its fifth edition.[85] Many more textbooks have appeared on the frankly easier subject of the Bible *and* literature, including my (with Stephen Prickett) *The Bible and Literature: A Reader* (1999), which threads particular passages from Genesis to the Psalms through a series of literary intertexts, and the more recent *Blackwell Companion to the Bible in English Literature* (2009), edited by Rebecca Lemon, Emma Mason, Jonathan Roberts, and Christopher Rowland, which offers a series of essays on the use of the Bible by specific authors, from Old English poets to modernist writers such as T. S. Eliot and Virginia Woolf.[86] Yet the continuing difficulty of critically appropriating the Hebrew Bible *as* literature, even while acknowledging the supreme examples of literary narrative and poetry within its books, lies in the deeply rooted sense, "whether we are fundamentalists or atheists,"[87] that it is essentially and ineradicably different from all other books both in its origins and in its traditions of reading. If the King James Bible remains as a classic of English literature, that was not the purpose of those responsible for it. This difficulty became apparent to me and my fellow editors, Andrew Hass and Elisabeth Jay, when we were working on *The Oxford Handbook of English Literature and Theology* (2007). For the most problematic part of that book was that entitled "Literary Ways of Reading the Bible," and the difficulty is summed up by Peter Hawkins in the opening sentences of his essay, "The Bible as Literature and Sacred Text": "Any consideration of the 'Bible as Literature and Sacred Text' must begin by recognizing the problematic nature of that deceptively simple conjunction, 'and.' Although it may imply an easy equivalency— the Bible is both a work of literature *and* the Word of God—these two identities have never rested easily with one another. For centuries, appreciation for Scripture's artistry sprang from the devout conviction that its divine Author would offer nothing less than perfection."[88]

No fewer than seven chapters in the *Handbook* deal with specific books of the Old Testament, from the Pentateuch to the Prophets. Tod Linafelt's essay on the Pentateuch expresses well the dilemma for the authors of these chapters. Linafelt suggests that the Pentateuch, regarded as a work of literature, is among the most "unliterary" of texts. Later poets and writers have responded creatively to the great narratives of creation and fall, the histories of the patriarchs, the poetic passages. Yet no less important are the cultic and legal texts—to literature far less attractive but to which Linafelt is "reluctant to give short shrift."[89] For the power and complexity of these texts lie in the depths of their religious sensibility, and this can be as profound in their legal ordinances as in the puns, wordplays, and alliterations that carry a theology and a religious vision that remain a troubling presence even when they also inspire the imaginations and genius of later generations of poets, from Milton to Joyce. We return to the issue of biblical literature as "poetry with a purpose," and as Harold Fisch once pointed out, writers and critics from Longinus onward have acknowledged the Hebrew scriptures as models of literary excellence, and yet "those writers who have had difficulty in accommodating the Bible to any normal aesthetic have also not been mistaken."[90] Such writers include Saint Augustine and Dr. Samuel Johnson, who was clear, as we have seen, that poetry and the Word of God cannot, finally, mix.[91] The Song of Songs may be "the most lyrical poetry in the Bible," but long ago Origen was clear that it is a wedding song, written in the form of a play but specifically expressing, for our instruction, the heavenly love of a bride for her bridegroom, who is the Word of God.[92]

Thus we are left with the issue expressed by T. S. Eliot almost eighty years ago in his essay "Religion and Literature," that the Bible *as* literature and within the great literature of the world remains powerful and disturbing because it is *different* from all other books in literature—it is, in Eliot's phrase, "considered as the report of the Word of God."[93] It stands resolutely apart and separate, while yet inextricably involved in the cultural and critical issues to which it often gives rise and which its reading reflects.

NOTES

1. S. T. Coleridge, *Confessions of an Inquiring Spirit* (London: William Pickering, 1840), p. 13.

2. Roland Barthes, "The Struggle with the Angel: Textual Analysis of Genesis 32: 23–33" (1972), reprinted in Stephen Heath, ed. and trans., *Image Music Text* (London: Fontana, 1977), pp. 125–41; Mieke Bal, *Death and Dissymmetry: The Politics of Coherence in the Book of Judges* (Chicago: University of Chicago Press, 1988); Jacques Derrida, "Des tours de Babel," in Joseph F. Graham, ed. and trans., *Difference in Translation* (Ithaca, N.Y.: Cornell University Press, 1985), pp. 165–248.

3. Lyle Eslinger, "The Wooing of the Woman at the Well: Jesus, the Reader and Reader-Response Criticism," *Literature and Theology* 1, no. 2 (1987): pp. 167–83, at p. 167.

4. Ibid.; emphasis added.

5. Peter S. Hawkins, "The Bible as Literature and Sacred Text," in Andrew W. Hass, David Jasper, and Elisabeth Jay, eds., *The Oxford Handbook of English Literature and Theology* (Oxford: Oxford University Press, 2007), pp. 197–213.

6. See David Norton, *A History of the Bible as Literature*, vol. 2, *From 1700 to the Present Day* (Cambridge: Cambridge University Press, 1993), pp. 277–85.

7. Ibid., p. 277.

8. Lowth, as was the custom for the Oxford Professor of Poetry well into the nineteenth century, lectured in Latin, his work being translated into German before appearing in English in 1787, more than thirty years after its first publication.

9. George Gregory, quoted in John Drury, ed., *Critics of the Bible, 1724–1873* (Cambridge: Cambridge University Press, 1989), p. 70.

10. R. G. Moulton, *The Literary Study of the Bible*, 2nd ed. (Boston, 1899), pp. 113–14.

11. James L. Kugel, *The Idea of Biblical Poetry: Parallelism and Its History* (New Haven, Conn.: Yale University Press, 1981), esp. chap. 2, "Poetry and Prose," pp. 59–95.

12. Sir James George Frazer, *Passages of the Bible Chosen for Their Literary Beauty and Interest* (1895; 2nd ed., London: Macmillan, 1909), pp. v–vi.

13. Ibid., p. viii.

14. T. S. Eliot, *Selected Essays*, 3rd ed. (London: Faber and Faber, 1951), p. 390.

15. William Ralph Inge, *Every Man's Bible: An Anthology Arranged with an Introduction* (London: Longmans, 1934), p. ix.

16. Erich Auerbach, *Mimesis: The Representation of Reality in Western Literature*, Willard R. Trask, trans. (Princeton, N.J.: Princeton University Press, 1968), p. 12.

17. T. R. Henn, *The Bible as Literature* (London: Lutterworth Press, 1970), p. 9.

18. Ibid.

19. Robert Alter, "Introduction to the Old Testament," in Robert Alter and Frank Kermode, eds., *The Literary Guide to the Bible* (London: Collins, 1987), p. 27. The same point is made by David Norton (*History of the Bible as Literature*, p. 386).

20. C. S. Lewis, *Fern-Seed and Elephants*, Walter Hooper, ed. (Glasgow: Fontana, 1975), pp. 104–25.

21. C. S. Lewis, "The Literary Impact of the Authorised Version," in *They Asked for a Paper* (London: Bles, 1962), p. 34.

22. John F. A. Sawyer, ed., *The Blackwell Companion to the Bible and Culture* (Oxford: Blackwell, 2006). See also such volumes as J. Cheryl Exum and Stephen D. Moore, eds., *Biblical Studies/Cultural Studies*, Third Sheffield Colloquium (Sheffield: Sheffield Academic Press, 1998); David J. A. Clines, *The Bible and the Modern World* (Sheffield: Sheffield Academic Press, 1997).

23. George Aichele, ed., *Culture, Entertainment and the Bible*, Journal for the Study of the Old Testament Supplement Series 309 (Sheffield: Sheffield Academic Press, 2000).

24. See Susan A. Handelman, *The Slayers of Moses: The Emergence of Rabbinic Interpretation in Modern Literary Theory* (Albany: State University of New York Press, 1982); and *Fragments of Redemption: Jewish Thought and Literary Theory in Benjamin, Scholem, and Levinas* (Bloomington: Indiana University Press, 1991).

25. Robert Alter and Frank Kermode, "General Introduction," in Robert Alter and Frank Kermode, eds., *The Literary Guide to the Bible* (London: Collins, 1987), p. 6.

26. See John D. Caputo, *The Prayers and Tears of Jacques Derrida: Religion without Religion* (Bloomington: Indiana University Press, 1997), p. xxvi.

27. Geoffrey H. Hartman, "The Struggle for the Text," in Geoffrey H. Hartman and Sanford Budick, eds., *Midrash and Literature* (New Haven, Conn.: Yale University Press, 1986), p. 3.

28. Ibid., p. 17.

29. Andrew Marvell, "On Mr. Milton's *Paradise Lost*," in Hugh MacDonald, ed., *The Poems of Andrew Marvell*, 2nd ed. (London: Routledge and Kegan Paul, 1956), p. 64. Harold Bloom adapted the phrase for the title of his Charles Eliot Norton Lectures (1987–88), *Ruin the Sacred Truths: Poetry and Belief from the Bible to the Present Day* (Cambridge, Mass.: Harvard University Press, 1989).

30. More recent, and slighter, examples include Howard Jacobson, *The Very Model of a Man* (London: Penguin, 1993), which explores the figure of Cain; Frederick Buechner, *The Son of Laughter* (San Francisco: HarperCollins, 1993), retelling the story of

Jacob; and Joseph Heller, *God Knows* (London: Jonathan Cape, 1984), an irreverent first-person narrative account of the life of King David.

31. Isaac Bashevis Singer, "Genesis," in David Rosenberg, ed., *Congregation: Contemporary Writers Read the Jewish Bible* (San Diego: Harcourt Brace Jovanovich, 1987), p. 7.

32. Hans Frei, *The Eclipse of Biblical Narrative: A Study in Eighteenth and Nineteenth Century Hermeneutics* (New Haven, Conn.: Yale University Press, 1974), p. 1. See also M. H. Abrams, "The Design of Biblical History," in *Natural Supernaturalism: Tradition and Revolution in Romantic Literature* (New York: W. W. Norton, 1971), pp. 32–37, at p. 35: "The design of Biblical history constitutes a sharply defined plot with a beginning, a middle, and an end."

33. See George W. Stroup, *The Promise of Narrative Theology* (London: SCM, 1981).

34. John Barton and John Halliburton, "Story and Liturgy," in *Believing in the Church: The Corporate Nature of Faith*, Report by the Doctrine Commission of the Church of England (London: SPCK, 1981), p. 79.

35. Robert Alter, *The Art of Biblical Narrative* (London: George Allen and Unwin, 1981), p. 21.

36. Frank Kermode, *The Genesis of Secrecy: On the Interpretation of Narrative*, Charles Eliot Norton Lectures, 1977–78 (Cambridge, Mass.: Harvard University Press, 1979), p. 61. To remain for a moment with the New Testament, the critical reading of the Bible as "fiction" continues to flourish. See, for example, Douglas A. Templeton, *The New Testament as True Fiction* (Sheffield: Sheffield Academic Press, 1999).

37. For example, Adele Berlin in *Poetics and Interpretation of Biblical Narrative* (Sheffield: Almond Press, 1983) explores character and multiple narrative perspectives in the books of Samuel and Kings. J. Cheryl Exum recovers the tragic vision of Judges, Samuel, and Kings in *Tragedy and Biblical Narrative* (Cambridge: Cambridge University Press, 1992).

38. Meir Sternberg, *The Poetics of Biblical Narrative: Ideological Literature and the Drama of Reading* (Bloomington: Indiana University Press, 1987), p. 85.

39. Ibid., p. 482.

40. Ibid., p. 155.

41. Harold Fisch, *Poetry with a Purpose: Biblical Poetics and Interpretation* (Bloomington: Indiana University Press, 1990), p. 1.

42. Christopher Smart, *Universal Visiter*, January/February 1756, quoted in Drury, *Critics of the Bible*, p. 70.

43. William Blake, *Complete Writings*, Geoffrey Keynes, ed. (Oxford: Oxford University Press, 1972), p. 621.

44. Robert Alter, *The Art of Biblical Poetry* (New York: Basic Books, 1985), p. 214. Such "substantive links" were famously acknowledged by S. T. Coleridge in his definition of the Primary Imagination in *Biographia Literaria* (1817), chap. 13, as "the living Power and prime Agent of all human Perception, and as a repetition in the finite mind of the eternal act of creation in the Infinite I AM" (*Collected Works,* vol. 7, James Engell and W. Jackson Bate, eds. [Princeton, N.J.: Princeton University Press, 1983], vol. 1, p. 304).

45. Shimon Levy, *The Bible as Theatre* (Brighton: Sussex Academic Press, 2002), p. ix.

46. Ruth, for example, is considered in a chapter entitled "Ruth: The Shrew-ing of the Tame." Chapter 13 is entitled "The (Unabridged) Play of David and Bathsheba."

47. For a discussion of the move toward "reader response" in biblical studies, see Mark G. Brett, "The Future of Reader Criticism?" in Francis Watson, ed., *The Open Text: New Directions for Biblical Studies* (London: SCM, 1993), pp. 13–31.

48. Phyllis Trible, *God and the Rhetoric of Sexuality* (London: SCM, 1978), p. 166.

49. Ibid., pp. 166–67.

50. Mieke Bal, a Dutch narratologist, describes this encounter as "transgressive": "The very dialogue between narrative theory and a body of biblical texts leads to a transgression of disciplinary boundaries." Mieke Bal, "Dealing/with/Women: Daughters in the Book of Judges," in Regina Schwartz, ed., *The Book and the Text: The Bible and Literary Theory* (Oxford: Blackwell, 1990), p. 16.

51. Alicia Suskin Ostriker, *Feminist Revision and the Bible* (Oxford: Blackwell, 1993).

52. J. Cheryl Exum, *Plotted, Shot, and Painted: Cultural Representations of Biblical Women* (Sheffield: Sheffield Academic Press, 1996), p. 236.

53. Bal, "Dealing/with/Women," p. 19.

54. A term used by Cheryl Exum in *Plotted, Shot, and Painted* (pp. 101–28).

55. See, for example, Timothy K. Beal and David M. Gunn, eds., *Reading Bibles, Writing Bodies: Identity and the Book* (London: Routledge, 1997), p. xi: "Biblical Studies exists in a ghetto. Isolated within the academy, the main body of biblical scholarship is not an active conversational partner within mainstream intellectual discourse."

56. Stephen D. Moore, *God's Beauty Parlor and Other Queer Spaces in and around the Bible* (Stanford, Calif.: Stanford University Press, 2001). See also Moore's earlier book, *God's Gym: Divine Male Bodies of the Bible* (New York: Routledge, 1996).

57. Regina M. Schwartz, *The Curse of Cain: The Violent Legacy of Monotheism* (Chicago: University of Chicago Press, 1997).

58. Jacobson, *Very Model of a Man*, p. 1.

59. R. S. Sugirtharajah, *Postcolonial Criticism and Biblical Interpretation* (Oxford: Oxford University Press, 2002).

60. Akiki Nyabongo, *Africa Answers Back* (London: George Routledge and Sons, 1936), p. 10.

61. Sugirtharajah, *Postcolonial Criticism and Biblical Interpretation*, p. 19.

62. Edgar V. McKnight, *Postmodern Use of the Bible: The Emergence of Reader-Oriented Criticism* (Nashville, Tenn.: Abingdon Press, 1988).

63. A.K.M. Adam, *What Is Postmodern Biblical Criticism?* (Minneapolis: Augsburg Press, 1995), p. 4.

64. Jean-François Lyotard, *The Postmodern Condition: A Report on Knowledge*, Geoff Bennington and Brian Massumi, trans. (Manchester: Manchester University Press, 1986), p. xxiv.

65. Stephen D. Moore, *Poststructuralism and the New Testament: Derrida and Foucault at the Foot of the Cross* (Minneapolis: Fortress Press, 1994).

66. Edmond Jabès, *Le Livre des questions* (Paris: Gallimard, 1963), p. 169, quoted in Jacques Derrida, "Edmond Jabès and the Question of the Book," in *Writing and Difference*, Alan Bass, trans. (London: Routledge, 1981), p. 68.

67. Derrida, "Edmond Jabès and the Question of the Book," p. 68.

68. Bible and Culture Collective, *The Postmodern Bible* (New Haven, Conn.: Yale University Press, 1995), p. 7.

69. Ibid.

70. Ibid., p. 23.

71. David Jobling, Tina Pippin, and Ronald Schleifer, eds., *The Postmodern Bible Reader* (Oxford: Blackwell, 2001).

72. Harold Bloom, introduction to *The Book of J*, David Rosenberg, trans., interpreted by Harold Bloom (London: Faber and Faber, 1991), p. 9.

73. Gerhard von Rad, *Genesis: A Commentary*, John H. Marks, trans., 3rd rev. ed. (London: SCM, 1972), p. 24.

74. Bloom, introduction to *Book of J*, p. 9.

75. Ibid., p. 12.

76. Ibid., p. 25.

77. Ibid., p. 44.

78. Derrida, "Edmond Jabès and the Question of the Book," p. 67, quoting Jabès, *Le Livre des questions*, p. 109.

79. Jabès, *Le Livre des questions*, p. 92, quoted in Derrida, "Edmond Jabès and the Question of the Book," p. 68.

80. Bloom, introduction to *Book of J*, p. 45. David Daniell, in his book *The Bible in English* (New Haven, Conn.: Yale University Press, 2003), with better reason, suggests that the KJV, as the work of a committee, is more of a diminution from the earlier translators.

81. Robert Carroll and Stephen Prickett, introduction to *The Bible: Authorized King James Version with Apocrypha* (Oxford: Oxford University Press, 1997), p. xi.

82. Robert Alter, "The Glories and the Glitches of the King James Bible: Ecclesiastes as Test-Case," in Hannibal Hamlin and Norman W. Jones, eds., *The King James Bible after 400 Years: Literary, Linguistic, and Cultural Influences* (Cambridge: Cambridge University Press, 2010), p. 47.

83. Gabriel Josipovici, *The Book of God: A Response to the Bible* (New Haven, Conn.: Yale University Press, 1988), p. 56. Much more recently, and more playfully, the linguistics scholar David Crystal has written on the literary effect of the King James Bible on the English language in *Begat: The King James Bible and the English Language* (Oxford: Oxford University Press, 2010).

84. Josipovici, *Book of God*, p. x.

85. See John B. Gabel and Charles B. Wheeler, eds., *The Bible as Literature: An Introduction* (New York: Oxford University Press, 1986); John B. Gabel, Charles B. Wheeler, and Anthony D. York, eds., *The Bible as Literature: An Introduction*, 5th ed. (New York: Oxford University Press, 2005).

86. David Jasper and Stephen Prickett, eds., *The Bible and Literature: A Reader* (Oxford: Blackwell, 1999); Rebecca Lemon, Emma Mason, Jonathan Roberts, and Christopher Rowland, eds., *The Blackwell Companion to the Bible in English Literature* (Chichester: Wiley-Blackwell, 2009). Both of these books are deeply indebted to the magisterial David Lyle Jeffrey, ed., *A Dictionary of Biblical Tradition in English Literature* (Grand Rapids, Mich.: William B. Eerdmans, 1992).

87. Josipovici, *Book of God*, p. 3.

88. Hawkins, "Bible as Literature and Sacred Text," p. 197.

89. Tod Linafelt, "The Pentateuch," in Hass, Jasper, and Jay, *Oxford Handbook of English Literature and Theology*, p. 215.

90. Fisch, *Poetry with a Purpose*, p. 1.

91. In his *Lives of the Poets*, Johnson asserts that the essence of poetry is invention, and from it the reader expects "the enlargement of his comprehension," while "whatever is great, desirable, or tremendous, is comprised in the name of the Supreme Being. Omnipotence cannot be exalted; Infinity cannot be amplified; Perfection cannot be improved." Samuel Johnson, "The Life of Waller," in *The Lives of the Poets* (1779–81), vol. 1 (Oxford: Oxford University Press, 1952), p. 203.

92. J. Cheryl Exum, "Song of Songs," in Hass, Jasper, and Jay, *Oxford Handbook of English Literature and Theology*, p. 259; Origen, *The Prologue to the Commentary on the Song of Songs*, Rowan A. Greer, trans., Classics of Western Spirituality (Mahwah, N.J.: Paulist Press, 1979), p. 217.

93. Eliot, *Selected Essays*, p. 390.

FURTHER READING

Robert Lowth's *Lectures on the Sacred Poetry of the Hebrews* (1753) remains a seminal text on the literary understanding of the Bible. Modern academic study begins with R. G. Moulton's *The Literary Study of the Bible* (London: Isbister and Co., 1896). A key text for reading biblical narrative, still much quoted, is the essay "Odysseus' Scar" in Erich Auerbach's *Mimesis* (1946; English translation: Willard R. Trask, trans., Princeton, N.J.: Princeton University Press, 1953). T. R. Henn was one of the first literary critics to write on the literary Bible, in *The Bible as Literature* (London: Lutterworth Press, 1970); and Robert Alter and Frank Kermode, eds., *The Literary Guide to the Bible* (London: Collins, 1987), remains a key text in such study. In direct opposition to its somewhat conservative stance is the Bible and Culture Collective, *The Postmodern Bible* (New Haven, Conn.: Yale University Press, 1995). Robert Alter's two books *The Art of Biblical Narrative* (London: George Allen and Unwin, 1981) and *The Art of Biblical Poetry* (New York: Basic Books, 1985) are accessible and provocative texts by a leading Jewish professor of comparative literature. More difficult but essential in the field of feminist criticism is the Dutch critic Mieke Bal's trilogy of books on the Old Testament and readings of the book of Judges: *Lethal Love* (Bloomington: Indiana University Press, 1987), *Murder and Difference* (Bloomington: Indiana University Press, 1988), and *Death and Dissymmetry* (Chicago: University of Chicago Press, 1988). The essays edited by Regina Schwartz in the volume entitled *The Book and the Text* (Oxford:

Blackwell, 1990) provide an excellent introduction to the Bible and literary theory. Among the many books concerned with the Bible *and* literature, the best introduction can be found in Rebecca Lemon, Emma Mason, Jonathan Roberts, and Christopher Rowland, eds., *The Blackwell Companion to the Bible in English Literature* (Chichester: Wiley-Blackwell, 2009). David Norton's monumental *A History of the Bible as Literature* (Cambridge: Cambridge University Press, 1993), in two volumes, is the best historical review of the subject.

20

❀

Theological Approaches to the Old Testament

R.W.L. Moberly

INTRODUCTION: THE MODERN PARADIGM OF OLD TESTAMENT THEOLOGY

The standard modern approach to theological study of the Old Testament (OT) has been to seek to understand the OT's religious language, thought, and practices both in themselves, as expressions of the life of ancient Israel, and in relation to the religions of Israel's neighbors, from Egypt to Mesopotamia. The quest for good historical knowledge about the religious content of these ancient texts in their Israelite context of origin, and in the context of the surrounding world of which ancient Israel was a part, has been the sine qua non for their better understanding. Whether one calls the result of such study "history of Israelite religion" or "OT theology" has usually related more to principles of arrangement (e.g., the former is chronological/developmental, the latter is often topical/thematic) than to significant differences in substantive content.

A paradigm of such scholarship is arguably the recent fifteen-volume *Theological Dictionary of the Old Testament* (*TDOT*), edited by Botterweck, Ringgren, and Fabry.[1] Although the *TDOT* is the prime reference work in the field, there are also other comparable theological dictionaries/lexicons, but on a lesser scale.[2] In *TDOT* all significant theological vocabulary is discussed in relation to ancient Near Eastern parallels, to nonreligious use, and to the variegated theological uses in the many texts and traditions of the OT (and, where appropriate, Qumran). However, there is no discussion at all of rabbinic or New Testament and patristic interpretations; the historic understanding and appropriation of the biblical material within Judaism and Christianity lies beyond *TDOT*'s frame of reference.

The characteristic concern in such scholarship—if one may present it in a simplified and schematic form, which is conceptually aligned with Gabler's famous 1787 oration[3]—has primarily been to *describe*, in analytical and sharply focused historical mode, the content of the biblical text. Such *description* is regularly, either explicitly or implicitly, distinguished from *prescription*. This corresponds to two distinct (and potentially confusing) uses of the term *theology*, which can be accounts both of *what people do/did believe* and of *what people should believe*. Although Israel's scriptures still function as religiously authoritative in both Judaism and Christianity—that is, they are in some way *prescriptive*, or *normative*, religious texts for both Jews and Christians—the task of the biblical scholar has not been understood to involve engagement with that authoritative religious function. Rather, the biblical scholar concentrates on clarifying what stands in the texts in their world of origin. The task of prescribing what should be believed or done in the light of what these ancient texts say falls to someone else, that is, the clergy and/or authoritative bodies (synods, councils) of the various religious communities, rather than the biblical scholar (though some biblical scholars do nevertheless point out, usually on ethical grounds, what they think should *not* be believed or done!). In other words, the biblical documents are studied as any other religious documents of any religious tradition might be studied, by anyone with the necessary interest and ability; adherence to (following the prescriptions of) the religion of which these texts form a part is an option that may or may not be adopted, according to individual preference, but it is not intrinsic to the scholarly quest for understanding the texts in themselves.

It is, of course, widely recognized that practice is rarely as neat and tidy as theory, for at least two obvious reasons. First, a majority of modern OT scholars, and probably all those concerned specifically with OT theology, have been religious believers (predominantly Christian but with a growing number of Jews academically studying their scriptures in recent decades), motivated in their study by their religious convictions and concerned that their study should not be without some value in relation to their faith. Indeed, until recently such scholars were usually ordained ministers, that is, recognized teachers in their faith community, and so officially combining within themselves both descriptive and prescriptive responsibilities. Walther Eichrodt, for example, concludes the 1957 preface to the fifth revised edition of his landmark *Theology of the Old Testament*: "It is the author's prayer that this new edition ... may meet with a friendly reception and, like the earlier editions, be of service beyond all confessional frontiers, both in the sphere of academic study and in the practical ministry of the pastor and missionary, to the glory of God and the happiness of the reader."[4] Gerhard von Rad concluded his landmark *Old Testament Theology* with a substantial section on the relationship between the Old Testament and the New.[5] Moreover, von Rad taught theological students the relationship between OT study and preaching, and the content of his *Biblical Interpretations in Preaching* is not substantially different from that of his major scholarly publications, even if it is presented more accessibly.[6]

Second, even if description can easily be distinguished from prescription, description cannot so easily be separated from *evaluation* in some form or other. What one says and how one says it tend to go closely together. Since substantive religious issues touch on basic questions of human self-understanding, identity, values, and priorities, the way in which people (nonbelievers no less than believers) depict theological matters usually reveals something of the stance they take toward those questions. This is often a matter of nuance, revolving around the possible resonances of the particular word that a writer chooses. But sometimes the difference can be stark. For example, one of the OT's most theologically generative passages is Yhwh's promise to David, through Nathan, to give him a perpetual dynasty (2 Samuel 7 // 1 Chronicles 17). While Gerhard von Rad depicts this as a "great new thing" that "became highly creative in the tradition" and as "the historical origin and legitimation of all messianic expectations," Robert Pfeiffer depicts its author as "ignorant" and "amateurish" and its content as "monkish drivel."[7] In other words, to describe is to interpret, and interpretation entails evaluation. Yet, perhaps curiously, in the modern discipline of OT theology, criteria for evaluation, other than the straightforwardly ethical, are rarely discussed—which may reflect a fear that such discussion will entail a lapse into the dogmatic/prescriptive concerns from which properly historical work seeks to be independent.

An influential raising of this issue in recent years appears in the essay of Jon Levenson, the Albert A. List Professor of Jewish Studies at Harvard, "Why Jews Are Not Interested in Biblical Theology."[8] Levenson highlights the way in which scholarly treatments of the OT may purport to be straightforwardly historical yet in fact be deeply shaped by unexamined evaluative judgments, which presume a Christian frame of reference but which are far from self-evident to those, not least Jews, who stand outside that frame of reference.

Nonetheless, difference of approach and evaluation could be argued to be intrinsic to all work in the humanities and to be more a sign of life and health than of any real problem. Why shouldn't scholarly study of OT theology simply continue in the kind of way that has been briefly sketched, which has been enormously fruitful for the better understanding of the content of the OT?

TOWARD THEOLOGICAL INTERPRETATION: A SOCIOCULTURAL CONTEXT FOR A NEW PARADIGM

In recent years there has been a rapid rise of new approaches to OT theology. These are diverse and difficult to catalog, and a short account such as this will necessarily be selective and impressionistic. Nonetheless, recent work tends to have certain characteristic phraseology—for example, *theological interpretation, reading* the OT *as Scripture*, a *canonical approach*—and the context of such concerns is sometimes called *postliberal.*

In general terms, the intellectual changes cannot be understood if they are isolated from the changing sociocultural contexts of Western society. The assumptions that undergirded the dominant modern paradigm of OT theology in the late eighteenth, nineteenth, and twentieth centuries arose in interaction with the sociocultural contexts of those times.[9] In general terms, England, Germany, and America were, in varying ways, Christian cultures, where the cultural significance of the Bible was not questioned and knowledge of its content was widespread. However, the historic churches in these cultures, which had enormous sociopolitical power, could for various reasons (not least to preserve both piety and power) restrictively constrain its interpretation, even though tragic conflicts between Catholics and Protestants tacitly undermined the respective claims of each church to understand the Bible rightly. This meant that the watchword for the biblical scholar became *freedom*, the right to scrutinize the text and pursue philological and historical evidence on its own terms, wherever it led, without constraint by established authorities.

Today, however, Christendom lies in the past. Contemporary Western culture is secular, and it is widely indifferent and uncomprehending, not to mention at times hostile, toward Christian faith and practice (although Christian faith and practice are still more extensive and publicly visible in the United States than in Europe). Things that once could be taken for granted can be taken for granted no longer. Insofar as societies have now moved away from their former Christian identity and self-understanding, and practicing Christians have become a minority, attitudes to both the status and the content of the OT, as of the Christian Bible as a whole, and the issue of which questions to ask and why, are being rethought.

Arguably the key question concerns God. Why should one privilege what the OT says about Israel's deity and suppose that Yʜwʜ has some ultimate reality as the one true God—God and not (a) god—if one makes no such supposition for any other deity of the ancient (or subsequent) world? As Richard Dawkins puts it: "I have found it an amusing strategy, when asked whether I am an atheist, to point out that the questioner is also an atheist when considering Zeus, Apollo, Amon Ra, Mithras, Baal, Thor, Wotan, the Golden Calf and the flying Spaghetti Monster. I just go one god further."[10]

Related to the question of God is the question of canon. Why should one in any way privilege the moral and religious content of the OT generally in relation to that of other religions in antiquity (or even in relation to those practices within ancient Israel of which the OT writers disapproved)?[11] Ancient historians in practice ignore the distinction between canonical and noncanonical texts and artifacts and appraise the content of what they study by other criteria. Why shouldn't those interested in religious content follow suit? In other words, why not reimagine and relocate the constituent documents of the OT as noncanonical documents, whose study would form part of the ancient history of the Mediterranean world, with no implication of enduring significance (which would presumably make them of interest only to a greatly reduced number of scholars)?[12] Alternatively, if one is concerned with the enormous impact of the OT in Western culture over the course of the last two millennia (an area in which biblical scholars are increasingly showing interest), then shouldn't the OT be located within some form of cultural studies setting, where the questions put will be other than those in mainstream biblical studies?

The underlying issue is simple. The privileged status of the OT as a bounded collection, with the historic understanding that the one true God is in some way revealed in its pages together with enduring wisdom and truth about the human condition (such that this material merits extensive theological study), represents a specifically Jewish and Christian perspective. These texts are privileged because Jews and Christians have privileged, and continue to privilege, them; and they have been formative in Western culture because Christian faith has been formative in Western culture. So deeply rooted has this privilege been that many are happy still to take it for granted: the contributors to *TDOT*, for example, refer to Israel's deity as God, not god, although neither contributors nor editors offer any account of why they do so. But where Christian or Jewish identity is not shared, Christian or Jewish understandings about what matters are not necessarily shared either. It is unclear how one can privilege the content of the OT, other than as a cultural artifact, without appeal to the perspectives of Christian or Jewish faith.

What difference should this changing cultural context make? In general terms, just as the conceptual assumptions of modern biblical criticism grew out of the intellectual world of the Enlightenment, so the conceptual assumptions appropriate to the contemporary task should build on more recent developments.[13] For example—to select a few of many significant thinkers—Wittgenstein reestablished how linguistic and conceptual meanings relate to practices of life; Gadamer drew attention to the difference that standing within the flow of reception history makes to the understanding of a text; Paul Ricoeur reflected on the relative autonomy of a text once it has left its author and has developed the interpretative significance of both suspicion and trust; Alasdair MacIntyre has emphasized the social nature of knowledge and has drawn attention to the importance of communal identity and practices over time as setting a meaningful context for certain ethical and conceptual issues to receive potentially constructive discussions and disagreements; Peter Berger has discussed how views of reality relate to the social worlds to which people belong. By way of contrast to the Enlightenment tendency to abstract reason from life and the individual from society, these (and other) recent developments tend to emphasize the relatedness of thought and life and the indebtedness of individual to communal understanding. So I suggest that two particular concerns become important for framing the changing debates about OT theology.

On the one hand, there is the *social nature of knowledge* (a keynote discussion of which is Jon Levenson's essay "Historical Criticism and the Fate of the Enlightenment Project").[14] In "liberal" contexts the emphasis tends to be on the freedom of the individual scholar to work honestly without prejudice or constraint; but comparable attention is not usually given to establishing a subject's value or a scholar's wider responsibilities. In a "postliberal" perspective, the question of what people value and perhaps appropriate as individuals relates to complex sociocultural, religious, and intellectual frames of reference that help form people's identity and understanding; individual integrity matters no less, but the ways in which such a quality is framed and directed are always shaped by the larger frames of reference that people inhabit. This also influences the question of which subjects are considered to deserve institutional resources of money, time, and space to be directed to them.

Thus to determine the OT (or Christian Bible) as a coherent and worthwhile object of study in itself (other than as a small part of ancient Mediterranean history or as a historic part of Western culture) is inseparable from enduring social and intellectual respect for, with the implication also of at least some significant public adherence to, Christianity and/or Judaism. However much one can conceive of ancient places and times when the documents now contained in the OT were first written and seek to understand them in such terms, these documents are of interest today primarily because of their historical and continuing reception and appropriation by Jews and Christians. *Original meaning and continuing significance are not identical, but they are in important ways inseparable.* Judgments and expectations related to the continuing significance of the OT make a difference not only to how the OT is studied but also to the OT being constituted as an object of study in the first place.

On the other hand, this changed sociocultural context suggests that, at least for those who wish in one way or another to maintain the privileged status of the OT, it becomes important in some way to take responsibility for articulating Christian or Jewish perspectives in relation to it, and not just leave these to someone else (e.g., religious authorities). Nicholas Lash, in the course of expounding the thought of Karl Rahner, puts it this way:

> In a Christian culture, a culture in which scholarly attentiveness goes hand in hand with contemplation, a culture quite at ease with prayer [Lash's shorthand for a human relationship with God], it is society as a whole that sings the song, that makes the music. In such a society, it is quite in order for the academic theologian simply to function as *technician*—as music critic, we might say, or as historian of musicology. However, in a culture such as ours (and, for this purpose, it matters not whether we call it "secular" or "pagan")—a culture lacking in contemplativity, finding prayerfulness a *problem*—in such a culture, *no* Christian can afford the luxury of sitting in the audience, but *all* are called to sing the song, to make the music of the Gospel. And this applies, not least, to theologians.
>
> Rahner's plea was not that our theology should become less rigorous in argument, less critically meticulous in treatment of the evidence, but that—irrespective of the level of technicality or accessibility at which a work is pitched—it should spring from and contribute to the articulation of that Word whose utterance, as *Christian* theology, it serves.[15]

Admittedly it is hardly self-evident what specific difference these considerations should make to the student of OT theology; and it is certainly no license for reducing scholarship to devotional reflection, homiletic application, or apologetics (even if all these may be appropriate in the right time and place). Nonetheless, in contexts where the OT is taken to be a foundational document of Christian faith, its theological study should hardly be exempted from Lash's concern. Rather, questions about the nature of, and basis for, truth claims about God and human nature and destiny, as not just ancient but also enduring issues, should appropriately be raised and discussed in relation to the biblical text. If the old watchword for the biblical theologian was *freedom*, perhaps a new watchword might be *responsibility*.

TOWARD THEOLOGICAL INTERPRETATION OF THE OT:
ADVOCATES OF A NEW PARADIGM

Probably the single most significant biblical scholar in the development of new perspectives on OT theology has been Brevard Childs (1923–2007). Childs taught at Yale Divinity School for many years, wrote extensively, and taught or influenced a new generation who themselves have gone on to make significant contributions as theologically interested OT scholars (for example, Christopher Seitz, Gerald Sheppard, Ellen Davis, Stephen Chapman). Also highly influential is Walter Brueggemann (b. 1933). Although Brueggemann is less wide ranging conceptually than Childs, he is probably more widely read, as he is even more prolific than Childs, and his OT discussions have a higher level of engagement with contemporary faith and life than do Childs's. Childs and Brueggemann tower over current discussions of the OT and theology, rather as Eichrodt and von Rad towered over mid-twentieth-century discussions (which is not to deny that there are other weighty contemporary contributors also).

Childs and Brueggemann differ substantially in their approaches (and sadly, over time, became distanced from, and less comprehending of, each other), but they share the conviction that the whole enterprise of OT theology needs rethinking in a contemporary context. Brueggemann speaks for both when he says, "It has slowly dawned on me that biblical exposition cannot be, in the context of the church, a scientific enterprise designed to recover the past as historical criticism has attempted."[16] For both scholars, dissatisfaction with conventional OT interpretation was a realization that developed over time even as they were being immersed in it during their early careers, and for both the key factor is the continuing role of the OT in the life of the church—the role that is invisible in *TDOT*. Childs likewise speaks for both when he says, "It is one thing to attempt to understand the Old Testament as the sacred scriptures of the church. It is quite another to understand the study of the Bible in history-of-religions categories. Both tasks are legitimate, but they are different in goal and procedure."[17] If the OT is to be related to the life of the church, then both the nature and the purpose of the scholarly endeavor need rethinking—not to deny the legitimacy and value of established philological and historical questions but, rather, to put further questions that may need different handling. Precisely what these other questions should be, and what difference they should make, is what is being steadily probed in current literature.

BIBLE AND CHURCH

As is clear from what has already been said, a core concern in theological interpretation is to rethink the relationship between Bible and church and to try to escape a long history of their polarization. The basic point is that the OT is a construct of Judaism and Christianity; if one does not continue to recognize ancient decisions, initially Jewish and subsequently Christian, to privilege and demarcate certain texts, then the OT simply dissolves. *Ancient canon and continuing communities are intrinsically related.* As Robert Jenson puts it, with reference to the Christian Bible as a whole:

> Apart from the canon's role as a collection of texts the church assembled to serve its specific needs, the volume comprising the canon is not a plausible literary or historical unit.... Apart from the fact that Israel's Scripture funded the initial church, and apart from the fact that the church collected writings of its own in one book with this Scripture, there would have been no "Holy Bible," and there would be no reason to treat the documents now bound together under that title as anything but sundry relics of two or more ancient Mideastern religions. It is only because the church maintains the collection of these documents, with the texts they presented, as the book she needs, that we are concerned for their interpretation.[18]

Similar issues apply, mutatis mutandis, in Jewish frames of reference.

As already noted, questions of canon and of God are closely related. Particular *assumptions* and *expectations* are brought to the study of the text by those who identify with, or are willing heuristically to go along with, Jewish and Christian perspectives—not least in relation to one's stance toward the deity depicted in the biblical text. Brevard Childs memorably says:

> I do not come to the Old Testament to learn about someone else's God, but about the God we confess, who has made himself known to Israel, to

Abraham, Isaac and to Jacob. I do not approach some ancient concept, some mythological construct akin to Zeus or Moloch, but our God, our Father. The Old Testament bears witness that God revealed himself to Abraham, and we confess that he has broken into our lives. I do not come to the Old Testament to be informed about some strange religious phenomenon, but in faith I strive for knowledge as I seek to understand ourselves in the light of God's self-disclosure. In the context of the church's scripture I seek to be pointed to our God who has made himself known, is making himself known, and will make himself known.[19]

Perhaps not all Christians today would speak with Childs's confidence, and biblical scholars who are not located in explicitly Christian contexts are often nervous about using such overtly confessional language; whether one is located in a secular university or in a theological seminary or in an ecclesial gathering makes a difference. Nonetheless, Childs articulates what surely has historically been the prime conviction underlying a Christian privileging of Israel's scriptures: whatever their difficulties, they give truth about the one God in a way that other ancient religious texts do not. The conviction is bound up with the continuing attempts by Christians (and comparably, albeit differently, Jews), in their many and varied ways, to live life in relation to God and to develop resources and practices that can help enable the content of the biblical text to be meaningfully engaged with and appropriated in a contemporary context. In sociological terms, the churches become *plausibility structures* for taking seriously the core conviction that the biblical God is the true and living God.[20]

Whether or not secular universities, as distinct from specifically Christian or Jewish institutions, will give space and resources to the study of Israel's scriptures as a canonical collection will depend largely on the social and intellectual respect commanded by church and/or synagogue in any given society. Just as the secular marketplace in principle gives space to religious groups to speak and act from their particular perspective, subject to the constraints of law, so the secular university in principle gives space to intellectual disciplines that are religiously constituted, subject to the religion having sufficient public significance and its academic practitioners observing appropriate academic disciplines.

RECONTEXTUALIZATION

Another cluster of concerns relates to the phenomenon of *recontextualization*. A basic principle of modern biblical study has been that one should "interpret in context." But this principle becomes harder to use well when it is asked, "Which context?" and "Whose context?" Because Israel's scriptures have a continuing history as authoritative material for both Jews and Christians, it becomes clear that issues of recontextualization are integral to their very nature as a canonical collection.

A characteristic concern of modern biblical scholarship has been to *look backward*, as it were, from the OT to the world that gave rise to it: the immediate world of Israel and also the wider world of the ancient Near East. This has meant, for the most part, a focus on times and places before there ever was an OT, although in recent years there has been increased interest in the processes whereby the various documents came together as a discrete collection. A characteristic move of recent theological approaches has been to *look forward*, as it were, from Israel's scriptures toward those faiths, both Jewish and Christian, that have continued from antiquity until today and which have consistently rooted their self-understandings and practices, in various ways, in this material. (Jews have tended to be primarily interested in the legal material and the commandments, while Christians have often focused more on narratives and prophecy; both Jews and Christians have extensively used those prayers that constitute the Psalter.) For this angle of vision, Israel's scriptures as an authoritative collection are more or less a given from the outset (whatever the historic disagreements over the precise boundaries of the canon).

The general point of principle is succinctly expressed by Jon Levenson:

> In the realm of historical criticism, pleas for a "Jewish biblical scholarship" or a "Christian biblical scholarship" are senseless and reactionary. Practicing Jews and Christians will differ from uncompromising historicists, however, in affirming the meaningfulness and interpretive relevance of larger contexts that homogenize the literatures of different periods to one degree or another. Just as text has more than one context, and biblical

studies more than one method, so scripture has more than one sense, as the medievals knew and Tyndale, Spinoza, Jowett, and most other moderns have forgotten.[21]

In some ways, this is not different from issues relating to all texts that come to be recognized as classics and that are appreciatively read, and perhaps enacted, in a wide variety of contexts: They acquire fresh resonances; and also people understand them differently in different places and times.

However, there are particular issues relating to the canonical context of the OT as part of the Christian Bible. For example, how should one consider the separation of the study of the OT from that of the New Testament? Until the early nineteenth century both testaments were usually studied together. Their separation came about in the context of biblical study becoming primarily a history of biblical literature and religion, when it became apparent that for historical purposes the literature of Israel could perfectly well be studied without reference to the literature of the early church. But when Israel's scriptures are studied as a canonical collection, the OT of the Christian Church, should they be studied apart from, rather than in dialectical relationship with, their reception in the New Testament and in subsequent Christian thought and practice? Given the enormous scholarly literature that exists today, there are, of course, obvious pragmatic reasons for limiting one's study to only one of the two testaments. But what about the issue of principle?

Here a prime complicating factor is renewed appreciation, especially post-Holocaust/Shoah, of the continuing religious role of Israel's scriptures as Bible/Tanakh for Jews—a factor that was simply absent in formative mid-twentieth-century OT theological interpreters such as Eichrodt, von Rad, Wolff, Westermann, Zimmerli, and Vriezen. However, Rolf Rendtorff, one of von Rad's most distinguished students, has argued that if "the interpreter consider[s] the pre-Christian (i.e. Jewish) meaning of the text to be theologically relevant," then "he must first view the Old Testament texts in their 'canonical' context, that is to say as a component part of the pre-Christian Jewish biblical canon, and he must also interpret them theologically in that context." He goes on to claim that "this leads to new hermeneutical tasks for which the previous history of Christian biblical interpretation offers no models and but few guidelines."[22]

Yet, even if the motivation of interpretative respect for Jewish religious identity and practice is largely unprecedented (though one should not forget regularly appreciative Christian responses to the Jewish voices of Martin Buber and Abraham Heschel in twentieth-century scholarship), the practical outworking of Rendtorff's approach may be less novel.[23] For an angle of vision that restricts the theology of Israel's scriptures to their pre-Christian context is historicizing in a way that is akin to the paradigm represented by *TDOT*, even if Rendtorff gives special attention to the interrelationship of the texts in their received form.

More promising to many, therefore, is Levenson's approach:

> Just as in medieval Europe there could be interreligious agreement on the *sensus literalis*, so in modern biblical criticism there will continue to be a broad base for agreement on the meaning of textual units in their most limited literary or historical settings. But when we come to "the final literary setting" and even more so to "the context of the canon," we [sc., Jews and Christians] must part company, for *there is no non-particularistic access to these larger contexts*, and no decision on these issues, even when made for secular purposes, can be neutral between Judaism and Christianity. Jews and Christians can, of course, study each other's Bible and even identify analogically or empathetically with the interpretations that the other's traditional context warrants, growing in discernment and self-understanding as a consequence. For the normative theological task, however, a choice must be made: Does the canonical context of the Abraham story, for example, include the Abraham material in Galatians and Romans or not? For Christians it must; for Jews it must not.[24]

The issues here are akin to those in interfaith dialogue. A common modern approach has been to seek maximal agreement by emphasizing ethical issues and downplaying theological/dogmatic issues. Yet in recent years there has been a flourishing of "scriptural reasoning," which takes an almost opposite approach.[25] Participants are encouraged to speak out of the fullness of their own tradition, especially in relation to their foundational scriptures where they are most at home, and to interact with those of other faiths with attention and respect, not so as to secure agreement but so as *to improve the quality of disagreements*. In relation to theological interpretation this means that both Christians and Jews engage dialogically with Israel's scriptures, not only as pre-Christian and pre-Jewish texts but also as Christian OT and Jewish Tanakh, in ways that are academically rigorous and also fruitful for each interpreter's religious frame of reference.

The point is that Christian faith only appropriates Israel's scriptures insofar as they are the Christian OT. However much it matters to hear Israel's witness in its own right, and to be open to being challenged and unsettled by it, this witness functions within a frame of reference larger than itself. Not least, the God of whom the OT speaks is known by Christians in and through Jesus Christ, as Father of the Son. This does not mean that Christians should be unaware that the OT writers did not themselves understand God in these terms. Rather, a Christian appropriation of the OT's witness to God recontextualizes as it appropriates, precisely because the ancient texts are read within a historic and continuing framework of life and practice.

THE RECEIVED FORM OF THE OT TEXT

A characteristic aspect of recent theological interpretation of the OT has been to work with the "final form" of the biblical text. Admittedly, the term *final form* is not entirely felicitous in relation to issues of text and translation; for there are problems involved in determining text-critically what counts as the text of the OT, and there are problems raised by the translation of the OT, already in antiquity, not only into Greek but also into Syriac and Latin, and its reception and appropriation by many churches in these linguistic forms. But the term *final form* (and comparably *canonical form* and *received form*) was developed by way of contrast to a theological focus on hypothetical earlier documents or pre-redacted voices, as reconstructed by scholars. A prime example is the older documentary analysis of the Pentateuch, according to which the Pentateuch was compiled out of four once-independent documents from differing authors of differing dates and outlooks (J, the Yahwist; E, the Elohist; D, the Deuteronomist; P, the Priestly writer). Major mid-twentieth-century OT scholars did significant theological work in relation to these supposed documents.[26] Alternatively, scholars have sought to recover the voices of Israel's histories and prophets apart from the traditio-historical overlays and editorial shaping they appear to have received. An emphasis on the final/canonical/received form of the text directs attention to the biblical text that undoubtedly exists rather than to hypothetical documents or putative earlier versions that, even if they did once exist (which, at least in current Pentateuchal criticism, is a distinctly moot point), do so no longer, other than as part of something larger into which they have been subsumed and thereby transmuted.

What is gained by this shift to basing theological interpretation on the received form of the text? For Childs, it is primarily to do with taking seriously the way in which Israel's traditions have been shaped in such a manner as to make their content accessible to future generations, to all those who by definition could not have been present at the text's point of origin: "The heart of the canonical process lay in transmitting and ordering the authoritative tradition in a form which was compatible to function as scripture for a generation which had not participated in the original events of revelation. The ordering of the tradition for this new function involved a profoundly hermeneutical activity, the effects of which are now built into the structure of the canonical text."[27] In other words, the OT documents have an intrinsic forward-looking function, to utilize material from the past to give theological understanding to those living in the future (as is also indicated by the numerous teachings and observances, both national and familial, that the OT specifies, especially in the Pentateuch). Of course, as a historical claim about the way in which the material developed this is as open to dispute as any other historical claim. Nonetheless, it accords in a general way with the actual use of the material by Jews and Christians down the ages.

A simple illustration for aspects of this issue can perhaps be seen in the possible different forms in which a believer may give a personal testimony. Over the course of time, a believer may reinterpret an experience of coming to faith, told initially in terms of the difference made by significant events and people, in terms that become more overtly theological, when what had felt at the time like a human initiative is reenvisaged as a response to a divine calling and aspects of the initial process are differently weighted. One then has two versions of the testimony, the later one more theologically explicit and reflective than the earlier one and perhaps presenting a somewhat different historical narrative. By analogy one might suggest that the scholar who wants to get behind the received form of biblical traditions is doing something fully legitimate;

but for the purposes of understanding life in the light of God, as articulated by Christians or Jews, attention is being directed to the less reflective account.

This forward-looking orientation to the OT text, with a concern for theological understanding of its received form, need not mean that nothing is to be learned from looking backward. Insofar as the origins and development of the text and its content have left traces in the text, some attention to these ought in principle to be illuminating. Childs, for example, regularly insisted that awareness of behind-the-text issues should add a "depth dimension" to theological interpretation, even while the final form represents a judgment of the inadequacy of earlier versions:

> The final form of the biblical text marks the end of a historical development within Israel's tradition.... It seems obvious that this final form can be much better understood, especially in its crucial theological role as witness, if one studies carefully those hundreds of decisions which shaped the whole. Thus it greatly sharpens one's vision of the final form of the Pentateuch which is the goal of exegesis if one first distinguishes between earlier and later levels within the witness.[28]

Childs's reference to "hundreds of decisions which shaped the whole" presupposes a degree of confidence in traditio-historical and redactional analysis that many scholars, even those less theologically inclined than Childs, might struggle to share today. But Childs's basic concern was that attention to the biblical text in its received form should not sacrifice awareness of, and learning from, all those behind-the-text issues that have featured prominently in OT scholarship.

A different way of angling this giving of priority to the received form of the text is to suggest, following the lead of theologians such as George Lindbeck in his *The Nature of Doctrine*,[29] that Israel's traditions have been shaped in such a way as to provide a kind of theological grammar of the life of faith.[30] On this account, just as a knowledge of grammar enables people to understand how languages work and to use them well, so doctrines, or in the OT context those theological norms that have shaped and are embodied in the content of the text, serve to show what does and does not qualify as meaningful language about, and valid action in response to, God. All sorts of things may have gone on in the religious life of ancient Israel. But only certain aspects are judged to be right, or normative, by those who formed Israel's scriptures; and many of these judgments remain normative for Jews and Christians.

There are at least two further reasons why recent theological interpretation focuses on the received form of the OT text. One is the growth of literary and narrative approaches.[31] Although these are not intrinsically theological, they are amenable to theological concerns. Especially if one recognizes that the OT regularly conveys its theological concerns in the form of dramatic narrative, rather than in the more abstract forms that have often predominated in Western theology, the potential value of literary readings for theological interpretation is not hard to see. So, for example, a good number of recent commentaries on the books of Kings have either made only limited use of or effectively ignored historical-critical concerns (composition, date, historicity, social function, etc.) in favor of narrative readings of the text as enduringly resonant in its received form, with a particular eye to the theological implications of the text, in which God and issues of human faithfulness and faithlessness feature prominently.[32]

A different reason for a theological focus on the received form of the OT text is that it enables the contemporary interpreter more readily to reengage premodern interpreters and their readings. Of course, there is a major growth of interest in reception history generally, in the study, say, of Greco-Roman classics as well as in biblical study. Often, however, the scholarly concern can be primarily that of a historical chronicle that compiles examples from the extensive reception history of all biblical texts and relates them to the contextual concerns of their authors. Of more theological interest is a hermeneutical approach to this reception history that reflects on the nature and purpose of the differing interpretative moves that have been made and relates them to the hermeneutical challenges still faced by contemporary readers of the biblical text. A suggestive example is John L. Thompson's *Reading the Bible with the Dead: What You Can Learn from the History of Exegesis that You Can't Learn from Exegesis Alone.*[33] Among other things Thompson shows that much OT content that troubles contemporary feminists troubled premodern Christian readers also, and he suggests that there is a wisdom in some premodern approaches from which one can still benefit today.

ON ENGAGING WITH THE THEOLOGICAL SUBJECT MATTER

In the biblical (and Jewish and Christian) frame of reference an understanding of God is inseparable from, although not reducible to, an understanding of humanity—as most famously expressed in the OT's opening chapter, that humanity is created "in the image of God" (Gen. 1:27). But how best can one do justice to such subject matter?

In this general context numerous aspects of recent theological interpretation can usefully be located. First is the widespread contemporary recognition of the role of the reader in understanding what the biblical text, like any significant text, is saying. The basic point is that where you stand, and what you are looking for, makes a difference to what you see. Scholarly disciplines and techniques still matter, but the issue concerns how they are framed and utilized. The general point is interestingly made by David Clines:

> My own set of distinctive beliefs—cultural, ethnic and religious commitments and inheritances—are what make me an individual. Call them my prejudices and presuppositions if you must, though I would rather call them the components from which I construct my identity. My integrity as a person lies in the way I balance these competing drives and desires. I can suppress them only at the cost of loss of personal integrity. I do not mean that my personal identity must be on show, in evidence, at every moment; when I go to pay for my petrol at the garage I conduct a formal transaction where I don't strongly feel the need to act as a human being with a distinctive identity. But in doing theology, or developing a literary interpretation of my texts, much more of my self is involved, and I cannot so casually screen out my identity.[34]

Or as Childs more briefly puts it, "The theological enterprise involves a construal by the modern interpreter, whose stance to the text affects its meaning."[35]

Second, there is a hermeneutical issue concerning what is necessary to understand any text, especially one from the distant past. Over against Krister Stendahl's famous distinction between what the text *meant* in the past and what it *means* today,[36] Nicholas Lash has argued:

> If the questions to which ancient authors sought to respond in terms available to them within their cultural horizons are to be "heard" today

with something like their original force and urgency, they have first to be "heard" as questions that challenge us with comparable seriousness. And if they are to be thus heard, they must first be articulated in terms available to us within *our* cultural horizons. There is thus a sense in which the articulation of what the text might "mean" today, is a necessary condition of hearing what that text "originally meant." ...

... It is no part of my argument that we should suppose it to be a straightforward matter to "make sense" either of the past or of the present, let alone to make a sense that would be recognizably Christian.... I am only concerned to insist, as a matter of general hermeneutical principle, that understanding what an ancient text "originally meant," in the circumstances in which it was originally produced, and understanding what the text might mean today, are mutually interdependent and not merely successive enterprises.[37]

This would suggest that, for understanding the theological content of the OT, some engagement with its subject matter in contemporary Jewish or Christian contexts ought in principle to be of value; there needs to be a dialectic between present and past understanding.

Third, the dialectic between reader and text raises fresh questions about what a reader most appropriately brings to the text. The dominant answer to this in modern biblical criticism has been a mastery of the necessary philological and historical disciplines: the interpreter as skilled technician. But if the premise of theological engagement is the enduring significance of the OT as Scripture for the church (or synagogue), then one needs to reconsider the characteristic sharp modern separation between exegesis and dogma, in which dogma is disqualified from exegesis for the sake of scholarly honesty and freedom to follow the evidence where it leads without prejudicial constraint by ecclesial authority. As Childs puts it:

I would argue that the relationship between exegesis and theology ... is basically dialectical in nature. One comes to exegesis already with certain theological assumptions and the task of good exegesis is to penetrate so deeply into the biblical text that even these assumptions are called into question, are tested and revised by the subject matter itself. The implication is also that proper exegesis does not confine itself to registering only the verbal sense of the text, but presses forward through the text to the

subject matter (*res*) to which it points. Thus *erklären* and *verstehen* belong
integrally together in the one activity and cannot long be separated.... In
itself the presence of a dogmatic decision accompanying the exegetical
task is of little consequence; rather, the crucial issue turns on the quality
of both the exegetical analysis and the theological reflection in relation
both to the text and the subject matter.[38]

Fourth, since judgment is influenced by context and character, there
are renewed questions about the appropriate context and character of
the theological interpreter. Much of the writing on theological interpretation has come from scholars located in explicitly Christian contexts
(seminaries, divinity schools), and there are complex issues about how
this should relate to the work of scholars, both Christian and other, in
explicitly secular contexts: What is appropriate to each context, and how
best do they interrelate? Over against the older tendency to set history
against dogma, description against prescription, arguably the basic issue
is how best to relate *knowledge*, as a shorthand for scholarly work in
general, to *wisdom*, in the sense of a knowledge that enables life to be
lived better. The prime epistemological principle in the OT itself is that
"the fear of YHWH is the beginning of wisdom" (Prov. 9:10), which directly links a certain kind of understanding (wisdom) with a moral and
religious way of living (fear of YHWH). The recognition of deep intercon-
nections between thought and life was a premodern commonplace that,
as already noted, is being rearticulated in a wide range of ways in a contemporary postmodern context.

Fifth, as has already become apparent, theological interpreters often
use the terminology of *witness/testimony* and *subject matter* (*Sache, res*)
to depict their approach to the text. This terminology was developed
in the twentieth century especially by Karl Barth and has been widely
adopted. Whether or not theological interpreters recognize the influence
of Barth, or align themselves with some or all of Barth's own concerns,
the legacy of the conceptual categories developed by Barth (himself in
dialogue with Christian theology down the ages) is weighty[39]—though
it should be noted that Eichrodt and von Rad were themselves arguably
no less influenced by Barth than have been Childs and Brueggemann.
Alongside the familiar notion that the biblical text constitutes *evidence*
for historical understanding, the category of *witness* represents a theo-

logical understanding of the role of the biblical text in relation to God—it points beyond itself to ultimate reality: the subject matter of the text is supremely God and the understanding of all life in the world in the light of God. To quote Childs again, "Old Testament theology cannot be identified with describing an historical process in the past ... but involves wrestling with the subject-matter to which scripture continues to bear testimony."[40]

Sixth, it is notable that the image of "wrestling" has proved valuable in providing a way of thinking about how contemporary theological interpreters may best engage with those aspects of the OT that are in some way problematic. For there is much within the OT that appears objectionable for various reasons, and an undifferentiated polarity of belief and unbelief that aligns with an undifferentiated polarity of acceptance or rejection of biblical content is not, despite its periodic adoption in some contexts, the most helpful way of making progress. The image of wrestling has been particularly important for Phyllis Trible, probably the most influential of OT feminist theological interpreters. Trible appeals to the archetypal story of Jacob as paradigmatic for her work: "I'm always struggling with the Bible.... The story that I use as a model is Jacob wrestling in the night (Genesis 32:24–30).... At the end, when the struggle is over, Jacob goes away limping. He gets a blessing, but he doesn't get it on his terms—and he limps. I see this as my struggle with the Bible, my wrestling with Scripture."[41]

Finally, it is worth commenting on the widespread preference for speaking of "theological interpretation of the OT" rather than "OT theology." The shift from a noun depicting what stands in the OT to an adjective that depicts the activity of the interpreter is of a piece with the other issues in this section. The point is to include the interpreter and the interpreter's ability to think and discuss theologically within the task of OT interpretation.

CONCLUSION

Although more could be said, I hope that a sufficient outline has been given of at least some of the most characteristic contemporary concerns that go under the heading of "theological approaches to, and interpretation of, the OT." It should be clear that there is substantive continuity with much twentieth-century work on OT theology in the concern to read the OT text in ways that are fruitful for Christian life and thought. However, the approaches outlined here seek, by way of response to changes in Western culture, to be more self-reflexive, more hermeneutically alert, and more responsive to literary developments than an older (and still continuing) style of OT theology that has been conducted within a historical-critical frame of reference and that has often seen no real problem in separating Israel's scriptures from their continuing validation and appropriation in both Jewish and Christian frames of reference. In important ways these newer approaches seek to reframe, rather than replace, the contributions from more ancient-historically oriented scholarship by adding other interpretative dimensions also. They emphasize that the continuing presence and public significance of Judaism and/or Christianity is a necessary concomitant, or plausibility structure, for recognition of the enduring truth content of Israel's scriptures—especially that Israel's deity is God and not just a god and that humanity should be seen to be in the image of God. Moreover, these approaches are reminders that Jews and Christians, in their differing ways, have, by virtue of living with the biblical text for a long time, developed important resources, both conceptual and practical, for engaging with and appropriating in a contemporary context that of which Israel's scriptures speak in their ancient canonical context.

NOTES

For improvements to this essay I am grateful to Richard Briggs, Anthony Bash, and my informal seminar of postgraduate students.

1. G. J. Botterweck, H. Ringgren, and H.-J. Fabry, eds., *Theological Dictionary of the Old Testament*, 15 vols. (Grand Rapids, Mich.: Eerdmans, 1974–2006; German, 1970–95).

2. E.g., E. Jenni and C. Westermann, *Theological Lexicon of the Old Testament*, 3 vols., Mark Biddle, trans. (Peabody, Mass.: Hendrickson Publishers, 1997); W. VanGemeren, ed., *New International Dictionary of Old Testament Theology and Exegesis*, 5 vols. (Carlisle: Paternoster, 1997).

3. J. P. Gabler, "An Oration on the Proper Distinction between Biblical and Dogmatic Theology and the Specific Objectives of Each," in John Sandys-Wunsch and Laurence Eldredge, "J. P. Gabler and the Distinction between Biblical and Dogmatic Theology: Translation, Commentary, and Discussion of His Originality," *Scottish Journal of*

Theology 33 (1980): pp. 133–58; also in the valuable anthology Ben Ollenburger, ed., *Old Testament Theology: Flowering and Future* (Winona Lake, Ind.: Eisenbrauns, 2004), pp. 498–506.

4. Walther Eichrodt, *Theology of the Old Testament*, vol. 1, J. A. Baker, trans. (London: SCM, 1961), pp. 15–16.

5. Gerhard von Rad, *Old Testament Theology*, 2 vols., D.M.G. Stalker, trans. (London: SCM, 1965).

6. Gerhard von Rad, *Biblical Interpretations in Preaching*, John Seely, trans. (Nashville, Tenn.: Abingdon Press, 1977).

7. Von Rad, *Old Testament Theology*, vol. I, pp. 310–11; Robert Pfeiffer, *Introduction to the Old Testament*, rev. ed. (London: A. and C. Black, 1948), p. 370.

8. Jon D. Levenson, "Why Jews Are Not Interested in Biblical Theology," in *The Hebrew Bible, the Old Testament, and Historical Criticism* (Louisville, Ky.: Westminster/John Knox Press, 1993), pp. 33–61.

9. See esp. Michael C. Legaspi, *The Death of Scripture and the Rise of Biblical Studies* (Oxford: Oxford University Press, 2010).

10. Richard Dawkins, *The God Delusion* (London: Bantam Press, 2006), p. 53.

11. A famous formulation of this challenge is Friedrich Delitzsch's 1902 and 1903 lectures in his *Babel and Bible* (Chicago: Open Court Publishing Company, 1906). See also Francesca Stavrakopoulou and John Barton, eds., *Religious Diversity in Ancient Israel and Judah* (London: T&T Clark International, 2010).

12. See Hector Avalos, *The End of Biblical Studies* (Amherst, Mass.: Prometheus Books, 2007).

13. See also Anthony Thiselton, *New Horizons in Hermeneutics* (London: Harper-Collins, 1992).

14. Jon D. Levenson, "Historical Criticism and the Fate of the Enlightenment Project," in *Hebrew Bible, the Old Testament, and Historical Criticism*, pp. 106–26.

15. Nicholas Lash, "Creation, Courtesy and Contemplation," in *The Beginning and the End of "Religion"* (Cambridge: Cambridge University Press, 1996), pp. 164–82, at pp. 175–76.

16. Walter Brueggemann, *A Pathway of Interpretation* (Eugene, Ore.: Wipf and Stock, 2008), p. xx.

17. Brevard S. Childs, *The Struggle to Understand Isaiah as Christian Scripture* (Grand Rapids, Mich.: Eerdmans, 2004), p. 321.

18. Robert W. Jenson, *Canon and Creed* (Louisville, Ky.: Westminster John Knox Press, 2010), p. 55.

19. Brevard S. Childs, *Old Testament Theology in a Canonical Context* (London: SCM, 1985), pp. 28–29.

20. For this insight of Peter Berger, see R.W.L. Moberly, "Theological Interpretation, Presuppositions, and the Role of the Church: Bultmann and Augustine Revisited," *Journal of Theological Interpretation* 61 (2012): pp. 1–22.

21. Jon D. Levenson, "Theological Consensus or Historicist Evasion? Jews and Christians in Biblical Studies," in *Hebrew Bible, the Old Testament, and Historical Criticism*, pp. 82–105, at p. 104.

22. Rolf Rendtorff, "Old Testament Theology: Some Ideas for a New Approach," in *Canon and Theology: Overtures to an Old Testament Theology*, Margaret Kohl, trans., Overtures to Biblical Theology (Minneapolis: Fortress Press, 1993), pp. 14–15.

23. See Rolf Rendtorff, *The Canonical Hebrew Bible*, David Orton, trans. (Leiden: Deo Publishing, 2005), pp. 415–715.

24. Jon D. Levenson, "The Eighth Principle of Judaism and the Literary Simultaneity of Scripture," in *Hebrew Bible, the Old Testament, and Historical Criticism*, pp. 62–81, at pp. 80–81.

25. See David Ford and C. C. Pecknold, eds., *The Promise of Scriptural Reasoning* (Oxford: Oxford University Press, 2006).

26. See Gerhard von Rad's 1938 essay, "The Form-Critical Problem of the Hexateuch," in *From Genesis to Chronicles* (Minneapolis: Fortress Press, 2005), pp. 1–58, esp. pp. 36–55; and his *Genesis*, 3rd ed. (London: SCM, 1972), esp. pp. 13–31, 152–55. The "Kerygma" essays on the different Pentateuchal strands are conveniently collected and contextualized in Walter Brueggemann and Hans Walter Wolff, *The Vitality of Old Testament Traditions* (Atlanta: John Knox Press, 1975; 2nd ed., 1982).

27. Brevard S. Childs, *Introduction to the Old Testament as Scripture* (London: SCM, 1979), p. 60.

28. Brevard S. Childs, *Biblical Theology of the Old and New Testaments* (London: SCM, 1992), pp. 104–5; compare his *Introduction to the Old Testament as Scripture*, p. 300.

29. George Lindbeck, *The Nature of Doctrine* (London: SPCK, 1984).

30. See Stephen Chapman, *The Law and the Prophets* (Tübingen: Mohr Siebeck, 2000).

31. A formative hermeneutical discussion appears in Hans Frei, *The Eclipse of Biblical Narrative* (New Haven, Conn.: Yale University Press, 1974), esp. pp. 1–16.

32. See, e.g., Richard Nelson, *First and Second Kings*, Interpretation: A Bible Commentary for Teaching and Preaching (Atlanta: John Knox Press, 1987); Iain W. Provan, *1 and 2 Kings*, New International Biblical Commentary (Peabody, Mass.: Hendrickson, 1995); Jerome T. Walsh, *I Kings*, Berith Olam: Studies in Hebrew Narrative and Poetry (Collegeville, Minn.: Liturgical Press, 1996); Terence E. Fretheim, *First and Second Kings*, Westminster Bible Companion (Louisville, Ky.: Westminster John Knox Press, 1999); Peter Leithart, *1 and 2 Kings*, SCM Theological Commentary on the Bible (London: SCM, 2006).

33. John L. Thompson, *Reading the Bible with the Dead: What You Can Learn from the History of Exegesis that You Can't Learn from Exegesis Alone* (Grand Rapids, Mich.: Eerdmans, 2007).

34. David J. A. Clines, "Possibilities and Priorities of Biblical Interpretation in an International Perspective," in *On the Way to the Postmodern*, vol. 1 (Sheffield: Sheffield Academic Press, 1998), pp. 46–67, at pp. 53–54.

35. Childs, *Old Testament Theology in a Canonical Context*, p. 12.

36. Krister Stendahl, "Biblical Theology, Contemporary," in G. A. Buttrick, ed., *The Interpreter's Dictionary of the Bible*, vol. 1 (Nashville, Tenn.: Abingdon Press, 1962), pp. 418–32; reprinted in Heikki Räisänen, Elisabeth Schüssler Fiorenza, R. S. Sugirtharajah, Krister Stendahl, and James Barr, *Reading the Bible in the Global Village: Helsinki* (Atlanta: Society of Biblical Literature, 2000), pp. 67–106.

37. Nicholas Lash, "What Might Martyrdom Mean?" in W. Horbury and B. McNeill, eds., *Suffering and Martyrdom in the New Testament* (Cambridge: Cambridge University Press, 1981), pp. 183–98; reprinted in Nicholas Lash, *Theology on the Way to Emmaus* (London: SCM, 1986), pp. 75–92, at p. 81.

38. Brevard S. Childs, "Does the Old Testament Witness to Jesus Christ?" in J. Adna, ed., *Evangelium, Schriftauslegung, Kirche: F/S Peter Stuhlmacher* (Göttingen: Vandenhoeck & Ruprecht, 1997), p. 60.

39. For Karl Barth's biblical hermeneutics, see Richard Burnett, *Karl Barth's Theological Exegesis* (Tübingen: Mohr Siebeck, 2001).

40. Childs, *Old Testament Theology in a Canonical Context*, p. 12.

41. Phyllis Trible, "Wrestling with Scripture: An Interview between Hershel Shanks and Phyllis Trible," *Biblical Archaeology Review*, March/April 2006, pp. 46–52, 76–77, at pp. 47–48; cf. Phyllis Trible, *Texts of Terror* (Philadelphia: Fortress Press, 1984), pp. 4–5.

FURTHER READING

James Barr, *The Concept of Biblical Theology: An Old Testament Perspective* (London: SCM, 1999), is the most extensive survey of the field, although unsympathetic to both Childs and Brueggemann. Stephen Fowl, *Theological Interpretation of Scripture* (Eugene, Ore.: Cascade, 2009), offers a short and sympathetic guide to recent reconceptualizations of both Old Testament and New Testament theology; see also Kevin Vanhoozer, ed., *Dictionary for Theological Interpretation of the Bible* (Grand Rapids, Mich.: Baker Academic, 2005). The best guide to Childs's work is Daniel Driver, *Brevard Childs, Biblical Theologian* (Tübingen: Mohr Siebeck, 2010; Grand Rapids, Mich.: Baker Academic, 2012). A good overture to Brueggemann is his *Disruptive Grace: Reflections on God, Scripture, and the Church* (Minneapolis: Fortress, 2011), where his work is sympathetically profiled by editor Carolyn Sharp.

There are detailed practical examples of theological interpretation of the Old Testament in R.W.L. Moberly, *The Theology of the Book of Genesis* (Cambridge: Cambridge University Press, 2009) and *Old Testament Theology: Reading the Hebrew Bible as Christian Scripture* (Grand Rapids, Mich.: Baker Academic, 2013). A distinctive voice in relating the Old Testament to contemporary issues is J. W. Rogerson, *A Theology of the Old Testament* (London: SPCK, 2009). Commentary series that practice theological interpretation of the Old Testament from a variety of perspectives include Interpretation: A Bible Commentary for Teaching and Preaching (Westminster John Knox Press), Brazos/SCM Theological Commentary on the Bible (Brazos/SCM), Westminster Bible Companion (Westminster John Knox Press), and Belief: A Theological Commentary on the Bible (Westminster John Knox Press). Journals that promote theological interpretation include *Ex Auditu* (1985–) and the *Journal of Theological Interpretation* (2007–), which also has a related monograph series, JTI Supplement Series (2009–).

Jewish approaches constitute a major development in the field. See Alan Levenson, *The Making of the Modern Jewish Bible* (Lanham, Md.: Rowman and Littlefield, 2011); and Isaac Kalimi, ed., *Jewish Bible Theology: Perspectives and Case Studies* (Winona Lake, Ind.: Eisenbrauns, 2012). A suggestive survey, which also offers a proposal in certain ways analogous to that of Christian theological approaches discussed here, is Benjamin Sommer, "Dialogical Biblical Theology: A Jewish Approach to Reading Scripture Theologically," in Leo Perdue, Robert Morgan, and Benjamin D. Sommer, eds., *Biblical Theology: Introducing the Conversation* (Nashville, Tenn.: Abingdon Press, 2009), pp. 1–53.

21

※

Political and Advocacy Approaches

Eryl W. Davies

Recent years have witnessed a variety of approaches and methods applied to the study of the Old Testament that aim to highlight its contemporary social and political relevance. To some extent, the rise of these approaches represented a reaction against the hegemony of the historical-critical approach to the Bible that had reigned supreme for almost two hundred years and which had generally been regarded as the only method of biblical interpretation recognized as legitimate within the academy. Toward the end of the twentieth century, however, the limitations of the historical-critical approach were becoming increasingly apparent. One of the perceived problems with this method of interpretation was its tendency to distance the biblical scholar from the social and political issues of the day. In focusing on interminable debates concerning the authorship, date, place of writing, and social setting of the various books of the Bible, the interpretive task had been locked in the past, and the Bible had often been viewed as little more than a relic of a bygone age, the primary aim of which was to inform the reader about the customs and practices of the ancient world. Moreover, the commitment of the historical-critical approach to the ideal of objectivity and value-neutral scholarship, untainted by political or personal interests, meant that biblical scholars had effectively been precluded from raising issues of contemporary concern, and thus the method, by default, appeared to lend legitimacy and support to the political, social, and religious status quo. Furthermore, the historical-critical approach increasingly came to be regarded as a method of interpreting the Bible created and deployed by white, male, Western, middle-class academics, and such an approach was regarded as far too restrictive in the multicultural world of the late twentieth century, when the Bible was read and studied by people from different geographic, racial, ethnic, and religious backgrounds. Not surprisingly, therefore, there was a growing consensus that the time had come to move beyond the traditional, established parameters of the discipline, and consequently, the historical-critical approach—long regarded as the litmus test of academic legitimacy—began to yield to fresh and exciting methods that sought to connect the study of the Bible to the social and political dynamics of the age.

For advocates of these newer methods of studying the Bible, the starting point for theological reflection was not so much the biblical text itself but the experiences of ordinary people who felt marginalized, excluded, or oppressed. Thus, for example, feminist biblical critics often approached the Bible from the perspective of women who had been marginalized by men and who had been denied access to positions of authority and influence within the academy and within the church. The point of departure for liberation theologians was the experience of economic poverty and political powerlessness suffered by the poor in the Third World. Postcolonial criticism was concerned with the cruelty and injustices suffered by those who had been on the receiving end of oppressive colonial regimes. Queer criticism took up the cudgels on behalf of those who had been discriminated against on account of their sexual orientation. The factor that united these approaches was the realization that study of the Bible must not remain a merely intellectual activity indulged in by comfortable academics; praxis was not an optional extra or a secondary, subsidiary enterprise but a vital part of the interpretive process itself. Making the Bible relevant was far more important than engaging in abstract theories about its formation and participating in abstruse theological debates about its content, for advocates of these newer approaches were only too aware that a scholarship that ignored the people would eventually be ignored *by* the people.

The various hermeneutical approaches discussed in this chapter share a common agenda, namely, a commitment to the social and political empowerment of the marginalized and oppressed. While advocates of these approaches recognize that the Bible has exerted a major cultural influence on the West, they also recognize that the methods of interpreting the Bible were themselves influenced by the cultural conditions that prevailed during the latter half of the twentieth century. In so doing, they exploit the subversive elements of Scripture and seek to release the liberating potential of the Bible by restoring memories of people and events hitherto suppressed and reclaiming voices that have too often in the past been silenced or ignored. Thus, for example, feminist biblical criticism came into its own with the rise of the so-called second wave of feminism in the late 1960s; the phenomenon of multinational capitalism, which dramatically increased the gap between rich and poor nations and exacerbated the fate of exploited classes and marginalized cultures, led to a rigorous rereading of the Bible from a liberation perspective; the emergence of mass global migration and the creation of multicultural societies that followed the collapse of the great European empires provided fertile ground on which postcolonial biblical studies could flourish; and ambiguity concerning the culturally accepted indicators of sex and gender gave rise to queer theory as applied to the Bible. Clearly, it would be impossible, within the remit of this chapter, to consider in detail all the methodologies applied to the Old Testament that have an avowedly political agenda, but by focusing on a few select hermeneutical approaches, it will be shown how they occasionally succeed in transforming the way in which we read the biblical text. The chapter will conclude by examining how some of these approaches might be applied to the book of Ruth.

FEMINIST BIBLICAL CRITICISM

Feminist biblical critics have long been committed to a particular social and political agenda, for they openly acknowledge that they are engaged in biblical interpretation in order to change entrenched institutional attitudes toward women and to realign the power structures present in contemporary society. Feminist scholars recognize that many of the values of Western culture have been inspired, directly or indirectly, by the Bible, and while they readily concede that various factors have contributed to the establishment of patriarchal power and influence in society, they believe that it would be wrong to deny or minimize the role that the Bible has played in shaping peoples' thoughts and perceptions and in reinforcing sexist attitudes and structures.

One of the first female scholars to call for a critical examination of the role that the Bible played in the subjugation of women in Western society was the political and social activist Elizabeth Cady Stanton (1815–1902).

She believed that the Bible, throughout the centuries, had inculcated in women an attitude of submission, dependency, and obedience and that it had been instrumental in denying them some of their basic rights and freedoms. Whenever women complained about their lack of citizenship or demanded equal access with men to theological training, opponents of women's suffrage used the Bible as ammunition against them: "When in the early part of the nineteenth century, women began to protest against their political and civil degradation, they were referred to the Bible for an answer. When they protested against their unequal position in the church, they were referred to the Bible for an answer."[1] The Bible, as a collection of male-authored texts, written in androcentric language and reflective of male experience, served to promote and sustain patri-archal values and normalize and legitimatize the inferior position of women. It was this realization that prompted Stanton, toward the end of the nineteenth century, to initiate the first "feminist" commentary on the Bible as a means to challenge the dominant male interpretation of Scripture and to highlight its invidious role in the oppression of women. She encouraged the female biblical scholars of her day to contribute to the project, reminding them that "your political and social degradation are but an outgrowth of your status in the Bible."[2] Much to her disap-pointment, however, few responded to her plea, no doubt concerned that if they participated in such a controversial venture, their scholarly ambitions might be thwarted.[3] Such a pusillanimous response merely fueled Stanton's suspicion that women were often complicit in the main-tenance of patriarchal structures, and it strengthened her resolve to see the project through to its completion. *The Woman's Bible* eventually ap-peared, in two volumes, in 1895 and 1898, and it contained a compila-tion of all the sections in the Bible that were of particular relevance to women, accompanied by appropriate, often acerbic, comments, most of which were written by Stanton herself.

Many of the concerns expressed by Stanton at the end of the nine-teenth century are reflected in the writings of more recent feminist bib-lical scholars. They, too, recognize that biblical injunctions such as those that stipulate that women should be silent in church (1 Cor. 14:34–35) and should not exercise authority over men (1 Tim. 2:11–13) have been used repeatedly to reinforce women's inferiority and to exclude them from positions of leadership and authority in the church. Similarly, within Judaism, women who feel called to be rabbis often find themselves barred from such a vocation and prevented from participating fully in the religious life of the Jewish people. For feminist scholars who adhere to the basic principles of the Christian and Jewish faiths, the Bible has inevitably proved to be very problematic, for they find themselves to be in the frustrating position of having to accept as binding and authoritative texts that appear to be incompatible with some of their basic beliefs and principles. Their predicament is well expressed by Letty Russell: "Are they to be faithful to the teachings of the Hebrew scriptures and the Christian scriptures, or are they to be faithful to their own integrity as whole human beings?"[4] Some feminist scholars, faced with such a dilemma, have opted to reject the Bible altogether, regarding it as irredeemably patriarchal and as a source of hindrance for women in their struggle for emancipation. Others have favored a more positive approach and have argued that the biblical text, once shorn of its androcentric trappings, is not as oppressively patriarchal as is often supposed and that a proper understanding of the *true* role of women in the Bible may have far-reaching implications for the rights of women in society generally. Yet others have opted for a more adversarial approach to the biblical material by challenging its assumptions concerning women's cultural marginalization and religious subordination, convinced that, in the process, the role of women in society generally and in the formal structures of institutional religion in particular can be radically changed.[5] Hence, feminist biblical scholarship is brought into direct contact with issues of contemporary concern, and feminist critics see their advocacy stance as part of a collective enterprise that has as its ultimate goal the elimination of sexual stereotypes and the transformation of cultural values.

In this regard, feminist biblical scholarship may be said to derive its impetus not primarily from the academy but from social and political movements promoting the virtues of justice and equality. Indeed, one of the factors that seems to have motivated much feminist biblical scholarship was the realization that traditional study of the Bible seemed distinctly uninterested and uninvolved in current affairs, often appearing to be detached from the various political, social, and economic developments in society. The point was made very effectively by Elisabeth Schüssler Fiorenza in her 1987 presidential address to the Society of Biblical Literature, when she observed that "since 1947 no presidential address has explicitly reflected on world politics, global crises, human sufferings, or movements for change."[6] Developing her argument at length in a later publication, she emphasized that if biblical research was to be relevant, it had to have application beyond the narrow confines of the academy and must strive to bring about "a different world of justice and well-being."[7] The notion that such an unashamedly political agenda might compromise the neutral, "objective" stance of the biblical interpreter was dismissed out of hand, for, as Schüssler Fiorenza has remarked, "intellectual neutrality is not possible in a historical world of exploitation and injustice."[8] Indeed, many feminist biblical scholars exhibited a distinct impatience with the rhetoric of disinterested and presupposition-less exegesis; on the contrary, they argued that biblical scholars should be encouraged to bring their own interests and commitments to bear on their reading of the Bible, for biblical interpretation must begin not with the biblical text but with a considered reflection on one's own experience in one's own sociopolitical location.

Feminist biblical criticism has not, however, been without its detractors, and many of the most telling criticisms have emerged from African American (or so-called womanist) and Hispanic American (or so-called *mujerista*) women's groups that have been anxious to distance themselves from the kind of biblical criticism developed by their Western counterparts. The main point of contention was that the white, middle-class context of traditional feminist biblical studies had been virtually oblivious to the hopes and aspirations of women who had experienced a history of colonialism, enslavement, and conquest. Feminist critics in the West mistakenly presumed that their experiences were universal and generic for all, and they failed to recognize that women's experiences varied markedly from culture to culture and that "feminist theology" was not a monolithic enterprise but one rooted in multiple communities and contexts. Renita J. Weems, for example, has forcefully criticized the universalizing tendency of North American and European feminist biblical scholars who tended to "homogenize women in general and women of color especially without regard to our differences of race, religion, nationalities, sexual orientation, and socio-economic backgrounds."[9] They focused almost exclusively on gender oppression and failed to recognize that women in the Third World were exploited, marginalized, and discriminated against not only on account of their gender but on account of their race or caste. Moreover, it was argued that white, middle-class feminist biblical scholars were mired in interminable debates about issues such as gender-inclusive language and the male bias of Scripture, whereas women in Africa and Asia were concerned with more immediate problems, such as the struggle for survival in the face of famine, malnutrition, and racial and ethnic strife. *Their* reading of the Bible took place not in the ivory towers of academia but in the context of their own sociopolitical situation, and for them, it was the urgent questions of the present that determined how the biblical text should be read and interpreted.

Feminist biblical scholarship in the Western tradition has generally been very sensitive to such criticism, and by now there is increasing recognition that feminist theology must cut across ethnic, cultural, and religious ties and that white, European feminist scholars must integrate non-Western approaches into their exegesis of the Bible. They must step outside a worldview steeped in narrow Eurocentrism and recognize that they are part of a global resistance movement concerned with the solidarity of women across racial, economic, and religious borders. No longer can the experiences of women in the Third World be left out of theological reflection, for women's experiences intersect and overlap in ways that demand an intercultural approach. In this regard, much valuable work has been done by postcolonial feminist biblical critics, such as Kwok Pui-lan and Musa Dube, who have emphasized that feminist theology must concern itself not only with patriarchy but with all forms of oppression and domination, including colonialism, cultural imperialism, and racism, all of which have contributed over the years to the violence perpetrated against women.[10] There is clearly room for further dialogue between feminist and womanist/*mujerista* scholars, as there is between biblical and nonbiblical feminist scholars and between all of these and mainstream biblical scholars, and the hope must be that in future feminist/womanist/*mujerista* biblical criticism will become "so integral to strategies of interpretation that it is no longer distinguishable as a separate genre."[11]

LIBERATION THEOLOGY

Liberation theology emerged in Latin America in the 1960s, though parallel developments were witnessed in other parts of the world, including Africa, Asia, and North America. Strongly influenced by Marxist social theory, liberation theologians emphasized that traditional biblical interpretation served the interests of the sociopolitically dominant groups in society, and they sought to counter this by advocating a "preferential option for the poor" and by focusing on the position of the weak, the vulnerable, and the powerless. They observed that the social and economic circumstances of peoples in Old Testament times were not unlike those of the poor in Latin America, who were similarly faced with oppressive landowners and avaricious merchants and who were ensnared in a social system that was manifestly unfair and unjust. The Bible could thus be held up as a mirror in which the poor and downtrodden could see a reflection of their own experiences of poverty, suffering, and deprivation. But the Bible also contained a message of hope for those who felt beleaguered and oppressed, for it suggested that their present difficulties could be surmounted and their present situation could be reversed. In this regard, liberation theologians pointed to the social critique of the prophets, who condemned in no uncertain terms the situation of injustice and exploitation current in their day. Jesus himself was viewed as a political revolutionary, deeply embroiled in the class struggles of his time and preaching a gospel of freedom and equality. But it was primarily the story of the exodus from Egypt that became a recurring theme in the writings of the liberation theologians, for this seminal event in Israel's history was regarded as a symbol of throwing off the yoke and breaking free from established institutions, enabling people who had been marginalized and oppressed to refashion a new life for themselves. Moses's words to Pharaoh, "Let my people go!" (Exod. 10:3), had a particular resonance for the poor and powerless in the Third World, and the story of Israel's release from bondage provided a message of encouragement and a beacon of hope for all those who were in despair.

As a theology born in the midst of a struggle for survival, liberation theology was intended, from the outset, to be a practical, action-oriented approach to the Bible. Its goal was not to provide a studied reflection on the nature of poverty but to actively seek its elimination. It was not a theology *about* liberation but a theology designed to *promote* liberation, and it was intended as a clarion call for the vulnerable to engage in the struggle for justice and to seek better conditions for themselves. Liberation theology thus had a clear political agenda, for it was intended to make a difference in the real world and to lead to meaningful social reform. As such, it proved highly successful in influencing groups working toward justice and equality, and it even had some sway over the manner in which social movements and international aid agencies came to view social policy.[12]

In recent years, however, the shortcomings of liberation theology have become increasingly apparent, and as a result, it has suffered something of a decline in its popularity. Some have tended to regard it as too narrowly focused and have wondered whether its "preferential option for the poor" is still relevant in the post-Marxist world. After all, wasn't the biblical message of liberation intended for everybody, irrespective of their economic circumstances? Moreover, the Catholic Church criticized liberation theologians on the grounds that their use of a Marxist analysis of social reality was hardly an appropriate frame of reference for reading the Bible. Surely, it was argued, a theology concerned with social and political structures of exploitation could not justifiably be based on a philosophy that was ideologically committed to atheism and materialism— and one that was, in any case, now widely regarded as outmoded and discredited? Marxism's denial of God struck at the very core of Christian belief and was therefore, unsurprisingly, viewed as potentially damaging to the Christian faith. But perhaps the most telling criticism of liberation theology came from those who felt that its one-sided emphasis on the liberating aspects of the Old Testament had led liberation theologians to overlook—or deliberately ignore—its more oppressive aspects. Their focus on the exodus narrative was a case in point. They manipulated the text to provide positive signals for the aspirations and desires of those whom they represented while exhibiting little awareness of, or sensitivity to, the plight of the victims who, according to the biblical tradition, were on the receiving end of God's liberating action. Scholars such as Gustavo Gutiérrez read the biblical narrative uncritically, without considering the event from the viewpoint of the Canaanites. He referred to the oppression suffered by the Hebrews in the land of slavery (Exod. 13:3, 20:2) and emphasized their repression (Exod. 1:11) and humiliation (Exod. 1:13–14) but said nothing about the oppression and humiliation suffered by the indigenous population of Canaan at the hands of those very slaves. He claimed that the liberation of Israel was "the beginning of the construction of a just and comradely society."[13] But a "just and comradely society" for whom? Certainly not for the Canaanites, who, according to the biblical text, were annihilated by the invading Israelites. While it was true that the exodus had inspired social movements of liberation, the traditions of the exodus and conquest contained elements that were arguably antithetical to the principles of peace and social justice. In South Africa, for example, the story of Israel's settlement in Canaan was used to justify colonial dispossession of blacks by whites, and the text merely served to undergird the interests of the oppressors. The same narrative served to justify the genocide of North American Indians and Aboriginal Australians and the expropriation of land from the Palestinians.[14] It was partly in order to deal with such troubling issues that a new mode of inquiry emerged in biblical scholarship, namely, postcolonial criticism.

POSTCOLONIAL CRITICISM

As a method of inquiry postcolonial theory is encountered in a variety of academic subjects, and although its application varies from one discipline to another, its basic aim is the same, namely, to uncover colonial domination in all its forms and to oppose imperial assumptions and ideologies. Its entry as a critical theory into the arena of biblical studies was comparatively late, for it was not until the 1990s that scholars in the Third World and those among racial minorities in the United States began to raise questions about the role of the Bible in the imperial cause and the extent to which colonial assumptions were embedded in the text. Postcolonial criticism engaged in oppositional or resistant readings of the Bible, viewing it from the perspective of the socially excluded and oppressed and exposing texts that appear to condone various forms of tyranny, domination, and abuse.

Colonialism was based on an overweening desire for power and domination, and the Bible provided the very ammunition that the colonizers needed to achieve their aim, for it proved to be a useful tool to undergird their imperial designs and to legitimate their expansionist agenda.[15] They argued that the distinction between master and servant, governor and governed, rich and poor, was something that had been authorized and sanctioned by Scripture itself (cf. Rom. 13:1–7), and thus the Bible became an instrument of domination that could be used to promote social structures that perpetuated an unjust and oppressive system. The Bible taught that everyone had a divinely given status in life, and as far as the colonizers were concerned, this meant that the status of the black indigenous population was subservient to that of their white European counterparts. Moreover, select passages from Scripture were used to justify political and military aggression by the West and to provide legitimacy for European expansion into regions and countries such as Latin America, South Africa, and Palestine. Biblical texts were also used to denigrate the indigenous culture as inferior and primitive, mired as it was in superstitious and idolatrous practices. The colonized were depicted as morally and spiritually degenerate and in need of salvation, and spreading the message of the gospel was intended to encourage them to renounce their corrupt and superstitious practices and to embrace, instead, the enlightened ethos and progressive values of the West. The Bible demonstrated the superiority of Christianity over the heathen culture of the colonized, and it served to instill in the natives the belief that the ruler knew better than the ruled and that whatever the colonial master did, however unpleasant or unpalatable, was ultimately for the benefit of the subject people. Emphasis was placed on the native-friendly and sympathetic face of colonialism, for its aim was merely to bring law and order to an unruly people and abolish practices—such as witchcraft and ritual sacrifice—that the civilized world had long outgrown. Far from being an aggressive imposition of one culture upon another, the colonial enterprise presented itself as a well-meaning and benevolent intrusion into the lives of the natives, and it emphasized that the subject peoples should be grateful for such generous and charitable intervention, for there was little doubt that, were the colonizers to leave, the natives would simply revert to their old, barbaric ways.

While some among the colonized were taken in by the ideology of those in positions of power, and even expressed gratitude and admiration toward the colonizer, others cast doubt on their supposed altruistic motives and were by no means convinced that colonization was the benevolent humanitarian enterprise that the colonizer would have them believe. The kind of propaganda disseminated by the colonizers—that the natives were basically a barbarous people who were quite incapable of ruling themselves—came to be regarded as patronizing in the extreme and smacked of cultural arrogance. While apologists for the colonial program regarded it as a positive development and claimed that there was nothing wrong with ridding the world of polygamy and human sacrifice and delivering the natives from the twin evils of ignorance and savagery, those on the receiving end of such supposed blessings were aware of the predatory, exploitative nature of colonial rule and its various strategies of domination. For them, the atrocities committed in the name of empire—including land seizures, forced resettlements, and economic exploitation—merely highlighted the rapacious nature of the colonial enterprise. They viewed the colonizers as a culturally disruptive force, intent upon imposing their own economic system and political rule on foreign nations, so that the natives virtually felt themselves to be strangers in their own land.

Such resentment inevitably led to a rebellion against the colonial masters, and the colonized came to realize that the Bible, which had been used as an effective tool to justify social and economic injustices, could equally well be used by the marginalized and oppressed to articulate their self-worth and empowerment. Texts that had been cited to promote an attitude of resignation and apathy in the face of exploitation could just as well be used to foment rebellion and to revitalize the life and culture of the indigenous people. Instead of being hapless consumers of imperial interpretations of the Bible, the colonized began to claim the authority to interpret Scripture from their own perspective, and when the Bible was read by those who had suffered repression, persecution, and exclusion, its message came to be understood very differently. The colonized discovered the revolutionary potential of the Bible and realized that, instead of being an instrument of oppression, it could become a vehicle of emancipation and that they themselves could be liberated, rather than subjugated, by the words of Scripture. There were biblical texts that opposed the oppression and exploitation of the vulnerable and that indicated God's solidarity with the weak and powerless members of society. After all, didn't the prophets challenge the gross abuses of power by the monarchy and the ostentatious greed of the prosperous merchants and landowners (cf. Amos 2:6–8; Isa. 5:8–10)? Didn't the law legislate against all kinds of socioeconomic injustice (Exod. 23:6–8)? Didn't the Psalmist and the authors of the Wisdom literature condemn those who were indifferent to, or complicit in, the oppressive systems of their day (Ps. 10:1–11; Prov. 14:31)? And didn't Jesus side with the oppressed against the officially constituted religious and political authorities of his time and speak out against injustice and exploitation in all its forms (Luke 4:18–19, 11:42–44)? Of course, the colonized had no theological training or exegetical expertise, but, for them, that hardly mattered; what was important was that the Bible spoke meaningfully to their own experience of struggle and oppression and that it was possible to extract from an ancient text a message that was relevant to their own situation. For the colonized, the purpose of Bible study was not to glean information about the past but to illuminate and inform the present, and by being read in this way the Bible instilled in them a new sense of national pride and purpose.

Postcolonial biblical scholars in the Third World viewed their task as being to scrutinize and expose not only the colonial assumptions of the biblical text but also the colonial assumptions of the biblical interpreter. They thus began to question the Eurocentric thinking that had hitherto dominated much biblical interpretation. Since Western scholars had traditionally controlled the interpretive agenda, their method of interpreting the biblical text had often been deemed to be *the* normative approach by which all other methods were to be tested and *the* benchmark against which all rival interpretations were to be judged. They considered themselves to be the true custodians of the interpretation of Scripture, and their implicit assumption was that interpretations emanating from Asia or Africa were somehow inferior, since they represented an emotional, spontaneous response to the Bible, far removed from the detached, "objective" interpretation of their European counterparts. While analysis of the biblical text emanating from the Third World might be interesting and, at times, engaging, it was regarded as lacking the required academic pedigree and therefore was not to be taken too seriously. If Third World scholars wanted their interpretations to gain credibility, they should conform to the rules, criteria, and conventions established within the Western academic paradigm.

With the rise of postcolonial criticism, however, scholars from the Third World began to resist the notion that their Western counterparts had the sole authority to determine the text's meaning, and they steadfastly opposed European hegemonic control over biblical interpretation. They realized that traditional biblical scholarship had its roots in the ideology of the ruling classes and that its ultimate aim was to rationalize and universalize what were, in effect, sectional class interests. They argued that the story of the Bible was *their* story and that the events recorded in the pages of Scripture spoke directly and constructively to their own situation. They perceived echoes in the Bible of their own beliefs and rituals, for both worlds were inhabited by spirits, demons, and angels and both shared similar practices, such as polygamy and libation. Such echoes, far from being an impediment to biblical interpretation, enabled them to enter the world of the Bible, which was populated with similar notions and customs, and the affinities between the cultural and religious practices of ancient Israel and their own led them to claim that they had a special access to the texts denied to their counterparts in the West. Their own experience in the religious, social, political, and economic realms could lead them to provide a distinctive and creative interpretation of the Bible and might even enable them to discover and appreciate nuances in the biblical text that the learned exegete in the academy may have missed. European scholars did not have a monopoly over the interpretation of Scripture. Indeed, the kinds of scholarly readings of the Bible that emerged from Western academies were deemed by people in the Third World to be largely irrelevant to their needs and alien to their lives and faith.

QUEER CRITICISM

During the last two decades or so, queer theory has been appropriated by a number of disciplines within the humanities, including literature, music, history, and art, and since the 1990s it has emerged as a distinctive and radical method of interpreting the Bible, as is evident from the burgeoning number of books and articles that have appeared in recent years with a view to examining the biblical text from a gay, lesbian, bisexual, or transgender perspective. *Queer theory* or *queer criticism* remains something of a contested term among some biblical exegetes; yet there can be little doubt that—ironically enough—the very word once used in a disparaging sense as a term of abuse aimed at those who indulged in same-sex relationships has now become a respectable term in the repertoire of biblical scholars. That queer criticism should have come to be applied so enthusiastically within the discipline is, perhaps, not surprising, for there is a long legacy of Bible-based hostility toward homosexual practice that has resulted in the marginalization and victimization of countless Jews and Christians on account of their sexual orientation. Since the Bible was commonly regarded as providing the normative guide for sexual conduct, those who indulged in same-sex relations were seen as acting contrary to God's will and contrary to both natural and moral law. Heterosexuality was considered to be the God-given norm, and all other forms of sexual relations were regarded as aberrations that would lead inevitably to depravity and moral dissolution. Advocates of queer theory have inevitably been left to ponder how gay and lesbian readers should position themselves vis-à-vis a sacred text that appears, on the surface at least, to be implacably opposed to same-sex relationships.

Among the biblical texts that are usually regarded as sustaining the ideal of heterosexual union are the opening chapters of the book of Genesis. The clear implication of such passages as Gen. 1:27–28, 2:24, and 3:16 is that heterosexuality should be the norm in human relations and that the divine intention for humankind was for male-female complementarity. Not surprisingly, then, the opening chapters of the Jewish and Christian scriptures have been regarded as creating "a heteronormative atmosphere against which the remainder of the scriptures have traditionally been read."[16] The heterosexual orientation of the Bible is compounded by a handful of texts that appear to adopt a distinctly antigay or antilesbian stance. In this regard, the main passages that have been the object of critical scrutiny are the narrative concerning Sodom and Gomorrah in Gen. 19, the Levitical prohibitions against homosexual acts in Lev. 18:22 and 20:13, and Paul's reference to both male and female same-sex relations in Rom. 1:26–27 and 1 Cor. 6:9. In order to ward off attacks putatively based on such texts, queer readers have adopted a number of different strategies. Some argue that these texts were composed in a very different cultural and historical context than our own and, consequently, biblical passages condemning same-sex relations have little or no relevance for contemporary debates about homosexuality. Others point to the double standards that appear to operate among those who use these biblical passages to denounce gay and lesbian relationships, for while they readily accept the biblical *prohibition* of homosexual activity (Lev. 18:22, 20:13), they are not similarly disposed to accept the *penalty* that should be inflicted (death, according to Lev. 20:13). Yet others detect a sense of hypocrisy among those who insist on the normative authority of the Old Testament when dealing with sexual morality but ignore it when it comes to teachings on other issues that they feel cannot and perhaps should not be observed.[17]

Many queer commentators, however, argue that the biblical passages that appear to condemn homosexual practices have regularly been misinterpreted and misunderstood by the dominant heterosexual interpretation of such texts. It is argued, for example, that Gen. 19 was never intended to be a diatribe against homosexuality but, rather, merely a condemnation of inhospitality toward strangers.[18] Thus (so the argument goes) it is the interpretation of Scripture rather than Scripture itself that is condemnatory of same-sex relations, and when the relevant texts are read through the filter of a queer reading and viewed in the light of their historical context, "the Bible is actually not saying what we have thought it said."[19]

While some are happy to adopt the defensive strategy of contesting traditional interpretations of biblical passages that appear to condemn same-sex unions, others prefer to focus on texts that seem to present same-sex relationships in a positive light in an attempt to correct the impression that the attitude of Scripture toward homosexuality is uniformly negative. Such gay-affirming readings of the Bible tend to highlight the passionate friendship between David and Jonathan, whose love for each other was "wonderful, passing the love of women" (2 Sam. 1:26), or the relationship between Ruth and Naomi (see below), or that between Jesus and the Beloved Disciple. Such texts suggest that there is more material in the Bible that is amenable to a gay or lesbian hermeneutic than has hitherto been supposed, and some have even argued that, in biblical times, same-sex relations between women and between men were "socially normative and divinely ordained."[20] Viewed in this light, the Bible can be used as a tool of liberation, rather than as a tool of oppression, in the lives of gay, lesbian, bisexual, and transgendered people. Of course, such bold, provocative, and controversial interpretations of the Bible have been criticized by some as strained, unconvincing, and highly conjectural, and it is argued that various biblical texts have been deliberately manipulated by queer readers in order to make them conform to their own expectations and desires. For their part, queer readers insist that they are merely exposing the heterosexual bias inherent in traditional biblical interpretation and that they are simply indulging in a "hermeneutic of hetero-suspicion."[21] Owing to their own experiences, they claim to be able to make visible aspects of the text that have long been suppressed and neglected and to discover subtle nuances in the text that may have been missed in traditional heterosexual interpretation of Scripture.

It must be emphasized that queer criticism is not merely about contesting the latent homophobia of particular biblical texts and their interpretation, nor is it merely about seeking to legitimate same-sex practices by pointing to canonical precedents; it is also concerned to promote an intellectual climate of tolerance toward gay, lesbian, bisexual, and transgendered people. It seeks to eradicate homophobia by opposing the "us" and "them" mentality and by striving for greater levels of understanding and inclusiveness in society. The binary division between male and female (underscored by such passages as Gen. 1:27) is contested, and the rigidity of sexual identity labels is resisted. Indeed, queer theory involves the transgressing of norms and the recognition that the categories of heterosexual/homosexual and straight/gay are too narrow, limiting, and polarized, for binary sexual differentiation takes no account of those whose lives do not conform to conventional gender norms. By opposing prevailing definitions of sexual identity, queer theory challenges what is commonly perceived as "normal" and questions the very notion of "compulsory heterosexuality." For biblical scholars who espouse a queer reading of the Bible, it is not enough to encourage Jews and Christians to reflect theologically on their own experience, for such abstract reflection is irrelevant unless it succeeds in changing institutional mindsets and transforming academic and ecclesiastical discourse. Of course, they recognize that many positive developments have occurred in recent years concerning the rights of gays, lesbians, and bisexual and transgendered people, who have all too often in the past been subject to prejudice, discrimination, and harassment.[22] Yet, despite the growing acceptance of gays and lesbians in contemporary society, an element of discrimination and stigmatization still persists within the church and, to a lesser extent, within the academy,[23] and consequently much work remains to be done to challenge oppressive systems that are still prevalent in society.

THE BOOK OF RUTH

At this point it may be helpful to consider how some of the methods outlined above might be applied to a specific biblical text. In this regard the book of Ruth may serve as a useful point of reference.

As one of the only two books in the Old Testament named after a female figure, the book of Ruth has understandably attracted much attention from feminist biblical critics. Some have even argued that the book was written by a woman; be that as it may, the worldview reflected in the biblical story is unquestionably thoroughly female. Ruth emerges as one who has freed herself from patriarchal constraints by making an independent decision to remain with her mother-in-law rather than returning to the land of Moab. Far from reinforcing the biblical stereotype of the submissive woman, the book portrays Ruth as a strong, confident, and courageous person who actively participates in shaping her own destiny. It is she who goes to the threshing floor at night to seduce Boaz, and it is she who takes the dominant role in insisting that he fulfill his duties as the next of kin (3:6–13). As for Boaz, he merely gives an assurance that he will do whatever Ruth wants: "And now, my daughter, do not be afraid, I will do for you all that you ask" (3:11). The women of the town, full of admiration for Ruth's bold and decisive action, tell Naomi that her daughter-in-law has proved more valuable to her "than seven sons" (4:15). Not surprisingly, feminist biblical critics have regarded the book of Ruth as valorizing the autonomy of women and extolling their initiative and independence in a male-dominated world, and this is taken as evidence that the Bible occasionally offers a more positive view of women than is commonly supposed.

The book of Ruth also provides an example of the way in which postcolonial criticism can enable us to read a familiar biblical text in a fresh light. Laura E. Donaldson, for example, reads the story from the perspective of a Cherokee woman, and in doing so she succeeds in reconceptualizing the role of Ruth and Orpah in the light of the predicament faced by Native American women who, as ethnic minorities, are continually faced with the temptation to assimilate themselves into mainstream white American culture.[24] Donaldson begins by recounting briefly the events that occur in the opening chapter of the book, which relates how a man named Elimelech, along with his wife, Naomi, and their two sons, decides to leave their home in Judah because of the famine in the land

and settle down in Moab. While there, the two sons marry Moabite women, Orpah and Ruth. Elimelech dies, and some years later, both his sons also die, leaving behind Naomi, the widow, and her two daughters-in-law. When Naomi hears that there is no longer a famine in Judah, she decides to return to her homeland, and Naomi, Ruth, and Orpah begin their journey. At one point, Naomi, realizing that her daughters-in-law may prefer to remain in their own country, encourages them to return: "Go back, each of you to your mother's house" (1:8). Initially, the two women insist on accompanying their mother-in-law (1:10), but after further encouragement from Naomi, Orpah takes her leave and returns to Moab, leaving Ruth and Naomi to make the journey together to Judah.

Laura Donaldson then turns to focus on Moab, the place in which Elimelech and his family had settled. According to the biblical tradition, Moab was the home of a "sexually promiscuous and scandalous" population,[25] and the Israelites regarded its female inhabitants as agents of impurity and evil (cf. Num. 25:1–5). Indeed, Deut. 23:3 expressly states that no Moabites would be accepted as members of the community of Israel, even to the tenth generation. Thus, by deciding to leave behind the wicked and evil country of her upbringing and accompanying Naomi to Judah, Ruth was (according to the traditional interpretation of the text) making a deliberate choice to renounce her own depraved and degenerate culture in order to embrace, instead, the superior culture of the Jews. As befitted the woman who was to become the direct ancestress of King David (Ruth 4:13–17), she was prepared to sacrifice her home, her kindred, and her native religion and become a God-fearing Jew. Not surprisingly, the later rabbis regarded her in a favorable light, seeing her as the paradigmatic convert to Judaism. Indeed, her faith was regarded as greater even than that of Abraham, for she left her home of her own volition, whereas the patriarch left Ur only in response to God's command.

Donaldson's reading of the book of Ruth, however, subverts the traditional interpretation of the narrative, and she reverses the usual scholarly focus on Ruth and Naomi by bringing Orpah to the center of attention. Although Orpah is mentioned only twice in the book (1:4, 14), it is she who is held out as the role model for aboriginal peoples everywhere, for she represents someone who was determined to preserve her ethnic identity and who refused to be assimilated to a foreign culture. She was not willing to renege on the traditions of her ancestors, nor was she willing to go to a land ruled by a deity other than the one she had traditionally worshipped. Ruth, on the other hand, is viewed in a more negative light, for she was prepared to relinquish her cultural background, forsaking her homeland in order to align herself with the very nation that had been instructed to destroy the religious heritage of her own people. Ruth is thus viewed as representing indigenous people everywhere who have assimilated themselves to the culture of the colonizer, and as if to emphasize the betrayal of her indigenous heritage, she is characterized as "Ruth the Moabite" several times in the story (1:22; 2:2; 4:5, 10). When the book of Ruth is read from the cultural and historical perspective of an American Indian woman, Ruth's action serves to symbolize the inevitable vanishing of the indigenes' culture, while Orpah's decision symbolizes minority cultures whose people steadfastly refuse to become assimilated to the traditions and way of life of their "civilized" white counterparts. Donaldson's postcolonial reading of the story enables us to appreciate the narrative in a fresh light, for she has succeeded in transforming "Ruth's positive value into a negative and Orpah's negative value into a positive," and she ends her essay by expressing the hope that she has provided an interpretation "that resists imperial exegesis and contributes to the empowerment of aboriginal peoples everywhere."[26]

Finally, we may examine how the relationship between the characters in the book of Ruth is viewed by those who advocate a queer reading of the text.[27] Such a reading inevitably focuses on the relationship between Ruth and Naomi, rather than that between Ruth and Boaz, and the two women are regarded as having formed a bond that transcended age, nationality, and religious tradition. The oath of loyalty uttered by Ruth to her mother-in-law is regarded as a declaration of a deep and abiding love and friendship:

> Where you go, I will go;
>   where you lodge, I will lodge;
> your people shall be my people,
>   and your God my God.
> Where you die, I will die—
>   there will I be buried.
> May the LORD do thus and so to me,
>   and more as well,
> if even death parts me from you! (1:16b–17)

This stirring oath of loyalty, described by Cheryl Exum as "one of the most beautiful and profound expressions of attachment of one human being to another in literature,"[28] is regarded as far more than a declaration of female solidarity; rather, Ruth wished her relationship to her mother-in-law to be a lifelong commitment, a bond that was so strong that not even death would separate them. That Ruth wanted her life to be bound up with Naomi's is further confirmed by the vocabulary of 1:14, which states that Ruth "clung to her." The verb used for "clung" here (*dbq*) is that encountered in Gen. 2:24, which states that a man will leave his father and mother and "cling" to his wife, and its appearance in the present context is regarded as lending "the women's relationship its marriage-like quality."[29] The intensity of the relationship between the two women is further suggested by the words of the women of Bethlehem to Naomi, referring to Ruth as the woman "who loves you" (Ruth 4:15).[30] The fact that Ruth eventually marries Boaz is not regarded as undermining this interpretation of the story, for there is no indication that the marriage severs her allegiance to Naomi; rather, this merely indicates that it was impossible for women to survive in biblical times without the protection and financial support of men.[31] Others, conceding that the threshing floor scene between Ruth and Boaz is suggestive of sexual intimacy between them, argue that Ruth was entangled in both same-sex and opposite-sex relations, and viewed in this light, the book of Ruth is regarded as destabilizing familiar gender categories. That traditional commentators have tended to focus on the relationship between Ruth and Boaz and have not usually recognized or acknowledged any hint of sexual desire on the part of Ruth for Naomi is regarded by queer readers of the book as an example of the heterosexual bias so often at work in biblical interpretation.[32]

CONCLUSION

It is important to recognize that the various hermeneutical approaches discussed in this chapter are by no means mutually exclusive; on the contrary, there is an easy rapprochement among them, and some share similar preoccupations and theoretical presuppositions. Moreover, advocates of these approaches are often engaged in a common interpretive vocation, whether this takes the form of resisting dominant interpretations of the Bible, opposing various forms of oppression (such as patriarchy or colonialism), or foregrounding the voice of the marginalized and excluded. In the process, they have enabled pertinent and incisive questions to be formulated and addressed to the Bible with the urgency they deserve. How has it been used as an instrument of social manipulation and control? How has it been utilized to marginalize women and legitimize racism? How has it been deployed to defend particular political systems and protect powerful interests? But, also, how *can* it be used to effect a change in social, religious, and institutional mindsets? Such questions are important, for the Bible is read not only for religious or theological edification but for its broader cultural and political impact in influencing the norms and values of society. Advocates of the approaches discussed above have recognized the need to move beyond the cloistered world of the guild of biblical scholars in order to engage with the complex realities of everyday life, and it is no coincidence that they also recognize that the interpretation proffered by the "ordinary" reader of Scripture can often serve to relativize—and sometimes even subvert—the type of reading produced in the academy. By involving those outside the accepted academic tradition of biblical scholarship they have enlarged and enriched the interpretive community and provided a welcome opportunity for minority and marginal voices to be heard. Of course, some seasoned interpreters of the Bible will no doubt find it difficult to disengage themselves from the traditional historical-critical approach and may well regard the type of approaches discussed in this chapter as no more than a quixotic indulgence in an interesting—but ultimately harmless—hobbyhorse. That must surely be a matter of regret, for if these approaches are summarily dismissed as a passing fad, it will only demonstrate how insular and self-serving traditional interpretation of the Bible has become.

NOTES

1. Elizabeth Cady Stanton, ed., *The Woman's Bible*, pt. 1 (Edinburgh: Polygon Books, 1895), p. 8.

2. Ibid., p. 10

3. Ibid., p. 9.

4. L. M. Russell, "Authority and the Challenge of Feminist Interpretation," in L. M. Russell, ed., *Feminist Interpretation of the Bible* (Philadelphia: Westminster Press, 1985), p. 137.

5. For a discussion of various feminist approaches to the Bible, see Eryl W. Davies, *The Dissenting Reader: Feminist Approaches to the Hebrew Bible* (Aldershot: Ashgate Publishing Limited, 2003), pp. 17–35.

6. E. Schüssler Fiorenza, "The Ethics of Biblical Interpretation: Decentering Biblical Scholarship," *Journal of Biblical Literature* 107 (1988): p. 9.

7. E. Schüssler Fiorenza, *Rhetoric and Ethic: The Politics of Biblical Studies* (Minneapolis: Fortress Press, 1999), p. 52.

8. E. Schüssler Fiorenza, *Democratizing Biblical Studies: Toward an Emancipatory Educational Space* (Louisville, Ky.: Westminster John Knox Press, 2009), p. 14.

9. R. J. Weems, "Re-reading for Liberation: African American Women and the Bible," in R. S. Sugirtharajah, ed., *Voices from the Margin: Interpreting the Bible in the Third World* (Maryknoll, N.Y.: Orbis Books, 2006), p. 31.

10. See Kwok Pui-lan, *Introducing Asian Feminist Theology* (Sheffield: Sheffield Academic Press, 2000); M. W. Dube, *Postcolonial Feminist Interpretation of the Bible* (St. Louis: Chalice Press, 2000).

11. A. Loades, "Feminist Interpretation," in J. Barton, ed., *The Cambridge Companion to Biblical Interpretation* (Cambridge: Cambridge University Press, 1998), p. 92.

12. For a useful collection of writings on liberation theology, see C. Rowland, ed., *The Cambridge Companion to Liberation Theology* (Cambridge: Cambridge University Press, 1999).

13. G. Gutiérrez, *A Theology of Liberation* (London: SCM Press, 1974; 2nd ed., 1988), p. 88.

14. See M. Prior, *The Bible and Colonialism: A Moral Critique* (Sheffield: Sheffield Academic Press, 1977).

15. See R. S. Sugirtharajah, *The Bible and the Third World: Precolonial, Colonial and Postcolonial Encounters* (Cambridge: Cambridge University Press, 2001); see, also, his *Exploring Postcolonial Biblical Criticism* (Oxford: Wiley-Blackwell, 2012).

16. D. Guest, *When Deborah Met Jael: Lesbian Biblical Hermeneutics* (London: SCM Press, 2005), p. 146.

17. As Adrian Thatcher has observed, "Almost all Protestants who are unwilling to abandon their biblical literalism about homosexuality become closet revisionists over divorce and remarriage (whatever Jesus might have said)" (*The Savage Text: The Use and Abuse of the Bible* [Chichester: Wiley-Blackwell, 2008], p. 30).

18. See E. Stuart, *Religion Is a Queer Thing* (London: Cassell, 1997), p. 42.

19. Guest, *When Deborah Met Jael*, p. 246.

20. Ken Stone, "The Garden of Eden and the Heterosexual Contract," in R. E. Goss and M. West, eds., *Take Back the Word: A Queer Reading of the Bible* (Cleveland: Pilgrim Press, 2000), p. 57.

21. Guest, *When Deborah Met Jael*, p. 128.

22. As Guest observes, by today "it is the homophobe who is being scrutinized and criticized rather than the women who identify as lesbian" (ibid., p. 231).

23. For example, there is still sustained opposition in many quarters to the appointment of gay and lesbian clergy in the Church of England, and, as Guest observes, the teaching of the Bible concerning homosexuality has forced many to reconsider their

religious affiliation: "When oppression is legitimated by the very scriptures to which one gives allegiance there is inevitably a sense of radical dissonance.... The dissonance is so strong that it can threaten to force individuals down two equally distressing paths: either stay with one's religious faith, live a life of enforced celibacy or secrecy and bear the severe consequences—or leave" (ibid., p. 103). Ken Stone, the editor of *Queer Commentary and the Hebrew Bible* (Sheffield: Sheffield Academic Press, 2001), has noted that various scholars invited to contribute to the volume felt that "institutional or ecclesial politics prevented their participation" (p. 7).

24. L. E. Donaldson, "The Sign of Orpah: Reading Ruth through Native Eyes," in R. S. Sugirtharajah, ed., *Vernacular Hermeneutics* (Sheffield: Sheffield Academic Press, 1999), pp. 20–36.

25. Ibid., p. 23.

26. Ibid., p. 36.

27. See, for example, Rebecca Alpert, "Finding Our Past: A Lesbian Interpretation of the Book of Ruth," in J. A. Kates and G. T. Reimer, eds., *Reading Ruth: Contemporary Women Reclaim a Sacred Story* (New York: Ballantine Books, 1994), pp. 91–96.

28. J. Cheryl Exum, *Plotted, Shot, and Painted: Cultural Representations of Biblical Women* (Sheffield: Sheffield Academic Press, 1996), p. 137.

29. Ibid., p. 145.

30. I. Pardes observes that this "is the only biblical text in which the word 'love' is used to define a relationship between two women" (*Countertraditions in the Bible: A Feminist Approach* [Cambridge, Mass.: Harvard University Press, 1992], p. 102).

31. See Alpert, "Finding Our Past," p. 95.

32. See Exum, *Plotted, Shot, and Painted*, pp. 140–41. Alpert is particularly critical of heterosexual commentators who regularly focus on the relation between Ruth and Boaz and "can't imagine that there is a theme of love between women written between the lines" ("Finding Our Past," p. 95).

FURTHER READING

For a readable introduction to the political dimension of the Bible's message, see R. Bauckham, *The Bible in Politics: How to Read the Bible Politically* (London: SPCK, 1989). A convenient overview of recent feminist biblical scholarship may be found in my volume, *The Dissenting Reader: Feminist Approaches to the Hebrew Bible* (Aldershot: Ashgate Publishing Limited, 2003). One of the most influential feminist biblical scholars of recent times is Elisabeth Schüssler Fiorenza, and her volume *In Memory of Her: A Feminist Theological Reconstruction of Christian Origins* (New York: Crossroad Publishing Company, 1983) is regarded by many as a landmark in feminist interpretation of the Bible. Other, more recent volumes by the same author include *Democratizing Biblical Studies: Toward an Emancipatory Educational Space* (Louisville, Ky.: Westminster John Knox Press, 2009) and *Changing Horizons: Explorations of Feminist Interpretation* (Minneapolis: Fortress Press, 2013). An introduction to feminist biblical scholarship from an Asian perspective is provided in Kwok Pui-lan's *Introducing Asian Feminist Theology* (Sheffield: Sheffield Academic Press, 2000). The Peruvian theologian Gustavo Gutiérrez (*A Theology of Liberation*, 2nd ed. [London: SCM Press, 1988]) was one of the pioneers of liberation theology and was one of the first to apply the exodus narrative to the oppressive situation in Latin America. For a fine survey of liberation theology as reflected in different parts of the world, see the various contributions in C. Rowland, ed., *The Cambridge Companion to Liberation Theology* (Cambridge: Cambridge University Press, 1999). It is generally recognized that the work that paved the way for postcolonial criticism was Edward Said's influential volume *Orientalism* (London: Routledge and Kegan Paul, 1978). Nobody has written more extensively or more eloquently on postcolonial theory as it relates to biblical studies than R. S. Sugirtharajah; see, especially, his volumes *Postcolonial Criticism and Biblical Interpretation* (Oxford: Oxford University Press, 2001) and *Exploring Postcolonial Biblical Criticism: History, Method, Practice* (Oxford: Wiley-Blackwell, 2012). Deryn Guest's volume *When Deborah Met Jael: Lesbian Biblical Hermeneutics* (London: SCM Press, 2005) provides an excellent introduction to lesbian readings of Scripture, while D. Guest, R. E. Goss, M. West, and T. Bohache, eds., *The Queer Bible Commentary* (London: SCM Press, 2006), focuses specifically on passages in the Bible that have particular relevance for readers interested in gay, lesbian, bisexual, and transgender perspectives.

22

❀

Textual Criticism and Biblical Translation

Carmel McCarthy

With a textual transmission history for the Bible stretching back over more than 2,200 years, biblical textual criticism is continually confronted with three distinct but interconnected challenges. The first concerns the task of identifying more accurate readings for those parts of the Hebrew Bible considered doubtful or in some cases corrupt. The second concerns the production of scholarly critical editions of the biblical text and the elaboration of the principles underlying such editions. The third concerns the objectives of biblical translation today and asks what text(s) should be the basis for the biblical translator's work.

1. THE NATURE AND GOALS OF BIBLICAL TEXTUAL CRITICISM

With regard to the first of these challenges, most textual critics would accept that the identification of errors and other doubtful readings introduced into the text either inadvertently or intentionally during the long process of its transmission constitutes a basic function of biblical textual criticism. But they would also agree that the art of textual criticism is far broader than this. They would see it as including all that can be deduced from the available textual evidence predating the stabilization of the Hebrew text. The stabilization process itself, often referred to anachronistically as the "canonization" of the biblical Hebrew text, appears to have culminated in the selection of one particular strand of the textual tradition to the exclusion of all others. The agents of this selection were an influential stream in Judaism in the early decades of the second century CE, most likely of pharisaic origin. While this particular textual strand was not necessarily the best in every respect, it was for the most part both sober and accurate. Because of the labors of a group of scholars called Masoretes who meticulously conserved this strand, it eventually became known in the early Middle Ages as the Masoretic Text (= M).

The two principal ways of accessing the Hebrew text in its prestabilization state are through the "biblical" texts from Qumran and the wider Judaean desert, on the one hand, and through the Septuagint, a Greek translation (= G) begun in the middle of the third century BCE, on the other. The Qumran texts are characterized by what scholars call pre-canonical textual fluidity. The variety in their readings gives some sense of the evolution of the text in its earliest attested forms. Together with the Septuagint they provide invaluable insight into the complex journey from textual pluralism in the last two centuries BCE into the stabilized proto-Masoretic form (= proto-M) at the beginning of the second century CE. Other ancient versions occasionally offer indirect glimpses of earlier forms of the Hebrew text than those preserved in the Masoretic tradition.

Faced with such a wealth of textual data, biblical textual criticism, in accordance with established principles, undertakes some form of evaluation of textual variants with regard to possible original form(s). This evaluation process of necessity involves some measure of subjectivity while striving to be methodically rigorous and self-critical. Nevertheless, textual criticism is not so much a science as an art form or historical inquiry, by means of which textual critics seek to define textual problems and to find arguments for and against the originality of readings. In tracing the history of each textual problem they attempt to identify the relationship between its variant readings and to indicate the most likely reason(s) for the variation.

Given this preliminary overview of text-critical concerns, it is not surprising to find differences among scholars as to how best to engage in this work. A significant number of biblical critics maintain that the key task of textual criticism concerns the identification of the earliest attested forms of the text. This would make it possible to propose readings that in some cases are older than and preferable to M. The textual pluralism evidenced by the biblical material in Qumran and its hinterland has uncovered a much richer picture of how the biblical text came to be, leading some scholars to ask what kind of text should be the object of the text-critical endeavor and what principles should guide the production of critical editions of the Hebrew Bible. Other textual critics maintain that M should be the standard against which variant readings in Qumran and the early versions should be evaluated. Yet others would maintain that the yardstick against which to measure textual variation should be the consonantal form of proto-M, which had become normative for Judaism at the beginning of the second century CE.

In order to better appreciate the complex challenges facing textual critics, a brief outline of the key textual sources for the Hebrew Bible now follows. These sources fall into three broad groups, the first of which contains the earliest direct textual evidence provided by the discoveries in Qumran and surrounding areas. This evidence dates from the third century BCE to the second century CE. The second textual source consists of the Masoretic Text, with its long history of evolution from its proto-M form already evidenced in a certain number of the Qumran manuscripts, to its climax in the great medieval codices of Cairo (Former and Latter Prophets), Aleppo (complete, apart from the Pentateuch up to Deut. 28:17 and certain other lacunae), and Leningrad (complete). The third group contains the indirect witness of the earliest versions, with particular emphasis on the Septuagint, the oldest coherent initiative to render the Hebrew Bible in another language (begun ca. 250 BCE in Alexandria).

a. The Dead Sea Scrolls

The discovery of the biblical scrolls in both Qumran and the wider Judaean desert has enormously enhanced our understanding of the biblical text in its earliest attested forms. One measure of the significance of this textual treasure trove lies in the vast amount of secondary literature that has emerged in the seven decades since its discovery, which shows no sign of decreasing. Of the 850 manuscripts found in Qumran, more than two hundred are biblical, not counting the various biblical citations embedded in the commentaries and rewritten texts peculiar to the community who lived there. With all the material now published, scholars continue to gain new insights into the earliest phases of the evolving biblical text. Coming from an era and a group in which no single form of the text was regarded as exclusively normative, the scrolls' most striking contribution to textual criticism lies in the fact that they give direct entry into the state of the biblical text in a specific group of Jewish believers almost a thousand years before the earliest complete Hebrew manuscripts (ca. 1000 CE). They give a strong indication of which biblical entities were most valued by the group, with those of Deuteronomy, Isaiah, and Psalms being among the most attested. The overall picture they paint is one of textual pluralism, with numerous variant readings and peculiarities in spelling, with certain scrolls nevertheless exhibiting a remarkable continuity with what was to become the full-blown Masoretic Text of medieval times.

Prior to the discoveries of 1947, the prevailing viewpoint was that M contained the closest extant form of a so-called original text, which could be consolidated through comparative analysis with the early versions. This approach was based on understanding a textual development of "one into three," that is, on the evolution of a presumed Hebrew original or "Urtext" into M, G, and the Samaritan Pentateuch (= SP). Against such a background, Frank M. Cross developed his theory of local texts.[1] He identified three main textual types in the Pentateuch, which, he maintained, owed their separate identity to their having been developed in different geographic milieus, reflecting the scribal schools of Babylon, Egypt, and Palestine. The first text type, Cross argued, was carried forward in what was to become M; the second he identified with the Greek tradition, and the third, with that of the SP. There have been various critical reactions to this theory, mainly based on the fact that, because it was formulated before all the Qumran biblical evidence became available, it is too narrow to account adequately for the complexity of the textual evidence. More mature analysis of the data shows that it is a matter not just of different text forms but also of a plurality of redactional traditions.

A second theory is associated with Shemaryahu Talmon.[2] He interpreted the textual pluralism of the scrolls as reflecting those Jewish communities who survived the turmoil of the time, and he suggested that the variety may have been even greater than what is apparent in Qumran. His approach could be described as a "many into three" situation. A third interpretation is that of Emanuel Tov, who maintains that, although some manuscripts at Qumran can be linked more clearly with the strands that were eventually to reflect M, G, and SP, each manuscript or fragment should be seen as having certain independent characteristics that are not easily categorized.[3] Accordingly, he proposed two further types: texts written in the Qumran practice and nonaligned texts. More recently, Eugene Ulrich has maintained that each biblical text or fragment should be viewed in its own right, with its own textual history, particularly those texts containing two or more literary "editions" side by side, such as Jeremiah.[4]

Given this textual pluralism, it is most important to avoid superimposing a postcanonical conception of Scripture on the Qumran scrolls, particularly since the terms *Bible* and *books* would not have been used or understood by these scholars. It is clear that the Qumran "biblical" collection as a whole as well as the literary structures of some of its "books" were still in a state of flux. The community would have been no more likely to eliminate one or another version of Jeremiah, for example, than Christians would have been likely to eliminate any one of the four gospels. The Qumran material reflects a compilation of sacred writing that was still open, with some "books" well established, others on the way, and still others on the margins. In sum, the Dead Sea Scrolls give a direct insight into the role of Scripture for a splinter group from mainline Judaism of the period.

Care must be taken therefore not to overexaggerate the contribution of these texts to the text-critical endeavor. Since most of the two hundred-plus biblical texts are in fragmentary form, some of them indeed consisting of a few words or verses, it can be misleading to imply that the Qumran scrolls witness to fresh and full antique forms for the entire Bible. Very few of the scrolls in fact contain a full book, the 1QIsa[a] scroll being the best example of an almost complete entity. To say that "all the books" of the Bible, apart from Esther, are represented in Qumran likewise needs to be qualified, particularly since the evidence for some of the other biblical entities such as Judges, Kings, Ruth, Song of Songs, Qoheleth, Lamentations, Ezra–Nehemiah, and Chronicles amounts to hardly more than a few verses in each case. Moreover, in this respect, it needs to be remembered that these biblical texts appear to have been copied and used for different purposes: some are careful study texts, some were perhaps used for liturgy, and others are excerpted texts, such as the tefillin and 4QDeut[n]. This variation in purpose, leading to disparities in the quality and care taken in the copying of the manuscripts, has direct implications for the text-critical relevance of variations in the text.

The principal contribution of the Judaean desert discoveries to the task of textual criticism therefore does not just consist in the number of readings that diverge from M. They also challenge scholars to be careful not to place M always or exclusively at the center of their textual thinking. The Qumran biblical manuscripts represent one example of pre-canonical fluidity already present in the Judaism of that era and show that, alongside popular texts marked by assorted corruptions, there also existed some carefully executed texts. These were restrained and conservative in orthography, and their scribes scrupulously preserved difficult readings that other manuscript traditions appear to have altered or eliminated or smoothed over. It is understandable therefore that most textual critics insist on the importance of contextualizing the various Qumran readings and of attending to the details of each fragment or scroll in its own right when evaluating its text-critical worth.

b. The Masoretic Text

If M in its most developed form subsists in the great medieval codices mentioned above, evidence of its earliest attested forms is present in some of the Qumran manuscripts (see 4QGen[b], 1QIsa[b], 4QJer[a], 4QJer[c]), in the second-century CE tefillin texts of Wadi Murabba'at, and in the revisions of G toward M by the first-century CE Jewish scholars Aquila, Symmachus, and Theodotion. These early attestations illustrate the emergence of what scholars retrospectively call the proto-M, a term that refers to the consonantal text authorized by influential circles in Judaism in the early second century CE. This particular form of the text was adopted by all Jewish communities thereafter and was in due course brought to its fullest form by the Masoretes in the ninth to eleventh centuries CE, through the insertion of vowel pointing, accentuation, paragraph markings large and small, and other paratextual elements.

The precise circumstances leading to the choice of this particular textual form that was destined to become M are not clear. That it was chosen by a particular stream in Judaism does not automatically imply that it represented the best available text of the Bible. As will be noted below, there are certain instances where the Hebrew parent text of G or some of the Qumran texts attest textual readings that are clearly superior to those attested by M. However, because of the care and meticulous attention given to preserving M in all its details through careful copying and by means of elaborate Masoretic notes developed over the centuries by the Masoretes, the text of M continues to be the most commonly used form of the Hebrew Bible.

The Second Rabbinic Bible of Jacob ben Hayyim, published in Venice by Daniel Bomberg (1524–25), became the most influential of the early printed editions of the Hebrew Bible. Based on a collation of late medieval manuscripts, it also contained the Aramaic Targums, together with comments taken from some of the outstanding medieval rabbinic commentators (Rashi, Ibn Ezra, Qimhi). It also featured the full Masorah, but in a collated form garnered from a variety of medieval manuscripts. It remained the standard printed text of the Hebrew Bible until the twentieth century. The first two editions of Kittel's *Biblia Hebraica* (1906, 1913) also used this mixed text (without the Masorah) and added a limited critical apparatus.

c. The Septuagint

Among the ancient versions, pride of place goes to G, commissioned in Egypt for the Greek-speaking Jewish community in Alexandria, most likely during the reign of Ptolemy Philadelphus (285–247 BCE). The term *Septuagint* originally referred to the Greek translation of the Pentateuch and was then gradually extended to include that of the Prophets and Writings, so that G was probably completed by the time of Ben Sira (ca. 190 BCE). Since the entire translation took more than fifty years, it would have required many translators, resulting in variations of style and quality of translation from book to book. Some books would have been the work of individuals, while others would have had more than one translator. Some translations may have been made outside of Egypt. In addition to translations of the books of the Hebrew Bible, G also contains the Apocrypha. These latter were positively excluded from the biblical corpus by the early second century CE because they were believed to have been written in Greek (though Hebrew originals have been discovered for some of them in Qumran, such as Sirach).

As a translation, G is generally competent and idiomatic. Prior to the discovery of the Hebrew Qumran manuscripts, the value of G for text-critical purposes was often undervalued or misunderstood. Presuming that its parent text was more or less identical to that of M, variations were taken to be either errors on the part of the translators or deliberate changes or interpretations introduced by them. The numerous variants in the Hebrew readings attested in Qumran have confirmed that many of the differences in G must be seen not as initiated by the translators of G but as witnessing to a Hebrew parent text that differed from that of M. Perhaps the clearest example concerns the book of Jeremiah. Here G's translation is approximately 20 percent shorter than M's Hebrew text; moreover, some of its chapters occur in a different sequence. In the past it might conceivably have been argued that G's shorter text was due to its translator. However, the Hebrew text of four different Jeremiah fragments from Qumran's fourth cave now demonstrates adequately that G's translation was based on a Hebrew parent text that differed from M.

Ulrich, among others, sees these Jeremiah fragments as providing evidence of two successive "editions" of Jeremiah, arguing that the fragments from 4QJer[b] and 4QJer[d] from the second century BCE attest in Hebrew the earlier, shorter edition, including an arrangement of the book that reflects the parent text of G, whereas by contrast the longer text of M is supported by the fragments from 4QJer[a] and 4QJer[c]. Even if caution should be exercised in applying the label "editions" to these fragments, lest the impression be given that such editions are complete documents rather than fragments, nevertheless, these four Jeremiah fragments confirm that the shorter Hebrew parent text of G differed significantly from the text of M.

d. The Daughter Versions

Of lesser value from the point of view of textual criticism are the so-called daughter versions, the Peshitta, Vulgate, and Targum, all three being independent translations of proto-M, each containing some interesting variations of relative text-critical value. Prior to the Qumran discoveries, such variant readings occupied a more central role in textual criticism than at present. Analysis of where they deviate from M seeks to determine whether or not they reflect original variants already present in their Hebrew parent text. Where there is no direct Hebrew witness for such variants, the retroversion (retranslation or reconstruction) of such elements into assumed Hebrew/Aramaic originals must remain tentative since such differences may be due to other factors such as exegesis or various translation techniques. Familiarity with the translation techniques of each of the versional witnesses is indispensable to the textual critic in deciding whether a variant presupposes a Hebrew parent text or whether it simply reflects a particular technique employed by the translator(s) in question. In other words, when we understand a version's relation to the proto-M, we can better discern the presence of a variant by retroversion.

The Peshitta or Syriac version is the second oldest of the ancient versions, with its origins reaching back into the second if not first century CE. The scholarly consensus concurs that it is an independent translation of a proto-M textual type, with some minimal later influence coming from G. Apart from Chronicles, its rendering of the Hebrew Bible is almost verbatim for the most part and reasonably accurate, with just a minority of unique readings.

The Vulgate is the name by which Jerome's fifth-century CE Latin translation became known in the sixteenth century. After initial work on rendering the Psalms from Greek into Latin, in 392 Jerome switched to working on the Hebrew text. Guided by the principle of preference for the *veritas hebraica* (the true Hebrew), and particularly for the renderings of Aquila and Symmachus, he completed his version in 405. Using the form of the Hebrew text known at his time, which was virtually identical to that of the medieval manuscripts, he also occasionally incorporated some readings from the Greek tradition.

The origins of the practice of translating the Hebrew Bible into Aramaic are clouded in uncertainty. It is impossible to know whether Ezra's bilingual reading and rendering of Scripture (see Neh. 8:1–8) became a regular practice. Since the Targums sought to give their readers and auditors a better grasp of the Hebrew original by rendering it in accordance with the exegetical traditions that were then current, it is often difficult to identify where translation ends and interpretation begins. Apart from Qumran, the earliest extant Targums date from the third century CE, while many are considerably later.

2. CRITICAL EDITIONS OF THE HEBREW BIBLE

With such an abundance of textual data now available, a practical way of experiencing contemporary textual criticism would be to compare three projects currently engaged in producing scholarly editions of the Hebrew Bible. A brief exploration of their aims and methods will reveal similarities and differences in their text-critical presuppositions.

a. *The* Hebrew University Bible

The first project is concerned with a diplomatic edition of the Aleppo Codex (ca. 930 CE), together with its full Masorah. A "diplomatic" edition seeks to reproduce a single manuscript as faithfully as possible and records textual variants in one or more critical apparatuses. Since the Aleppo manuscript is incomplete, the lost Torah section (up to Deut. 28:17), together with other lacunae in the Prophets and the Writings, will have to be reconstructed from other medieval sources. The *Hebrew University Bible* project was founded in 1956 by Moshe Goshen-Gottstein, who served as its editor-in-chief until his death in 1991. Chaim Rabin and Shemaryahu Talmon worked as editors under Goshen-Gottstein, all three being considered "founding editors." After Goshen-Gottstein's death, Talmon served as editor-in-chief from 1991 until his own death in 2010. He was succeeded by Michal Segal, the current editor-in-chief. At some point in the 1970s–80s, work on the project was divided across two teams: Goshen headed the Isaiah team (and, after the completion of the collation work in the 1980s, continued with Ezekiel and then the XII), whereas Talmon and Rabin (joined later by Emanuel Tov) headed the Jeremiah team. Three books have been published so far: *Isaiah* (1995), *Jeremiah* (1997), and *Ezekiel* (2004). The first half of the Twelve Prophets volume, which is nearing publication, has been edited by Talmon (posthumously) and Segal, while the second half is under Segal's editorship.

By means of six critical apparatuses each volume reports as fully as possible on (i) variations in the ancient translations; (ii) the Judaean Dead Sea Scrolls and rabbinic literature; (iii) medieval Bible codices, such as Leningrad and Cairo; (iv) variants in spelling, vowels, and accents that do not affect sense; and (v) and (vi) the editors' comments on the text in English and Modern Hebrew, respectively. A detailed description of the project's nature and aims is given by Goshen-Gottstein in the Isaiah volume.[5] Since the *Hebrew University Bible* aims at being factual in reporting on the data, very little evaluation is made regarding the text-critical worth of the variants. The wealth of detail given in the apparatuses is impressive, but the absence of editorial judgment or adequate evaluation of the raw data can be overwhelming for the average reader. Some of its critics maintain that it is unrealistic to suppose that textual criticism can be totally objective.

b. The Biblia Hebraica Quinta

Biblia Hebraica Quinta (*BHQ*), with Adrian Schenker of Fribourg as president of its editorial committee, is so called because it is the fifth edition in the *Biblia Hebraica* tradition. The first two editions of *Biblia Hebraica* were published in Leipzig in 1905 and 1913, respectively. Like the 1929–37 *Biblia Hebraica* edition of Kittlel and the 1967–77 Stuttgart edition, the *BHQ* is a diplomatic edition, conforming as closely as possible to the Leningrad codex (= *Leningradensis*), which, while it is less than ideal in some respects, remains the earliest known complete manuscript of the Hebrew Bible (ca. 1008 CE). (See Figure 22.1.) Recent developments in understanding the origins and development of the biblical text (especially the contribution of the Dead Sea Scrolls), and the concomitant shifts in appreciation of the aims and limits of textual criticism, have occasioned this new edition. Seven volumes are already in print: *Megilloth* (2004), *Ezra–Nehemiah* (2006), *Deuteronomy* (2007), *Proverbs* (2008), *The Twelve Minor Prophets* (2010), *Judges* (2011), and *Genesis* (2015), with *Ezekiel* and *Leviticus* nearing publication.

Aware of contemporary discussion of the relative merits of an eclectic edition, that is, an edition in which its editors feature what they judge to be preferable readings in the Hebrew text itself, the *BHQ* editorial committee chose to maintain the format of a diplomatic edition for three reasons. First, it considered that as yet not enough is known about the history of the development of the text of the Hebrew Bible and its various textual traditions to give a sound basis for constructing an eclectic text. Second, an edition presenting an eclectic text of the Hebrew Bible

Figure 22.1. *Codex Leningradensis,* fol. 98v (Deut. 1:1–21). Photograph by Bruce and Kenneth Zuckerman, West Semitic Research, with the collaboration of the Ancient Biblical Manuscript Center. Courtesy Russian National Library (Saltykov-Shchedrin).

must choose to reconstruct that text at a particular point in its development. Given the current lack of consensus about the appropriate stage of the text to aim at in such a reconstruction, the committee deemed that an edition that will be widely used by students and nonspecialists should not present as its running text a reconstruction based on one of the positions in the debate. Third, the committee was of the view that, since an eclectic text ought to be based on the presentation of all variants found in the surviving witnesses, such a presentation would be beyond the limits inherent in a one-volume edition. These observations and the principles underlying *BHQ* are set forth in a "General Introduction" in the *Megilloth* fascicle.[6]

The Masorah of *Leningradensis* is reproduced in full, together with translations and brief comments given in a commentary section. A single text-critical apparatus contains a selection of textual cases, with emphasis on those that are of significance for translation and exegesis. The function of *BHQ*'s critical apparatus is to present and evaluate the evidence for the text's transmission. Two general criteria for the selection of cases are detailed in the "General Introduction": (i) a variant reading arguably, but not necessarily, represents a Hebrew text differing from the edition's base text, and (ii) it should be potentially significant for translation or exegesis.[7] All the evidence is given for each case entry, both that supporting *Leningradensis* and the readings from the other sources reflecting the variant(s), so that readers are free to draw their own conclusions as to the significance and merit of the variation. The apparatus does occasionally propose that a witnessed reading other than the one found in the base text is to be preferred. Such judgments imply a necessarily subjective component, but, as has often been pointed out, such a subjective component is unavoidable if one engages in textual criticism.

Characterizations are often included in the apparatus to indicate the editors' interpretation of the data, and for certain complex cases a textual commentary is also given. The characterizations fall into eight broad categories, with various subdivisions, all of which are explained in the introduction. For example, in the third category, a reading may be characterized as a "conflation" (confl), as a "gloss," or as an "omission" (om), all three representing types of change from another reading, but without including the motivation for the change. By contrast, in category six, various types of facilitation in reaction to some difficulty in the source text are listed, such as grammatical, lexical, semantic, stylistic, or syntactic facilitations. Conjectures are kept to a minimum and are presented in the apparatus, not as "preferred readings" but explicitly as conjectures, with their rationale explained in the textual commentary. Thus the editors see their task as the presentation of the evidence in a way that allows readers of other viewpoints, or readers studying other aspects of the transmission of the text, to draw their own conclusions, without necessarily having to agree with a given characterization.

c. The Hebrew Bible: A Critical Edition

This last edition, *Hebrew Bible: A Critical Edition* (*HBCE*), initially called the *Oxford Hebrew Bible*, differs fundamentally from the above two in that it seeks to be an eclectic edition, that is, a critical text with an apparatus presenting the evidence and justifying the editorial decisions.[8] There will be one volume for each book of the Hebrew Bible, apart from the Minor Prophets, the Megilloth, and Ezra–Nehemiah, which will be edited in three single volumes, respectively. The editor-in-chief, Ronald Hendel, presents this project as responding to the challenge of integrating the knowledge gained in the post-Qumran era with the aims and procedures in constructing a new scholarly edition of the Hebrew Bible. Hendel argues that a key advantage of such a critical eclectic edition is that it will require its editors to exercise their full critical judgment concerning the variant readings and textual problems of the Hebrew Bible. He also sees it as being capable of representing multiple editions of biblical books in cases where such multiple editions are recoverable. A third advantage, he argues, concerns the fact that, to the best of the editors' ability, primary readings will be distinguished from secondary readings in the apparatus. The rationale for the *HBCE* presupposes that the goals and procedures in the textual criticism of the Hebrew Bible are not unique; indeed, many scholarly biblical commentaries present eclectic critical texts in their translations and notes, and many modern translations (as will be noted below) construct their own eclectic translations.

The *HBCE*'s practical goal is that of approximating in its critical text the textual "archetype," that is, "the earliest inferable textual state," and in the case of literary editions, the archetype of each edition. Hendel is clear that the *HBCE* does not set out to be a definitive text; rather, he presents it as a provisional work of scholarship. Approximating the archetype, he notes, is a step toward the "original text," however that original is to be conceived, since each biblical book is the product of a complex and often unrecoverable composition history.

Two major types of text-critical decisions are envisaged, of which the first is the more typical: (i) adjudicating among variants to determine which reading is the most likely archetype or is ancestral to the other(s) and (ii) proposing a reconstruction or conjecture of the archetype where none of the variants is likely to be the archetype. Each volume will have a text-critical commentary that will analyze in fuller form the rationale for complex textual decisions.

There have been varied reactions to the *HBCE*'s project of an eclectic scholarly edition of the Hebrew Bible. Aside from the fact that it does not appear to take into account the different linguistic levels that are amalgamated in M, perhaps the other most controversial concern is its use of the notion of "copy-text." Hendel maintains that a legitimate distinction can be made between substantives and accidentals in the textual history of the Hebrew Bible and so proposes the concept of copy-texts to undergird this distinction. The focus of *HBCE*'s critical work, Hendel maintains, will be on the substantive readings, while reproducing the accidentals (orthography, vocalization, accents) of a copy-text. He (not surprisingly) selects *Leningradensis* as the "most reasonable choice" of copy-text, and in those places where the critical text differs from the copy-text in its substantive readings, the critical text will lack the vocalization and accents of the copy-text—but will maintain its orthographic style. The result is that this new scholarly eclectic edition will have a reprint of *Leningradensis*, but in those cases where the editors judge that a variant or emendation is to be preferred, the word or words in question will appear with neither vowels nor accents. In a critical analysis of the *HBCE* project, Hugh Williamson fears that this will result in a totally un-unified text,[9] which would contradict the very notion of a critical edition. A fundamental weakness for Williamson is that this project appears to gloss over serious issues arising from the fact that the so-called copy-text is itself the combination of linguistic levels that are as much as a millennium apart.

3. BIBLE TRANSLATION TODAY: RECENT ENGLISH VERSIONS

The brief overview of three current scholarly projects engaged in producing critical editions of the Hebrew Bible outlined above illustrates a considerable diversity of understanding regarding the nature and aims of textual criticism. It is not surprising therefore that, where modern translations are concerned, there should be an even greater diversity in both approach and end result. This is because the translational choices facing translators are endless, particularly in those places where the Hebrew text is obviously corrupt or at least ambiguous. What text, therefore, should form the basis of the translator's work, and what should be the aim of biblical translation today?

Preliminary Comments

Before attempting to explore these two aspects of contemporary Bible translation, some preliminary comments regarding the nature of Bible translation in general may be in order. No language is fully translatable. All translation involves making choices that spell out the meaning of the original in ways that never exactly correspond to or fully capture the meaning of the original. Each language is limited by its own cultural, historical, and other socially determined conventions. Words change their meaning over time. This is because human experience, which comes to expression in language, changes and adapts over time in varying cultural and social contexts. New Bible translations will continue to be needed because changes in the above-mentioned variables are ongoing. New translations are needed from time to time also because our knowledge of Hebrew lexicography continues to be enriched by the discovery of other Near Eastern nonbiblical literary sources.

Bible translation must not be based on a literalist approach, since translation is not merely a process of identifying in the dictionary of the host language verbal equivalents to words in the source language. Rather, it is a matter of "carrying over" (trans-lating) meaning from one linguistic world or culture into another. In this "carrying over" translations may be located anywhere between two poles: those of formal equivalence (literal) and dynamic equivalence (free). A strictly literal translation, on the one hand, would be unintelligible, whereas, on the other, a totally free rendering would no longer be a translation and could even betray the sense of the original text. Translations also differ because of their target readership or audience. It is unlikely that one and the same translation will suit scholar, teacher, liturgist, and young person alike.

Given the complexity of the textual origins of the Hebrew Bible, and the existence of double literary traditions for certain passages and even books (such as Jeremiah), a basic question facing translators concerns how to decide on the form of the text to be translated. This is a complex issue for which there is no simple answer. Up to the present, it would seem that in both theory and practice, among Hebrew texts, M has been chosen as the base text for translations, whether those undertaken for scholarly purposes or those undertaken for religious or denominational purposes. Up to the middle of the twentieth century Roman Catholics relied on the Latin Vulgate, itself believed to be a translation of the Hebrew, whereas Greek and Russian Orthodox Christians continue to look to the Septuagint.

In the case of translations based on M, the principal argument in favor of selecting M is that this is a text tradition with an illustrious history, the main elements of which have been handed down with extraordinary care and fidelity from the early second century CE onward. That M offers a text that actually existed and which constituted the Bible for a believing community or communities is a further argument favoring its choice as the basis of the translator's work. Nevertheless, even when using M as their base text, translators have no option but to incorporate various translational preferences based on one or another variant reading in those cases where it is clear that M's text is either unintelligible or secondary. In this sense no translation can avoid being eclectic to a greater or lesser extent. Indeed, as will be illustrated briefly below, it would be impossible to translate M exactly as it is in every respect because of those passages, relatively few though they may be, where the text is indeed unintelligible or corrupt.

M also has the advantage of being a complete Hebrew (and Aramaic) collection of the texts that make up the Hebrew Bible, in contrast to either the incomplete nature of the Qumran scrolls or the translational nature of the early versions. Moreover, it is also more or less accurate to say that a good, critical translation will in the main agree with M more often than with any other single textual source. Once the fundamental issue as to which base text to translate has been settled, a good biblical translation should have three foundational supports: a sound knowledge of the language and cultural world of the original, a broad familiarity with the language and cultural context of the target audience, and a solid grasp of the content and meaning of what is being translated.

Comparative Analysis of Four English Translations

To illustrate some of the difficulties and challenges facing modern translators, four contemporary English translations will be examined with
regard to their translational options in a select number of Old Testament
passages: the Jewish Publication Society Bible (JPS, 1985), the New Revised Standard Version (NRSV, 1989), the Revised English Bible (REB,
1989), and the New American Bible, Revised Edition (NABRE, 2011).
Because each of these versions represents the work of a translation committee rather than of a single individual, it is inevitable that there will be
some differences of approach within each version.

Four categories of translational challenges will be briefly explored below.
They range from passages where M's text appears to be corrupt or secondary to those where M's reading has been changed for ideological motives.
Also considered will be passages where M's text is relatively coherent but
has given rise to varied modern renderings or interpretations. Some general comments will be added concerning passages where M's text is not
problematic but where the renderings of one or another of the modern
translations are improvements compared with traditional renderings.

A. PASSAGES WHERE M'S TEXT APPEARS TO BE CORRUPT

Deuteronomy 33:2c
The end of v. 2 of Deut. 33 is problematic, as is evidenced by the variety
of modern translations. A literal rendering of M would be "from his
right hand fire law for him/for them," which does not yield much sense.
JPS renders it as "lightning flashing at them from His right," adding in a
footnote that the meaning of the Hebrew is "uncertain, perhaps a place
name." NRSV renders it "at his right, a host of his own," noting that this
rendering is conjectural and has some links with G and that the Hebrew
is "uncertain." REB's rendering, "streaming along at his right hand," lacks
a footnote or comment, while NABRE's attempt, "at his right hand advanced the gods," adds a note: "Gods: the divine beings who constitute
the armies of the Lord, the heavenly hosts." These four different attempts
illustrate the unavoidable eclectic nature of modern translations when
confronted with obscure passages.[10]

Deuteronomy 33:21b

The meaning of Deut. 33:21b is uncertain. This is due in particular to the corrupt status of its middle strophe, with regard to the eighth (*sāpûn*, "reserved/hidden") and ninth (*wayyētē*ʿ, "and he came") words of the verse. These were originally a single word (*wayyitʾassᵉpûn*, "and they assembled together"), as reflected in G's rendering, but in the course of transmission this single word was inadvertently divided into two, with its sequence then transposed. Rejoining the two transposed words into their original form, the second strophe should read: "For where the portion of a commander was, there the chiefs of the people assembled together." The respective renderings of NRSV and NABRE attempt to make sense of M as it stands and, without any note, are more or less identical in meaning: "For there a commander's allotment was reserved; he came at the head of the people." Although JPS and REB note that the Hebrew is obscure, they, too, attempt a literal rendering of M. Only REB alludes to G, but without recognizing the corrupt and transposed nature of M, since its rendering presupposes two words (*sāpûn*, "allotted" as well as "and were assembled"): "For to him was allotted a ruler's portion, when the chiefs of the people were assembled together."[11]

B. PASSAGES WHERE M'S TEXT APPEARS TO BE SECONDARY

Hosea 6:5c

The final phrase of v. 5 of Hosea 6 may be translated literally as "and your judgments light shall go forth." JPS renders it as "and the day that dawned [brought on] your punishment" and notes that the Hebrew is uncertain. NRSV and REB translate it as "and my judgment goes forth as the light," which is substantially NABRE's rendering also. Of these three, only NRSV carries a note at *my*, indicating that this is the reading of the Greek and Syriac versions, instead of the Hebrew reading, *your*. This case illustrates how JPS, in remaining as close as possible to M, misses the obvious flow of the verse, while the other three, in following the text of G and the early versions, are closer to what can be described as "the earliest attested text."[12]

Judges 15:16

Samson, the speaker in Judg. 15:16, describes how "with the jawbone of a donkey, heaps upon heaps." This is a literal translation of the Hebrew consonantal text together with its Masoretic vocalization and accents. However, if the consonantal text is vocalized differently, we get "With the jawbone of a donkey, a crushing I have crushed them." This rendering makes more sense of the Hebrew play on words here and neatly mirrors the first-person verb in the second part of the refrain ("With the jawbone of a donkey I have slain a thousand men"). In other words, the consonantal text is sound; it is the vocalization that is secondary. Nevertheless, JPS and NRSV follow M's current vocalization, with JPS rendering this phrase "With the jaw of an ass, mass upon mass," while NRSV has "With the jawbone of an ass, heaps upon heaps." NABRE has "With the jawbone of an ass I have piled them in a heap." REB's translation is closer to the consonantal text, in that it features a first-person verb plus suffix, but its rendering of the idiom as "I have flayed like donkeys" is somewhat inventive.[13]

C. PASSAGES WHERE M'S READING HAS BEEN CHANGED FOR IDEOLOGICAL MOTIVES

Deuteronomy 32:8

The Song of Moses in Deut. 32:8 contains a scribal intervention, the aim of which was to render this poetic description of Israel's coming into being as the Lord's special people in a more theologically acceptable way. The verse speaks of the Most High organizing the division of peoples within their various territories, fixing their boundaries "according to the number of the sons of Israel" (= M). A different form of v. 8b, "according to the number of the sons of God," occurs in Qumran (4QDeutʲ). This is also the reading of a section of the Greek tradition: "sons of God." M's reading, "sons of Israel," is generally accepted as a later theological correction, a textual intervention aimed at avoiding any possible hint of polytheism or suggestion that the Lord was simply one of the lesser gods in a pantheon presided over by "the Most High." Only JPS follows M—"He fixed the boundaries of peoples in relation to Israel's numbers"—without further comment. By contrast, the remaining three modern translations adopt the reading of 4QDeutʲ and G, in varying formulations. NRSV renders it as "the number of the gods," REB has "the number of the sons of God," and NABRE reads "the number of the divine beings." All three include a footnote explaining the origin of their preferred reading.[14]

1 Kings 10:8

The Queen of Sheba expresses wonder at Solomon's great wisdom, exclaiming (according to M's text): "Happy are your men" (1 Kings 10:8). In the Greek version it is Solomon's "women/wives" who are deemed happy by the visiting queen. The difference between the two textual traditions can be reduced to the presence or absence of an initial ʾalep, and the motivation for this ideological change in M's text most likely would have been to suppress reference to the ill-reputed wives of Solomon in a context that appears to express approval of them. What did the modern versions make of this variation? Both JPS and NABRE follow M, the former with "How fortunate are your men" and the latter with "Happy are your servants." Neither carries a note. By contrast both NRSV and REB opt for "Happy are your wives" and explain their choice in a footnote.[15]

D. PASSAGES WHERE M'S TEXT IS RELATIVELY COHERENT BUT GIVES RISE TO VARIED MODERN RENDERINGS OR INTERPRETATIONS

Psalm 84:6b

Psalm 84:6 is usually understood as the prayer of a pilgrim celebrating the beauty of God's house, the goal of pilgrimage. Verse 6b is very succinct; its two Hebrew words can be translated literally as "[the] highways [are] in their heart." The rendering of JPS, "whose mind is on the pilgrim highways," adds *pilgrim* to clarify *highways*. Both REB and NABRE also add *pilgrim*, the former reading "whose hearts are set on the pilgrim ways," and the latter, "in their hearts are pilgrim roads." The rendering of NRSV goes further with "in whose heart are the highways to Zion" and notes that the Hebrew lacks "to Zion," a rather strange way to qualify an addition that has no textual basis in either M or the ancient versions.

Qoheleth 3:11

Qoh. 3:11 is enigmatic with regard to what the deity has placed in the human heart/mind. The full verse can be translated as "He has made everything beautiful in its time; also he has put 'ôlām in their heart, because of which no one can find out the work God has done from beginning to end." JPS renders 'ôlām as "eternity" and adds the following note: "He preoccupies man with the attempt to discover the times of future events; cf. 8.17." The renderings of NRSV and REB resemble each other in that they both expand 'ôlām to "a sense of past and future." NABRE translates it as "the timeless" and notes that "others translate 'eternity,' 'the world,' or 'darkness.'" How best, therefore, can 'ôlām be rendered in the context of chap. 3 of Qoheleth? If it has the more usual sense of "eternity," wouldn't this in some way contradict what follows: "so that humanity cannot find out ...."? The Hebrew root 'lm, which underlies 'ôlām, can mean "ignorance," "darkness," or "concealment," interpretations that fit neatly in this context with the clause that follows: "God has made everything beautiful in its time, but has put darkness/ the unknown into their hearts so that humanity cannot find out." This type of reasoning fits well with the questioning mind of Qoheleth. See Qoh. 12:14, where this root also occurs and is variously translated as "secret," "unknown," or "hidden."

E. PASSAGES WHERE M's TEXT IS NOT PROBLEMATIC

Finally, there are numerous instances where M's text is not problematic but where the renderings of modern translations are a considerable improvement compared with traditional renderings. Such instances illustrate well how changes in the meaning of English over time lead to the need for new translations. One such illustration concerns biblical passages in which God is described as "jealous." The rendering of JPS in using either *impassioned* or *passionate* in these contexts would seem more meaningful to modern ears than *jealous*. In the Decalogue passages of Exod. 20:5 and Deut. 5:9, JPS reads: "For I the Lord your God am an *impassioned* God." By contrast, NRSV, REB, and NABRE all feature *jealous*. This is also the case in Exod. 34:14: "Because the Lord, whose name is *Impassioned*, is an *impassioned* God"; and Deut. 4:24: "For the LORD your God is a consuming fire, an *impassioned* God." Furthermore, at Deut. 6:15, while NRSV and REB feature the traditional *jealous*, JPS renders "an *impassioned* God," and NABRE has "a *passionate* God" (emphases added).

Biblical Translation: A Complex and Evolving Art

The above examples represent the tip of a very large iceberg regarding the diversity of translational choices made by the four modern English translations selected for this brief comparative analysis. To go through each version in detail would uncover thousands more. Nonetheless, it should be apparent from the foregoing paragraphs that the art of biblical translation is complex and requires both skill and wise judgment. It should also be evident that, given the evolving nature of textual criticism and ever deepening insights into the textual stabilization and transmission history of the Hebrew Bible, there will never be a perfect or definitive translation. Other factors that would make such a goal difficult to realize include growth in the study of comparative Near Eastern philology and a deeper grasp of the cultural context of the ancient biblical world. Insights gained from the ongoing production of new critical editions of the Hebrew Bible, the Dead Sea Scrolls, and the ancient versions of the Bible also have their part to play. A final challenge lies in the evolving nature of the target readership of contemporary Bible translations.

NOTES

1. F. M. Cross, *The Ancient Library of Qumran and Modern Biblical Studies* (New York: Doubleday, 1958; 2nd rev. ed., 1961).

2. F. M. Cross and S. Talmon, eds., *Qumran and the History of the Biblical Text* (Cambridge, Mass.: Harvard University Press, 1975).

3. Emanuel Tov, *Textual Criticism of the Hebrew Bible* (Minneapolis: Fortress Press, 1992; 2nd ed., 2001).

4. Eugene Ulrich, "The Jewish Scriptures: Texts, Versions, Canon," in John J. Collins and Daniel C. Harlow, eds., *The Eerdmans Dictionary of Early Judaism* (Grand Rapids, Mich.: Eerdmans, 2010), pp. 97–119.

5. M. Goshen-Gottstein, *Isaiah* (Jerusalem: Hebrew University Bible Project, 1995), pp. xi–xxxiv.

6. Adrian Schenker, Yohanan P. Goldman, Arie van der Kooij, Gerard J. Norton, Stephen Pisano, Jan de Waard, and Richard D. Weis, eds., *Biblia Hebraica Quinta. Fascicle 18. General Introduction and Megilloth* (Stuttgart: Deutsche Bibelgesellschaft, 2004), pp. vii–xxv.

7. Ibid., pp. xii–xv.

8. See Ronald Hendel, "A New Critical Edition of the Hebrew Bible," August 2014, http://www.bibleinterp.com/opeds/2014/08/hen388019.shtml.

9. H.G.M. Williamson, "Do We Need a New Bible? Reflections on the Proposed Oxford Hebrew Bible," *Biblica* 90 (2009): pp. 153–75.

10. For a fuller discussion of the text-critical problems in this verse, see Adrian Schenker et al., eds., *Biblia Hebraica Quinta, Fascicle 5: Deuteronomy*, prepared by Carmel McCarthy, pp. 155–56*.

11. For further analysis of the corrupt nature of this verse, see ibid., p. 164*.

12. For an explanation of the corrupt nature of M's text, see Adrian Schenker et al., eds., *Biblia Hebraica Quinta, Fascicle 13: The Twelve Minor Prophets*, prepared by Anthony Gelston (Winona Lake, Ind.: Eisenbrauns, 2010), p. 60*.

13. For a fuller discussion of the vocalization issues in this verse, see Adrian Schenker et al., eds., *Biblia Hebraica Quinta, Fascicle 7: Judges*, prepared by Natalio Fernández Marcos (Winona Lake, Ind.: Eisenbrauns, 2011), p. 95*.

14. For further analysis of this text-critical question, see Schenker et al., *BHQ: Deuteronomy*, pp. 140–41*.

15. For further analysis of this text-critical question, see C. McCarthy, *The Tiqqune Sopherim and Other Theological Corrections in the Masoretic Text of the Old Testament* (Freiburg: Universitätsverlag, 1981), pp. 232–33.

FURTHER READING

The most comprehensive recent manual on biblical textual criticism is Emanuel Tov's *Textual Criticism of the Hebrew Bible*, 2nd ed. (Minneapolis, 2001); while James A. Sanders explores the subject concisely in "The Task of Text Criticism," in H.T.C. Sun and K. L. Eades, eds., *Problems in Biblical Theology* (Grand Rapids, Mich.: Eerdmans, 1997), pp. 315–27. An excellent overview of current thinking resulting from analysis of the biblical Dead Sea Scrolls is provided by Eugene Ulrich, in "The Jewish Scriptures: Texts, Versions, Canon," in J. J. Collins and Daniel C. Harlow, eds., *The Eerdmans Dictionary of Early Judaism* (Grand Rapids, Mich.: Eerdmans, 2010), pp. 97–119. For an understanding of the principles underlying the *Hebrew University Bible*, see M. Segal, "The Hebrew University Bible Project," http://www.academia.edu/4350024/ The_Hebrew_University_Bible_Project. The "General Introduction" in Adrian Schenker, Yohanan P. Goldman, Arie van der Kooij, Gerard J. Norton, Stephen Pisano, Jan de Waard, and Richard D. Weis, eds., *Biblia Hebraica Quinta: General Introduction and Megilloth* (Stuttgart: Deutsche Bibelgesellschaft, 2004), pp. vii–xxv, presents the rationale and working principles of the *Biblia Hebraica Quinta* and is indispensable for a correct understanding of the aims and methods of this edition. The principles underlining the proposed *Hebrew Bible: A Critical Edition* (formerly called *Oxford Hebrew Bible*) are presented by Ronald Hendel in "A New Critical Edition of the Hebrew Bible," August 2014, http://www.bible interp.com/opeds/2014/08/hen388019.shtml; and in an earlier version in "The Oxford Hebrew Bible: Prologue to a New Critical Edition," *Vetus Testamentum* 58 (2008): pp. 324–51. These principles are illustrated in pp. 352–66 of the same volume using three sample texts (Deut. 32:1–19; 1 Kings 11:1–8; Jer. 27:1–10[34G]) prepared by Sidnie White Crawford, Jan Joosten, and Eugene Ulrich, respectively. Some fundamental reservations regarding this new edition are expressed in Hugh G. M. Williamson's analysis of the *Oxford Hebrew Bible* (= *Hebrew Bible: A Critical Edition*): "Do We Need a New Bible? Reflections on the Proposed Oxford Hebrew Bible," *Biblica* 90 (2009): pp. 153–75.

23

To Map or Not to Map?

A Biblical Dilemma

Adrian Curtis

The biblical writers, when telling the stories of the people of Israel and Judah, and of those claimed as the ancestors of the later inhabitants of those lands, gave accounts not only of what had been done but also of where events were said to have taken place. So should maps be provided to aid the Bible reader's understanding? It is sometimes claimed that the provision of maps to accompany biblical accounts suggests an unwarranted confidence in the historicity of those accounts. This is especially true of those that purport to show such things as military campaigns, such as Joshua's conquest of Canaan; or battles such as that of Barak and Deborah against Sisera; or routes traveled, for example, by Moses and the Israelites from Egypt, through the Wilderness, to the Promised Land or by Abraham to the land of Canaan from Ur of the Chaldeans.[1] But the phrase just used cautions against this assumption because "of the Chaldeans" (Gen. 11:28, 31; 15:7) is perhaps a geographic description, designed to help the reader to know the city's location, rather than a historical statement of the city's inhabitants in a putative patriarchal period. And of course fictional works can be set in "real" settings, and maps can be drawn of fictional locations. (It should also be noted that maps can convey a sense of confidence that sites have been correctly identified, unless they are furnished liberally with question marks!)

It is not only in narratives that a geographic awareness is shown. The beginning of the book of Amos contains oracles against foreign nations, but it is only when it is read in consultation with a map of the area that the possibility emerges that the final arrangement presents a sequence in which God's judgment is being described as gradually coming nearer and nearer until it finally reaches the northern kingdom of Israel (a designation that in itself implies a geographic perspective). The point of the psalmist's plea to God to restore the people's fortunes "like the watercourses in the Negeb" (Ps. 126:4) is lost without an awareness of the location of the Negeb region, what the area was like, and what happened to the usually dry riverbeds when they occasionally became raging torrents. And in passages such as Ezek. 47:1–12, we move from physical geography to theological geography, as the Temple in Jerusalem becomes the source of life-giving waters that transform the Dead Sea itself. Without an awareness of the physical geography the theological claim being made might not be appreciated.

ANCIENT MAPS IN PICTURES AND WORDS

What has already been said suggests that the biblical writers did have geographic awareness and interests. But they did not supply maps, as usually understood, to accompany their writings! Examples of "pictorial" maps from the ancient world in which the biblical stories are set are very limited. A small clay tablet, now housed in the British Museum in London, dating from about 600 BCE, contains what might be more appropriately called a diagram than a map, purporting to show the world as then known, with the city of Babylon on the River Euphrates at its center, the Persian Gulf depicted as a river surrounding the land, and beyond that, strange places far from Babylon.[2] The "map" accompanied an account of the campaigns of Sargon, king of Akkad, in the second half of the third millennium BCE. From much later than the period that is the setting of the Hebrew Bible's narratives and other types of writing comes the famous "Madaba Map," found toward the end of the nineteenth century in a Byzantine church at Madaba in Transjordan, thought to date from the sixth century CE.[3] The floor of this church is decorated with a mosaic that represents the lands of the Bible, including a depiction of Jerusalem that shows several features of the city as it was at the time, including the domed Church of the Holy Sepulcher and other churches, including the Nea Church, and the impressive main thoroughfare (the Cardo) lined with columns, leading across the city from the Damascus Gate. The fact that this "map" incorporates a number of biblical quotations points to an interest in relating biblical events to geographic locations. And both the maps mentioned above may share an additional feature that goes beyond a purely geographic interest, in that they appear to be indicating the special status of Babylon and Jerusalem, respectively.

Before turning to another type of "mapping" it is relevant to note that caution may be needed in assuming that those who produced the ancient sources shared the same geographic perspectives as the modern reader may have. For example, the modern reader will tend to assume the customary north-south perspective, whereas the Madaba Map has an east-west orientation. One very specific instance of orientation being an issue relates to discussions as to whether Khirbet Qumran, the site associated with the Dead Sea Scrolls, was an Essene community. The first-century CE writer Pliny the Elder, in his work *Natural History*, book V, says that "below the Essenes was the town of Engedi." The modern reader might naturally understand this statement as implying that Engedi, on the western shore of the Dead Sea, lay to the south of the Essene settlement, assuming a north-south perspective, a fact that would be correct if the reference is to Qumran. However, Pliny's words *could* be understood as meaning that the Essene settlement was located somewhere in the hills above Engedi.

It is noteworthy that for the Hebrew Bible writers, the equivalent terms to our points of the compass included references to geographic features or relative positions. In Ps. 89:13, the Hebrew phrase *ṣāpôn wᵉyāmîn* is usually understood as meaning "north and south." The former term is thought to derive from the name of Mount Saphon, near the Mediterranean coast in what is now Syria (associated with the god Baal in particular in the texts from ancient Ugarit).[4] The term translated "south" can also mean "right (hand)," suggesting that directions were envisaged from the perspective of someone facing east (the dawn?). This is supported by the use of the word *qedem*, associated with the root "to be in front of," to mean "east." The word *yam* (sea, i.e., the Mediterranean) can be the equivalent of "west," and *negeb* (Negeb) is another way of indicating "south." Four of these terms occur together in Gen. 13:14 (*ṣāpôn, negeb, qedem,* and *yam*), each with a suffix indicating "toward," when Abram is instructed by God to look northward, southward, eastward, and westward.

Of course the biblical writers have not left us any maps in the conventionally understood sense. But there are a number of passages that might be thought of as providing a type of mapping—but in words. Genesis 10 contains what is sometimes known as the "Table of the Nations."[5] It is presented as a genealogy comprising a list of the descendants of the sons of Noah. But what soon becomes clear is that many of the named persons are in fact nations or peoples, and sometimes there is an indication of the extent of the territory where they lived (see verses 19 and 30). The chapter concludes with the comment: "These are the families of Noah's sons, according to their genealogies, in their nations; and from these the nations spread abroad on the earth after the flood" (Gen. 10:32). The chapter can be read as an attempt to "map" the ancient world, now placed strategically between the primeval "history" and the stories of Abraham and his descendants, in order to provide the context in which the latter are about to be played out.

A somewhat different type of verbal map is to be found in the book of Joshua.[6] In between the opening accounts of battles and conquests of cities such as Jericho, Ai, and Hazor (the bulk of chapters 1–12) and Joshua's farewell discourses in chapters 23–24, much of the material comprises lists, particularly of towns and of boundaries, presented as the allocations of land to the various tribes by Joshua after the land had been captured. The precise origin of these lists has been much debated but remains uncertain. However, it is inherently likely that they reflect some ancient attempt to define boundaries and territorial possessions rather than being fictional creations. These chapters demonstrate that the biblical writers, or those responsible for whatever underlying sources they may have been drawing upon, were aware of how parts of the land related to one another geographically. And in their canonical context, the chapters now serve a theological function in that they show how God's promise to Abraham and his descendants, that they would have a land in which to dwell (Gen. 17:8), was fulfilled.

If the book of Joshua's "map" may reflect some sort of reality, the same can hardly be said of the verbal map that is to be found in the final chapter of the book of Ezekiel.[7] Chapter 48 envisages a future "Israel," restored to its maximum extent (or perhaps even beyond), after the successive destructions of the northern kingdom (Israel) by the Assyrians and the southern kingdom (Judah) by the Babylonians and the subsequent exile in Babylon. The divisions of the land are arranged in a highly schematic fashion, the tribes being allocated successive latitudinal ("from the east side to the west") strips of land, from Dan in the north to Gad in the south. Between the territories allotted to Judah and Benjamin there is to be a "sacred" or "holy" portion, distinguished from the rest of the land, at the heart of which would lie the reconstructed Temple. I have already noted that the previous chapter makes a remarkable claim about the future Temple (Ezek. 47:1–12), namely, that from its threshold there would flow a river whose waters would gradually get deeper and deeper as they flowed eastward until they reached the Dead Sea, where they would give life to its waters, enabling fish to live there and plant life to flourish around its shores. God's Temple in Jerusalem would be at the heart of God's land and be a source of life in the most remarkable way. The nature of such an idealized picture, to be understood as theological geography, can only be appreciated with some awareness of the physical geography of the region.

MAPS AS AN AID TO THE STUDY OF THE HEBREW BIBLE

Relatively early in the Hebrew Bible, the traditions passed on about the ancestors of Israel set their activities in the wider world of the ancient Near East. The stories of Abraham envisage travel from southern Mesopotamia in the east to Egypt in the west. The Jacob traditions envisage travel to and fro between the southern Levant and Upper Mesopotamia, and much of the Joseph story is set in Egypt. So a map encompassing that region can provide the setting envisaged by some of the Genesis traditions (see map 23.1). This area includes what has come to be known as the Fertile Crescent, an approximately crescent-shaped swath of land that was relatively fertile thanks to rivers and rainfall. (J. H. Breasted, who coined the term *Fertile Crescent*,[8] did not include Egypt within its ambit, but for an understanding of the region it is important to be aware of the significance of the inundations of the Nile, as well as the Tigris and Euphrates.) As already noted, there can be difficulties with any attempt to mark routes taken by such figures as Abraham. But information about what is known of ancient roads and trade routes may shed light on the perceptions of the ancient writers. Given the importance of the results of archaeological excavations for the study of the Bible, an awareness of the locations of major archaeological sites is also important.

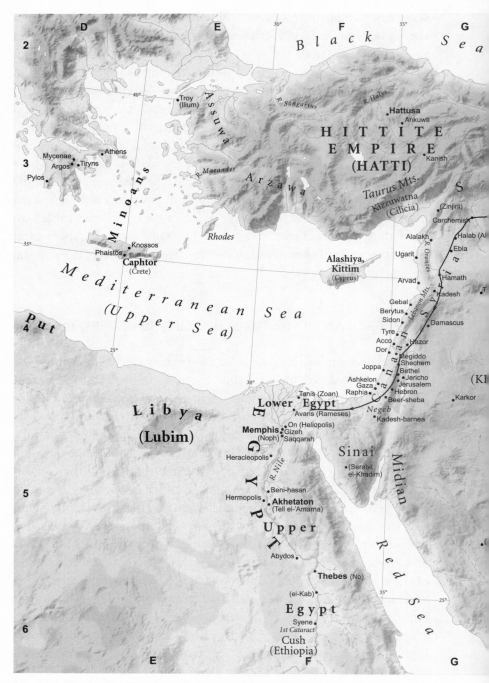

Map 23.1. The Ancient Near East: The Setting of the Genesis Stories

ARAT (URARTU)

Lake Van

Lake Urmia

Caspian Sea

50°

40°

H   J   K   L

3

Halaf)
R. Habor

Nineveh
Calah   Gt. Zab
Arbela
ASSYRIA   Zab
Asshur   Little
Nuzi

Zagros Mts.
GUTIUM

MEDIA
(MADAI)

Ecbatana

A RTU

NNI

Mari

River Tigris
R. Adheim
R. Diyala

Euphrates

BABYLONIA

Eshnunna

(Akkad)

Sippar
Cutah
Babylon   Kish
Borsippa
Nippur
Isin
(Sumer)
Lagash
Erech (Uruk)   Larsa
Ur
Eridu

ELAM

Susa

(Malamir)

ancient coastline

RABIA

Persian Gulf
(Lower Sea)

Dilmun

50°

55°

25°

4

5

6

⟶ Route reflected in the
story of Abraham

0   100   200 Miles

0   100   200 Kilometres

b)

(Mahd edh-
Dhahab)

H   J   K

© Oxford University Press

Map 23.2. Palestine

The term *Palestine* is used here as a convenient geographic designation of that part of the southern Levant that is the focus of much of the Hebrew Bible and is the setting of the kingdoms of Israel and Judah (see map 23.2). (None of the terms conventionally used to refer to this area is without its difficulties. Some carry religious or political overtones, while others lack precision—notably *Israel*, which has several different meanings within the Bible itself.) An awareness of the main geographic regions aids an understanding of the characteristic types of vegetation and where crops could be grown or domestic animals could be reared. The locations of mountains and hills, narrow valleys and wider plains, perennial streams and deserts, and the main roads and valley routes can help the reader to understand, for example, why Solomon fortified certain cities because of their strategic importance (see 1 Kings 9:13–19). For the reader with a geographic awareness, the account of the battle between the troops led by Deborah and Barak and those under the command of Sisera (Judg. 4–5) first raises a question and then provides a clue to a possible answer. It is easy to understand why soldiers on foot would be gathered on the slopes of Mount Gilboa, with its commanding views over the surrounding Plain of Esdraelon, but why would they take the apparently suicidal decision to leave relative safety and come down onto the plain where Sisera's iron-clad chariots would pose a major threat? The prose account in Judges 4 gives no explanation, but the old poem preserved in the following chapter suggests that a storm made the land so muddy that the chariots got stuck, resulting in the ignominious picture of the great commander Sisera running away on foot to hide in a woman's tent. This awareness of the setting renders the story even more dramatic.

The area whose physical characteristics have just been discussed provides the setting for much of the story told in the Former Prophets (and some of the Writings) and of the activity of those whose oracles are a major component of the Latter Prophets. It is here (see map 23.3) that the biblical writers set their accounts of tribal settlement; the establishing of a monarchy, initially on a small scale but reaching its maximum extent under King David; the division of the so-called United Monarchy into the separate kingdoms of Israel and Judah; the fall of Israel to the Assyrians and subsequently the fall of Judah to the Babylonians; and the reestablishment of Judah/Yehud under the Persians. It is therefore important to have an appreciation of the approximate areas occupied by the people of Israel and Judah and their proximity with some of their immediate neighbors, such as the Phoenicians, Philistines, Edomites, Moabites, and Ammonites. Awareness of the locations of key cities is also relevant to an appreciation of their significance. Mention has already been made of the strategic positioning of Solomon's chariot and storage cities. The choice of Jerusalem as the capital of the United Monarchy, and subsequently just of the southern kingdom of Judah, and the successive capitals of northern Israel (Shechem, Tirzah, and Samaria) owed much to their location and strategic potential.

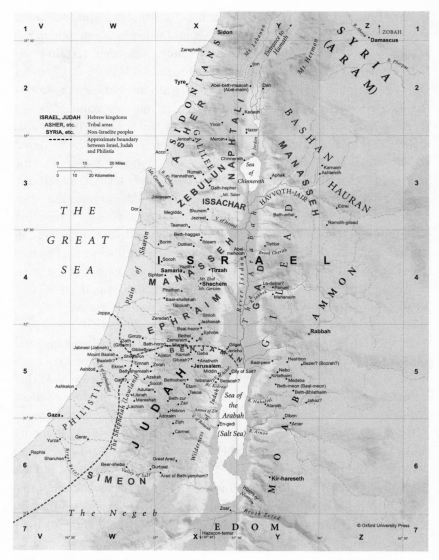

Map 23.3. The Lands of Israel and Judah

It was not just specific cities that were of strategic importance. The whole of the region of "Palestine" was of strategic significance since it occupied part of a narrow bridge of land at the crossing point between the continents of Africa and Asia (see map 23.4). Control of this strip of land meant control of the major trade routes and military routes between Egypt, the Arabian subcontinent, and Mesopotamia. From the perspective of Egypt and Mesopotamia, it formed a sort of buffer state between the two great powers, so its fortunes were often bound up with the relative strengths of its major neighbors. Just occasionally, perhaps under David, for example, it may have been able to enjoy relative independence, but more often it was under Egyptian, Assyrian, Babylonian, or Persian control during the period reflected in the Hebrew Bible. The likely scenario of events shortly before the fall of Judah illustrates this point. With the threatened ending of Assyrian dominance under the advance of the Babylonians, and the fall of Nineveh in 612 BCE, the Egyptian pharaoh Neco seems to have decided to march north to try to bolster up the remnants of Assyria against this new threat. For some reason (suggestions include that he was making a bid for independence or that he was siding with the Babylonians as the rising power) King Josiah of Judah made an ill-fated attempt to intercept Neco at Megiddo in 609 BCE but lost his life (2 Kings 23:28–30). Neco was unsuccessful, so for the time being he consolidated Egyptian control over the territory to the west of the Euphrates (2 Kings 23:33–35). (The choice of Megiddo as the place in which it was most likely that Josiah might be able to stop the northward march of Neco underlines its strategic significance as the fortress controlling a major pass through the Carmel hills.[9])

The city of Jerusalem served as both a political and a religious focal point of the United Monarchy and subsequently of the southern kingdom of Judah and of the restored postexilic community (see map 23.5). The original city was established on a small hill, just south of the present Temple Mount/Haram esh Sharif area, flanked by the Central (or Tyropoeon) and Kidron valleys. The story of its capture by David suggests that its previous inhabitants thought it virtually inviolable (2 Samuel 5:6), and the precise means by which David's troops gained entry is unclear. The key Hebrew word ṣinnôr (2 Sam. 5:8; its only other use in the Bible is in Ps. 42:7) is often thought to refer to some feature of the water supply system and may suggest that entrance to the city was initially

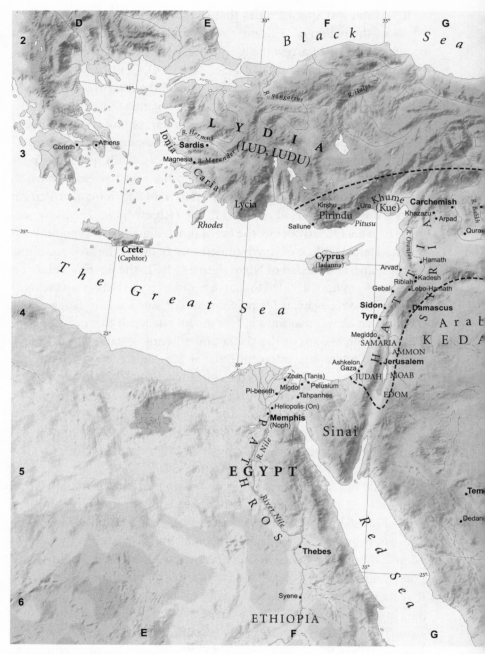

Map 23.4. The Babylonian Empire

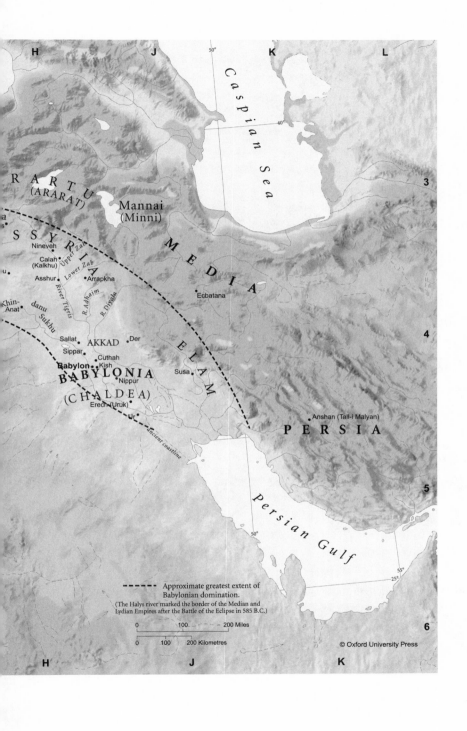

H   J   50°   K   L

Caspian Sea

40°   3

R A R T U
(ARARAT)

Mannai
(Minni)

a.

S S Y R I A

Nineveh

Calah
(Kalkhu)

Khin-
Anat   danu

Sukhu

Asshur   Arrapkha

Upper Zab

Lower Zab

River Tigris

R.Adhaim

R.Diyala

Ecbatana

M E D I A

Sallat   AKKAD   Der

Sippar   Cuthah

Babylon   Kish

Susa

E L A M

B A B Y L O N I A

(C H A L D E A)

Nippur

Erech (Uruk)

Ur   ancient coastline

Anshan (Tall-i Malyan)

P E R S I A

4

5

Persian Gulf

50°

55°

25°

6

- - - - -   Approximate greatest extent of
Babylonian domination.
(The Halys river marked the border of the Median and
Lydian Empires after the Battle of the Eclipse in 585 B.C.)

0   100   - - - -   200 Miles

0   100   200 Kilometres

© Oxford University Press

H   J   K

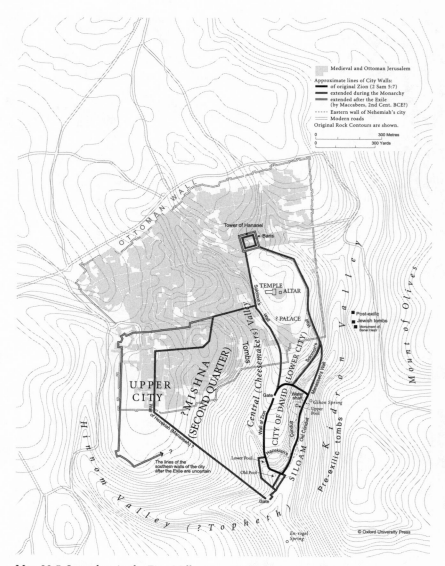

Map 23.5. Jerusalem in the First Millennium BCE

gained by stealth before other troops were given access. The biblical account suggests that the city was strengthened under David and further developed under Solomon, notably by the construction of a palace and its crowning feature, the Temple (1 Kings 9:15). The subsequent stages of the city's development during the period of the monarchy have been the subject of much debate. One particularly noteworthy feature of its development is King Hezekiah's decision to ensure a safe and defensible water supply, to which end he ordered that a tunnel be hewn through the rock to bring water from the Gihon Spring to the newly prepared Pool of Siloam, which lay inside the city's extended fortifications (2 Kings 20:20; 2 Chron. 32:2–4, 30). This tunnel was rediscovered in 1880. An inscription carved into its wall (now in Istanbul) suggests that two gangs of workers started at either end of the tunnel and worked toward each other and that they might have missed each other had not noises from one tunnel been heard in the other so that they changed direction to join the tunnels. Jerusalem was destroyed by the Babylonians in the sixth century BCE. The biblical narrative credits Nehemiah with taking the initiative in the subsequent rebuilding of the city's walls after the return from exile and overseeing the work of construction (Neh. 2:17–6:19). This restored city was probably quite small and may have occupied just the City of David and Temple Mount areas.

Relating the successive stages of Jerusalem's development to a map that shows the contours of the hills and valleys, and the location of the water supply, can be important in appreciating, for example, the strategic considerations underlying its role as a royal capital city. But it can also serve another function. The reader of Mic. 4:1 will realize that statements such as "The mountain of the LORD's house shall be established as the highest of the mountains and shall be raised above the hills" are envisaging a remarkable change in the very nature of things. Clearly the hill on which the Temple was built is not as high as some of those overlooking the city, such as the Mount of Olives. This is again theological geography, which can be appreciated thanks to an awareness of the actual physical geography, so the question "To map or not to map?" must, with appropriate caution, be answered affirmatively.

NOTES

1. See Map 23.1 above, where the marked route is intended to reflect the story of Abraham as told in Genesis rather than an actual journey.

2. For a picture, see Adrian Curtis, *Oxford Bible Atlas*, 4th ed. (Oxford: Oxford University Press, 2009), p. 9.

3. For a picture, see ibid., p. 10.

4. For a picture, see M. Yon, *The City of Ugarit at Tell Ras Shamra* (Winona Lake, Ind.: Eisenbrauns, 2006), p. viii. See also Adrian Curtis, "The Divine Abode: Ugaritic Descriptions and Some Possible Israelite Implication," in J. M. Michaud, ed., *Le Royaume d'Ugarit de la Crète à l'Euphrate*, Proche-Orient et Littérature Ougaritique 2 (Sherbrooke: GGC, 2007), pp. 295–314.

5. See, e.g., Gordon J. Wenham, *Genesis 1–15*, Word Biblical Commentary (Waco, Tex.: Word Books, 1987), pp. 213–15.

6. See Adrian Curtis, "Joshua: Historical Mapping," in George J. Brooke and Thomas Römer, eds., *Ancient and Modern Scriptural Historiography/L'Historiographie Biblique, Ancienne et Moderne*, Bibliotheca Ephemeridum Theologicarum Lovaniensium 207 (Leuven: University Press/Peeters, 2007), pp. 99–108.

7. See Paul M. Joyce, *Ezekiel: A Commentary* (New York: T&T Clark, 2007), pp. 219–21, 239–41.

8. J. H. Breasted, *Ancient Times: A History of the Early World*, 2nd ed. (Boston: Ginn and Co., 1935), p. 135.

9. See Curtis, *Oxford Bible Atlas*, pp. 96–97.

FURTHER READING

The "classic" work on biblical geography is George Adam Smith, *The Historical Geography of the Holy Land*, 25th rev. ed. (London: Hodder and Stoughton, 1931; first published 1894).

Other important older treatments include Yohanan Aharoni, *The Land of the Bible* (London: Burns and Oates, 1967); Denis Baly, *The Geography of the Bible*, new and rev. ed. (Guildford: Lutterworth Press, 1974).

A number of Bible atlases are available, some of which have appeared in several editions, for example, the *Oxford Bible Atlas* and *The Carta Bible Atlas*. Adrian Curtis, *Oxford Bible Atlas*, 4th ed. (Oxford: Oxford University Press, 2007; rev., 2009); Yohanan Aharoni, Michael Avi-Yonah, Anson F. Rainey, Ze'ev Safrai, and R. Steven Notley, *The Carta Bible Atlas*, 5th ed., rev. and exp. (Jerusalem: Carta, 2011).

Other atlases include James B. Pritchard, ed., *The Times Atlas of the Bible*, rev. ed. (London: Times Books, 1987); John Rogerson, *Atlas of the Bible* (Oxford: Phaidon, 1989); David Girling, Simon Hall, Nicholas Jones, and Fiona Plowman, eds., *The Essential Bible Atlas* (London: SPCK, 1999).

On Jerusalem, see Dan Bahat, with Chaim T. Rubinstein, *The Illustrated Atlas of Jerusalem* (New York: Simon and Schuster, 1990).

On historical mapping, see Ariel Tishby, ed., *Holy Land in Maps* (Jerusalem: Israel Museum, 2001).

Index of Scripture

Index of Modern Authors

Index of Subjects

512–13; impetus of from social and political movements promoting justice and equality, 511; increasing recognition of the importance of integrating non-Western approaches into biblical exegesis, 513; and the rise of the so-called second wave of feminism, 509; stances of toward the Bible, 511; and *The Woman's Bible*, 510

Fertile Crescent, 561

flood, the, 281; *Atrahasis* as a conceptual model of, 116, 117–18; *Epic of Gilgamesh* as a conceptual model of, 117; the two flood accounts, 117, 120

food rules complex, 380–86, 399, 401n13; and the bringing together of food rules, purity, and sacrifice, 380; food rules concerning mixtures of milk and meat/blood, 380–81, 383–86; food rules concerning types of animals (those that can be eaten and those that are forbidden), 380–83, 384; the pig as emblematic of the system of food rules, 381–82, 387, 390. *See also* animals, categorization of in the Old Testament as permitted or forbidden (for food)

foreigners/foreignness: Greek terms for, 55–56; Hebrew terms for, 55

Gemara, 419

Genesis, book of, 109; date of, 4; genealogies and lists of descendants in, 302; the Joseph story in, 129, 198; legal texts in, 162; use of *'ādām* in the early chapters of, 295

genres, biblical, 340–41, 348–49. *See also* law; narrative; poetry; prophecy; wisdom literature

Gezer, 37, 38, 39, 40

Glassius, Salomon, 436–37, 450

Gnostics, 14

gods. *See* divine beings, in the Old Testament

Greek, 11, 11–12

Greek religion, classical, 241

Grotius, Hugo, 437–40, 440–41, 441, 446

Habakkuk, book of, 151

Haggai, book of, 150, 212

Halevi, Yehuda, 463

Hammurabi, laws of, 167, 173, 174, 255, 311n21, 344; prologue to, 258

Hananiah, 137

Harper's Song from the Tomb of King Intef, 194–95

Hazor, 37, 38, 39, 40

Hebrew, 7, 11; linguistic shifts in, 7–8; Mishnaic Hebrew, 7; Modern Hebrew, 7, 9; as a Northwest Semitic language, 7; relation of to Aramaic, 8–9; and vowel points, 9–10; writing of, 9

Hebrew Bible: A Critical Edition (*HBCE*), 545–46; approximation of the textual "archetype" in, 545; as an eclectic edition, 545; initial title of (*Oxford Hebrew Bible*), 545; rationale for, 545; types of text-critical decisions envisaged in, 545–46; use of the notion of "copy-text," 546

Hebrew University Bible, 541–42; absence of editorial judgment and adequate evaluation of the raw data in, 542; as a diplomatic edition of the Aleppo Codes, 541; nature and aims of, 542; six critical apparatuses of, 541–42

Herbert of Cherbury, 441–42

hermeneutics, 406

Herodotus, 259

Hesiod, 256, 258, 260

Hezekiah, 35, 36, 96; and the extension of his life by fifteen years, 303

Hillel, and the *middot*, 423

Hinduism, 241

historical criticism, 91–92, 102n25, 410, 431–51 *passim*, 497, 507; abandonment of the biblical time frame and story line in modern historical criticism, 444; abandonment of "salvation history" in modern historical criticism, 444; aiming of for knowledge and understanding, 431; and the concept of mythology as an explanation of biblical primeval history and apocalyptic imagery, 446; early modern historical-critical scholars, 431–44; historical assumptions gained through historical-critical inquiry, 445–51; limitations of, 507–8; and the philosophy of religion, 445; and the poetic books of the Old Testament, 449–50; and the prophetic tradition in the Old Testament, 448–49

history: as a portrayal or version of the past, not an accurate "record" or description, 26; presentations of the past in the Old Testament, 27–32, 38, 44–45, 102n9; the problem with "history," 25–27; as a social construct, 59. *See also* history, presentations of the past in biblical scholarship